CULTURES AROUND THE WORLD: FIVE CASES

THE TIWI/ULITHI/THE SWAZI
THE NAVAJO/THE VICE LORDS

edited by GEORGE AND LOUISE SPINDLER

Stanford University

HOLT, RINEHART AND WINSTON   New York   Chicago   San Francisco   Atlanta
Dallas   Montreal   Toronto   London   Sydney

Library of Congress Cataloging in Publication Data

Main entry under title:

Cultures around the world.

   (Case studies in cultural anthropology)
   Bibliography: p. 499
   Includes index.
   CONTENTS: Spindler, G. and Spindler, L. Introduction.
   Useful Reading.—Hart, C. W. M. and Pilling, A.R.
The Tiwi of North Australia. [etc.]
   1.   Ethnology.   I.   Spindler, George Dearborn.
II.   Spindler, Louise S.   III.   Series.
GN378.C84   301.2   76–20447
ISBN 0–03–018396–0

The Tiwi of North Australia by C. W. M. Hart and Arnold R. Pilling
Copyright © 1960 by Holt, Rinehart and Winston, Inc.

Ulithi: A Micronesian Design for Living by William A. Lessa
Copyright © 1966 by Holt, Rinehart and Winston, Inc.

The Swazi: A South African Kingdom by Hilda Kuper
Copyright © 1963 by Holt, Rinehart and Winston, Inc.

The Navajo by James F. Downs
Copyright © 1972 by Holt, Rinehart and Winston, Inc.

The Vice Lords: Warriors of the Streets
Copyright © 1969 by Holt, Rinehart and Winston, Inc.

CONTENTS

iii

Introduction

SINCE 1959 students of anthropology have learned about diversities and commonalities in human culture from the Case Studies in Cultural Anthropology Series. Until now they have been available only in single copy editions. For the first time, for the convenience of students and teachers of anthropology, we have brought several together in one volume. The culture cases included have been carefully selected to represent major culture areas of the world. They also represent major subsistence types and different levels of sociopolitical complexity. And they have been selected for their readability and for the ethnographic competence their authors have displayed in these and other works. These are time-tested studies and are among the most widely used in the series. Any student reading these five studies will have acquired a background in world ethnography that will help him or her to understand better what human cultures are, how they work, and how anthropologists interpret them. As fellow anthropologists and teachers of anthropology this background seems to us to be an essential starting point for the ordering of anthropological thought and for its communication.

With these purposes in mind, we have focused upon intact cultures, recognizable on their own terms, rather than on changes, or on adaptations to the modern world. This does not imply that the ways of life as described were unchanging, or uninfluenced by the outside world. We know that virtually no culture described by anthropologists is free of influence from the post-Renaissance world of exploration and exploitation, and none are static, unchanging entities, existing in a social, political, economic, and relational vacuum. It is a matter of emphasis. For this volume we felt that the culture as a relatively intact working system was what was important.

The essence of the anthropological position is the cross-cultural perspective. This perspective is involved, explicitly or implicitly, in nearly every statement made by an anthropologist talking or writing about human behavior. This volume gives concrete meaning to this perspective.

The Tiwi

The Tiwi live on Bathurst and Melville Islands just offshore from northern Australia. They cannot be held as representative of the whole of the subcontinent. Nor can they be discarded as unrepresentative. Tiwi culture is unique, as all, each, and every culture is unique. Tiwi culture also shares with every human culture a great number of categories of behavior, but displays the greatest affinity in culture content with other native Australian cultures.

1

The complexity of social organization, ritual, and cosmology among Australian native cultures, made all the more dramatic by the simple hunting and gathering technology, is well known to anthropologists and is used by them in their teaching. Hart and Pilling choose to focus upon the exchange of women and the competition among men for prestige and influence through their control of women. In this system there are no illegitimate children, no unmarried females of any age, and wives are either very much older or very much younger than their husbands. A vivid picture of Tiwi life, as viewed from within the culture, emerges. The reader is not left an outsider to peer into a dimly understood, formalized, alien way of life. He or she becomes a witness to angry quarrels, a participant in involved machinations aimed at success—as defined by the Tiwi.

Ulithi

The people of Ulithi Atoll, island of Mogmog, the northernmost of the islands of the Carolinian archipelago, are Micronesians and as such represent one of the most important cultural divisions of the Pacific. In contrast to the Tiwi, who are foragers with no settled abode, the Ulithians are horticulturalists, living in villages, for whom the coconut, taro, sweet potato, breadfruit, banana, and sugar cane, supplemented with an abundance of fish, are staples. Their way of life is represented in various versions on small and larger islands and atolls throughout the vast reaches of the Micronesian Pacific and exhibits some affinities with Polynesian and Melanesian cultures. The Ulithian design for living is exotic by Western standards. The people engage in a form of ancestor worship. Most of the deceased become ordinary ghosts and are quickly forgotten. Others become prominent ghosts who, through possession of a medium, can provide information on the feasibility of an ocean voyage, the safety of relatives, or the cause of illness. Such a ghost may acquire great prestige over a wide area of Micronesia. On Ulithi Atoll magic is also very important. There are typhoon, navigation, community, fish, house, and grave magicians. Ulithians engage in what appears to be a free sex life and yet there are many restrictions applied to sexual behavior. But homosexuality, impotency, and frigidity as well as voyeurism, exhibitionism, and bestiality are virtually unknown. Sexual behavior is placed in the context of social and legal obligations and family life so that its interdependence with these other areas of life may be understood.

The Swazi

The Swazi represent a most important type of society—the African centralized state with a dual monarchy—the king and the queen mother, with a pastoral, traditional "cattle complex" as well as cultivation. The interlocking of clans and lineages, the function and meaning of the homestead with its patriarchal headman, his wives, and other dependents, and the relations of these units with the royal lineage and household are all interrelated into a complex system that the author of this study makes very clear. The full meaning of the Swazi way of life becomes most dramatically apparent in the description of religion, magic, sorcery, and ceremonial. The analysis of Swazi society and culture are developed in the functional mode, in keeping with the author's British training, but history is not left out. This centralized state society stands in sharp contrast with a band society such as the Tiwi, and makes interesting comparisons with the situation among the Ulithians, where the chieftainship has importance.

The Navajo

The Navajo are a pastoral people, but they were not always so. About 250 years ago their ancestors were Athapaskan-speaking hunters in the western sub-arctic. The Navajo still speak an Athaspaskan language, but since migrating to the Southwest they have become pastoralists. Sheepherding plays a most important role in the history of the Navajo and remains the most important focus of the recent culture of Nez Ch'ii, the specific community described. Other important aspects of the culture are treated, for the most part, within the framework of relationships existing between the maintenance of the herds and the sociocultural system. The relationships between the Nez Ch'ii families and their herds are described in detail. Other basic themes of Navajo culture as represented at Nez Ch'ii, such as the importance of females, the inviolability of the individual, the prestige of age, and the reciprocity principle are interpreted within this framework.

There has probably been more written about the Navajo than any other Native North American people, and for this reason, as well as the intrinsic qualities of the Navajo way of life, this case study is particularly important in this volume. It is especially significant for American students, for the Navajo, in our own country, represent the tribal world that was inundated by the flood of European expansion during the nineteenth century. Though this case study is not cast in historical terms, it makes apparent the fact that the Navajo have been able to adjust to new situations and to Anglo culture without losing their identity and pride.

The Vice Lords

The home of the Vice Lord "nation" is "the streets, alleys, and gangways of Chicago's major Black ghettos." The Vice Lords were the first urban group to be represented in the case study series. The Vice Lords not only represent an important sociocultural type, the delinquent gang, a segment of complex urban society and a species of adaptation to the conditions of life in depressed areas of American (and other) cities, but also an anthropological approach to a kind of field research that is becoming more and more important. Urban anthropology has sprung into prominence within the past decade and particularly during the past five years. Much anthropological fieldwork is being done in urban environments and many ethnographies are being written. *The Vice Lords* is a pioneer work. It has been read by many thousands of students and cited widely. The strengths and weaknesses of a participant-observer style of field research in an urban context are apparent. Probably most compelling to student readers will be the direct reporting of life on the streets among the Vice Lords and rival gangs. It will become clear that "gang" life is not disorganized. In fact, the organization of behavior is the object of study. This in itself is a major challenge to the kind of thinking about social disorganization that has prevailed for so long in many quarters, and still does in some.

Using This Book

We suggest that you read these case studies, the first time, as though you were reading a novel. You should get a feel for the way of life without getting bogged down in details. The second time you can go over the studies for a better understanding of the ways in which each of the cultures works as a system. You may find it useful to do some systematic comparing among the five cases, or between pairs of them. Keith Otterbein's book *Comparative Cultural Analysis* could be very helpful. It lays out quite explicitly just how a comparison can be made. Another useful aid to getting the most out of this volume is the book *Being an Anthropologist*, edited by G. Spindler. Chapters by C. W. M. Hart, the senior author of *The Tiwi*, and Lincoln Keiser, author of *The Vice Lords*, describe their fieldwork from a personal point of view. The case studies really come to life when you have an understanding of what it was like to work and live in the place, and with the people, described. It can help you also to see how the case study may be biased by the personal experience and viewpoint of the author. There are also textbooks in introductory anthropology that use case materials, many of them from the Case Studies in Cultural Anthropology. Reading them will help you to interpret the case studies in *Cultures Around the World* and will put them into the broader perspective of anthropological concerns. Those most directly related to the case studies series are Ernest Schusky's *The Study of Cultural Anthropology* and Alan Beals' *Culture in Process*. The various books mentioned in this introduction are listed under Useful Reading at the end.

There are many excellent textbooks in cultural and social anthropology with which this volume can be combined. The text should provide a conceptual ordering that can be applied to the interpretation of culture cases. Though not all parts of culture and society are represented equally in the five case studies included in this volume, for they were not written according to blueprint, there is scarcely any aspect of society or culture that is not represented in one or more of them. Questions formulated on the basis of textbook and lectures can be pursued through *Cultures Around the World*, treating the cases as primary sources. In this way the meaning of concepts and theory can be discovered and extended.

Many students will want to increase their knowledge of cultures. To this purpose we have included a brief list of further readings at the end. Of course other anthropologists might well select quite different readings, but these will help to get into interesting territory.

We have also provided an index to all five of the case studies. It should prove especially useful because entries will indicate the individual case studies for which page references are provided. This will facilitate the use of *Cultures Around the World* for comparative exercises and problems, preparation of reports, discussions, and term papers.

George and Louise Spindler
General Editors

THE TIWI OF
NORTH AUSTRALIA

C. W. M. Hart

Arnold R. Pilling

Wayne State University

C. W. M. Hart (1905–1976) was born in Australia and became an American citizen in 1953. He studied at the universities of Sydney, Chicago, and London. He taught anthropology at the University of Toronto, London School of Economics, University of Wisconsin, University of Istanbul, and most recently at Witchita State University. Hart did fieldwork with the Tiwi, with a minimum of personal equipment and with no transportation other than his two feet, for about two years. He was associate editor of the *American Anthropologist*, president of the Society for Applied Anthropology, and founded the first chair of social anthropology at the University of Istanbul.

Arnold R. Pilling, a Californian, studied at the University of California, Berkeley. He was a Fulbright Fellow to Australia in 1953 and 1954 and spent most of that time studying the culture of the Tiwi. He is now professor of anthropology at Wayne State University in Detroit.

5

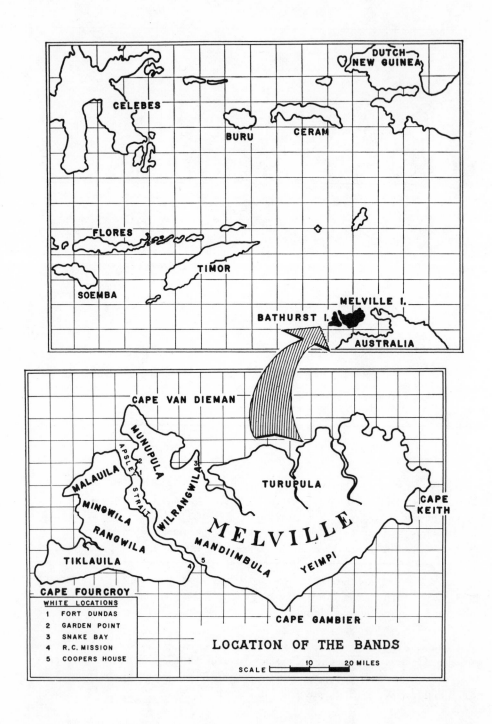

CELEBES

BURU   CERAM

DUTCH NEW GUINEA

FLORES

TIMOR

SOEMBA

MELVILLE I.

BATHURST I.

AUSTRALIA

CAPE VAN DIEMAN

MUNUPULA

APSLEY STRAIT

MALAUILA

MINGWILA

RANGWILA

TIKLAUILA

WILRANGWILA

TURUPULA

CAPE KEITH

MELVILLE

MANDIIMBULA

YEIMPI

CAPE FOURCROY

CAPE GAMBIER

WHITE LOCATIONS
1   FORT DUNDAS
2   GARDEN POINT
3   SNAKE BAY
4   R.C. MISSION
5   COOPERS HOUSE

LOCATION OF THE BANDS

SCALE   10   20 MILES

Contents

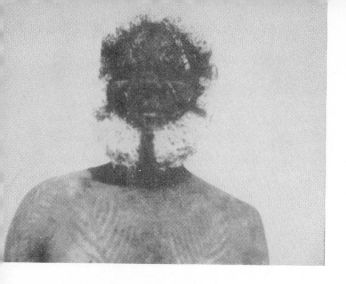

Top to bottom: Timalarua, the canoe maker; Tiwi spears; mourning ceremony around graveposts.

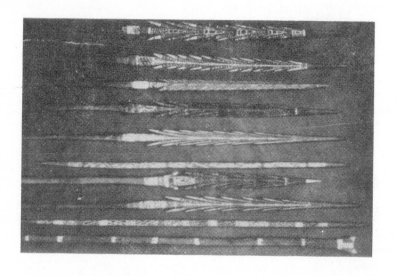

Introduction:

The Australian Aborigines

The First Men in Australia

THOUGH EUROPEAN SEAFARERS, particularly the Portuguese and the Dutch, had sighted and even landed upon the shores of Australia at much earlier dates, the first real knowledge of Australia and what it contained was brought back to Europe by the great English explorer, Captain James Cook, as a result of his voyage of 1769-71. During that voyage, Cook surveyed and mapped most of the long eastern coastline of the island continent, and since he was a keen scientist himself and also had on board several naturalists, including the noted botanist Sir Joseph Banks, the wonders of the new country—its peculiar flora and fauna and its strange, primitive human inhabitants—were carefully examined and described for the first time. We may therefore fix the bringing of the Australian native peoples to the attention of the Western world as dating from Cook's discovery of 1770.

By that date, most of the rest of the world was known and at least some rough notions of what the existing races looked like were held by educated Europeans. Captain Cook and the naturalists with him were therefore quick to realize that the Australian natives, both in their physical appearance and way of life, were distinct from any people elsewhere. Dark skinned and wide nosed as they were, their low brows and wavy hair (including luxuriant beards) clearly differentiated them from the African Negroes, while the general crudity of their culture distinguished them from the dusky islanders of the Pacific. Physical type different from anybody else, culture simpler and more primitive—these were the two predominant impressions which the Australian natives made on the first Europeans to associate with them and they are still, to modern anthropologists, the two basic features that must be used when trying to place the Australians within the racial and cultural history of mankind.

Why the Australians—when finally discovered by the Europeans—should be so different in physical type and so primitive in culture compared with most of the world is usually explained by employing the same concept that scientists use to account for the continued survival in Australia of eucalyptus trees, kangaroos, koala bears, and the duck-billed platypus—namely, the long-continued isolation of early forms, which elsewhere have either died out or changed into something a little more modern. Australia is a large and geologically an ancient country, but in relation to the other large land masses on the earth, it is very "cut-off" and remote. Recent white settlement in Australia has built up large modern cities which are similar in many respects to those in America. During World War II, American troops stationed in these Australian cities were astonished to find so many of their cherished American institutions —department stores, drug stores, movie theaters—located in a country "so far from everywhere." It is this isolation that accounts for the preservation in Australia of plants, animals, and a native race which, deprived of contact with the rest of the world until recently, developed or retained characteristics which are unique in the modern world.

Most of what we know about the first entry of men into Australia is based on probability and inference. Since Australia is in such an out-of-the-way corner of the earth's surface, man is not likely to have originated there. He must therefore have migrated—probably accidentally—from somewhere else. A glance at a world map will show that this migration can hardly have been from any continent other than Asia. The long chain of islands stretching down into the Pacific from the neighborhood of Singapore suggests the obvious migration route. There was a time in the geological past when many of these islands were joined to each other by land bridges which also tied them to Asia and Australia, so that early animals such as marsupials were able to walk (or hop) from Asia to Australia without getting their feet wet. But these land connections disappeared under the ocean long before the appearance of man on earth, and therefore the early ancestors of the Australians, in moving down from Asia through the islands, must have encountered stretches of open ocean on their route. Such inferences pose the general shape of the problem. The early Australians came from Southeast Asia; they came, part of the way at least, by water, and they must have remained isolated in Australia after their arrival.

How early in terms of years these first humans reached Australia can be inferred from indirect evidence. The crucial point is the simplicity of the Australians' tools and weapons. Present-day anthropology does not subscribe to the idea that human technological development has only been along a single line (the doctrine of unilineal cultural evolution), but nonetheless in a rough sense the presence or absence of certain basic pieces of human technology can be used as time indicators. When the Europeans first encountered the natives of southeastern Australia in the 1700's, the following items of technology were completely lacking among them: all use of metal, agriculture, domestic animals (except the dog), pottery, and the bow and arrow. As they had none of these in 1700, the belief is that their ancestors had none of them when they first arrived. Since those ancestors came from Asia via the islands, they must have left Asia before these items of culture were invented or known there. Agriculture, pottery, and metal using were developed comparatively late in human history, but the absence of knowledge of the bow and arrow in the southern parts of Australia is particularly notable since this weapon is relatively ancient and very wide-spread among hunting and gathering peoples. Moreover, its value to hunters is so great that it is unlikely to be given up. Hence, we infer that the earliest Australians migrated down from Southeast Asia at a time so early that knowledge of the bow and arrow had not yet reached that area. Evidence regarding the origin of the bow and arrow is still not certain. In Western Europe this weapon is usually dated as first appearing in the Mesolithic Period (roughly 20,000–6,000 B.C.). Dr. Kroeber includes the bow among the artifacts which the first ancestors of the American Indians carried across Bering Straits around 15,000 B.C. This last date will suffice as an approximation. By 15,000 B.C. the bow and arrow were present in Northeast Asia (that is, the section lying towards Bering Straits) and probably were also known in Southeast Asia. We may hazard the conclusion, therefore, that the ancestors of the Australians must have already left the vicinity of the Asiatic mainland by that date. This leads to the inference that when discovered by Captain Cook in 1770, the Australians had been in Australia for something like 17,000 years,[1] having drifted down from the mainland of Asia possessing only the primitive technological equipment that the rest of the world had evolved at that time. Having arrived "at the end of the line" in Australia, they could go no further, and survived there in isolation, keeping, but not improving upon, the simple technology they had brought with them.

But why were they left alone while other peoples, at later dates, with improved tools and weapons (including the bow and arrow) occupied the islands behind them and beyond them? For today the island chain from the mainland of Asia down to New Guinea and the numerous island groups further out into the Pacific (Melanesia, Micronesia, and Polynesia) are occupied by peoples who not only differ from the Australians in physical type but also possess such cultural items as the bow and arrow, agriculture, domesticated pigs, pottery, and many others, which were unknown in Australia. The answer to this second part of the problem seems to hinge upon the types of ocean transportation employed by these early migrants.

In reconstructing the early culture history of the Pacific region, it is impossible to operate without one general assumption—namely, that the type of tools (including the type of canoe) possessed by a given native people when the white man first arrived was approximately the same as that which the early ancestors of those people brought with them when they first entered the area in question. (This assumption can, of course, only be made if there is strong supporting evidence that changes in the tools (and canoes) *after arrival* were minimal or superficial.) On this assumption the early Australians

---

[1] So far, very little archaeological investigation has been carried out in Australia. The earliest dated cultural material from the continent is about 8,500 years old. However, Australian archaeologists have located human artifacts which apparently are earlier than this dated culture.

are thought to have arrived in the type of canoes that were still in use by their descendants in the 1700's. These craft, mostly in use in Cook's time on the northern and eastern coasts and the inland waterways, were called canoes by courtesy but were incredibly frail. They consisted of a single sheet of bark bent roughly into the shape of a boat, laced together at the ends, caulked with wild honeycomb or some vegetable gum, their sides held apart by a few sticks. Such "canoes" are little better than rafts; even in calm water they are likely to swamp, capsize, or disintegrate, and the only thing that can be said for them is that when swamped or capsized, the bark will still float, enabling the occupants to cling to the remains, at least briefly. Hanging on to a swamped sheet of bark is not an activity that merits the name sea-faring, and in the shark-invested waters around the Australian coastline and in the crocodile-infested rivers of the north it is not conducive to survival. Such canoes were until recently in use here and there by Australians as these craft could be very quickly constructed. But today where the natives use canoes, those made of bark have been replaced by the dugout canoe.[2] No Australian would willingly have ventured very far from land in a bark canoe, and therefore, as we said earlier, the crossing of open stretches of ocean by the first Australians on their migration down from Asia through the Indonesian islands must have been accidental and involuntary, by being blown or carried on, whether they liked it or not. In short, they finally reached the Australian coastline as castaways drifting in from the islands to the northwest or north.[3]

When they arrived on the North Australian coast, their sea wanderings were over, for they possessed no boats which could carry them onward to the far-off Pacific Islands. These first human occupants of Australia had to make the best of the inhospitable country they found. They moved into the large, empty land mass before them and their descendants remained there without much alteration in their way of life for succeeding millennia. Those who stayed near the coast or found rivers to settle along retained the use of crude bark canoes, while those who reached the desert interior forgot about them entirely.

Such a pattern of reasoning brings us to the final question: Why were these Australians left isolated from the influence of later migrants who came by way of the same series of islands? The answer is that all later migrants—whose descendants we know today as Melanesians, Polynesians, or Micronesians—had much better canoes when they left Asia. Hence they could control where they went and had greater freedom to move on further if they did not like an area where they had landed. Evidence seems to suggest that the bulk of these later peoples, and certainly the Melanesian peoples, came from the direction of Southeast Asia around the *northern* side of New Guinea

---

[2] Lloyd Warner and others have established that the Australian tribes along the northern coasts learned about dugouts from Malay visitors in relatively recent times. (Warner 1937)

[3] See Andrew Sharp who has recently demonstrated this to be true for the Pacific generally. (Sharp 1957)

and therefore never approached the northern coasts of Australia at all, being carried on past the eastern end of New Guinea toward the Solomons and the New Hebrides. If any such later peoples did sight or land on the northern coast of Australia, they stayed only briefly, leaving no trace, probably because the region appeared uninviting. More recently, others have also found the northern coastline of Australia unattractive; these include the Japanese Navy, in World War II, which carefully by-passed it and followed the route of the Melanesians along the northern shores of New Guinea, through the Bismarcks and the Admiralties toward the Solomons and Guadalcanal. Thus the early Australians were left in isolated possession of an empty continent during the fifteen thousand or more years following their arrival.

For those who maintain that human progress is an inevitable movement, it should be noted that all the evidence indicates that during those long centuries the Australians remained at almost the same technological level as they were when they first landed.

Australian Culture When the White Men Came

The continent of Australia varies a good deal in such matters as climate, rainfall, and amount of vegetation, but in general it may be said that well over half of it is country in which keeping alive is fairly easy, even for people of such a low level of culture as that represented by the first Australians. In particular, there were no dangerous animals (except snakes), and much of the climate being like that of Southern California, the country was mostly free of tropical jungles and the diseases that are associated with them. For a primitive hunting and gathering people, the main problem of existence in Australia was lack of water, as indeed it still is today, despite modern technology. At least one-third of the continent, comprising about a million square miles, is arid desert or semidesert where rain rarely falls, and the so-called river beds are bone dry for years at a stretch.[4] Elsewhere there are well-watered areas which provide an adequate food supply for a hunting and gathering people. The Murray River Valley in the southeast and the coastal strips along the east, southeast, and north coastlines are the best watered regions, and these were the areas that supported the largest native populations when the white man arrived. But even in such favorable tracts the population was spread very thin. The best estimate of size of the native population for the whole continent before the arrival of Europeans is that within the total area of approximately three million square miles there lived slightly above a quarter of a million people, giving an average density of one person to every twelve square miles. Since over one-third of the continent is almost waterless and could support, then or now, very few humans, the density for the livable parts is more re-

---

[4] It rained in Alice Springs in Central Australia on New Year's Eve, 1929-30. According to their parents, white children six to seven years old were then seeing rain for the first time in their lives.

alistically estimated at about one person to six and a half square miles, and for the best watered sections as about three persons to every ten square miles.[5] Some detailed corroboration for this last figure is supplied by the Tiwi of Melville and Bathurst Islands who are dealt with at length in this monograph. The Tiwi are one of the few tribes occupying a well-watered and favorable environment for hunting and gathering who have been left in continuous occupation of their native habitat down to the present day. A careful and exhaustive census of them (by Hart) in 1928-29 showed that the approximately 2900 square miles comprising the two islands were occupied and used by 1062 people.

Thus between the time of their first arrival and approximately 1770 when the white men first got to know them, the original group of primitive castaways had multiplied to a population of between 250,000 and 275,000. This relatively small number (for the size of the continent) was thinly spread over most of the land, but was more numerous in the areas where the water supply was good and where the natives had available adequate sources of meat—marsupial, reptile, and bird—and fish, as well as a considerable quantity of wild plant foods.

Basically, all Australian tribes had cultures of the same general type, although local variation had developed as the original emigrants spread out into different geographical environments and their descendants lost contact with each other. The question of how many tribes there were at the beginning of white settlement is almost impossible to answer since "tribe" in Australia meant little more than a group of bands with a distinct language. There were at least five hundred distinct languages (all belonging to the same linguistic family, but most of them mutually unintelligible) which in the total population of a quarter of a million gives an average of about five hundred speakers for each distinct linguistic group. This seems a low figure for a so-called tribe and is probably brought about by the large number of very small linguistic units ("tribes") which early writers report in some areas such as coastal New South Wales and parts of Victoria. Certainly the linguistic units ("tribes") which survived down to modern times and could therefore be studied by twentieth-century anthropologists, such as the Arunta, Murngin, and Tiwi tribes, were considerably larger than five hundred people, but probably even the biggest "tribes" did not exceed two thousand in population.

Scattered in small local groups (bands) over enormous areas of country and armed only with boomerangs, crude stone-pointed spears, and spear throwers, the Australian natives were in no position to resist the white settlers. They were simply brushed aside by the early British colonists[6] who began arriving in 1788, and in the course of the next century and a half, the natives

---

[5] Radcliffe-Brown 1930.

[6] There is an interesting link between American history and the first white settlement in Australia. Prior to the Revolutionary War, Great Britain deported her worst criminals to convict settlements in the colony of Georgia. After American independence, she had to find a new dumping ground to relieve the overcrowding in the British jails and established her new convict settlement at Botany Bay near the present city of Sydney on the east coast of Australia.

disappeared entirely from much of the landscape. Since the British settled first in the well-watered fertile areas of the east and southeast, it was the tribes of these regions who disappeared earliest, so that in the present state of Victoria which once contained a comparatively dense native population, an aborigine at the present time is about as rare as a full-blood Indian in Massachusetts and for much the same reasons.

White settlement in Australia since Cook's discovery of the fertile southeast corner has tended, however, to be very localized and uneven. The lack of water in the desert and semidesert areas has continued to hamper or inhibit white occupation. Moreover, even in some places where the rainfall is relatively high, such as the northern and northwestern coastlines, isolation has continued to make these regions unattractive to any heavy white intrusion. In American terms, such lands have remained until the present day as frontier areas ("The Outback" is what the Australian city dwellers call them) and in such regions the native or aborigine ("abo" in Australian slang) can still be found, often in surprisingly large numbers and in many cases still practicing and adhering to many of the traditional customs of his ancestors. In the central desert regions the western neighbors of the Arunta continue to practice something not far removed from their aboriginal tribal life on land which the white man regards as useless for settlement purposes. Further north, in the area called Arnhem Land, on the western side of the Gulf of Carpentaria, there exists an enormous stretch of inaccessible but not at all hopeless country in which the whites have shown very little interest and in which native tribes such as the Murngin (studied by Lloyd Warner) still retain much of their traditional culture. Similarly, to the west of Arnhem Land, along the coastline and on islands lying offshore, isolation and lack of white settlement have permitted a number of tribes to continue down to the present time relatively untouched by European influences. Since the annual rainfall along the northern coast is appreciable and reliable, some of these tribes live in country that is much more favorable to hunters and gatherers than is the desert area inhabited by the Arunta and their neighbors. Among these north-coast tribes the people occupying Melville and Bathurst Islands and who call themselves Tiwi have twice been studied by modern anthropologists—by Hart in 1928-30 and by Pilling in 1953-54. The brief account which follows is presented with two main objectives in view: first, to explain how this Australian culture operated as a going concern in aboriginal times, and second, to analyze what has happened to it as it was brought into contact with the modern world.

Tiwi Marriage

Cultural Isolation

PEOPLE WHO LIVE in the congested cities and towns of the modern world have difficulty in realizing how different life can be at the hunting and gathering level of human existence. The basic fact about the life of hunters and gatherers is the thinly spread-out manner in which they live and the isolation of families and households from each other. In the case of the Tiwi, these conditions of isolation and dispersal were accentuated by their island habitat. Melville and Bathurst Islands lie off the northern coast of Australia some fifty to eighty miles from Darwin, which is the administrative capital of the empty north. They are separated from the mainland by about twenty-five miles of open sea at the narrowest part. This distance is slightly greater than the distance that separates England from France at the Straits of Dover, and just as the dim outline of coastal France can be seen from England on clear days, so the dim outline of the Australian mainland can be seen from the southern edges of the islands. However, Tiwi tradition is firm and certain that before the white man's arrival there was no contact between the islands and the mainland. To them, the dimly seen coastline of Australia was *Tibambinumi,* the home of the dead, to which all Tiwi souls went after death. It follows from this they they regarded the inhabited world as composed of their own two islands, and on those islands they lived a self-contained and exclusive existence. Occasionally outsiders appeared, either castaways from surrounding areas, including presumably the Australian mainland, and in recent centuries, fishing boats and pirates from Indonesia, loosely called "Malays" in the literature. To such visitors from outside, the Tiwi were consistently and implacably hostile. Their own traditions and what little written history there is of "Malay" penetration into the Arafura Sea both tell the same story. Outsiders who landed on the islands were massacred or vigorously resisted. Whether they were classified as *Malai-ui* ("Malays") or *Wona-rui*

(Australian aborigines from the mainland) they were not Tiwi and hence not real people, or at least not human enough to share the islands with the chosen people who owned them.

Thus, the word "Tiwi" did not mean "people" in the sense of all human beings, but rather "we, the only people," or the chosen people who live on and own the islands, as distinct from any other alleged human beings who might show up from time to time on the beaches. This exclusion of outsiders from real "us-ness" and hence from real "human-ness" was continued when the Europeans began to arrive in the early nineteenth century, and certainly as late as 1930 the Tiwi continued to call and think of themselves as Tiwi, *the* people, and to use other words for all non-Tiwi, whether they were mainland aborigines, Malay fishermen, Japanese pearl-divers, French priests, or British officials, who penetrated into their exclusive little cosmos.

Their firm tradition that the twenty-five miles of ocean were adequate to isolate them from the mainland is confirmed by certain objective distributional evidence. Several characteristic features of mainland native technology were absent on Melville and Bathurst Islands, notably the spear thrower and the curved (or return) boomerang. To anthropologists, the idea of an Australian tribe lacking spear throwers and curved boomerangs is almost a contradiction in terms, and the only feasible explanation is isolation and hence failure of these mainland traits to diffuse to the islands.[1]

That no culture stands absolutely still in its technology no matter how isolated it may be is suggested by the fact that the Tiwi, while lacking the spear thrower and curved boomerang of the mainland, elaborated their wooden spears to a complexity of design and a degree of decoration unknown on the mainland, and also developed a much greater assortment of straight throwing sticks, made of hardwood, than any mainland tribe. Moreover, their carved and elaborately painted grave posts are unique among Australian tribes, and point up both the Tiwi isolation from the mainland and the favorable food situation which permitted the leisure time necessary to manufacture the elaborate posts as well as the elaborate ceremonial spears. In the nontechnological aspects of their culture we find in many respects the same absence of mainland traits and the same elaboration of traits that were distinctively or even uniquely Tiwi. Male initiation ceremonies on the mainland focus upon circumcision or subincision or both; neither custom was practiced by the Tiwi, who instead included in their initiation ritual the forcible plucking out of the pubic hair of the novice. The degree of plural marriages achieved under their marriage rules was far greater than anything reported for the mainland; the absolute prohibition of any female, regardless of age, being without a husband was unknown elsewhere in Australia; certain features of the kinship system fail to conform to any of the mainland norms, and so on. Wherever we look in their culture we get the strong impression of an Aus-

---

[1] A toy spear thrower, played with by children, was in use, but this may be the result of post-white contact. Its native name—*pani*—seems most un-Tiwi, and a likely guess is that it was introduced by Cooper's mainlanders, being accepted as a toy for children but scorned as childish by the adult men.

tralian tribe that was able to develop within the general Australian type of culture a number of distinct features, some of them unique, while at the same time lacking entirely other features which were widespread on the mainland. Tiwi isolation from the mainland explains the differences and the lacks; their favorable environment explains why they were able to develop certain traits along their own unique lines.

The Tribe and the Bands

Because they were isolated and few outsiders came near them, they did very little as a united tribe. Everybody on the two islands was a Tiwi, and the Tiwi world stopped at the water's edge. Fuzziness on the edges of tribal territory—a chronic headache to anthropologists working with mainland tribes —did not exist, nor did the problem of marriage outside the tribe. All Tiwi, of course, spoke the same language and practiced the same customs and regarded themselves as *the* people; these were almost the only respects in which they could be said to do anything as a tribal unit. There was no tribal government, there were no tribal officials, and no occasions which required the whole tribe to assemble together as a collective entity. For daily and yearly living, the important group was the band or horde,[2] of which there were nine. The total area of the two islands is about 3000 square miles, but some of this is swampy, some of it waterless, some of it mosquito-infested mangrove jungle, and the suitability of the rest for native living varies a good deal. Hence, the actively used and lived-in areas for each band probably averaged about two hundred square miles each and, in any case, there was not a very close relationship between band size and area occupied. Details of band size at various times are given in a later chapter, but, typically, Tiwi bands probably varied in size between a hundred and three hundred people.

The band was the territorial group with which a man most closely identified himself. Though the band lived from day to day spread out over a wide area and a man might not see many of his fellow band-members for weeks at a time, the average Tiwi thought of the two or three hundred square miles of band territory as his "own country" and of his fellow members as his own people. This is why the tribal name—Tiwi—so seldom needed to be used at home on the islands. It did not identify one group as distinct from another, since all locals were Tiwi. Just as in a New York suburb one does not say that there are some Americans in the house next door, but may say that there are some Texans or some Californians or some people from Michigan next door, so a Tiwi, seeing a group of visitors arriving in his band territory, would immediately identify them as Malauila or Rangwila or by whatever band they belonged to. A father would say casually, "I have betrothed my daughter to a

---

[2] Radcliffe-Brown, the great authority on Australian tribal society, tried to introduce the word "horde" for the Australian local group, but probably because of its suggestion to the popular mind of a dense concentration of people, it has never become established and in these pages we have used the more neutral word "band."

Tiklauila" or "My wife is a Munupula woman"; a mourner would say, "He died when visiting the Munupula and therefore we will have to go to Munupi for the funeral"; an old man would reminisce about being brought up as a youth by his mother's brother, who was a Turupula, and the good times he had in Turupi; and another would recount details of big battles between the Munupula and the Malauila. All of these were band names or band territories. The nine bands thus acted, psychologically, as small tribelets or semisovereign groups, since it was with one of them that every Tiwi most closely identified in his day-to-day life on the islands. It is only when, as nowadays, he leaves the islands to go to work for the white man in Darwin that he has to think of himself as a Tiwi, since there he mingles with men of other tribes. Even then, work and residence in the white man's town does not entirely obliterate band identification. A Tiklauila in Darwin prefers to work with and to consort in the evenings with other Tiklauila, and Malauila with Malauila.[3]

Because of certain peculiar features of Tiwi domestic life, to be discussed below, it is difficult to sum up the Tiwi band in any simple formula. People, especially women, changed their band residence frequently in the course of their lives, and being born into a band did not at all require permanent residence with that band, either for males or for females. Thus the district (for example, Tiklaru or Malau) was a firm, fixed, known quantity, but the people who "owned" the district (for example, Tiklauila or Malauila) were a flexible and constantly shifting collection of individuals.

The territorial boundaries between bands were clear and well known to everybody, though they were not the sharp lines on a map such as we regard as essential for a frontier or a land boundary. All pieces of country—clumps of jungle, stretches of grassland, sections of thick woods—had names. One such piece of country, say a thickly wooded area, belonged to one band, while the more open country that began where the woods thinned out belonged to another; thus the boundary was not a sharp line but a transitional zone—perhaps of several miles—where the change from trees to open savannah became noticeable, with the band territories thus fusing into one another rather than being separated by sharp lines. The Tiwi, so to speak, thought of the landscape as a sort of spectrum where a man moved gradually out of one district into another as he passed from one type of horizon to the next. Since rivers, and even Apsley Strait, a very narrow arm of the sea separating Melville from Bathurst Island, usually have similar types of vegetation on *both* sides or banks, none of the island rivers nor Apsley Strait was a boundary or frontier between bands. The Mandiimbula, predominantly a Melville Island

---

[3] In the early 1930's the situation at the Government Hospital in Darwin offered a good illustration of this. The hospital authorities said they gave preference for houseboy jobs to "Melville Islanders because of their greater intelligence and reliability." In point of fact, some of the younger Tiklauila had established a monopoly on hospital jobs and no Tiwi other than a Tiklauila was ever hired there. The whites thought they were hiring Tiwi but the Tiklauila saw to it that they hired only Tiklauila and felt no vestige of obligation to other Tiwi to help them get these desirable jobs. The alleged greater intelligence of the islanders was undoubtedly due to the fact that the Tiklauila, having had a Catholic mission in their territory since 1911, were more used to white requirements.

tribe, owned also the country on the opposite side of Apsley Strait at the southeast corner of Bathurst, while the Malauila, the band in the northern half of Bathurst Island, conversely overlapped their ownership across the strait to take in a thin strip of coastline on the northwest corner of Melville.

These details illustrate the fact that the band was the land-owning, workaday, territorially organized group which controlled the hunting, the food supply, and the warfare. Until the white man arrived in force in the coastal waters of North Australia, the average Tiwi regarded the nine bands as the main functional units of his existence, and his loyalty to and identification with his band were given much greater opportunity for exercise than any loyalty to or identification with the whole Tiwi tribe. He did many things as a member of a band, but he did little as a member of a tribe. Only when an outsider turned up did he need to think of himself as a Tiwi, and outsiders were very rare. For the rest of the time he thought of himself as a member of his band, thought of his band as his people, and of his band territory as his country.

The Household

Since the band consisted of anything from one hundred to three hundred people, it could not live together in one place, except for very short periods of time. Hunting and gathering in almost any part of the world (except the northwest coast of America in pre-white times) require the human population to disperse itself very thinly over the countryside and live from day to day in small hunting and camping units. Such small primary groups are usually in one sense families and in another sense households, and this is the case among the Tiwi. We propose to call such units households rather than families for reasons that will soon become apparent. It is true that Tiwi "houses," especially in the long dry season (from March to October), were the flimsiest and most temporary of structures, but the group of people in question was the group who lived together day after day, hunted as a unit, pooled the results of their food getting, and ate and slept together. Functionally this group is identical with an American household, even though the "house" they used was nothing more than a few piled-up tree branches, used as shelter for a night or two and then abandoned. Like the American household also, the Tiwi household usually consisted of a man, his wife (or wives), and their children, though in many would also be included a few leftovers or extras, common to all cultures, such as bachelor uncles, visiting cousins, ancient widowers, and ambiguous "men who came to dinner" and were still there. (Tiwi households did not, however, include maiden aunts, female orphans, or ancient widows, since these could not exist in Tiwi culture.)

Thus the Tiwi household was more or less the same thing as the Tiwi family group, but Tiwi family organization had such a number of unusual twists that we find it desirable to insist upon calling such a group the household rather than the family. There was no ambiguity about its "living together" aspect; there were many ambiguities about its kinship aspects. To some of these unusual domestic usages we now turn.

Marriage by Betrothal

In many nonliterate societies, including most, if not all of the mainland Australian tribes, there is a tendency to believe that the main purpose in life for a female is to get married. The Tiwi subscribed to this idea, but firmly carried it to its logical conclusion; namely, that all females must get married, regardless of age, condition, or inclination. They (and they almost alone among human societies) took the very slight step from saying "All females *should* be married" to saying "All females *must* be married." As a result, in aboriginal times there was no concept of an unmarried female in Tiwi ideology, no word for such a condition in their language, and in fact, no female in the population without at least a nominal husband. Their own explanation of this unique situation was connected with their beliefs about conception and where babies come from. Anthropologists have long been aware that the Australian aborigines generally (and indeed some of the Melanesians, such as the famous case of the Trobriand Islands) ignored the role of the male in human conception and firmly believed that a woman becomes pregnant because a spirit has entered into her body. The Tiwi were no exception, but went a step further than the mainlanders in dealing with the dangerous situation created by the unpredictability of the spirits. Since any female was liable to be impregnated by a spirit at any time, the sensible step was to insist that every female have a husband *all the time* so that if she did become pregnant, the child would always have a father. As a result of this logical thinking, all Tiwi babies were betrothed before or as soon as they were born; females were thus the "wives" of their betrothed husbands from the moment of birth onward. For similar reasons, widows were required to remarry at the gravesides of their late husbands, and this rule applied even to ancient hags who had already buried half a dozen previous husbands in the course of a long life. It can readily be seen that these rules—prenatal betrothal of female infants and immediate remarriage of all widows—effectively eliminated all possibility of an unmarried female from Tiwi society. They also eliminated any possibility of an unmarried mother or a fatherless child. No matter where the unpredictable spirit chose to create a baby, whether it was in the body of a pretty young woman, a toothless old hag, or a little girl of six or seven, the pregnant female would have a husband, and the children when born would have a father. The Tiwi were thus probably the only society in the world with an illegitimacy rate of zero.

The practical application of these two unusual rules had certain unusual consequences. The rule of prenatal betrothal obviously gave a great deal of power to the person with the right to betroth, and in Tiwi this right belonged to the husband of the pregnant woman. We carefully say "the husband of the pregnant woman" rather than "the father of the child" because the right resided in the male head of the household at the time of the birth. Although he was ordinarily both the father of the child and the husband of its mother, there were naturally occasions when a child was born after the death of its father, in which case the right of betrothal unquestionably belonged to the mother's new husband. The clearest statement of this rule is to say that the right of betrothal of all newly born females resided in the husband of the mother at the time of the girl's birth. "He who named the child bestowed it."

In most human societies the proportion of males and females in the population is approximately equal, except in the older age-groups where women predominate owing to their tendency to live longer than men. The Tiwi conformed to this norm biologically, but their cultural insistence that all females of every age be married resulted in further unusual features of the domestic situation. No such compulsory marriage was required or expected of males. Hence, the total female population, but only part of the male population, was married. Mathematically this permitted, indeed required, a high degree of plural marriage. The men who held the right to betroth—namely, the fathers of the female babies—could, within certain limits imposed by the kinship system, bestow their about-to-be-born or newly born daughters where they wished, and they certainly did not bestow them on about-to-be-born or newly born males. On the contrary, they bestowed them, generally speaking, where some tangible return was to be anticipated. Put bluntly, in Tiwi culture daughters were an asset to their father, and he invested these assets in his own welfare. He therefore bestowed his newly born daughter on a friend or an ally, or on somebody he wanted as a friend or an ally. Such a person was apt to be a man near his own age or at least an adult man, and hence perhaps forty years or so older than the newly born baby bestowed upon him as a wife. Or, the father might bestow an infant daughter on a man—or some close relative of such a man—who had already bestowed an infant daughter upon him, thus in effect swapping infant daughters. Obviously, the fathers who did the swapping, even if they were not quite the same age themselves, were bound to be many years older than the infant wives they thus received from each other. Or, thirdly, a father looking for a suitable male upon whom to bestow his infant daughter's hand might decide to use her as old-age insurance—in which case he selected as her future husband not one of the older adult men who would be old when he himself was old, but a likely looking youngster "with promise"; that is, a youth in his late twenties or thirties who showed signs of being a good hunter and a good fighting man, and who was clearly on his way up in tribal power and influence. Such a youth, in his late twenties at the time of betrothal, would, with luck, be in his prime as "a big man" in about twenty years—a time when the father of the infant daughter would be getting old and decrepit and much in need of an influential son-in-law who was obligated to him.

There were other bases upon which infant daughters were betrothed, and indeed the father was seldom an entirely free agent, since he not only had to make his choices for his daughters within the limits imposed by the kinship system, but he was also caught in an intricate network of previous commitments, residual interests, and contingent promises made by other men who had had some prior interest in the baby or the mother of the baby. To mention only the most common limiting situation of this sort, the mother of the baby might have been given to him in the first place on the understanding that when she grew up and had a female baby it was to be bestowed on so-and-so or even returned as a *quid pro quo* to its mother's father, either as wife or as ward.

We have oversimplified the situation, but it should be clear that Tiwi fathers, in an overwhelming number of cases, bestowed their infant daughters on husbands a great deal older than those daughters. It is hard to strike an average, but the overall situation is best expressed by saying that no Tiwi father, except in the most unusual cases, ever thought of bestowing an infant daughter upon any male below the age of at least twenty-five. Taking this lowest limit for illustration, this meant that a youth of twenty-five had his first wife betrothed or promised to him at that age but had to wait another fourteen years or so before she was old enough to leave her father's household and take up residence and marriage duties with him. By this time he was about forty and she was fourteen. An age gap between husband and wife at least as great as this, but usually greater, was a necessary and constant result of the Tiwi betrothal system.

No Tiwi young man, then, could expect to obtain his first resident wife through betrothal until he was well into his thirties, at which time this first resident wife would be around fourteen, having been betrothed to him at her birth or before. But it was likely that his first wife's father, who spotted him in his twenties as a "comer," was not the only older man to want him as a son-in-law. As in our own culture, where the first million is the hardest to make, so in Tiwi the first bestowed wife was the hardest to get. If some shrewd father with a daughter to invest in a twenty-year-old decided to invest her in you, his judgment was likely to attract other fathers to make a similar investment. As a result, for *some* Tiwi men, the arrival in residence of the first wife, an event for which they had to wait until their late thirties, was quickly followed by the arrival in residence of a second, third, and fourth (at least), all of them bestowed very shortly after the bestowal of the first. Thus a successful Tiwi, having had no resident wife at all until his late thirties, would accumulate perhaps half a dozen between his late thirties and his late forties as his various betrothed wives reached the age of puberty and joined his household, and from then on he was practically certain to accumulate still more wives as later bestowals grew up and as he was able to invest the daughters borne by his first crop of young wives in transactions which brought in a later crop.

That this is not an exaggerated or overdrawn picture of the number of wives that could be accumulated in the course of a long life by a successful

Tiwi household head is shown by the genealogies of the grandfathers of the present generation. Turimpi, who was born in the 1830's and died in the early 1900's, was at his death the most powerful old man among the Tiklauila. Some of his sons are still alive, and all of them were in the prime of life around 1930.[4] A complete list of Turimpi's wives, not all of them living in his household at the same time or necessarily alive at the same time, contains more than twenty names. But Turimpi was outshone in this regard by several of his contemporaries in other bands. A prominent Turupula of the same generation had a list of twenty-five; the father of Finger of the Wilrangwila had twenty-nine; the father of Tamboo and Puti had twenty-two. As late as 1930, men with lists of ten, eleven, and twelve wives were still plentiful, and Tu'untalumi, who was aged about seventy in that year and was a man of great influence, had by then accumulated no less than twenty-one.[5]

Such numbers of wives as these per husband are very much higher than usually prevail even among the most polygymous hunting tribes. Obviously, a domestic unit with twelve or more wives in it makes for a very large household. Among the Tiwi, a household even of such men as those just named did not contain all these wives at the same time, mainly because of the very great variation in the ages of a man's wives. As far as bestowed or betrothed wives were concerned, such wives arrived at their husband's household to take up wifely duties therein when they reached the age of about fourteen. Hence the first of them to arrive (typically when their husband was nearly forty) would be women of nearly forty by the time the latest of them arrived (typically when the husband was well into his sixties). Even when the husband died, let us say at the ripe old age of seventy-five, there would probably be some of his bestowed wives still under the age of fourteen who were as yet too young to join his household. Tu'untalumi, the man of twenty-one wives, was already about seventy in 1930, yet in his list of twenty-one wives five were still *ali'inga*—that is, little girls not yet approaching puberty—and two were still babies at their mothers' breast. On the other hand, some of his earliest bestowed wives, who had taken up residence with him when he was in his late thirties, were already dead.

Because of this wide variation in the ages of a man's wives, it is necessary to distinguish between a "list" of a man's wives and those actually in residence in his household at any given time. The resident or active wives— one might almost say the working wives—were always fewer than the listed wives. This would necessarily be so even if marriage by betrothal were the only way by which a Tiwi man could obtain a wife. But while it was the most prestigeful form of marriage and the only respectable way in which a man could obtain a *young* wife, there were other ways of setting up a household

---

[4] See Hart 1954.
[5] Finger, Tamboo, and Puti were elders prominent in tribal affairs at the time of Hart's fieldwork. Puti was still alive in 1953-54 and well known to Pilling. Tu'untalumi, held in great affection by Hart, but anathema to the Mission Station, died in 1935.

The most important way is one which we have already mentioned—namely, widow remarriage.

Widow Remarriage

To become "a big man" a Tiwi had, among other things, to accumulate a lot of wives. This required time, in addition to everything else. A rising star who accumulated by bestowal seven or eight wives by his middle forties and then died, merely left a lot of widows to be redistributed at his graveside, and by the process of wealth attracting more wealth, or capital creating more capital, these widows were most likely to be redistributed among his rivals and competitors of his own age group or among men even older than he. Hence, the largest number of wives ultimately accrued to the successful man who lived longest, since he was likely to gather up at least a few of the widows of each of his contemporaries or seniors as they predeceased him.

There was thus a close correlation between increasing age and the number of wives a man had, and the largest households belonged to a few surviving old men in each band. The two conditions, therefore, which were necessary to accumulate a large household were (1) to attract prospective fathers-in-law to invest their infant daughters in you while you were a young man, and then (2) to live long enough to reap the dividends. The longer you lived, the more dividends would accrue to you from one source or another, provided you started off right by attracting betrothals in your twenties and thirties.

But what about the unimpressive young men, the "noncomers," who somehow failed as young men to attract any prospective fathers-in-law to invest an infant daughter in them? As we have seen, even the most highly regarded and well-connected Tiwi young man had to wait until his late thirties or longer before his first bestowed wife was old enough to join him in domestic bliss, but at least while waiting he knew the time was coming. The overlooked or unbetrothed young man had no such prospects. Since the only source of supply of new females was through the birth of female infants whose hands only their fathers could bestow, it would appear as if a young Tiwi male overlooked or ignored by all fathers of bestowable female daughters had no alternative except permanent bachelorhood. Doubtless Tiwi fathers, as a class, would have regarded this as an ideal situation and would have said that permanent bachelorhood was a proper fate for such friendless and hence useless young men, but no social system of such rigidity has ever been discovered by anthropologists. Tiwi fathers were able rigidly to control the marriages of their infant daughters, but they were not able to control with the same rigidity the remarriages of their own widows, and it was widow remarriage that supplied the loophole in the system, or the cultural alternative that took care of young men.

A Tiwi husband was unavoidably and necessarily always much older than a bestowed wife. Therefore he usually died much earlier than she. A girl of fourteen who entered into residence with her first husband when he was fifty was likely to be left a widow by him within the next fifteen years, and even if she remarried a man of the same age as her first husband, she could easily be widowed for the second time while still herself a comparatively young woman. There were several different patterns, most of them intermingled in the same household, for a female matrimonial career, but the situation may be illustrated by the concrete case of one of Turimpi's widows, an ancient crone (in 1930) named Bongdadu. Born about 1865, she was betrothed at birth to a powerful old man named Walitaumi who was at least the same age as her father, if not older. Not unnaturally, he died while she was still a child and well before she was old enough to join his household. Her betrothal was then reassigned, so to speak, to Walitaumi's half-brother, Turimpi, then in his early forties. About seven years later, she joined Turimpi's household as a blushing bride of fourteen, her husband then being close to fifty. In the next twenty years she became Turimpi's most prolific wife and bore numerous children, three of whom, Antonio, Mariano, and Louis, all born between 1883 and 1900, were men of importance in Tiwi politics in 1930, and one of whom, Louis, is still alive today.[6] Around 1900, when Bongdadu was still only about thirty-five, she passed to M., a middle-aged Tiklauila, and was his wife until his death around 1925. By this date, Bongdadu was over sixty and had borne ten children, four of whom died young. Not unnaturally, she was beginning to approach the hag or crone stage of Tiwi womanhood. Nonetheless, she had to remarry, but by now all of the people who might have claimed any rights of bestowal in her were long since dead, her eldest sons were adult men of some importance and able to protect their mother's interests, and clearly she was unlikely to produce any more children.[7] Her chief value was as a food producer and housekeeper and female politician, roles for which she had been well trained in her long years as wife of Turimpi and M.

Old women in Bongdadu's position had to remarry, but they were in a good position to exercise some choice of their own as to whom they remarried, especially if they had strong influential sons to support them in their wishes. There was a frequent pattern in such cases for the widow, aided and abetted (or perhaps even forced) by her sons, to arrange a marriage of convenience with some obscure nonentity much younger than herself and usually a friend or contemporary of her sons. In 1925, then, Bongdadu, widowed three times already, married as her fourth husband one Dominico, a man of no importance whatever, as was shown by the fact that at this time he was nearly forty and had not been able to attract even one bestowed wife. He had, however, already married one widow, so that his marriage to Bongdadu gave

---

[6] Tiwi personal names are polysyllabic and hard for the reader to remember; hence, wherever possible, we have used "whiteman names" for individuals. The frequency of Spanish names among these "whiteman names," such as Mariano or Dominico, derives from the fact that the original buildings for the Mission Station were built by a number of Filipino workmen whom the priests brought with them.

[7] The Tiwi saw no inconsistency between believing in spirit impregnation and believing at the same time that an old woman was unlikely to bear children. It was to them a matter of probabilities, and of course with them as with us, occasionally an elderly lady did—disconcertingly—have a baby, proving the logic of their position.

him a second wife, also, of course, a widow. This marriage is of further interest when we discover that Antonio, Mariano, and Louis, the main sons of Bongdadu by a previous marriage, had some influence in arranging this marriage of their mother to a contemporary and satellite of theirs, and that a year or two before, Antonio had married the ancient mother of Dominico when *she* became a widow. In other words, Antonio and Dominico had married each other's mothers; Antonio while waiting for his oldest bestowed wife to grow up, Dominico with no bestowed wife in sight. The approximate ages of the parties at the time of these marriages were:

Antonio	37	Dominico's mother	55
Dominico	38	Bongdadu (Antonio's mother)	60+

Earlier, we mentioned the practice of fathers swapping their daughters within the infant bestowal system; here we find sons swapping their mothers within the widow remarriage system.

This is a relatively simple example of the complexity of Tiwi domestic arrangements, and we hesitate to complicate matters further. But clearly the last remarriage of Bongdadu (to Dominico) and the remarriage around the same time of Dominico's mother to one of Bongdadu's sons, a friend of Dominico, raise some important issues of social structure, particularly the question of whether widow remarriages of this type are to be regarded as a subspecies of bestowal marriages, with the sons having a right of bestowal over their mothers parallel or similar to the right of bestowal possessed by fathers over their infant daughters. Space does not permit any adequate discussion of this fascinating theoretical issue, but we can point out two factors which strongly deter us from regarding Tiwi widow remarriage as a special case of bestowal marriage. One is the self-evident and empirically observed fact that Tiwi widows, who remarried as Bongdadu and Dominico's mother remarried in the quoted case, were usually highly vocal and pretty tough old ladies who were not easily pushed around by anybody, even by their adult and ambitious sons. Whom they remarried in their old age was a matter upon which they had themselves a good deal to say. Secondly, to any anthropologist familiar with the kinship structures of Southeast Asia and the Pacific countries, there is a great deal of difference, in a society with matrilineal clans such as the Tiwi had, between a father making marriage decisions for his daughters, who do not belong to his clan, and sons making marriage decisions for their widowed mothers, who do belong to the same clan as their sons. We prefer, therefore, to view the overall Tiwi marriage situation and the interrelationship of their two forms of marriage as essentially a system wherein the matrilineal clan had lost its right to make marriage decisions for its female children, that right having been taken over (usurped) by the fathers of those children. The daughters of the clan were disposed of, not where fellow clansmen decided, but where an outsider (the father) decided—thus, bestowal or betrothal marriage. But when the female no longer had a father—that is, when she was old and could only be remarried through widow remarriage—then the right of her clansmen and more specifically her sons (in consultation with her own wishes) to arrange her remarriage became restored as a sort of residual or reanimated right. Moreover, as we shall see, it was in line with their own political interests for the sons to insist on exercising such a right.

Naming Rules

Such a way of integrating the two forms of marriage is supported by the Tiwi rules for naming children, which are very relevant to the issue. We mentioned earlier that the right to bestow a daughter was vested, strictly speaking, not in the actual father, but in the man who named her. Personal names were important in the Tiwi value system[8] and were given to every child a few weeks after its birth by its father or the man currently married to its mother. But whenever a husband died and the widows remarried, all the personal names given to their children by the dead man became strictly taboo, and the new husbands of the widows had the duty (or right) of providing all the children with new names. Since most women were widowed several times in their lives, most children were thus renamed several times in *their* lives, and the names given them by the earlier husbands of their mother dropped completely out of use.[9] Logically under this system nobody would get a permanent name until his or her mother was dead, since as long as she were alive she would remarry and her new husband would rename all her children, no matter how aged they might be. The Tiwi insisted that logically this was how the naming system was supposed to work, and, in fact, the personal names of even prominent senior men did become taboo whenever their mothers' current husbands died. But convenience proved stronger than logic and the personal names of most men and women became well established in their early adulthood as people became used to them. While such names did become taboo when the man who had given them died, the taboo in such cases was temporary rather than permanent, and after a decent interval the name would creep back into use replacing some new and unfamiliar one which might be bestowed by the widow's new husband. In general, the name which thus became permanently or irrevocably attached to a person was the name which a person held when he or she first emerged into tribal prominence or first began to get talked about. For a male, this was most usually the name he was bearing in his late twenties and early thirties; for a female, the name she was known by in her early adolescence when she first left her father's household to take up residence with her earliest husband.

That convenience thus overbore logic in the Tiwi naming system by

---

[8] See Hart 1931.

[9] It can easily be seen what headaches this naming system created for an anthropologist trying to collect genealogies. Individuals would occur in one genealogy under one name and in another under another name, making the task of cross-indexing and cross-checking enormously difficult.

attaching some one semipermanent name to a person despite the rules of name taboo should not cause us to overlook the importance of these rules. In theory, at least, every new husband renamed all his wives' children by all their previous marriages—thus, at least symbolically, canceling out the signs of title of all the previous "fatherhoods" in those children and asserting his own fatherhood right as a new and exclusive one. A widow's new husband was the new household head for all her children, and he took over this position by renaming them all, thus becoming their legal father. If we can stop thinking of "father" as a biological or kin relationship, and think of the word as meaning only "head of the household," the Tiwi concept will become understandable. We will also realize that there is no contradiction or illogic involved in the Tiwi beliefs that male parents were not necessary for conception, but that every child born must be born to a woman with a husband. All they meant was that every child must be born into a household with a male at its head who belonged to a different clan from its mother—in other words, a "father," in Tiwi context.

The renaming of the children by the new household head was not, of course, sufficient to wipe out the commitments made by previous titleholders. Although the new father could and did change his step-daughters' names, he could not change their bestowals. The men upon whom the daughters had been bestowed by the previous father made sure of this. The new father was compelled to carry out the marriage arrangements for the daughters made by his predecessors in the fatherhood role, and there was sure to be a terrific row if he tried to alter them. Nevertheless, he acquired some power over the future of the daughters. The man to whom one of them had been promised by the previous father might die, thus making redisposal of the girl possible for him, or some new deal might be arrangeable in which he could use his new assets— for these new step-daughters were assets, regardless of the fact that their immediate matrimonial future was already settled. The new father could delay his decision as to whether they were yet old enough to join their betrothed husband or even drop a few hints that he did not think the betrothed husband's right to them was quite as certain as was generally believed. Such actions, of course, were liable to lead to violent reprisals by the betrothed husband, but there was always a chance that he would be open to a deal; for example, by giving an option on one of the women in whom he had an interest, he would seek to hasten the appearance of the girl in his own household or seek to clear whatever shadow upon his title to her the step-father sought to cast. Even the last husband of an elderly widow who had already passed through the hands of six or eight husbands and all of whose daughters were grown up and married two or three times already, gained some shadowy rights in the future remarriages of those daughters by marrying their ancient mother. And the validation of these shadowy rights was the fact that as their mother's new husband he had renamed the daughters and he who named them could bestow them. The only catch was, that while he could wipe out all the names bestowed by his predecessors, he could not equally readily wipe out their commitments. All he could do was maneuver within the network created by their commitments so as to try and advantage himself as much as possible by a skillful use of whatever shadowy right in the daughters he had obtained by becoming their current "father."

It is within such a context that the apparent swapping of mothers by Dominico and Antonio must be viewed. By marrying Bongdadu in her dotage, Dominico had acquired some rights in the future remarriages of her daughters, the sisters of Antonio, but since his marriage to her had been, partly at least, arranged by Antonio and her other sons, he would have to share with them his disposal rights to their sisters. Similarly, the marriage of Dominico's ancient mother to Antonio (part, so to speak, of the same "package deal") meant that Antonio as current father had some say in the future disposal of Dominico's sisters when they became widowed, since he had the power of renaming them.

What in effect occurred in this, as in many other cases, was that men of different clans and of about the same age formed a partnership or close alliance wherein "sons" and "husbands" cooperated in arranging the remarriages of their "mothers" and "sisters" by acting as quasi-fathers and treating their mothers and sisters as "quasi-daughters." The partnership or "firm" of Dominico (of the Crane clan) and Antonio, Mariano, and their brothers (of the Red Paint clan) had already arranged the remarriages of Bongdadu (Red Paint clan) and of Dominico's mother (Crane clan), and stood ready to take care of all future remarriages of any of Bongdadu's daughters (Red Paint) or Dominico's sisters (Crane) whenever any of these women became widowed. Each member of the firm was trying to maximize his own self-interest in this and all the other alliances he had a share in, but operations had to be carried out in this partnership form because the marriage of any woman had to be arranged by her "father," and the father, in the Tiwi rules, had to be a non-clansman of the woman whose marriage he arranged. Hence the Red Paint men needed Dominico, a Crane, as a front man to arrange the remarriages of their sisters, and he in turn used Antonio, a Red Paint man, to arrange the remarriages of his sisters. When clansmen made decisions about the remarriages of their sisters, they could only do it by using agreeable nonclansmen as nominal "fathers" and cooperating with them—and the agreeable nonclansmen would of course only come in on the deal if there was something in it for them, as there was for the obscure and unimportant Dominico in the present case. In return for acting as a front for the Red Paint brothers, he got himself a second wife, an excellent food provider though no longer beautiful; he became the ally, even if junior, of some men with assured futures; and he acquired some shadowy residual rights in the future remarriages of several potential widows. Dominico did himself a lot of good by marrying Bongdadu; if he hadn't married her, he would never have attracted much tribal notice and hence would not have warranted mention in these pages.

We find that the whole complex situation makes most theoretical sense if we see it as essentially an institutional struggle between clan rights and the father's rights in women. Tiwi fathers, as suggested above, had taken away from the clan the right to make marriage decisions for newly born female members of the clan. As mechanisms validating this success of father's rights against clan rights there existed two rules: he who bestowed the name had the right to dispose in marriage; and all names given by a woman's previous husband were cancelled by his death and a new set of names given to all her children by her new husband. Strictly and universally enforced, such rules would put *all* control over the marriages of *all* women, of every age, in the hands of their mother's husbands—that is, men from outside the clan of the women being disposed of, in other words, fathers in the Tiwi sense. But the Tiwi system failed to achieve such a result though their rules are pointed toward it. They achieved something close to it as far as infant or even young girls were concerned, since the fellow clansmen of such girls were either (as brothers) too young and unimportant to have any power to resist this alien control over their sisters' hands, or (as mothers' brothers and hence older men) too involved and absorbed in their own activities *as fathers* to take any position asserting clan rights as against fathers' rights. To be successful in tribal life, an ambitious young Tiwi male was best advised to forget his mother and his sisters' daughters (all members of his clan) and concentrate on getting wives for himself. Only by getting wives could he have daughters, and only by having daughters could he build alliances and obtain influence, power, and more wives. To get wives for himself, he could not use his mother or his sisters or his sisters' daughters, since their disposal was in the hands of the men who had named them—that is, their fathers. But there came a time in the life of an older man when his mother was old, and *her* mother was dead, and there-fore the rights of the last man to name his mother had lapsed. And a similar situation would arise in the case of his sisters when their mother's last husband died. By this age, a man so situated was likely to be powerful enough and skilled enough in the rules of the game to exert some control over the late remarriages of his elderly sisters and even of his mother, were she still alive. Whenever this occurred, although the resulting situation might have the super-ficial appearance of clan solidarity—with sons, mothers, brothers, and sisters all acting and planning together as a partnership—such a surface appearance was illusory. The motivations involved in it were scarcely altruistic desires on the part of the brothers to look after their mothers and elderly sisters, but rather efforts by the brothers to use to advantage, in their intricate political schemes, some women of their own clan (their mothers and elderly sisters). Earlier in life these men had been prevented from such manipulation by the control over those women exercised by nonclansmen (their husbands or fath-ers) through the naming rules. Put another way, we might say that Tiwi men as a group had acquiesced to the system wherein "the father" had control over all marriages of his "daughters," because every Tiwi man hoped to be a "father" himself; but having acquiesced, every Tiwi male tried to beat the system, especially as he became older and more influential, by intriguing in the remarriages of his mother and elderly sisters—matters in which, according to the strict letter of the law, he had no right to interfere, since bestowal rights resided with the "father" or "fathers" of these women. One factor which greatly contributed to the setting aside of the rights involved in the naming system was the fact that since, on the whole, old men married young women and young men married old women, in many cases the nominal "father" of an elderly woman was very much younger and less influential than were her brothers, or her sons by an earlier husband. The brothers and/or sons, therefore, were able to override the wishes of their sisters' nominal father since the seniority system was on their side in such contests, even though the renaming rules were not.

Although it was very rare indeed for any Tiwi male to have a resident young wife until he was nearly forty, long before that age he was likely to acquire an ancient widow or two. In at least ninety out of every hundred cases a man's first resident wife was a widow very much older than himself. According to a complete genealogical census carried out in 1928-29, nearly every man in the tribe in the age group from thirty-two to thirty-seven was married to an elderly widow. Many of them had two elderly widows and a few had three. But very few of them, and certainly not more than one out of five of them, had a resident *young* wife. About half of them had bestowed wives, but these were mostly toddling infants who would not come into residence with them for another ten years or more. Even for the most promising and rapidly rising young man, the first young bestowed wife was not likely to arrive until several years after his marriage to a widow.

To get a start in life as a household head and thus to get his foot on the first rung of the prestige ladder, a Tiwi man in his thirties had first of all to get himself married to an elderly widow, preferably one with married daughters. This was the beginning of his career as a responsible adult. The widow did several things for him. She became his food provider and housekeeper. She served as a link to ally him with her sons. As her husband, he acquired some rights in the future remarriages of her daughters when they became widowed. And she, as the first resident wife in his household, stood ready to be the teacher, trainer, and guardian of his young bestowed wives when they began to join him after they reached puberty.

Levirate, Sororate, and Cross-Cousin Marriage

We have emphasized infant bestowal and widow remarriage because it was the elaborate development of these two matrimonial mechanisms that brought about the unusual, perhaps unique, character of the Tiwi household. Other matrimonial mechanisms, more usual in preliterate societies, were also used by the Tiwi but always in combination with or as minor adjuncts to the two basic mechanisms. Thus, a man often remarried his dead brother's wives, or at least some of them, within the institution of widow remarriage. Such a practice is known to anthropologists as the levirate, and tribes are said "to have" the levirate or "not to have" it. The Tiwi, with their pluralistic approach to the whole area of marriage relationships, can hardly be said to fall into either category. To them, every widow had to remarry and among the many possible candidates for her, the brothers of the dead husband were recognized as having a reasonable, but far from automatic, claim. Whether the brothers jointly, or any one of them singly, were able to translate that claim into marriage depended on the other claims. Brotherhood in itself gave no exclusive right to widows, but of course a brother, being necessarily of the same clan and frequently of the same band as the deceased husband, was well in line to assert a claim to the widow if he could make the claim good. Cursory inspection of the genealogies reveals, however, a surprisingly small number of cases of men taking over the widows of their deceased brothers. At best it was a very minor factor in Tiwi marriage customs.

The parallel custom of the sororate—that is, of sisters being married to the same husband—was more common. It occurred both in connection with infant bestowal, by a father promising *all* his daughters by a particular wife to the same husband, or in connection with widow remarriage, whereby two or more full sisters, previously married to the same husband, passed together on his death to the same new husband. The sororate occurred more frequently in the first form than in the second, largely because, as already mentioned, widows had more say in their own marriages than baby girls had, but there was nothing obligatory nor required about it, as is shown by the frequent cases in which a father bestowed all his daughters by one wife on the same man but on the early death of that man rebestowed them *seriatim* on several different husbands. One got the impression, though no Tiwi ever made the point explicit, that within the Tiwi bestowal system the prevailing high rate of infantile and child mortality was an important factor in sustaining the sororate principle to the extent that it did exist. A father who bestowed upon a man the first daughter borne by a certain wife was almost obliged to bestow upon the same man the second daughter of the same wife if the first one died in infancy. Moreover, since most fathers bestowed their daughters with an eye to their own advantage, it was clearly desirable if he wanted to cement the goodwill of a prospective son-in-law, to promise him *all* the daughters produced by a certain wife, so that even though most of them died in infancy, at least one or two would be delivered in good condition at the age of puberty. The aim of bestowal was to win friends and influence people, and a bestowal of a child who died before she reached the son-in-law did a father little good. A shrewd father could avoid this risk by following the sororate principle; a stupid or feckless father who scattered his daughters widely could well end up with as many disappointed sons-in-law as friendly ones, as the infantile and child mortality took its heavy toll of his young daughters. In the genealogies, sororate marriages in some form occur much more frequently than levirate marriages, but nonetheless their incidence is such as to indicate that they were a relatively minor feature in Tiwi marriages and that their occurrence was most frequently due to careful fathers trying to insure sons-in-law against disappointment, and themselves against charges of nondelivery.

No account of marriage in any Australian tribe can go very far without raising the difficult matter of the kinship system, since all the accounts we have of mainland Australian tribes tell us that all marriages there took place within a rigid kinship framework which required everybody to marry somebody who was automatically his or her cross-cousin (for example, a man and a daughter of his mother's brother).[10] Enough has been said already to indicate that in Tiwi marriage nothing was automatic. Females were given in marriage by their fathers, or (to a lesser extent) by their brothers, or (to a still lesser extent) by their sons. But fathers died and were succeeded by the men their widows remarried, and these men renamed all the widow's children, and by renaming them established some rights to make marriage decisions for the females. Therefore, cross-cousin marriage in Tiwi was merely part of the total system of marriage and had to adjust itself to the rest of the system. In theory, fathers could only bestow their infant daughters on men who stood to them in the relation of sisters' sons. Conversely, every man who received a bestowed wife received her from a man who was technically his mother's brother and of course the girl's father. To this extent the Tiwi were a tribe who practiced cross-cousin marriage and their kinship system belonged to one of the commonest Australian types, that which Radcliffe-Brown called Type I, having investigated it among the mainland tribe called the Kariera.[11] But a kinship system of the Kariera type could not accommodate all the complexities that had been introduced into Tiwi life by the emphasis on infant bestowal and widow remarriage. In particular, the generations kept getting badly mixed up, as for instance in the very common case of old men bestowing their infant daughters on other old men of their own age group, and in return receiving as infant wives (or wards) daughters of those old men. With this happening constantly, it was difficult to maintain the kinship principle that recipients of wives were always sons of the donor's sister and donors were always brothers of the recipient's mother. Which was mother's brother and which was sister's son in the case of two old men busily swapping daughters was a problem that put a severe strain on a Kariera-type kinship system. And widow remarriage introduced further complexities. We have already mentioned the case of two young men, Antonio and Dominico, who through a judicious use of widow-remarriage had ended up married to each other's elderly mothers. This was no isolated case; many pairs of men of like age were married to each other's mothers. Who called whom "father" and who called whom "son" became an insoluble riddle in such cases.

To avoid further involvement in the labyrinthine complexities of Australian kinship organization, all that we need say here is that the Tiwi had unscrambled the potential confusion introduced into their kinship categories by inventing a few new terms which, superimposed upon their Kariera-type system, kept everything straight. In Kariera, and generally among all the mainland tribes, no kinship distinction was made between potential wife and actual wife or between potential "in-laws" and actual "in-laws." A Kariera male called all the girls who were eligible for marriage to him by the same term (*Nuba*, usually translated mother's brother's daughter); all the fathers of such girls

---

[10] The definitive work on Australian kinship systems is Radcliffe-Brown 1930-31, and there is a large technical literature on the subject. See also Elkin 1951; Berndt 1955 and 1957; Murdock 1949.

[11] See Radcliffe-Brown 1913.

by the same term (*Kaga,* usually translated as mother's brother); and all the mothers of such girls by the same term (*Toa,* usually translated father's sister or mother's brother's wife). When he married one of these girls he still called her *Nuba,* he still called his wife's father *Kaga,* and still called his wife's mother *Toa.* But not in Tiwi. For them, all potential wives were, in theory, mothers' brothers' daughters and all potential wives' fathers were mothers' brothers. But when a man married any such girl, he immediately called her by a new and different kinship term which can only be translated as "wife," and corresponding new and separate terms were used for the actual wife's father, actual wife's mother, and even for the actual wife's father's sister. Thus marriage introduced for a Tiwi a new set of relatives with new kinship terms different from those he used toward his general run of cross-cousins, mother's brothers, father's sisters, and so on, and these "relatives by actual marriage" terms, being based on actual marriages rather than kinship categories, were capable of handling in a fairly orderly manner all the complexities introduced into Tiwi domestic life by such customs as old men exchanging infant daughters or young men marrying each other's mothers. We may sum it up briefly by saying that Tiwi marriages operated within a general framework of cross-cousin marriage kinship categories identical with the categories of the Kariera, but that females had become such important assets in power and prestige relationships among the senior men—marriage had become, so to speak, such a political affair—that a new set of kinship terms based on actual marriages had to be superimposed on the terms geared to cross-cousin marriage; in cases of conflict or anomaly or confusion in the cross-cousin terms, the terms based on actual marriages were controlling or took precedence. Which is only another way of saying that in theory all Tiwi marriages were rather idealistically approximated to marriages between cross-cousins, but in practice they departed quite far from such an ideal; so far, in fact, that extra kinship terms had been introduced to take care of the relationships created by such departures.

"Disputed" Wives

There is still one more category of wives to be mentioned, a category for which the Tiwi had no name in their own language but which in pidgin English they referred to as "stolen" wives. A few women so labeled were likely to turn up in the "list" of the wives of most big men, but analysis of the circumstances in each case makes it clear that "stolen" was an unsuitable label and that wives so designated were most often in a status that should be called either "disputed" or "shared." In legal terms they were wives in which there was or had been a divided interest. To explain fully the nature of these cases would carry us over into both the Tiwi legal and sexual systems, and here we are trying to confine our analysis to those aspects of marriage that have consequences for household organization. Since these disputed or shared wives had to at least reside in some household and had at least a nominal current husband at any given moment of time, all we need to note about them at this point is that in any listing of a man's wives we have to include "disputed" wives in addition to all the other categories of wives mentioned previously.

The Household: An Overview

In the discussion so far we have selected only those aspects of the Tiwi family complex that had close bearing on the nature of the household. These aspects can be briefly summarized as follows:

1. the high number of wives per husband that a successful man was likely to acquire if he lived long enough.

2. the two distinct mechanisms by which wives were acquired—infant bestowal and widow remarriage.

3. the operation of the bestowal system in such a way as to prevent even the most promising young man from achieving coresidence with a bestowed wife until he was at least nearly forty years old.

4. the tendency for success to lead to more success, whereby *some* astute men received into their households a number of young wives in rapid succession after the age of forty.

5. the tendency of younger men and of nonbetrothed younger men in particular to marry elderly widows while waiting for betrothed wives to grow up or, in the case of those with no bestowals in sight, to enable them to start a household of their own.

6. as a result of the integrated operation of all these customs, the strong tendency in Tiwi households for husbands to be very much older than their wives (as a result of infant bestowal) or very much younger than their wives (as a result of widow remarriage) or—what was commonest of all in the bigger households—some combination of both. Hence many a Tiwi husband had some wives much older than himself, including some already dead (but still counted), and some very much younger than himself, including some who were still babies in their mothers' wombs (with their sex still undetermined). All these dead wives, current wives, nominal wives, "disputed" wives, not-yet-joined-the-household wives, and not-yet-born wives were still counted in a husband's list, and the length of his list was a measure of his influence, power, and importance as a household head.

It is now perhaps clear why we chose to begin our account of Tiwi culture with some discussion of Tiwi marriage. Compulsory marriage for all females, carried out through the twin mechanisms of infant bestowal and widow remarriage, resulted in a very unusual type of household, in which old successful men had twenty wives each, while men under thirty had no wives at all and men under forty were married mostly to elderly crones. This unusual household structure was the focal point of Tiwi culture. It linked together in an explicable unity the kinship system, the food-gathering system, the political and prestige system, the totemic system, the seniority system, the sexual system, and the legal-moral-religious system of the tribe. Or perhaps all these should be labeled as subsystems under the household structure, the master system which unified them. We turn therefore to consider the Tiwi household as it affected the food-gathering and leisure-time activities of the people.

2

Life in the Bush

Organization: Band and Household

THE PRECEDING CHAPTER should convey something of what a Tiwi band really was. The casual way in which people left one band and joined another shows that the band was in no sense a tight political or legal group. Old men preferred, on the whole, to bestow their daughters on men in other bands, but far from this indicating any tendency towards patrilocality, there was at the same time a strong tendency on the part of such selected sons-in-law, especially if they were young and mobile, to move into the band of the father-in-law, partly, at least, to ensure that the donor did not change his mind. Even the faint prospect of a wife was sufficient to cause young men to change bands, and change of band residence by senior men was not at all rare.

The emphasis on widow remarriage was another factor that influenced band residence and made the whole matter of band affiliation extremely fluid and arbitrary. For widow remarriage not only caused elderly women to move perhaps several times in their lifetimes, but also caused their younger sons to move with them. Such unmarried sons preferred home cooking and followed their elderly mothers outside the band if remarriage required the widows to move. Almost invariably the question "Why is So and So (a youth of 15-25) living in Turupi if he is really a Malauila?" evoked the response (obvious to a Tiwi) "Because his mother is there." Conversely, mothers often followed their sons, especially when the son began to acquire young wives who needed senior female supervision. Such mothers divided their time between the household of the son (or even several sons) and the household of the nominal husband, and if such part-time residence in two (or more) households involved part-time residence in two (or more) bands, the arrangement did not provoke any comment, nor was it thought to be in any way odd.

The fluidity of band affiliation was so constant a feature of Tiwi life that almost the only firm generalization that can be made about it is that when "a big man" with a large household had lived most of his adult life in the territory of a band, and had been up to the time of his death one of the dominating elders of that band, his children, both male and female, would be regarded as "really" members of that band during *their* lifetimes, regardless of where marriage took the girls, or where their own life careers or the remarriages of their mothers took the boys. Thus in 1928 the three oldest men of Malau—Ki-in-kumi, Enquirio, and Merapanui—were regarded as core members of the Malauila band. Reference to their family trees reveals that the latter two had been born in Malau to a big man of that band in the previous generation and had resided in Malau all their lives. Ki-in-kumi, however, always thought of as equally a Malauila, in fact had been born in Rangu to a Rangwila father and had moved to Malau as a youth when his marriage prospects had seemed to him best in that district. This move had happened so long ago that only old people remembered it, and as a result all three old men were generally regarded as "real" Malauila and the children of all three would so be regarded all their lives. Such identification would hardly carry over for more than one, or at best, two generations. In explaining the matter, we have had to use the English word "really" in quotation marks because the Tiwi themselves had no corresponding concept. If one asked "Why is he a Malauila when he never seems to live there?" the answer would be "Because his father was, and he grew up there." It was only in pidgin English that one could talk of a "real Malauila" or a "real Rangwila." In Tiwi language and thought, Malau or Rangu was a firm, fixed, unchanging piece of country; the Malauila or Rangwila were the households, of constantly changing personnel, who hunted there, and a man had to belong to one of those households practically all his life and have his father before him also a permanent resident of the same district before his identification with that district was sufficiently close to approximate the degree of identification that is implied in the European concept of a "real" Malauila or "really" a Rangwila.

The crux, then, of Tiwi territorial organization was not the band but the household.[1] A band was merely the temporary concentration in one district of semiautonomous households which were the food-collecting, living-together, and sleeping-together units of Tiwi life. People were not members

---

[1] There has been a prolonged argument in the anthropological journals about the Australian territorial unit, especially as to whether it was patrilineal or matrilineal. For the Tiwi, such a problem could not arise. A father bestowed his daughters where he wished and at puberty they joined their husbands. Where his sons found wives was no concern of the father, and hence where they established their households was of no interest to him either. The father would wish, however, that they would establish their households as far away from his as possible since then he would not have to worry about them interfering with his young wives. On the other hand, it was thought to be "unfatherly" actually to throw sons out. See G. P. Murdock and A. R. Radcliffe-Brown and A. P. Elkin in *American Anthropologist* (*passim*) for the main contributions to the mainland argument, which we think becomes pointless when dominance of the household ties over band ties existed, as it did among the Tiwi.

of bands as part of any political or legal system; they were members of households as part of a domestic system. What held the unit together was the central position and dominance of the father or husband, and hence the life of a household was only as long as his lifetime. When he died, the household broke up and the surviving members joined other households, perhaps in the same district, perhaps in some other band territory. Such change of household was carried out by the individuals concerned, not quite at will, but certainly not with sufficient uniformity for any political or legal label to be put upon it.

Uniformity was derived from the fact that every Tiwi had to live in a household. The universal prohibition on unmarried females was obviously one expression of that requirement. For men, the requirement was less firm, and if a young man wanted to live entirely alone he was free to try—although there is no record of any man having tried it for more than a few weeks at a time. Even if his mother were dead and his father or step-father did not welcome him, he attached himself to some household since, apart from any question of loneliness, this was the only way by which he could eat regularly. For Tiwi households were primarily autonomous food-producing and food-consumption units. A household made its own decisions, camped where it saw fit to camp, moved on when the food quest made it advantageous or necessary to move on. A large household, such as that of Ki-in-kumi or any other big man, was a complete community in itself, with the old man as executive director. He laid down the daily, weekly, and monthly work and travel schedules for the women, the young men, and the children. Most of the time the work went automatically because all the adults and the older children knew their jobs.

Daily Activities

By shortly after dawn each day, the household was up, and after a light breakfast, usually of leftovers from the previous night, everybody left camp to go to work. The women and children (except perhaps the five- to ten-year-old boys, who were rather useless at that age) scattered in every direction from the camp with baskets and/or babies on their backs, to spend the day gathering food, chiefly vegetable foods, grubs, worms, and anything else edible. Since they had spent their lives doing it, the old women knew all about gathering and preparing vegetable foods, and they supervised the younger women. This was one important reason for men marrying widows, and even a man with many young wives was quite likely to remarry an elderly widow or two nonetheless. A husband with only young wives might have a satisfactory sex life, but he still needed a household manager if he wished to eat well. The supervision of the female members of the household was left to the old women and, provided the returns were good, the husband did not attempt to interfere nor to give orders concerning the details of women's work.

After the women had scattered out in a wide circuit from the camp, the husband might hunt, but only if he were not too old. In hunting kangaroos,[2] wildfowl, and other game, keen eyesight is essential, hence Tiwi men did very little hunting once they were past about forty-five, though they hated to admit their hunting days were over. The meat, fish, and game provided for the large household of an old man was obtained by the young men, and this was about the only thing an old man thought his sons or his step-sons were good for. Typically the young man, when he returned at nightfall with a kangaroo which he had spent most of the day tracking down and spearing, would ignore the old man and dump the carcass at the feet of his mother as if to say, "I brought this back for you, not for that old So and So."

As the women straggled back to camp toward sundown with the results of their day's gathering and the young hunters brought in their bags, cooking began and the main meal of the day (usually the only hot meal) was eaten. The Tiwi themselves had no doubt about the close relationship between plural marriage and good eating. "If I had only one or two wives I would starve," the head of a large household once told the missionary who was preaching against plural marriage, "but with my present ten or twelve wives I can send them out in all directions in the morning and at least two or three of them are likely to bring something back with them at the end of the day, and then we can all eat." This was a realistic appraisal of the economic situation and it is to be noted that he put the emphasis on the food obtained by the women gatherers rather than that supplied by the male hunters. Based on the observations of 1928-29, it would appear that the Tiwi ate pretty well, especially in the larger households. Kangaroo and other marsupials, and some of the larger lizards (for example, the goanna) were very plentiful in the bush, as were fish and turtles and dugong on the coasts and wild geese in many districts. But all these were extras or dividends; the staple everyday foods were the vegetable foods gathered day after day in apparently unending quantities by the women. For most months of the year there was always plenty of *kwoka*, a porridgelike dish prepared by soaking and mashing the small nuts of a native palm. These nuts grew in such quantity that in every large camp baskets or dishes of *kwoka*, at various stages of preparation, were always available, even for midnight snacks if anybody woke up hungry. *Kwoka* was about as dull and tasteless as Scotch porridge, but equally filling, and naked small boys full of *kwoka* had stomachs distended like balloons. In the wet season the place of *kwoka* was taken by *kolema*, a yam whose ripening and growing season was much shorter than that of the nuts from which *kwoka* was made. It was on the abundance of the *kolema* yams during January and February that the Tiwi supported the more elaborate of their collective ceremonials.

The abundance of these and other vegetable foods, plus the ample supply of game and fish in many places, meant that under aboriginal conditions the Tiwi lived at a food-consumption level much further above the near-

---

[2] Actually there are no kangaroos on Melville and Bathurst Islands; the chief meat animal is a slightly smaller species of marsupial technically called the wallaby. As the distinction is important only to zoologists, and as many of the so-called kangaroos in American zoos are in fact wallabies, we prefer to use the more familiar word.

starvation level than was the case with many of the mainland tribes.[3] Even to talk about the Tiwi in near-starvation terms seems quite incongruous, for there was an abundance of native food available the whole year around and their only problem was to collect or catch it. We regard the development of their large multiple-wife household as essentially their own evolutionary solution to the problem of finding the most efficient unit of food production. Abundant food was there in the bush in its raw state; the most efficient way to extract it was by a work unit represented by such households as those of Ki-in-kumi, or Tu'untalumi, with the old remarried widows directing the young women and the hunting and fish spearing being done by the younger males.

Even the smallest households nearly always contained at least one old female veteran of the food quest who knew the bush like the palm of her hand and could wrestle some food out of the most inhospitable district. The only households that ever went hungry—and they only overnight or at worst for twenty-four hours or so—were the small households of only one or two wives, especially if both wives were young and inexperienced or young and flighty or both. Such households were uneconomic and were rare. On the other hand, the apparently absurd households such as those in which two young men shared their respective elderly mothers as wives, made good economic sense. Any attempt by two such young men to substitute two young wives or even four young wives for the two old ladies would have drastically reduced the standard of living of the household. When young wives arrived in Tiwi households they were not regarded as replacements for the old crones but joined as reinforcements and apprentices to the skilled workers—the veterans. The sexual aspects of marriage were necessarily subordinated to the housekeeping or food-production aspects, which is why in the previous section we spoke of every young man laying the foundation of his household by marrying an elderly widow usually long before there was any young wife in sight.

Since the bigger the household the more food it produced for its own consumption, there was a tendency for the smaller and therefore hungrier households to hang around the fringes of the bigger ones. Though every household was autonomous and could camp and collect food anywhere in the band territory in which it roamed, it was rare to find all the households in a band distributed evenly over the available territory. In Malau, Enquirio's household and that of Merapanui were usually to be found camped together, since the two men were full brothers and not in competition with each other. Also camped with or near them on any given occasion would be a few other small households. Such a combined group as this would, all told, amount to between forty and fifty people camping at the same spot and remaining together for weeks at a time. Under mainland conditions in most areas, a gathering of forty people for ten days at a time in the same locality was unheard of, except on

---

[3] As was pointed out earlier, the best-watered and most fertile areas of the mainland were the areas attractive to white settlement, and the tribes who inhabited such areas (for example, Victoria or coastal Queensland) were wiped out quickly. Most of the mainland tribes who survived long enough to be studied by modern anthropologists were tribes whose habitats were unfavorable both for native and for white occupation.

special rare ceremonial occasions, because of the poverty of the food supply. The prevalence of such large camps among the Tiwi supports our general thesis that their native food supply was, for Australia, unusually plentiful, and that, in this sense, the Tiwi were a "rich" Australian tribe.

When camped together thus, the various households kept their distance, with the main fires and shelters of each separated by some twenty or thirty yards from the others, and during the day when everybody (except the old men) was out food collecting, the camps were almost deserted. When the food gatherers returned in twos and threes in the late afternoon, each household would cook and eat at its own fires as a unit, but if they wished, members of the smaller households, in which food returns for the day were probably smaller per capita than those of the bigger households, would "drop in during supper" upon the latter and supplement their own slender meal. Such hospitality was always extended on an individual basis; some member of the bigger household, usually a senior wife, would offer to one of the visitors a piece of meat or a dish of *kwoka* and if rebuked by her husband she would justify her act by mentioning her own kin relationship to the visitor, as if to stress that the kindness was her own individual gesture and did not commit the whole household to friendliness. Heads of large households were, however, generally very permissive if such handouts were made by senior females of their household to women or children of other households; it was handouts to adult male outsiders, especially young male outsiders, that were likely to provoke snarls or reprimands from the old man. This was in line with the general hostility of all old men to all young unmarried men that ran through all aspects of Tiwi culture.

After darkness fell, such a camp, with three or four households all resting within easy hearing distance of each other, became highly animated with men visiting from fire to fire as the women, who were not encouraged to walk about after dark, gossiped around their own fires. Little productive work could be done after dark, though a few cooking chores and food-preparation activities were performed, and most people went to sleep early unless the shouted conversations from fire to fire earlier in the evening had started an argument. If an argument did arise, the participants might go on abusing each other at long range for hours, with many of the listeners becoming involved and the rest remaining awake to enjoy the row.

Such rows were almost invariably outgrowths of the constant suspicion with which older men regarded younger men. This suspicion was in turn part of the price the Tiwi had to pay for the efficient type of food-production unit that they had evolved. This production unit, to reach maximum economic efficiency, required the vast majority of all females to be concentrated in the households of a very small number of husbands; namely, the very oldest men. As a necessary correlate, men under twenty-eight had no wives at all and very few men under forty had any wife except elderly and physically very unattractive widows. The efficient economic organization thus obviously created a moral and social problem—the problem of how to keep the unmarried young men away from the young women. The old head of the household had a double role:

he was at the same time the executive director of a work unit which he expected to work for him, and the husband of many of its members whom he expected to be faithful to him. The young wives were willing, under supervision, to meet his first expectation, but found it difficult, even under the strictest supervision, to meet the second. Successful supervision of the morals of young wives was easy to achieve at night because each camp was then gathered together and it was relatively easy for the husband and his senior wives to guard the young wives closely. But during the daytime matters were different. Then the young women of the household were widely scattered through the fairly dense bush and it was impossible for the old wives to watch them every minute of the day. And the young men of other households, or even of their own household, were hunting game in the same neighborhood. Encounters, whether by chance or by previous arrangement, were likely to occur and probably occurred with a high degree of frequency. We say "probably" because no anthropologist working with a tribe which has neither courts nor written records can ever know how often casual extramarital offenses take place. (There is even some difficulty in obtaining reliable statistics on such matters in our own society, as the attacks on the late Dr. Kinsey's statistics indicate.) We therefore make no statement about how common the act of adultery was in Tiwi culture, but we can say that, judging by the public accusations of adultery, its practice must have been widespread indeed. In any Tiwi camp comprising more than two households, few weeks went by without an outraged and angry old husband shouting accusations at one of the younger men sitting by another camp fire a few yards away. The young man accused would (usually) deny it; the old women of both households would enter the argument, the young man's mother protesting his innocence, the old man's elderly wives (who had of course been the informers) giving details of time and place and circumstance; the young man would produce, or try to produce, an alibi and appeal to a friend to bear him out; the old man would call the friend a liar and the youth's mother an old witch; the youth's mother would retaliate by shouting things she knew (but had never before revealed) about the private lives of everybody in the old man's household, including the old man himself when he was a young bachelor. A good time would be had by all, including the listening anthropologist, but nobody would get much sleep. Such nocturnal uproars, always starting with accusations hurled by an older husband against a younger man and always involving incidents that had allegedly occurred while the young wife was somehow left unchaperoned for a short period during her daytime wandering in search of food, were a commonplace of nightlife among the Tiwi; but no case was ever reported, observed, or hinted at in which even the most adventurous and enterprising bachelor had succeeded in seducing, or had even attempted to seduce, a young wife when she was back in camp after nightfall. The deeds were always done in the secrecy of the bush during the daytime; it was the recriminations and accusations that occurred in the public glare of the campfires at nighttime.

Sometimes these disputes or accusations went no further than the nocturnal shouting of charges. Often the young man accused the previous night quietly slipped away to some other camp and was not seen the following morning. The matter might then die, depending largely on whether the old husband wanted to carry it further or was content to drop it. If the young man was still in camp the following day, the old man might insist on a duel then and there, but it would take place only if the camp were large, since Tiwi duels were essentially legal actions and as such needed a sizable audience for their correct staging. Disputes between men, of which old men accusing young men of seduction were by far the most common type, usually remained at the verbal level until a large body of spectators was available. Since such large concentrations of many households were necessary for the performance of the main collective ceremonials, it was at the time of these ceremonials that most verbal arguments were pushed by the aggrieved party to the action level.

During the dry season (April to November) when travel was easy, the only collective ceremonials sufficiently important to draw together a large number of households were those held for the funerals of big men. In the wet season (November to March) when the grass and bush were high and travel was difficult, the main collective phases of the male initiation ceremonies were held (see Chapter 4), and these brought together for a few weeks at a time large numbers of households. The funeral ceremonies for adults were always held some considerable time after the death and burial of the deceased. How long a period elapsed between the death and the funeral ceremonies depended on the expected size of the gathering, and this figure correlated, at least roughly, with the importance of the deceased. Here again the overriding consideration was food supply, since the chief mourners (that is, the deceased's closer relatives) had to feed everybody who came to the funeral while the ceremonies lasted, which might be almost a week. The more important the dead person the bigger the crowd at his funeral, and hence the greater the amount of time needed by the mourners to arrange the catering. As much as a year might elapse between the death and the time when the mourners felt that the funeral arrangements—especially the food supply, but also the ceremonial preparation —were sufficiently well in hand to permit them to set a date and send out invitations for the funeral ceremonies. Funerals, therefore, were not held at regular times but were individually scheduled at times fixed by the chief mourners. They were always held in the dry season, however (except those of young children, to which nobody came in any case), and therefore an old man who had a dispute to settle or a case to try publicly could always depend on a few big funerals being held in the not very distant future which would provide the large audience necessary to make the settlement of the dispute legal. During the wet season the *kolema* phases of the initiation ceremonial always drew a large attendance; the annual time of these was pretty definitely fixed by the ripening of the *kolema* yams.

Hence the verbal wrangles in the small scattered encampments at night, about seduction during the day, could have any one of three outcomes, depending largely upon the determination of the old man-accuser and the demeanor of the young man-accused. If by the following morning the young man had disappeared and showed no further interest in the old man's menage, the matter might end there. Or the old man might let matters rest until the time of the next big gathering of people at a funeral or at the *kolema* rituals, and then revive the issue under such public circumstances that the accused young man could not slip away unpunished. If he followed this second course, the old man went to the gathering covered from head to foot in white paint, the Tiwi uniform for anybody who came in anger and intended to pick a fight with somebody. The decision between these two lines of action lay, of course, with the old man, and while that decision was to some extent determined by how vindictive and revengeful he felt, nonetheless it was also influenced by how this dispute was related to all the other feuds, disputes, deals, marriage exchanges, and so forth, in which both parties were already involved. Like a good lawyer in our own culture, the old man had to consider, before he took the matter to court, who the young man was and who his friends and relatives were, and had to ask himself whether in seeking vengeance for the blow to his pride he might not be doing himself more political harm than the injury was worth.

In arriving at his decision, the old man was influenced to some extent also by another variable, the attitude of the young man. If the alleged offense occurred only once and the young man denied it and thereafter kept his distance, the accuser would probably let the matter drop. Offenders were very rarely caught *in flagrante,* and the evidence of seduction was almost always circumstantial or hearsay. In every case there was some element of doubt as to whether the right young male was being accused or whether the whole story had not been invented by some of the old wives out of sheer spite toward a young wife. The old man had to take such factors into consideration, not out of any abstract sense of justice, but because, naturally, he didn't like to be made a fool of, either by young men or his own spiteful old wives. But he was most suspicious and unbelieving of his own flighty young wives, and sometimes the accused young man was defiant and persistent in his attentions to the same young wife, or wives. In effect, such a young man was daring the old husband to do his worst. Such continued defiance of the seniority system could not be permitted; it became a case not of simple seduction but of subversive activity, since it was a threat to the whole social structure of the tribe, centered as that was around the marriage of old men to young women. When confronted by such action, a Tiwi elder said (as people of other cultures might), "What would happen if everybody did that? We'd have complete anarchy and free love." Hence an old husband, so defied, was almost duty bound not just to seek satisfaction for the private injury done to himself, but to defend the public weal by hauling the offender before the bar of public opinion and denouncing him before as large a crowd as possible, as a public enemy. If the situation became so flagrant that he could not wait until the next big funeral or the next *kolema* gathering, he began calling in surrounding camps or going himself, dressed in white paint, to summon them to assist him in meting out public justice to the violator of the system. When a sufficient number of upholders of the right (that is, senior heads of households) had been collected together, the usual one-sided duel (see below, Chapter 4) was staged and this was usually sufficient to incapacitate the offender and make him decide to move—at least for a while—into some other district. The group thus hastily convened to mete out public justice seldom numbered more than sixty or seventy people (seven or eight households) and having been convened *ad hoc* would remain camped together only for the forty-eight hours or less needed to deal with the emergency.

Joint Activities

This discussion of the alternative lines of action open to an outraged household head enables us to specify the relatively rare occasions during the year when the dull, quiet, day-by-day, food-gathering routines of the dispersed household camps were interrupted by events that required many households to gather together in one place and indulge in joint action. Foremost among these occasions were big funerals and the *kolema* ceremonial, both of which were mentioned above. These were the main religious events of the year, full of dancing, singing, wailing, and excitement. The excitement was the psychological result of so many people being together at the same time, a rare experience in the life of any Tiwi. Since the *kolema* ceremonial was an annual event and even the most enthusiastic funeral goer did not attend more than three or four really big funerals in the course of a year, we may reckon that even an old and important man, much concerned with ritual observances, would probably find himself a participant in such crowd activities on not more than some six occasions per year. For less important men and for women and children the number of such occasions was less than six. The *kolema* ceremonial lasted two weeks or more, big funerals, even when they became the occasion for carrying on other public business, did not last more than four or five days each. Hence we may reckon an average of about a week each for the half-dozen times a really big man spent in the company of a sizable crowd of fellow tribesmen, giving a total annual average of about six or seven weeks at most out of every fifty-two—or a little less than 10 percent of the year spent by an old important man in large ceremonial activities or what Durkheim calls the collective life of the tribe.

In addition-there were the smaller gatherings, such as the funerals of younger men and most women, and the calling together of a number of households to settle a dispute in the manner we have described above. These were collective occasions also but they brought together a considerably smaller crowd. A really big man's funeral was likely to draw over three hundred people or even as much as one-third of the whole tribe.[4] Not only did many

---

[4] Tamboo's funeral in May 1929 (he died in the previous August) drew practically the full band membership (men, women, and children) of the four Bathurst Island bands; almost all the Munupula; many Mandiimbula; and large delegations from the remaining three bands. With such a crowd, an actual head count was difficult, especially of the children, but there must have been over four hundred people present. Needless to say, excitement was intense; more fights occurred, more insults were exchanged, more ancient feuds revived and new ones started, and more food consumed than at any funeral in living memory. At least that was the opinion of Tamboo's chief mourners, but since it was they who threw the party and had to pay for it, they may have been biased.

people come to such a funeral to express their kinship with, and pay their respects to, the deceased, but as mentioned above, many men with disputes to settle or fights to pick let such matters ride until the next big funeral was called and then took advantage of the large crowd to provide the necessary witnesses for the transaction of the outstanding legal business. Gatherings of many households for purely legal affairs, without funerals or *kolema* ceremonial as the main *raison d'etre* for the gathering, were comparatively rare and when they did occur they were usually called by one man, to settle one case only, and hence did not promote the attendance of very many households. Similarly, the funerals of most women and of younger and therefore less important men drew together at most ten or twelve households and a few other individuals, so that the crowd was usually not above one hundred people at the most. A single *ad hoc* legal duel, even when an episode in a long-drawn out and notorious dispute, seldom drew more than this number. Duels always attracted some spectators who came for the excitement, even though not personally involved, provided of course they were camped somewhere in the vicinity.

This second type of collective gathering, of which the smaller funerals and the single duels were the main occasions, might then require the attendance of a household head, accompanied by some or all of his household members, perhaps five or six times a year. These gatherings wou'd each last less than forty-eight hours, and since the people the household head met at them would mostly be people of his own band or of closely adjoining bands, the excitement of seeing unfamiliar faces—people not seen for over a year perhaps—would be absent. We may reckon that attendance at these smaller, more localized gatherings, and the participation in group activity which they entailed, took up two more weeks, all told, out of the yearly round. When these two weeks are added to the six or seven already estimated for the time spent by a busy public man at the large gatherings, we find that even the busiest and most gregarious senior elders spent less than ten weeks out of the fifty-two in collective activity outside their immediate households.

To complete the list of occasions which called for joint activity by the members of several households, we must include the joint kangaroo hunt. This activity was very localized and very spasmodic, occurring only when and where conditions were right and somebody felt sufficiently energetic to organize it. Much of the Tiwi country is a mixture of dense scrub and relatively open savannah; kangaroo are relatively easy to hunt in the latter but very hard to get near in the denser types of vegetation. The native method of hunting was based on getting as close as possible to the animal before it saw or heard the hunter. If it detected the hunter, it fled, and no Tiwi in his senses ever threw a spear or a throwing stick at a moving kangaroo.[5] Only when the animal was standing still and the hunter was close enough to aim carefully at a vital part was the spear thrown. At certain seasons of the year, particularly after the end of the wet and early in the dry season, many sections of good kangaroo country gave very poor hunting returns because the grass had become

---

[5] The up-and-down movement of a hopping kangaroo in flight makes it an extraordinarily difficult target even for skilled white hunters armed with shotguns or rifles.

so high and rank that the hunters were unable to get near the kangaroo. In this event, a senior man of the district might decide to convene a grass-burning posse. To it he invited more or less whom he pleased, so long as he included other household heads of the same band and other senior men from outside it whose ancestry gave them some claim to be invited. At the appointed time the hunters assembled, perhaps ten or fifteen adult men, with younger ones doing the actual hunting and the older ones supervising. The women and children acted as beaters; the grass was set on fire over a big area, and the kangaroos rounded up and killed while dazed by the smoke and the noise. The bag of animals killed in such a concerted hunt sometimes ran higher than one kangaroo per participant, so that every man, woman, and child present was able to gorge himself on kangaroo meat for a day or two. This sudden glut of meat was not, however, the main object of the burning, but a dividend. Even though few kangaroos were caught in the smoke and confusion, the burned-over area would provide good visibility for kangaroo hunting during the rest of the dry season, since the new tender shoots that sprang from the burned-over grass were a favorite food of the kangaroo and served to lure them out of the denser scrub areas and the mangrove swamps where hunting them was always difficult.

These occasional joint hunts, like the occasional small fights and the funerals of unimportant people, usually brought together only the members of households who lived relatively close to one another, so that while they are included in the list of events which interrupted household isolation, they did not, as a rule, involve any interaction between members of any wider group than the neighboring households. Perhaps the whole matter of activity beyond the household and the band can be illustrated best by an actual case. We have already mentioned the venerable Tu'untalumi, an old man resident among the Tiklauila, who as late as 1929, and despite the fact that by then the Tiklauila were the band most subject to mission influence, nonetheless had a list of twenty-one wives. In other ways besides his record of polygamy, Tu'untalumi was a pillar of the old culture. Though past seventy and much too old to hunt, he was a most enthusiastic and indefatigable song and dance composer, and in his zest for ceremonial he made a point of attending every big festival and as many smaller ones as he could get to. The whole tribe respected Tu'untalumi as a big man, liked him as a person, admired him for his steadfast support of Tiwi traditions, and most of all accepted him as a sort of leading authority on ritual matters. When dubious or disputed points of ceremonial were submitted to him, his decision, given clearly and firmly and with much citation of precedent and the distant past, was accepted without demur. His presence at a gathering located outside his own district was always a source of gratification to the household which had convened the gathering. The fact that Tu'untalumi had seen fit to attend not only made that household feel important but also provided its members with a technical guide and arbiter for unofficial help in running the rituals. The old man loved going to parties—and he was always a welcome guest—and years of such activity had given him such a sturdy, wiry constitution that despite his near-seventy-five years he could outdance and out-sing and out-party most of the men fifty years younger than himself.[6]

Since Tu'untalumi was a senior Tiwi household head who spent more of his time attending festivals, funerals, fights, and other collective occasions than did most of his contemporaries, it is instructive to examine his movements over a full year. If he had kept an engagement book during 1928-29, it would have looked something like this:

Early April (end of wet season): Leaves his home base in Tangio where he has spent most of the wet season and visits the Mission station to attend a few small funerals (children who have died at the Mission in the preceding months). During these funerals a series of fights and duels also takes place. Total people present: perhaps fifty or sixty. Time thus spent in helping to wind up public business: five days. Returns home to Tangio and remains there for rest of April.

End of April: Goes to Rangu with a big party of other Tiklauila for a funeral (junior elder). Fairly big funeral, lots of people, lots of disputes. Time away, including leisurely journey to and from Rangu, about two weeks. Gets back home about middle of May.

Middle of May—end of June: Lives quietly at home with his household in Tangio.

About July 1st: Goes to Mission for a few days, "visits" with whoever is there. Tries out a new composition of his own (song and dance) on group camped at Mission. Returns home for rest of July.

Last week of July: Taking his younger wives and their children with two senior wives in charge of them, sets out for Malau for a big funeral with lots of people and fights. There he performs his new dance; is much consulted on ceremonial matters by the Malauila; gets into a few fights himself but handles them with dignity and honor; remains in Malau two weeks; stops off to visit and attend a small funeral with the Munupula on his way back; has a fight with a Munupula while there; returns to the Mission; stays there a day or two dispensing all the news from Malau and Munupi to those camped there; issues invitations for a grass burning in some sections of Tangio which were not burned in April or May. Goes on home to Tangio where some of his older wives have remained during his absence. Total time away: about three weeks.

End of August: Is joined in Tangio by several other Tiklauila and Rangwila households whom he has invited. Grass burning and joint kangaroo hunting goes on for four or five days. Dancing and partying at night. After five days most of visiting group leave and he and his household remain alone in Tangio until well into October.

---

[6] There is no suggestion that Tu'untalumi was in any way an official ritual leader. All old men, by virtue of their years, were to some extent ritual leaders; he had merely worked harder and longer at it than most of them. His tirelessly joyful personality had a good deal to do with his success in the self-established role. In a culture that might be thought likely to make all its men gloomy, anxiety-ridden introverts, he was a warm, happy, dignified old extrovert and he was widely admired.

Middle of October: Rains about to commence. Last chance for travel before the wet season. Goes to another district for the naming ceremony of a new baby (he is its mother's father, having bestowed the mother on the man now naming the child). Goes on from there to the Mission. Finds a large party there about to visit the Mandiimbula on Melville Island, ostensibly for a funeral but really for a big argument since Tiklauila-Mandiimbula relations were badly strained at this time.[7] Joins this party. They go in force to the Mandiimbula country. Big fight. He is not much involved in the fighting, concentrates on the dancing.

End of October: Returns to Mission. War party disbands. He returns home to Tangio and remains there until the initiation ceremonies begin in late January. During this period (November-January) makes occasional very short visits to neighboring households and is occasionally visited by neighbors who drop in on him from no great distance away.

End of January: *Kolema* phase of initiation begins. As guardian of ritual, he is in much demand by the various groups with boys of suitable age. All the Tiklauila and Rangwila households gather together (about 300 people) for nearly four weeks to conduct these ceremonies. Much feasting, much dancing, he in the center of everything. Very few fights or disputes, which is the way he likes it.

End of February: Finish of *kolema* season. Finish of ceremonies. Households disperse. He and his household return to Tangio and remain there for the balance of the wet season, which usually ends toward the end of March.

During the year for which we have listed the details, Tu'untalumi attended three big funerals, one big *kolema* ritual, and several small funerals, and made a few other miscellaneous visits to other districts. In addition, he was the host at a joint kangaroo hunt in his own district and attended the naming ceremony of one of his daughters' children. He also was a member of one war party. Although this hectic social whirl totals up to about thirteen weeks spent away from home or with a large party of guests in the home, even the busy and popular Tu'untalumi spent about thirty-nine weeks out of the year living alone with his household and seeing nobody except members of that household. Since there were few other Tiwi as gregarious as he, we may take this figure as an outside limit and conclude that the great majority of "big men" spent at least four-fifths of their time in the isolated environment of the single household, engaged largely in the daily routine of getting a living and supervising their wives and children in their unending food quest.

---

[7] We have tried to keep out of the text those factors in the 1928-30 situation which were clearly due to post-white influences, and this friction was of that order. Briefly, Mandiimbula fathers with daughters bestowed on Tiklauila husbands were failing to deliver the girls at puberty to those husbands, hoping instead to hire them out as prostitutes to the Japanese pearling boats which periodically visited the Mandiimbula and Yeimpi beaches in search of women. See Chapter 6 for a full discussion of this outside influence as well as that of the Mission, which (for different reasons and motives) was also in the girl-buying business at this time.

The mobility of people other than household heads was much less. Women and children could move only with the permission, and usually in the company, of their lord and master. Occasionally old and trusted wives might be sent, unsupervised, on a journey by their husbands or their brothers, usually to carry messages and bring back gossip, but young wives were never trusted to be out of sight either of the husband or of elderly female supervisors. Young men were less subject to their fathers' orders and hence were fairly free to come and go as they pleased, but the universal suspicion which all husbands bore toward wandering young men put severe restrictions on their mobility and prevented them attaching themselves to any household or camp in which they did not have some close relative.

The fact, then, that a man like Tu'untalumi was (in Tiwi terms) very mobile did not necessarily mean that members of his household shared his degree of mobility. When he took most of his large household with him on his journeys away from home, as he often did, it was always because he was going a considerable distance and was traveling slowly, living off the country as he went. In such cases he liked to have a large retinue to feed him on the way and also to permit him to entertain in fitting style when he arrived. For while it was true that at a funeral or at an initiation the relatives of the deceased or of the novices were supposed to take care of the feeding of all the visitors, nonetheless, wealthy and generous men like Tu'untalumi believed in taking along with them a bevy of young wives, with a couple of efficient elderly widow-wives in charge of them, to contribute to the food-getting and food-preparing activities. Of course the supervision of the young wives' morals in the strange environment was often difficult, especially in the hectic atmosphere of a big ceremonial, but this worry was compensated for by the fact that the visitor who came so attended was contributing a number of extra food providers to the labor force of the harassed hosts and thus making a generous gesture, and also by the fact that such a visitor was not dependent upon the hospitality provided by the hosts. Having his own food-producing unit with him, he could live better and stay longer than if he had come alone or only as one of a party of men. In this respect, as in so many others, a Tiwi household head's decision had to be reached by balancing against one another the two competing motives of, on the one hand, the desire to eat well and, on the other, the desire to keep his young wives safe from prowling bachelors. Ki-in-kumi, the wealthiest man of the Malauila band, usually decided not only to leave his wives at home but also not even to go himself. But Ki-in-kumi was a gloomy, pessimistic old man. Tu'untalumi usually decided to do the thing in style, travel with a large retinue, have all the comforts of home while in strange districts, and take his chances on the strange bachelors. He clearly believed that a good booming ceremony with lots to eat and himself in the center directing the dancing was well worth the risk of a few of his young wives being seduced off-stage. Men like Ki-in-kumi thought Tu'untalumi an old fool for not leaving his young wives at home, and Tu'untalumi probably thought that old Ki-in-kumi might as well be dead, especially since his death would be the occasion for a really magnificent funeral.

The matter of men traveling to distant camps for ceremonials illuminates again, and from a new angle, the great value of elderly widows in the household. Tu'untalumi, during his visit to Malau in August, was able to split his household efficiently by taking a couple of old wives with him to supervise his young wives on the journey and leaving other old wives at home in Tangio to begin storing up food for the grass-burning project which he intended to stage on his return. It will be noticed in the account of his movements that he began issuing invitations to the grass burning on his way home from Malau, showing his confidence that the elderly wives he had left at home would have the preparations well in hand during his absence. A big man with a big household really needed three or four elderly widows because these enabled him to split his work force in various ways as his various political and social obligations required and to be sure of trustworthy supervision of each of the segments. A man without widows in his household, or with only one, could not do this; in fact, it was hard for a man without widows to attend ceremonials at all, or even to receive a large party of visitors to his household. And, as we have already pointed out, since such a man would probably go hungry very often because he would not dare to send his unsupervised young wives into the bush to gather food, there were practically no such men nor such households. Widows were indispensable to a senior Tiwi, both in his public and in his private life.

Making Things

Throughout this chapter we have been stressing the contrast between the dull routine of life in an isolated Tiwi household during the greater part of the year and the sort of life typical on those relatively rare occasions when something special—a festival, a funeral, a fight, a grass burning, a naming ceremony, some collective phase of men's initiation—required the assembling together of several households for joint activity. Before leaving the daily life of the isolated camp, we should mention one other area of activity—namely, the manufacturing activities of the tribe. The Tiwi did not manufacture much, but spears, throwing sticks, canoes, digging sticks, baskets, bodily ornaments, graveposts, and all the miscellaneous paraphernalia used in ceremonials had to be made in whatever leisure time people could find during the long weeks and months when each of the households lived more or less in isolation from the others. Crude and simple as these artifacts were, their construction required time, and only the older men had the time and the skill based on experience to make the more important of them.

Largely because of their failing eyesight, the older men hunted very little and hence tended to remain in camp all day while the young men were hunting and the women were gathering. There were, of course, some old men who took advantage of this time to do little except doze in the shade, but most of the household heads spent a fairly active day in camp engaged in making things. Here we find another aspect of Tiwi culture that results from the relatively favorable food supply. Some of the Tiwi artifacts, particularly the highly decorative graveposts and ceremonial spears, are unique among Australian tribes, and the carving and painting of these graveposts and spears were skills possessed only by the senior men. They were provided with the leisure time necessary to develop and use these skills by the efficiency in food production of the large household which all old men were expected to accumulate with age, and which many old men did succeed in accumulating. We said earlier that the bigger the household, the better its members ate. We now add the further correlation that the bigger the household, the more leisure time was provided for its head to engage in manufacturing and artistic production. Tu'untalumi has been cited as an example of a large household head (twelve resident wives and thirteen children at home in 1928-29) who loved ceremonial affairs. It would be wrong to infer from this that Tu'untalumi only loved going to parties. He also loved preparing for them, and this preparation (for him as for all other senior men) included the manufacture of ceremonial spears, the preparation of graveposts, and the composition of songs and dances. In the long dull periods between trips outside his home district, he spent most of the days and many of the nights in the creation of these ceremonial necessities. He was not a full-time specialist in the sense that he made spears or posts to exchange with other men who had neither the time nor the skill—the rules of kinship required that every senior man make his own ceremonial spears and contract for his own posts. Tu'untalumi manufactured his graveposts to meet his own ritual obligations, but he took a more magnanimous view of those obligations than did most men. Put in our terms, we might say that he was wealthy enough (in the size of his household) to be generous with his own productions. One example of this attitude was his attendance at funerals that other men of equal kinship to the deceased did not find it necessary to attend; his frequent contribution of an extra gravepost to those provided by the chief mourners of the deceased was a similar gesture. "Tu'untalumi not only came to our mother's funeral, he also made a gravepost for it" was a very gratifying reflection for an obscure group of mourners to cherish among their memories, and of course it was acts of this sort that made the old man so well liked and admired. The economic point of the matter, however, is that only a man with as large a household as his could afford the gesture of giving away, in a situation where kinship obligations did not demand it, a gravepost that required about a week's full-time work.

It was, however, sad to observe that as an artistic producer Tu'untalumi, like many intellectuals in other cultures, tended to operate in too many media. His work as a composer of songs and dances was universally admired, but his graveposts, while appreciated, were not regarded as being as outstanding, technically speaking, as those of another old man, his crony Timalarua. In personality, Timalarua, a successful household head (eleven living wives, ten children at home), was quiet spoken, placid, and only mildly gregarious, and he is mainly of interest because in his leisure-time activity he paid but routine attention to song and dance compositions and concentrated rather single mindedly on making canoes, ceremonial spears, and graveposts. Fre-

quently, on the banks of some creek or river in Tiklauila territory, a party
wanting to cross would scout around and find a canoe hidden in the weeds.
Everybody would use it to cross, and the question "Whose canoe is it?"
would elicit the reply, "Oh, it's always there and everybody uses it who wishes
to cross." But if the question were "Who made it in the first place and put it
there?" the answer would be, "Probably Timalarua. He likes making canoes;
he makes them all the time." He also liked making spears and posts, though he
was not as generous with them as Tu'untalumi. When one of his posts appeared
at a funeral, people would point it out admiringly saying, "Timalarua made
that one" and the speaker would trace the lines and designs on it with his
finger, using much the same gestures as an art critic in a modern gallery.
When a post by Tu'untalumi was identified and admired, however, the admiration was for Tu'untalumi the generous person rather than Tu'untalumi the
artist. One was a wonderful craftsman, the other was a wonderful man. But
acclaim given to the song and dance performances of the two men was just
the reverse: the dances of Timalarua were adequate but not outstanding, those
of Tu'untalumi were in a class by themselves.

Comparison of the activities of these two old men illustrates the im-
possibility of drawing any line, in the simpler cultures at least, between artistic
production and technological production. The canoes and the posts manufactured by Timalarua and the posts manufactured and the new dances created
by Tu'untalumi were all, so to speak, in the same category, as far as the Tiwi
were concerned. The distinction we might make between the canoes as "useful"
products and the posts and dances as ceremonial or artistic products never
occurred to them. All were objects or products which only successful old men
had the required skill and leisure to make. The fact that one old man liked to
make canoes and leave them around for other people to use, and another old
man liked to compose dances and perform his compositions widely for other
people to enjoy, to them merely indicated individual taste and choice; it did
not make the first a craftsman and the second an artist. This point has been
overlooked in most of the theorizing about primitive art; perhaps a necessary
first step in the development of primitive artists is for a society to be able to
provide a few men with enough leisure time to be able to cultivate what might
perhaps best be called hobbies, since a hobby can equally well be something
"useful" to society, like canoe making, or something personally satisfying, like
dancing or decorating graveposts.

The huge, heavy, painted spears made by these old Tiwi men were
mainly used only for display, and even the oldest men were positive that
this had always been the tradition. In fact, they seemed a little shocked at the
implication that such beautiful and valuable objects could ever have been used
for such mundane purposes as hunting or warfare. The cutting and painting
of such spears took time and skill—more time than a gravepost—and no important man went to the smallest gathering without bearing on his shoulder at
least half a dozen of these symbols of his importance. If on his way through
the bush he sighted a kangaroo, he dropped his painted spears and stalked
the animal with an ordinary spear, or more probably left it to the young men

in the party who carried only ordinary ones. The painted spears were symbols of wealth and status and roughly corresponded to white tie and tails in our culture. No important man could afford not to have them, even though for most of the year they were unused. Before leaving home on a journey, it was often necessary for a man to renew the paint on his spears, for it rubbed off easily. Since paint was an aspect of ritual, its use, even the renewal of old paint, was senior men's prerogative; women were not supposed to touch it.[8] The analogy with formal dress even extended to the borrowing of ceremonial spears. An important man, caught short of them, might borrow some from a contemporary who had plenty, and though everybody would know that his spears were borrowed, he at least was properly dressed for the occasion, though stark naked otherwise.

Baskets made of bark with gummed sides were made by the women, but the painted designs upon these baskets were applied by the men, in line with their monopoly on all work that required paint. These baskets of various sizes but little variation in shape were used for all domestic tasks involving the collection, storing, transporting, and preparing of vegetable foods, and were sufficiently watertight to enable water also to be carried in them. Ordinary wooden spears (without barbs or painted designs) and a great variety of throwing sticks were made by all men, young or old, but important old men bothered with them very little, considering such routine manufacture beneath them. These workaday spears and throwing sticks lay around every camp in abundance, and a man who needed spears or sticks in a hurry could always gather up a bundle in a few minutes. Small boys picked up the techniques of making spears and throwing sticks by spending time with older boys who in turn improved their skill both in making and using hunting weapons by spending time with the local young men.

Although much of this learning was fairly random, other instruction was not. During his initiation period a youth spent long intervals isolated in the bush with a couple of older teachers from whom he received training in religious and ritual matters. At the same time, of course, it was inevitable that the novice absorb some of the older men's experience in bushcraft. There was no corresponding initiation period for girls. What they learned, they learned first from the older women of their childhood household and later from the older women of the husband's household into which they moved as child-brides after puberty. In all households the supervision by the elderly women of all younger women included the training of both female children and young wives in the things all females should know—things which were mostly concerned with collecting and preparing vegetable foods and the making of baskets.

In pre-white times Tiwi males wore no clothing whatever. The Mission insisted on calico loincloths, but, at least in the 1928-29 period, one could

---

[8] Female mourners were required to daub their bodies with white clay as a sign of mourning, but this paint was smeared haphazardly over their bodies and faces without any attempt at regularity or design, in contrast to the careful paint designs on the men's bodies.

observe the spontaneous gesture with which men, on leaving the Mission, automatically threw off their loincloths at the Mission fence and headed for the bush as naked as the day they were born. Women, in pre-white days, habitually carried a piece of bark which they held in front of themselves whenever they met a male. As soon as string or rope was introduced by the early white contacts, the women found it more convenient to tie some sort of band around their waists and double the piece of bark over this waistband. This was much handier since it left the hands free, but the bark, being stiff and unsecured, was at best a very capricious covering, and old women in the midst of public arguments often tore off their aprons and threw them at their opponents as a gesture of contempt.

Young women were more decorous and fussed modestly with their bark aprons when young men were present rather in the same way as American coeds fuss with their skirts in crowded classrooms. Theoretically, young women were supposed never to meet either young men or men outside their own household, and so the bark apron, carried in the hand, was in aboriginal times merely something to have in case of emergency. It was noticeable in Tiwi ceremonies that when the women danced, they did nothing with their hands. We think this was because, in pre-white days, their right hands, at least, were needed to hold their bark aprons in front of their pubic regions, since at dances they were in the presence of strange men.

This brief account of the daily and yearly life of the Tiwi households enables us to draw a few important conclusions about their economic life:

1. Compared with many of the mainland tribes, the Tiwi were economically rather well-off, in that the bigger household units were usually able to produce a food surplus.

2. This food surplus varied directly with the number of working wives that a household head possessed.

3. A household head with many wives was therefore, in Tiwi terms, a wealthy man who could retire entirely from the food quest and devote his time to other activities.

4. Such men were able to devote full time to other activities such as manufacturing useful and ceremonial objects and participation in ceremonial affairs and public life.

5. Wealthy men, active in one or all of these pursuits, were the "big men" of the tribe. In each band there were two or three such men, and in the whole tribe perhaps less than twenty had attained full success or were ranked by public opinion as being the most admired and influential. The next chapter examines the career patterns by which every male Tiwi sought to become, and a few succeeded in becoming, a big man.

3

The Prestige
and Influence System

To BECOME a really big man, or even a minor figure among the elders,
a Tiwi had to devote all his adult life to that goal. Careers were built
up and influential positions gained not by executing spectacular coups
at any one time, but by slow, devious maneuvering and dealing in influence
throughout adulthood. Men in their early thirties invested their very small
assets in the hope of large returns twenty years later, and if the anthropologist
witnessed the initial investment he was not around to witness the final return;
or if he witnessed the return he found it difficult to reconstruct all the relevant
details of the initial investment. A man in 1928 bestowed his daughter in a
certain direction because of some deal back in 1900, arranged by men many
of whom were now dead. And the bestowal in 1928 was done in such a way
as to bind the hands of men negotiating in 1960, some of whom were infants
in 1928.[1]

The Tiwi influence and career patterns can best be compared to a sort
of nonstop bridge game wherein the scores were never totaled up nor a new
game ever started on a clean slate.[2] Whenever an observer came in, he always

---

[1] A typical illustration of this situation arose during the writing of this
book. In 1928-29 Hart had observed Padimo beginning to acquire a number of bestowed
wives. Being interested in the status of Padimo twenty-five years later, he included
Padimo in a list of inquiries to Pilling. Pilling's reply: "Re Padimo. I am almost certain
that he was the 'Paddy' who died leaving several widows, in February, 1953, about
three months before I got to the Islands. The natives did not like to talk much about
him while I was there (because of the taboo on dead men's names) and his widows were
still being fought over. The fights over his widows did not end until the week I left (if
they really did then)." Thus the deals which Hart saw in 1928-29 were having delayed
repercussions when Pilling was there in 1953-54.

[2] We use bridge rather than poker as our analogy because nobody ever "went
broke" in Tiwi influence competition and nobody ever "won the pot," because there was
no pot to win. The scoring was always, so to speak, on a comparative basis and everybody,
even the most unsuccessful man, had some score relative to his competitors.

entered in the middle of the game and found the current hands being played with all the old scores back for at least two generations influencing the play of the present hands. The game never had a beginning or an end; every new player had to start in the middle and make the best of whatever assets he had by way of kinship, clanship, household membership, and help from older players. Similarly, any attempt to describe the operations involved or the "rules" of the game must perforce start in the middle.

The "game" was one of trying to win friends and increase prestige and influence over others. The "assets," in a tribe with such minimal material possessions as the Tiwi, were mostly intangible ones such as friendship, "help," goodwill, respect of others, control over others, importance, and influence. Even in our culture such things are difficult to express in concrete or tangible symbols. The most concrete symbol of Tiwi success was the possession of surplus food, for this not only permitted its possessor to make gifts to others and throw large parties for which he picked up the check, but also gave him lots of leisure time to devote to social and political life. Since a man required a large number of women in his work force if he was to build up a surplus of food, in the final analysis it was control of women that was the most tangible index of power and influence. Women were the main currency of the influence struggle, the main "trumps" in the endless bridge game.

It should be noticed that we stress the value of women as women rather than as wives or bestowable daughters. To a smart Tiwi politician, wives or daughters were assets but so was his mother—if submissive to her son's wishes. So were his sisters—if amenable. A bachelor at the age of thirty who had several sisters was a lucky young man, especially if those sisters already had daughters to their current husbands. As successful old men used their infant daughters to gain influence and buy satellites, so young men used their mothers and their sisters—if they could.

Thus the psychological line between the attitude of a man toward a wife and his attitude toward a sister or a daughter was a very thin one. A Tiwi elder had many women related to him in some way—as wives, as daughters, as step-daughters, as sisters, as sisters' daughters, as wards, and as mother—and all of these were part of his assets or capital. The fact that he had sexual rights to the wives and not to the daughters or the sisters was only of minor relevance. What was of major relevance was that they were all women whom he could use—or try to use—as investment funds in his own career of influence seeking. The devious details of Tiwi prestige and influence operations are much easier to follow if one keeps in mind the crucial fact that the Tiwi men valued women as political capital available for investment in gaining the goodwill of other men more than they were interested in them as sexual partners. Some of the more senile elders were quite vague about the young girls in their household; such an old man was sure only of the fact that a girl, by being in his household, was part of his capital. Which were his daughters and which were recently joined young wives was a question that had to be referred to the old wives who kept track of such academic details.

Women were, however, a form of capital that possessed the power of talking back to the investors. As daughters or as wives they were quite thoroughly subordinate to the wishes of their fathers or husbands, and Tiwi wives were as frequently and as brutally beaten by their husbands as wives in any other savage society. But as mothers and as sisters the women were not coerced by their sons and their brothers. On the contrary, sons or brothers wishing to use their mothers or their sisters in their political schemes (typically when those mothers or sisters became or were about to become widows) could only do so with the active collaboration of the women concerned. Tough-minded young widows could drive a hard bargain with their brothers as to where they remarried, since each needed the other to make the remarriage acceptable to the tribe at large and to beat down the other competitors (the dead husbands' brothers, for example) who wished to control the remarriage of the widows. Young girls thus had no bargaining power but young widows had a good deal. Old mothers with influential senior sons were extremely powerful. Any affront to an old woman was an affront to her sons, and some of the strongest influence networks were alliances of several senior brothers, in which their old mother seemed to be the mastermind and the senior sons largely the enforcers of what the old mother and her middle-aged daughters (their sisters) had decided among themselves.

Thus, for women, as for men, age and political skill were the crucial factors in determining their position. Young girls were chattels and as such were passed around from husband to husband. But with increasing age, smart young women, especially in alliance with their smart young brothers, could control their own fate with some firmness, and if they and their brothers had a shrewd old mother (also with powerful senior brothers still alive) to advise them and support them, then the decisions of such a group as to where the girls remarried were very difficult decisions for anybody else to combat or oppose. Not as independent operators, but as behind-the-scenes allies of their sons and brothers, Tiwi mothers and sisters enjoyed much more essential freedom in their own careers as often-remarried widows than would appear at first sight in a culture which ostensibly treated all women as currency in the political careers of the men. No matter how males, both old and young, might connive, they were constantly aware that no remarriage of a widow could ever be arranged and made to stick unless the widow herself was agreeable.

In the limited space available, all we can offer are a few samples of how the influence game was played by a few selected individuals of various ages. Age was of great importance in Tiwi careers and therefore we select our samples from all the adult male age-groups. We have selected them all from the same band—the Malauila—so as to show as clearly as possible the interplay between one career and another for men of the same band. And finally we select men of the Malauila band for our examples because in 1928-29 it was a band little affected as yet by the outside influences—Catholic missionaries and Japanese pearl divers—which were beginning to modify Tiwi marriage customs among some of the other bands.

The Beginning of Tiwi Careers

The Malauila in 1928-29 consisted of forty-nine males and sixty females of all ages. The males were divided into the following age groups:

20 years and below	28
between 21 and 30	7
between 31 and 42	7
between 43 and 55	4
over 55	3
	—
Total	49

Of the twenty-eight males aged 20 or below, none had a wife of any kind, and none of them expected or were expected to have one. This group comprised the male children—boys and youths—and such males were of no importance whatever in the Tiwi scheme of things. They lived in the households of older men and were ignored by the male elders.

The next group, the seven men between 21 and 30, was the group of young men whom the elders were just beginning to take seriously. The younger of them were almost indistinguishable from the "youths," while the older of them were beginning to be watched by the seniors with some interest. Of the seven, six were neither married to a wife of any sort nor promised a wife. One, called Banana by the whites, was a man of about 28 and married to an ancient crone who was childless by three previous husbands, but she was in the category of "disputed" wife since her young husband had only been able to acquire and hold her because of abnormal circumstances arising from the presence of white buffalo-hunters on Melville Island some years previously. Under pre-white conditions, none of the seven men under 30 would have had a wife of any kind.

The years between 30 and 40 were the crucial years for Tiwi men in their establishment of households and careers. It was during this period that men normally married their first ancient widows and the "likely to be successful" became sorted out from the less-likely. As they passed into their thirties, men were allowed to enter for the first time into the influence game and, as the most junior players, they entered it by becoming subordinates and satellites of the bigger and more senior players, or by making alliances among themselves so as to pool their small individual assets.

In this age group in 1928-29, there were seven Malauila men ranging in age from around 31 to 42. One (Tiberun) was still unmarried and unpromised. He was thus (at age about 33) the oldest bachelor in the band. Not unnaturally he spent a good deal of time with other bands or at the Mission in the hope that his failure to get started in Malau might be remedied by elders of other bands or even by the priests. Tiberun was an older full brother of Banana, the 28-year-old married irregularly to a woman whom he had "stolen." A glance at their family tree revealed one potent reason why Tiberun was still a bachelor and why Banana had acted so impulsively and thereby gotten himself in the bad graces of the elders. The two men were the eldest of four brothers without any full sisters and as such they were necessarily handicapped in their career struggle. Elders seeking satellites or contemporaries seeking allies looked askance at men without sisters, for such men could have no sisters' daughters to use in the marriage-arrangements struggle. The mother of Tiberun and Banana was dead, but even were she still alive, few men would have been interested in marrying a widow whose only living children were sons. Widows without daughters and bachelors without sisters rated very low in the scale of desirable assets sought either by elders or by contemporaries.

Tiberun was thus the only bachelor in the 30-42 age group. Of the remainder we select Teapot as an example of another man who failed to get started. Teapot was at least 35, and about seven years previously he had "stolen" a wife from an elder. This wife was no ancient and shop-worn widow like the wife Banana had "stolen," but a young girl who had been betrothed in due form to an elder by her father. How Teapot had managed to get away with her is too complicated an incident to unravel here, and in any case it hadn't done Teapot much good. After presenting Teapot with a baby boy the young woman died, and Teapot, with a now six-year-old son, was more or less an outcast among the Malauila. No elder wanted him as a satellite and none of his contemporaries wanted him as an ally. His mother was dead and his only sister was married to a Munupula elder. This sister in Munupi was his only asset and one which a different man might have used as a means to better himself. But Teapot, instead of using this small asset to get started on a career, had chosen to defy the rules and "steal" an elder's bestowed wife. "Stealing" an old widow was reprehensible conduct in the eyes of the elders; stealing a young bestowed wife was unforgivable. Hence Teapot, since his crime, had received no bestowal, had been able to marry no widow, and was wanted by no one as an ally.

A complete contrast to these two unsuccessful men in their thirties was provided by the case of Gitjara, who was about the same age as Tiberun. Gitjara, it is true, had sisters, and that was always a help. Using his sisters (already married and bearing children to an elder) as bait, Gitjara when he was about 28 proposed an alliance to L. F. B., a rather feeble man about five years older than himself, who was not doing very well in the influence race. The gist of the proposal was that, since both their mothers were still alive and each married to an old man who could not last much longer, Gitjara should marry the ancient mother of L. F. B. when she became a widow, and L. F. B. should marry Gitjara's mother when that old lady became a widow. Perhaps the idea originated with the two old women rather than with either of the young men. Since such arrangements were essentially plots or schemes, it is impossible to determine who conceived them in the first place—old women ambitious to aid their sons or young men ready to use their mothers as long-term gambits to ultimately provide themselves with young wives. Mother-exchange operations were probably first conceived at high-level strategy conferences in which smart mothers and dull mothers, smart sons and dull sons were all present, and the final plan emerged from consensus.

In this case the former husbands of the two old women both died conveniently soon and within about three years of each other and, according to plan, there came into existence a household of two men in their thirties each married to the elderly mother of the other. Gitjara and L. F. B. thus set up jointly the foundations of their households and began their careers as a joint enterprise.

Gitjara had two sisters, both married to White Man, an elder, and already the mothers of daughters to him. By marrying Gitjara's mother, L. F. B. automatically became the nominal father of these women, and in the event of White Man's death would have, as such, some say in where they remarried. But the right of the step-father to redispose widowed step-daughters was always disputed by the brothers (or even sons) of the step-daughters, provided those brothers (or sons) were old enough or influential enough for their wishes to be taken seriously. Thus we may say that in putting L. F. B. into position as his own step-father, Gitjara's main object had been to get a satellite or henchman of his own into the position of step-father of his sisters (the wives of White Man) so that when they became widows there would be no conflict between the wishes of their brother and the wishes of their step-father as to whom they should remarry. L. F. B. as step-father was, so to speak, a stooge for Gitjara the brother.

Conversely, L. F. B. had two sisters both married to Ki-in-kumi, the most powerful elder in Malau. By marrying the mother of L. F. B., Gitjara became the step-father of two of Ki-in-kumi's wives, thus immediately (despite his youth) becoming technically the father-in-law of that powerful old man, and a man with some say in where those two wives of Ki-in-kumi would remarry on Ki-in-kumi's death. As step-father of such widows, Gitjara would have to make his wishes prevail as against the wishes of their brothers, but the only brother was L. F. B. and his vote was obviously in Gitjara's pocket.

By engineering this double shuffle of two elderly widows, each with daughters, Gitjara had launched his career as a marriage manipulator. Almost before it was concluded he became involved in another widow operation. We will omit the intricate details, but can say that he emerged from this with a second wife for himself, this one (naturally) also a widow but quite a young widow. This woman had already borne four sons and one daughter to her previous husband but was still young enough when Gitjara took her over in 1926 to bear him a son (her last) in 1927. In Tiwi terms the acquisition of this widow by Gitjara was a real achievement for the young man, not because of her comparative youth nor because of the son she bore him but because among the children by her previous marriage was a daughter aged about nine at the time she remarried Gitjara. To become the step-father of such a young girl was a real asset for the young operator. Her dead father had bestowed this child on Summit, another of the same Malauila age group of 30-year-olds and hence one of Gitjara's rivals and competitors in the influence struggle.

This created an intriguing situation since Summit, having had this child be-stowed on him at her birth some nine years previously, had thus acquired a bestowed wife at about age 27; Gitjara now 33 or so still had not received a bestowal. By remarrying the mother of Summit's young bestowed wife, Git-jara had turned the tables on one of his chief competitors among his age group. He could not, of course, alter the bestowal; in five or six years' time the girl would take up residence with Summit. But as the step-father who renamed the girl and the head of the household in which she would live for the next five years, Gitjara was in an excellent position to make Summit enter into a deal or two with him. He could drag his feet as to the time of the delivery of the girl to Summit; he could drop hints that there was something irregular about the bestowal to Summit in the first place, and so on; but whatever form of pressure he chose to exert on Summit, the latter well knew that all Gitjara wanted was to be cut in on some of Summit's deals and to be included in the network of Summit's alliances. The next move was now clearly up to Summit.

If Summit wished the nine-year-old girl now in Gitjara's household to be transferred promptly and without argument, he would be well advised to give some consideration to Gitjara, perhaps even the promise of one of his still-to-be-born daughters either as a wife or as a ward. Although not neces-sary, it would be a politically wise gesture. If he did so, both men would be gambling in futures. Since Summit's young wife was now nine years old, it would be at least six or seven years before she could produce a daughter (if at all) and another fourteen or fifteen years before any such daughter (if she lived) would be old enough to join Gitjara's household either as a wife or ward. Hence, under any such arrangement between the two young men, Summit would be giving something to Gitjara but in such a way that the latter could not collect for at least twenty years and might never collect.

Anthropologists will note that such arrangements still conformed to the patterns of cross-cousin marriage. Gitjara as de jure father delivers his "daughter" to Summit and thus becomes technically Summit's mother's brother or wife's father. Twenty years later (if all goes well) Summit delivers his daughter (by Gitjara's daughter) to Gitjara, thus becoming technically the mother's brother or wife's father of Gitjara. Gitjara himself might marry this daughter of Summit by his own step-daughter or treat her as a ward given to him by Summit and bestow her on some other man selected by himself; in the latter case he would be acting as father to his step-daughter's daughter. There were no clan barriers to such an arrangement, since fathers had to belong to clans different from those of their wives and of their daughters, step-daughters and daughters' daughters.

There were, of course, alternative actions or "deals" open to Summit and also to Gitjara, depending upon their plans in other directions. The pattern described above, however, was extremely common in Tiwi marriage arrangements, and often it was the reason why some very old man would receive some female infant as a wife: an agreement of this type had been made twenty or thirty years before, when the now senile old man was in his thirties and when the mother of the baby he was now receiving was married to some man long since dead. The circumstances were certainly right for such an arrangement in the Gitjara-Summit case of 1928.

If we now pause and look at the marriage career of Gitjara at the point it had reached by the time he was 33, we can separate out three distinct types of operation in which this admirable young man had engaged. His first marriage, with L. F. B.'s elderly mother, had brought into existence a joint household of young men and elderly widows which not only was a very satisfactory housekeeping arrangement but also put Gitjara and his ally, L. F. B., in a position to exert some influence on all the subsequent remarriages of their respective sisters.

Gitjara's marriage a few years later to a second widow put him in a position to enter into marriage arrangements even more directly, since the second widow had a daughter promised to Summit but still too young to take up residence with him. By dragging his feet on the fulfilment of this promise, Gitjara could put pressure on Summit and extract from the latter some sort of consideration to facilitate the delivery of the girl. Gitjara was thus well in the marriage-broker business before he had any children of his own and indeed before he had received any bestowal. This was the second type of operation for an up-and-coming young man, and it was one wherein a shrewd and aggressive operator would use the daughters of other men (that is, of a widow's previous husbands) in such a way as to attach all sorts of codicils and contingent interests and second mortgages to the original bestowal of those daughters, many of these collectable in full only in the far distant future, after all prior interests had been satisfied or had lapsed.

The third type of operation engaged in by Gitjara was, of course, to try and attract bestowed wives of his own. His vigorous operations, by age 33, in the widow remarriage field, were not only ends in themselves but also were the type of operation that attracted the approval of older men with daughters to bestow. Hence it is not surprising to find that by 1929 Gitjara, married to the two widows already mentioned, had received two bestowals. The older of these was a girl of ten rebestowed on Gitjara in 1927 when the man died upon whom she had been bestowed at birth. The second was a baby born in 1927 whose father was Tomitari of the Rangwila. (The choice of Gitjara as a son-in-law by Tomitari was so interesting that we shall discuss it later in this chapter.) Both these bestowals were made *after* Gitjara had engineered his remarriage of the two widows and as far as kinship was concerned had no connection whatever with these widows or their close relatives. We conclude, therefore, that widow remarriage could be used by alert and aggressive men in their early thirties for three purposes: (1) to establish households and obtain elderly housekeepers; (2) to establish low-priority rights in the daughters of the widows' previous husbands; and (3) to attract attention to themselves as smart operators and gain the attention and approval of older men. As an outgrowth of the third purpose, they were likely to attract bestowals. Hence we may say that among the Tiwi the best road to obtaining a young wife or several young wives was for a young man to be first successful in the manipulation of the remarriages of elderly widows, who were always in large supply. If a man showed skill and know-how in his early thirties among the widows, then in his late thirties and early forties young wives would be bestowed upon him in abundance. Such a lesson could not have a better exemplar than Gitjara. By age 33 he had done so well among the widows that his first *young* wife would be joining his household by the time he was thirty-eight or thirty-nine, and another was already a year old. Clearly he was a young man of promise and one to be watched—and cultivated.

Summit, a man slightly older than Gitjara, must be dealt with very briefly, since the reasons for his success would take us too far afield. In 1929 he had a list of six wives, the only resident one being an elderly widow. The other five were bestowals and the eldest of these was the girl of ten whom we have already mentioned as being in the household of her step-father, Gitjara. Two more, younger than the ten-year-old, were in the household of Padimo (see below) and the remaining two were in the household of one of the elders of the Rangwila band. Summit, in Tiwi reckoning, was a Rangwila himself and had only moved to Malau a few years before. Some four years previously he had been a young Rangwila with no less than five bestowed child-wives. Three of these had been given him by an elder in Malau, two by an elder of his own band. The Malauila girls were older than the two Rangwila girls and his Malauila father-in-law was older than his Rangwila father-in-law. Summit therefore moved north to supervise personally his interests in Malau. He had, however, been out-maneuvered when the Malauila father-in-law died, since Gitjara had then been able to remarry the mother of Summit's eldest child-wife and Padimo had been able to remarry the mother of the other two little girls. Having thus moved to Malau to be near to and a satellite of his elderly Malauila father-in-law, Summit now found himself the technical son-in-law of two young men of his own age group who were among his keen competitors in the influence struggle. To ensure that his three promised Malauila child-wives joined his household when old enough, he now needed to make some arrangements with Gitjara and Padimo. Summit had gotten his bestowals rather early and rather easily but he still had the problem of nailing them down.

While thus engaged in acquiring five bestowed young wives and trying to promote their safe delivery when ready, Summit had married a widow not much more than forty years old but childless by her two previous husbands.[3] Such a widow at least provided him with a food-getter and housekeeper and enabled him to establish a household into which his five bestowed wives would enter as they successively reached the proper age. Thus Summit's household in 1929 consisted only of himself and his *palimaringa* wife. Within the next fifteen years it would be increased by the addition of at least five young wives,

---

[3] Such women who had reached middle age without surviving children were called by a special term, *palimaringa,* in Tiwi and the term referred to childlessness rather than barrenness. Summit's widow, for example, had borne two children, both of whom had died in infancy, and she was classified as a *palimaringa.* When a *palimaringa* became very, very old indeed, the word changed to *timaringa.*

plus any new bestowals, plus any further widows Summit might find it to his interest (and power) to remarry.

Padimo, who thus enters our story as one of Summit's rivals and one
of his nominal fathers-in-law, was also a Rangwila who had moved to Malau
at the call of an elderly father-in-law. He presents another pattern of Tiwi
upward mobility and one that was statistically more frequent than the rather
tortuous road followed by men like Gitjara. Padimo had been chosen as a
nephew worth supporting by old Ki-in-kumi, the wealthiest of the Malauila.
The earliest proof of Ki-in-kumi's patronage of Padimo had come in 1925-26
when an old man died, leaving eight widows of very diverse ages. Three of
these "widows," aged respectively 17, 13, and 9 at the time of the death of
their first husband, were daughters of Ki-in-kumi. Being so young and their
brothers being equally young, their father's right to arrange their remarriage
was unchallenged and Ki-in-kumi reassigned[4] them as wives to young Padimo,
then aged about thirty-three. The eldest of the three girls had already borne
two female children to the dead man, these being the two girl babies mentioned
above as having been promised to Summit.

As well as the three young widows, Padimo had also obtained at the
same redistribution the oldest and most haggish of the dead man's eight wives.
It was at the same redistribution that Gitjara had obtained his second widow
(the mother of the girl promised to Summit). Thus through Ki-in-kumi's
influence, Padimo had obtained four "widows" of the eight left by the man
who died in 1925-26; Gitjara, working without a powerful patron, had been
lucky to obtain one.

Ki-in-kumi had subsequently followed up this initial selection of Padimo
as a favored sister's son by giving further daughters to him as they were born.
Consequently, by 1929 Padimo's wife list consisted of the following:

A. One extremely ancient widow.
B. One wife aged about 20, daughter of Ki-in-kumi, mother already of two
   daughters by a previous husband who, before his death, bestowed these
   daughters on Summit.
C. One wife aged about 17, daughter of Ki-in-kumi; had just had her first
   child (who lived only a week); had previously been bestowed on the dead
   husband of wife B, but was too young to join his household before he died.
D. Three more girls, daughters of Ki-in-kumi, the eldest about 12 and hence
   old enough to have been bestowed on the same previous husband as wives
   B and C; the other two aged 2 and 1 and hence born since his death. All
   three of these were still resident in their father's household.

-----

[4] It is difficult to decide whether such reassignments of female children by their
father, on the death of the man to whom he had first betrothed them, should be called
"rebestowals" or "remarriages." We prefer the first word since such "child-widows"
were usually reassigned by their fathers (if still alive) without any challenge to his
rights to do so. They therefore do not differ from original bestowals at birth except
for the awkward semantic fact that the man to whom such a "child-wife" was reassigned
was technically her second husband.

With a lineup such as this by the time he was thirty-six, Padimo was clearly in process of going places in Tiwi society. The only weakness one could see in his position was that it all derived from the favor of one patron, and no old man with daughters, other than Ki-in-kumi, had seen fit to bestow a girl upon him. It should be noted that in 1929, though Padimo had two young wives resident in his household, he still had no children of his own. His first child, born that year, lived only a few days. The only children in residence were the two girls promised to Summit by the previous husband of their mother. Their bestowal on Summit was a matter beyond Padimo's control though he could use them to force some concessions from Summit just as Gitjara could with the girl in his household. But as Padimo's young wives began to bear daughters of his own, his bestowal of them would be less encumbered by the commitments of any predecessor. While Ki-in-kumi lived, Padimo would have to consider his obligations to that old man and at least consult with Ki-in-kumi as to how he should bestow his female children, since any such children would be the daughters' daughters of the old man. Nor would the death of Ki-in-kumi leave Padimo entirely free to bestow his own daughters anywhere he wished. Many of the girls already given to him as wives by Ki-in-kumi had mothers who possibly, and brothers who certainly, would outlive Ki-in-kumi. On the old man's death, all of his numerous wives would remarry—some of the older ones probably to ambitious younger men—and these new husbands of the widows of Ki-in-kumi would begin interfering with and trying to alter the arrangements made for his daughters by the old man during his lifetime. Thus Padimo would find himself stuck with a group of new and antagonistic fathers-in-law in place of the old, indulgent father-in-law who had been responsible for his success so far. Padimo's problem was basically how to hold, after Ki-in-kumi's death, the favored position he had gained during the old man's lifetime through the old man's favor.

In the meantime, with Ki-in-kumi still alive and powerful, Padimo had the biggest and fastest expanding household among the Malauila men in their thirties. The only remaining man in this age group was Boya who was the oldest of them all, being at least 42 years old in 1928. As might be expected, his career illustrates some new facets of the Tiwi influence struggle.

Structurally the position of Boya was simple but politically it was complex. His father had been a henchman and satellite of Ki-in-kumi in the early career of that old operator and roughly had had somewhat the same relationship to the young Ki-in-kumi as L. F. B. had to Gitjara. Boya's father, the satellite, left only two widows (an indication of his mediocrity) and these two widows had been remarried by Ki-in-kumi, the patron. One of these widows was Boya's mother, and Boya was too young at the time to have any say in where his mother remarried. Ki-in-kumi's interest in marrying Boya's mother was not of course because he thus acquired Boya as a step-son, but because he acquired Boya's sisters as step-daughters. Step-sons were liabilities which new husbands had to take over in order to get rights in the real assets —the step-daughters.

Some years later, when Boya had reached a reasonable age like 30, Ki-in-kumi had arranged for him to marry a very ancient and childless widow (*palimaringa*) more than twenty years older than himself. This was all that Ki-in-kumi considered he needed to do for his step-son, and in Tiwi terms it was almost a gesture of contempt and an open indication that Ki-in-kumi, by providing him with an old woman who was childless but could cook, was not interested in helping Boya toward a career. Since the joining up of Boya to the crone took place shortly after the death of Boya's mother, who had lived with her sons in Ki-in-kumi's household, Ki-in-kumi by producing the old widow for Boya was telling him in effect to get out and start his own household now that his mother was dead.

In 1928 we found Boya aged about 42 married to the crone of 65. But he, she, and Boya's younger brother of 24 were still living in Ki-in-kumi's household. Ki-in-kumi's detestation of him was notorious and yet Boya had by now no less than four young bestowed child-wives growing up elsewhere. No one of these bestowals had come from Malau but were bestowals from different fathers of baby girls in other bands. At first sight this presented a curious situation. Within his own band Boya appeared a complete failure, suffering so severely from Ki-in-kumi's hostility that he had received no bestowals and at age 42 did not even have a separate household of his own. But how could this judgment be squared with the four bestowals from elders of other bands? Clearly none of the causes of success so far analyzed fitted the case of Boya.

Further research into who lived with whom as distinct from who was married to whom revealed that not only was "the household" of Boya, his elderly wife, and his younger brother an integral part of the Ki-in-kumi "establishment," but also that Padimo with his "household" was part of that establishment. Padimo, like Boya, had one elderly wife but he also had five bestowed wives, all daughters of Ki-in-kumi. We said above that the two eldest of these five girls being now aged 20 and 17 respectively were in residence with their husband, while the three youngest, not having reached puberty, were still "with their father." Actual observation showed that this was an academic distinction, since the households of Padimo, the son-in-law, and Ki-in-kumi, the father-in-law, were parts of the same establishment. When one of Ki-in-kumi's daughters bestowed on Padimo became old enough to "leave her father and join her husband," she did not have to move her residence or even change her daily work routines. She merely sat at night around the campfire of her older sisters (Padimo's wives) instead of around the campfire of her younger sisters (Ki-in-kumi's daughters). She remained part of the same establishment.

Padimo, it will be remembered, was the young man whom Ki-in-kumi had attracted from Rangu to Malau by liberally bestowing him with child-wives. Padimo had thus moved into the northern band and by 1928 had moved right into Ki-in-kumi's camp, where he functioned as a sort of executive officer and heir apparent to the old man. In the same camp, though in a very different capacity, was Boya, the 42-year-old despised step-son. Many roads thus led to Ki-in-kumi's household, but before discussing the large establishment of that wealthy elder, we will first summarize, in Table I, the marital conditions of the eight young men we have been discussing.

TABLE I
THE MALAUILA YOUNG MEN IN 1928-29

Name	Age	Resident Old Wives (Ex-widows)	Resident Young Wives (Bestowals)	Promised Wives (Under 14)	Own Children
Tiberun	33	0	0	0	0
Banana	28	1	0	0	0
Teapot	35	0[a]	0	0	1
Gitjara	33	2	0	2	1
L. F. B.	38	1	0	1	0
Summit	36	1	0	5	0
Padimo	36	1	2	3	0[b]
Boya	42	1	0	4	0

[a] Teapot's "stolen" wife was dead.
[b] Padimo's first child, born in 1929, lived only a few days.

This table presents a summary of many of our earlier attempts at generalization. The only Malauila under the age of 43 who had a bestowed young wife old enough to live with him was Padimo, who was thus exceptionally lucky. Leaving out young Banana, five of the seven men between the ages of 30 and 42 had young females promised to them, but these were mostly babies or children who would not come into residence for several years. Six of the seven had married widows, mostly elderly widows, well in advance of the arrival of young wives and before any father had bestowed a daughter on them. Finally, and a point not made before, men of this age group rarely had any children of their own. The only entries in the last column of Table I are the irregularly born son of Teapot; Padimo's first daughter who died virtually at birth; and the 1-year-old son of Gitjara who was the last child born to his second ex-widow. Tiwi men rarely had young wives until they were around forty; they even more rarely had any children of their own before that age. Padimo's dead baby and Gitjara's 1-year-old son were exceptional; the zeros in the last column against the names of Boya (42), L. F. B. (38), and Summit (36) represent the normal situation for Tiwi men of such ages.

In terms of success (as measured by bestowals) Padimo and Summit (largely through the patronage of elders) and Boya and Gitjara (largely through their own operations) were the coming young men among the Malauila. Of the others, L. F. B. was approaching forty with few assets and no influence, and the other three, Tiberun, Banana, and Teapot, had not even got started in the influence race.

A Very Successful Elder: Ki-in-kumi

The most influential man in Malau and the head of the biggest household was Ki-in-kumi. Since he had been born around 1863-64 and had been a "young operator" somewhat before 1900, the deals by which he got his career launched were difficult to reconstruct. The results of them, plus the fact that he lived long enough to draw full dividends from them, gave him by 1928-29 a wife-list of twenty-one. These had been accumulated as follows:

When around 30 years old he remarried two elderly widows and a year or two later received his first bestowal. Thus by age 33 he had three wives. On that foundation he went ahead thus:

		Total
At age 33		
Had two widows and one bestowed wife		3
Between age 33 and age 43		
Remarried two more widows and had three more bestowed wives join him	+5	8
Between age 43 and age 53		
Three more bestowed wives came into residence	+3	11
(During these twenty years at least five bestowed wives died in infancy or childhood)	+5	16
Between age 53 and age 65		
Two more bestowed wives joined him and he married 2 more widows (one the mother of Boya)	+4	20
Now at age 66 there is still one more bestowed wife, aged about 9, in her father's household	+1	21

Thus his list of twenty-one wives was made up of six elderly widows and fifteen bestowed or rebestowed young wives.

By 1928-29 five of his bestowed wives had died before puberty and one was still with her father. Three of his six widows were dead. Subtracting these nine women, we find that his current household contained twelve resident and active wives: the oldest about sixty, two in their fifties, four in their forties or thirties, three in their twenties, and the two youngest around seventeen or eighteen years of age. Almost all of them had borne children since joining his household, but the death rate had been high among Ki-in-kumi's children and from all of his wives he had only eight living children of whom six were girls. Five of these six daughters he had bestowed or rebestowed on Padimo (see above) and the sixth on a middle-aged Rangwila. His oldest living daughter was the girl of 20 married to Padimo. His oldest living son was a boy of 18, despite the fact that Ki-in-kumi had been "a married man" for over thirty-five years. This was a situation which many Tiwi elders found themselves in at the close of long and successful lives. With numerous wives, numerous step-sons, large households to be managed, and large estates to be liquidated after their deaths, their oldest real sons (as distinct from step-sons) were still boys or youths and as such quite unsuitable as executive assistants while the old man lived or as heirs or executors after the old man died. Quite apart from kinship considerations, the Tiwi emphasis on age and seniority made it impossible for Ki-in-kumi to utilize in any capacity his 18-year-old son. A youth of that age was a nonentity, whoever his father.

TABLE II
KI-IN-KUMI'S ESTABLISHMENT

(Ages in brackets)		Males	Females
Head (Ki-in-kumi	66)	1	0
Oldest step-son (Boya	42)	1	0
Sister's son (Padimo	36)	1	0
Old wives (of all three adult men)		0	5
Young wives (including Padimo's 2)		0	11
Young males (sons and step-sons)		8	0
Young females (daughters and step-daughters)		0	5
Totals		11	21

Confronted by this situation, Ki-in-kumi in his advancing years had summoned Padimo, a sister's son in his early thirties, to come from Rangu and become his chief lieutenant. The youth of his own son had been a factor in his selection of Padimo. The presence in his camp of an older step-son, Boya, had been another factor. Boya, the step-son, was more than twenty years older than the son, and at least six years older than Padimo, the chosen instrument. Padimo, as we have seen, moved right in, fused his own small household with Ki-in-kumi's large one, and became Ki-in-kumi's Man Friday. Boya, the step-son, though married to a widow, refused to move out. Thus, among other things, we have to distinguish between Ki-in-kumi's household of twelve resident wives enumerated above, and Ki-in-kumi's establishment which contained Padimo, Boya, and the various people attached by marriage or kinship to them. Padimo had an old wife and two young wives (daughters of Ki-in-kumi). Boya had an old wife and a younger brother. There were a number of younger step-children of both sexes also resident with Ki-in-kumi. The full size and make-up of his establishment is given in Table II.

The Establishments of Malau

There were, besides Ki-in-kumi, six other elders of the Malauila band. Two of these, the brothers Enquirio and Merapanui, were well over sixty and deserve, both by age and by success, to be labeled senior elders. The remaining four ranged in age from about 45 to nearly 60 and since none of them were particularly successful we call them the junior elders. In Table III we have listed the seven "establishments" in which lived all the members of the band. We mean by an establishment a food-production and food-consumption unit. Ki-in-kumi's establishment contained three married men—himself, Boya, and Padimo—and therefore contained three households. Economically it was one establishment, since the sixteen wives it contained worked as a team and the food they produced was consumed by the thirty-two total members of the establishment. For comparative purposes in Table III we list Ki-in-kumi's establishment as Unit I and give the personnel breakdown of the other six establishments that made up the total population of Malau. Unit II is the joint enterprise maintained by the other two senior elders, the brothers Enquirio and Merapanui. To this we have added the pathetic and ostracized Teapot and his motherless son, since when they ate at all they ate as hangers-on of the Enquirio-Merapanui menage. Unit III is the establishment jointly maintained by the brothers White Man and Ku-nai-u-ua. Since the oldest wife of Ku-nai-u-ua was Summit's mother, that young man, together with the elderly ex-widow who was so far his only resident wife, lived in this establishment. Units IV and V present no difficulty; they are the small households of the other two junior elders Pingirimini and Tipiperna-gerai respectively. Unit VI is the joint enterprise of Gitjara and L. F. B., containing largely old ladies and young men. Unit VII is the remarkable menage that had gathered round the elderly widow whom young Banana had illegally "married." To this couple

TABLE III

THE FOOD PRODUCTION UNITS OF MALAU

Unit	Married Males	Unmarried Males[a]	Old Wives[b]	Young Wives	Girls Under 14	Total Persons
I	3	8	5	11	5	32
II	3	9	1	7	11	31
III	3	2	2	3	5	15
IV	1	5	0	1	1	8
V	1	2	0	1	2	6
VI	2	5	3	0	1	11
VII	1?	4	1	0	0	6
Total	14	35	12	23	25	109

a Unmarried males include all males from male infants to men around 30, or more.
b The division between old wives and young wives is arbitrary. Several of the young wives were 40, others only 14 or 15.
? The question mark in Unit VII refers to the difficulty of deciding whether Banana should be classified as married.

had attached themselves Tiberun (Banana's unmarried older brother), two younger brothers, and another male orphan who had apparently moved in for want of some better place to eat. The Banana menage thus had somewhat the appearance of a case of economic polyandry and somewhat the look of a fraternity house with an elderly housemother in residence. We include it as Unit VII since by so doing we are able to include in Table III all the hundred and nine people who made up the Malauila band in 1928-29 and allocate all of them to the economic units in which they functioned as food producers and food consumers.

The data in Table III merit close study. These seven establishments illustrate in capsule form several of the more significant emphases in Tiwi career patterns; indeed each might be said to illustrate some time point in the life careers of adult men and/or some degree of success or lack of success in becoming an influential man.

The Politics of Widow Remarriage

Ki-in-kumi's large establishment was the sort of set-up that every Tiwi sought to achieve but few accomplished. An establishment such as his meant wealth, power, prestige, and influence for its head, and, in Malau, Ki-in-kumi was the only man with such a household. With eleven males, many of them food producing; sixteen women, all of them food producing; and several of the girls under fourteen able to assist the older women, the amount of food this unit could collect in a day provided an ample food surplus for the establishment. A man whose household was a surplus food producer was a successful man. Moreover, since the large work force that produced the food surplus contained numerous young wives who (usually) could be relied upon also to produce numerous female babies, he was doubly blessed with both the requisites—surplus food and surplus daughters—necessary to increase his influence and make more people beholden to him or dependent on him. Of the thirty-five married women in Malau, sixteen, or over 45 percent, were in this one establishment.

By comparison, the other old men of Malau were less successful.[5] Through pooling their work forces, Enquirio and Merapanui had achieved an establishment (Unit II) almost as big as that of Ki-in-kumi, and probably its members ate almost as well as the members of his, but their effort was a shared effort and their influence and prestige had to be divided between them. They had been lucky with daughters but, divided between the two fathers, the eleven daughters in their establishment were less impressive than Ki-in-kumi's eight, and the total of seven young wives between them was quite overshadowed by Ki-in-kumi's nine. The two old brothers were successful men and headed a successful operation, but their prestige and success must be rated at least one whole degree below that of Ki-in-kumi.

Another pair of elderly brothers, White Man and Ku-nai-u-ua, had also joined forces (Unit III), but the results can be judged as only fair. They were at least the best off of their age group, the 45- to 55-year-olds, but the competition in that age group was weak, as can be seen by comparison of their establishment with Units IV and V, the households of Pingirimini and Tipiperna-gerai. Perhaps the best indication of the respective success in life of the seven oldest men is that given in the column of Table III headed "young wives." Of the twenty-three such women in the band, eighteen were in the establishments[6] of the three oldest men (Units I and II); the next five men in age shared the remaining five (Units III, IV, and V).

It might be thought that the small establishments of the unsuccessful junior elders like White Man, Ku-nai-u-ua, Pingirimini, and Tipiperna-gerai could be expected to increase sharply in size and these men to grow in relative prestige and influence when death removed the three old men at the heads

---

[5] It will be noticed that as we move into the older group of men we have to use their native names, since most of them had no "whiteman" names.

[6] Two of these eighteen were of course actually married to Padimo, but still part of the establishment of their father, Ki-in-kumi, since Padimo's wives all lived with Ki-in-kumi's wives.

of Units I and II and made their wives available for redistribution. The working of the Tiwi system made this possibility unlikely. Unsuccessful junior elders could not expect to step into the shoes of successful senior elders merely by outliving them; nor could one rise to power in the gerontocratic system merely by living past fifty-five. What was necessary was age *plus* ability, and the time to demonstrate the ability was in one's thirties. If it was not demonstrated and recognized by then, a man could not forge ahead in his middle forties and early fifties, for by then it was too late. This fact gave a certain cyclical quality to the transfer of influence in Tiwi. The influence of successful senior elders, to the extent that such an intangible thing was transferable at all, tended to skip a decade and bypass the men currently in the junior elder category in favor of the men in the current "young operator" category. Since Ki-in-kumi was already quite old, there was in 1929 a great deal of political maneuvering going on in Malau and elsewhere in anticipation of his death, and it was clear that the people most likely to profit by his death and the redistribution of his twelve resident wives (one-third of all resident wives in the band) were the men aged from thirty-two to forty-two such as Padimo, Boya, Summit, and Gitjara, all of whom were jockeying for position to take advantage of the death of any old man, especially such a wealthy elder as Ki-in-kumi. Some of the widows would undoubtedly remarry into other bands, but these younger Malauila, living with or near the old man's establishment, were already taking advantage of their strategic location to make some preliminary deals and marriage arrangements for the old man's widows even before his death. Neither Padimo, as Ki-in-kumi's son-in-law, nor Boya, as his nominal "son," could themselves marry any of the widows, but as resident members of his establishment and the only two men so situated, each was in an excellent spot to act as an honest broker in the disposal of Ki-in-kumi's large estate. Anybody interested in obtaining a widow or two at the death of Ki-in-kumi was well advised to have a few quiet words with either Padimo or Boya well ahead of time. Both of them had wives who lived and worked every day alongside Ki-in-kumi's womenfolk and thus they each had ideal communication systems to the women's side of the band. This was why they had held off setting up their own separate establishments though they were both married men. Neither were "heirs" of Ki-in-kumi in any strict Western use of that word, but it was obvious that it was their careers that would be promoted and their spheres of influence that would be enhanced by the death of Ki-in-kumi. The junior elders, all approaching or past the age of fifty with only small establishments and small spheres of influence, were being bypassed in the transfer of the old man's assets.

Every Tiwi anxious to obtain a Ki-in-kumi widow recognized the strategic positions of Padimo and Boya; the problem was to decide which broker to retain, since the positions of the two men in relation to Ki-in-kumi were so different. For the past four or five years Padimo had been the right-hand man and trusted lieutenant and undoubtedly it was he upon whom Ki-in-kumi was relying to carry out his own wishes about the distribution of his widows. We said earlier that old men found it difficult to control the remarriage of their widows with the same unchallenged authority with which they bestowed their daughters. Nevertheless they tried hard in many cases to do so. Ki-in-kumi was one who tried hard to make the decisions for his widows, by selecting Padimo as his trusted executor. If Padimo faithfully carried out the old man's wishes after he died, then the widows were not likely to come on the open market; they would be redistributed in accordance with the terms of Ki-in-kumi's will (in both senses of the word "will").

Though, of course, Padimo might prove to be a dishonest executor of the estate, there was a safeguard provided in that the new husbands whom Ki-in-kumi had selected for his wives were all aware of his wishes and hence if Padimo tried to depart from those wishes the cheated heirs would bring charges of double dealing and broken promises against him. But regardless of Padimo's honesty after the death, his position as Ki-in-kumi's trusted lieutenant clearly made him an unsuitable agent before the death for those numerous men who wanted some of Ki-in-kumi's future widows and who had not seen any indication that Ki-in-kumi had included them among his beneficiaries. The obvious young man for such men to use as their go-between and agent was Boya. Ki-in-kumi was hostile to him and had given him nothing willingly. Boya's presence in the old man's establishment was based on the nominal tie of Ki-in-kumi being the last husband of his mother to rename him before she died. Viewed thus, the two young men in Ki-in-kumi's household can be said to have become agents for two different networks of intrigue. Padimo was the manager and agent for all the men, including Ki-in-kumi himself, who wanted to perpetuate and continue the existing alliances and arrangements that Ki-in-kumi had built or helped to build during his long and successful career; Boya was the natural agent for all the men who, being outside that set of alliances, had nothing to gain from Ki-in-kumi's death unless his death dissolved the network of alliances and arrangements of which Ki-in-kumi had been the main architect. Padimo's responsibility was necessarily a sort of holding-together and preserving operation as the executor of an existing estate; Boya's clients were men hoping for fragmentation and subdivision not only of Ki-in-kumi's widows but also of the alliances and deals of which the widows were a part.

It is incidentally amusing, and also indicative of how the ever-present kinship ties affected all such deals and redeals, to note that if some of Boya's clients succeeded in grabbing off some of Ki-in-kumi's widows—despite the opposition, before his death, of Ki-in-kumi and the presumed opposition, after the death, of Padimo the executor—they were very liable thus to become automatically fathers-in-law of Padimo, since several of Ki-in-kumi's wives already had daughters who were bestowed on Padimo.

The question then of which agent was employed by the numerous men yearning to acquire one or more of Ki-in-kumi's widows was fairly well settled by the respective roles which the two young men occupied in the household. Men already well inside the Ki-in-kumi-centered alliances were relying on Padimo; men outside those alliances were relying on Boya to engineer a fluid situation and a more open market. In choosing an agent in this as in any other "deal," there was also the question of fee. Neither Padimo nor Boya would become involved or make any soundings among the widows unless there was something in it for them. Hence the client had to find out whether a promise of general goodwill and friendship was all that Boya (or Padimo) would ask in return for his services or whether the price would be much higher—perhaps as high as the bestowal of the client's next baby daughter. It was in such ways that widow-remarriage arrangements and infant bestowals were intertwined; a much-delayed bestowal to an apparently unrelated individual would be the ultimate pay-off to the broker or agent who had engineered a widow remarriage for the bestower years before.

This role of agent in the disposal of a dead man's widows was a type of operation best suited to men in the first stages of their own married lives —that is, to men in their middle thirties or very early forties who had perhaps married their first or second widows and who had as yet no young wives of their own in residence. Having no young wives to guard, they were able to get around easily on diplomatic missions and they had their own listening posts inside the world of women in the person of their own mothers (if still alive) and in the elderly widows whom they themselves had married. The ambitious young brokers were tipped off by their mothers and elderly wives as to how the young wives wished to be distributed and what the competing young brokers were trying to arrange. Thus when a wealthy old man like Ki-in-kumi died, the redistribution of his wives through remarriage was a matter that had been decided beforehand by an extraordinary complex tangle of semisecret arrangements and deals and promises, but the people most influential in arranging the redistribution were the young brokers who usually got few, if any, of the young widows for themselves but who collected their rewards in reputation, influence, alliances, and future bestowals from the men for whom they had acted as agents.

Thus the death of Ki-in-kumi or of any other old man with many wives tended to disperse the wives all over the tribe, with only one or two, or at most three, going to any one new husband. A large estate was almost always fragmented by the death of the old man who had built it up, and any one of his contemporaries was able to take over only a very small fraction of it at best. The levirate and sororate principles, though present, worked very feebly. The men who benefited most—not immediately, but eventually—were the young operators.[7] In such a manner Padimo and Boya were sure to be the long-term beneficiaries of Ki-in-kumi's death though neither of them could remarry any of his widows. The real heirs of the wealthy old men of sixty and over were the young men who happened to be between thirty-two and forty-two when those old men got near to death. The men between forty-five and fifty-five whose brokerage business ten years earlier had not been very skillfully

---

[7] At least some of the so-called "stolen" or disputed wives were widows who had insisted on marrying the younger agent instead of the older client, which put the young broker in the embarrassing position of saying to his client, "I cannot make delivery of the widow I acquired on your account; she insists on marrying me instead." Such an incident did not do his agency business much good but tended rather to frighten off clients.

handled, or who happened to be at the brokering age when no big households were being liquidated, found themselves in the position that Pingirimini and Tipiperna-gerai occupied in 1928-29. We know they had not been successful dealers in their thirties because we found them around the age of fifty with only one resident wife each and relatively few bestowals in prospect. Their earlier dealings in widows had not laid the right foundations for successful careers as elders. Even before he was forty, Padimo had five or six bestowed wives either in residence or in prospect, and Boya, not much over forty, had several already promised. The death of Ki-in-kumi in the near future would bring both of them more reputation and ultimately more bestowals in return for their skill (if they showed it) in the disposition of the estate. The inferiority of Pingirimini and Tipiperna-gerai to these younger men in the marriage and influence struggle was already apparent and would be even more accentuated by Ki-in-kumi's death.

The Politics of Bestowal

The above discussion of how younger men were indirectly benefited by the deaths or impending deaths of wealthy older men does not pretend to give an exhaustive list of all the considerations that went into the reallocation of a dead man's widows. We built our analysis around those factors which were paramount in the case of Ki-in-kumi's household. Other cases were different to the extent that there were real adult sons involved in them rather than a nominal "son" like Boya, or because in them the old man had not chosen a clear-cut executor as Ki-in-kumi had chosen Padimo, or because an old man had surviving brothers close to him in age and alliance who would emphasize the levirate principle and seek to have it followed in the relocation of their dead brother's widows. The few points we are seeking to emphasize among the many that might be emphasized in any exhaustive treatment of Tiwi widow remarriage are: 1) that widow remarriage was a very flexible area in which the ultimate disposition of the widows was decided by the manipulations and wishes of a wide range of individuals including both relatives and nonrelatives. The dead man himself; the fathers of the wives, if still alive; the brothers of the widows, if adults; the widows themselves, if strong minded; the executors of the dead man, if clearly nominated; and the numerous dealers and brokers on behalf of remote clients or even on their own account—all tried to make their own wishes prevail. The result was that no two cases were ever alike, but on balance 2) it was younger men rather than older men who were most likely to enhance their reputations and increase their assets in the long run as the results of these widow redeals, even though in the short run it was the older men who remarried most of the widows, especially the younger widows.

We have briefly discussed what we have labeled the politics of widow remarriage before discussing the politics of infant bestowal, although logically it might appear that infant bestowal should be taken up first. We have followed this order because, in Tiwi life, infant bestowal was reserved for fathers, and a Tiwi was at least a middle-aged man before he became a father at all. Before he could have a daughter to bestow, he had to be the father of one; and before he could become a father, he had to have a baby girl bestowed upon him and wait for her to grow up to child-bearing age. The much-married Ki-in-kumi did not have his first actual daughter (as distinct from wives' daughters begotten by previous husbands) until he was forty-five, and En-quirio was closer to fifty than to forty when his first real daughter was born. We are inclined to call such daughters free or unencumbered daughters since the step-daughters brought into a man's household by widows, even young widows, were already bestowed by act of the widows' previous husbands and the new husband's control over their marriage was therefore encumbered by the dispositions made by his predecessors.

Thus most men did not have and could not expect to have any free or unencumbered daughters to bestow until they were well into their forties. By that time a man was a prisoner of his past. When at last he had free daughters he was no longer a free man but a junior elder with a mass of obligations both to older men and to younger men, which he had contracted in the previous twenty or thirty years. Even his initiation, which had started when he was only about fifteen, left him under obligation to the older men who had initiated him. Any bestowals he had received had almost necessarily come to him from older men. In his thirties, it is true, he had operated in the widow remarriage area and put some older men under obligation to him by acting as their agent. But in his agency activities he had also contracted debts, usually in fee-splitting or log-rolling agreements with other agents of about his own age. Thus all his past activities, from his initiation at fifteen until the arrival of his first free daughter at (let us say) age forty-five, were on balance a story of obligations contracted and debts of gratitude assumed in his career of upward mobility. The more successful he had been up to now, the stronger the pressure on him to begin paying off those who had helped him, since it was assumed that his very success was a clear indication of how much obligation he must have to other men, especially older men and contemporaries.

If this line of reasoning had been the only relevant one, a Tiwi of age forty-five just presented with his first free daughter would have had problem enough deciding which of his many obligations to liquidate first by his bestowal decision for that daughter. Unfortunately he was at the age when he had to consider the future as well as the past. Some of his old obligations were to men who were very old and unlikely to live much longer. Others were to men of his own age with whom he had been partners ten years before, but by now it was clear that some of these would never amount to much and paying them off would reap no dividends for the future. Failure to meet the obligation might incur their enmity, but in view of their lack of success, perhaps their hostility was a lesser evil. In 1929, Gitjara, who had needed L. F. B. to get his own career launched, was ready to drop him as a partner now that Gitjara had attracted favorable notice in the form of two bestowals. The junior elders, though obligated to older men like Ki-in-kumi, were not bestowing their scanty free daughters on the older men but upon each other while waiting for the power alignment in Malau to change with Ki-in-kumi's death. Perhaps the clearest case of the pull between the obligations of the past and the planning for the future in the bestowal of free daughters was provided by Merapanui. He was a man who owed or thought he owed very little to his elders. None of them had ever bestowed a girl on him, and he reached fifty with nothing but an ancient widow. The fortunate death of an elder brother had suddenly provided him with bestowable daughters rather later in life than the average. By 1929 he had been able to bestow no less than four, and every one of them went to men much younger than himself and in other bands. Merapanui, being relatively free of old debts, was investing his daughters in young men with a future, but unlike Ki-in-kumi who had invested most of his daughters in one younger man, Padimo, old Merapanui believed in diversifying his investments.

Thus the politics of bestowal marriage were just as complicated as the politics of widow remarriage but, since a man was ten or more years older when he became involved in the former than when he became involved in the latter, a rather different set of motivations prevailed. At thirty-five as a mobile operator in the widow field, a man was trying to launch a career, and if he had no obvious assets—no living sisters or mother or important mother's brothers—he was often trying to launch it on a shoestring. By forty-five the same man was well along in his career and was a junior elder—the head of a household with at least one young wife in residence and a man beginning to have bestowable daughters of his very own. He now saw tribal politics and reputation building in different perspective from the way they had looked to him ten years earlier. Then he had put his services and his wits and his diplomatic skills at the disposal of older men in order to gain favorable notice from the elders. But now that he was an elder himself, albeit still low in the pecking order of elders, he was no longer their satellite but rather one of them and therefore in competition with them. Now he no longer wanted to build up his client's business; he wanted to build up his own household and his own influence. With the arrival of his first free daughters he was no longer content to work for and accept the leadership of older clients; he was in business as an elder for himself. His free daughters were therefore bestowed not as acknowledgments of his obligations to older men but as inducements to younger men to accept him as their patron. With his first free daughters a man was in position to become emancipated from the dominance of the elders because with the arrival of those daughters he could start bidding against them for the allegiance of men younger than himself.

One of the neatest examples of the switch in life career was provided in 1928 by the case of Tomitari. All Tiwi life careers and marriage arrangements were so tangled that one was delighted to find a relatively open and shut case. Some of the principals involved were relatives of Padimo, who was originally a Rangwila before Ki-in-kumi, his patron, lured him to Malau. Padimo and three sisters were the children of a Rangwila man and woman whom for simplicity's sake we will call Padimo's real father and real mother. The father bestowed the three girls on another Rangwila named Inglis who was about the same age as himself. (If we tried to answer *why* he did, the case would no longer be simple.) Padimo's father died while the four children were still young, and their mother remarried a relatively young man named Tomitari. This occurred in about 1914 and the situation then was as follows:

GENEALOGY I
THE INGLIS-TOMITARI RELATIONSHIP 1914
(Males are in italics; ages are in brackets)

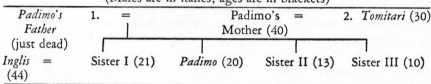

Padimo's Father (just dead)	1. =	Padimo's Mother (40)	=	2. *Tomitari* (30)

| *Inglis* = (44) | Sister I (21) | *Padimo* (20) | Sister II (13) | Sister III (10) |

Fifteen years or so later, all parties were still alive; the two youngest sisters had joined Inglis as wives and all three sisters had borne children to him, including girls. Thus the situation in 1928-29 was:

GENEALOGY II
(1928-29)

Padimo's Mother (55) = *Tomitari* (45)

Padimo

Sister I wife of *Inglis*   (59)
Sister II wife of *Inglis*
Sister III wife of *Inglis*

Daughter A (11)
Daughter B (8)
Daughter C (5)
Daughter D (2)
Daughter E (1)

The three sisters of Padimo had borne five daughters to Inglis and as they were successively born Inglis had bestowed the first three on Tomitari. He did not bestow the fourth or fifth nor any of his daughters by other wives.

The master clue to the whole matter was the marriage in 1914 of Padimo's widowed mother to Tomitari, then little more than thirty. His function had been to act as trustee or stand-in for Inglis' interest, not in the widow but in her daughters who had been bestowed on Inglis by their dead father. The young Tomitari as step-father of the girls had to ensure their safe delivery to Inglis' household. (One was there already but the other two were not.) Tomitari accomplished his mission, acquiring the widow, of course, as a wife in the process; the girls arrived safely in Inglis' household and Inglis paid off handsomely by bestowing their daughters on his honest agent who had held off the competitors.

But by 1923 or thereabouts Inglis had stopped paying off. Tomitari by then had received three bestowals from Inglis. (Actually he had received about six, but three died in infancy). Moreover, he was no longer a young man but was entering the junior elder class and, having received wives from other sources than Inglis, was getting to the point where he would soon have free daughters of his own. He had no intention of performing any more services for Inglis who was now nearly sixty. Hence Inglis had not bestowed any daughters on Tomitari since 1923; those of his daughters who had been born since that year were bestowed on men other than Tomitari and men who were younger and less successful than he.

As we see it, the deals involving widows, particularly the pay-offs to young agents for acting to promote the interests of older men, had distorted what might be called the pure theory of Tiwi bestowal. According to the pure theory, mothers' brothers bestowed their daughters on selected sisters' sons, and the older man who gave a young man a wife and became his wife's father, was performing a kindness toward a favorite nephew for which the nephew should be grateful. But the Inglis-Tomitari operation shows how the theory had become distorted in practice. In order that Inglis might have some young daughters whom he would be free to bestow on his favored young nephew, Tomitari, in 1914 he had had to arrange the young man's marriage with an elderly widow to ensure safe delivery to him (Inglis) of some young wives who would bear him those daughters. Everything went smoothly and no slip-up occurred, yet by the time Inglis was in a position to give a wife to his favored young nephew, he found that the latter was no longer a dependent young man but a successful junior elder competing with him in his own field of identifying and using talent among the younger men. Tomitari's first daughter, born in 1927—not to any daughter of Inglis but to an older wife— was bestowed by its father on the distant but very promising Gitjara, a man of thirty-two. Gitjara was thus selected by Tomitari as a promising satellite at about the same age as Tomitari in 1914 had been selected by Inglis. Moreover, Tomitari by this time, far from being the grateful nephew of old Inglis (as the theory stipulated), was looking forward with anticipation to the old man's death, since when that occurred, among the widows of Inglis would be the three sisters of Padimo of whom he was still the nominal father. It was by acting as their step-father when they were children that he had got his own career started. They were indeed the foundation stone of his own career and, having profited so much from them as children, he was keenly interested in their redisposition whenever Inglis' death should put them on the market again. Thus he was simultaneously the husband of some of Inglis' daughters and nominal father of some of Inglis' wives. In the first status, he was expected by the theory to be a grateful son-in-law of Inglis; in the second status, the facts of Tiwi life required him to see Inglis' death as providing him with an opportunity to derive some new benefits for himself from his position as nominal father of the three wives of Inglis whose delivery to Inglis' household he had himself engineered.

Thus the politics of bestowal cannot be separated from the politics of widow remarriage. Every case of one had endless repercussions in the other. Sisters' sons who were promised young wives by their mothers' brothers were always too old to be grateful by the time the bestowal occurred or by the even later time when the bestowed child was old enough to come into residence.

Mothers' brothers, in turn, were unable to endow their nephews any earlier because they as younger men had been caught in the same trap. The only way out was by deals in which older men and younger men collaborated. Ideally such collaborative efforts should always have been between mothers' brothers and sisters' sons, but amid such fierce competition and endless log rolling this was not possible, and in many cases the mother's-brother—sister's-son relationship was a *result* of collaboration between older man and younger man rather than a cause. The bond arose from the deal rather than from their original kinship, particularly when the two men involved were very close in age.

The collaborative deals between older men and younger men were essentially designed to compensate for the older man's inability to bestow a young wife upon the younger man at a reasonable age. As was stated before, not until he was about forty-five would the older man have a free or unencumbered daughter. By then his younger collaborator and satellite had attracted the attention of older and wealthier men with many unencumbered daughters. After performing all his services to Inglis, young Tomitari had not had to depend on him for his first bestowal. A wealthier man than Inglis had reached over Inglis' head, so to speak, and bought Tomitari's allegiance by the bestowal of a young wife who provided Tomitari with a free daughter several years earlier than any child the daughters of Inglis could provide. With this first unencumbered daughter, Tomitari promptly bid for the allegiance of Gitjara. Put in terms of allegiances, Tomitari had from 1914 until about 1923 been the henchman of Inglis. During those years he passed from about age thirty to age forty, and his main patron was Inglis, who passed from about forty-four and on the fringes of the elder group to about fifty-four and accepted among the elder group. Then—and this was typical of the shift of allegiance that occurred in most life careers—a senior elder more wealthy in wives and daughters than Inglis bid for Tomitari's allegiance, and Tomitari became his henchman. Five years later, in 1928, Tomitari was a coming junior elder in Rangu and a man of influence in his own right. His oldest bestowed wife had already borne him a daughter whom he used to make Gitjara *his* henchman. The three wives (daughters A, B, and C) of Inglis were nearing the stage when they would join his household and he had other bestowals from other quarters. His relation to Inglis was no longer that of henchman but of rival, since they were now both successful elders in the same band and competitors in the struggle to make younger men dependent on them. Far from bestowing any more daughters on Tomitari, Inglis was bestowing his daughters (now plentiful) on men of Gitjara's generation (though not on Gitjara). Having more free daughters than Tomitari, he had more men of that generation to patronize, but since Inglis was sixty and Tomitari only forty-five, time was obviously on the side of the latter.

Thus the crux of the Tiwi system of influence-satelliteship-marriage arrangement-wealth centered around what happened to a man in his thirties. This is what we meant when we said earlier that old men with many daughters bestowed them on young men who looked to them like "comers." Old men with many free daughters were usually men well over fifty. "Comers" were men in their thirties. In so choosing the "comers," the old and wealthy men reached right over the junior elders and the forty-year-old group down to the ranks of the young operators. In this way we may say that the real power group, the successful old gerontocrats, chose their own successors. They chose young men twenty or more years younger than themselves (as Ki-in-kumi chose Padimo) because men at such an age were not rivals or competitors. A man so chosen in his thirties could be already powerful and fairly wealthy by his middle forties (like Tomitari in 1928) and very wealthy in his fifties. Such men went up fast because of their selection by the group in power. Those not so chosen had to go up the hard way by accumulating what position and influence they could by manipulations of the few available females not controlled by the wealthy old men. The "haves" left a small minority of women available to the "have-not" men to keep them quiet, but the great majority of females were concentrated in the hands of a few old men and these old men chose their own successors. Thus the Tiwi system actually deserves to be called a primitive oligarchy as much as it deserves to be called a gerontocracy. It was run by a few old men who ruled it not so much because they were old but because as young men they had been clever and then had lived long enough to reap the rewards of their cleverness. These rewards made up Tiwi wealth— many wives, much leisure, many daughters to bestow, many satellites and henchmen, and much power and influence over other people and tribal affairs.

4

The Collective Life

Legal Affairs

THE MOST SATISFACTORY overall view of Tiwi culture is that, within the general framework of mainland patterns, it had developed along its own distinctive lines. Some of these distinctive lines of development are traceable to the relatively favorable food and rainfall situation; others are traceable to the absence of neighbors. The unusually large polygamous households are, we think, attributable to the good food supply. But the large households of the Tiwi, economically efficient as we judge them to have been, involved certain social costs, the most obvious of which was the enforced celibacy of the younger men. This compulsory celibacy did not, of course, mean chastity. Not only were there the endless charges of seduction against young men, but there was also the more objective fact that most young wives continued to become pregnant with monotonous regularity, no matter how ancient and senile their husbands. (The Tiwi belief that babies came from spirits prevented pregnancies from being used against young wives as proofs of unfaithfulness.) Despite the numerous cases of seduction or alleged seduction, few young men ever took the most straightforward way of escaping from their state of compulsory celibacy—namely, abducting a young wife and running off with her. Here we encounter the other factor of the Tiwi natural environment that explains so much about their cultural development—and that is the absence of neighbors. Young men did not elope with young wives because there was no place to elope to. On the mainland such elopements were common, and the couple sought refuge with a neighboring tribe. But an eloping Tiwi couple could only take refuge with other more remote Tiwi bands where the system was the same as that which they had rebelled against back home, and the people with whom they sought shelter were interrelated with those whom they had defied back home. Hence, no matter where they fled, the Tiwi system, embodied in a war party of the girl's husband's friends and relatives, soon caught up with them. Several cases of such elopements occurred during the period of fieldwork, including the case of one young couple (Peanut and Jumbo's wife) who made repeated attempts to elope over a period of several years. But despite the relaxation of standards that white contact had brought, as long as they remained on the islands these violators of the system were soon forced back into conformity by outraged public opinion and its punitive sanctions. Unless he fled to the mainland with his girl, the young bachelor who stole an old man's young wife had to restore her sooner or later to her rightful husband. Under pre-white conditions they could not flee to the mainland; if they tried, they both probably drowned on the way or at least were never heard of again.

Thus the isolation of the Tiwi made the rule of the gerontocracy much more absolute, and the enforcement of it much more effective than was possible for any of the mainland tribes where violators of the rules could skip across the border. Tiwi bachelors had to be satisfied, by and large, with casual and temporary liaisons and even in these, because of the constant suspicion of the old husbands and the constant spying and scandalmongering of the old wives, they had to be prepared to be often caught and, when caught, to be punished. Thus we come to another of the main emphases in Tiwi culture—the enormous frequency of disputes, fights, duels, and war parties arising directly or indirectly out of cases of seduction. If we may call this area of life the legal area, then over 90 percent of legal affairs were matters in which women were in some way involved.

THE DUEL   The Tiwi formula for handling seduction was very straightforward and clear-cut in its formal outline. Since senior men had young wives and young men had not, seduction was necessarily viewed as an offense by a young man against a senior man. Hence the charge was always laid by the senior and the younger man was always the defendant.[1] At night in camp the accuser hurled his charges at the offender. We described earlier the alternatives available at this stage to both parties. Two of those alternatives were for the old man to press the matter to a public "trial," either the next day, if the camp was already a large one, or else on the next occasion when both men were present in a big gathering.

The basic shape of all Tiwi trials was standardized in the form that we have been calling the duel. Everybody present—men, women, children, and dogs—formed a rough circle in an open space, sitting or standing according to their degree of excitement at the moment. At one end stood the accuser, the old man, covered from head to foot in white paint, with his ceremonial spears in one hand and a bundle of the more useful hunting spears in the

---

[1] Under pre-white conditions this had to be so. After the arrival of the Catholic missionaries, some young men through Mission manipulation got a young wife at an age that would have been impossible earlier. This resulted in an occasional case around the Mission where a *young* husband charged a man older than himself with seducing his wife. The resulting duel, with an older man as defendant, was regarded by the Tiwi as both embarrassing and ludicrous, perhaps analogous to the average American's attitude toward female professional wrestlers. (See Hart 1954 for a case of this sort, the duel of Bob v. Louis.)

other. At the opposite end stood the defendant, with little or no paint on him, perhaps holding a hunting spear or two in his hand (a sign of insolence), perhaps holding only throwing sticks (less defiant, since the stick was an inferior weapon more appropriate to young men), or perhaps entirely weapon-less (a sign of proper humility and the deference to his seniors that all bache-lors ought to show in such situations). The accuser, with many gestures, par-ticularly with much stamping of the feet and chewing of the beard, told the young man in detail precisely what he and all right-minded members of the community thought of him. This angry, loud harangue went into minute detail, not only about the actual offense, but the whole life career of the defendant, and paid particular attention to occasions in the past when the old man even remotely, or some of his relatives, even more remotely, had performed kind-nesses toward either the young man or some of his relatives. It is difficult to summarize briefly one of these harangues, but the general formula, subject to much variation by each individual accuser, appeared to be the building up of as much contrast as possible between the criminal or antisocial character of the young man's actions and the fact that he was a member of a network of interpersonal relationships in which mutual aid and reciprocal obligations were essential. The Tiwi orators, of course, did not put the matter in such abstract terms. They listed the long catalogue of people who had done things for the young man since his birth, and for his ancestors and relatives, until the cata-logue took in practically the whole tribe—past, present, and future. And what had he done to repay his obligations to all these people? "Why, the miserable, ungrateful wretch spends his time hanging around my camp, etc., etc. And not only my camp, but last year it was widely believed that he was indulging in similar actions around the camp of my esteemed fellow-elder, So and So." We do not think that we are overintellectualizing the content of these harangues if we say that they involved the old man's reminding the young man of his debt to society, and his attempting to convey the idea that social life needed mutual aid and trust between all its members.

After twenty minutes or so of this sociological abuse and blame pinning, the old man threw aside his ceremonial spears and began to throw his hunting spears at the defendant. This active phase of the duel conformed to a stereo-typed pattern which in some respects resembled baseball. The old man stood about ten feet farther away from the young man than the pitcher stands from the plate. The young man had to avoid being hit by the spears. To do this he was permitted to jump from side to side or into the air, or to duck, but he was expected always to land on approximately the same spot as he had been standing on when the first spear was thrown. Thus there was no marked strike zone, but an implied one. If the accused jumped well away from the strike zone, he was jeered by the crowd. If the old man was wild, he was jeered too, but more respectfully. Under such rules a modern baseball hitter, having no bat in his hand to worry about, would almost never be hit by a pitched ball, and the Tiwi young men were similarly never likely to be hit by an old man's spears. The main danger was the spear that pitched in the dirt. Although clearly outside the strike zone and hence an indication that the old man was really wild, such a spear was apt to carom off the ground at an unexpected angle and inflict a severe wound before the spectators (as collective umpires) had time to call it—in which case the duel was over and the accused was punished.[2]

Apart from those that unpredictably deflected off the ground, or even off a neighboring tree, the young man could dodge the old man's spears indefinitely if he wanted to. He was much younger and hence almost invariably in much better shape than the older man. But if he did this, the old man soon began to look a little ridiculous, and Tiwi society thoroughly disapproved of young men who made old men look ridiculous in public. Continued dodging and jumping and weaving of the body, no matter how gracefully they were done, were not prolonged by any young man who hoped in time to become a respected elder himself. The elders in the last analysis controlled bestowals, and holding one of them up to public ridicule was sure to antagonize all of them. So the young man, having for five or ten minutes demonstrated his physical ability to avoid being hit, then showed a proper moral attitude by allowing himself to be hit. This took even greater skill in bodily movement. Trying to lose a fight without making it too obvious to the crowd and without getting hurt too much oneself is a problem that confronts some professional athletes in our own culture, and few of them do it with as much skill as the younger Tiwi in the same situation. A fairly deep cut on the arm or thigh that bled a lot but healed quickly was the most desirable wound to help the old man inflict, and when the blood gushed from such a wound the crowd yelled approval and the duel was over. The young man had behaved admirably, the old man had vindicated his honor, the sanctity of marriage and the Tiwi constitution had been upheld, and everybody went home satisfied and full of moral rectitude. Seduction did not pay.

This was the Tiwi duel as it ideally should be conducted, and in perhaps as many as two-thirds of all such disputes it was so conducted. Divergences from this form clearly arose from the unpredictability of human beings and their fondness for trying to exercise choice instead of following a set pattern. Though the dice were heavily loaded against them, some Tiwi young men chose defiance instead of repentance. There were various avenues of defiance open to them. The mildest was to refuse to allow the old man's spears to hit the target. Slightly more brazen were the young men who turned up at the beginning of the duel with throwing sticks or hunting spears in their hands, even though they used these not to throw but to knock aside contemptuously the spears of the old man. More brazen still was the young man, rare but not unknown, who went so far as to throw missiles back at the older accuser. All such attempts to defy the traditional pattern of the duel met with the same response, and that very quickly. The duel began as usual with the two antagonists facing one another inside the circle of spectators. As soon as it became apparent that the young man was not conforming to the normal pattern of meekness and nonretaliation, there would be immediate activity on the

---

[2] Two cases of broken legs below the knee within six weeks of each other in 1928 give some indication of the force with which such badly aimed spears would bounce off the ground.

sidelines. Two or three or four senior men would leave the spectators and range themselves alongside the accuser, spears in hand. Other senior men would quietly leave their seats and sit down in the audience alongside close relatives of the young defendant, particularly his full brothers or his father, if they were present, and gently lay restraining hands upon them. Within a few minutes there was no longer an old man facing a young man but as many as four or five old men facing one young man, and no sign of support for him. His close male relatives would keep their seats or (more often) allow themselves to be led away as if they did not want to witness what was coming next. Never, in any of these cases, did any supporter of the young man step into the ring and line up with him. He remained an isolate, faced by several older men, and of course he had no chance. It was easy to dodge the spears of one opponent, since they had to be thrown one at a time; it was impossible to dodge the spears of more than one, since they could be thrown more or less simultaneously.

Usually this baring of its teeth by society-at-large was enough. The group of elders did not need to throw many spears simultaneously. The accused capitulated by throwing aside his spears or throwing sticks, or if the defiance had been only of the mildest form—namely, an undue prolongation of the dodging—he allowed his accuser to score a direct hit and the duel ended in the normal way. In the rare cases of the accused refusing to give up, even when confronted by a menacing line of several elders, a concerted volley or two from them quickly knocked him out, and in pre-white days, usually killed him.[3] Crime thus paid even less for the accused who chose defiance than it did for the accused who allowed himself to be wounded in a duel by a doddering ancient three times his age. The greater the amount of defiance, the more clear it became that the doddering ancient, acting ostensibly as an outraged husband, was the responsible agent of society dispensing public justice. If he needed help, all responsible elders went to his aid, and the kinsmen of the accused stood aside and let justice take its course.

WARFARE   Apart from the occasional castaways and the very occasional other visitors such as "Malays," the Tiwi in pre-white times had nobody to fight with except each other. Duels of the type we have just described were their only formula for settling disputes, and these occasionally became sufficiently broadened to warrant being called warfare. The expedition of Tiklauila and Rangwila to the country of the Mandiimbula which was listed in Chapter 2 among the travels of Tu'untalumi in 1928 was an example of this sort of activity. At least half a dozen senior members of the two first-named bands had disputes with various individuals among the Mandiimbula. Some of these were seduction cases but some of them involved charges by elder against elder,

---

[3] Since the coming of white administration, the Tiwi have found that when a man is killed in a native duel, there is a strong likelihood that white policemen will appear and will drag some of them off to Darwin where incomprehensible proceedings called murder trials then take place. To avoid such nonsense, since about 1925 they have tended to use throwing sticks rather than spears in their fighting. Throwing sticks, while dangerous, seldom kill people outright and as long as nobody is killed, the police in Darwin show no interest in native fights on the islands.

of nondelivery of bestowed daughters, or other types of broken promises. Some of these cases had been going on for years, and settlement of them at the level of the individual duel had failed. The aggrieved individuals in the two Bathurst Island bands therefore pooled their grievances, persuaded many of their relatives and friends who were not aggrieved to join them, and a large party of men of all ages set off for the Mandiimbula territory.

This party, comprising about thirty fighting men all heavily armed and all wearing the white paint indicative of anger and hostile intent, was a "war" party, and its coming to their territory was recognized as such by the Mandiimbula. On arrival at the place where the latter, duly warned of its approach, had gathered, the war party announced its presence. Both sides then exchanged a few insults and agreed to meet formally the next day in an open space where there was plenty of room. After a night mostly spent by both sides in individual visiting and renewing old acquaintances, the two armies met next morning in battle array, with the thirty Tiklauila-Rangwila warriors drawn up at one end of the clearing, and about sixty local warriors at the other end. Immediately the familiar patterns of the duel imposed themselves. A senior individual on one side began a harangue directed at an individual on the other. When he ran out of breath, another individual began his complaint. Since each accused Mandiimbula replied individually to the charges made against him, the whole proceeding remained at the level of mutual charges and replies between pairs of individuals. Angry old men on both sides often seemed to be trying to find a basis that would justify or provoke a general attack by one group upon the other, but always failed to find it because of the particularity of the charges. The rules of Tiwi procedure compelled the accuser to specify the sources of his charges and his anger, and these always turned out to be directed not at the Mandiimbula band, but at one, or at most two or three, individual members of that band. And when another old man took the center of attention, his anger would be directed at quite different individuals. Hence when spears began to be thrown, they were thrown by individuals at individuals for reasons based on individual disputes. Unlike the seduction duels, however, these duels occurred mostly between two senior men, and the danger of a direct hit was much reduced because of the poor marksmanship of both parties. On the other hand, the danger of somebody getting hurt was increased because a fight between two old men was likely to spread as other old men were drawn into it to support one or the other side—in which case, a wild melee occurred with badly thrown spears flying in all directions. This was probably a good thing, because soon somebody was bound to be hit, thus ending the fight. Not infrequently the person hit was some innocent noncombatant or one of the screaming old women who weaved through the fighting men, yelling obscenities at everybody, and whose reflexes for dodging spears were not as fast as those of the men.

As soon as somebody was wounded, even a seemingly irrelevant crone, fighting stopped immediately until the implications of this new incident could be assessed by both sides. For the crone was never really irrelevant; she was somebody's mother and somebody else's wife and somebody else's sister and therefore the question of who threw the spear that wounded her gave rise to a new series of wrangles which had to be integrated into all the old ones. A man who had been quietly sitting, minding his own business and having no quarrels with anybody, would suddenly leap into the center of the stage and announce that the damaged old lady was his mother and therefore he wanted the hide of the rat that had damaged her, and a whole new argument was in progress.

If the person wounded in the first flurry of spear throwing was a senior male, that similarly led the arguments off in some new direction since his kinsmen in *both* war parties felt compelled to support him or revenge his wound or inflict a wound on his wounder. Frequently it appeared that the original matters of dispute, which had brought the two war parties together in the first place, were forgotten and lost in the new disputes and fights that originated on the field of battle. Such a view was supported by the frequency with which one found at the end of the day that the main casualties and the main headline performers had been people who had gone to the field of battle in the morning with no quarrel with anybody, and not even wearing white paint. Even the most peaceful spectator in the most remote corner of the gallery was likely to find himself in the center of the ring before the day was over at a Tiwi "battle."

Despite this apparent confusion and near anarchy of procedure, however, the main outlines were quite clear. The bands were not firm political entities and therefore could not do battle, as bands, with each other. Everybody, on both sides, was interrelated in the same kinship system. An angry old Tiklauila, abusing and throwing spears at an angry old Mandiimbula, might have as the basis of his complaint the fact that the Mandiimbula father had promised but not delivered one of his daughters. Since Tiwi bestowals were from mother's brother to sister's son, the spear throwing was patently a case of a sister's son abusing his mother's brother, and the fact that the two men belonged to different bands was not germane to their dispute. The angry Tiklauila elder could not demand support from other Tiklauila *as Tiklauila* in the case at issue for it involved a dispute between kinsmen whose band affiliations were irrelevant to the subject matter. Mainly for this reason the so-called war party of one band against another band turned out to be only a loose collection of individuals, each with his own case to argue, who found it convenient, and safer, to travel together into the territory of another band and argue all their individual cases on the same day at the same place. Tiwi interpersonal relations were primarily kin relations between members of all bands; territorial loyalties were shifting ones, temporary and necessarily quite subordinate to kin loyalties. Hence warfare, in the sense of pitched battles between groups aligned through territorial loyalties, did not occur and could not occur among the Tiwi.

The confusion of the so-called battle itself was also due to the primacy of kinship and friendship ties. When a man with a grievance started his harangue on a battlefield, he was never quite sure of what support he would get or where it would come from. He was pretty much on his own, even though he had arrived there as a member of a large war party. This situation stemmed from the coexistence, on the one hand, of the intricate web of kinship that united everybody present and made the problem of who would support whom unpredictable enough, and, on the other, the intricate network of deals and promises and personal alliances and obligations that every senior Tiwi man had woven inside the kinship system. A Tiwi elder did not, for example, have one category of relatives called his mother's brothers; he had at least three different categories of mother's brothers. There were those mother's brothers who had given him nothing, those who had given him wives, and those who had promised him a wife but were dragging their feet on delivery, or even trying to renege on their promise. In pressing a case against one of this third category, an elder might quite conceivably alienate some of his mother's brothers of the second category. Nor could he be sure of the support of even his own brothers, since they were certainly cultivating, and possibly undercutting him with, the same donors of daughters as he was involved with. Perhaps the nondelivery, which was the whole basis of his case against the mother's brother, had been instigated by his own brother trying to engineer a rebestowal of the girl to him. Because of the two networks, that of formal kinship obligations and that of marriage deals, two Tiwi seniors engaged in a dispute had no impartial body to whom they could submit their arguments about breach of contract. Disputes between a young man and an elder could be submitted to the publicly witnessed duel, since these were not breaches of contract but cases of trespass by the young men, and as such were crimes. Impartial public opinion upheld the old men and punished the young men every time. The old men's arguments with each other, however, could not be so adjusted, since they involved marriage deals (as distinct from seduction) and in marriage deals everybody was involved and nobody was impartial. Where any senior stood on any marriage deal in dispute depended on how that deal fitted into his own conniving. In that area of life, every adult man had his own axes to grind and a disinterested group of umpires was impossible to find.

Thus Tiwi battles had to be the confused, disorderly, inconclusive things they always were. They usually lasted all day, during which about two-thirds of the elapsed time was consumed in violent talk and mutual abuse between constantly changing central characters and satellites. The remaining third of the time was divided between duels involving a pair of men who threw spears at each other until one was wounded, and brief flurries of more general weapon throwing involving perhaps a dozen men at a time, which ended whenever somebody, even a spectator, was hit. As a result of this full day of violence, perhaps a few of the cases would be settled that night—by a father handing over his delayed daughter, or a man with a disputed wife relinquishing her to her rightful husband—but when the war party left next day to return home, the number of cases settled was likely to be less than the number of new feuds, grievances, and injuries that had originated during the day of battle. For not only did the participants carry away from the battlefield a vivid memory of all the physical wounds, intended or accidental, inflicted by whom on whom, but they also brooded long and suspiciously upon who had supported whom and why, either verbally or with spear in hand. In addition, all the incidents of the battle, in minute detail, were relayed to the rest of the tribe who had not been present, and many of these absentees would discover, among the proceedings, things they did not like or suspicious-looking actions on the part of some of their competitors or putative friends. These they would weave into their own strategies and store up for future use. An elder frequently found some basis for a new grievance against somebody in the events of a battle at which he had not even been present.

Finally, through all these disputes and hostile actions between senior men ran their united suspicion of bachelors. The only "battle" in two years between large groups drawn from distinct bands that had a clear-cut and definite final act was one fought in Rangu in late 1928. On that occasion, after disputing and fighting among themselves from early morning until mid-afternoon, all the old men present from both war parties gradually channeled all their anger toward one unfortunate young Mandiimbula bachelor whom they finally accused of going around from band to band creating misunderstandings between various elders. Several elders on both sides testified publicly that their mistrust of each other had started shortly after the bachelor in question had begun hanging around their households; whereupon the senior warriors of the two opposing armies had no difficulty in deciding that most of their suspicions of each other "were all his fault," and with great unanimity ganged up on the bachelor and quickly clubbed him into unconsciousness for being a troublemaker and a suspicion spreader. In the midst of battle the gerontocracy had reasserted its solidarity by finding a bachelor scapegoat upon whom to unload all their mutual suspicions and aggressions.

Religious Activities

If by religious activities we mean those beliefs and practices which pertain to unseen or supernatural forces, including rituals whose performance somehow affects those forces, then Tiwi religion readily crystallized around three focal points. These were: 1) their elaborate system of day-to-day taboos; 2) the elaborate set of beliefs and rituals pertaining to death; and 3) their complicated initiation ceremonies for young men. Add to these their myths and folklore about creation and their tribal past, and the whole of Tiwi religion has been covered. Space permits only brief mention of these three focal points.

TABOO   In earlier chapters we have pointed out several aspects of life in which Tiwi culture diverged sharply from what anthropologists have come to regard as Australian mainland norms and we have suggested that these differences from the mainland are most reasonably to be attributed to either Tiwi isolation or favorable food supply, or some combination of both factors. In their religious life this same line of explanation continues to have validity. To those familiar with the cultures of Australian tribes, perhaps nothing is so startling as to be told that the Tiwi almost completely lacked what we must call "positive" magic. Such familiar mainland practices as bone pointing or "singing" a man to injury or death were completely unknown on the islands, and though references to people dying through supernatural agency were often made, it was very hard to find any positive techniques or known practitioners of such techniques. Briefly the Tiwi may be said to have believed that magical acts were possible but to have lacked any knowledge of how to perform them. If, as anthropology is wont to teach, magic is used in the simpler societies to handle and control the unpredictable or mysterious areas of life, then this absence of magic among the Tiwi needs an explanation. Our hypothesis is that the Tiwi did not use magic in human relations because they had never invented magic for use in other unpredictable areas of life—for example, to control the natural world. And they had never invented magic to control their natural world because their physical environment was on the whole a satisfactory and not a hostile universe.

If we run through the areas of life that many of the simpler peoples use magical means to control, we find that many of them were not problems for the Tiwi. The rainfall and water supply were more than adequate; the food supply was good, needing only people to come and gather it; wild animals (except snakes and crocodiles) were unknown; tropical diseases (except yaws) scarcely existed; cyclones, tornados, and earthquakes were very rare, and thunder and lightning were no more frightening there than in, say, Chicago. Death, of course, is mysterious and unpredictable everywhere, but to handle that they had most elaborate burial and mourning customs that were not magical but collective rituals. Perhaps the most favorable feature in the whole friendly Tiwi universe was the absence of any neighboring tribe. Their cultural isolation removed all fear or suspicion of what the foreigners next door might be up to, and one gets the impression from the literature, though it has not been systematically explored, that the hotbeds of magic making and sorcery were areas of the primitive world, like Melanesia or Central Australia, where people were acutely conscious of their neighbors and always expecting magic and sorcery to be directed by them across the village or tribal boundaries. The Tiwi, having no neighbors, had nobody to be suspicious of except each other, and their suspicions of each other were mostly rational suspicions, of men motivated like themselves and using the same political tricks against each other.

The strongest support for the hypothesis that the Tiwi found their environment a friendly and reassuring universe to live in comes from their wide elaboration and reliance upon the negative form of magic called taboo. As a tribe they were magic free but taboo ridden. Their generic word for anything sacred or forbidden or untouchable was *pukimani,* a word which in its most common form referred to a state of special being in which a person or thing temporarily was. Thus mourners were *pukimani* for the period of their mourning, youths undergoing initiation were *pukimani* during the cere-monies, a woman who had just given birth was *pukimani* for a week or two afterwards. Dead bodies were *pukimani* until buried; graveposts were *pukimani* once erected on the grave; the names of dead people immediately became *pukimani* on their deaths and could not be used, and the same was true of all the names bestowed by a dead man on the children of his household and all the other words in the language that sounded similar to the name of the dead man.[4] All ceremonials and rituals were *pukimani* as were the main performers and the armlets, neck ornaments, and other ceremonial objects. People in a *pukimani* state had to observe all sorts of avoidances of and abstentions from everyday actions, particularly with regard to food and sex. Close relatives of dead people could not touch food but had to be fed by nonmourners. That pillar of rigid orthodoxy, Tu'untalumi, was virtually never able to feed himself but was in a *pukimani* state almost the whole year round and needed one of his wives to feed him. (Another advantage of a large household.) Certain spots in the bush or on the banks of streams were *pukimani* places; the dimly seen outline of the Australian coast was *pukimani* as was the ocean near Cape Keith where the Tiwi ancestors had first created the Tiwi world; and finally, the violation of a *pukimani* restriction rendered the violator *pukimani*.

Pukimani as thus applied to people, places, things, names, words, restrictions, and avoidances, meant both sacred and taboo, and was clearly one of that widespread class of words and concepts that is almost standard among the simpler societies. The only noteworthy thing about its Tiwi form is that *pukimani* was a state which people did not actively seek to enter but which happened to people regardless of their wishes. Furthermore, when a man found himself in a state of *pukimani,* his behavior was automatically prescribed for him and for the duration of his *pukimani* condition he observed his avoidances and his abstentions just as automatically as he dropped them when his *pukimani* period expired. When he became *pukimani,* he punctiliously fulfilled the requirements because if he did not, he was likely to be unsuccessful in his enterprises. Big men simply did not dare to be casual about the requirements lest their reputations suffer and they lose face and influence. Less successful men were occasionally explained as probably being secret violators. "His wives and daughters all seem to die young; he must have broken some *pukimani* restrictions sometime" was a reason often given for somebody's failure to be as successful as he might have been. It was noticeable in such explanations of nonsuccess that the failure, or in our terms the bad luck, was attributed to the violation of the taboos, never to the active displeasure of the spirits. The spirits simply did not figure in the picture.

Apart from the big ceremonial occasions, a Tiwi did not have much concern with religion in his everyday life except through some aspect of the *pukimani* system. It was only through *pukimani* that the sacred world impinged upon him at all for most of the year. Since *pukimani* was a condition that could not be actively sought but "just happened" to a person every so often by such common events as the death of a relative, his wife giving birth, or his

---

[4] When a man named Tibuki died in 1928, a crisis occurred at the Mission where the natives were supposed to make their requests in pidgin English. How could they now ask for tobacco, since that word was now *pukimani?*

sister's son being initiated, the attitude of a Tiwi toward the whole *pukimani* state was essentially a passive attitude. *Pukimani* behavior was something one accepted and conformed to when required; it was in no way an active attempt to change nature, people, food, gods, spirits, or anything else in the universe. It is therefore not unreasonable to conclude that since their *pukimani* system offered them no handle by which to seek actively to alter the universe in which they lived, the Tiwi found that universe to their liking as it was. Unlike the tribes of central Australia who lavished a lot of thought upon magical methods of improving the food supply or the rainfall, the Tiwi believed and acted on the belief that as long as they observed their *pukimani* taboos, the food would continue to be as abundant and the rains as regular as they had always been. The central Australians, by seeking to coerce nature through magic, suggest that they found nature unsatisfactory; the Tiwi, by relying upon passive taboo-observance alone, suggest rather that their relationship to nature was an acceptable equilibrium that they wanted to preserve, not change. And if everybody observed his *pukimani* taboos when required, that equilibrium would remain undisturbed. Hence the antisocial man in Tiwi was not the maker of individual magic (he was unknown, anyway) but the nonobserver of taboo. By his nonobservance he threatened to upset the normally satisfactory equilibrium between man and nature. For a senior Tiwi male to be charged publicly with breaking *pukimani* rules was a disgrace and a blow to his prestige and his position in public opinion. His behavior was possibly a sin against the spirits but it was certainly a shame in the eyes of his fellows. *Pukimani* observance was thus a matter of respectability to a much greater degree than it was a matter of pleasing the spirits.

DEATH   As was mentioned above, death is the natural phenomenon around which the Tiwi had woven their most elaborate web of ritual. The most frequent and most important Tiwi ceremonies were the mourning ceremonies, and they came in three sizes—small, medium, and large—depending on the age, sex, and importance of the dead person. The mourning ceremonies which drew the crowds were not held until some time after the death and burial. All bodies of dead persons were buried within twenty-four hours of their death by digging a hole near the camp where the death had occurred and placing the body, wrapped in bark, in it. Near most well-used camping spots there was already a graveyard marked by old graveposts, and the latest corpse was buried there or near there. Seldom was the body carried any distance for burial. If a person died even less than a mile from an old burial ground, there was little inclination to carry the body that far. He would be buried, instead, within perhaps a hundred yards of where he died. This had certain awkward repercussions for social organization, since occasionally a person died while away from his home district and, being buried where he died, his ceremonies were held and his posts erected in a district in which his immediate family did not live. Young men often used this to validate a change of residence, giving as their reason for living in a band territory in which they had not grown up, the location there of their father's graveposts.

To avoid constant use of the awkward phrase "mourning ceremony," we refer to it as the funeral though it took place some considerable time after the burial of the body. How long a time elapsed between the burial and the funeral depended upon the importance of the dead person. The more important the deceased, the longer it took after his or her burial to prepare for the funeral, both ceremonially and practically. Babies frequently had no funeral ceremonies at all, especially if they died very young and unnamed. Children were given small funerals, held within a month or so after the death, and the people present were merely the members of the local households. Young adult men and all adult women had funerals of medium size, and old men had the biggest funerals of all. Big funerals were rarely held in the wet season because of the height of the grass and bush and the consequent difficulty of travel. The season after the end of the rains (April-May-June) was a favorite time for funerals since by then people were moving again and there was then an accumulated backlog of funerals to be held for people who had died late in the previous dry season or during the wet. The mourning ceremonies of two or more people were sometimes held together; this obviously required that they be buried close together, although they need not have died at the same time. Seeking as usual to increase his importance in the public eye, a man might hold the medium-sized funeral of one of his children at the same time and place as the big funeral of an important elder—provided their graves were close together—even though two or three months had separated the two deaths.

The actual burial of the body immediately after death was usually a small affair attended only by whatever people happened to be in the vicinity. But some Tiwi ancients were on their last legs for months before they finally expired, and it was typical of Tiwi psychology that people should maneuver to be present when a death occurred. Until the anthropologist understood that even death had its political aspects, he could not understand why the Tiwi were always so anxious to hang around the camp of an old man who was taking an awfully long time to die. Since so very little happened at the actual time of death, this desire to be on the spot seemed merely morbid curiosity.[5] But it was not. A death immediately divided the whole tribe into two groups: a small group of relatives who automatically became mourners and therefore in a state of strict taboo, and the rest who were not sufficiently close to the deceased to have to assume a state of *pukimani*. The mourners, being *pukimani*, could do scarcely anything except weep and wail and gash their heads with stone axes. They could not touch the body or wrap it in bark; nor could they dig the grave, nor put the body in, nor fill in the hole. They had to ask non-mourners to carry out these tasks and thus became obligated to those non-

---

[5] How else was one to interpret the reluctance of Hart's party to move on, after spending three weeks waiting for old Tamboo to die, and the old man still lingered on? "Let's wait another day; maybe he'll die tomorrow" was the invariable response to suggestions that we move. "And if he does die, what will happen?" "Nothing; we'll move on then." But this was early in the fieldwork period, before Hart realized the all-pervasive character of Tiwi opportunism.

mourners for their services. Death, in other words, incapacitated the relatives, so the nonrelatives swarmed in to "help" them—that is, take advantage of their incapacity. A man who could say, "I helped to dig your mother's grave" had a hold for the rest of his life over the man or men to whom he could say it. Such a hold was not as strong, of course, as that of a man who could say, "I helped you get your first bestowed wife," but the difference of obligation was only a difference of degree. The Tiwi were always "helping" each other, but the man who was "helped" therefore "owed" something to his helper. At deaths, mourners mourned and nonmourners did the work; therefore the mourners "owed" the nonmourners, and such debts were carried on the same mental ledgers as other debts, such as marriage debts.

When deaths occurred suddenly and unexpectedly, the mourners had to choose their helpers for the burial from the relatively few people present at the time, and were thus often forced to become obligated to men they did not much relish being under obligation to. At the funerals the same bookkeeping mentality prevailed, but since these were not held until months after the death and burial, the chief mourners had time to select their helpers with care and political finesse. Satellites were very useful in this connection, since a man could ask his satellites to perform the necessary ceremonial services and thus get a return from them for the debts of gratitude they already owed him. This was one reason why a skillful Tiwi politician did not by any means select only close kinsmen for satelliteship. A death which made him *pukimani* was likely to make his close kinsmen *pukimani* also, hence he needed some satellites who were not close kinsmen.

In the interval between the burial and the funeral, the chief mourner, on behalf of all the mourners but fairly independently if he were a big man, allocated all the jobs that had to be done in preparation for the funeral. Everybody who came had to be fed by the mourners, and the collection and hoarding of the necessary food devolved on the women of the mourning households. Thus the mourners provided the food, but everything else necessary had to be prepared by nonmourners. The chief item among the ceremonial necessities was the graveposts. The prohibition on mourners approaching the body and the grave extended to the posts, and therefore the cutting, carving, erecting on the grave, and painting of these central features of the funeral ceremonies had to be carried out by nonmourners, "asked to cut the posts" by the chief mourner. Here there was much room for influence maneuvers. A big man acting as chief mourner for a dead relative wanted the funeral to be as lavish as possible, to show his own importance. But the more important the nonmourners he selected to cut the posts for him, the more he owed them for their services. Such a request was in the nature of asking a favor, and to ask a favor was to put oneself in a subordinate position, in terms of influence. The Tiwi power orientation was so ingrained that, even when acting as chief mourner, an elder could not avoid making his requests and allocating the ceremonial tasks so as to gain ground if possible, or at least not lose any ground, in the influence and prestige race.

The mourning ceremonies, though prolonged for several days of constant dancing and singing, were rather dull and monotonous, considered as ceremonial. The gaily colored posts erected right on the grave served as a sort of central altar. Every senior male sang and danced in turn " his own dance" and the rest of the men standing in a large circle acted as a major chorus. A large gap was left in the circle of men and into this gap and out again danced the women in a disorderly clump, as a sort of minor chorus. Most of the day was taken up with endless repetitions of these individually owned and individually performed dances which had no relation whatever to death or the deceased, but which each "owner" used on every ceremonial occasion. In addition, there were a few ritual performances that were special to the fact of death, including the grand finale of every mourning ceremony, when everybody present, led by the mourners, collectively charged the posts and then roared past them into the surrounding bush. This was done to drive the spirits away from the grave finally and forever and thus end the mourners' state of *pukimani*.

We have no space for further details of ceremonial, but enough has been said to indicate that mourning ceremonies, the biggest collective occasions of the Tiwi dry season, were as much political affairs as they were religious occasions. The connecting link was the state of *pukimani* in which death put the relatives. Men in a state of *pukimani* were at a disadvantage in social and political life while that state lasted. They had to ask other people to do things for them. They had to "pay" for these favors. At the same time they could not afford to be niggardly in running their relative's funeral. If they were, they would never live it down. In such an atmosphere we have to conclude that the spiritual welfare of the deceased was relegated to a minor place and that for the mourners the real climax of the days of frenzied grief around the posts came when the spirits were driven away from the grave into the bush and thus their own *pukimani* state, which had been such a political handicap to them for many months, came to an end.

INITIATION   Space permits only the barest mention of initiation, which was, along with mourning, the chief vehicle of Tiwi ritual. For females there were no initiation ceremonies, but for males it was a long drawn-out and elaborate affair, marked by successive stages or grades which began with the status of *Marukumarni,* which a boy entered when he was about fourteen, and did not end finally until he was around twenty-four. Here again we meet the ideology of debt and obligation. The group of men, necessarily older than himself, who initiated a youth thereby put him under obligation to them for the rest of his life. They "did something for him" and years later would bring it up if his subsequent behavior seemed to be directed against their interests. The obligations contracted in initiation, like obligations contracted at burials or mourning ceremonies, were woven into the kinship and influence systems; indeed the relation of a youth to the men who initiated him was often the beginning of a satellite-patron relationship that lasted half his life.

The initiation of a boy had to be undertaken by a group of men who were already fully initiated themselves and who stood to him in the relation of male cross-cousins. Preferably such men were either married to or likely to marry the boy's sisters, an easily met requirement since girls were "married" so much earlier than their brothers. Very senior and successful men did not bother as a rule with initiation sponsorship because it took too much of their valuable time. Hence in practice, most boys at the *Marukumarni* age were taken in hand by a group of men around 40 years of age who were at least betrothed to, if not already married to, the boys' sisters. Such men justified or rationalized their actions by stating that, as the husbands of the boy's sisters, they wanted their little brother-in-law to be made into a man in proper form. In fact, they were usually given the job by the boy's father, who, having bestowed daughters upon them, regarded it as a legitimate request to make of them. It was the duty of male cross-cousins to initiate their wives' little brothers, but in true Tiwi style the father had to request them to do it, and they counted it in their tallies of what they owed him and what he owed them.

Though the father instigated and stage managed the whole affair, he and his household were always thunderstruck when the cross-cousins—armed to the teeth and painted like a war party—arrived at his camp one evening and proceeded to carry off forcibly the yelling 14-year-old.[6] He had to be dragged literally from the bosom of his family, with his mother screaming and trying to hide him and the father pretending to resist the invaders of his household. From then on, until the final stage (*Mikingula*) at age 24-26, the boy was completely under the authority of the men who carried him off. During these approximately ten to twelve years, he spent much of the time alone with them in the bush where the group lived a monastic existence, as a small band of isolates, speaking to no one (especially not to females) and obtaining their own food. During these phases the tutors guarded the boy as if he were literally a prisoner and taught him all the things—chiefly ritual matters—that grown men should know. At intervals the youth was allowed to go home, on week-end leaves so to speak, but when at home he had to observe all the silences, the modest demeanor, the taboos and the austerities of the isolated life. In monastic language, he was under a strict rule of obedience to his tutors.

Breaking in on the long years of austerity, spent either in seclusion in the bush or in *pukimani* at home, were periodic collective ceremonies when the youth was ritually advanced from one stage of initiation to the next.[7] These were public ceremonies, witnessed by large crowds, and the more important of such transition ceremonies took place in January and February when the *kolema* yams were ripe. At these ceremonies the youths were handled in batches or classes, all the boys of one grade being ritually advanced to the next grade, and the top grade or final class being formally graduated as fully initiated men. The crucial grade—when the pubic hairs were forcibly pulled out and he was at last allowed to talk back a little to his tutors—was usually reached by a youth somewhere between his eighteenth and twentieth years, but

---

[6] See Hart 1955 for some further details of the tearing away of the boy from the bosom of his family.

[7] A full list of initiation grade names and their duration in years is given in Hart 1931.

he still had six years to go after that, not finishing the final grade of *Mikingula* until somewhere past the age of 24 or 25.

In contrast with the mainland initiation ceremonies, we think the most interesting point about Tiwi initiation resides not in the formal ceremonies but in the removal from the food-production units, for long periods of the year, of all the young males between the ages of 14 and 25. It is true that they did not spend *all* their time in seclusion and that after the age of twenty they remained mostly in their household camps, where they contributed to the household food production. Nonetheless, it remains clear that only a very well-off tribe could afford to allow so much time off from food production to all its young hunters. Tiwi fathers, it would seem, in arranging for the initiation of their sons to begin just when they were becoming productive hunters, were willing to sacrifice that productivity for less tangible advantages. The youths, secluded and guarded in the bush while getting an education, were not only out of the work force but were also out of the predatory-bachelor force. A Tiwi elder made sacrifices to "send his sons to college" but he breathed easier to know that the sons of the other elders were all there too.

All males without exception had to go through the full initiation cycle, and from the time of their first forcible seizure at the age of 14-15 to their final graduation at 24-26, they were in a state of *pukimani* and their personal names were strictly taboo to everybody in the tribe. Each youth was referred to only by his grade name, *Marukumarni* for the first year, *Mikingula* for the last four years, and so on. And here we return finally to a point which was mentioned much earlier—namely, the complete unimportance in tribal eyes of all males below the age of twenty-five. Until they had completed the final stage of initiation, Tiwi males were still boys; they did not even have names. Occasionally, when collecting genealogies and coming upon a reference to a young man, the innocent anthropologist would ask, "Is he married?" In tones of the deepest contempt the informant would reply, "That kid, how could he be married? He's still *Mikingula*." Though *Mikingula* was the stage typically reached by a man at about 20-21 and lasted for the next four years, to the Tiwi it was still a stage in the life of a boy. Not until he had finished as *Mikingula* could he step out into the world and life of men. How he spent the years immediately after finishing initiation decided how soon some senior man would think sufficiently highly of him to aid him in acquiring his first ancient widow.

References Cited

Historical References

CONIGRAVE, C. PRICE, 1936, *North Australia*. London: Jonathan Cape.

EARL, GEORGE WINDSOR, 1853, *The Native Races of the Indian Archipelago*: *Papuans*. London: Hippolyte Bailliere.

HEERES, J. E., 1899, *The Part Borne by the Dutch in the Discovery of Australia 1606-1765*. London: Luzac & Company.

MANDER JONES, PHYLLIS, 1948, *The Tasman Map of 1644*. Sydney: The Trustees of the Public Library of New South Wales.

TINDALE, NORMAN, 1956, The Peopling of Southeastern Australia. *Australian Museum Magazine*, Vol. XII, No. 4.

Anthropological References

BERNDT, R. M., 1955, "Murngin" (Wulamba) social organization. *American Anthropologist*, 57: 84-106.

———, 1957, In Reply to Radcliffe-Brown on Australian Local Organization. *American Anthropologist*, 59: 346-351.

ELKIN, A. P., and R. M. and C. H. BERNDT, 1951, Social Organization of Arnhem Land. *Oceania XXX*, No. 4, 253-301.

HART, C. W. M., 1930, The Tiwi of Melville and Bathurst Islands. *Oceania I*, 167-180.

———, 1931, Personal Names among the Tiwi. *Oceania I*, 280-290.

———, 1954, The Sons of Turimpi. *American Anthropologist*, 56: 242-261.

———, 1955, Contrasts between Prepubertal and Postpubertal Education. In

Education and Anthropology, G. D. Spindler (ed.). Stanford, Calif.: Stanford University Press.

MOUNTFORD, CHARLES P., 1958, *The Tiwi, Their Art, Myth and Ceremony*. London: Phoenix House.

MURDOCK, GEORGE PETER, 1949, *Social Structure*. New York: Macmillan.

RADCLIFFE-BROWN, A. R., 1912, Three Tribes of Western Australia. *J. A. I.*, XLIII, 143-194.

――――, 1930, Former Numbers and Distribution of the Australian Aborigines. In *Official Year Book of the Commonwealth of Australia*, No. 23.

――――, 1930-31, The Social Organization of Australian Tribes. Oceania Monographs No. 1. *Oceania I*, Nos. 1-4.

――――, 1956, On Australian Local Organization. *American Anthropologist*, 58: 363-367.

SHARP, ANDREW, 1957, *Ancient Voyagers in the Pacific*. London: Penguin Books.

SPENCER, BALDWIN, 1914, *The Native Tribes of the Northern Territory of Australia*. London: Macmillan.

WARNER, W. LLOYD, 1937, *A Black Civilization*. New York: Harper.

ULITHI: A MICRONESIAN DESIGN FOR LIVING

William A. Lessa

University of California, Los Angeles

William A. Lessa, professor of anthropology at the University of California, Los Angeles, obtained his graduate degrees from the University of Chicago. He did fieldwork with the Ulithians in 1947, 1948–1949, and in 1960 and 1961. His topical interests include religion and mythology.

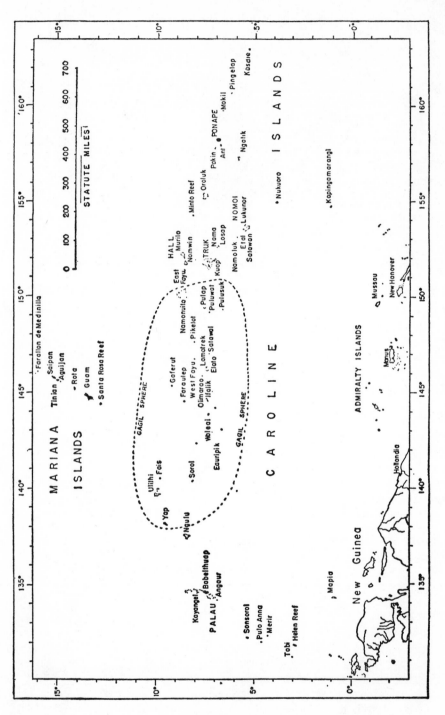

Islands of the Yap empire. Ulithi is in the northwest.

Preface

You must not seek to find the Ulithi described in this book, for it does not exist. To be sure, you can locate the atoll on the map, and if you can procure the permission of the proper authorities to visit the islands, you will find that there is indeed such a place. But the community as here depicted has undergone such a rapid metamorphosis since my first visits in 1947 and 1948–1949, as well as the later ones of 1960 and 1961, that once I was asked by a young native to clarify a point about the old culture. There might have been some merit in writing a work describing cultural change, but I chose not to do so because I have already written on this subject in connection with a great typhoon I studied in 1961. Instead I have assembled from my field notes, and occasionally from the older literature, a picture of Ulithi (pronounced roughly as if it were YOU-li-thee) as it was when first I went there—projected back, in fact, even a decade or two before that.

Almost all my work was under the generous auspices of the Office of Naval Research and the Pacific Science Board of the National Research Council. If it has been successful, much is due to my great informant and wonderful friend Melchethal, who died only recently. He asked for little (that I order a can of paint for him) and gave much (almost a solid year of time). A man of greater native erudition and integrity I have never known. At least twenty-five or thirty other informants were of considerable help but cannot be listed, except for Iamalamai. He became my assistant at the age of eighteen. Occasionally he writes to me and is my chief link with a little world whose kindly people never questioned my motives or lost patience with my presence. It is my fervent hope that my writings can in some measure repay a gift of human warmth that cannot ever be wholly repaid.

WILLIAM A. LESSA

Sherman Oaks, California
January 1966

Contents

Above: The men's council on Mogmog, 1948.

Below: A fish magician, on the right, distrains a canoe.

Above: A women's menstrual lodge.

Below: Young adults. They mingle if not within the incest range.

1

Background

ULITHI ATOLL, located at 10°05′N and 139°43′ E (on the island of Mogmog), is a cluster of low islets of carbonate rock near the equator in the western portion of the Pacific. It is the northernmost of all the islands of the Carolinian archipelago, although nearby Yap and Fais are at only slightly lower latitudes. Guam is about 400 statute miles to the northeast, and New Guinea double that distance to the south. If one were to travel due west for almost a thousand miles one would hit the Philippines, an archipelago not unfamiliar to Ulithians who are often stranded there after being lost in the sea.

A Place To Live

Much is revealed about the mode of life of a people to know that they live on an atoll, for such islands are located in tropical or near-tropical latitudes, have little surface area, are composed of calcareous soil, rely heavily on the sea, and support only small populations.

Strictly speaking, atolls are not primarily coral in composition, being built up also from other organisms that similarly leave deposits of calcium carbonate. The corals, however, are a conspicuous feature. They manifest great variety in size and shape, as well as in color; most are gray or white, but many are tinted beautiful shades of blue, green, yellow, orange, pink, and red. It is the skeletons of these fleshy polyps that assist in atoll formation.

Ulithi is made up of over thirty islets, the number being indeterminate for several reasons. Some islets are no more than sandy excrescences out of the sea. Others may disappear temporarily because of the erosive effects of typhoons and tidal waves. Still others, strictly speaking, are not geologically a part of the main atoll. These fine distinctions need not concern us, except that one of the elements usually included as part of the atoll is in fact a submerged atoll in its own right and includes two islets, Gielap and Iar, which have never been inhabited but have some economic and political significance. This element, to the east, will not ordinarily enter into our considerations.

It is customary to indulge in poetic imagery when describing the outlines of an island or island group, so one may say that Ulithi looks like a broken mushroom whose stem has been slightly detached from its cap. Although this configuration departs from the ideal circular outline of an atoll, it is by no means aberrant, for fewer atolls conform to the ideal than depart from it. Ulithi's characteristic outline is of course largely a function of the outer contours of the volcanic cone forming the basement foundation of the atoll. More immediately, its shape is closely connected with the reef characteristics of the rim of the island group.

Space resources are tiny, the atoll contrasting sharply with the immensity of the sea surrounding it. The land surface of the main atoll, including the detached island of Falalop, is a mere 1.80 square miles. The largest islet is only a mile long and less than that wide. Yet Ulithi is the biggest of all the atolls in the western region of the Carolines, with a great lagoon or "lake" and extensive zones of living reefs, both of these conditions being conducive to fish production. At the same time its large size is a factor in making transportation and communication time-consuming and sometimes arduous, causing some islets to be relatively isolated from the others. The greatest length of the lagoon is about 24 statute miles and the greatest breadth about 15 statute miles, with a surface area of 183 square miles, a marked contrast to the surface of the land. The maximum depth of the lagoon, 210 feet, places it among the deeper lagoons of the Pacific.

The lagoon plays so vital a part in the native culture that it is well to know that its marine life is greatly influenced by special conditions resulting from its shallow waters and enclosed circulation. The water, which is shallow only by contrast with the surrounding ocean, is circulated mainly by the winds, with additional movements created by waves, tides, and the north equatorial current. The exchange of water between ocean and lagoon is greatest in the winter months when the northeasterly winds, aided by the tides, exert strong action and help effect the exchange of water between ocean and lagoon. One cannot help noticing the stagnant appearance of the water of the lagoon during the summer months, in contrast to the cleaner, crisper appearance of the water in the months of the northeasterlies.

The weather and climate are those characteristic of the Pacific atoll realm, which is to say that there is continuous warmth. Air temperatures, according to a spotty survey, show a yearly average of 83° F, but this may be a degree or two higher than the average over many years. Although a difference of about ten degrees exists between day and night averages, there is little change from one month to another. The mean relative humidity, about 84 percent, is so high that it makes the climate seem very hot in terms of sensible temperature. Clear days are not frequent, a general high degree of cloudiness prevailing most of the time. Fog and haze are virtually unheard of, and visibility is exceptionally good at all times except when it rains. There are occasional thunderstorms, due in large part to the fact that convection attributable to the presence of the atoll is kept down by the smallness and lowness of the land surface. These same factors prevent the production of orographical rainfall.

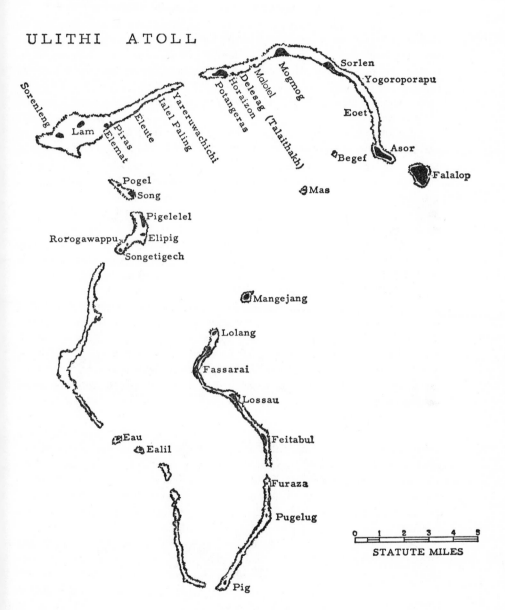

ULITHI ATOLL

Sorenleng

Lam

Piras
Elemat
Eleute
Ialel Paling
Yareruwachichi

Potangeras
Horaizon
Delesag
Malolel
Mogmog

Sorlen
Yogoroporapu
Eoet

Begef
Asor
Falalop

Pogel
Song

Mas

Pigelelel
Rorogawappu
Elipig
Songetigech

Mangejang

Lolang

Fassarai

Lossau

Feitabul

Eau
Ealil

Furaza

Pugelug

Pig

0   1   2   3   4   5
STATUTE MILES

While the northeasterly winds and the easterlies are dominant, the winds show a good deal of variability, with the humid southerly and southwesterly winds almost equally as important as these. Ulithi is not in the trade wind realm; rather it is in the typhoon circulatory region bordering the monsoon realm.

Tropical typhoons, which are of course greatly dreaded and have played a large part in shaping the culture of the atoll, may occur during any month of the year, but almost two thirds of them occur in the four months from July to October. However, the two greatest typhoons to strike within living memory came in March (1907) and November (1960). Ulithi is in the incubating area of tropical cyclones, most of which start a few degrees above or below ten degrees latitude.

Ulithians have no strong concepts concerning the length of the solar year but do maintain a system of lunar months. Their primary interest in the seasons is in the changes in the winds, which are so vital for canoe travel.

Topographically, the flatness and lowness of the islets is their most striking feature. Except for the trees, the very highest point in the atoll is on the island of Falalop and is only about 22 feet. Even this is considerably higher than the average for other islands. As is characteristic of atolls, the lagoon shore is lower than the outward shore of each island, and there is often a depression in the middle of an island, which may be converted by the natives into a swamp garden, especially for the cultivation of taro. The shores of the lagoon side of each island are sandy; the opposite sides are rough. Reefs surround individual islands or groups of islands, with channels where the reefs are not continuous. At low tide it is possible to walk from one island to a neighboring island, but the trip is difficult because of the necessity for wading through water about waist high with rough coral under foot. Natives do not often negotiate it.

Water of brackish quality accumulates in the fresh-water lens (Ghyben-Herzberg lens) formed by rain water seeping down through the rock and sand. This water makes contact with marine water that has infiltrated through the porous rock from the sea, and instead of mixing with it will float upon it because of its lighter density. The body of fresh water floating on the body of salt water assumes the form of a lens which is replenished anew by rainfall. On some islands the water is potable, and natives dig wells to reach it. Surface water does not remain standing very long, and that which is held in capillary openings in the soil soon disappears by evaporation and transpiration through shallow rooted plants. Most water for drinking and cooking is collected from roofs and tree trunks when it rains.

The soil, being coralline, does not support much variety of vegetation. While on the atoll I collected a total of sixty-seven useful species of wild flora, this apparently representing the lot, which may seem large but is not. The number of varieties and species of plants that could be successfully cultivated is small.

The wild biota is poorly represented on land. Small lizards are numerous and varied, and there is the very large monitor lizard. Snakes are absent, except for a small, worm-sized burrowing snake that lives in the ground. There are numerous rats, of three kinds. The only other indigenous mammal is the fruit bat, which attains large size. Insects abound. Scorpions, centipedes, and spiders are present but not as common as millipedes.

Permanent birds are few in species; transient birds are much more numerous in numbers and species. The economic value of the avifauna is trivial.

Fish, arthropods, shellfish, and other sea biota constitute the richest group of fauna, numbering in the hundreds, but no effort will be made to name even the more important of them. They have great economic value to the natives.

It would be injudicious to suppose that an ecologic system with the above-mentioned features has shaped the Ulithian design for living into what it is. We must assume that the culture is not a purely indigenous adaptation, and that much of its nature finds sources in antecedent lands. Nevertheless, the environment has offered certain kinds of resources and been devoid of others, and has had at least some say in the way the people can live.

Those Who Stopped By

Ulithi was caught up early in the voyages of exploration made by Europeans searching for a water route to the East Indies after the old route to the Spice Islands had come under Turkish control. We cannot be sure of the first contacts between natives and Europeans, but there is some chance that a Portuguese captain, Diogo da Rocha, was the first to come to Ulithi, the time being October 1, 1525. He had arrived in the Indies via Africa and was on an expedition from Ternate to Celebes, to which the commander of the Moluccas had sent him in search of gold. The problem as to the identification of the islands visited by da Rocha is his failure to locate them longitudinally, for longitudes had not yet been adopted in those days. The latitude is about right.

There are some who think that Ulithi was sighted by the Spaniard, Alvaro de Saavedra, in 1528, as he was making the third crossing ever made across the Pacific by Europeans. The truth is that the islands he saw are in the Marshalls and that he never got to Ulithi at all.

There is much to support the possibility that Ulithi was sighted in 1543 by Ruy Lopez de Villalobos, a Spaniard. On January 23 of that year he came across a small island that appears to have been Fais, a short distance east of Ulithi. He did not anchor there, but the natives came out in boats, making the sign of the cross and saying in Castilian, "Buenos dias, matalotes!" or "Good day, sailors!" He reports that at the same latitude and 35 leagues to the west he encountered another large island, and there is good reason for us to feel it was Ulithi. But who taught the natives to make the sign of the cross and utter a Spanish greeting is a mystery. There is interest in the Fais episode because it indicates that the natives of this area had met and, possibly, for a while entertained a party of Spaniards.

Interest in the Carolines was whetted by the arrival in the Philippines of many shipwrecked natives, some of them apparently from Ulithi. The Jesuit missionaries were particularly aroused by a group stranded on Samar in 1696, and proceeded to make plans to go to the islands for the purpose of converting

the natives to Christianity. A frigate financed by the Jesuits was lost in a typhoon in 1698 as it was preparing to leave. Work had to stop because no help
was forthcoming from the government, so one of the Jesuits went to Europe in
order to procure funds. He was given moral support by Pope Clement XI and
financial support by Philip V, king of Spain. A galiot was accordingly able to
set out for the Carolines in 1707 but came back empty handed. Another vessel
was similarly unsuccessful in 1709 in locating the islands, although it did come
close to Ulithi. In 1710 a patache, the "Santissima Trinidad," succeeded in putting some missionaries ashore at Sonsorol but they were killed by the natives
while the vessel was away in the course of discovering the Palaus.

Finally, Don Bernardo de Egui y Zabalaga succeeded in reaching Ulithi
on February 6, 1712, on the patache "Santo Domingo." The Spaniards induced
some natives to come aboard and tried to make them drunk so that they could
detain them as guides. They also gave them presents of food, as well as nails,
which they seemed to value most. But all the natives except an old man left the
vessel. The next day there was an encounter over an effort at kidnapping some
young men, and three of the natives were hit by gunfire. The Spaniards then
left. A report on the visit mentions, among other things, that the natives "seem
to be a very gay race." Another report states that the reception given the Spaniards on their arrival was "friendly," and that the natives treated the visitors as
though they were "old acquaintances."

All these events considerably fired up the enthusiasm of a Jesuit destined
to be a major figure in the history of the atoll. Father Juan Antonio Cantova,
stationed on Guam, where he had interviewed some natives shipwrecked there
in 1721, set out for the Carolines in 1722, but after a futile search for the islands his ship was driven to the Philippines and only he survived. The indomi-
table priest undertook to learn navigation against the day when he would try
again, which he did in 1731, arriving at Ulithi on March 2 with a fellow priest,
12 soldiers, 8 cabin boys, and a Ulithian who had been wrecked on Guam. Soon
he had baptized 127 children and was proceeding to teach the gospel to the
adults. Cantova has left us a fine set of records concerning Ulithi, preparing
them both before he left Guam and after arriving at Ulithi.

In May of the same year Cantova prepared to leave the atoll for Guam
in order to procure supplies and additional help for his work. He had planned
to leave his fellow missionary, Father Victor Walter, to carry on in his absence,
but as the vessel was getting ready to sail, he sensed that something was wrong
and sent Walter in his place while he remained behind to handle any possible
emergency. His premonition was justified. As revealed later, some Carolinians
had arrived in the meantime and related to the Ulithians the mistreatment being
administered to the Carolinians marooned on Guam. This, and a smouldering
resentment already existing among some of the men against interference with
their religion and customs, caused them to turn on the missionary party and kill
all of them except a Filipino boy. The murders took place on June 9, 1731, ten
days after Father Walter had left for Guam. Walter did not return until after
he had drifted to the Philippines, remained there a year, had his vessel founder

near the Marianas, and spent nine days on his return voyage to the atoll, all of which took two years.

The fate of the Jesuits not only on Ulithi but on Sonsorol before that caused the Church to call a halt to further efforts to Christianize the western Carolines. These two places, as well as many other islands of the archipelago, had acquired such bad reputations among seafarers that they were subsequently avoided. It is a matter of interest that neither on Sonsorol nor on Ulithi is any memory of the Spanish visits preserved in the historical traditions.

For almost a century Ulithi remained forgotten and unvisited. The atoll was again sighted on June 7, 1823, by a Captain John Mackenzie; the event was treated as a new discovery and the islands were named after him. The British captain, who was on his way to India from Mexico after stopping at Guam, stayed only long enough to exchange some gifts and take some soundings, but he did observe that "the natives were well featured, and seemed particularly inoffensive."

Next came Fedor Petrowitsch Lütke, a distinguished explorer leading a Russian circumnavigation of the world. He was interested in Ulithi because it had been shut off since the Cantova tragedy, but his arrival in 1826 came after Mackenzie had already been there. He praised the kindliness of the atollers and noted that they were very timid, although friendly and "decent."

On December 29, 1838, Ulithi was sighted by two corvettes under the leadership of Dumont d'Urville while exploring the Pacific for the French government, but no landing was made.

The significance of these encounters with Europeans should not be overlooked. The atollers were learning something of a vast unknown world from which strangers came with huge vessels, gunpowder, iron and other wonderful materials, artifacts, and ways that were different. Much of what they found out also came from secondhand sources, from other islanders who had seen Europeans. It must not be supposed that between the time of the Cantova episode and the arrival of the later explorers Ulithi had been living in a world sealed off from European influences. The atoll was kept in continual indirect contact with Spaniards through the lively trade being carried on with the Marianas by natives of other Carolinian islands. These natives would return with iron tools, glass beads, and cloth.

Following these first European visitors came the traders, the most important being the German, Alfred Tetens, and the Irishman, David O'Keefe. An anthropologist, Johann Kubary, of the Museum Godeffroy in Hamburg, was a casual visitor about 1870, making some observations on tattooing. Still another anthropologist, the Russian Nicolas von Miklucho-Maclay, stopped very briefly in 1876.

Behind these seemingly desultory events, a pattern of German interest in the area was emerging, and eventually it ran up against the question of Spanish sovereignty, which was tenuous indeed. After several years of litigation, Pope Leo XIII was asked to adjudicate the dispute, and he ruled in favor of the Spaniards, but Germany eventually acquired the Carolines in 1899 after the

Spaniards had been defeated in war by the United States. Ulithi was visited in 1901, 1904, and 1905 by a district officer by the name of Arno Senfft, who left some good ethnological observations. It was during the German administration that a member of the famous Hamburg Südsee Expedition did research on Ulithi, for a little over two weeks in 1909. He gathered excellent ethnographic notes for so short a stay. It was the policy of the German government to disturb native custom and authority in the area as little as possible, although at the same time expanding the copra trade.

The Japanese took over Ulithi and the rest of the Carolines in 1914 after declaring war against Germany. In 1920 they were given a class C mandate over the islands. Because of Japan's military interest in Micronesia, Ulithi and the other islands were virtually sealed off from the outside world. The principal effects of Japanese control were in travel, trade, and education. The administration tried to observe the conditions and spirit of the mandate. As far as Ulithi is concerned, the greatest single impact was on the economy, for the Japanese set up a local branch office for a while to look after the copra and trading interests of the South Seas Trading Company. During this period, some missionary activity was carried on from Yap by Spanish Jesuits. About 1937, one of these missionaries began to make the first sizable conversions to Catholicism among the Ulithians. However, as the tide of war began to turn against Japan after the events at Pearl Harbor, the Japanese attitude stiffened, the two missionaries on Yap were beheaded, and the natives were treated with greater severity than had been the case before.

The first Americans to arrive on Ulithi during the war were troops of the 81st Army Division, landing on September 20, 1944, in search of nonexistent Japanese. They were greeted in most friendly fashion by the people, even though a useless bombardment had killed five natives. Naval military government soon took over and Ulithi was converted into a huge advance base for the invasion of Okinawa and the Philippines. The natives were confined to the islands of Fassarai and Lossau, and given excellent medical and other attention, free from unwanted intrusions by the military. Naval administration continued after the military had left, and was replaced by civilian control in 1951. From that time on, change has been very swift. Ulithi is now a part of the Trust Territory of the Pacific Islands, under the Department of the Interior.

Those Who Came To Stay

It is usual to attribute an ultimately Asian origin to the Micronesians, and there is no reason to dispute this. Contacts with the mainland were apparently terminated long ago. How many centuries Ulithi has been occupied, and whether it has been a continuous sojourn, cannot be said. Tradition has it that the people of the atoll came "from the east." This does not contradict the idea of a more ancient western provenance for the people of the area as a whole, for it is possible that the low-lying atolls were originally bypassed and then occu-

pied by people who filtered back westward. Certainly the people are closer culturally to the eastward-lying islands extending to the area of Truk than they are
to the western islands of Yap and Palau. The languages spoken by these eastern
islands are mutually intelligible.

Linguistic studies show that Ulithian is a dialect of Trukese, a subdivision of Micronesian, which in turn forms part of the farflung Austronesian
(Malayo-Polynesian) language family. It differs sharply from the language of
nearby Yap, which, although Micronesian, is greatly aberrant from the nuclear
forms of that subdivision. Ulithian is an agglutinative language using extensive
suffixes. The grammar is fairly simple and the word order is similar to that of
English. Only two verb tenses exist: past-present and future-imperative. The
number of consonants is not large but there are many vowels, not always distinguishable to the outsider. Generally, consonants do not follow one another, and
one of the devices to overcome the "taboo" against double consonants is to in-
sert an excrescent vowel, such as Mogemog for Mogmog. Accent is fairly even.
The language is spoken rapidly but has a pleasing sound. It is capable of being
honeyed or whining and may come close to singing.

As Micronesians, the people manifest physical characteristics that have
led many anthropologists to think of them as trihybrids composed of more or
less equal ingredients of an ancient white strain mixed with Mongoloid and Negroid elements. This is not the place to speculate on the racial history of these
natives, who show much variability among individuals, but it is safe to assume
that they are closely allied to the Polynesians, although they are less massive and
much shorter. Nor, if the hybrid theory is valid, can we say with any assurance
whether the mixing took place before leaving the Asian continent, or en route,
or even as the result of successive waves. In the light of this, it would be futile
to look at Ulithians as embodiments of human racial adaptations to the island
ecosystem. Having raised the question, it is best quickly dropped.

Due to measurements and observations taken by me in 1947 and 1948
on fifty-nine males, it is possible to describe the men, at least, with some degree
of objectivity. One of the most noticeable features is their small stature, which
approximates no more than 5 ft 4⅓ ins. Old-timers insist that in the past the
people were much taller, and statements recorded by early voyagers seem to bear
this out. Certainly, in the few years that have elapsed since the measurements
were taken, there has been an unmistakable spurt upwards, so there might have
been a depressing effect as the result of dietary factors. Body proportions, as determined with instruments, show that the men have long trunks, broad shoulders, and narrow hips. The impression one gains is that the men are well propor-
tioned, as well as heavily musculatured and strong. Relying again on measurements, it is found that the head form is longish, with a dolichocephalic index of
74.6. Head size and head height are above what might be construed as average.
Noses are broad, but at the same time long.

The skin as described by use of a color scale is seen to be predominantly
light brown on the upper inner arm, with a fair share of individuals showing
reddish brown and medium brown coloration. The hair is predominantly black,
with a moderate degree of dark brownishness. Only in old age does greyness

manifest itself. One cannot help but remark on the frequent presence of blond hair among children, which I am inclined to feel is due not to any connection with the blondism reported for the archaic Caucasoid element constituting the aboriginal population of Australia, but to sporadic admixture over the centuries with Europeans. Hair form is mostly wavy, with occasional frizziness and infrequent straightness. Mostly the hair is coarse. Baldness is seldom seen. Facial and body hair is generally small. The eyes have brown to dark brown irises, and I have the impression that the total size of the eyeball is quite large. Eye folds are infrequent, but when they do occur they are usually slightly epicanthic or moderately lateral. The lips tend towards thickness.

There are individuals who give one the impression that they are merely tanned Caucasoids, while others look like frizzly-haired Melanesians. None look as if they were Mongoloids, but many have individual features suggestive of that stock. It is interesting that 45 percent of the men examined had median and lateral shovel-shaped incisors. Dental caries in the males examined in 1947–1948 was markedly infrequent, with almost one third the subjects having all their teeth.

Ulithians are remarkably free of infectious disease. Based on my own observations and some records made by a visiting hospital ship, the following seems to be a fair report. Either completely absent or virtually nonexistent are dengue, malaria, rickettsioses, typhus, typhoid fever, smallpox, measles, and syphillis. There have been epidemics of poliomyelitis during the period of Japanese administration but apparently none since. Intestinal parasites, particularly trichuria and hookworm, do occur and are not uncommon. Tuberculosis, especially pulmonary, is infrequent, although respiratory diseases that do not involve tuberculosis are very common. Yaws, until the advent of the American military in 1944, used to be prevalent throughout the population; its incidence is now zero. There is some filariasis, and its manifestation as elephantiasis can be seen among older men and women. Gonorrhea was unusually prevalent until treated in the postwar years with the newer drugs; now it seems to have been largely eliminated. Deficiency diseases are lacking. I am unable to comment on the incidence of cardio-vascular, gastro-intestinal, neurological, dermatic, carcinomatous, and other diseases. I knew of only one blind man, but encountered no one who was deaf.

Demographic data, although often neglected in research among the simpler peoples, can be extremely valuable in determining not only population size and structure, but other facts vital to interpreting social structure, marital patterns, extent of migration, fertility, and the like. I took complete censuses of the atoll in 1949 and again in 1960 and am able to make detailed reports for those years. However, neither of these times was "typical," for the first census represents a people still in the throes of decline, possibly due to culture contact, and the second shows it in the beginning of a great upward spurt, probably the result of Western medicine. Nevertheless, the figures are not without value in trying to describe what the atoll was approximately like before the disruptions of foreign administrations; therefore, they are offered as crude indicators.

The first thing one wants to know is how many Ulithians there are, and the answer is, not many. In 1949 there were 421 residents, of whom 200 were males and 221 females, but we know that, as with other island populations, there can be and has been a wide fluctuation. Over two centuries ago an estimate by a missionary placed the count at almost 600, and another one made in the opening years of the present century placed it at almost 800. Immigrants have come to the atoll to stay, and about 20 percent of the parents of Ulithians have been counted from other islands of Micronesia. Marriage with persons outside the atoll is stimulated by the strict and wide rules of incest, which often make it necessary for a Ulithian to fetch a wife from elsewhere. Movement into, as well as away from the atoll, has also been dictated by the consequences of typhoons.

At the time of the 1949 census, only five islands were inhabited: Mogmog, 142; Falalop, 126; Fassarai, 69; Asor, 53; and Lossau, 31. In the past, several other islands have had settlements. Ordinarily, the greatest population is on Falalop, the largest of all the islets, but typhoons and disruptions resulting from the war between Japan and the United States have caused it to decline.

Distribution of the population by age cannot be given with the assurance that it is representative, so the figures for 1949 and 1960 will be omitted. It should be said, however, that the earlier sex ratio of 90.5 males for every 100 females was aberrant and suggested the possibility of male infanticide, which in point of fact does not exist. Eleven years later the masculinity ratio had assumed more typicality; indeed, it showed a disproportionately high number of males.

Statistics relative to the marital state of the inhabitants shows that virtually everyone marries, unless he is a psychotic or has some other gravely detrimental handicap. In 1949 there were only seven bachelors and spinsters, all of them with mental or physical defects, except one, who later married. Even after becoming widowed or divorced, there is little disposition to remain unmarried. Age at marriage could not be determined but is only moderately early.

Divorce is common, so that of all persons who had ever married, each had been divorced on an average of 2.05, the figure running to 2.46 for all those who had married and reached the age of fifty or more. The rate of divorce was probably higher in the past.

An inordinate high rate of adoption was revealed by the census, these adoptions all having occurred, as is customary, before the actual birth of the child. The percentage was 45.0, showing only a slight drop by the time of the next census.

Having been told all this, the question still remains: What are Ulithians like? That is, what traits of personality do they have? Fortunately, to the impressions gained from living with them I am able to add the results of Thematic Apperception Tests, or TATs, administered by me to ninety-nine persons of both sexes and almost all ages, and interpreted "blind" by a psychologist. Observations and tests showed much agreement.

These are a mild people who feel and move emotionally in a low key. They experience the gamut of human emotions, including anger, sadness, and pain, and, to a lesser extent, loneliness, guilt, and excitement. Yet they do not give strong expression to their inner feelings. In their thinking they veer away from fantasy and abstraction, and towards the concrete and literal. It can be said that they are not escapists but maintain an essentially ougtoing, optimistic view of life. There is no tendency towards introversion and introspection, brooding and morbidness. There is no sense of vindictiveness. The people do not show a preoccupation with death, nor with suicide, which is something known to have occurred only by hearsay. According to test results, all of which were interpreted in terms of manifest content alone, Ulithians have, as their main goal, food and oral gratification. One might view this as associated with childhood frustrations, but a more likely explanation is that at the near-subsistence level at which the people live they have to exercise a good deal of attention and effort in procuring enough to eat. The tests show less concern with libidinal interests than one might expect. Perhaps one reason for this is that the separate category of amusement really includes the predominant Ulithian notion of "play" in the sense of dating and petting. Certainly, prudery does not conceal concern with sex. As for means to goals, these are dominated by work, group activity, and cooperation. In an atoll ecology, enlightened self-interest demands communality and sharing of work and responsibility. Individuality and personal striving are greatly deprecated, and so are its concomitants—bragging, strutting, and any ostentatious display. This may account for the weak expression of artistic endeavor, but so may the generally concrete attitude towards the environment.

What Is There To Eat

The adaptation made by the people to their environment is limited by pervasive ecological factors that prevent the economy from rising very far above a subsistence level. The small size of the population, the paucity of raw materials, and the simple state of technological competence have worked against the development of a prestige economy. Yet subsistence activities proceed at a sustained and adequate level.

With the raw materials for artifacts limited to little else than wood, shell, carapaces, coconut shell, sennit, and hibiscus bast, it is surprising that so many specialized tools and other objects can be made. Using adzes, drills, and files, the natives make, for example, a large number of kitchen artifacts: scrapers, graters, grinders, knives, spoons, ladles, taro crushers, boxes, beakers, dishes, bowls, baskets, and hanging hooks. Without the help of flint or steel tools, which came in only with the Europeans, native carpenters have been able to fashion good looms, fine houses, and superb canoes.

Subsistence activities are confined mostly to gardening and fishing, with less attention given to the raising of domesticated animals. There is a small amount of gathering, confined for the most part to reef fauna and the products of wild plants and trees. Fowling is inconsequential.

Before devoting our attention to food procurement, some brief words are needed to explain the system of landownership. The system is unusually complicated. This results from the clash of two opposing principles. Matrilineality is seen in the ownership of land plots, whereas a sort of patrilineality exists in the actual tenure of the land. That is, matrilineages have the right to dispose of land and exchange it as they see fit; but they allocate it to individuals who pass it on to their descendants in accordance with a patrilineal emphasis having bilateral overtones. The land plots are of two kinds: those in the swamp gardens and those outside, the latter being much the larger. Boundaries defining the plots are poorly marked, usually by trees, and disputes arise from the consequent ambiguity. Even more serious are the endless disagreements as to rights of inheritance. It is said by Ulithians, with some justice, that land causes more conflict than any other thing in their lives. It is valuable not only for horticulture but, of course, for dwellings, cook houses, work space, and pigpens as well. Certain fishing grounds are owned by districts and there seems to be no problem of trespass from people of other districts.

The staple foodstuffs are certain plant crops. These are simply cultivated.

As in many tropical islands, we must begin with the coconut, which is probably the most valuable tree in the world. Certainly, it is the principal source of food not only for its nut, which is eaten plain or cooked in all stages of maturity, but also for the water in its nut and the toddy yielded by its sap. The planting and servicing of the coconut trees are the responsibility of men, especially since the climbing of these trees is considered inconsistent with canons of feminine modesty. Those trees set aside for toddy do not bear fruit and have to be climbed three times a day to keep the tree bleeding and to collect the sap. The toddy is made into a drink for adults and children, and is nowadays left sometimes to ferment into a wine. Aside from their value in supplying leaves for thatching, baskets, mats, hats, and skirts for prepubescent girls, their trunks are used to make beams for houses, and their roots and other parts to concoct medicine. The flesh of the nut furnishes an oil useful cosmetically and important as a religious and political offering.

Three aroids are next in importance as a source of food. True taro, *Colocasia esculenta,* is grown in swampy pits on those few islands geologically suited for digging down to the Ghyben-Herzberg lens. The cuttings are planted in plots by women early in the morning, and the taro can be harvested in eight months. A long flat digging stick is used to dig up the tubers, which are eaten boiled, as are the leaves. Care must be taken to cook both leaves and tubers sufficiently to dissolve the harsh, glasslike crystals contained in them; if this is not done, the throat can be severely irritated. Magico-religious taboos surround the cultivation of taro, as we shall see in our discussion of things supernatural. The natives have a passion for another aroid, *Cyrtosperma chamissonis,* sometimes known as "elephant's ear." There are four varieties. This, too, is grown in the swamp garden. Less prized but used extensively because it grows so easily is the aroid *Alocasia macrorhiza,* sometimes known to us by its Hawaiian name "ape." It seems to be grown anywhere in the coralline soil and attains great height. Because it is so bitter, it is marinated in palm toddy before being cooked and eaten.

The sweet potato, with nine varieties, has long had great importance in the diet and is highly prized, not only because of its palatability but because it can be planted at any time of the year and harvested within about three months. It is planted from cuttings and dug up with a wooden spade. Cooking is by boiling in a pot, after which the potatoes are mashed into a pulp and covered with grated coconut. Most of the varieties are not sweet to the taste. The leaves of the tuber may be eaten by cooking with an herb and then blending with palm toddy or grated coconut.

Valuable and held in great esteem is breadfruit, which is to be found in twelve seeded and seedless varieties. It does not grow as readily as the natives would like. It is planted without seeming pattern and bears fruit seasonally. The first fruits are the object of ritual attention. Of all foods it is the only one whose preservation is important.

Bananas and sugar cane are eaten raw, but are not important sources of food. They must be cultivated.

Several kinds of wild plants are also sources of food. It is perhaps of interest to know that although pandanus grows fairly well in the atoll its fruit is not eaten.

Some foods of obviously recent vintage are squash, papayas, watermelons, and lemons. There was at one time a tremendous use of squash, which grows well and to great size, but its production has declined in recent years.

All this may give the impression that there is much variety in the Ulithian cuisine, but in point of fact the lament of the natives that their food has a certain monotony is justified. If it were not for food from the sea, things would be far worse.

The utilization of the resources of the sea is easily the most complex of the exploitative activities of the islanders. It demands much time, a variety of techniques and equipment, and great familiarity with the habits and location of the fauna. The proliferation of fishing techniques is necessary for supplementing land-oriented subsistence activities, not only to provide variety and supplementation to the diet but a certain degree of insurance when there is a food shortage, such as follows in the wake of a typhoon.

Spectacular catches come seasonally, when certain kinds of fish come in huge schools to the outer reef and are caught by large numbers of men, working communally, who use long nets to herd the fish together as they wade through the shallow water with the slowly shrinking net. Lagoon fishing is by far the most common of all and has many methods. The most successful involves the cooperation of a large number of men in canoes who assemble in traditional fishing grounds to catch fish with seines. This is the most reliably consistent kind of fishing. Some individuals go out into the lagoon alone or in small groups, using hooks, usually made of tortoise shell or coconut shell, or nowadays steel. Dip nets are often employed in fishing. Some angling is done with gorges made of mussel shell. Composite trolling hooks are used for pelagic fishing, especially to catch bonito, but Ulithians are not fond of leaving the safety of the lagoon, which in any event is the more convenient place to fish. Fishlines are made of sennit or coconut string. Basketry traps and stone weirs are occasionally employed in the lagoon. The traps are usually tied to a drifting log. As much for a sport as anything else, men and boys occasionally indulge in torchlight fishing from the outer reef at low tide, walking along with huge torches whose flames attract the fish, which are then gathered with small nets or clubbed into insensibility. A small amount of fishing is done with metal spears by men swimming under the surface of the sea. Some men fish with throw nets weighted with lead. In further exploiting the maritime aspect of their environment, the women of the atoll engage in littoral shellfish gathering. They also pick up such reef and lagoon fauna as crabs and any fish left stranded in pools by the ebbing tide.

The importance of fishing is attested to by the number of taboos surrounding the fisherman and his techniques, as well as the folklore accounting for the origin of fishing itself. Many of the songs and dances of the people center around fishing, especially of the exciting or hazardous kinds.

Cooking is done in various ways. Thanks to the earthen pots brought in from Yap, boiling and stewing are possible. Roasting and broiling are done on a grid placed over live coals. The earth oven, so characteristic of Oceania, has a prominent place and requires some attention. First, a shallow trench is dug and filled with firewood, which is then burned and superimposed with coral rubble. On top of that are placed coconut leaves, and on these are put the raw food, wrapped in leaves. Additional leaves and mats then cover all these underlayers, and the whole complex is allowed to stand for some time until cooking is completed. Food not prepared in the earth oven is usually cooked in sheds and eaten out in the open. Meals are highly irregular, but usually there is an evening meal participated in by a group which I call the "commensal unit." There are no restrictions as to the age and sex of the members.

Food plays an important part in almost all ritualistic events and is often the only occasion for the event. One does not need psychological tests to realize that nothing makes the people happier than to eat or talk about eating. Only three times over the space of twelve months have I ever seen Ulithians as a community in a state of ecstacy, and each had to do with some huge hauls of fish when thousands of the creatures had been caught by net. On one of these occasions, a fat enthusiast gorged himself with 45 six-inch mackerels, eaten raw, before the formal division of the catch had been completed.

$$\boxed{2}$$

Basic Social Relations

T HE ULITHIAN COMMUNITY comprises all the people of the atoll, with their common territory, common activities, common interests, and interdependent relationships. Its life is structured and organized into readily recognizable groupings of people who maintain intensely personal and intimate relationships, and experience strong social solidarity. For the most part, the community is locally autonomous and self-contained, but by no means entirely so, for it has a certain dependency on social and political arrangements with other islands. For our present purposes, the wider complex can be ignored.

In the social alignment of the community, it is the village, the family, and the corporate kin groups that are the basic units of social interaction. They will be considered first. Later, other organizing principles of social differentiation and behavior will be considered, particularly the political and religious elements of the social structure.

The Village

The Ulithian village is a highly nucleated subunit of the wider community, and within it its members interact especially intensely with one another, for they are few in numbers and live within the confines of a small area. The average size of a village fluctuates over the years, but at the time of maximum population for the atoll the number of inhabitants for a village came to eighty-eight. That was in 1903. Since then the figure has declined and then increased. There is great difference between the size of the smaller villages and the larger ones.

The Ulithian village, always located on the shore of the lagoon, is compact rather than scattered. Its dwellings are close together and people are thrown into close proximity. This is no place for families who like to be by themselves. The patches of ground surrounding each dwelling are planted in flowers and random crops, such as sweet potatoes, coconuts, aroids, bananas, and lemons. Breadfruit trees grow here and there. Women sit outside their houses, usually in groups, and perform most of their household chores there in the shade of a tree. With them they have their small children, the older ones being at play somewhere on the island, usually at the beach or in the water. Adjacent to each house is a cooking shed of small size and unpretentious appearance.

Canoe houses, better referred to as sheds, line the shore and provide not only shelter for their canoes but a clubhouse for the men of the lineages that own them. Friends often visit them and join in the gossiping and lounging. Some men may be found performing a light chore, such as twisting coconut husk into twine or carving out a loom sword. Children like to dart in and out but may sit still long enough to listen to the conversation and yarns of the men. A canoe shed is a cool place to be, as it catches any breeze off the lagoon and is fairly free, therefore, of flies and day mosquitoes. Men often sleep here at night.

Flanking the villages are the burial grounds, identifiable as clusters of above-surface tombs made of slabs of coral broken off the reef. Cemeteries are simple and unadorned.

The remainder of the island is wooded except for small gardens here and there. Chickens wander into these outer places and scratch around for food. People do not have much occasion to go into the woods, unless they want to gather up some firewood, berries, wild fruits, or leaves. The woods are avoided at night because of a fear of evil spirits lurking there, and if it is necessary to pass through them in the dark, a person will take along some friends and a torch. In the center of four of the islands are the swamp gardens necessary for raising taro, and here a few old women can usually be seen puttering about.

The outer reef is a place for women to gather up shellfish, crabs, and trapped fish. Herons and other marine birds make this their hunting ground. Children seldom play here because the slope is steeper than the repose angle of loose sediments and there is no sand; moreover, it is a little lonesome to be that far from the activities of the village. Men do not have much occasion to be here, except when they engage in their hauls of fish coming in from the sea in schools.

Except for the island of Falalop, where there are two villages, no island has more than one village. The Falalop villages are contiguous, however, and for many purposes may be regarded as a single unit with bonds of common interest. Unless otherwise specified, we shall treat them as one.

The nerve center of the village is the *metalefal,* or men's house. It is large and imposing, as well as conspicuous to visitors arriving from the lagoon, for it is located near the shore in the middle of the village. It has a high pitched roof made of thatch, and is raised well above the ground on a platform built up of slabs of coral. Its very appearance tells one that it embodies the authority and pride of the community.

Its visibility from the lagoon helps guide the visitor immediately to it. And it is well for the stranger to recognize it, for certain amenities must be observed by all visitors, especially those hailing from a land beyond the confines of the atoll. Even passengers in a local canoe returning from a voyage to another island must go through the ritual. As soon as a canoe has anchored, at least one of the passengers must proceed immediately to the house and recite certain words expressing the fact of arrival and prefacing the news that is to follow. To violate this necessary gesture is considered to be an outrageous breech of proto-col, punishable in drastic ways. Should the passengers, especialy if they are visi-tors, find no one present at the house, which would be extremely rare, they must address their brief ritual, without the ensuing accounts, to any child nearby, and should not even a child be in evidence, they would still have to apostrophize the "spirit" of the house. Usually, however, a canoe is spotted long before it arrives and a group of men will await it, especially so if the canoe is recognized as coming from outside the atoll; in this event the whole village may assemble be-fore the house, with the women and children, however, preserving a discrete distance, for this is a solemn occasion. As the representative of the canoe ap-proaches, even though he may be a member of the community itself, he is met with conspicuous silence and a studied air of indifference, for emotions must be controlled and hidden. There is certainly no hilarity, even among close friends.

The effect of all this is to impress on everyone the seriousness of the ar-rival. When the passengers come from other communities they tacitly acknowl-edge by their submission to the rites that they are visitors who hope to be offered welcome and hospitality by the residents. The gesture also serves to in-form the village, especially if it should be night, that people have arrived. Fail-ure to go through with the ritual is prima facie evidence that hostile intent or concealment is behind it. However, the main practical effect is the transmission of news. This is supported by the fact that even passengers returning to their own village after a voyage will recite the recent events on the island from which they have come. A villager may have great concern, for example, over the health of a relative, or may want to know if a friend has married or a sister given birth. The strange part of this ritual of arrival is that the opening words are al-ways the same, *"Tor kaptal wai,"* or "My canoe has no news." I found no one who could explain this contradiction and I finally stopped asking. Tradition has a mystique of its own.

Some explanation should be given for the presence of more than one men's house on two of the islands. These are the islands with the greatest popu-lation.

One of them, Falalop, has two villages, so there are two *metalefal*, each serving as a clubhouse, dormitory, and meeting place for the men of the village where it is located. But over and above these two is a third *metalefal* whose function is primarily political. Here the chiefs and elders of both villages meet when matters concerning them are to be deliberated upon.

The island of Mogmog similarly had three houses until about a century ago. The main one, called the Rolong, served all the island, which is divided into halves, each of which has its own chief and was probably once a recogniza-bly distinct village. The Rolong served also as the atoll-wide meeting place. Its name is still applied to the site where it formerly stood, and although the house is gone, kings are still invested there. The site has a sacred aura, supported by taboos against trespass and disrespect. No houses may be built on it, so it re-mains unused, except for an important politico-religious ritual wherein turtles are slaughtered and their flesh apportioned according to a highly formal proce-dure. Nowadays, the only *metalefal* left on Mogmog is one that in former times used to be simply a clubhouse. The other clubhouse has disappeared, having been destroyed in the great typhoon of 1907, so that the present one consolidates all the functions of the three. It serves also as the atoll-wide council house.

The presence on all other islands of only one *metalefal*, and no tradition of any more than that, suggest that they have never had more than a single village. Each of these houses performs all the functions of both kinds of *metalefal*.

As one walks through a Ulithian village, he will notice that all the houses are built at right angles to the shore—that is, all but one. It is located on the beach and is parallel to the shore. This is the menstrual house, where women retire to have their babies or wait out their menses. Whatever the original reason for this orientation, its position certainly serves to warn the male visitor of its nature and to remind him to observe the strict rules against trespass. Women spend a good deal of time here, and the men often suspect that they use this as an opportunity to shirk their domestic responsibilities. I have heard complaints.

Where there are two villages on an island, there is a menstrual house for each. In the days before the apparent merger of its villages, Mogmog used to have a pair.

This counting of houses, those for men and those for women, may seem tedious and unnecessary, but there is a certain diagnostic value in doing so. Such houses are clues to territorial and political divisions. The fact that the island of Fassarai has two menstrual houses and only one village reveals the rise of an important territorial cleavage there. Fassarai already has manifested a tendency toward bifurcation, as seen in the two named divisions that are beginning to emerge. It is my understanding that the chiefs of the atoll have been petitioned to give assent to the political distinctions that may adhere to such bifurcation.

Further symbolic corroboration of the notion of duality on some islands is to be found in the persistence of a certain kind of house known as the chief's house. Where an island is divided in two, there is a house for each division. It belongs to the lineage which heads the division, and is ordinarily named after the lineage itself. The chief in question is the head of that lineage. The houses are used as meeting houses for the lineages to which they belonged. We know that they also served as meeting places for the territorial division, differing from the *metalefal* in that both men and women could assemble. Despite their loss as formal meeting places, they are still used today on more informal occasions.

Where an island is structured into two divisions, a good-natured rivalry exists and finds expression in competitive dances and sports. The individuals belonging to each half feel a sense of solidarity, and a good deal of mutual assistance is given in the performance of work that requires the efforts of many persons. Cooperation within and competition without find especial expression in two semiannual feasts, one given by men for women and the other by women for men. One division tries to outdo the other in accumulating fish and plant foods for the island.

As a consequence of the frequent and repetitive, as well as direct, social interaction within the village, the pattern of social relations is stable and predictable. The great need for economic cooperation helps shape this pattern, and so does the presence of kinsmen with their strongly structured and almost unalterable social relations.

While the village *esprit de corps* is high it is not unduly exaggerated, and there is considerable exchange with other villages of the atoll. According to tradition, in the past sometimes there was conflict to the point that intervillage warfare burst out. Various forces, however, serve to counteract any real antagonisms between villages. What helps to bind them together in a relatively harmonious single community is not only the mitigating need for economic exchange, but also intermarriage, residence rules, sprawling kin groups, and tributary obligations to the island of Yap.

A further word may be useful concerning the wider cohesion promoted by the rules of residence and of descent. Since these are father-oriented and mother-oriented, respectively, lineages cannot have a real territorial base. That is, even if spouses are discounted, the members of a Ulithian village cannot comprise a single kin group, for although women are the perpetuators of the lineages, they have to move to the residences of their husbands, and this often involves a change of village. To be sure, most marriages take place between residents of the same village, but over the years the dispersive effect of the kind of patrilocality that requires the wife to change villages becomes cumulative.

Countering this centrifugal effect, however, is a modification of the residence pattern, whereby wives who move from one community to that of their husbands regularly return for long stretches of time to their natal villages, principally in order that they and their spouses may cultivate lands that have been assigned for her use through the prevailing system of land tenure. Coupled with a pattern in which most marriages are between members of the same village, certain lineages tend to be identified with one village more than another and for this there are historical factors, for a rule of matrilocality probably prevailed in the past. This is suggested not only by the fact that islands closely akin culturally to Ulithi practice matrilocality or some related kind of residence, but by the presence of lineage houses, hearths, parcels of land, and other things on traditional islands. The transition in residence has obviously been only partially consolidated.

A factor almost as pervasive in social behavior as kinship is the territorial propinquity provided by the village. Exploitative activities are often pursued not by kinsmen but by the village subcommunity, for here large numbers of men beyond the capacities of kinsmen are often necessary. This was hinted at in the discussion of fishing techniques. Again, while the distribution of food at festive rituals is often nominally a responsibility of the relatives concerned, in practice the distribution usually becomes village wide. Once again, some hereditary factors notwithstanding, village political organization is based on the territorial principle, for the group that controls the village is the council of elders, and it is drawn from the entire male membership of the village and not according to kin group representation. In social control, the strength of the village is obvious, for while individuals are curbed by their relatives and punished by them when they transgress the moral code, the members of the village play an appreciable part, through criticism, ridicule, and the threat of ostracism, in inducing them to conform or reform. The village also participates in many of the religious phases of social behavior within the village, even though much of the rest of it is private or kin-based. Finally, the village offers social outlets not possible within kin groups. It permits the exercise of friendship relations, clique behavior, sexual exploits, and such recreational activities as dancing, canoe-racing, and games, in a context providing welcome relief from the often austere character of kinship relations.

The Family

The Ulithian family is based on monogamous marriage, more by reason of economic limitations than moral stringency, for the natives maintain that they see nothing wrong in plural marriages but do realize the inability of a man to maintain more than one wife.

The nuclear family is strongly dependent in character, for it must compete with three other kin groups—the extended family, the commensal group, and the lineage. These other groups assume some of the roles of the nuclear family, which may be, and often is, scattered among other units for purposes of eating and sleeping. Adding to these impinging influences are the extremely common practices of adoption and remarriage. These practices cause shifting about of the personnel of the family, with the result that biological members are often replaced by purely sociological ones. The result of all this is that the feeding, sheltering, training, and other services which the family provides the individual are so dissipated that his nuclear family loses much of its importance in his life. However, it would be wrong to think of it as playing an unimportant role, for the sexual, economic, reproductive, and indoctrinational functions of this kind of family, even though rivalled by other kin groups, are never surpassed by them.

The nuclear family does not usually exist in its ideal form. Attached to it for purposes of residence may be any of various kinds of kinsmen. At the other extreme are residential units consisting merely of husband and wife, with no children or other persons. A canvass of households in the village of Mogmog reveals that only one fourth consist of a husband and wife and their offspring. Almost another fourth of the households are made up simply of husband and wife. The remaining consist of either extended families, composite families, or units not involving a marital pair.

Complicating the picture of the nuclear family is the fact that its members do not always eat together even when domiciled under one roof. In Mogmog's village there are twenty-six commensal units; they do not represent simple combinations of residential units, for an individual may eat in a group in which there are no individuals whatsoever with whom he lives. The average number of people in an eating unit is 5.2. Commensal units tend to revolve around nuclear families, but not invariably so. The members of the nuclear family, then, do not always eat together.

Descent is matrilineal; that is, a child is affiliated with his mother's group of relatives. But this by no means implies that the genealogical relationship with the father is overlooked. Indeed, the father is considered to have more rights than the mother with respect to the child, for in the event of divorce it is he who has custody over him. The effect of matrilineal descent, then, is to affiliate the child with his maternal kinsfolk for certain social purposes but not to deny the genealogical tie to his father's kinsfolk. Accordingly, we find that incest taboos are extended bilaterally, marriages to paternal relatives being forbidden to the same extent as marriages to maternal ones.

Marital residence is patrilocal, a statement that must soon be qualified. The postnuptial location of the couple is with the husband's kinsmen, not necessarily in their household but at least in a dwelling nearby. However, as previously noted, a man must periodically perform bride service for his wife's parents, and if his spouse comes from another island, this may require him to establish temporary residence there. Actually, residence is of an alternating character, but nevertheless fundamentally patrilocal; after the wife's parents die and there is no longer any need to support them, the couple usually goes back permanently to the husband's community to live. This alternation of residence is a concession a man may make to his wife's family when he takes her, a productive worker, away from its midst. However, the matter is not entirely this simple, for the wife may have garden plots in her own community and she and her husband may wish to exploit them for their own interests.

Further clarification must be made of the term "patrilocal." As loosely employed here—aside from the matter of alternation—it does not have the strict meaning of residence by a couple with the husband's parents. Rather, it refers to the tendency for the couple to live in the vicinity of the husband's male kinsmen. When the couple come from the same village, the change is not particularly dislocating for the women; but when they come from different villages, located on different islands, the woman makes a big change. Further complicating the picture is the fact that analysis of actual residence histories shows that in addition to patrilocality as here defined, there is some matrilocality, and also some avunculocality, neolocality, and combinations of these forms of residence. For any given point in time, the mode of residence of a couple may not be what it has been in the past or will be in the future.

It is futile, then, to discover rules of residence from a static census of houses alone. The history of residence must be carefully worked out for each actual case. My own use of the term "patrilocality" is based not on an analysis of the forty-two dwellings on Mogmog, but in terms of the ideal depicted by informants and, even more, the fact that when an intervillage marriage takes place, the wife moves to the husband's community. In addition, we know that when a man's parents-in-law have died he is no longer compelled to spend part of his time living in their village with his wife and children.

Speaking of Kinsmen

The terms used to designate social relationships arising from marriage and parenthood constitute a terminological system of great internal consistency whose character is to a large extent shaped by the system of reckoning descent through the female line. These terms are extended to relationships going beyond the nuclear family. They belong to the so-called Crow type of terminology, and involve not only much use of the classificatory principle but the ignoring of generational distinctions for certain relatives.

The basic kin terms are reduced to a mere seven: father, mother, sibling-of-Ego's-sex, sibling-of-opposite-sex-to-Ego, child, spouse, and sibling-in-law-of-Ego's-sex. The classificatory pattern is seen not only in the overriding of generations but in the ignoring of sex in the term for child and its various extensions. Classificatory terms are also produced by applying all the consanguineal terms, except one, to affinal relatives. It should be noted that only two terms are exclusively affinal. A further reduction in terms is accomplished by ignoring collaterality and merging blood relatives of different degrees of biological relationship to Ego. Put another way, a kin term always embraces secondary and tertiary relatives in addition to primary ones.

Not all societies address a relative by the same term he is referred to, but Ulithi does allow one system of nomenclature to serve both purposes. That is, for example, if you talk about a man as "my father," you then address him also as "father," rather than have to employ some special term.

An explanation concerning sibling terms is useful to know. There really are no absolute terms for "brother" and "sister." Instead, one talks about a sibling-of-same-sex, the term for which is *bwisi*. If it is a male who is referring to his *bwisi*, then the relative in question is his brother. If a female is speaking, she is referring to her sister. So there has to be a term for a sibling-of-opposite-sex. There is one, and when a male uses it he is talking about a sister; when a female uses it, she is talking about her brother. In either event, it's the same term, *mwangai*.

One could easily get to thinking that the Ulithian child has to have a prodigious intelligence and memory to know how he must refer to a relative. Nothing could be further from the truth. For one thing, there are lots of relatives and they are near at hand, so the child has constant opportunity for learning. For another, the number of terms are few, and in any event the child has no need to confuse himself by undoing another system, such as our own, in learning his. The Ulithian system has great logicality and consistency. It follows clear-cut principles.

Nowhere is this better illustrated than in the influence of lineal descent in determining how a relative will be addressed. What could be simpler than to have to remember that everyone in your father's lineage is called your father and mother (see Figure 1). That applies to the oldest and most decrepit man or woman and the youngest baby boy or girl. Age has nothing to do with it. As

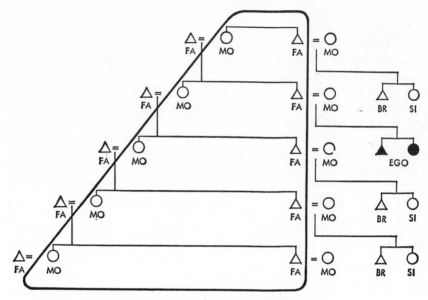

Fig. 1. Father's lineage (male or female Ego).

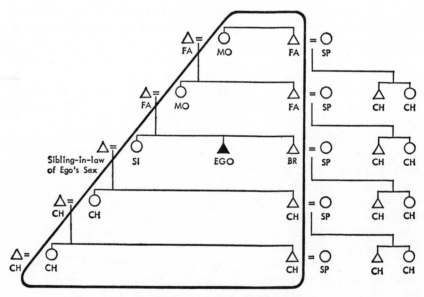

Fig. 2. Mother's lineage (male Ego).

indicated in Figure 2, those relatives in your own (your mother's) lineage are known as your father and mother if they belong in any generation above your own, as your sibling if they are in your generation, and your child if in any generation below that. Knowing that, then the people they marry and the children they have are called by terms consistent with the way they are addressed. So if you call a man your brother, it follows logically that you will call his children your children, because brothers are considered to be equivalent to one another. If you call a woman your mother, then unless she is in your paternal lineage you will usually call her children your siblings.

With matrilineal descent the guiding principle in Ulithian terminology, it turns out that certain first cousins on the paternal side are one's parents, and certain first cousins on the maternal side are one's children—at least, terminologically they are.

If the reader has persevered until now and mastered at least the general idea behind the terminology, he may show initial disgust upon being told that in daily life one hardly uses these terms. Instead, one talks about or addresses all his relatives by their personal names, such as "Melchethal," "Sorekh," "Iamalami," "Chuoior," or "Rukhlemar" (which happen to be the names of my chief informants). But all is not lost; the individual has to know the kin terms for each individual relative he deals with. And so, in order to give life and meaning to the system, we may now turn to a consideration of the relationship between kin terms and behavior.

We may preface our remarks by saying that it is axiomatic that behavior between kinsmen can largely be predicted from terminological categories expressive of their genealogical relationship. This is not the place to trace out these patterns in full. They occur in economic activities, the inheritance of property, the relationships within the nuclear family, political status, social control, religious structure, ritualistic obligations, child training, mourning, and many other activities in which kinsmen are expected or required to exercise customary roles. However, at this point we may examine only those kinds of behavior outside the nuclear family that are parallel extensions of sexual behavior within it. These extensions are remarkably consonant with kin terms.

Just as real brothers and sisters practice strict avoidance, so do any other relatives who address one another as "sibling-of-opposite-sex." As long as a man refers to a woman as his sister, he may not be in her company alone, use sexual language in her presence, sleep under the same roof with her, have intercourse with her, or marry her. The number of kinds of sisters falling under these taboos is large: females of the man's lineage and generation, father's brother's daughter, daughter of any man of the father's lineage. But where the biological relationship is actually very distant the rules may be relaxed to some extent.

If a man calls a female his "child," she comes under slightly reduced restrictions. However, as such females are his children, he may not marry or have sexual relations with them, and must avoid coarse language in their presence. Many females come under this category, including, for example, the daughters of his own brothers and sisters, and the daughters of any men in his own lineage. Many affinal relatives too are referred to as "child," but marriage or sexual relations with them is strongly disapproved rather than prohibited. People regard such relationships with ridicule and even some anger. For instance, a man living on Falalop had intercourse with the daughter of his wife's sister, a terminological "child," and his wife became so embarrassed (not over the adultery) that she left him in a rage.

Toward females whom a man calls "mother," the forbidden behavior embraces sexual joking, sexual relations, and marriage but, as with real mothers, does not require the avoidance of classificatory mothers or sleeping in houses other than the ones in which they sleep. This means that there is no mother-in-law avoidance. Relations are thus a notch more permissive than with terminological sisters and terminological daughters. The women who fall within this vast classificatory range, to mention only a few, include parents' sisters and any females of the father's lineage. Affinal relatives classified as "mother" are not as strictly included under the rules, for with such females sexual relations, marriage, and off-color language are considered bad form rather than the violation of a code of prohibitions. An illustration will make this clear.

In an episode related to me by a man, he told of a "son" who was in fact his sister's son. The informant had a young wife and this son had adulterous relations with her, she being his "mother" by virtue of her marriage to his classificatory father. In Ulithi, sons do not make love to mothers, but since the relationship was one through marriage, no incest was involved. But the feelings of my friend were. He was angered not so much by the seduction of his wife—after all, he had dismissed her simulatenous infidelity with a nonrelative as an indiscretion—as by the affrontery of his son, who, incidentally, was older than he. It was a matter of disrespect, and he never forgave him. Umbrage might have lasted indefinitely, except that the offender was later lost in a storm at sea.

It is interesting but logical within the framework of the Ulithian point of view that there is no avoidance by a man towards a female who is his terminological "spouse." Indeed, there is much freedom, as there is with a real wife. He need not sleep under a separate roof from her, although in practice this privilege is not extended except when the husband is away, the idea being that she is better off with him than outsiders. It is all in the family.

Thus, just as kinship terms are mutually correlative or reciprocal in that the use of one term implies the use of another or even the same term, so is the social behavior between the relatives involved similarly correlative and reciprocal.

The Corporate Lineage

Though biological descent is traced bilaterally on Ulithi, an examination of a genealogical chart will usually show a skewing in favor of relatives in the mother's line. This is because there are groups of persons who trace affiliation with one another through females. The most important of these exist in the atoll as corporate groups, which we have already referred to as lineages. There are also a few intrusive, noncorporate groups which we shall refer to as clans. In

native terminology, one term encompasses both, but there are important economic and political distinctions between the two, and it is necessary to know when
we are dealing with one and when with the other.

The lineage is a group of people with a common name, a common ancestress traced through the maternal line, and an identity beyond that of its constit-
uent members. Its corporate nature is best expressed through the ownership of
common property, as well as through its formal organization. The lineage has no
totem. It is strictly exogamous.

There are twenty active, landowning lineages in the atoll. There are
twenty others that are really defunct but maintained through the custodianship
of members of active lineages. In addition, there are some immigrant lineages of
recent vintage coming from nearby islands, having no local lands and still maintaining an identity with their homeland. They are represented by a few lone individuals, who sponsor them and look after their interests.

The active lineages are small enough so that the members of each can
trace their relationship to one another through actual genealogies, as well as
through identification with a traditional ancestress whose name is preserved as
founder of the lineage.

Ideally, lineage affiliation can never be changed. Once a Hamathakh, always a Hamathakh. Once a Lipipi, always a Lipipi. But in practice it occasionally happens that a change is made. When a male is adopted he retains the name
of his true lineage but interacts mostly within his adoptive parent's lineage.
However, when a female is adopted there are complications. She, too, retains her
lineage identity, but there is a difference. While the children of the adopted
male will belong to his wife's lineage, the children of the adopted female may
make a switchover to the adoptive lineage that is complete and permanent.

Most adopted individuals, however, do not change their lineage affiliation. This is understandable when one bears in mind the enormous percentage
of newborn infants who are adopted. It would be impossible to maintain any
semblance of order if, in reckoning descent, almost half the population were
constantly involved in complete absorption into another lineage. An examination
of the genealogies of all the people of Mogmog shows that seldom is a change-
over made.

Some rank order may be detected in Ulithian lineages, probably having
something to do with the sequence followed in the genesis of local lineages
through the centuries. The most important unilineal group is the one that furnishes the hereditary chief or king of the atoll, while the next important lineage
is that which supplies the headman of the men's council on the island of Mogmog. Their rank is almost coequal. Other lineal groups have varying places of
importance, with some so small that they seem really to be sublineages.

The structure and function of these corporate groups are simple and
clear. To begin with there is a headman, or leader, known as the *mal,* or male.
He is automatically the oldest capable man of the group and derives his prestige
mostly from the power he holds in making decisions for the group. His importance also derives from the knowledge of the past that he has accumulated over
the years, for such information, especially as it pertains to genealogies and land

tenure, is used to back up his decisions. He acts for his lineage when granting or withholding approval for the marriage of younger members. True, considerable personal freedom of choice is permitted in marriage, yet the rules of incest are so pervasive that only a person such as "the man" is in a position to know the sociological eligibility of the prospective spouse. The headman also speaks for the lineage when allocating work and ordering the preparation of food for lineage rituals. He has a strong responsibility, too, in divorcements, especially because of his duty to accumulate the compensatory gift which a divorced lineage mate may be required to give to his or her former spouse upon remarriage. But his main role is in the control and allocation of lineage land and other property.

The female counterpart of the headman is the *fefel,* or female. Her duties and responsibilities do not match his. They include the supervision of gardening, the weaving of fiber garments, and such other tasks as have lineage rather than personal connections. In addition, she has something to say about the marriage of junior members of the lineage. She acquires her position by virtue of seniority, and when she dies or becomes incapacitated, she is replaced by the next oldest woman.

In a society in which there are numerous ascribed statuses, it is not surprising to find that within the lineage there is another kind of position that should not be confused with that of the headman or headwoman. It pertains to generational differences within the lineage. The oldest man or woman in his generation is called by a certain term regardless of sex. Technically, if a lineage had members belonging, let us say, to four generations, there would be eight such persons, a male and a female for each generation. These persons have no duties and obligations beyond a diffuse exercise of authority over the younger persons of their own sex within their generation. Obviously, the very eldest generations have heads who are at the same time the headman and the headwoman of the whole lineage.

Each lineage has its traditional lands. The plots are not always contiguous, for they may have been acquired by exchange with other lineages. But most plots are close together on the particular island where the lineage has its historical seat.

Each lineage also has its traditional house, named after the group, and is the official residence of the headman, as well as the seat of the ancestral shrine. The plot on which the house is built is located within the village proper and is considered to be the most important of all.

Each lineage has its common hearth, where all the members resident in the village eat on various occasions. The lineage hearth does not supplant the family hearth, being activated only when the members of the body eat together on certain ritualistic occasions.

Lineages have their own canoe sheds, the functions of which have already been described. If one were to pick out the place of greatest lineage activity, it would be the shed. This is where things are usually going on.

Tradition has it that in the past, each lineage had its own menstrual house. Such individualism has now given way to communalism.

A very important piece of property, the canoe, always belongs to a lineage, unless it is small and without sails. Some lineages have as many as three canoes, whereas others are so small that they have none of their own. A superficial observer might get the erroneous impression that canoes can be used freely, and that when a man wants to go somewhere he simply puts out to sea. Nothing could be further from the truth. The lineage engages a man, who may not even belong to it, to look after the canoe and grant permission to those who wish to use it. Such borrowers may not even be members of the group, having to make their request because their own lineages have no boat available. The carpenter who constructs the canoes may not be a member of the descent group, either, having merely been commissioned to do the job. The headman is the one who decides when a canoe is to be built and when a new pandanus sail is to be woven by the women of the lineage. He has the curious responsibility of making the sennit rope used on a canoe, but no one knows the origin of this obligation. As a reward for this ritualistic chore he receives two fish from any catch made by the users of the canoe if it has been in private service; otherwise, he receives none.

Finally, each functioning lineage has its pool of ancestral ghosts and a shrine for the sacrifices made to these spirits. The shrine is in the traditional lineage house and is cared for by the headman, who receives the offerings.

The profound importance of lineal descent groups should at once be obvious. A person owes much of what he is and what he can do to his membership in a lineage.

By contrast, the clan in Ulithi is of little consequence. Clans are intrusive and unimportant locally. They are noncorporate and unorganized. They do not have a local clan hearth, house, headman, or shrine, nor do they possess their own canoes or ghosts. The members of each of the six clans represented in the atoll bear a common name with alleged common ancestry from such animals as the porpoise, eel, rat, and a shellfish. That is sufficient to make the clan exogamous. Members of clans fit into the Ulithian scheme of things by becoming absorbed into local lineages, which is done either through marriage or adoption. In time, such people may take over a moribund lineage and completely control it and its lands, at the same time dropping their old identity in favor of the new. The hospitable acceptance of clan members into Ulithian society is further testimony to the tolerant and outgoing nature of the natives.

Relatives Right and Left

Figuratively speaking, and following the structure employed by genealogical charts, people have maternal relatives on the right-hand side and paternal relatives on the left. Can we in any sense think of them as a unity?

Yes, but not in the sense that they are a discrete group. They are a unity only as a category—a category of cognates or persons related to an individual by ties of blood relationship, affinals being excluded. Ulithians call these kinsmen the *ieremat*. In a society in which the principle of descent is unilineal it should not be overlooked that recognition must be given to kinship ties on both sides.

Ulithians do not precisely define the members of one's kindred, who, theoretically, are all the people who are his cognates. In practice, out of this vast pool only the following are usually included: one's parents and their parents, one's parents' siblings and their children, his own siblings and their children, his own children and grandchildren, and the members of both parents' lineages, unless they are distantly related. Cognatic kin of this sort lack a corporate character because of their inherent inability to perpetuate themselves as a formal and autonomous group. Because the *ieremat* shift composition for any individual and his siblings, they have fixity only for Ego.

Since the kindred cannot perpetuate itself as a body, it cannot have a house, headman, headwoman, ancestral shrine, or property.

Yet, for Ego, the kindred is real. He knows that he cannot marry anyone within this category, and that relatives on both sides will assemble and come to his aid when necessary, or participate in some rite on his behalf. At the same time they will criticize his behavior when it merits criticism. Members of the *ieremat* have a hand in raising him and when he visits any of them they make him feel welcome to food, shelter, and any other kinds of hospitality. They will present him with small gifts on such occasions. When the individual needs labor to complete an enterprise they stand ready to assist. Obviously, these cognatic relatives have functions duplicating or overlapping those of the lineage, but they are real roles, performed by a fairly well-defined group.

In conclusion, Ulithian society is not bilateral, but within its unilineality it provides ample room for noncorporate kin groups drawn from all the individual's cognates. It has seemed necessary to point this out lest one gain the impression that no social function adheres to biogenetical consanguinity.

Political Organization

CONSIDERING THE SMALL SIZE of the territory and its population, the political system of the atoll presents unexpected complexity. Some of the complications are due to the political overlordship of nearby Yap, for this dominance shapes the local organization in a fashion designed to make it mesh with the caste and landownership system of the Yapese.

There can be little doubt that viewed from the historical perspective the Ulithian system of government grew out of a kinship foundation. This accounts for the mildly gerontocratic tinge to political power, for political officers and representatives are drawn from lineages in accordance with the principle of seniority. At the same time it accounts for the strongly democratic nature of political authority, for all lineages have some voice in government, at least in internal affairs.

The political system is so influenced by kinship principles that at many points it tends to become identified with it. One notes that at the level of local government, quasi-political authority is lodged with the family and the lineage. Each exerts great social control over its members and acts as an informal punitive body. In addition, the lineage regulates marriage, land tenure, and various other matters affecting its members. The *mal,* or lineage headman, is the instrument for the exercise of whatever political power is held at this level. It is he who calls meetings of the lineages and presides over them.

But true political organization is not encountered until one goes beyond the kin groups and examines the way in which villages, districts, and the whole atoll are administered.

The Village Council

The everyday affairs of a village rest in the hands of a council of elders. This body is headed by a chief known as a *metang.* To become a member of the council requires no qualifications of wealth, lineage, heredity, or anything more

145

than middle age and a measure of intelligence and responsibility. Young men are not admitted into the deliberations of the council, unless hereditary factors have already caused them to become district chiefs. There is no objection, however, to any man's sitting to one side as a spectator. No formal action or ritual is involved in becoming a member of the council. It is merely a matter of tacit understanding and assent.

The council meets several times a week, sometimes daily, in order to confer on community affairs and reach decisions. Its deliberations are concerned with economic and political matters, such as catching fish, constructing and repairing council houses and menstrual huts, policing the island, and any other tasks requiring communal effort on behalf of the whole village. The council also acts when it receives orders emanating from higher authority, either inspired locally by the paramount chief or relayed by him from sources outside the atoll, usually Yap. The *metang* presides over meetings, and does so with impartiality, dignity, and decorum. He allows free discussion by members and is guided and corrected by them. But if he has a strong personality, he may greatly influence the decisions ultimately agreed upon by shaping the agenda and the discussion along lines that he knows are compatible with the wishes of the district chiefs and the king; but as a rule these latter are above the relatively routine matters being dealt with, and so remain passive.

The *metang* can be a dynamic and influential leader, but since he attains office by virtue of membership in a traditional lineage he may be weak and ineffectual, so that the people of the village will have to put up with him until he retires of old age or dies. It is unthinkable that an incompetent man should be ousted, especially if he has not yet fallen into the decrepitude of the aged.

The council is a hardworking body, highly sensitive to the common good. Every effort is made at fairness. Thus, the *metang* is always drawn from a different village from the district chief, so that a balance of power can partially be maintained. Individual members are heard with respect, and there is no shouting or excitement. Ulithians are fond of decorum. A person with a desire for fame has no place in the society and would be withered with silence should he disport himself with passioned oratory or anything else that might appear to be ostentatious.

The District

Beyond the village, the next larger political unit is the district, of which there are eight in the atoll. The district is composed of a village and one or more lesser islands, most of them uninhabited but nevertheless economically useful.

Each district, including some that are no longer inhabited, is headed by a chief. His jurisdiction does not extend over any village in his area but rather over the district as a whole. The nature of this jurisdiction is vague but is principally concerned with the interests of the district as a whole in matters involving the entire atoll. A district chief, as such, does not have the right of eminent domain over the land that he controls politically, although he may exercise such control if he is simultaneously a landownership chief.

Succession to chieftainship is matrilineal and occurs through certain hereditary lineages. The oldest male member succeeds any chief who dies or becomes incapacitated, but Yap must give its approval to the succession.

Districts, which bear no names and are identified only by the name of the principal island dominating each, are ranked in a crude fashion that does not seem to follow any consistent principal. Mogmog is at the top, which is understandable, but the districts of Mangejang and Sorlen, which are relatively unimportant, come next, each being co-equal in status with the other. At the third level comes Falalop, with both Fassarai and Lossau occupying a fourth order of rank. Finally, at the bottom are Losiep and Asor. A definite chain of authority exists among these districts and this is tangibly expressed in the way in which orders at the top are transmitted to inferior districts by envoys. These messengers, or envoys, are men of chiefly status and follow a pattern that need not be discussed here. The rank order of the districts has its origin in the past and cannot be explained. Propinquity or considerations of transportation do not enter in, for some of the lower ranked districts are nearer to Mogmog than are some of the higher ranked ones.

No larger units than the political districts exist on the atoll; however, there are two other kinds of districts, one pertaining to landownership and the other to the caste system of Yap. The functions of these are not truly political.

Most likely, district chiefs, like other chiefs, commanded great respect in the past and a certain degree of subjugation. Father Cantova, observing castaways who had reached Guam from the general area, wrote in 1722 before going to Ulithi that their chiefs "govern with authority, speaking little and affecting a grave and serious air." When a chief granted an audience he sat on a raised table, and the people approached him bowed almost to the ground. "His words are as so many oracles that are venerated; a blind obedience is rendered to his orders." When some favor was asked of him the people kissed his hands and feet. Mind you, all this was on Guam where the Carolinians were virtually prisoners of the Spaniards.

It is not likely that chiefs on Ulithi, or nearby islands, have manifested such marks of regality for some time. Foreign domination through aggressive traders, such as O'Keefe, or through government control, as after the Germans came in, probably irrevocably undermined the splendor and power of the chiefs. Unfortunately, when Father Cantova got to Ulithi in 1731 he failed to speak of the chiefs and their lofty status. But when pieces of evidence are carefully assembled, the picture they present is one of a "nobility" approximating that of the Polynesians.

Chief of Them All

Ulithi is under the jurisdiction of a paramount chief, referred to in a loose way by Europeans as a king. He has some judicial authority but exercises it moderately. As executive head of the atoll he exists mostly to coordinate atoll-wide affairs and preserve interdistrict harmony. In most instances, he does not originate many orders, leaving the affairs of the people mostly to their own lineage chiefs and village councils. The outstanding exercise of his office is in external matters, principally involving relations with Yap and other islands of the western Carolines. When grave matters are to be settled he summons a kind of supercouncil made up of chiefs representing each of the villages and districts. The deliberations are conducted in the same democratic and restrained manner as in meetings of the village council, with the paramount chief seeking to gain a consensus of his subordinates. The council house on Mogmog is of course the forum for these discussions.

Succession to the paramount chieftainship is hereditary within the Lamathakh lineage. The man who succeeds to office is ordinarily the oldest son of the oldest daughter of the outgoing head, unless the latter has a younger brother to succeed him. A king cannot, of course, pass on his office to a son since his children never belong to his own lineage.

One would hardly think that so tiny a community as Ulithi would have a "coronation," but it does and it is both solemn and religious. Before the investiture, the consent of Gagil district in Yap must be obtained, consent seldom being denied. After endorsement from Yap, the district chiefs of Sorlen and Mangejang are notified through envoys, and these chiefs in turn notify all other chiefs and lineage heads throughout the atoll that a convocation is to be held. The assembly is not designed to express endorsement of the candidate but only to witness and participate in the investiture.

The ritual involves certain spatial arrangements of the participants, with the chiefs and headmen gathered in a circle in front of the atoll-wide council house on Mogmog known as the Rolong, and the spectators, always males, seated behind them. In the center of the circle sit the two chiefs from Sorlen and Mangejang. On this occasion, only they are allowed to wear the combs that distinguish chiefs from others, fastening the feathers of a black bird to the comb. By prearrangement, one or the other of these chiefs officiates. The incoming king is placed in the center of the circle with these two men. The officiating chief begins the ritual by holding up a special type of loincloth over his head and, addressing the great spirit of the Sky World, Ialulep, and the great spirit of the Earth World, Solal, announces to them that a new king is being installed. He implores these great gods to give long life to the chief should he rule well, but to cause his death should he rule badly, so that he may be replaced by someone more worthy. The ceremony is brief but by this simple gesture and these few words not only is a new king inducted into office but he is at the same time transformed into an individual of sacred character who henceforth must live a life apart. The special loincloth, accepted but never worn by him, is disposed of in any way he sees fit, often being sent to the paramount chief of Gagil district in Yap as a token of good will.

Upon assuming his new status, the paramount chief has to live an ascetic life, being enjoined for five years from sexual relations and from sharing his food with anyone else. Afterwards, he is allowed to share his food only with religious specialists of the highest order—diviners, typhoon magicians, fish magicians, and navigators. At no time may he eat food prepared by women still in the menarche. Many more taboos give testimony to his sacred nature. No one may share his drinking water, coconuts, palm toddy, tobacco, turmeric, and coconut oil. His palm toddy may be collected from his trees only by the major religious personages; all others are forbidden to touch the trees. No one may sleep in the same house with him, except his wife, and then only after the original period of taboo against coition has expired. In fact, no one else may even enter his house except the religious specialists and the woman who cooks his food. During the five-year period of taboo no one may so much as touch his person, and even after that he may not be touched by children, young men, or women who have not reached the menopause. Perhaps the most conspicuous concession to his high status is the requirement that all persons walking past him must crouch or crawl, calling out the words *"Soro! Soro!"* as they go by. To be sure this gesture of respect is required toward all chiefs but they themselves do not perform this gesture to anyone else except the king. The five-year period of taboo obviously imposes considerable inactivity on the paramount, for during that time he may not work, or climb trees, or dance, except solo. However, he may fish. One kind of fish, *hathekh* (unidentified), is reserved exclusively for him at all times. It should be apparent that the investiture and the observance of the taboos endow him with an aura that goes a long way towards maintaining his position of authority and responsibility.

Relations Without

This seemingly tight little world is in reality enmeshed with many other islands of the Carolines. Interaction with some of them is informal, but with the great majority it is structured along hierarchical lines, in which not only political but economic and religious factors play a part. The islands with which these formal relations are maintained lie within the domain of Gagil district on Yap. They constitute a miniature empire.

Does this mean that Ulithi is not a state? This depends on your point of view. The political entity that is called the state has been defined in many ways. Some insist that it be exclusively invested with the final power of coercion. Others stress the delegation of power and control to a few members of the society. In both instances the idea of force is never far away. The approach I favor is one that thinks of the state as a sovereign territorial group. How does Ulithi meet this succinct definition? Certainly, without stopping to argue whether or not the enforcement of rules is a function of a differentiated system or organs within the community, Ulithi is a human group, having a distinct territory, and possessing a government of a sort. The crucial question is whether it has sovereignty. In general, yes. Yap steps in to threaten and demand, but it is significant that Yap does not perform what is the chief function of the state—the maintenance of social order. Yap has almost nothing to do with internal events in Ulithi; it is mostly concerned with relations between the two communities.

In view of this, the dilemma may perhaps be resolved by thinking of the atoll as a satellite state.

From the point of view of Ulithi, as told to me by knowledgeable old men there, the Yapese empire may be seen as constituted of three blocks: Yap (Gagil district), Ulithi, and the Woleai (see Figure 3). The name ''Woleai'' is the one given by Ulithians to all the islands to the east, except nearby Fais, that form part of the Yapese sphere. These islands are subordinate to Ulithi, and both these units are in turn subordinate to Yap. Ulithi generally acts as an intermediary. How Yap came to control these islands is a mystery lost in the distant past.

To start with Yap, it is necessary to know that there exists internally in those islands a strong caste system in which the upper caste controls the lands used by the lower caste. Marriage between the two groups is forbidden.

What the Yapese have done is extend their caste system to Ulithi, so that Ulithians are serflike inferiors who may not intermarry with the Yapese and must at the same time send them political tribute, as well as payment for use of their own land and as offerings to certain spirit beings. In this system, the Yapese are known as "fathers" and the Ulithians as "children," a fictive kinship terminology also employed between the two Yapese castes. Much of the behavior between the people of Gagil district on Yap and the people of the atoll is epitomized by these terms, for the former are under a certain kind of obligation to look after their so-called children, while the children are obligated to show respect and gratitude towards their parents. The relationship may be described as symbiotic to the extent that it involves reciprocally advantageous relations between dissimilar participants. If anything, the inferior unit has more to gain than to lose through the arrangement.

Yap exercises indubitable political control over Ulithi. It demands and receives tribute in the form of mats, rope, fine textiles, and food. This tribute goes only to the paramount chief of Gagil district, although in accordance with the prevailing system of economic distribution it eventually finds wide distribution throughout Yap as gift exchange. The demands from Yap for tribute, which comes about every two or three years, follows a regular chain of authority, being given first to the paramount chief of Ulithi and then, through him, to the chiefs of the various political districts of the atoll. Protocol must be strictly observed in communicating the demand, with envoys meticulously consulting the proper lineage heads and the districts they represent. Political tribute is not given regularly but may be ordered on any one of the annual visits to Yap required of the paramount chief of Ulithi.

An aspect of dominance that has greater practical significance in the economic sphere is the payment by Ulithians of a kind of rent to certain lineages in Gagil district. Ulithians are considered to be tenants of land owned by absentee landlords in Yap. The Ulithian lineages are locked with those of Yap in what is known as a *sawei* relationship, and although the precise etymology of the word is not known, it refers in effect to not only the system of tenancy but to the kinship units involved, as well as the goods exchanged. The word "exchanged" is used advisedly, for after the tenants have delivered their payments of foodstuffs

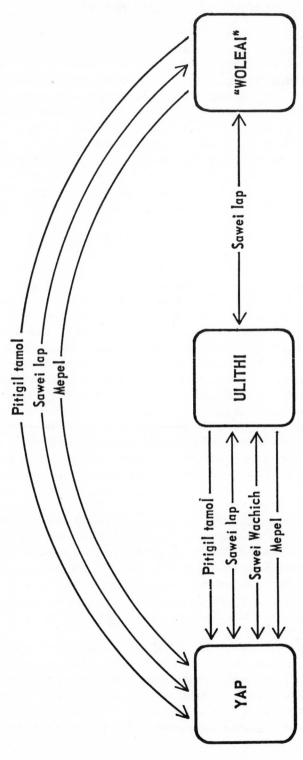

Fig. 3. The flow of tribute (pitigil tamol), gifts (sawei), and religious offerings (mepel) within the Yap empire. Some gifts are big, or lap; other gifts are small, or wachich.

and goods, they are given return gifts by their landlords, and these often, if not usually, exceed the payments! Because of this reciprocity it is hard to justify use of the term "rent" but the fact remains that while payments made by tenants are obligatory, the gifts given in return are optional. Ulithians usually find the arrangement so much to their advantage that they do not mind humoring the Yapese by calling them fathers or mothers and being called children in return. Nor do they mind too much the restrictions imposed on them when they visit Yap, for when they go there they are given shelter and food and permitted, if they so desire, to build canoes using the large local mahoganies lacking on the atoll. In return, they must show deference, refrain from making sexual advances towards Yapese women, observe numerous food taboos, and perform a certain amount of work. Some might find this degrading, but people living on impoverished islands do not find the choice difficult to make. Yap is a land of variety and abundance, and going there is a kind of exciting adventure for people who live on tiny, flat islands devoid of many resources.

The subordination of Ulithi is further seen in a final kind of tribute that must be sent to those lineages on Yap with which the atoll lineages are paired in the *sawei* relationship. These are religious offerings made to the lineage ghosts of the Yapese. It is not clear why people with their own ancestral ghosts should have to send coconut oil, pandanus mats, and finely woven loincloths to alien spirits. However, it has been suggested that since Yapese lineage ghosts are beneficent not only towards their own descendants but the wards of their descendants as well, the Ulithians should be acting out of gratitude for the services rendered by such ghosts. Mitigating the necessity for making these religious offerings is the fact that the major one of the ghosts is claimed by Ulithians to be one of their own—at least he was born on Ulithi, of a Yapese mother.

There remains the connection between the second and third units of the Yap-Ulithi-Woleai complex, and here we find some replication of the above scheme. Certain Ulithian lineages are the parents and landlords of the filial islands of Fais, Sorol, Earipik, Woleai (atoll), Ifaluk, Faraulep, Lamotrek, Elato, Satawal, Puluwat, Pulap, Pulusuk, and Namonuito (see Figure 4). These eastern islands must give *sawei* to Ulithi and in turn they receive gifts and hospitality. There is no implication here of caste; indeed, intermarriage between Ulithians and these neighbors is frequent and relations fairly relaxed. All indications are that the replication has its source in Yap's ultimate political control over the islands of Woleai, in which Ulithi acts as intermediary between the first and third units by looking after the interests of the lineages of Gagil district. Ulithi's right to *sawei* from the eastern islands seems to be compensation for its administrative services.

Replication does not extend to political tribute and religious offerings. True, Woleai must send these to Yap but Ulithi's role is simply to pass on orders for them and supervise their transportation. This is done according to a strict chain of authority that is scrupulously observed, so that a small island will not comply with orders from Yap unless they have been sent in accordance with the proper pattern. The importance of Ulithi's position is better understood

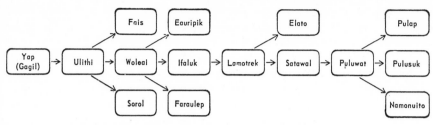

Fig. 4. The chain of authority within the Yap empire.

when it is realized that there is no direct communication between chiefs on Yap and the Woleai.

Turbulence occasionally marks Ulithi's relations with Yap, usually over sexual rivalry and the breaking of taboos, but also over real or imagined insubordination. Since Yap always holds the ultimate upper hand in the form of natural resources not found in the atolls, it prevails. But when the symbiosis is working smoothly, which is to say when the children are showing proper respect and gratitude towards their parents, then the people of the atoll have the advantage. For, to repeat, in this whole relationship the upper caste usually exercises a benevolent paternalism over the lower caste. From the point of view of the Ulithian, where else can he get yams, betel nut, Polynesian chestnuts, big timber, ochre, and other prized goods? Not unless he were to risk distant voyages of hundreds of miles instead of a mere eighty-five, and then he would not be sure of success for his efforts. He would have little more to offer in return except services in transporting goods in their own canoes.

Evidence of the persistence of the Yapese empire over time comes from the pen of Father Cantova, who, writing in 1731 from Ulithi, stated: "These islands [Ulithi] like so many others of this archipelago are subjects of the king of Yap."

Outside this political complex there are other islands, and Ulithi has intercourse with many of them, particularly Ngulu, where many Ulithians settled some time ago. Contacts are maintained, too, with Sonsorol, Pulo Anna, Merir, and Tobi, a group of distant atolls where some Ulithian lineages are represented. Occasional visits are made to Truk and Palau. Ponape and Kusae are known mostly by name. The Marianas have some affinities with the atoll on account of the refugees once located there after a typhoon, but also because of contacts established centuries ago. But political influence is entirely lacking once one leaves the Yapese sphere.

There are traditions of warfare between islands. These apply to a period too remote to speak of authentically. Yet warfare has existed and cannot be discounted as one of the characteristics of this island world.

4

Aspects of Law

I N ADDRESSING OURSELVES to the question of law we are not interested
merely in customs or morals but in those social norms whose violation in-
vokes the use of systematic and coercive procedures of formal nature.
Ulithian modes of conduct which are legal, or at least incipiently legal, cannot
however always be clearly distinguished because they do not conform to law in
the sense that it exists in more complex societies.

The Stuff That Makes Law

In a society that values conformity and deprecates controversy, there is
little opportunity for law to be formed, for law requires the processes of litigation for its development. The truth is that contentiousness is not favored by the
mores of the people.

I am reminded of a comment made by a young Ulithian who, after considerable hesitation, consented to relate to me the details of his recent divorce.
On asking him what proof he had had of his wife's infidelities, he replied that
after receiving hints from reliable sources he had crept up one night outside the
house where he knew that she and a young man were alone. He heard enough
to know positively that they were engaged in the most ardent of intimacies. I
pressed him to recount what had happened next. "I went home," he said. I protested that in America he would probably have burst through the door and as-
saulted the lovers. No, he insisted, that would have been bad. "When my wife
came home I told her she must stop doing this. I did not speak to the man
about it." There is not much chance for law to be formed in an atmosphere of
such exquisite restraint.

If litigation is weak, the answer is to be found in the structure of the
society and the whole way of life. The relationships that people have to one another have been worked out over many years and are predominantly personal
and kinship in character. The thrust for conformity comes mostly from outside

the law, for the very nature of legal procedures and sanctions is contrary to the prevailing spirit of so minuscule a society. Pressure to conform of course comes in part from the dread of criticism, public contempt, ridicule, and ostracism.

It comes also from the sheer need for cooperation. In an insular environment where life is not easy to sustain and the catastrophic effects of typhoons are always menacing, one cannot dare risk the loss of the reciprocal aid so needed to carry on. Conformity is vital for economic activity, which has a highly cooperative character in the atoll. But it has other rewards: companionship, affection, and status. The pressure to conform comes mostly from one's kinsmen, for they above all others offer not only these inducements but food, clothing, shelter, and property rights as well.

Finally, pressure to conform comes from the fear of supernatural retribution. It might be insisted that the punishment of delicts by supernatural agencies is actually a part of Ulithian law. While it is true that such punishment serves as an important force of social control, it is by no means to be construed as a kind of law. Even though the sanctions of supernatural agencies are thought to bring about misfortune, illness, or death, they do not involve procedure or a scale of punishment. They are structureless and vague. This may be seen, for example, in the total lack of judicial procedure for the punishment of sorcery, a delict rated as highly antisocial and yet, aside from public scorn, punished only by Ialulep, the chief deity of the Ulithians, and by countersorcery by the intended victim. Nevertheless, supernatural sanctions are effective and as a consequence additionally inhibit the development of law. An intriguing use of sorcery is its employment by an individual against persons who defecate on his land. One might speculate on the extent to which the threat of contagious magic serves to promote sanitation in the atoll.

The structure of the law is as crudely developed as its concept. Codes are unclearly defined, procedures for the mediation of disputes are sporadic, and courts are absent.

Although code is weakly developed, it is not altogether negligible. There are brief reports in the literature, concerning this atoll and other islands in the area, of a principle of talion or equivalent retaliation in effect early in the century. They pertain to bodily injury. If a victim lost an arm or a hand, his relatives could inflict the same damage on the assailant. If he lost one or both eyes, they could inflict a like injury on the culprit.

But we cannot be sure if the principle of the *lex talionis* was always applied exactly. For example, in addition to retaliation against the person of the offender, there could be seizure of his house and other belongings. Moreover, a lesser offense, such as the tearing of an earlobe, was punished by payment of a ball of turmeric, no mention being made of the tearing of the earlobe of the offender. Evidence of code is seen in the penalty for loss of both legs, but here loss of land rather than equivalent retaliation was involved. It is said that a man who had mutilated the sex organs of another man would be put to death by the whole village, yet once more the details are lacking. There can be little doubt, however, that in the western Carolines there once did exist a code of indemnity of varying degrees of precision.

If, then, we display any indecision as to the strength of the Ulithian judicial code, it results from our difficulty in finding regularity. Law implies regularity, and regularity must be seen in litigation. Lacking litigation, even a hypothetical answer as to what constitutes the law cannot always be framed.

Numerous acts which in many societies would be considered delicts fail to qualify as involving the juridical for the simple reason that they are nonexistent. Thus, abortion and infanticide are not practiced, so any reaction to them can only be stated in hypothetical terms. Homicide, according to the oldest inhabitants, has never occurred within their memory, although, to be sure, in 1949 a demented youth found a loaded wartime carbine and killed two men with it. This is obviously a special situation in which no culpability was charged against the youth because of his acute psychosis. Sodomy, bestiality, and prostitution are unknown in the atoll and consequently, again, there has been no formation of juridical concepts and procedures regarding them.

As for the mediation of disputes, here again there is little regularity. The society does not exercise its authority or even its prestige in terminating litigation. Perhaps the area of most persistent and gnawing controversy pertains to land rights; grudges may be carried on covertly or even openly during the whole of men's lifetimes. Yet here there is no instrumentality to decide disputes one way or another and the complexity of the problem constantly increases. Some of the cause behind the lack of procedure obviously lies in the kinship character of sanctions. With kinsmen applying punishment in their customarily diffuse fashion against transgressors who are members of their group, process fails to receive encouragement for its development. Incest, adultry, thieving, lying, and quarrelling, for example, are essentially handled by the kinsmen of the offender, who may berate, beat, or otherwise punish him and—though this is inconsistent—seek to appease the kinsmen of the aggrieved party with gifts if they belong to another group.

It has been commented that courts are absent. They can be said to be present only in the sense that they are made up of the plaintiff and public opinion. Thus, where a plaintiff takes such action as the imposition of a distraint, without the intervention of a third party, the only tribunal is that of public opinion, which may recognize that the complaint of the aggrieved party is just, his procedure proper, and his assessment of damages reasonable. If the defendant feels the force of public opinion so strongly—as he usually does, for distraint is not exercised lightly—that he accepts the charges and makes compensation, then we may say that in a very loose sense there are courts in Ulithi. But this is perhaps going beyond the bounds. Actually, if we are to admit the presence of incipient courts at all it is in the deliberations of the men's councils; yet even here cases are adjudicated in a legal sense only by stretching the definition of the word legal.

The most fundamental aspect of law, which is to say the systematic and formal application of force by the state for the support of explicit rules of conduct, is as weakly represented as is concept and structure, for the use or threat of coercion is ordinarily neither impersonal nor delegated to parties acting on behalf of society. The cold neutrality of an impartial judge is nowhere to be found. Instead, the use or threat of physical force is mostly exercised by private parties acting in their own behalf. In such contexts, glimmerings of law in the stricter sense come from the tacit support given the aggrieved party against the actions of the defendant, these actions being diffusely felt as injurious to the general social interest.

Yet occasional exercise of a kind of sovereign, impersonal force must be conceded. As will be duly documented in the next section, the king wields the threat of force in certain matters infringing on him as the head of his miniature state. Allied to this is the authority exercised by the men's councils. The implication of force is vaguely felt behind their verbal chastisements of individuals who offend the community by such acts as shirking communal chores, disrupting the successful termination of a communal fishing effort by their thoughtless incursion into the area, defecating in unseemly public places, and ignoring prohibitions broadly referred to as *etap,* or taboos.

There can be no question but that the use of force is repugnant to Ulithians. The prevailing attitude is irenic—operating toward peace or conciliation.

While exile is apparently unknown nowadays, it seems to have existed in the past as a method of avoiding trouble rather than punishing one for making it. During his voyage around the world early in the last century, Kotzebue heard from his informant, Kadu, a man originally from Woleai but picked up by the Russians in the Marshalls, of an act of banishment intended to repress further delinquency. Kadu says that on the island of Mogmog in Ulithi the trees were regularly robbed of their best fruit, and when it was at long last discovered that the thief was a boy, they first merely scolded him, then tied him up at night and shut him up so he could not go on his depredations. But "the sly thief knew how to frustrate all these precautions, and continued as before." In despair, several persons rowed the young man to a remote, uninhabited island of the group, but the trees were robbed as before. The boy had used the trunk of a tree as a boat. They destroyed this and then enjoyed some respite. But once, when a party sought to discover how he was faring alone on the isle, they could not find him. As they searched, he stole their canoe and set out for the atoll of Sorol. Here he talked the chief of the atoll into sending a war party to Mogmog to seize and murder the chief and take the supreme power. But the people were frustrated on landing. "The instigator was punished by death. The people of Sorol returned uninjured to their island." The point Kotzebue tried to make is that everything was done to prevent misdeeds. The ultimate retribution was forced on the people. The example is interesting but does not answer many questions. Were the people who tied up the boy and later rowed him into exile acting on behalf of the village? Probably not. They could have been his kinsmen. Was exile a habitual practice?

In a letter written in 1722 while he was on Guam interviewing some castaways before his voyage to Ulithi, Father Cantova writes: "Criminals are not punished by either imprisonment or corporal punishment. It is enough to exile them to another island." Perhaps exile was a kind of sanction in those days, rather than a preventive. But again, who ordered the exile? Who executed the order?

Closely related to law, yet only quasi-legal, is the conventionalization of such diffuse sanctions as public contempt, criticism, and withdrawal. Here one does not find the systematic and impersonal application of force in the maintenance of individual rights and in the public interest. Nevertheless, the results are similar to those of law and act in its place. They have much the same effect as naked force.

Perhaps the best example of this is the bizarre exposure to ridicule offered through the *hamath* song, which bears the same name as the *hamath* dance. While the dance is connected with female puberty rites, it is seized upon as an occasion for redressing a grievance. The person who launches the procedure enlists the aid of his friends to compose and sing songs of derision and exposure while performing the dance, which, apart from its use in this context, is always frankly erotic or even lewd.

Let us say that a woman wishes to end her husband's philanderings with other women. She will secretly arrange with some women friends to make up a song to accompany the *hamath* dance. In this song reference may be made to the inadequacy of the man's sexual organ, to his clumsiness in his relations with women, or to his preference for eating chicken instead of catching fish—a mark of laziness. The man is humiliated and sets about trying to discover who initiated the *hamath* against him. He summons his men friends to retaliate in kind, whether or not the identity of his specific critic is known. If known, the men sing obscene words about the woman's easy virtue and deprecate her anatomy. If unknown, the men chant songs against women in general, taunting them as so sexually inadequate that the men must find solace with women on other islands. The next night, the women reply with new songs directed against the man. The contest continues sometimes for many days and may end when the women pick up stones and throw them at the men dancers. The original center of all this attention is usually chastened sufficiently for him to mend his ways. The effect goes even further than this; it may clear the air between men and women in general by allowing them to unburden themselves of pent-up grievances, and it may also serve to put all of them on the defensive lest as individuals they are exposed to the blasting words of the *hamath*.

Another conventionalization of criticism along lines that are quasi-legal is to be seen in the formalized song directed by a group of women against a member of their sex who shirks the performance of communal labor ordered by the men's council through the council of female elders. As the tardy offender approaches the cluster of women already at work, they initiate a lugubrious, slow chant naming the culprit and specifying her indolence. They keep repeating the chant until the guilty party has settled into the full swing of her duties. An air of merriment seems to pervade the gesture but there can be little doubt of its ultimate efficacy, at least for a time.

Leaves of Distraint

The most developed legal institution in Ulithi is indubitably the *harme-chung,* or distraint. It is an act designed to insure that an offender will make restitution for a wrong. Ideally, according to Anglo-Saxon common law, the distrainer takes the property of the wrongdoer into his own custody as a pledge that satisfaction will be forthcoming. In Ulithian practice, we may view the distraint as sometimes doing this, but sometimes acting without actual seizure of property. An act is performed with leaves to signify that the reputation and well-being of the offender, as it were, are now in the hands of the distrainer, who will redeem this reputation and well-being on payment of gift fines.

The word *harmechung* seems to be generic for "young leaves," but in actual practice the young leaves are always the young white ones of a growing coconut tree. These leaves, called *ubwoth,* always have highly ritualistic connotations, being used in magic and religion by specialists who wear them tied around the head, neck, arms, and ankles. They are also used by performers in either sacred or secular dances. The term *ubwoth* is often used as a synonym for the *harmechung.*

As an object, the *harmechung* are the leaves, fastened either to a stick planted in some appropriate place, often the locale of the transgression, or else tied directly to some property belonging to the offender. When it is thus displayed it means that a person has declared a sanction against another person.

The unusual feature of the distraint in Ulithi is that it is imposed unilaterally, without the benefit of a hearing or court, and yet has the support of the society. The assumption is that the distraint is not exercised frivolously, and that due reflection and adequate evidence have preceded the decision to resort to it. The object of the levy is expected to acknowledge his guilt, either implicitly or explicitly, and to atone for it by the payment of an indemnity or the forfeiture of property, which may be destroyed by the distrainer instead of being put to use.

Some hypothetical examples will bring out the multifaceted character of this legal institution.

The most serious application of the *harmechung* is in offenses against sovereignty or political authority. Such offenses may impinge on the king as the symbol of sovereignty, and include lese majesty. They may also encompass offenses against a village, whereby the council head initiates punitive action. Unwarranted intrusion into a territory is one of the most common occasions for resentment, and such trespass is regarded as an offense when it is committed by an outsider, either foreign to the atoll or to the district. For example, if a canoe from outside of Ulithi comes to the atoll and fails to report to the council house on Mogmog, that canoe will have leaves tied to one end of its hull as a sign that it has been confiscated for failure to observe the ritual. Should a canoe within the atoll arrive at another island in Ulithi and fail to perform the ritual, it too will be tied with young coconut leaves and be confiscated or even destroyed. Should a canoe pass through the area of one district on its way to another district without stopping to pay its respects, it again is subject to the penalty of the distraint. So is a canoe that has fished in grounds not belonging to its district.

It sometimes happens that an offending canoe cannot be seized. The act of *harmechung* cannot be performed literally but word will be sent to the lineage owning the canoe that it has been declared confiscated. The lineage must accept the decision.

Since sailing canoes are owned by lineages, the latter are culpable. It is possible to procure the return of a canoe that has been confiscated by making gift payments to the injured party, that is, either the king or a district chief. These payments are colorfully called "untying the young coconut leaves." It is no mere coincidence that canoes play so large a part in the law, for they are not only the instruments by which trespass is effected but constitute extremely valuable property as well.

The king also imposes the leaf sanction against any district that fails to send first fruits to Mogmog when certain kinds of plant foods are being gathered. He may also impose it for failure to contribute fish for a certain annual ritualistic feast given for the two leading chiefs of Mogmog.

The leaf sanction is seriously invoked when a district secretly kills a green turtle instead of sending it to Mogmog to be killed and distributed ritualistically. Green turtles have sacred connotations, and in any event are under the control of the island of Mogmog, which is to say, the two district chiefs there. It happened that for some years the turtle ritual had not been performed. The reasons for this are highly involved but go back ultimately to the suspension of the pagan ritual investing the king. The island of Fassarai, knowing the ritualistic killing of sea turtles had not been perpetuated, killed some of the huge reptiles clandestinely. The chiefs of Mogmog, one of whom was the king, sent word of a distraint to Fassarai, forbidding anyone at all from that island to carry on any kind of fishing whatsoever. Since fish is the most prized of foods, this was a severe blow. After two or three months of deprivation, the people of Fassarai brought an "untying" to the offended chiefs. It consisted of garments, dried leaves to make into sails, turmeric, rope, cloth, and hawksbill carapaces (not taboo). The two chiefs on Mogmog accepted the indemnity and shared it with each of the two council chiefs on the island. As is customary, although the payments were nominally made to them, they distributed the goods to all the people. An apology had to accompany Fassarai's indemnity.

The island of Mogmog holds a privileged position in the *harmechung* system by virtue of its being the seat of sovereignty. In a dispute with another island, it may distrain but not be distrained against. However, in civil cases involving challenges against Mogmog lineages, this immunity does not apply.

Behind the leaf sanction is the threat of force, and it is here that the main ingredient of law manifests itself. It is not necessary to use force against the chief of an offending island, since he would not think of ignoring a *harmechung*. Tradition and public opinion are too strong for that. However, in private cases an individual may choose to defy the imposition of a leaf sanction. Should he do so, his own village would punish him by damaging his house or canoe, if he has one, and confiscate any movable property. It should be pointed out that such action is not taken in ordinary civil cases but only when the individual has been the object of a leaf sanction imposed by his lineage or some chief.

Recourse to distraint in civil cases, as opposed to public or criminal types, seems predominantly to involve disputes between lineages rather than individuals, even though the lineages are represented in the dispute by their chiefs. A typical litigation might involve the payment of *momwoi*. This payment is a kind of compensation made after a divorce to one's former spouse if one is the first to remarry after the termination of the marriage. In a way, the payment signalizes the complete divorce, for prior to that a couple is actually only separated. It does not serve as acknowledgment of guilt in the dispute that led to the breakup. In actuality, the payment is made by one lineage to another. Should a lineage fail to make payment of the *momwoi,* it becomes the recipient of distraint. If its delinquent member is a woman, the land she has brought into the marriage is distrained by tying young coconut leaves to a stick, which is then implanted on the land in question. Her ex-husband keeps the land. If the offender is the man, his land may not be distrained. Instead, verbal distraint is declared by her lineage against all of his property in movables: rope, pots, knives, pigs, chicken, and so on. So obvious to all is the failure for an ex-spouse, man or woman, to pay the *momwoi* that the objects of the distraint make no retaliation. Their guilt is acknowledged by their silent yielding to the seizure.

The leaf sanction is obviously an effective institution in preventing the indefinite extension of conflict. While it substitutes for physical force, the ultimate recourse to physical coercion is implied. Being recognized by the society as a just and valid procedure it brings finality into a dispute, so preventing deterioration into a feud. The leaf sanction is indubitably at a higher level of the juridical than is most rudimentary law in the atoll.

Liability

Ulithians make full and reasonable allowance for deviations resulting from lack of comprehension between what is right and what is wrong. Even though many violations of the legal norms can be attributed to the feebleminded or insane, it is considered that those individuals who are mentally incompetent should not be held responsible for their acts. While on the atoll, I was deeply impressed by the solicitude with which the people treated a young manic who damaged property, refused to work, struck his father, pursued women threateningly, and menaced small children with fishing spears. They tolerated an old woman who was accustomed to steal, spread falsehoods, hoard food, and shirk communal chores. These psychotics were shown every consideration and sympathy. Effort was made to draw them and others like them into the pattern of daily life.

Children are often held unresponsible for their acts, their culpability depending on their age and the nature of the offense. Children who offend within the family are held responsible to the family but not beyond that. Those who transgress against a neighbor and are of an age sufficiently advanced to know they have done wrong, must have have their parents compensate the injured party with some item of goods. If the child is too young to have realized his culpability, the family may extend a gift to the injured party in order to demonstrate its regret.

Involuntary or unwitting transgressions do not incur liability. Should a man accidentally damage a canoe belonging to someone else, or unintentionally break a borrowed knife, or injure a bystander while lifting a heavy object to his shoulders, he is considered blameless. Indeed, the injured party may be considered to be the victim of a spirit or other supernatural power that has simply used the offender as an instrument for performing the damage or injury.

The owners of animals that inflict damage, bite, steal food, or commit a nuisance in a man's house or garden may be liable for the act if it is due to negligence in controlling the animal, usually a dog or a pig. But if the damage or injury can be traced to such actions on the part of the injured party as teasing the animal or unleashing it when tied, then the owner is not liable. If a third party has teased or unleased the animal, he is the one who is responsible.

Rank as such conveys no immunity for violation of the law. If anything, a chief or other person of high status is held especially culpable in any transgression, as he should serve as a model of comportment. However, there is no evidence that this ideal is given expression in practice. There is no doubt, however, that the force of public opinion is such that it serves to exact of its chiefs a spirit of *noblesse oblige.*

5

The Transcendental World

I T IS NOT POSSIBLE to characterize Ulithian religion in holistic terms, for it is overwhelmingly eclectic. It is as if the people, having been exposed throughout centuries to myriads of other people's adjustments to the supernatural, have incorporated anything in their armamentarium that suggests the possibility of reward. No haughty disdain of alien creeds or rituals, no smug satisfaction with indigenous creations marks the Ulithian attitude towards the transcendental. Consequently, side by side with ancestor worship is a belief in a pantheon of celestial and terrestrial gods, an involvement with animistic spirits, a concern with the other world of punishment and reward, a recourse to mediums, a reliance on magic and divination, and a guide to things taboo.

Included in this conglomerate is a belief in totemic beings; but totemism has not caught much hold in the atoll because it belongs to the alien clans that have established precarious residence there, and in any event is more social than religious in character.

Ancestors Who Care

Father Cantova, a remarkably reliable informant, wrote in 1722 about Carolinian religion and tells us enough about the worship of ancestors to reassure us that the practice has endured long and without much change. The ensuing account, however, is not drawn from him and refers specifically to Ulithi.

At the basis of the system of ancestor worship is a recognition that some spirit beings have an originally human origin rather than the impersonal one of the spirits of nature.

Ancestors are of course people and consequently are possessed of souls. The soul of the living person is lodged in the head, and ingress and egress take place where the bregmatic fontanelle of infancy is located. This unossified membranous interval in the frontal portion of the cranium is the spot where the soul enters the baby at birth. The soul is not a prisoner; it may, especially in dreams and illness, leave the body and wander or fly about and then return. When a person dies the soul leaves forever and is then called a ghost. Ghosts hover in the vicinity of their graves for four days after death and subsequently fly away to the island of Angaur in the west, where they bathe. They then proceed to make their way upward through various levels to the Sky World, where a decision is made by the chief deity there as to their fate. The ghosts of the dead do not lose interest in the living; in fact, they are an extension of society because of the interest they take in human activities.

Of the vast pool of departed ancestors, most are soon forgotten by the living, while others achieve varying degrees of prominence and remembrance. Since ordinary ghosts are of little practical consequence and quickly achieve the oblivion that is the destiny of the undistinguished, they may be immediately dismissed.

The ghosts that are remembered are of various kinds, but all have a link with lineages. A lineage ghost is one who has returned from the Sky World to possess a lineage mate. Of course, such a spirit is known by name and gains a certain amount of ritualistic attention and respect. But if in the course of his or her necromantic career he begins to falter in the performance of the services expected of him, he becomes neglected and ultimately forgotten. His memory to be sure is not as transient as that of a new ghost who has failed completely to make his presence known through a medium; on the other hand, it endures so briefly that after the passage of a few generations his lineage cannot recall his name.

A more important type of lineage ghost is one who has made so great a contribution to members of his lineage that he is elevated to the uppermost position for that kin group. In the course of his ascendancy he supplants the extant number one ghost, who is thereby demoted and relegated in the course of time to oblivion. Oddly enough, this exalted type of spirit is known as a "little ghost," but only by comparison with two individual ghosts of wide renown who will be examined later. All lineages, except very minor ones, possess a little ghost and provide a shrine for him, located in the house of the head of the lineage. The shrine consists essentially of a bamboo grid from which are suspended offerings of coconut oil, leis, loincloths, and turmeric. The oil is left there indefinitely and the leis until they have withered, but the loincloths and turmeric are removed after about ten to twenty days and given to members of the household to use. Neither of these may be employed in connection with a corpse or a funeral. There is a pragmatic tone to the arrangement. The offerings are essentially payments for services performed. Usually, no offering is left for a ghost until he has made an appearance; however, on occasion a family will present offerings in anticipation of a visit, discontinuing the offerings should the ghost fail to manifest himself through a medium. The principal gainer seems to be the custodian of the shrine, who is normally the eldest male member of the lineage but may come from the patrilineal side of the little ghost. He is the only one who may receive the offerings and look after the shrine. He may or may not be the ghost's medium. In any event, many of the offerings ultimately come into his hands.

Lineages may on occasion adopt a little ghost from another lineage on the grounds that they do not have a successful one of their own. The intrusive clans on Ulithi have similarly borrowed the services of little ghosts. Thus, through borrowing as well as replacement there is some fluidity in the system, yet as documentary evidence has shown change is not characteristic. The mobility of the system is rather a sign of the great democracy prevailing in the atoll, for anyone's ghost may achieve a position of eminence, eminence depending not on one's rank while alive but on accomplishment after death. In his lifetime a little ghost may have been a chief or an ordinary man, a female as well as a male, an infant as well as an adult.

In ancestor worship, the medium plays an important role, for it is through him that the ancestors provide the kind of information sought by the living in the conduct of their lives. The medium is the means by which advice, warnings, and facts are transmitted. While in a state of possession he trembles a good deal and on occasion may go into an epilepticlike fit. He utters the words of the spirit in clear and intelligible language, rather than strange verbiage or incomprehensible mutterings. The information imparted in trance communication pertains to the things that most concern the Ulithian: the feasibility of an ocean voyage, the safety of relatives away from home, the cause of an illness, the attitude of a loved one, the approach of a typhoon, and the like. The experience of having been possessed by the dead is a trying one. When the ghost leaves, the mouthpiece emerges from his trance and is given water and a massage. He recovers from his feeling of malaise but has no recollection of his experience and cannot repeat what the spirit said during that time. The seance is not on this account wasted, for the medium's relatives have been listening attentively to all that has been said.

One might suppose that attaining the rank of principal ghost of a lineage would be the pinnacle of success for an ancestral spirit, but there is a status beyond that. There exists a social class of lineage ghosts called "great ghosts," of which there are only two in number. Ulithians are adamant as to their historicity and do not confuse them with spirits of high eminence who are not thought of as having once been mortals. True, these ghosts have reached such heights that they have journeyed a long way on the road to apotheosis, and their fame has spread throughout a vast area of the Carolines. Nevertheless, they have human origins. This is hard to verify for the great ghost called Iongolap. It is easier to document for the other, named Marespa.

Early mention is made of Iongolap in the literature. The Russian explorer Kotzebue was told by Kadu in 1817 of his great importance at that time not only in Ulithi but Yap, Ngulu, and Fais as well. The information is scanty but discloses to us that the god "visits distant islands where he is acknowledged," and that several "temples," where offerings are made, are built for him at Ulithi, Yap, and Ngulu.

Iongolap, according to Ulithian informants and mythology, was born in the atoll a long time ago of a woman who had left her home on Yap in anger because of a quarrel, and had created the islands of Ulithi by strewing sand on the surface of the sea. Iongolap's father was a Yapese, and when the boy left

Ulithi to visit him on Yap, his father gave him most of the islands of the Carolinian archipelago, and some others besides. One day Iongolap wanted to leave Yap to visit his mother on Ulithi but the people would not let him go. Instead, they sent some men to the atoll, instructing them to bring back gifts to present to Iongolap. That is why, it is said, Ulithi continues sending religious tribute to Yap even today. But occasionally Iongolap does visit his birthplace, joining the crews of the Ulithian canoes as they return home after paying tribute to Yap. Statements in the literature indicate that when he is at the atoll he "lives" at the house of the Fasilus lineage, the head lineage of the atoll and the one that supplies the paramount chief. These statements also assert that early in the present century a grandson of Iongolap lived in that same house. At any rate, despite the fact that the Yapese claim the ghost-become-god as their own, the people of Ulithi have other ideas and once a year hold a feast in his honor, with all islands of the atoll participating. He is turned to in time of need, especially when famine threatens. Obviously, notwithstanding the changes introduced by the process of myth making, the people of Ulithi consider Iongolap to be an ancestral ghost. Though we hear nothing regarding his necromantic accomplishments, the tacit assumption is that as a great ghost he surely must have reached such status because of his talent in providing information, presumably at first to members of the Fasilus lineage, later to the people of the whole atoll.

But the process of apotheosis has proceeded so far, as long ago as 1817, that it is hard to recognize in him a mere ancestor. Iongolap is the stuff of which gods are made. In one myth he sends a bird from Yap to Ulithi to look after his sister. The bird gives birth to a girl, who lives with this sister until they have a serious quarrel over food. Iongolap's sister deserts the girl and returns to Yap, but the girl gives birth to a son—grandchild of the bird. The son lives in the heavens but returns each day to earth to do the cooking. One day he went to Yap in a canoe that had been transformed by magic from a stone, and the stone canoe may still be seen in a channel there. This myth, collected in 1909 by a German anthropologist, is supplemented by another in which Iongolap sends a spirit to a man on Ulithi to teach him how to make a fishhook and to fish with it. Another myth, this time from Yap, has Ionglap born there near a village in the district of Gagil, which it will be recalled is the overlord of Ulithi and the islands further to the east. These myths explain not only why a series of complex festivals are held on Yap throughout the year in honor of the deity but also why he has a relationship to Ulithi that is expressed through political subordination and various rituals.

In the course of time a new great ghost named Marespa appeared on the scene. He is completely Ulithian and has largely supplanted his predecessor. Regarding his historicity there is little or no doubt. I have gathered his genealogy and certain anecdotal materials that not only authenticate his existence but help us place his date of birth at about 1868. Like Iongolap, he is said by Ulithians to belong to the dominant Fasilus lineage. His birthplace is the island of Lam, and his grave on that island still stands.

Marespa died when he was only a few weeks or months old. Soon afterwards he possessed one of his relatives and continued to use him for a time as his mouthpiece. Speaking in the high-pitched voice of a baby, he communicated forthcoming events, it is said, with such startling accuracy that his fame soon spread throughout the atoll. But it did not stop at the verges of Ulithi; it jumped rapidly to Yap, where, in Gagil district, he became second only to Iongolap in importance. In view of the fact that Gagil considers Ulithians to be low caste people, this concession to their great ghost attests to the eagerness with which people of the Carolines seize upon any supernatural phenomenon that has promise of success.

It did not take long for Marespa's fame to spread further afield. He became the leading ghost of the eastward islands called the Woleai. Undoubtedly, the receptivity he encountered was partly inspired by the superordinate position of Ulithi with respect to these islands in the Gagil domain, but it is likely that his great talents as a ghost were even more persuasive. To the west, he caught the fancy of Palau, where it is said that one lineage, possibly originally from Ulithi, asked for and received permission from the atoll to build a shrine for him, just as the people of Ulithi and the Woleai had already done. Beyond Palau, at the westernmost limits of Micronesia, the islands of Sonsorol, Pulo Anna, Merir, and Tobi are reputed to have found a place for him despite their recognition of a certain local ghost as the most powerful of all. Ngulu, a satellite of Yap outside the Gagil sphere and closely allied to Ulithi by virtue of certain common historical, cultural, and linguistic relations, is said to have adopted Marespa as its chief ghost. In all these islands, he became so identified with the people that they built their own local shrines for him and did not take offerings for him to Ulithi. It is possible that the facts about Marespa have been exaggerated in Ulithi's favor by local informants and that the places in the extensive area to which his fame and activity traveled may be only those where Ulithians have been present as immigrants or visitors, but there can be no doubt of his importance. A Polish anthropologist recorded some details in the last century concerning his presence in Palau, and a German anthropologist provides fuller information garnered in 1909 on Ngulu atoll. In 1947 an American anthropologist working on the atoll of Ifaluk collected some songs in which the ghost is several times mentioned.

With such talent in predicting typhoons, warning of impending epidemics, revealing the loss of voyagers at sea, describing events in distant places, forecasting the arrival of schools of fish, and other choice morsels of information so dearly sought by anxious people, Marespa was destined to go beyond the status of a great ghost. Like Iongolap before him, he began to have woven about him a tissue of mythology that set in motion the metamorphosis towards godhood. Then suddenly his progress was halted by the encroachments of alien creeds and administrations, and he lost his position of pre-eminence where previously he had been shown honor and deference. But on Ulithi there are those who still remember his halcyon days of glory.

Little has been said here of the role of the dead in participating in human affairs. Like solicitous parents they provide blessing and protection, but at the same time are not averse to inflicting ghostly retribution against transgressors of the moral order. Such parental-like involvement makes them, in a sense, active members of society. For they are never very far from the dreary inter-course of daily life.

Ancestor worship is not a unique local phenomenon. Despite inadequate reporting, it is obvious that throughout Micronesia all the conventional criteria of ancestor worship are met: the historicity of the ghosts of ancestors, the trans-ference to them of an attitude of reverence, and the employment of ritualistic practices designed to effect interaction between the living and the dead. Nor is the apotheosis experienced by Iongolap and Marespa unknown elsewhere. Similar instances have been noted, for example, in the Gilbert Islands, and it is likely that the process of deification of mortals was once not uncommon in all of Mi-cronesia. Ancestor worship fits the prevailing culture, with its strong emphasis on kinship, and is consistent with the highly personal character of social rela-tions.

Demons Who Menace

Ulithians take cognizance also of superhuman beings who lack human origins. The generic name for such beings is *ialus*, which may be translated as "spirit." They range from lowly to lofty.

The less elevated of these spirits live in close intimacy with mortals and lack the dignity of gods. They are not the object of a cult. Some are benevolent but most are malevolent, and in any event demand attention and respect, even though they do not merit worship. For want of a better word they may be re-ferred to as demons.

Demons are reported in vague and conflicting ways by the natives. Some say they have one large eye, others say two, and still others say four. They are variously depicted as anthropomorphic or balls of fire, male or female, clothed or nude, and transparent or nontransparent. Some say they are black, whereas others depict them as brown, blue, or white. Demons have been observed sit-ting, standing, walking, swimming, or suspended in air a few inches off the ground. Some have pursued people and even wrestled with them. They have been heard to moan, whistle, sing, and talk. They have been seen in various haunts—houses, groves, beaches, and the sea. They have been observed during the daytime and at night.

For the most part demons are anonymous. They are classified in four main categories, depending on whether their habitat is a tree, a burial plot, the earth, or the sea. People do not ordinarily think of them as being male or fe-male. They are well aware of the demons' sinister attitude toward human beings and are quick to attribute illness, misfortune, and strange happenings to them. *Ialus* of this type threaten men constantly and force them to maintain a constant vigil against them. So they are not simple pranksters; rather, they are the source of much of the misery afflicting mankind.

Some demons are known by name and their personal traits. One, a tree spirit, causes blindness, stomach pains, and a sickness that enormously distends the abdomen. Another tree spirit is responsible for gonorrhea. Another demon, who lives in the coral holes of the sea surrounding the island of Lam, has a bad reputation and is greatly feared, yet no one knows what causes him to be angered, or can say if he has in fact ever injured anyone. A curious spirit, whose name is greeted with laughter even though he is feared, is held in low esteem by the people because he employs an absurd method of catching fish and lobsters. He uses his penis as a light to attract these sea fauna in the dark. He has been seen walking at night along the reef and on the surface of the water. On account of the delicate nature of his fishing technique one refrains from mentioning him by name in mixed company; instead, a euphemism, "the spirit that uses a torch," must be employed. Finally, although the list of named demons is not exhausted, there is a female spirit who has jurisdiction over the sacred swamp gardens. These are sacred to the extent that many taboos must be observed by persons with respect to entering these gardens. Not permitted to enter are: people who have eaten or defecated during the day; people who are in mourning for a close relative, or have washed a corpse, or dug a grave in the past five months; women who are menstruating; women who are barren; persons who have had sexual relations during the previous six days; men who have fished with a line during the previous four days; fish magicians who have used a certain type of hook during the five previous lunar months; and, lastly, medical practitioners who are currently engaged in treating a patient. This demon, whose hair and skin are reputed to be gray in color, always carries a basket. Her very appearance frightens people, even when they are innocent of any wrongdoing. She lives in all four of the swamp gardens, and if she feels that their sanctity has been violated she punishes the offenders by inflicting on them such diseases as yaws, filariasis, and small boils, as well as other maladies. Her anger may be expressed in a broader way by sending insects to attack the plants growing in the gardens, causing them to die. It is plain that the great concern which the natives have with the food supply is reflected in the numerous precautions they must take to see that nothing will endanger the productivity of the gardens.

Named or not, then, demons cause many of the tribulations that humans must face, and this includes insanity, too. They cannot be won over through prayer but fortunately they can sometimes be coaxed or bribed with gifts and sweet talk. Certainly they serve a positive role in causing the community to maintain proper concern with certain aspects of daily living. In any event they help explain away perplexing phenomena not otherwise explicable, and in doing so lift the gnawing worry that comes from the uncertainty of not knowing the source of one's woes.

A special kind of demon is the ogre. Spirits of this genre eat human beings but they are so outlandishly stupid that ultimately they get their comeuppance from a mortal of greater guile and courage than they possess. Ogres play no part in the religious system, being found principally in the folklore. In a way one must feel a certain compassion towards their fumbling efforts to fill their stomachs with human victims. Though they may terrorize the land, they are fated to end ignominiously, sometimes at the hands of a boy or even a madman.

Gods Who Control

In less intimate contact than either the ancestral dead or the demons infesting every nook and cranny of man's habitat are the gods of sky and earth. True, they are awesome and powerful, yet they are not always concerned with daily life and are not the object of as dynamic a religious cult as are the spirits of the dead. Their worship and propitiation proceeds in irregular fashion.

The gods play no part in the creation of the world. Myths do not tell us how the world originated; at best they tell only how particular islands were formed. In doing so they presuppose the existence of the world and certain supernaturals within it. The lack of cosmogonic myths may be no more than the effects of cultural erosion, for other islands of the Carolines sometimes have accounts telling of the creation of the world, trees, grass, people, and so on.

The pantheon is bifurcated into gods whose realm is the Sky World and those who dwell on earth. The former are more involved with the after-life of mortals, the latter with the present life and its instrumentalities. There is no important distinction in their nature and both branches come under the rubric of *ialus*. They are not affiliated with kin groups; instead, they belong to all the society.

A better appreciation of the spirits of the sky can be gained by looking first at the structure and features of their domain. The Sky World, called Lang (*cf.* Hawaiian Lani) is conceived of as constituted of four levels, the fourth being the one where the great deities live. Each plane has distinctive features and, although these are fairly well delineated in the mythology of other Carolinians, they are, except for the top level, vaguely known to Ulithians. Souls on the way to their final destinations must traverse these levels.

In the highest level of Lang there is an enormous house where the chief deities of the sky branch of the pantheon live. To it come all the fresh spirits of the dead in order to be judged by Ialulep, the greatest *ialus* of them all. For a figure of such pre-eminence strangely little is known about his personality and experiences. He is said never to bother to come down to earth, as do other celestial spirits on occasion. His main role is to listen to the newly arrived spirits as they are being interrogated at the great house by his son, Lugeilang. He listens and decides the fate of each spirit.

Ialulep, which means Great Spirit, is known elsewhere in the Carolines and is generally portrayed as of enormous size and tremendous age. His hair is white. So old and weak is he that men must help him to open his mouth and keep his upper lip from hanging down too far when he wishes to eat. His eyelids are so heavy that when he wishes to look over the world two men have to lift his eyelids. When the door of his house slams there is thunder on earth. In some places, he is believed to control life itself. In his hands he holds the thread of life of each human being, and when he decides that a man is to die he utters words to that effect and tears the thread extending to the brain of the person in question.

Much more is known on Ulithi about Lugeilang, his son. He is a color-ful god who used to be in the habit of maintaining trysts on earth, where once he met a woman who subsequently gave birth to their son, the famous trickster god of the Carolines known as Iolofath.

Iolofath is perhaps the best known of all the characters of Carolinian mythology. He has many of the traits of the Polynesian Maui: brashness, crafti-ness, precocity, mischievousness, and lustiness. A Ulithian version of the Iolo-fath cycle has it that he was born when his mother, mistress of Lugeilang, tugged on a lock of her hair and he issued forth from her head, with all his teeth erupted, and able to walk and talk. Against his father's wishes he ascends to the Sky World on a cloud of smoke to visit him. At each of the four levels of Lang he has experiences that provoke him into performing mischievous deeds. Thus, at the first level he sees several boys playing with a scorpion fish. Annoyed because they will not let him into their circle, he causes the fish to de-velop spines which prick the boys' fingers and make them cry. At the second level he is again rebuffed by some boys playing with a shark. He causes the fish to develop teeth and bite the boys. Their parents beat him and he flees to the third level, where several boys are playing with a sting ray that is without sting-ers. He causes stingers to appear and jab the boys, for they too have rejected him as a playmate. Reaching the fourth level he finds men fetching timber to build the great house of the Sky World known as the Farmal. They are all fish but have human attributes, gliding back and forth, imperceptible in their ap-pearance between the piscatory and the anthropomorphic.

The people of the fourth level are digging a hole into which to plant the great housepost of the Farmal. On seeing Iolofath they decide to kill him be-cause he is a stranger. They induce him to go into the posthole and then they ram the post down on him. Red and green fluids squirt upwards and the people think this is his blood and bile, but he has tricked them by taking refuge in a pocket he has dug to the side of the hole. The fluids are merely red earth and green mountain apple leaves that he has put in his mouth. Our ingenious hero escapes from his subterranean prison by having termites eat a hole upward through the great housepost. He has ants bring him small morsels of coconut meat and an arum, and magically causes these to attain full size. He increases the size of a grain of sand until it becomes a rock. Dashing the coconut against the rock he cries out *"Soro!"* to the workmen below. They are astounded and immediately realize he is the son of Lugeilang. Thenceforth they treat him with deference.

The following day the young trickster goes from house to house dis-tributing certain turtle meat. At the home of the procupine fish he scolds him for having spines. He next scolds the cornet fish because his head has no flesh; then the swellfish for having a big belly. When he arrives at the home of the halfbeak he does not find him in and so proceeds to make love to his wife. The halfbeak returns, catches the pair in the act, and kills Iolofath. It takes the efforts of his father, Lugeilang, to bring him back to life.

Another major theme in this myth cycle deals with the conflict between the trickster and his half-brother, whose mother is the true wife of Lugeilang and not a mortal mistress. No love is lost between the two brothers. In a cruel episode Iolofath kills his brother by severing his head but is persuaded by his father to put it back on. Later, this brother puts the trickster in his place by teaching him a lesson in magic.

In later episodes of the cycle, the trickster has mellowed considerably, and in a major episode acts as conciliator between a youth and the wife he has spurned.

Iolofath is not a god in the conventional sense. He mediates between the worlds celestial and terrestrial. After all, he is half-mortal and his behavior has many of the frailties of earthlings, which is probably what endears him to the natives. But still, he is one of the three principal figures in the Sky World and should not be looked upon simply as an unusual mortal. Although in some islands of the Carolines he imparts fire to mankind and decrees that men shall be mortal, he is neither a creator nor culture hero in Ulithi.

Other celestial figures are trivial in importance, acting principally as supporting actors in the myths of the three great gods.

Parallel to the celestial gods is a branch of the pantheon made up of deities of closer relationship to the people than are those in Lang. These gods enter more intimately into the lives of humans, who are keenly aware of their presence and influence. Chief among them are several deities connected with navigation and the sea.

Many of the terrestrial gods, who are far more numerous than the ones in heaven, are characters in a strange myth in which their progenitor exiles himself and his family from the Sky World where they originally lived and takes up permanent abode on earth. In making the transition they forsake their former names and adopt the names of gods in the world they have just deserted. Henceforth, they are identified only by their assumed names.

The father of the brood is Palulap, or Great Navigator. He is said to have brought knowledge of navigation and canoe building to mankind. However, the patron gods of these arts are two of his six sons. Some credit him also with teaching men the art of palm-leaf-knot divination, a practice of utmost importance not only in Ulithi but the rest of the Carolines as well.

His youngest son is Ialulwe, who, because he was born on earth, has a name of his own rather than a borrowed one. He is in practice the deity closest to the people of the atoll. He is the patron of navigators—men of great consequence in the society. Ialulwe is feared because of the punishment he metes out to violators of the mores of the society, and in this respect rivals any of the ancestral ghosts. But his attitude is generally a benevolent one. Of the two cabins constructed on the large seagoing canoes, one is devoted principally to him. In this little cabin, located over the booms of the outrigger, are placed offerings of turmeric, oil, carapaces, mats, and belts. Also included are an effigy of the god himself with two or more stingray stingers as legs. The effigy is used to fight off any sorcery that may possibly be directed against the navigator and his crew. Amulets and other objects of magical character are also placed in the cabin. The mixed nature of Ulithian supernaturalism is reflected in the intermingling in one place of religious and magical objects.

The other cabin, located on the leeward side of the canoe, is secular in nature, being used to store food and supplies, yet some objects of the same kind left for ancestral ghosts at their shrine are put in the cabin. It is not clear if some appeal to the ancestors is thereby intended; at any rate, no connection with Ialulwe is made.

Ialulwe has more than two eyes. Some say he has eyes all over his head, others say he has four eyes in all. There is always at least one eye at the back of his head, as his effigies reveal, this having to do with navigational techniques.

There is something undefinably strange about this god. He gains his knowledge of navigation while still being carried in his mother's womb. This he does while his father is instructing the other sons, of whom there are five. By the time he is born he is already a grown boy with a strong mind of his own and capable of unusual deeds. He is a loner who creates an island out of sand and then lives henceforth on it. When one of his brothers is wrecked at sea and attempts to crawl wearily on the island, he rebuffs and even blinds him because of his insubordination and the violation of certain maritime taboos. Yet while the brother is still in his blindness Ialulwe teaches him the art of navigation. The brother eventually returns to his family, after which he experiences the castigation of his own people because they do not recognize him as he sits at the beach, and are impatient with his gloomy forecasts concerning the suitability of the weather for an ocean voyage they are planning. Despite his warnings they make the trip, and all aboard, including his father, sister, and three of his brothers, perish. The myth that recounts these adventures gives expression to many of the ritual prohibitions of the sea observed in Ulithi.

A brother, also of patronlike character, is Solang, who dwells in canoes and is prayed to by canoe builders to enlist his help in making a good craft. Canoe building is an important and prestigeful art, surrounded by many prescriptions and taboos. Solang insists that none of his carpenters work late in the afternoon. Men who fail to heed this rule run the risk of intervention, as a result of which they mishandle their adzes and cut themselves. Solang permits no one to build a house or repair one on any island where the building or repairing of a canoe is already in progress. Violators, who run the risk of death, are simultaneously threatened from another quarter by the house deity, Thuchera, who has a parallel resentment against such dual activity. This god is the patron of house carpenters. He is not a member of the family to which Ialulwe and Solang belong.

The completing of a canoe is an important occasion, and the owners present gifts to Solang. These, consisting of such goods as turmeric and loincloths, are placed in the canoe and a prayer is uttered for the success and sturdiness of the vessel. In actual practice, the gifts come into the hands of the canoe builder, who turns them over to the master who taught him his art. Should his teacher be dead he keeps them for himself.

There are other terrestrial deities, but of lesser importance. Some of them are the remainder of Palulop's children, as well as his wife, but none of them seem to figure outside of mythology except the only daughter in the family, Ligafas. Like the other members of the family she has a connection with the sea. Her part in dooming the canoe in which members of her family were traveling serves to remind people that it is strictly taboo for a menstruating woman to undertake a sea voyage.

The only other terrestrial deity worth mentioning is Solal, not to be confused with Solang. He is merely referred to as lord of the nether regions, yet information from other islands of the Carolines suggest that he is coequal with the great celestial god, Ialulep. Apparently his high status has not been perpetuated in Ulithi. Nevertheless, he is the patron of the public fish magicians of the atoll, who pray to him to gain success in their complex and hazardous annual ritual to create an abundance of fish for the people. They do this just before they begin to drag their magical medicine bundles through the waters of Rowaryu channel.

6

Rituals That Tap
Supernatural Power

ULITHIANS DO NOT RELY solely on their complex of souls, ghosts, and gods to resolve their relationship to supernatural power. In addition, they envisage an essentially technological approach which uses ritual itself as the agent for the accomplishment of ends not achievable through the ordinary world of experience. The key to power rests not in the spirits but the rite.

At first glance it may seem a contradiction to discover that spirit beings are involved in much of this kind of ritual. They are often appealed to obsequiously. According to myths, they may even be the authors of the rites, teaching them to mankind. The problem is resolved, however, if one bears in mind that if the spirits are invoked it is not because they are expected to grant the desired end; rather, it is in order to receive their blessing and encouragement. The verbal portion of the rite is to be seen, then, not as a prayer petitioning the spirits to take action but as a means for accomplishing a desired result in its own right. Whatever partakes of the nature of prayer in the incantation is prefatory or ancillary to the main drive for results.

Many of the rites make no such allusion to spirit beings. The natives do not distinguish conceptually or terminologically between those that do and those that do not. They gather all these techniques under a single rubric that distinguishes them from prayers to ancestors and deities. This rubric is equivalent to our word "magic."

The ends for which magical techniques are a means are more egocentric than those of religion. Magic has less effect in supporting the moral order than in satisfying an immediate specific objective on the part of the magician himself, his client, or the society he may be called upon to serve. The magician is little concerned with the ethical system as such. If he observes taboos it is because they are regulations necessary for the success of his effort and not because they are requisite for a good life. To abstain from the use of certain wood to build a fire, to prevent people from touching his person, to sleep apart from his wife—these have nothing to do with what is morally right in social behavior but what is expedient for the success of his ritual. Violating the compulsive rules of his art has little to do with incurring the disfavor of the gods; it is relevant mostly to the extent that it renders his efforts ineffective.

This might seem to imply that there is some speculation over the source of power. Such is not the case. Just as the power with which the spirits are endowed is taken for granted, so is the abstract force that the magical rite is intended to draw upon. People do not inquire into their nature. This simple acceptance of supernatural forces contrasts conspicuously with the complex proliferation of spirits and the elaboration of magical procedures.

Traits of the Rituals

The magic is not elaborate, requiring ordinarily the activity of but a single person. Even in the rituals of the fish and wave magicians, the assistants to these men take no hand in carrying out the techniques of the ritual. The assistants to the fish magicians paddle the canoe and fish; those who help the wave magicians hold on to a rope fastened around the waist of the performer so that he will not be dragged into the sea as he does his work at the shoreline. Their actions do not constitute part of the magic. Even where assistants are required to observe various taboos, it is only so they will not spoil the work of the magician, who must keep himself and his ritual free of contamination.

The magic never involves interaction with a responding audience. While spectators may look on, they are not encouraged to do so. In certain kinds of ritual the client may be on hand merely as an interested party.

The simplicity of Ulithian magic is also seen in the brevity of its duration. Most magic is performed in a matter of minutes or a portion of an hour, and is not repeated over and over. The longest ritual is that of the fish magician, who carries on his efforts for one to two months, but this is an exceptional length of time.

An examination of the techniques of magic reveals still further the simplicity with which they are endowed. Verbal symbols in the form of threats, powerful words, and imagery constitute the principal technique. There is a pleasing use of alliteration and a dramatic use of intonation. The language employed is often strongly garbled and archaic, so that it may be partially or completely unintelligible. What has been called the "coefficient of weirdness" in magical spells is high, and many of the persons who have memorized and used a spell are unable to translate or understand it. Yet most incantations are brief, and so, despite their quality of strangeness, they are not hard to memorize.

Next to linguistic symbols, the most important element in the magical techniques is the use of bodily ornaments. Strictly speaking, these objects are not really ornaments at all, and if they embellish, this is incidental to their true significance. Ritualistic ornaments are not instrumental in themselves, having no power without the incantations recited over them. Made of coral, plants, and other materials, they assume their dynamics through the spells spoken over them. An exception is the *ubwoth,* or young coconut leaf, referred to previously in connection with the placing of a distress against an accused party. Such young leaves are tied into formulistic knots and loops, and worn on the head, neck, shoulders, waist, biceps, wrists, and ankles, especially when the magician is actually performing his rite. They give an impressive appearance and inspire confidence.

Another technique of magic involves the use of certain bodily gestures, such as tapping one's body, either in one spot or in many, with a magical object. This is done while the incantation is being recited. There are other body gestures, too, which are not as widely standardized. For instance, there is the tapping of a canoe with a coconut, the rubbing of the belly with a love charm, and the clapping of the hands.

Less important techniques are concerned with direction, space, weapons, food gathering, fire, and symbols of transportation. These are found only sporadically, as in jabbing at the wind or waves with a spear in battling meteorological phenomena, or fishing ritualistically to promote fish for the people of the atoll. In one minor ritual some leaves are burned.

The conventional categories of magic, such as contagious and imitative, have little importance here, for the overwhelming emphasis is verbal. Contagious magic does make an appearance, as when in sorcery a man's rope or clothing is put under a spell, but the use of exuviae, nail parings, hair, or other parts of the intended victim are either uncommon or rare. Imitative magic is more common, as when a magician pretends to step with impunity on sea urchins and fish spines, these being symbolic of the barbs of the black magician; yet it is subordinated to the technique of language.

The Practitioners

Magicians are always part-time specialists and usually men. Women are permitted to be general practitioners in white magic but are denied admittance to the specialized fields, except doctoring. For various reasons, magicians are not often young, this being due in part to the cumbersome character of the taboos imposed on specialists and in part to the jealous guarding of esoteric knowledge by the older men.

In many instances an ordinary person knows magic for his personal use rather than as a profession, and for that reason is scarcely a magician in the strict sense. He is not hired by anyone. He chants to the wind to make it pick up to drive his canoe, and to fish to make them bite. He performs a ritual to cause a girl to love him, and another to make a baby stop vomiting. Magic of this low level is learned from any friend or relative, and in gratitude one rewards him with the usual gifts. The amateur performer of the magic is under no taboos, his person is not sacred, he is unspecialized.

When, on the other hand, white magic is being performed for the benefit of a client, he and the magician are both under constraint to follow certain taboos. In some instances, especially where any of the major categories of magic are being worked, the magician observes additional ones, but ordinarily the following are the general proscriptions that the two must observe: They may not eat certain foods, such as bananas, two kinds of arums, breadfruit, certain small coconuts, chickens, octopuses, land crabs, and certain kinds of fish. They may not enter the sacred garden. Emphasizing the gravity of the situation are still further proscriptions. Neither the specialist nor his client may have sexual intercourse, though ordinarily the latter keeps the taboo even longer than the magician, unless the latter is one of the major kinds of specialists. They may not wash a corpse, dig a grave, or, in certain instances, act as pallbearers. A female client, according to the rules of some magicians, may not visit a menstrual house or be experiencing her menstrual period when the magic is being performed for her benefit. Sometimes a magician demands that his client refrain from coming in contact with salt water or riding a canoe for the duration of the rite. The nature of the taboos and the time they endure are a matter to be decided wholly by the individual magician, but in practice a customary pattern is observed.

One wonders what impels a man to undertake to become a magician when the life he must lead is often extendedly ascetic. In a cultural environment marked by an easy attitude towards life it is incongruous to find men willing to renounce the conventional life for one that is almost monastic. Personal motivations may vary but there is no doubt that two things are operative. The first is a sincere desire to be of service to one's relatives and neighbors. The second is more self-centered and revolves around the great opportunity offered by magic to acquire a "profession" and so bring some distinction to the practitioner. The magician is a man of prestige, and he knows it. His talents enable him to rise above the usual run of people, especially when he does not have inherited political status. He gains considerable satisfaction in the knowledge that he is a person to whom others must go for help. The material compensations are there, too, but they are not the mainspring behind the decision to learn the magical art.

If it can be said that religion is largely dependent on "whom" you know, then it can be said that magic relies on "what" you know, for it is knowledge of the suitable thing to do that brings about the results intended. And so the prospective practitioner must undergo training at the hands of a person versed in the art he wants to acquire.

The relationship between master and pupil is a highly personal one and the ties continue even after the death of the teacher. Magic is a form of property known only to those who have been given a right to share it by virtue of training, friendship, and the payment of gifts. The teacher is either a friend or relative of the pupil. He carefully rehearses his procedures with him. During the period of training, many taboos have to be observed, especially if the magic is of major importance. When finally the student goes out to practice on his own, he may preface his incantation with an appeal to the ghosts of all the men now dead who once knew and used the formula. Here is how one navigator opened his incantation for protection against sorcery:

> You, Weg!
> Look this way from yonder;
> Inform Pul.
> Pul, inform Wasioi!
> May all of you make your wisdom
>   effective for me.

The man's teacher was Weg, whose teacher was Pul, whose teacher in turn was Wasioi.

An abbreviated example of the steps undergone in the training of the palm-leaf-knot diviner, a man of uppermost stature, will serve as an illustration of the training of all major magicians. The divination involves the interpretation of combinations of knots tied at random in coconut leaflets. There are 256 possible combinations, each with a meaning for the question posed by the client. The student must learn all the combinations, which are made more complex by the fact that the social status of the client requires varying interpretations, as may also the kind of information asked. The lessons last from one to three months, depending on the aptitude of the learner and other circumstances. Superior intellectual endowments are needed not only to memorize the codes but also to accommodate the answers to given situations. The knot diviners whom I have known—in fact, all the major kinds of magicians I have worked with—displayed impressive mental endowments. The pupil must always compensate his teacher with a gift and continue to show him deference, not only during his lifetime but afterwards as well.

During an apprentice's training to be a diviner he must observe numerous taboos that will remain with him forever. These pertain to menstruation, eating, making fire with wood from a certain species of tree, and approaching a woman drying pandanus leaves over a fire. Certain other taboos last a shorter time. For ten months after the inception of training the pupil may not have sexual relations. For five months, in addition to the permanent taboos mentioned above, there are certain taboos relative to the persons with whom he may eat. The observance of taboos during training is so vital that when a diviner makes errors in his judgments one of the chief causes to which this is attributed is that he failed to observe the taboos. (The failure of any magic, in fact, is often said to be due to the pupil's errancy, although, of course, there are other possible explanations, too.) Not only may the diviner's information to his client be false, but the practitioner may develop depigmentation of the skin and ringworm. The most serious breach of taboo is to indulge in sexual relations. All the taboos pertaining to the diviner are more strictly observed on the island of Mogmog than any other, for this is the center of prestige and authority. The diviners there outrank all others.

Like other major specialists, the knot diviner's status implies a certain degree of sanctity, and no better illustration of this is the inviolability of his person. No one may touch his head, face, and back. If he is seated, it is forbidden for anyone to walk near him in an erect position. Mostly, he eats in solitude, for he may sit down to a meal only with other magicians of primary rank. The fact that a woman has reached the menopause does not exempt her from the taboos of contact. One is reminded of the psychological phenomenon of *noli me tangere,* "do not touch me," sometimes manifested by neurotics. However, the taboos on the person of the magician are designed to protect his power from being endangered by contact with persons of lesser sanctity—a power that is not immanent or charismatic but stems from the possession of knowledge—the knowledge of a ritual. This, in the final analysis, is the source of any magician's power, for to know what to do is the key which unlocks supernatural forces for men.

Areas of Concern

The things that inspire recourse to magic are those about which Ulithians are most anxious.

One of these is the sea. The ocean is a highway for travel and a major source of food, yet at the same time it is inconstant and menacing. So there have to be procedures for minimizing its deleterious phases. Some of the dangers of the deep stem from typhoons; therefore, typhoon magicians exist. Some result from heavy wave action against the shore; for this there are wave specialists to soothe the surface. A constant hazard is present when a vessel tries to achieve a landfall, for not only do storms threaten destruction but the tracklessness of the vast sea presents enormous difficulties in maintaining a proper course; consequently, navigators must fortify themselves not only with help from the god Ialulwe and the ancestral dead but with rituals, talismans, and amulets as well. And then the sea often withholds its fauna from men who search it for fish; to counteract this there are spells, especially in the public interest, for insuring the release of marine creatures.

It is noteworthy that of the four types of primary magicians recognized by Ulithians as being the most elevated of all, each has some involvement with the sea. The typhoon magician is concerned with the effects of giant winds on canoes at sea and in churning up the waters surrounding the islands so that they are threatened with erosion and engulfment. The navigator, half of whose training is in magic, is even more closely oriented towards the sea. The third type of specialist, the community fish magician, has an equally obvious involvement. And the fourth major type, the palm-leaf-knot diviner—engaged in discovering hidden events in the past, present, and future—devotes himself in large part to answering inquiries about the advisability of a voyage, the welfare of sea travelers, and the prospect of catching fish. He encourages decision.

It is firmly believed that much if not most of the threat of the sea originates with men of ill will, residing either within the atoll or without, especially on Yap. Against their nefarious spells, countersorcery must be hurled and objects worn or carried to fend off evil of this nature. The navigator is one of the chief targets of black magic; consequently, he fortifies himself in diverse ways. Here is how a man, who by the way was also a custodian of a shrine for Mares-pa, endowed a leaf belt with power to protect him:

> I am making an amulet
> Underneath the sky,
> I, the man Chuoior,
> So that I will not die.
> Wave away and empty out (the bad),
> Wave away and put in (the good),
> So that I will not die.
> Where I am standing?
> I stand radiant, glistening radiantly.
> I am a babe in arms,
> The child of Iolofath.
> My food is the incantation,
> My food is the spider lily,
> My food is the coconut offering,
> Of men (who incant against me)
> Anywhere in the islands of Ulithi;
> I will outlive them all.
> Wave away and empty out (the bad),
> Wave away and put in (the good),
> And fence in the shark,
> Make him secure,
> Sew up the tip of his mouth,
> Sew up his bite,
> Sew them up twice.
> The sky is my safeguard,
> The sky is my shield,
> I step on the reef
> And it is shattered.

This was only one of his precautions. Navigators have recourse to many.

Illness is of course a source of much anxious concern, and the native medical practitioner or doctor is understandably ranked high among the specialists in the magical arts. Like the navigator, he employs empirical skills in addition to his supernatural ones, and this may account for the slightly lower ranking that both of them have as compared with the typhoon specialist and the diviner of knots. Besides, much illness is handled by procedures that are neither medical nor pseudomedical. Thus, the diviner has much to say concerning the etiology of a disease and, in addition, he is important to therapy because he often will designate a suitable doctor—a primitive system of referral. Ancestors, as well as a general kind of secondary magician, also to some extent rival the work of the doctor.

The magical aspect of Ulithian medicine stems from the fact that many diseases are believed to be due to sorcery, taboo violation, or other supernatural causes. Most older people have some knowledge of curative spells and so may treat members of the family or friends on an amateur basis. But for graver cases the doctor is summoned. Although he himself is competent to make a diagnosis, he realizes the great importance of etiology in knowing how a disease should be treated; consequently, he may require the help of a knot diviner or a medium to discover the source of the illness.

Anxieties about food account for the plethora of taboos surrounding the swamp garden and the elaborate ritual of the communal fish magician. Of the proscriptions attendant upon the garden, nothing further need be said, but of the fish magician there is much that can be told.

Communal fish magic is carried out once a year by any one of several available men commissioned on behalf of the atoll by the king or the next highest chief on the island of Mogmog. The ritual is always begun on Mogmog, when the moon is full, during either one of two native lunar months corresponding closely to November and December. After preliminaries in which the magician takes a loincloth to the shrine of the ghost of Marespa and another loincloth to the house of the Fasilus lineage, he works magic over the canoe he is going to press into service and then sails across the northern end of the lagoon with four or five assistants until he comes to the island of Song. There he fulfills a duty inspired by a myth explaining the way in which a certain spirit, grateful to a woman for finally yielding to him her yellow wrap-around skirt, reveals the secret of fishing to her in a vision. The spirit is unusual in that he is kind and mellow, whereas sea spirits as a class are greatly feared. His father, however, runs true to form and, being a chief, takes great umbrage at this betrayal. He threatens to harm the woman, so she hides on Song with her husband and two boys. Following the instructions of the kindly spirit, she trains her children in the magic of fishing. Henceforth, all communal fishing magicians must go to Song at the beginning of their extended rite in order to leave her and the sea spirit an offering of two coconuts to help insure the success of the rite, which from this point on departs from the tale and proceeds independently, except to the extent that the magic produced is a fulfillment of the procedures learned from the spirit.

The work of the magician and his assistants is unusually arduous and lasts for two lunar months. They first drag through the water at night a small bundle suspended from the back of the canoe, and attract flying fish to them by light from huge coconut leaf torches. The ingredients of the bundle constitute a strange melange: fruits, roots, bark, the spathes of the coconut and pandanus trees, flowers from the breadfruit tree, soil from a swamp garden, the heads of an eel and scorpion, and termites. Another bundle, filled only with black ants, remains in the canoe. For four days the crew fishes for albacore and tuna in the turbulent waters of Rowaryu channel, facing all weather conditions short of a tropical storm. For the remainder of the two months the fishing continues, but instead of remaining away from Mogmog on the island of Pigelelel, the men return daily to their base in Mogmog. They are surrounded with numerous taboos, the observance of which is eloquent testimony to the unselfish dedication of these men to the common good. The minimal restrictions that all must observe for two months prevent them from walking near any female whatsoever, or having intercourse; going near the menstrual house or talking to its occupants; touching a corpse or digging a grave; eating preserved breadfruit, the fruit of a species of Allophyllus, or the husk of a certain variety of coconut palm; allowing persons who have been in contact with a corpse or have dug a grave during the past five months to handle their food; giving their leftover food to anyone to eat; and sleeping at home. For five months subsequent to the ritual, the men must remain sexually continent. They must continue to live for several days or even months in the men's house, the period of time being optional and a conscious self-abnegation for the benefit of a more successful denouement of the magic. As for the magician himself, his taboos are all of these and many more, and must be observed for four to seven months after the first fishing at the channel. He is virtually a prisoner of his profession. Small wonder that most fish magicians serve a term of only two or three years and then willingly turn over their duties to the next designee.

The gravity of the fishing rite and what it symbolizes may further be seen in the attitude of the community, for during the performance several taboos must be observed by those who merely wait: no one may shout in the men's house, no one may troll for fish in the lagoon, no one may go to Rowaryu channel, and, for the first five days, no relatives of the magician may cut down a live tree.

All these exertions and restraints, briefly alluded to here, speak eloquently of the apprehensions of the people of the atoll towards fish as a source of food, but still more is done than this. Individuals setting out to fish on their own may call for the services of a minor-type fish magician, who performs a simple rite on the canoe to be used and exhorts the fish to come forth to be caught. The performer gets a portion of the catch.

To allay the doubts and frustrations of the lovesick there is a modest body of magic. There are no love magicians as such; instead there are general practitioners in magic who will take on a client with a problem. Most commonly, to insure success in amatory affairs recourse is had to charms. These are usually worn, although sometimes they are kept in one's carrying basket or left in one's house. Men have charms to persuade women, women have similar objects to persuade men. Love charms may take the form of chest bands, head wreaths, neckpieces, and earpieces; the materials used being vines, flowers, leaves, twigs, and roots. Accompanying each charm is an incantation, usually pleading for the charm to cause the loved one to reciprocate one's affection. One might speculate that the relative paucity of magical means for inducing love may be due to the relative ease with which sexual favors are exchanged in the permissive erotic climate of the atoll.

Remaining anxieties are revealed through other minor magicians. Reference has already been made to the wave magician, who soothes the waters if they are too rough for a canoe or if they endanger an island. Measured by his training and the taboos surrounding him he has more stature than other secondary magicians.

Then there is the specialist in spirits such as reside in the larger trees.

His clients are men who are about to cut down a tree and want to have the spirit coaxed into leaving. But it is not clear what anxiety in the realm of reality is relieved by this action, except a generalized fear that disease is often due to the action of tree spirits, who are stubbornly malevolent towards the human race. In 1731 Father Cantova confounded the Ulithians by chopping down a tree whose spirit had killed ten successive people wanting to fell it.

Ulithians are enormously reliant on palm toddy, made from coconut trees. A certain beetle can spoil the sap as it is being allowed to drip into a container fastened to the inflorescence. Therefore, to prevent the awful prospect that one's trees may yield toddy that is ruined, a specialist is impressed into service. Sometimes, if the situation is grave and a whole islet is beginning to feel the effects of the insects, the king may commission the magician to exert his power on behalf of the community.

Canoes constitute valuable property which, because of their fragility and the dangers to which they are exposed, are given the protection of magic exerted by the canoe carpenter, who doubles up in his craftmanship with a knowledge of the suitable rite. The rite is lengthy, which is as it should be, for lineages prize their canoes beyond mere pride of ownership. Although the material accoutrements and body gestures are magical, the rite contains some ingredients of prayer because Solang, who it will be recalled is the patron god of canoe carpentry, is implored to make the vessel lucky, spare it from damage, and cause no one to so admire it as to want to use or even acquire it. Should the canoe, despite the palliatives employed, encounter misfortune, it is believed that Solang is either angry with the canoe carpenter for having violated taboos during the construction of the boat, or with the owners for having failed to give the carpenter proper compensation for his work. Obviously, this way of looking at things serves to promote a satisfactory fulfillment of contractual obligations.

To give peace of mind to owners of a newly built house, a house magician is engaged to bring it good fortune. Some gifts are presented to Thuchera, the god of house carpentry, but as with all gifts offered to spirits, there is always a human who gathers them ultimately into his fold.

Because of a diffuse fear of spirits who moan at night either in the village or the woods, a man who is knowledgeable in these matters protects himself and his family with a spell, which includes throwing a stone in the supposed direction of the spirit.

> *Litingingi! Litingingi!*
> *Letanganga! Letanganga!*
> *Litingingi! Litingingi!*
> *Letanganga! Letanganga!*
> If thou, O spirit, come here
> Near my house
> You will cry out
> *Litingingi! Letanganga!*

There is no use asking what *Litingingi* and *Letanganga* mean. The user of the spell does not know. Chalk it up to the coefficient of weirdness.

Next, there is the grave magician trained to free a burial plot from the spirit residing there so that a corpse may be interred. This again is a response to a generalized fear of spirits as the cause of illness and death. The magician chants,

> Scatter from the ground!
> Scatter from the ground!
> Spirits everywhere,
> Whoever you are.
> O spirits, halt
> Outside my house;
> Barracudas of the night,
> Sharks of the night,
> Halt and soar,
> Soar westwards to Palau.

He says this as he circles the ground and jabs it with a dried coconut leaf to whose rib have been tied *ubwoth* leaflets. Part two of the rite involves more pounding with a rock to which more *ubwoth* has been tied. The accompanying words are specifically directed towards the spirits at the grave site.

> O Limkhei!
> I arrange the ground of
> This grave of mine;
> Now sleep, sleep, O grave spirits,
> Sleep, sleep, O island!
> Sleep, sleep, sleep.

Limkhei is variously called the sister of Iolofath or his mother. It is again interesting that a god is drawn into the ritual, but the proposed result is achieved by the performance of the magic, not the salute to the spirit.

Finally, covering all contingencies not specifically embraced by the primary and secondary magicians is a general practitioner, already alluded to, who will work for clients beset by sundry perturbations. Sometimes his work overlaps with that of others who are more specialized. In any event it cannot be said that in Ulithi any area of human anxiety is left unguarded.

Antisocial Rites

Black magic or sorcery is the recourse of men who wish to castigate others whom they feel are guilty of ill will or overt action against them. Such men may not have the power to inflict punishment directly, or may simply wish to conceal their actions from the intended victim and the community. Not much is revealed about the black art because by definition it is criminal in character, and no practitioner is willing to admit his guilt by revealing his knowledge and practice of the forbidden techniques. Still, we are by no means left completely in the dark about the details of sorcery, especially when "reformed" sorcerers are willing to discuss them as if they were hypothetical cases. Insofar as one can focus on so shadowy and outlawed an art, it is utterly conventional.

When a prospective client wishes to engage the services of a professional he must set about cautiously, dropping hints here and there to persons he believes are sorcerers or who may have knowledge of the identity of one. The first man he approaches may pretend not to be a practitioner when in fact he is, so the conversation proceeds cautiously, with much sparring about. If finally the client decides he is indeed talking to a man who practices the art, he delineates his complaint. The sorcerer may decide the aggression is either unwarranted or too severe and will dissuade the person, who will then give him a gift payment in exchange for his silence. The rejected individual may then go off to find someone else to accept his commission. This is not easy, for the sorcerer not only fears the ostracism that would follow exposure but the anger of his intended victim and relatives as well. Besides, there is the danger that the great sky deity, Ialulep, may frown upon his work and inflict harm on him. Once the sorcerer consents to perform, he must be paid in advance with the traditional gifts given to specialists. He then sets out to do what he has been hired to do— cause disease, miscarriages, accidents, death, or other deplorable misfortunes.

The ritual and paraphernalia used, because of their secrecy, are not well known. Yet it seems apparent that the rigmarole is not basically different from that of the white magician. Strangely enough, the sorcerer not only addresses prayers to his teacher's ghost and those of close departed relatives, but to the great god Ialulep as well. The items he uses in his technique may include magical starfish, live lizards, and coconut oil, over which incantations are uttered before the object is buried near the house of the intended victim or, better still, in the floor of the house. Some contagious magic is used, as when the specialist puts a concoction on the person's comb to cause him to contract ringworm, or places it on the garment of the man so that when he puts it on and goes swimming he will be bitten by a shark.

Father Cantova casually mentions while on Ulithi that "there are a few sorcerers, who give us something to do," although he seems to have discredited them. One of them tried to drown the priest and his party by creating a storm as they were returning from an islet where they had taken a census. The typhoon did not materialize. The sorcerer probably did not regard himself as really a sorcerer but as a defender of the pagan faith.

Political sorcery from Gagil district in Yap menaces the atoll when the chiefs there get it into their heads that the people of Ulithi are not being sufficiently obsequious. From the point of view of the Yapese their magic is not truly black, for it is envisioned as a kind of negative sanction against wrongdoers outside their society; from the point of view of their apprehensive vassals, however, nothing could be more darkly tinted.

If this nefarious practice can be epitomized, it can be done through an understanding of certain magical locales, whose generic name need not concern us here. There are three such spots, one on each of the islands of Falalop, Asor, and Sorlen. Ulithians are hazy on the details but say that long ago some men came to the atoll from Gagil and selected these places for their performance of magic. They were empowered by their chiefs on Yap to wreak vindictive magic there whenever they were told to do so. The effects of their sorcery are greatly feared by Ulithians, who attribute to them visitations of respiratory diseases, infestations of crops by insects, and other calamities, including typhoons. The magicians of Yap are considered to be very powerful and are held in considerable awe. In all fairness to the Yapese, however, it should be pointed out that whereas for our present purposes we have stressed the evil side of their magic, they use the same spots and the same magicians to reward Ulithians for being good. This is expressed, for instance, in producing for them an abundance of plant foods or a plethora of fish. However, the lingering impression is not one of gratitude for services of this sort, but dread of the other ones.

Happily, against all the machinations of evildoers in the atoll or without, there are measures to thwart one's enemies. One need not remain a passive victim. There exists a kind of countersorcery that anyone may employ, although in practice it is utilized mostly by the navigator and the communal fish magician. However, the most common device is the amulet, developed to an elaborate degree in the atoll.

When one knows or suspects that sorcery is being directed against him he uses one kind of amulet, and when he merely feels it contingent he uses an amulet belonging to a different native category of such things. The amulet against known sorcery is designed as a specific defense; that against contingent sorcery is a general defense.

Of course sorcery being the clandestine thing that it is, in most instances one can merely defend against the possible rather than the known, so the contingent amulet is the more common. Here there is great variety in the materials used: spider lilies; turmeric; coral, of which there are various colors and shapes; sea urchins; stingers of the stinger ray; leaves of an arum, and so on. The materials are painted in various ways, as with crosses or bands, and are put in various places, depending on the status of the person defending himself. Let us take some examples. A patient is being treated by a magician for an illness resulting from eating tabooed fish while on Yap. The amulet is placed along either of his sides, not to protect him, but to counteract any sorcery being possibly employed against the magician as he works. A canoe carpenter places an amulet under each of the two coconut tree trunks used to support a canoe while it is being built, to ward off any possible threat directed against the execution of his work. One can well imagine how jittery a navigator is about a journey to a distant place, so it should occasion no surprise to know that every navigator worth his salt has at least an amulet tied to the weather platform of his canoe. He cannot afford to take chances against magic. Communal fish magicians are inveterate users of amulets, and, as one might suppose, they place one or more of them in some part of the canoe, such as under the lee platform or the struts on which the sail of the canoe is rested. Ulithians are prone to say that the sorcery they are guarding against emanates on Yap, and to a large extent this is true, but of course it is not considered discreet to imply that Ulithians themselves may be the offenders.

Amulets against sorcery that is known or strongly suspected to be in action against a person are made of the usual materials and are decorated in much the same manner as general amulets.

But the really vital thing about amulets are the incantations that go with them. Amulets for one specific defense and those for another may bear a good deal of resemblance to one another. Anyway, they are not concealed and are often worn on the body, so they can be duplicated or imitated. But the verbal part of the amulet is the secret and powerful part, and employs all the characteristic features of Ulithian magic: the appeal to teacher ghosts, weird words, alliteration and other effects, defiance, boldness, symbolization, and so on. Every incantation is accompanied by appropriate actions.

Social Effects of Magic

If one thinks of magic as a special instrument that supplements the experiential techniques by which life is made possible for Ulithians, it becomes clear that it operates only as an adjunct rather than a primary means. Even then it does not permeate all of life, for it is invoked only as a complement to practical procedures or as a last resort when these utterly fail. If a man makes a journey across the great lagoon, it is enough for him to have a sound canoe and such ordinary nautical skills as paddling, hoisting and lowering a sail, tacking, bailing, and steering. He must know something about currents and the location of protuberances in the reef. Whatever help he uses comes only from someone who assists him in managing the canoe. Even though his destination lies beyond the horizon, he always has some landmarks within his line of vision. Why in the world should he use supernatural aids? He does not. When that same man journeys to Yap or beyond, he must navigate with the stars, worry about set and drift, cope with dead calm or contrary winds, face possible typhoons, and all the other hazards attendant upon a voyage in which there are no guiding landmarks, no chance of paddling or swimming to safety, no help from shore, and possibly not enough food and water to sustain life beyond a week or two. The mariner lacks a compass and a chronometer. All he has besides his craft and skill, as well as the possibility of help from the spirits, is a body of magic and countermagic. He memorizes his spells with meticulous care. He observes all taboos. He takes action beyond the mere exercise of the maritime art.

If one combs further through the areas in which magic is employed, he will find the same consistent strain throughout it all. Take love, for instance. Here there seems to be a reign of unreason. A man may desire a woman who rejects his attentions in favor of an emaciated youth with no particular talent or redeeming personality. He himself is strong, handsome, industrious, loyal, and particularly successful as a fisherman. He has all that a girl would want, or so he thinks. In frustration, since coaxing and appealing to reason have not changed her mind in the least, he takes to consulting an expert in these things and ends up wearing what he hopes will be an amulet to overcome her unreasoned resistance. Instead of suffering the despondency of the unrequited, he now feels he has at least a fighting chance. For reasons that cannot always be fathomed, his suit may eventually turn out to be successful. So he becomes convinced in the efficacy of magic and recommends his specialist to a friend.

Other areas of magic yield similarly to inquiry. A woman wants to gather shellfish and crustaceans stranded on the reef at low tide. No hazards or anxieties beset her and her companions as she walks out and picks them up. They are always there and present no difficulties. To my knowledge, there is no such thing as magic to promote the successful gathering of shellfish and crustaceans on the reef. But for obvious reasons there is elaborate magic to aid in pelagic fishing. The same applies to horticulture. There are some things that grow easily and yield abundantly, so they are raised in routine fashion, but there are others that though prized are unreliable, so they are surrounded with taboos and prescribed rituals. A few effective procedures have been developed to treat illness, but most disease, understandably, resists the impoverished art of the native doctor. Therefore he has to depend a good deal on a superstructure of belief in which, among other things, the etiology, prevention, and therapy of illness lies in the sphere of the magical.

For the Ulithian, when his ordinary cultural techniques and knowledge cannot give him satisfaction, magic rescues him from despair. It seems to bring about results often enough to insure that the principle of extinction through nonreward is not realized. Men do reach distant destinations in safety, lovesick swains do find that the object of their affections reciprocates, fishermen do catch fish swarming onto the reef after months of frustration, one's palm toddy does evade spoilage by invading beetles, and patients do recover from their illnesses. Never mind the failures. They were due to faulty ritual, violation of taboos, or powerful enemies. By providing a course of action, as well as an explanation for misfortune, a man or a whole community can face life with less doubt, less confusion. People may be able to take steps to accommodate themselves advantageously to events revealed by divination. True, there is a price to pay for all this. Many of the anxieties have no basis in reality; instead, they are the very products of the belief in supernaturalism. Furthermore, magic diverts men from the pursuit of logically and pragmatically sound means of overcoming their problems. But until something better comes along, it is good to know that one can tap a power over and above the natural means at one's command. A crew far from home and buffeted by a turbulent sea does not want to be told that its amulets are ineffectual; it cannot wait for the development of secure devices forthcoming in the uncertain future. People must make do with what they have, and if what a Ulithian has are only his palm-leaf knots, his piece of painted coral, and his sting ray effigy to fill out where all his nautical skills and lore have failed him, he is going to turn to them with a confidence that logic cannot demolish.

The magical solution is not the easy one. Magic is a hard master requiring training, the expenditure of human resources, and self-abnegation. It may plunge a whole society into a period of enforced restraint in the firm belief that ritual gains strength when people are willing to deny themselves of their comforts and desires. To be sure, the logic behind a taboo may be lost, as when certain fish are proscribed and certain areas restricted for reasons no one can any longer justify, yet the effect of the whole system of negative rules is to provide such an atmosphere of determination that one can feel every effort is being made to ensure that a rite will not be endangered. Fortified by conformance with the spirit and letter of the restrictive code, the people have an assurance, either individually as clients or collectively as a society, that no stone is left unturned. This gives them the resolution to carry on life instead of lapsing into the paralysis of fear and despondency. Further than this, the taboos of magic serve to emphasize certain important values or areas of life that are not readily apparent or consciously speculated upon.

7

Sexual Behavior

TWO SEEMINGLY OPPOSITE and yet not uncongenial attitudes pervade sexual behavior among the people of the atoll. One is a position of permissiveness; the other is one of restraint.

Sexual abstinence is not viewed as a virtue to be idealized by young people, consequently they do not experience a feeling of shame or guilt when they engage in intercourse before marriage. Women, especially, do not have to satisfy societal moral demands or fortify their chastity by weaving a tissue of ugliness around the sex act. When later they marry they do not carry into their marital union an attitude of revulsion against sex. No ideal is maintained that there is greater happiness and deeper love if the partners in a marriage, especially the wife, have been hitherto completely continent. Lacking such aversion to sexual activity, it consequently follows that there is nothing to inhibit the derivation of pleasure from it. Ulithians maintain ignorance of the phenomena of frigidity and impotence.

When sexual desire is suppressed it is chiefly in conformance with the conviction that there is magic in abstinence. Sexual abnegation fortifies one's effort to harness supernatural forces. The logic behind this is not specifically worked out but would seem to be based on the widely held human premise that self-denial of any kind is a form of sacrifice, and that sacrifice is a price to be paid in return for the use of supernatural power. If sexual self-denial is particularly valued, it may be because of the recognized power of sex in procreation.

Other than ritualistic restraints there are those having to do with marriage, kinship, and reproduction, as well as political status *vis-à-vis* Yap. They are aimed not at sex as such but in preventing the disruption of the balance of social relationships through competition for sexual partners.

And so, despite the leniency with which sexual gratification is viewed, sexual license or promiscuity, even among the unmarried, is far from being a socially sanctioned custom of the society.

Views on Sex and Decency

The Ulithian does not speculate a good deal on the matter of sex. He has built up almost no explanations or rationalizations regarding the differences between men and women and their impulses and genital organs. He is well aware of the reproductive role of sex but thinks little more about the matter than to notice the connection.

To him, love is an emotional attachment ranging over a wide spectrum, so that it encompasses an attitude towards a sweetheart, a child, a parent, a dog, or even a canoe. The seat of love is vaguely localized in a spot just below the ensiform process of the sternum. When the emotion has sexual connotations it travels down to the genitals. The unerotic feeling of love that one has, however, for other persons or things does not go down to the genital area, because the attraction is different. It is said that the sensation of sexual love which men and women have towards one another is due to a spirit, but the spirit is never identified or described, and no ideas are held as to its sex or place of abode. As far as terminology goes, then, no distinction is made in terms of logic, except that sexual love extends to the primary erogenous zone.

Sex is not clearly idealized. There is not even a consistent concept as to what the ideal sex partner ought to be like. Personal taste rather than a cultural ideal seems to dictate what is desirable. Outright ugliness is of course recognized by everyone, but whether a slender or heavy person, a tall or short one, has more appeal depends on the individual. It is worth mentioning that there is no cultural ideal concerning the pneumatic breasted woman. In fact, Ulithian men wonder why foreigners make such a to-do over breasts; they claim not to find them stimulating.

Definite ideas are maintained regarding decency and decorum. Men always wear a loincloth, but an upper garment is considered improper and is nonexistent. However, to guard against rain a cape as well as a leaf hat may be employed. Men never expose their privates in the company of women and are even reluctant to do so freely among men, being especially careful not to be seen naked by their children.

Women wear a short wrap-around skirt of woven hibiscus and banana fiber extending to the knees, and nothing more. To attempt to wear something covering the breasts is an act of immodesty or a breach of convention; in any event it is not done. Prior to puberty a girl wears a "grass" skirt made of shredded coconut leaflets or pandanus. Undergarments are not part of traditional dress. As for exposure, women are expected to exercise more care than men in keeping themselves covered in the proper places. It is not immodest for women to expose themselves in one another's presence, but it is not commonly done.

Nudity among children is the rule, continuing until about the age of five or six. People are utterly indifferent to nudity in children of such early age, but are insistent on scrupulous observance of modesty in clothing after that.

Decency must be maintained in other ways. It is considered highly improper for certain persons of opposite sex to be seen together. Such persons include especially those who stand in a real brother and sister relationship. They must avoid one another if they are the only ones present in a place, and, in a group, they may not sit around if matters of sex are under discussion, either seriously or jokingly. The rule of avoidance is a severe one, and if a sister stumbles upon a brother in the woods or must pass by him unavoidably, she must signal her presence with a certain phrase and pass by at as discreet a distance as possible. Patterned avoidance behavior is also expected of brothers and sisters whose relationship is only classificatory, except that the avoidance is less stringent. In such tiny islands, where so many people call one another by sibling terms, such relaxation of the rules is clearly imperative. Aside from brothers and sisters, it is considered bad taste for an unrelated man and woman to be alone in places where others may see them. If they want to be together, this is permissible as long as they are discreet about being detected; there is no inquiry into the motives of couples who meet in secret.

In bathing and elimination, complete care must be taken to see that one is not observed by a person of the other sex. Women who bathe in the sea, as they often do several times a day, do so in broad daylight, but always wearing their skirts. Those who bathe on land do so just before daybreak or after sunset and, unless their privacy is completely assured, they keep their skirts on. Women may bathe in concert, experiencing no feeling of shame or immodesty in doing so. Even in eliminating, women feel no shyness in the presence of other women; but they do take precautions not to be seen by men. As for men, all the precautions expected of women are also to be taken by men, except that they are not expected to exercise quite the care as a woman in intruding on a person who is bathing or eliminating. Women, whether they are the intruders or the intruded upon, feel the greater embarrassment. Notwithstanding, even though it is considered improper for a person of one sex to witness a person of the other sex in the act of bathing or eliminating, such an offense is not the traumatic event it would be in some other societies.

Women watch out for their modesty in other ways too. They do not climb trees, because of the possibility that a passing male might glance upward and espy their intimate anatomy. When women sit down, they keep their skirts adjusted and their legs crossed or close together. When men and women are in the confining quarters of a canoe at sea, the matter of preserving modesty becomes a difficult one. In getting on a canoe, a woman must not climb; she must give a short leap upward and land on the edge of the canoe in a seated position. Women become expert at doing this gracefully. When she gets off, she slides off with her legs close together. The matter of elimination is a special problem during a trip. Should a women have to urinate during a short trip, she must do everything she can to restrain herself, but if that is not possible she takes other measures. She sits down in the bottom of the canoe and throws sea water over her body, pretending to be bathing, and while doing this she urinates. Then she bails out the water. On a short trip a woman does not defecate. The rule appears to be immutable, and a woman must take meticulous care to see that when she boards a canoe she has forestalled the possibility of later embarrassment. When women accompany men on long voyages they stay in a cabin over the leeward platform and eliminate through a specially built hole in the platform.

As for a man, when starting out in a small canoe for a short trip, he takes all precautions ahead of time to see that he does not have to eliminate during the voyage if women are to be present. Should he be forced to urinate, he dives into the water on one pretext or another, such as to recover an oar or a bailer. On long trips, since large canoes are equipped with cabins, men have the women stay in the cabins and they then eliminate over the side of the canoe from a squatting position on the edge of the hull.

In mixed company there are numerous restrictions on the use of words connected with sex and elimination. In many instances, euphemisms and circumlocutions may be substituted. Thus, one does not mention the bat, because this is a figure which is tattooed on women's legs; instead, one speaks of the rat. One does not use the word for dark red, because this is the color of the vagina; instead, one uses the general term for red. One does not speak directly of a loincloth, which may be either the garment of a man or a woman; instead, one speaks of banana bark when referring to a man's breechclout, and hibiscus when speaking of the female garment, these being the names of the materials utilized in their manufacture.

Again, in mixed company, certain words involving sex and the organs of sex have no substitutes and must be altogether avoided. They include the words for penis, vagina, clitoris, semen, testes, coition, masturbation, and many others. Terms pertaining to elimination have such substitutes as "going to the beach" or "lightening oneself" for defecation, and "standing water" for urinating. However, there are no substitutes for feces or urine, unless these refer to the excrement of children, in which instance certain special terms are used.

In the presence of elders, towards whom Ulithians always maintain an attitude of enormous respect, many of the terms pertaining to sex and elimination must similarly be avoided, even if the company is not mixed. They include the words for the sex organs and their areas, as well as terms for the rectum, feces, urine, petting, coition, masturbation, and breaking wind.

When a person violates the restrictions on coarse words, he is met with a disapproving silence. A repeated offender is regarded as a foul-mouthed sort of person, improperly brought up. He may be scolded by his elders or a chief.

In conformity with their subordinate status, women are expected to observe a certain etiquette towards members of the opposite sex. They do not intrude in groups where men are working or talking. In walking with men, they follow submissively at the rear. If it is necessary for them to sit with men, they make themselves unobtrusive and do not enter into conversations unless necessary. At any rate, they must always act shy and modest in public, because forward women are bad women. Even in the intimacy of the sexual act, they must remain passive. Much of the bashfulness that women display in public, however, is a cultural pose. What passes for outward shyness may only be assumed coyness. In conversation this often is expressed in the form of a soft, whining tone —almost a falsetto. Another pose that women may assume in public when men are about, is one of great boredom or indifference to their surroundings.

Erotic Expression and Stimulation

In inquiring into the extent to which the people express themselves with regard to sex, one finds a complete absence of direct sexual symbolism in their representative art. It must be borne in mind, however, that there is almost no representative art, anyway. But the small amount that does exist is devoid of phallic symbols and sex themes.

It is a different story with women's tattooing, which while confining itself to geometric designs tends to have strong sexual connotations. This stems from the fact that women tattoo their thighs, groins, and labia minora. The tattooing of the last is done with a solid black pigment and is purportedly done for modesty's sake, to conceal the red membrane of the vaginal orifice during sex play. Regardless of the veracity of this explanation, which seems farfetched but is stoutly insisted upon, the fact remains that women's tattooing is not a subject to be discussed in public. As for men's tattooing, there is no erotic counterpart, for it is never done in the more intimate parts of the anatomy and is completely unconcealed. It has no sexual connotations.

Preoccupation with sex manifests itself clearly in the dance. There are three main categories of dances in which eroticism is apparent. These dances utilize almost twenty standardized movements, each with a name. Some of these movements are clearly erotic. Thus, the slapping of the buttocks, the thrusting of the pelvis back and forth with the legs wide apart in a deep bend, and the twisting of the hips from one side to another, are unmistakeably sexual in intent. Other movements, in which the biceps are slapped, the arms outstretched to simulate a bird in flight, or the head shaken or nodded, have no sexual meaning of themselves but may be executed in an erotic setting. Only one category of the dance, except for a stick dance alleged to have been imported from Yap, is devoid of sex or obscenity, so that it is safe to make the generalization that dancing is commonly concerned with sex. This is corroborated by the fact that the dances in question, with one notable exception, are performed segregated, so that women are enjoined from viewing men and vice versa.

Songs accompany the erotic dances, and these are bolder than the gestures that accompany them. It is likely that the words are more influential than the movements in requiring the separation of the sexes during the performance of the restricted dances.

Ulithians have love songs that do not necessarily accompany the dance, and most of these are essentially poetic and tender, though more straightforward than would be conventional in Western society. Such songs may be sung publicly or in the intimacy of two lovers' company. When sung by a group, the group is either all male or all female. Songs of this nature are sometimes sung by a person as a means of whiling the time away while at work or sailing in a canoe.

An outrageously indecorous dance with lewd words has already been referred to in connection with the quasi-legal conventionalization of diffuse sanctions against persons in need of castigation. It is the *hamath*. This dance is performed on peculiarly disparate occasions, having an interconnection through their relationship to the great god Iongolap. When used as a corrective it employs songs of criticism by men against women, and vice versa. It is a battle of derogatory taunts which may start against a single individual but ultimately widens its scope so as to become part of the war of the sexes. The words are straightforward, bitter, and obscene. Thus, if a woman is being attacked, her name is mentioned without evasion, and she may be accused of having an odd-sized sex organ or a large rectum. The dancers may tell how often they have creeped up to her as she lay asleep, and tickled her vagina. She may be accused of masturbating and performing *fellatio*. As the song is being sung, the reason for the attack on the woman is revealed, be it for laziness, shrewishness, adultery, and so on. When women take their turn with the dance they retaliate in kind. Sexual alignments and sexual ridicule play the main part in the performance.

Ulithian curses and profanity are overwhelmingly lewd. When a person is provoked and wishes to vent his aggression on another, he resorts to obscenity rather than to supernatural damnations or blasphemy. Typical insults are: "Your father's rectum!" "Inside your mother's eye!" "Come eat my behind!" "Go lay with your sister!" "Your mother's pubic tattooing." Such expressions may be hurled in anger by a man or a woman, modifications of course being made to suit the sex of the person under assault. Men use profanity more than do women. It is not uncommon among children, even when they are but a few years of age. Actually, the epithets are so highly stereotyped that their content is not as important as the anger behind them. They do have a certain amount of force, but it would be a mistake to impute excessive aggression to the people of Ulithi on account of them. The notable thing is that instead of expressing a desire for the death, sickness, or damnation or a person they taunt him with obscenities.

Reference may be made to the sexual content of traditional narrative, where love, incest, and lewdness are by no means uncommon. There is no particular concern over the presence of children in the audience; indeed, most often the ones to whom the tales are told are children. Scatology runs rampant in a story centering around a "heroine" called Feces Girl. As the story is told, the word for feces is mentioned incessantly without euphemism. Feces Girl is ugly and when she walks she is followed by flies. For some inexplicable reason, some men come to fetch her to be the bride of the son of a chief. As she leaves her island she must bid farewell to every pile of ordure there, and her adieu is carefully repeated by the narrator for each pile. She overlooks one pile, however, and later on it vengefully causes her to turn completely into excrement. Laughter greets the details of this odiferous narrative. In a story that apparently stems from a true incident, a hero lies unconscious in a refuse pit, where he had been thrown and beaten by some men, and he is revived when during the night a woman comes there and urinates on him. He returns to the atoll of Ifaluk, his home, and there he causes his penis slowly to become erect, and as the people watch, they see that it points in the direction of Woleai. This is his way of informing the people where they are to go to do battle against his assailants. A story about an ogre ends with two young sisters pulling his guts out of his anus as they sing a song taunting him about his breaking wind. Another one has a father discover that his daughter has been eaten by an ogre, after he has felled the monster; as the latter lies there the father sees his daughter protruding from the ogre's anus.

One should not get the impression that the tales are excessively colored with such coarse details. Many of them are yarns delineating amusing amatory episodes. Some deal with incest, at times lightly, as when two brothers trick their sister into sleeping with them, and at times seriously, as when the parents of two exceedingly handsome children decree that they must marry one another because they will be unable to find mates equally as handsome as they. An oedipal story, probably genetically related to the Greek story of Oedipus, has an incest theme, but here, as in other accounts involving sexual relations between those within a proscribed range, matters are always resolved in a pleasing manner.

Many erotic tales told on Ulithi are candidly romantic in nature. One, involving a youth separated from his sweetheart, who dies from pining while he is away on a voyage to Fais, is marked by compassion and tragedy, for he himself dies grieving for his loved one. Another, in which a youth marries a girl who has descended from the Sky World in a swinging bed, is filled with the pangs of frustration and separation because a covetous chief sends the husband away in order to seize the wife for his own lecherous designs. In the end, after some tender episodes in which she endeavors to hint to her despondent husband that she has returned to him, they are tearfully reunited and the evil chief is killed by a friendly spirit. Ulithi has a "swan maiden" type of story, in which a young man marries and then loses a girl who has come ashore as a porpoise to watch a dance and becomes transformed into a woman by removing her tail. Not to prolong these examples unduly, one final story may be mentioned. In it a young man is ordered to marry an old and ugly woman, and he does so without showing any sign of resentment. Indeed, he treats her with every consideration, and one day, in reluctant response to her cryptic urgings, he cuts off her head and she stands there a dazzlingly pretty girl. Another man has been ordered to marry an even older woman but does so with bad grace. When he learns about the transformation of his friend's wife, he cuts off his own wife's head, but not at her demand, and she turns out even older than ever and too feeble to walk, so he must carry her through the village on his back, to the derision of the people.

In these stories, then, sex appears in a wide range. In some of them words are not minced and are even injected for shock effect. For the most part, sex is treated routinely, and certainly without prudery. There is a constant theme of marriage, pregnancy, and birth, followed by another marriage, pregnancy, and birth—as if this were a way of marking the passage of time. The heroes and heroines may be far from perfect, and often, as in the case of Iolofath, are adulterous, but to compensate for this there are lovers whose ideals, emotions, and travails are not at all unlike those of Western romances.

Turning back to reality instead of fantasy, sex is a common subject for jesting and conversation, and when young men are with others of their age they are apt to expand upon their past exploits and their future aspirations in the arena of love. Young girls do the same. The anecdotes that are told are not standardized pieces of fiction to entertain one's friends; despite embellishments, they are true accounts. My chief informant told me an experience he was fond of relating to others. Once, when his wife was confined to a menstrual house away from their isle, and he felt a desire for feminine companionship, he encountered an unfamiliar girl on a path and arranged for a tryst that night. But while waiting for darkness he fell asleep in the clubhouse. A friend of his, also on the prowl for a girl, stumbled upon her at the appointed place and realizing that she was looking for his friend, imitated his voice and succeeded in making love to her without her discovering he was an imposter. Then he returned exultantly to the clubhouse and told the sleepy friend of his success of the evening. My informant denied that he had made arrangements for a rendezvous, but then confessed, whereupon his friend told him that all was not lost as he had arranged a meeting for the next night and my informant could keep the appointment. He did. He made love to the unsuspecting girl. Then he told her the details of the previous night, and she became so angry she would not accept his apology and refused ever to see him again.

This story is repeated here only to give some flavor of the kind of anecdote that amuses Ulithians. Two more may be added in more condensed form. The same men in the previous escapade made love one night to two girls in their house. Exhausted, they fell asleep, but one man awoke in time to leave, while my informant remained asleep. About daybreak he cried out in his sleep and people came running posthaste to see what the trouble might be. They entered the house and saw the bewildered young man. Later, the two friends met and after some preliminary recriminations on the part of the embarrassed youth, he and his friend fell into convulsions of laughter. Another anecdote, involving a different young man, tells how he overslept in his girl friend's house after making love to her during the night. The other people in the house saw them at daybreak but left quietly so as not to embarrass them. But the boy had to remain indoors the rest of the day, hiding up in the rafters, so no visitors would see him, and was not able to leave until nightfall. Such are the precious experiences that Ulithians like to swap with one another, and they do so with the feeling that sex can be droll.

Psychosexual stimuli are of course initiated, in varying degrees, by dances, songs, storytelling, and jesting. These activities may serve successfully as stimulants for sexual congress, and at the same time in some instances present the opportunity for furthering amourettes. Thus, a dance may start out as a village affair, but when it is over the younger people will linger on into the night and often wander into the woods in pairs.

There is an institutionalized occasion for sexual stimulus, however, that goes beyond anything so far discussed. It is the holiday known as *pi supuhui,* or a hundred pettings.

This holiday involves all persons of the village who are not excessively old or young. It occurs at no set intervals, and is unconnected with a feast or other event; rather, it takes place at the suggestion of a group or individual.

What happens is that couples of opposite sex, regardless of age, pair off and go into the woods for picnicking, relaxation, and merriment. If it is night, as it more commonly may be, the pairs prefer canoe sheds. Married couples are not allowed to go off together. One's partner, who may be unmarried or married, is never a relative. However, one does not remain with the same partner throughout the occasion, and "tagging" is practiced so that it will not seem, however true it may be, that two persons are particularly attached to one another. If visitors from other communities happen to be present at the time, they are invited to join in. Men invite female visitors to be partners, and females invite males. Should there be a discrepancy in the sex ratio, a man or woman is shared. Small children pair off, too, but they are usually made to keep at a discreet distance from their elders. The play of these children is noncoital and considered to be innocuous, as it usually is, but it may go so far as to imitate the amorous words, caressing, and embracing of men and women. Youngsters may even explore one another's genitals. Group dances sometimes take place, but they are spontaneous and not instigated by someone in authority. Either before or after the main part of the holiday there is a group feast, fish having been caught beforehand by the men and cooked by the women. The *pi supuhui* is one of the rare occasions when erotic dances are performed in mixed company. No conflict results from this institutionalized departure from conventional behavior, and while certain liberties may be taken, the prevailing spirit is one of affection rather than license. The people describe it as "nice play" and make no apologies for it.

Heterosexual petting is of course most commonly pursued outside this sporadic institutionalized setting. It involves many kinds of physical contacts producing sexual arousal. The male undertakes the preponderance of the action, which usually begins with hugging and close body contacts of a general nature. There is no lip or tongue kissing; instead, there is a rubbing of noses, which may be construed as a mild equivalent. Nor is there oral or manual manipulation of the female breasts. Ulithians maintain that neither the mouth nor the breasts are erogenous, and have backed up their conviction, misguided as it may be, with failure to develop erotic techniques employing them. Moral reasons are not involved, and it is noteworthy that the same people who raise queries about the lips and breasts have no objection to genital appositon. There is, however, moral objection to oral-genital activities, which are considered lewd. The one positive function of premarital petting is that it provides young people with an opportunity to learn something about sexual arousal and the art of love. In a society which does not consider erotic feelings sinful, it is educational because it permits them to adjust both sexually and socially to a person of the other sex without the inhibiting force of social condemnation. Early petting provides young people with a chance to sample a variety of persons of the other sex and to arrive at some kind of preference that will ultimately be of use in selecting a marriage partner. Marital petting of course serves different functions and is most often employed as enjoyable coital play, but it does not substitute for coitus as a source of orgastic satisfaction.

Sexual stimulation of a mild sort comes from another source, namely, the use of ornaments, clothing, and fragrant odors. A person makes himself appealing by wearing a wreath or covering himself with turmeric. Pleasant smelling flowers, leaves, fruits, and plants are worn to attract members of the opposite sex. Women are allowed almost no latitude in the color and design of their skirts but they may tighten them or loosen them for desired effects on men. Tattooing of the groin or labia minora is considered to be not only something to promote modesty, but, as claimed, a sexual stimulant for men, and women are said to be very well aware of this.

The use of love charms has already been alluded to. Women sometimes perform love magic over food which a man is about to eat. Men may whisper an incantation over tobacco being presented to a loved one as a cigarette. There is no concept of aphrodisiacs.

Certain acts may be interpreted, in the proper context, as sexual overtures. There is nothing startling about them, but they are fairly common techniques. Suggestive gestures consist of rolling of the eyes, a quick raising of the eyebrows, a wink, an outward flick of the tip of the tongue, a sly click of the tongue, a faint toss of the head, a stare, a scratch of the head, a scratch of the palm or pinch of the hand when exchanging an article, and so on.

Coition and Its Rules

Coition is regarded as a highly pleasurable activity and is not beclouded with feelings of guilt or disgust. It is considered as something necessary, not only to satisfy a natural desire for physical and emotional gratification, but also to have children. Some believe it leads to colds, laziness, weakness, retardation of growth, discoloration of the skin, and other undesirable conditions, but this attitude is by no means a prevalent one and prevails usually when extraneous factors creep in. Under certain conditions, of course, sexual congress is regarded as ritually unclean. So, despite its acceptance as a desirable experience, it is felt that certain rules regarding it should be observed.

In the regulation of coition, place and time are matters to be taken into account. Intercourse is carried out either in the house or in the woods, whether or not the couple is married. Unmarried lovers may sleep in one another's houses, though this is done secretly and under cover of darkness. Some parents become angered if lovers are discovered in the house, but others ignore their presence. The really essential precaution, as with everything else in Ulithi, is to be discreet. It is strictly forbidden to have intercouse in the men's council house, and it is unthinkable to perform the act in the menstrual house.

The time of copulation is controlled by certain regulating factors. One type of restriction is the magico-religious taboo. These limitations, which have been amply described in connection with the performance of magic by specialists and their clients, may be severely restrictive. Another set of limitations is operative in connection with the washing and burying of a corpse. The same period of sexual restraint must also be observed by all close relatives who are in mourning. Taboos exist for a woman during a lengthy period following parturition. They are also in effect during the time of her menses, when she is confined to the menstrual house. Certain restrictions of course exist with respect to kinship. As for rules concerning the time of day when copulation may occur, none exist, although practicality makes it more common during nighttime, when greater privacy is assured.

In coitus the man is expected to take the initiative. It is improper for the woman to make advances, and should she do so her actions would be regarded as evidence of excessive pruriency. Preliminary petting is usually resorted to before the act is consummated, especially with young lovers. The play element is stressed, with the boy perhaps teasing the girl by pulling out a pubic hair or the girl assuming a pretense of untoward hostility. A practice found elsewhere in the Carolines is present here and consists of the male prodding the female clitoris with his phallus over a prolonged period of time before making entry. The practice is not, however, developed into the kind of game reported for Truk.

Circumstances may dictate the coital position, but the one that is preferred is a recumbent one with the partners face to face and the man superior. Sometimes an averse position is used, with the woman lying ventrally or with both partners positioned laterally. But common for couples pressed for time or without the comforting reassurance of proper concealment is an averse position in which entry from the rear is effected while the woman is standing bent over or kneeling.

Extravaginal coitus is known but not common, being regarded with ridicule and disapprobation. Penile-vaginal copulation is considered normal and best.

The duration of coitus is short and lasts approximately the length of time it takes the male to reach his climax, no attempt being made to prolong the act. However, coitus may be repeated several times at one session. It may very well be that the unfavorable circumstances prevailing on a small island, where privacy is not easily gained, have militated against extending the act unduly and that this has caused the development of a pattern or rule that might never have come into being if matters were otherwise. Women seem to have no difficulty in achieving the climax. The man makes no special effort to time his movements so as to induce simultaneous orgasmic satisfaction, and there is no particular premium placed on the order in which the climax is reached. The women heightens her partner's satisfaction by contracting her vaginal muscles, an act referred to as "spirit."

There is no recourse to contraceptive measures. No mechanical or medicative devices for preventing conception exist, and coitus interruptus is not practiced. Informants are insistent on this score, and there is no reason to doubt their veracity.

Impotence is rare, and its presence has even been denied. Frigidity among women is not common, and in discussing this matter with some men, one of them doubted the possibility that it could exist in a female population so ardent. However, his sampling may have been biased.

Heterosexual explorations begin early in the preadolescent years among companions of approximately the same age. With nudity the rule for all children in their first years, genital differences as well as differences in urination postures, are observed from the very beginning. Genital exhibition is thus rendered meaningless, and the children proceed directly to the inspection of one another's sexual parts. Manipulation is usually confined at first to mere touching and does not ordinarily develop into truly mastabatory contacts. Where there is manual manipulation the erotic implications of the sex play may go unrecognized. Mouth-genital contacts appear to be rare, but genital apposition is not uncommon. Having in many instances witnessed copulation by their parents, the children may make clumsy efforts at penetration, but vaginal entries are rare and limited for the most part to finger insertion. Much of the sex play of young children comes when they are in mixed groups and have occasions to pair off, as when playing a game of hide-and-seek. There may be some hugging and tickling, and by the time of adolescence this may become a light petting.

When coition itself is eventually engaged in, it is again at an early age. It is not thought of as associated with any necessary commitment to marriage; indeed, it is regarded as a thing apart. Courting follows a pattern, in which tentative advances are followed up with an exchange of gifts and declarations of affection. Ordinarily, one's first partner is an experienced person; novices do not often initiate one another. Adults attempt to restrain children from engaging in sexual activity only to the extent that their actions would violate the rules of incest and decorum. Their surveillance is strictest when enforcing the rule of brother-sister avoidance, which is aided by enforced segregation in sleeping. Otherwise, it is largely confined to building up a general climate of discretion that will enable the young people to avoid inviting the barbs of derogation, which may come from the community if the boy or girl act too boldly or intemperately.

It may be said that premarital liaisons are so common that they constitute the rule. The number of people who enter into a marriage with at least one sex experience behind them is overwhelming. Only because of some unusual circumstance, as in the rare event that a girl has been betrothed while still a child, would one of the partners in a marriage be virginal. Premarital affairs, then, are socially accepted and, in fact, even advocated by many people on the grounds that, if confined to a single lover, they reduce conflict within the community. Promiscuity is frowned upon; it is believed to promote barrenness in a girl and to betray a defect of character. Even if quite attractive, an indiscriminate girl is less desirable as a marital partner than one who shows a certain degree of fidelity toward her lover. The same applies to a promiscuous boy. It is said that not only will he prove unfaithful but may become sterile through his inconstancy.

Formal sanctions are never imposed by the community against premarital liaisons. However, if the boy or girl involved is lazy, irresponsible, and uncooperative, he or she may be the recipient of unfavorable gossip. In some instances the boy is censured by the council of male elders and the girl by the council of women, the action of these bodies being the closest approach to a public expression of disapprobation. The immediate family, too, may express its disapproval if the person is very young or excessively promiscuous, giving him a stern warning or a tongue lashing, or even a beating.

Rivalry is common in premarital sex relations, but good taste dictates that the matter shall not end in blows. At most, there may be a quarrel or a prolonged grudge. Rivals for a girl may talk over the matter and decide that one of them will leave the field clear for the other. Should it be impossible to reach an agreement, the rivals may compete for the girl's favor by giving her gifts and added attention, as well as trying to outdo one another in dress and ornamentation.

Extramarital relations are common, but while ordinarily they are frowned upon by society there are situations in which they are permitted. Two men may promote and cement their friendship by an occasional exchange of spouses, the wives consenting. The attitude of the community toward this practice is a tolerant one.

Instead of such exchange, sexual hospitality may be practiced when visitors come from other islands and are without women, whether because they are separated, divorced, or widowed, or their wives are indisposed. The man lending his wife is a close friend of the recipient, who does not make a payment for the favor but is disposed to present a gift of appreciation to the husband. The whole practice is regarded as a splendid gesture and is not disparaged in principle.

Less nobly motivated than this is the surrendering of a wife to a man in exchange for a gift payment, the two men not necessarily being close friends. The wife is usually especially attractive and the man desiring her more or less homely. The practice never rises to the full status of prostitution, and in any event the wife's permission is always necessary. Her husband does not offer her for payment more than once or twice a year, especially since her family would not tolerate it if it should learn about the transaction. Sometimes the couple is not particularly interested in one another, and so the wife is indifferent about the morality of the situation, as is her husband. While this occasional, part-time kind of prostitution has been reported to me as a possibility, no one seems to have heard of its practice in many years. Certainly, it is not institutionalized.

Adultery is so common as to seem to be within the range of permissibility, but it is not. Virtually all married people are guilty of it. It is said to be committed for the thrill which accompanies variety and the forbidden, but often it is a way of evening a score with an adulterous spouse. Adultery is not looked upon any more lightly in the case of a man than in that of a woman. It constitutes grounds for divorce as much for the one as the other. The community takes no steps to punish it, except indirectly through gossip. The family of the guilty party takes a more direct interest, and the parents or older brother may even resort to a beating. In contrast to this, the injured spouse is surprisingly restrained and may at first do no more than issue a warning to the paramour and a tongue lashing to the spouse. On rare occasions, where there is persistent adultery, blows may follow, but it is hard indeed to document this recourse in a society so deprecatory of violence. To prevent adultery, few steps are ever taken. One spouse may watch over the other with special care, but he or she places few restrictions on the other's movements. Chaperoning is unheard of. It is not in good taste to act as informer against guilty persons. Unless they are very close friends or relatives of the injured party, informers are considered troublemakers.

Matters of adultery are kept within private bounds as much as possible, it being especially indiscreet to speak about them publicly, for despite the frequency of extramarital relations, marital fidelity is the social ideal.

The grand rule above all others limiting sexual gratification is that of incest, a practice viewed with thorough revulsion by Ulithians. All blood relatives, unless they are so distantly related to one another that the relationship is vague, come under this restriction. All lineage mates fall under the taboo, and so do relatives by adoption, even though they are not blood relatives. Included are all classificatory parents, siblings, and children—a wide range of people. But affinal relatives are not included, so that it is not incestuous to have sexual congress with a wife's mother, sister, or daughter by a previous marriage, though such sex relations are forbidden on other grounds. Incest is indeed rare, and when it occurs is usually found on the outermost ranges involving classificatory relatives rather than close ones.

According to native belief, the physical results of incest are illness in either the offenders or their close relatives. This illness is the result of the work of ancestral ghosts and takes the form of headaches, boils, or yaws. It is said that the child of an incestuous marriage will be mentally deficient, its toes webbed together, its fingers twisted and bent, and its buttocks shriveled. The overt social penalties of incest are minimal, with no physical action on the part of society, which is content to satisfy itself with resentment and ridicule. I knew of one incestuous marriage, in which the partners were only distantly related, yet the couple was ostracized. In an unusual display of resentment over the incestuous activity of a married man, the men of the village of Mogmog considered killing the culprit—a rare reaction for a people as restrained as the natives of the atoll. Children born of incestuous unions are treated with the customary sympathy extended to all children born of illegitimate liaisons. Ulithians feel that illegitimate children are guilty of no wrongdoing and should be cared for just as other children, and be allowed to take their place in society without penalty to them.

Looking back over all these attitudes and practices, the question may be raised as to the effects of such permissiveness. In replying to this query it should be kept in mind that despite the leniency with which sexual activities are viewed, there are always controls. These exist even for unmarried adolescents, who must observe not only the regulations pertaining to incest but those of decorum and moderation as well. Extramarital relations are not at all permitted to go uncontrolled. Though wife lending is allowed, it is always with the consent of both the husband and the wife. Sexual relations between a man and his wife's sister is permitted under some occasional circumstances. Postmarital affairs are conducted mostly by older people in the society and therefore are not viewed with disapproval, except to the extent that they involve married partners. For such persons as mourners, lactating mothers, supernatural specialists, and others in a special ritual status, there is an even more excessive burden of continence and avoidance. So on the one hand there is the bait of permissiveness, and on the other the cold facts of regulation.

There is more, too. Rivalries, frustrations, unrequited affection, and lack of privacy put obstacles in the way of simple sexual fulfillment. Take the matter of privacy. It is sometimes difficult to consummate the sexual act in the woods, for there is not a good deal of concealment in the daytime and there is a fear of spirits at night. Houses do not afford a good deal of privacy, visual or aural. Frustration also comes from the separations brought about by the frequent moving about of Ulithians. They go from one island to another for extended periods of time, and often leave the atoll to visit distant places, being gone for months or even years. This discourages an incipient alliance, and usually terminates one that is in full bloom. A further situation conducive to frustration is the customary segregation of the sexes outside the family circle. Women work and amuse themselves in their own groups, and men in theirs. There is not a good deal of commingling in public.

A fact of demography conducive to the absorption of the mind in sexual matters is the inordinate limit on potential sexual partners. In a society where kinship is extended to include a very wide range of persons, and where there is almost no single person beyond teen age, the number of individuals available as sex mates is severely circumscribed. One young man wanted to remarry after a divorce but had only three women in the whole atoll available to him. He rejected two because they were pretty and would probably prove unfaithful, and married the third, an older and unattractive widow with a child. With individuals forced by circumstances such as this to enter into opportunistic or arranged marriages, a man may later feel impelled to find satisfaction with a woman more desirable to him than his wife. She may similarly feel that she can gain greater satisfaction in an extramarital relationship. The sense of excitement going with an illicit relationship is an additional incentive spurring people into adultery.

Thus, amidst an atmosphere of sexual leniency there are rules of restraint, but they do not impose abstinence to the extent that it has deleterious effects on the normal functioning of the organism. Abstinence is not idealized and is practiced only to a moderate degree by most people, particularly the young. This has the effect ultimately of reducing sexual phantasies among them and probably is instrumental in reducing physiological and psychological disturbances as well. In substantiation of this point of view, it is pertinent to inquire into the prevalance of atypical sexual behavior, on the assumption that it is a measure of sexual maladjustment.

Atypical sexual behavior does not find a congenial setting in Ulithi. Its lack may provide a clue to the extent to which permissiveness, despite controls and frustrations, has brought about what might loosely be called a normal attitude towards sex. "True" homosexuality seems to be unknown. Boys sometimes indulge in mutual masturbation, as do girls, and for this they are scolded and occasionally even beaten by their parents. Women of mature age, usually because of involuntary continence, are said sometimes to resort to mutual masturbation, but only as a substitute for the normal sexual congress being denied them.

Voyeurism and exhibitionism, the latter only among children, are present to a slight degree. Bestiality, necrophilia, sadism, and masochism are completely absent, insofar as can be determined.

Rape, a kind of atypical sexual behavior of a different sort, seems to have been not uncommon in former times but apparently is unknown today. The native definition of rape would have it include the ravishing of both virgins and nonvirgins, the married and the unmarried. The seriousness of the offense varies. In reply to a hypothetical question, it is said that the worst offense would be the ravishment of a married woman. Less serious, in decreasing order, would be the rape of a widow, a virgin, a nonvirginal single woman, and a divorcee. At least these are the responses that informants place on the various possibilities mentioned. Apparently, there is no concept of statutory rape, the rationale being that if consent is given it does not matter what the girl's age may be. In view of the current absence of rape, there is no precise way of measuring social repugnance against it. In the past, it is said, the offender would be greeted with censure and ridicule, but not retaliation. Present-day views can be amusing. One informant, on being asked about the prevalence of forcible coition, simply replied, "But why doesn't the man just ask the girl?" The implication is that he would not be spurned. More telling is a response to a Thematic Apperception Test I administered to 100 persons (one later was deleted for lack of identification of the subject). Of the first 65 persons tested, all interpreted a woodland setting with a man crouched behind a tree and looking at a passing woman carrying plant foods as more or less of a benign scene, usually involving a woman and her husband out gathering food for the family. The artist who drew the picture had tried to suggest in a mild way that this was a situation of potential ravishment. He drew the girl to look attractive, the man evil. Finally, an informant offered the explanation that here was a woman walking through the woods with a bad man hiding behind a tree. The man leaps forward and knocks the woman to the ground—and then steals her food. The answer is not strange, for while we cannot positively document the absence of the idea of rape, we know from the test results that there is far greater concern with food than with sex among the people of the atoll.

8

From Womb to Tomb

W HAT MOULDS an individual into a social personality in Ulithi? How does he experience growth, maturity, and final dissolution? The people of the atoll distinguish five epochs in the lifetime of a person: babyhood, childhood, young adulthood, middle age, and old age. Their terminology not only distinguishes all these stages by sex but also gives a label to the status of the individuals in each of these epochs. It should be plain that much thought is given to the phases of the life cycle. And should one look back into the past to consult the brief but perspicacious notations of early commentators, one would be impressed with the constancy in these matters over the years. Storms, epidemics, and conflicts have battered these little islands without effacing a basically enduring pattern of individual development.

Babyhood

Roughly speaking, babyhood encompasses the period of nakedness. A young child dons clothing at the age of five or six, so it is with his life before this event that we are concerned.

A baby is said to belong to both the father and the mother, social recognition of that fact being afforded by an exchange of food between the father's and the mother's families one month after the mother has returned to the menstrual lodge with her baby. The sea is always associated with masculinity, so the man's family presents a gift of fish to the woman's female relatives. After several days or even weeks, these relatives make a return gift of plant foods to the men on the husband's side. No magic and no ritual drama accompany this rite, which, significantly, is not performed for the babies of unmarried mothers. A Ulithian tale, "The Poor Lizard Girl," makes the ritual exchange of food an important part of its plot. It concerns a beautiful girl whose mother was a lizard but whose family was human. The son of a chief falls in love with the girl and succeeds in marrying her, without knowing of her mother's reptilian nature. After a child has been born to the couple, he sends fish to her mother, and in return the lizard solicitously collects plant foods from her own human relatives. She had previously worked just as doggedly to fulfill not only this legitimizing obligation but a similar one required when the couple was married. The story has a happy denouement.

Although during marriage a child belongs to both parents, the father is said to be "more important" to it in many ways. Should there be a divorce, he has custody over the child, regardless of culpability or remarriage. Moreover, the father is more important than the mother in the eventual passing down of usufruct tenure rights to land. But as far as descent is concerned, an opposite situation exists, for a child belongs to the lineage of his mother.

When a child is adopted he belongs in a socio-legal sense to the adoptive parents, but it is very important to know that he continues to be domiciled with his real parents until the age of five to ten, these being the most crucial of the formative years in his life.

The infant is given the breast whenever he cries to be fed or whenever it is considered time to feed him, but sometimes only as a pacifier. He suckles often, especially during the first three to six months of his life, when he may average around eighteen times during the day and night. The great stress placed by Ulithians on food is once more given eloquent expression in nursing practices. Thus, if both the mother and child should happen to be asleep at any time and it seems to someone who is awake that the baby should be fed, both are aroused in order to nurse the baby.

If the mother is alive and well, she ordinarily does all the nursing. However, should her milk be insufficient, a lactating relative on her side of the family is asked to help. A relative on the father's side is usually avoided on the grounds that the baby of that woman, even though he may no longer be feeding at the breast, will be jealous. Such jealousy is not believed to be present on the mother's side. Indeed, on rare occasions, sisters may make an exchange in the nursing of their children.

Because fish and coconuts are thought to be milk producing, a mother eats as much of these as she can. If the first milk is reluctant to issue forth, the flow is stimulated by resorting to medicine or magic. The magic is secretly handed down from mother to daughter, with rare exceptions being made to its secrecy and then only on payment of a substantial gift in exchange for the formula. Jealousy on the part of mothers is assigned as the cause for the reluctance to give such information to persons outside the family. The failure of a mother's milk to flow immediately after childbirth is said to be because the pains and effort of parturition prevent its release, and that the situation will ordinarily be remedied as soon as the mother begins to feel better. No explanation is forthcoming as to why some mothers, even when recovered, are still unable to provide milk for their babies.

Feeding supplementary to nursing begins in a moderate way at the age of two months, at which time the baby may be given coconut cream and a leafless yellow parasitic plant which is first masticated by the mother and then put directly from her mouth into that of the infant. Expanded supplementary feeding begins about the fourth month, although the mother may choose to delay it for several months longer. She usually masticates the foods first and then feeds them to the baby with her fingers.

Weaning begins at varying ages. It is never attempted before the child is a year old, and usually he is much older than that. Some children are suckled until they are five, or even as much as seven or eight. Weaning takes about four days, one technique being to put the juice of hot pepper around the mother's nipples. Physical punishment is never employed, though scolding may be deemed necessary. Ridicule, a common recourse in training Ulithian children, is also resorted to. The child's reaction to being deprived of the breast often manifests itself in temper tantrums. The mother tries to mollify the child, saying that what she is doing is for the best. She may hold the child in a comforting embrace and try to console him by playing with him and offering him such distractions as a tiny coconut or a flower. To increase the little one's interest she may say the object is a tiny baby and that he should take care of it, or she may suggest the object is a canoe. Another way to distract the child is with foods that are especially agreeable to him. The mother tries to heighten the child's desire for the substitute for her breast by verbalizing on the delights of the food. Should these comforting devices fail, the mother may lightly castigate the child, or set him aside to let him cry himself out, although in such an event she remains within sight of the weanling so that he does not feel he has been deserted. As a substitute for the mother's breast, a child is never given anything to suck upon.

The reactions to weaning are not extreme; children weather the crisis well. In fact, a playful element may be observed. A child may quickly push his face into his mother's breast and then run away to play. When the mother's attention is elsewhere, the child may make a sudden impish lunge at the breast and try to suckle from it. After the mother has scolded the weanling, he may coyly take the breast and fondle it, toy with the nipple, and rub the breast over his face. A man told me that when he was being weaned at the age of about seven, he would alternate sleeping with his father and mother, who occupied separate beds. On those occasions when he would sleep with his father, the latter would tell him to say goodnight to his mother. The boy would go over to where she was lying and playfully run his nose over her breasts. She would take this gesture good-naturedly and encourage him by telling him he was virtuous, strong, and like other boys. Then he would go back to his father, satisfied with his own goodness.

The care of the baby is marked by much solicitude on the part of everyone. One of the ways in which this is manifested is through great attention to cleanliness. The infant is bathed three times a day, and after each bath the baby is rubbed all over with coconut oil and powdered with turmeric. Ordinarily, bathing is done by the mother, who, as she holds the child, rocks him from side to side in the water and sings:

> Float on the water,
> In my arms, my arms,
> On the little sea,
> On the big sea,
> The channel sea,
> The rough sea,
> The calm sea,
> On this sea.

Suddenly the mother whisks the baby from the water and makes a quick tossing motion with him, uttering a mock threat,

> Shark! Here is food for you!

The child does not cry at being bathed unless the water is cold, as often it is.

An infant is never left alone. He seems to be constantly in someone's arms, being passed from person to person in order to allow everyone a chance to fondle him. There is not much danger that if neglected for a moment he will harm himself. He cannot fall, for he is already at ground level, where he has been placed to rest. However, safeguards must be maintained against his suffocating, or putting objects in his mouth, or crawling away. He must be protected, too, against inquisitive chickens, dogs, and cats.

A baby should not be taken out of the house at night and carried through the village, for evil spirits will make him ill. If it is imperative that he be taken out after dark, the baby is safeguarded by an amulet over which an incantation has been recited. This kind of magic, already alluded to in Chapter 6, is called "fence" magic because it acts as a barrier in keeping the spirits from seeing the baby or coming into contact with him.

The care of the baby is mostly the concern of the mother. A close female relative is sometimes asked to look after a baby for a while, and, on occasion, the father may mind and feed him, unless the baby is still in the suckling stage. When the child can walk, teen-age children may carry him astride their hips. Mostly they are girls. An infant is usually carried about in a long coconut leaf basket slung from the mother's shoulder.

A sick baby is the cause of great anxiety. Often a practitioner is called in to treat him, but any person may be summoned who has had special experience in dealing with infants' ailments. The most common symptoms of illness are stomach noises and tremors, diarrhea, constipation, vomiting, fever, and rapid pulse. No distinction is made between symptom and disease; that is, the symptom itself is treated, without concern for its ultimate origin. An exception to this attitude occurs in diseases in which spirits have had a hand. For instance, stomach-ache is believed to be due to a spirit. A diviner may be called in to identify the spirit and through his magic he can tell whether it belongs to the category of trees, the sea, or anything else. The diviner then suggests, on the basis of the nature of the spirit implicated, which doctor in the atoll would be most effective in curing the child. Magical therapy may be applied, too, by nonspecialists, such as a mother or relative who knows some magic. In any event, the spell invites the spirit to go away from the baby. One example involves a plea to the demon Hosola, who, it is said, in his great loneliness tries to kill babies so that he may have them for himself.

> May you feel compassion
> O spirit, Hosola,
> Towards this baby.
> Ride, ride away
> On the waves.

But in Ulithi, magic is seldom used without medicine in curing disease, and so we find many concoctions being used, none of which seem to have any real empirical value. It is interesting that the etiology of a disease may often be attributed to the violation by the mother of the taboo against sexual intercourse before the proper lapse of time after parturition.

The great tenderness with which babies are dealt with is again seen when the mother puts her child to sleep. Lullabies are soft and gentle, but most often the songs that are sung are merely dance and love songs with slow rhythms.

The physical development of the child proceeds in a casual way. Folktales, however, often speak of magic applied to heroes to make them grow rapidly—sometimes to manhood in a few days—but the recourse to such means in real life is small. Parents do not like to intervene in a process which they feel will proceed well enough on its own. It is interesting that they do not use "baby talk" when addressing a child, even though they may be amused at the baby's faltering efforts to utter a word and will mimic it with delight.

Toilet training begins late in infancy, not being attempted until the child has some comprehension of what he is being told. The techniques employed consist of punishment, scolding, material rewards, praise, nose rubbing, and conditioning. The person most responsible for toilet training the child is the mother, but his father always stands ready to exert manly pressure when the efforts of the mother go unheeded. Patrilateral relatives are more important than matrilateral ones, allegedly because the baby "belongs" to the father's family. This seems incongruous in a matrilineal society but is insisted upon by the natives.

The feces of an infant are often disposed of by placing them in the hollow of an old tree, the rationale behind this being that otherwise they might be burned by mistake or even maliciously, causing the infant to become ill and perhaps die. When the child has achieved sphincter control he eliminates anywhere near the waterline of the beach, so that when the tide rises it will wash away the excreta. The islets are remarkably free of the odor of urine or fecal matter—eloquent testimony to the inculcation of judicious habits that are carried into adult life. The frequent rains also help. The attitude of the people towards excreta per se is not colored with strong emotions and if there are objections they are based on esthetic rather than moral grounds. Careless or indifferent persons who eliminate near another person's house run the risk of having a concoction placed over their ordure, after which an incantation is recited and the feces burned. The effects: the guilty person's intestines will be permanently forced out of his body. Such magic is only employed when the offender is unknown. When known, the injured party merely forces him to remove the nauseous substance.

The training of the baby, then, is mostly concerned with matters of feeding, speech, locomotion, and elimination; but this is linked with the beginnings of an awareness of sex. It also involves the formation of fundamental patterns in the basic personality of the child, and by the time he is five or six he already has been indelibly oriented into his society. These first years are naturally ones of great concern for the parents and they solicitously do all they can to guide their offspring through to a safer age. Often they are unsuccessful and mortality is high. Should a child die the mortuary rites are the same as for an adult, except that infants are not given formal burial.

Childhood

Childhood is the second stage in the life of the individual, and by native reckoning comes comparatively late. It does not follow immediately upon what we would call infancy, but only after weaning, which we have already noted comes as a long delayed process. The child can now walk, talk, and control elimination. Actually, he has proceeded much beyond all this, for he has now donned clothing and therefore has attained the age of five or six. Boys wear a long grasslike garment made of hibiscus bast that is shredded and made to hang down over the genitals and the buttocks. Girls abandon their nakedness by putting on a bulky "grass" skirt made of shredded coconut leaflets. Children fidget a lot when first they put on clothing and must be trained through scoldings, warnings, and rewards to keep from discarding them.

The education of the child broadens out in earnest during this period. Boys learn how to fish, climb trees for coconuts and palm toddy, make rope, and otherwise assist their elders. Girls learn something about cooking, weeding, gathering wild plants, and how to be of general usefulness to their mothers. However, the learning of economic skills is informal and is gained mostly from observing older people at work. Children are not expected to do a good deal, this being a time when it is thought that their chief concern should be with play.

Sex training is now initiated. The fingering of the genitals is fairly common among both boys and girls and in the course of time usually develops into masturbation, but ceases for the most part with the commencement of coition, usually at the time of puberty. Children are never masturbated by adults. Parents try to keep children from handling their genitals, as well as those of others, but do not always succeed in arousing aversion against it.

The attitude of society is tolerant in matters of sex, and the child soon senses this state of affairs. He comes to realize that the concept of sex is one which should be regarded with modesty rather than guilt. Much latitude is permitted children in hearing about pregnancy and its consequences, and the omnipresent menstrual lodge can scarcely conceal the function which that house serves. Children learn early that premarital coition does not seriously outrage the community, so that when they reach puberty the act is expected. Yet, despite the prevailing tolerance in these matters, avoidances and restraints are exercised. Sexual precocity is regarded with disfavor. A precocious boy is warned that he runs the risk of wasting away his muscles and being unable to resist colds or to grow. The same is said to be true of girls. The objection to sexual precociousness seems due as much as anything else to the disapproval by elders of anything indicative of forwardness. Significantly, the danger of pregnancy does not seem to be raised as a deterrent to the sex act. The one real dread is that a child will violate the strong taboo against incest.

The chief means of actively training the child in matters of sex is through scolding. Should this fail, some kind of punishment is resorted to. Positive sanctions in the form of praise or rewards can scarcely be given, for it is hard to single out an occasion for rewarding a child in such matters. Frequently, adults will make some vague reference to "the spirits" in admonishing a child, without however speaking with much conviction. An ingredient of fear is sometimes injected in different terms, a boy being warned that if he plays with a girl's genital she will bleed, sicken, and die; a girl is warned that if she handles the phallus of a boy he may be injured and perhaps die.

The channelizing of aggression begins in childhood. Aggression often is manifested by a child against his elders through crying and throwing temper tantrums in order to irritate them. For the same reason, he will utter obscene remarks or words, throw stones, or make a commotion. During a tantrum a child may stamp, hit himself on the head with a stone, strike his head against the ground, roll over and over, or merely cry to excess. Often, the real means of expressing aggression is through the mere threat of doing certain things that the child knows the parents object to. He may stand at a distance and taunt them. These threats are made when the child is still so young—five to seven—that the parents will not take excessive umbrage. Although temper tantrums begin back in the period of babyhood, they continue until the child is about eight. The objects of these aggressions are usually the father or mother or, to a lesser extent, an older sibling. The consequences for the child are occasionally advantageous, for he may get his way; but mostly the affair ends in his being punished. A child in a tantrum may simply be ignored by all those about him.

Physical aggression is infrequent among children. Although clashes between them do occur, they strike one another surprisingly little. Fighting takes place mostly at the ages up to eight, and rarely after that. Girls seldom fight with anyone. Boys engaged in a quarrel are quickly separated by other boys or by adults. They are not egged on by other children, who on the contrary may quickly run to tell an adult if a fight has begun.

Aggression manifests itself more commonly in words rather than blows or bites. One child may ridicule a physical defect in another child, or merely hurl obscene words that he has heard others use. Children may even accuse one another of sex play, foul body odors, or dirtiness. Verbal aggression against an adult is not common, and in any event is punished by the adult after a warning, or is reported to the parents if the person offended is not a close relative. The verbal aggressions of children usually cease at about the age of nine; at least, beyond that age they are committed with less frequency and greater caution.

Willful disobedience is infrequent, yet a child may resort to it if he cannot have his way or is forced to do something he does not want to do. He may threaten a parent, saying he will injure, drown, or hang himself, or, perhaps, leave home and become another's child. The results of disobedience are not rewarding, for instead of winning his way the child is almost invariably punished, usually by the mother. Insubordination ends about the age of nine or ten; thereafter, it is virtually absent.

Early in childhood there may be some wanton destruction of property. Small youngsters will scatter things, break baskets and kitchen utensils, and tear apart what they can. Since this sort of display manifests itself when the child is about five and ends when he is about six or seven, it is obviously of short duration. It comes not as the result of brooding or vindictiveness but as a reaction to frustration or scolding.

The person most important in aggression training is the child's mother; next comes the father and the older siblings. When a child is adopted he usually spends his early years with his natural parents, and his adoptive parents consequently do not play a strong role. As a reaction to the control of aggression the child resorts to various outlets, sulking being the most usual, leading occasionally to a general regression. Older children may resort to subterfuge, this being common enough that Ulithians have a name for it. If thumb sucking and nose picking are reactions to training, then they are common in that connection, but there is little fingernail biting and hair twirling. Night terrors are almost unknown, it being said that any crying at night is the result of physical pain of some sort or a desire to eliminate.

Dependency training, already begun of course in infancy, continues throughout the whole period of childhood. The child has previously learned to walk and talk; but children, more as a form of coddling than a means for transporation, are often carried about until they are about six, usually piggyback.

Children play in groups independent of the supervision of adults after they reach the age of five. Their play is spontaneous and carefree, with little competition or aggression. Much time is spent near or in the water, and mothers as well as other adults occasionally cast an anxious eye in their direction and call to them if they venture too far out. Some of the great freedom given to children in their play is because on a small coral islet there are not many hazards, and older children are usually close enough to younger ones so as to be of assistance if necessary. Children play mostly in peer groups, particularly as they grow older, and may even form small cliques. Smaller boys and girls make no special effort to isolate themselves from one another, but older ones do not mingle, except on certain occasions. Children play with adults mostly in connection with certain dances held at night in which everyone participates. They often choose to play in areas where men are lounging about or working in groups, trying sometimes to get recognition from them, but they do not press or sustain their efforts. Indeed, play is so haphazard and relaxed that it quickly melts from one thing to another, and from one place to another, with little inhibition. There is much laughter and chatter, and often some vigorous singing. One gains the impression that relaxation, for which the natives have a word they use almost constantly, is one of the major values of Ulithian culture.

The attitude of society towards unwarranted independence is generally one of disapproval. Normal independence is admired because it leads to later self-reliance in the growing individual, dependence being scorned if it is so strong that it will unfit him for future responsibilities. Ulithians talk a lot about homesickness and do not view this as improper, unless the longing is really for a spouse or a sweetheart, the suspicion here being that it is really sexual outlet that the person wants. Longing of this sort is said to make a person inefficient and perhaps even ill. Homesickness is expected of all children and is not deprecated. I was greatly touched once when I asked a friend to tell me what a man was muttering about during a visit to my house. He said he felt sad that I was away from my home and friends and wondered how I could endure it. Ulithians do not like people to feel lonely; sociability is a great virtue for them.

The learning of traditional knowledge, beliefs, and values proceeds steadily during childhood. Children spend long sessions with older people and like to listen to them recount stories or just talk about anything. Mention has already been made of the acquiring of technical and economic skills. Elders of course are constantly demanding obedience and respect, and they are quick to deprecate shouting and foul language. Older people will not tolerate running through the village paths or trespassing in tabooed areas. They scorn crying and forbid quarreling in their presence. Begging is intolerable. Honesty is insisted upon with almost a passion. All in all the standards of behavior are simple and always moderate. Fortunately, the training of the child is in such harmony with these ideals that there is a minimum of discrepancy between expected and actual behavior.

Adulthood

The mild concerns of ordinary life begin to catch up with the individual in the early years of adulthood and he can never again revert to the joyful indifference of his childhood.

Attaining adulthood is marked by a ritual for boys and another for girls, neither of which is featured by genital operations. The same term, *kufar,* is used for each of the initiations.

The boy's *kufar* is much the less elaborate and important. It comes about when he begins to show secondary sex characteristics and is marked by three elements: a change to adult clothing, the performance of magic, and the giving of a feast. All this occurs on the same day. The boy changes from the long grasslike hibiscus "skirt" to the banana fiber breechclout of men. This is followed by a rite performed by one of the parents, or any relative or friend knowing the formula, in which an incantation is recited over the youth, while at the same time two young coconut leaflets, tied at their ends, are snapped together before his face. The chant is designed to bring good luck to the adolescent in his choice of a mate and in his marriage. Upon completion of the incantation, the leaves, which are categorized as a talisman by the natives, are placed around the boy's neck for him to wear a day or more before hanging it in his house for an indefinite period of time. The feast follows the magic and is merely a small domestic affair, joined in by all the members of the immediate family except the youth's sisters, who are forbidden not only to share in the food but even to witness the rite. The boy undergoes no hazing or tests of manliness.

The outstanding consequence of the boy's ritual is that he must now sleep in the men's house and scrupulously avoid his postpubertal sisters. Not only may he not sleep in the same house with them, but he and they may not walk together, share the same food, touch one another's personal baskets, wear one another's leis or other ornaments, make or listen to ribald jokes in one another's presence, watch one another when doing a solo dance, or listen to one another sing a love song. The youth is expected to prevent anyone in a mixed group from using obscene words in a sister's presence. If a man and his sister have even to approach one another, the woman must give warning that she is coming close by, and when she passes her brother she must do this in the crouched position of respect used towards superior and elders. There is no further seclusion from women than this.

The *kufar* for girls is much more prolonged and important than that for boys, having two aspects, one of which signifies the physiological coming of age and the other the sociological attainment of adulthood. The onset of the menarche has unusual importance because of the great preoccupation manifested by Ulithians towards the catemenial discharge. A woman spends about a fourth or more of her procreative life in isolation from her husband and the community. Conversely, the effects of the catemenial cycle are inevitably felt by the men, who must make compensatory adjustments in their own behavior. Extraordinary precautions are especially taken to see that a menstruating woman does not ritually contaminate magico-religious specialists. Indeed, she must avoid all men, and to insure this she is confined to a menstrual house until three days have elapsed after the completion of her period. Men are strictly forbidden to trespass on the grounds surrounding the house, except in the event of grave emergency.

As soon as the girl notices the first flow of blood she knows she must immediately repair to the women's house. The current inmates have usually had some warning of the event, and as she approaches they all chant slowly but loudly enough for the village to hear: "The menstruating one, ho-o-o! The menstruating one, ho-o-o!" Other women, hearing the commotion, may come from all directions to join the chanting. Certainly, no attempt is made to conceal the event; indeed, someone may race through the village announcing it to everyone within hearing. It is interesting that the chanting of the women is said to keep the spirits from sending rain, since menstruation is somehow related to sea spirits and the weather.

The first act of the girl after entering the lodge is to take a bath, still clothed in her grass skirt, in the lagoon near the house. She then changes this skirt for a dry one. At the same time she places a wrap-around skirt on top of her head, for should she fail to do this it is said that the sun would become so hot that everything would be scorched. For four days she goes about with the skirt folded on her head, after which she transfers it to her shoulders for another four days, and then sets it aside. There then follows the same kind of magic used to initiate boys into adulthood. Her mother or, if she does not know the words, a close female relative will recite a spell designed to bring good luck in finding a mate and enjoying a happy married life. As the words are intoned, young coconut leaves, *ubwoth,* are snapped before the girl's eyes. The leaves are a talisman and are worn for a day or more, and then hung up near her sleeping quarters. It is in connection with this phase of the long rite that the change to adult clothing occurs.

On the first day of the girl's confinement the special dance called the *hamath,* already alluded to in connection with institutionalized ridicule, is performed by men dancing in the village and women on the grounds of the lodge. The girl does not participate. The dances are begun during the day and resumed at night, the alleged purpose being to prevent the coming of a typhoon. Ordinarily, this dance may not be witnessed by persons of the opposite sex, the only other exceptions being in connection with criticism and with catching turtles.

The newly initiated girl must observe many taboos that not only restrict her movements but forbid her to cook her own meals, eat with other people, or touch their food. These *etap* keep her from coming in contact with men and at the same time separate her to a great extent from other women confined to the house. To assist in keeping the taboos, a prepubertal girl becomes her constant companion and assistant for a long period of time, doing her cooking and other chores. She alone is exempt from the prohibition of eating with the initiated girl.

After the initiate has been in the menstrual lodge for eight days, some *etap* are lifted by a rite of the same kind generally used to lift other taboos in Ulithi. It is performed either by a diviner or a typhoon magician. The magician does not perform his rite in the presence of the girl, for she is strongly taboo to him. He does it in the safety of his house, using two kinds of leaves tied into two bundles. After reciting the incantation over them, in which he beseeches the spirits to relieve the girl of the taboos, he sends the bundles to the menstrual house, where a woman, any at all, takes them and waves them in a circle around the head of the seated or standing girl. Henceforth, she may have more freedom of movement in the grounds about the house, and she may do her own cooking. All the other taboos imposed on the first day remain in force as long as the girl stays at the house. To celebrate the lifting of the taboos, raw food contributed by her relatives is distributed in her honor, but none of the primary magico-religious specialists may partake of it—so potentially dangerous to them is any association with catemenial impurity.

The girl ends her confinement when six days have elapsed since the taboo-lifting rite—fourteen days after she first entered. She lives in a private hut of her own, built for her near her parents' house, her young companion staying there with her. Most taboos still remain in force and cause her to avoid not only men but often women as well. The hut is not a substitute for the menstrual house, to which she must repair whenever her discharge begins. While in the women's house she has greater restrictions than older women who are not newly initiated, being given more freedom only after she has completed ten confinements. After a total of twelve confinements, she has the same status as other women at the house, but not when she leaves it to return to the village. During a period of three years after her first menstrual discharge she may not go near any of the primary magicians, and must wait ten years in all before she may even touch one of them, unless she is married to him. This is usually unlikely because of the relatively greater age at which men of this sort are admitted to their profession.

Adolescence and adulthood come rushing together at young Ulithians, and the attitude of the community towards them undergoes a rapid change. The boy and the girl are admitted to a higher status, to be sure, and they are given certain rights and listened to with more respect when they speak. But a good deal is expected of them in return. Young men bear the brunt of the heaviest tasks assigned by the men's council. For their own parents they must help build and repair houses, carry burdens, climb trees for coconuts, fish, make rope, and perform all the other tasks commonly expected of an able-bodied man. Young women are similarly called upon to do much of the harder work of the village and the household. Older people tend to treat these very young adults with a sudden sternness and formality lacking when they were in their childhood. The missteps of young people are carefully watched and readily criticized, so that new adults are constantly aware of the critical gaze of their elders. They may not voice strong objections or opinions, and have no political rights whatsoever, accepting the decisions of the men's and women's councils without murmur. Altogether, they are suddenly cut off from children and must undergo a severe transition in their comportment towards others about them. Only in the amatory sphere can they find release from the petty tyranny of their elders.

Marriage is permitted upon reaching adolescence but is usually deferred for a few years, during which the young man or woman is free to carry on premarital sex relations. Marriage is considered to be the natural condition for every adult, there seldom being any individuals who never marry at all. If a man were to avoid marriage, it would be said that he is both selfish and lazy.

A romantic kind of love often enters into the selection of a mate, especially the first. Good appearance is one of the foremost ideals, but the possibility of finding a handsome mate is often limited by reason of the small population and the rules of incest. Industry, kindness, and compatibility are esteemed virtues. Wealth is a secondary consideration; indeed, it is hardly a consideration at all, since there is little inequality in this respect. Marriage to the son or daughter of a chief is not especially sought after as it confers no extra rights or rank in a matrilineal society. Aside from the limitations imposed by the hard rules of incest, there are few restrictions on marriage. Insanity is the chief obstacle, followed by some great physical handicap. Ulithians marry freely within or without their villages. They often find spouses outside the atoll, except for Yap, where it is not permitted to marry into these higher "caste" classes.

It is after the several liaisons that come before marriage that a boy and girl discover that they have a deeper interest in one another than one based on sexual relations alone. They may express their interest through a series of small gifts exchanged informally. The decision to marry is not forced by pregnancy; indeed, the boy has no obligations if his sweetheart becomes gravid. No serious stigma attaches to the illegitimate child or its mother, and there are always those eager to care for both. The child is adopted before it is born, and the mother has no difficulty in finding a husband.

The initiation of marriage negotiations, then, arises out of the probings so freely permitted young people. The initiative rests with the boy, although exceptions occur when the girl is particularly ardent. Only seldom do parents arrange marriages; they ordinarily give consent to what is practically an accomplished fact. On rare occasions a couple may find it necessary to elope.

There is no wedding ceremony. As soon as the young couple have decided to marry, they arrange to sleep together, and the public demonstration of their intent is made known to everyone by simple cohabitation. Postnuptial events are few. A few days or even a month after the marriage, the groom's family puts turmeric on the body of the girl and dresses her in a new skirt. Several weeks later, his family goes fishing and donates the catch to the girl's family, and the latter divides the fish among lineage mates on both sides. The gesture is not one-sided, for the girl's family makes a return gift of plant foods at the same time it receives the fish.

There is no bar to polygyny and occasionally there are marriages of this sort, but for the most part such marriages are considered so impractical economically that it does not enter into a man's mind to take on another spouse. There are no moral considerations involved. Aside from the need for a man to be possessed of enough "muscle," as one native put it, to supply two wives and their children with food, he would also have to be endowed with enough "smartness" to keep harmony within the family. The customs of the levirate and sororate are occasionally carried out, however, without being enjoined.

A marriage is crowned with success if a wife becomes pregnant and bears a child. The desire for children is strong. One might take the skeptical view that the desire for children is motivated by economic considerations, but this would ignore the obvious delight that a man and a woman take in having young ones about them. No preference exists for a baby of a particular sex, except in individual instances; people think in terms of wanting babies rather than wanting a boy or a girl. Sometimes women resort to magic or take a medicine to induce pregnancy, but the belief in their efficacy is not sustained by the results. No effort to prevent conception is made, and the people say it would be ludicrous to control birth, for it would deprive parents of the great comfort a child can bring to them. Consistent with this attitude is the acceptance of twin births as a fortunate turn of affairs rather than a matter of regret, for here the mother has a double share of happiness.

The pregnant woman is treated with solicitude. In a world in which food taboos seem to be ubiquitous, it comes as a surprise to find that not only is she not placed under any restrictions but is on the contrary allowed anything she desires. There is a cultural pattern whereby she is asked to express some special preference, and she may say she wants a pig, chicken, certain fish, or anything else not ordinarily a part of her diet. In actual practice the food she gets is distributed as a gift among her relatives. For this reason, the granting of this pregnancy wish is really not the gratification of a real food craving as much as it is another one of those countless occasions that serve as a distributive mechanism for food. If the woman has a real craving, it is catered to in routine fashion.

The lack of taboos surrounding the gravid woman's food extends to all other areas of life, with two exceptions. She may not enter the sacred swamp garden or have coitus once past the first three or four months of pregnancy. Yet, as if to emphasize the concern of her relatives, they are not allowed to carry on activities connected with canoe or house building, and may not eat any of the food supplied while the canoe or house is being built or when a feast is given at their completion. Her husband's relatives have lesser taboos in the same context. This is not to imply that not enough is being done to see the woman to a successful termination of her condition. In view of the perilous character of parturition, she is given medicines to help her in a general way and other medicines to make delivery easy. Miscarriages are believed to result either from natural causes—overstraining, fright, corporal injury—as well as supernatural ones—violation of any of the taboos associated with pregnancy. A woman who has had a miscarriage must retire to the menstrual house and remain three full moons, just as if the baby had been born and lived. The dead foetus is buried in simple fashion in a hole on the menstrual house grounds.

Abortion, like the prevention of conception, is not practiced. This can be explained in part by the tolerant attitude toward illegitimate births, and in part by the great desire for children. Moreover, there is no feeling that babies will tie down a woman, obstruct her extramarital amours, or reduce her desirability as a sexual partner. As for infanticide, there is not any evidence whatsoever that it has ever existed in Ulithi.

Unless unusual circumstances interfere, parturition always takes place in the menstrual house. Should labor begin unexpectedly and the woman delivers her child away from the house, this not only is not considered an ill omen but instead a fortunate circumstance that shortens the period of waiting. The ancestral ghosts are said to have intervened in favor of the woman.

At the menstrual house, the expectant mother is assisted by everyone present. She now observes a food taboo for the first time; it forbids her to eat food grown in the swamp garden. When delivery approaches, all children are cleared out of the area. Women experienced in these matters, but not "professionally" trained, help in the delivery; most commonly it is the girl's mother who plays the chief role. Labor is facilitated by massage and the use of native medicines. Respiration in the newborn babe is induced by massaging the arms and legs in a direction always towards the trunk. The head, too, is massaged, and should all this fail, an attendant will put water in her mouth and spray it on the head of the infant. The umbilical cord and afterbirth are buried in the grounds of the house near the beach. Should a woman die in labor, the child is given to a lactating relative to nourish. Maternal mortality is high.

Unusual births are not common, nor is there much speculation regarding them. A caul birth is said to be due to the disregard of the mother for the avoidance of fishnets. It has no other significance, good or bad. Triple and other multiple births beyond twins are claimed never to have occurred within the memory of any living inhabitants. Twins of course are welcomed.

The new mother must spend three full moons at the menstrual house, and during this time the father may not see his offspring. The woman is under no taboos, although other women are forbidden to trespass upon her sleeping quarters. She is expected to devote all her energies towards the care of her baby. During her confinement, she never drinks ordinary water—only water from the coconut. Other women try to be of service at every turn.

After three full moons have elapsed, the mother goes home with her child. She is expected to avoid strenuous exertion, for otherwise this will make her infant sick and "the spirits" will be angered. At this time a severe taboo is placed on her having any sexual relations with her husband, so she does not even sleep with him. It is not until the child is able to walk unassisted to the beach and duck his head in the water that marital relations may be resumed. It takes as long as four years for this to happen, so that any intercourse before then must be avoided to keep the child from becoming sick and dying. However, the father may have relations with other women without harm to the baby if the child sleeps apart from both the parents. An examination of census records shows that the spacing of a woman's children does not conform to the taboo, and for this there are several possible reasons. Discounting the fact that the taboo has lately been less operative than it used to be, it is likely that the woman either has broken the rule against relations with her husband or has engaged in adulterous affairs. As far as I could ascertain, there is no societal rule against her having sexual relations with someone other than her husband—at least, no more than would be the case if her child were beyond the early developmental stage.

Sterility or barrenness never constitute grounds for divorce, but adultery, frigidity, sexual incompatibility, desire to marry another person, desertion, laziness, failure to fulfill economic obligations, thievery, and insanity are sufficient for either spouse. A man may divorce a wife who attempts to conceal her menses in order to avoid going to the menstrual house. Conjugal infidelity is not as overpowering a reason for divorce as in many societies. While the dissolution of marriages is easy and common, and without formal procedure, it tends to occur early in the first marriage before any children are born. Most Ulithians get married about three times.

A divorced couple has to make certain adjustments. The spouse on whose lineage land the house in which they have been living has been built retains residence there, and the other spouse, most often the wife, leaves to live with his or her family. In practice, the unmarried man must actually sleep in his home. He must take up sleeping quarters in the *metalefal,* where all other unmarried men are required to stay. There is no penalty against a guilty party in a divorce. However, the first of the spouses to remarry must pay a gift to the ex-spouse. Should that party and his or her relatives not make the payment, the relatives of the aggrieved party are entitled to arrive en masse at the home of the delinquent and confiscate anything in sight. No protest is made and no resistance is offered because public opinion is outraged by failure to make the gift payment. It is interesting that when the second spouse remarries, no gift indemnity is made. The need to pay compensation is apparently not designed to prevent a hasty divorce, and in any event does not accomplish such a result even if so intended.

The children of a divorced couple do not suffer harshly. Although the father has technical custody, in practice they live with the mother, with occasional residence with the father. A woman who is divorced while pregnant has full claim on the child born to her. It is unusual, however, for a man to terminate a marriage under such circumstances since for selfish reasons he may want to claim the child as his, which he cannot do if he is divorced before the child is born. The maintenance of a child whose parents have terminated their marriage is up to the persons with whom the offspring is living.

Avoidance between divorced couples is mostly a personal decision, and the two parties may even be friendly enough to have sexual connections. They must, however, in any event avoid one another's families. Eventually, the ill feeling engendered by a divorce may be eroded and friendly relations on the part of all concerned may be renewed. In view of the smallness of the community and the frequency of divorce, it would be impractical for divorced couples and their respective families to maintain a permanent grudge.

The ever-running years advance these young people through later adulthood into middle age, the fourth period in the Ulithian division of life.

There are no criteria of middle age beyond the silent touches of time, when the physiological transformations that come at the end of the fourth decade can be noted. For a woman, this fourth stage is not necessarily connected with the ushering in of the menopause, which in any event is not marked by either a rite or other symbol. As with a man, the signs are the beginning of loss of muscle tonus, the appearance of graying, and all the little indicators that a people must employ when they do not count the years. Almost every man and woman has been married by this time. Bachelorhood and spinsterhood are deviant statuses, forced on individuals only by mental or physical disability. A widow or widower, or even a person divorced, is under pressure to remarry as soon as possible, if only for predominantly economic reasons.

The middle-aged person commands the respect of all those younger than himself and wields authority over them. This is especially true when he or she has become a member of the men's or women's council, a status not inevitably attained, however, by everyone. The elders keep younger people in check mostly through criticism and ridicule, as well as occasional threats. Young adults must show their deference by bending down as they pass in front of them, uttering the formulistic words, *"Soro! Soro!"*

In their evaluation of the personality of the middle-aged individual, Ulithians are guided by certain standards. The ideal man is, first of all, industrious and capable in the arts of men. He is intelligent, handsome, muscular, and healthy, as well as faithful, honest, cooperative, kind, jovial, and impartial. Such a man loves his family and has fathered many children. Neither wealth, lineage, nor political position are important or necessary in the Ulithian concept of what a man should be like.

The ideal woman, more than anything else, is industrious. She is intelligent, too. She obeys her husband, caters to his wishes, and remains ever faithful to him. She is pleasant and sociable, and neither gossips nor creates friction. She is attractive and healthy, but not too robust, for this would detract from her charms as a woman. She is fond of children and has raised a large family. It is not necessary that she belong to a particular lineage, or possess many rights to land. The status of an adult woman is lower than that of a man, but in practice she may take the initiative from her husband in many subtle ways. By force of personality, a woman may make her wishes felt in the men's council by influencing her husband, who then follows her suggestions at meetings. However, he would never admit to himself or anyone else that she had swayed him.

Middle-aged people may lean heavily on the younger in economic and technological activities but they still have much to occupy them. Aside from attending council meetings, a man is expected to aid in gardening and other small chores. Although he makes no effort to keep up with the young men, he still goes out fishing or climbs coconut trees. He spends more time than before in lounging at the men's house or a canoe shed, but while there and conversing with his friends he justifies himself by working leisurely at making rope, parts of a loom, fishhooks, and the like. Nothing strenuous, but enough to avoid criticism. A middle-aged woman spends her time in the area of her hut, engaged either in some domestic chore or tending small children while their mothers are away. She also is expected to continue with light gardening. Women do not seem to have the leisure of men, but when they are engaged in work their efforts are by comparison more desultory and slower-paced. They sit on the ground a good deal, legs extended before them, and I have more than once remarked that when a Ulithian woman reaches middle age she seems rooted to the ground, never again to regain her feet unless absolutely necessary. It is mostly in the realm of the supernatural that a woman has highest standing, and then only in a limited sense. A woman is excluded from practicing the magic of the more prestigeful arts, but she is allowed to learn many of their techniques in order to pass them on to her sons. She is, however, allowed to practice the healing art, with all that this implies for the manipulation of supernatural forces. She can work sorcery and countermagic, and make amulets and good luck pieces. Much of the minor magic of everyday life, including that associated with the puberty rites of boys and girls, may be exercised by her. A middle-aged woman may even be a medium, but always for a female ghost—never a male.

Middle age ends approximately at the termination of the sixth decade of life. Because men suffer from a greater rate of mortality, they are clearly outnumbered by women of this age period.

The years, as a writer once said, may steal fire from the mind and vigor from the limb, but Ulithians consider that on the whole middle age is the best time of life. It is then that a person enjoys the most stability and the greatest prestige in the community, as well as the strongest authority. Mental and physical faculties have not yet declined to the low ebb of old age.

Senescence and Death

Old age is dreaded not so much because people do not want to die but because they do not want to live to be senile dependents. Sickness is feared when it means the termination of life for a man who is still in control of his senses, with perhaps many years of vigorous participation ahead; but sickness is not dreaded so much in old age, for it can always be cured by death. When death comes, people meet it with all the palliatives at their command. They are not introspective about it; they do not brood.

This last stage of life is not, by native standards, a good period, for it is then that people are ugly, mentally clouded, inactive and dependent. So distasteful is the contemplation of senility that people would rather die in their late sixties or early seventies than continue on in a helpless and childlike condition. As people grow old, they long for some way of rejuvenating themselves, but they have no theories or procedures for bringing about such an effect. Even the traditional narrative has no stories regarding the renewal of youth.

The aged earnestly desire to be of service, and consequently many of them carry on activities with the vigor of the middle-aged. Chieftains may perform their administrative duties in addition to gardening, weeding, carpentry, and fishing. I knew of a high chief who was regarded as indolent, but I discovered he was about eighty-four years of age. It was pointed out in rebuttal that an old man on Falalop continued to make himself useful, even though he was about ninety-two. Aged women may similarly continue to perform domestic duties and attend to babies.

Within the household, the authority of the aged is not challenged by the younger men and women. They may continue to give orders concerning the running of the household. In the men's council, old men may exercise even greater power and authority than when they were only middle-aged. The opinions of old men and women must always be listened to and not deprecated as the babblings of people who have outlived their usefulness. However, in matters of training and disciplining the young, they yield to others, except for an occasional expression of advice or criticism. They are very indulgent toward children, but less indulgent towards persons past puberty.

The ones chiefly responsible for the care and support of the aged are their children, who make every sacrifice to ease their condition. Aged couples do not always live under the same roof with their children, preferring to have their own houses, to which sons and daughters come and spend considerable time with them, moving in if necessary. At any rate, parents do not forsake their own houses in order to move in with their children. Should they have no children, a relative would fill the role of caretaker and provider. In Ulithi, this is not a problem, as a person always seems to have at least a few relatives. I once inquired into this matter and was told that only in one instance could it be recalled where an aged person had had no kinsmen. This concerned an old woman who had outlived all her relatives, including everyone in her lineage, but others stepped in to look after her.

When one is so stricken with age that death hovers about, he is granted any favors he may wish. Any pronouncements he may make regarding the disposal of his body and property are respectfully listened to, and there is no air of incredulity or indifference. A dying man or woman is surrounded by all the relatives who can betake themselves to his house, even if they have to travel long distances from other islands beyond the atoll. I have observed relatives, especially older ones, remaining for weeks and even months at the side of a person believed to be near death.

Ulithians feel that ordinarily death comes to the aged as the result of natural causes and not, as with younger people, because of sorcery, taboo violation, or the hostility of spirits of ghosts. The cessation of life is detected by touching the abdomen just below the ensiform process, and if there is no movement this is a sign the soul has left. There is a relationship between the soul and breath. With the last breath the soul leaves the body, usually through the top of the head, but through the legs if the last breath is exhaled rather than inhaled. In either event, it goes from the body and hovers about on earth for a brief time.

After four days the corpse is interred and the soul flies away to the island of Angaur in the Palaus, where it takes a bath. Notions regarding the particulars vary, but in general Angaur is not a place of tribulation. Rather it is a mere stopping point along the journey to Lang, the Sky World. Though Lang is in the heavens it is not a pleasant place for all. A decision is made regarding the ultimate fate of the soul, this being left up to the great god, Ialulep. Those who have led unsatisfactory lives are consigned to a place known alternatively as Gum Well or Garbage Well, infested by such obnoxious animals as eels and snakes. Here the ghost must remain forever, being unable to escape because of the stickiness of the gum in which it wallows.

Ialulep rewards the worthy by sending them to either of two paradises, one of which is in the northern half of the afterworld, the other in the southern. It is not known by informants why the god decides in favor of one against the other, since both are equally delightful. There are no troubles; people are continuously happy, spending all their time dancing and playing. Marriage is permitted and babies are conceived and born, as in earthly life. It seems incongruous for a people whose lives are so focussed on eating that ghosts feed only on the leaves and flowers of plants, as well as the fragrance that they emit. New arrivals are feted by old residents so as to relieve them of homesickness and any desire to return to earth to see their relatives.

But ghosts may, and do, return to earth for visits. People cannot see them, detecting their presence only when they possess a person and cause him to transmit their words. The experience of possession is the only direct contact which mortals have with ghosts. For this reason relatives watch out for visits from the departed. Before a person is actually possessed he receives a warning in which the ancestor enters him momentarily and instructs him to prepare certain gifts, such as loincloths, turmeric, and wreaths. The ghost then returns to Lang, where it remains for four days. In the meantime, the family of the individual who has received this warning eagerly prepares the gifts and deposits them in a special spot in the house reserved for this purpose. On the first day the gifts are deposited; on the second, third, and fourth, wreaths are left in the morning and in the evening. All during this four-day period of preparation and expectation, the relative who has been selected as his medium feels ill, and his family makes wreathes for him and sings a song for him. This is done in order to gain the favor of the ghostly ancestor so that when it speaks it will reveal valuable information. When possession finally occurs, the medium may be caught unawares. He may be sleeping, eating, or walking. To be sure, he has usually ingested a concoction to induce possession, but he never can be sure of the time when the ghost will actually visit him. During a seance he loses consciousness of all about him and trembles throughout his whole body. This continues for an hour or two, during which time the ancestor, who may be only a child, reveals what he has to say.

Our digression into the career of the dead ancestor's soul has led us away from the living who have been attending the dying person before final dissolution. They have gathered about. They have summoned doctors and magicians, and appealed in final desperation to Marespa or ancestral ghosts of their own lineage to postpone death. They have listened to the admonishments of the sinking individual to younger people: be honest with one another, come to one another's aid when in need, and live in harmony. During his last moments, if the dying person has taught any of the sacred professions or arts to others, he will be visited by his living pupils, who come into his room and recite formal requests for the ghost of the dying person to help them afterwards in the exercise of their work.

When death finally comes, relatives and friends set up a formalized wail. The songs of lamentation are not created for the specific occasion but are traditional songs handed down from some incident in the more remote past. The dirges are deeply moving laments, and even though they are ritualistically determined they are sincere and motivated by a real sense of loss. I have had women sing songs of lamentation for me in order to record them, and the memories aroused have been so keen that the women have shed copious tears.

The corpse is washed, covered with turmeric, and decorated with flower garlands about the neck and head. Sometimes a portion of the deceased's head hair is cut off as a souvenir by a close relative and is stored in a wooden box. Ulithians are great sentimentalists. The corpse is always disposed of by interment, and must be wrapped in a special mat kept handy by a family for any such eventuality.

The preparation of the grave is attended with many taboos and much magic, some of which has already been described briefly. The funeral procession and the actual burial follow a good deal of ritual procedure and symbolism. The head of the corpse is always placed at the lagoon side of the island, with legs extended. In the right arm of the deceased are placed a loincloth and turmeric, so he can present them as gifts to the custodian at the entrance of the other world as soon as he reaches there. Grave goods are placed with the dead person; these consist of some of his or her personal belongings, such as knives, coconut graters, cups, bowls, sleeping mats, loincloths, combs, necklaces, and the like. Gifts brought by relatives and friends, as well as persons using the deceased's land on loan, are also buried with the dead.

For three days lamentations continue at the grave, and on the fourth a permanent stone slab memorial in the shape of a four-sided tomb is erected over the grave. The slabs are bulky and heavy, and are cut with great difficulty from the coral bed of the reef. The next day the soul leaves the earth and begins its journey to Lang, this being on the fifth day (but only after the lapse of four full days).

Cemeteries are numerous and are located along the lagoon. At one time burials were alongside the houses, allegedly to alleviate the grief of the survivors, for then the deceased would somehow be close by. Burial places are not weeded or otherwise tended to because of a taboo against trespass, except on the occasion of a new burial. They are also avoided because of the fear of certain demons who appear at night in various forms, such as balls of fire, and can be heard moaning. They are not the ghosts of the dead but malevolent spirits living in the graveyards.

The period of mourning varies according to circumstances. In any event, the whole village observes a ten-day period of respect, when everyone must comport himself with appropriate decorum. No one may laugh, shout, dance, wash too freely, or put on adornments. Mourning is more stringent for close relatives, however, and they observe certain practices for five full lunar months: no sexual relations, no entering the sacred garden or eating of food grown in it, no entering the men's house, and so on. Men and women must cut off all their hair.

Those who have washed the corpse and dug the grave are under even greater restrictions and for a longer period of time. They must sleep in special quarters away from all others for a period of ten days and otherwise keep segregated from the rest of the village, especially men belonging to the more important categories of supernatural practice. The taboos they observe are designed to keep from contaminating others with the effects of contact with the corpse.

Finally, when close relatives have ended their five-month period of mourning, a rite called "pay stone" is held to reward those who rendered services in connection with the funeral. In practice, all the village is invited to participate in the distribution of food prepared by the close relatives of the deceased. The food, both cooked and raw, is not eaten on the spot but taken home for consumption. A variant of the "pay stone," known as the "think chief," is held when mourning is ended for a chief.

Death is not complete dissolution for the Ulithian. While the name of the dead person may not be mentioned by relatives and friends, his or her memory is not effaced. For a while it is preserved through sentiment, taboo, and ritual; more lastingly, it endures through the system of ancestor worship. Ghosts come back to visit their loved ones and even guide their lives. Although death often strikes harshly at children, women in labor, or men at sea, and disease always lurks at every door, the people are not morbid or defeated by death. Their rituals afford them some victories and their mythology the hope for a happy life in another realm. Though their gods are somewhat distant they assure that the world has an enduring structure, and their ancestral ghosts stand by to give more immediate aid when it is merited. So, after their bereavements, they spring back resiliently into their lives of work and exuberant enjoyment of life. They do not retreat.

Glossary

AFFINAL: Related by marriage.

AMULET: An object that gives supernatural protection for the possessor.

CASTE: A division of society into which nonmembers may not marry.

CLAN: An allegedly consanguineal, unilinear group whose members trace descent through an imaginary ancestor (usually a totem).

COGNATIC: The relationship between people who share ancestry traced through both males and females.

COMMENSAL UNIT: A group that customarily eats together.

CONSANGUINEAL: Related by "blood" or common ancestry.

CORPORATE: Referring to a body of individuals having an identity over and above its individual members and capable of succession.

CROSS-COUSINS: The children of one's father's sister or one's mother's brother.

DISTRAINT: An act, usually involving the seizure of property, designed to insure that an offender will compensate for a wrong.

EGO: The designator in the naming of relatives by their kin terms, or the reference point in discussing them.

EXOGAMY: A rule or practice whereby marriage takes place outside a given group.

KINDRED: A kin group composed of the consanguineal relatives on both the father's and mother's side.

LINEAGE: A unilinear consanguineal kin group which traces descent through known genealogical ties.

MAGIC: A complex of beliefs and techniques for manipulating supernatural power.

MATRILINEAL: The mother-daughter line of descent determining the inheritance of kin membership, property, and authority.

PATRILINEAL: The father-son line of descent determining the inheritance of kin membership, property, and authority.

PATRILOCAL: Involving residence in or near the dwelling of a groom's parents.

POLYGYNY: The marriage of one man to more than one woman.

RITUAL: Those forms of prescribed formal behavior which have no direct technological consequence and are symbolic.

SIBLING: A brother or sister, irrespective of sex. Ulithians designate siblings according to whether they are of the same sex as Ego or of opposite sex.

TABOO: A sacred prohibition whose violation entails usually vague supernatural sanctions.

TALISMAN: An object that produces supernatural effects of advantageous character for the possessor.

UNILINEAR: Traced through either a male or a female line of descent.

THE SWAZI: A SOUTH AFRICAN KINGDOM

Hilda Kuper

University of California, Los Angeles

Hilda Kuper is a professor of anthropology at the University of California, Los Angeles. She was born in Rhodesia and studied anthropology in Johannesburg and London, where she obtained her doctorate at the London School of Economics. She spent two years doing field research in Swaziland and has revisited since then. She has published much on the Swazi, including a well-known book, *An African Aristocracy*. Her play, "A Witch in My Heart," has been translated into Zulu and published by Shooter and Shooter.

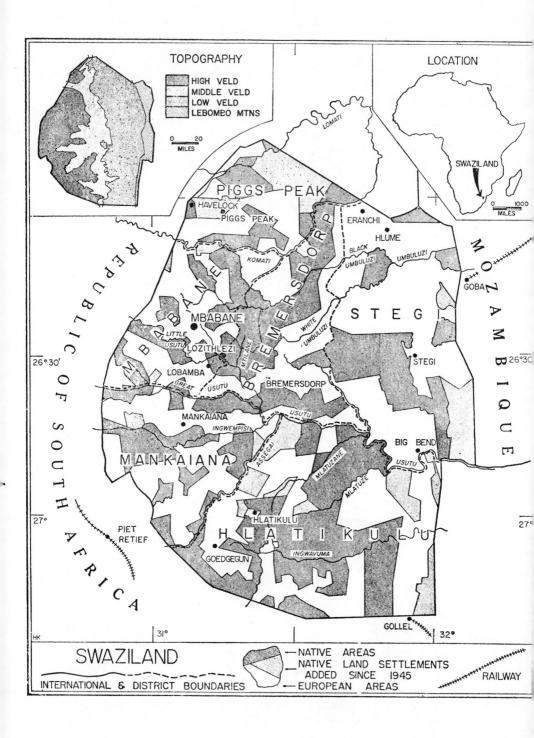

TOPOGRAPHY

HIGH VELD
MIDDLE VELD
LOW VELD
LEBOMBO MTNS

0   20
MILES

LOCATION

SWAZILAND

0   1000
MILES

LOMATI

PIGGS PEAK

HAVELOCK
PIGGS PEAK

ERANCHI

HLUME

MOZAMBIQUE

KOMATI

BREMERSDORP

BLACK
UMBULUZI   UMBULUZI

GOBA

MBABANE

STEGI

LITTLE
USUTU
LOZITHLEZI

WHITE
UMBULUZI

MTILANE

STEGI

LOBAMBA

GREAT   USUTU

BREMERSDORP

26°30'   26°30

MANKAIANA

INGWEMPISI

USUTU

BIG BEND

REPUBLIC   OF   SOUTH   AFRICA

MANKAIANA

ASSEGAI

MLATUZANE

USUTU

27°   27°

PIET
RETIEF

MLATUZE

HLATIKULU

HLATIKULU

GOEDGEGUN

INGWAVUMA

HK

31°

32°

GOLLEL

SWAZILAND

NATIVE   AREAS
NATIVE   LAND   SETTLEMENTS
ADDED   SINCE   1945
EUROPEAN   AREAS

RAILWAY

INTERNATIONAL & DISTRICT BOUNDARIES

Contents

The (late) Queen Mother, Lomawa, in leopard-skin cloak, at the ceremony of ingship.

A senior age group in full egalia.

Carrying the framework of a hut to a new site.

Mpundla Maziya, a chief of the ol
order.

The reluctant bride.

Introduction

T HE SWAZI are part of the millions of Bantu-speaking peoples of Africa who migrated at different times from places farther north and eventually arrived in the southeastern region between the Drakensberg Mountains and the Indian Ocean.* From their homelands they brought cattle and seed for cultivation, and handmade products of iron, wood, skin, and clay. They did not use their cattle for transport, and, being their own beasts of burden, they probably traveled light. But they carried with them the heritage of all immigrants—the knowledge, memories, and experiences of the past from societies they had left behind. With this, they were able to shape their lives anew, adapting as they forgot.

The country they traversed was inhabited by peoples—hunters and pastoral nomads—whose ways of life were different from their own, and there was also infiltration from non-African outsiders along the eastern seaboard, where they settled. Long before the arrival of white settlers in the southeast, there was contact, to the point of intermarriage, between different groups. The modern Swazi, a handsome people, are predominantly Negroid in appearance, but with skin color ranging from dark brown to honey gold; occasional individuals have profiles reminiscent of friezes from ancient Egypt and others show Bushmanoid features. Distinct from physical mingling there occurred cultural diffusion and borrowing, and social adjustments, which may account for some of the striking similarities in both culture (material goods and the less tangible aspects of social beliefs and behavior) and social structure (ordered systems of relationship), found in areas far apart on the vast African continent.

Traditional Africa presents several models of political systems, ranging from large-scale states and highly centralized chiefdoms to small local commu-

---

* *Bantu,* literally "People," is a linguistic label derived from the root *ntu,* "person," and the plural prefix *ba.* There are over 400 Bantu languages and many dialects, but their structure is sufficiently characteristic and distinctive to postulate a common origin.

237

nities, knit primarily by kinship and without defined political leadership. In the process of historical growth, the Swazi developed their particular system, a dual monarchy that was unique in some respects but which fits into the general category of centralized chiefdoms. At the head was a hereditary king, titled by his people *Ingwenyama* (Lion), and a queen mother, *Indlovukati* (Lady Elephant).

Beginning in the nineteenth century, boundaries drawn by white colonial powers cut through existing African political units. Swazi tribesmen found themselves dispersed in territories controlled by British, Boer (Afrikaner), and Portuguese. At present, the claim to Swazi identity remains based on allegiance to the two traditional rulers, but Swazi living in the Republic (formerly the Union) of South Africa and in the Portuguese province of Lourenço Marques fall outside their effective control. This book is limited to the way of life of those Swazi whose homes are in the small British High Commission Territory of Swaziland, where the *Ingwenyama* is recognized as the paramount chief in the new bureaucracy, and the *Indlovukati* is titled queen mother.

Swaziland, a lovely country of 6704 square miles—roughly the size of Hawaii—offers the challenge of considerable regional variation. In the west are rugged highlands where grass is short and sour, trees grow mainly in deep ravines, and the weather is cold and exhilarating. The mountains slope into the undulating plains of the more fertile and warmer midlands, which, in turn, gradually give place to bush country where cattle thrive throughout the year on green foliage. Between the lowlands and the eastern seaboard, the windswept Lebombo Range forms the fourth topographical region.

Of great cultural importance to the Swazi is the abundant supply of water. Rain comes with the beginning of spring, in August or September, and falls in heavy showers, saturating the land and filling four large rivers and many tributaries, until the end of summer, in January or February. Throughout southern Africa, the Swazi queen mother is famed for her rain medicine. Her people do not consider floods and droughts acts of God or nature, but signs of royal displeasure or punishment from royal ancestral spirits. In more arid areas it is safer for the rulers to employ others as rainmakers. In Swaziland rain supports the traditional monarchy.

Its temperate climate, fertile soil, and potential wealth have made Swaziland an area of white settlement. In 1946 the population was approximately 184,750, of whom 181,000 were Africans, 3000 Europeans ("whites"), and 750 EurAfricans, ("coloreds," people of "mixed" descent). The whites own roughly half the territory, and the majority of Swazi are concentrated in scattered reservations, called "Native Areas" or "Swazi Areas." Swaziland illustrates graphically the point that geographical conditions and natural resources are subservient to social controls. The territory presents an economic patchwork, reflecting largely a pattern of land distribution between whites and non-whites, irrespective of the four major topographical belts into which the country falls. All major advances in mining, agriculture, industry, and commerce are concentrated in "European areas." Like most of modern Africa in which Europeans have settled, there are striking contrasts between the traditional African and the Western way of life.

Superficially, the most conspicuous symbols of difference are buildings and clothing. In Swazi areas, most of the people live in huts that are clustered together into homesteads and linked by winding footpaths. The huts are of three types, representing three main Bantu-speaking groups that have been absorbed into the Swazi Kingdom: Nguni, Sotho, and Tonga. The predominant style is set by the Nguni, the group of the royal Dlamini clan. Nguni huts are shaped like beehives with plaited ropes radiating from neat ornamental pinnacles and binding down the thatching grass. There are no special air vents, and the doorways are so low that even children have to crawl to enter. Sotho huts, which are increasing in number, have pointed, detachable roofs placed on walls of mud and wattle, or sometimes of stone; wooden window frames can be built in and there are higher doorways. Tonga buildings, which are restricted to the eastern region, have overhanging eaves as their main characteristic. In some homesteads more than one style is found, but this represents no difficulty in adjustment, no conflict in level of development. In all, the central structure is the cattle byre. The relative uniformity is maintained by the absence of special functional buildings for trade, administration, education, health or worship. The whites introduced a variety of domestic architectural styles ranging from simple brick bungalows to Hollywood-inspired mansions, and also built clearly distinguishable shops, offices, schools, hospitals, and churches. The contrast in the the exterior of the buildings corresponds to a considerable extent to differences in interior equipment and furnishings. In conservative Swazi homesteads, there are no chairs or beds. The people sit and sleep on grass mats and use Egyptian-style wooden headrests as pillows. There are no stoves, tables, or cupboards. Cooking is done on an open fire in the hut, or in the yard. Utensils are limited, and wooden meat platters and clay drinking bowls, designed for group, not individual, portions are kept on the floor, which is of stamped earth smeared with moistened cow dung, to make it smooth, clean, and sweetsmelling.

Clothing, a more personal demonstration of cultural identification than buildings, always reflects major distinctions of sex and age. Small Swazi children are decked only in narrow waistbands of beads or plaited grass, with tiny charms to protect them against various evils. Older boys flaunt their manliness behind triangular flaps of animal skins, and later wear these over materials tied like a skirt and reaching to the knees. Young unmarried girls wear gay prints tied around the hips with a separate piece of cloth knotted over one shoulder. Married women are conspicuously set apart by heavy skirts of cowhide and aprons of goatskins, so tied that it is easy, with practice, to swing a baby from the back and suckle it at the breast. Whites, particularly missionaries, condemned traditional clothing as immodestly revealing, and Western clothing became for some Swazi synonymous with "Western civilization" and a first essential of Christianity.

Striking differences tend to mask the extent of borrowing and adaptation resulting from over a hundred years of white settlement. The effects are most visible on the outskirts of urban centers developed by Whites, where Swazi live in simple Western-styled-and-furnished houses, but even in the isolated backwoods of the bush country, woolen blankets, beads, tin trunks, and bottles are conspicuous clues of contact. Perhaps most significant, although also less conspicuous, are the pieces of paper symbolizing the penetration of the written word. We find in modern Swaziland a small group eager to imitate the ways of the whites and, at the other extreme, a group that rejects all things Western and longs for an idealized golden age; between the extremes are the mass, whose choices are not consciously or deliberately made in terms of whether they are "traditional" or "Western." The need for cash crops drives many Swazi to work for long periods in the world of the whites, but they do not live there as white men, and when their period of service is over, they return to their homes, unaware of the extent to which they may have been changed by their experiences.

Very few Swazi attempt deliberately to live in both worlds at the same time. The exception to this general rule is the present *Ingwenyama*, Sobhuza II, an educated conservative, with a deep pride as well as a vested interest in the traditional culture of his people. Applying the crude cultural indices of building and clothing, we find that he is the head of the most conservative homestead in Swaziland, but that he has also bought two of the most modern houses in the country. He retains the heavy drapes and solid furniture of the original white owners in the front rooms, where he serves hard liquor, and tea from bone-china cups. The rooms at the back have acquired a more traditional atmosphere; here one sits on mats on the floor with Sobhuza's wives and drinks beer from the common bowl. Sobhuza's clothing, like his housing, mirrors a conflict of cultures. When he interviews white officials in their own offices, he wears a tailored suit and polished shoes, and when he goes visiting, he usually carries a cane and a hat. But in his own homes he dresses in cloth and loinskin and walks barefoot and bareheaded with conscious majesty. Sobhuza typifies the dilemna of many a hereditary African ruler. He is a king at the crossroads—and for him there is no green light. The clash of cultures is part of a more basic conflict between two social systems: one, a small-scale monarchy with a rather feudal economy, the other a colonial structure based on expanding capitalism.

I met Sobhuza for the first time in 1934 in Johannesburg, where we were both attending an education conference. He agreed to help in a study of his people which was being sponsored by the International African Institute. When I arrived in Swaziland a few weeks later, he arranged for me to live at the tribal capital, Lombamba, in the care of his mother, the *Indlovukati*, Lomawa. He also introduced me to his closest kin and to the national council, publicly gave me permission to attend meetings and ceremonies, and delegated one of his own trusted men to act as interpreter, cook, and liaison officer. When I visited other areas, I usually stayed in the homes of local chiefs who were informed by runners of my intended arrival. I mention the cooperation received from Sobhuza because there is little doubt that without it an anthropologist would not have been able to obtain accurate information on the kingship, especially its ritual, which is at the core of the traditional system. But it was necessary to draw informants from groups of varying status, or position, and who fulfilled different roles in the kingdom. Chiefs and commoners, men and women, specialists and laymen, adults and children, educated and uneducated, view their society from different levels, which together, make up the social whole that the anthropologist studies. Although the majority of Sobhuza's subjects are less Westernized and less educated than he is, there are a few with higher scholastic qualifications and more radical ideas of progress.

In spite of Sobhuza's friendship—in some cases even because of it—the general attitude towards me, particularly in the early months, was one of suspicion and even fear. His mother, Lomawa, a shrewd, illiterate woman, acknowledged my presence with a formal courtesy characteristic of Swazi behavior to guests, but she allowed me entry into her huts only because of her son's instructions. To most Swazi I was *umlungu,* a white, who had to prove herself before she could be received as *umuntu,* a person.

Anthropological field technique is designed to obtain the necessary information from its human laboratory, but its recognized instruments—genealogies, village censuses, case histories, texts, questionnaires—cannot be applied with the objective precision of a pure science. Each society requires its own approach, since each has its specific points of entry related to its structure and values. A basic requirement of all field work is an adequate medium of communication. Anthropologists have long recognized the importance of language as a means of controlling behavior and expressing ideas. One of the great barriers that had to be overcome in Swaziland was the absence of a common language. English associated with alien masters was never spoken by Swazi when on their own, even by the few who were well schooled in it. I had therefore to learn *siSwati* or the more widely recorded *siZulu,** a language sufficiently similar to serve adequately as the medium in schools and as the official vernacular. Both Swazi and Zulu are typical of the vast family of Bantu languages made melodious by significant tonal patterns and alliterative concords that indicate, in a complicated classification of noun prefixes, a particular outlook on things concrete and abstract, on people, and on the universe itself. People laughed at whites who spoke "kitchen Swazi" but they became interested and sympathetic when they watched me strive to acquire the "deep" language with all its nuances and melodies, and they expressed their joy when I was finally able to follow what was being said, and sufficiently fluent to take part without embarrassing my audience or myself.

In the process of mastering the language, the field anthropologist learns other essentials of social behavior and joins in various routine activities until he or she becomes a familiar figure whose presence is no longer disturbing. Gradually I broke through the fence of noncommunication, and field work became a richly rewarding human experience. In Swazi society I found all types of people—proud, humble, generous, mean, gentle, talkative, shy, lazy, industrious. I recognized old friends in new shapes so that the familiar became strange as the strange became familiar. The human matrix remained universally com-

---

* The *si* is the characteristic prefix of this noun class.

plex but the cultural imprint varied and the qualities were often differently rated. The Swazi themselves have a number of ideal personality types, and, with an increasing differentiation between the traditional and the modern, these types sometimes conflict with each other.

This case study is but an introduction to one small group of people in a so-called "underdeveloped country." Since anthropology became a recognized discipline over a hundred years ago, there have been many approaches to the study of society, each making a contribution, no one really definitive and final, each stimulated by ideas current at a particular period. The following analysis is primarily influenced by the structural and functional approaches developed mainly by British schools of anthropology. The presentation of the material would have been different had I used a purely ethnographic, or a more comparative, or a psychological approach. Though much material has been omitted, that which has been selected covers the main aspects of Swazi life—political, economic, legal, religious, and social—as expressed in institutionalised systems of behavior.

Anthropologists analyze a society at a particular period of its history, and this book deals primarily with the Swazi in the years from 1934 to 1945 when I did my most intensive field work. Shaping this period, which I will treat as the ethnographic present, was a living past—starting with the first of the remembered kings and moving dramatically, rather than historically, through the period of contact with whites until the present time. Like other Bantu-speaking tribes, the Swazi had no script by which they could transmit their past to paper, and their approach to time was episodic rather than chronological. Famine, wars, epidemics were rememberd in isolation. The major unit of time is a reign, the duration of which is obviously not as accurate a measure as a decade or century, but is an index of social time. In the reign of some kings very little occurred; under others there were major events and crises.

Swaziland in 1962 is in many respects a different society from that of 1945. Since World War II, there has been a more positive approach to the political rights, the economic development, and the educational needs of the people. These will be indicated in the final chapter in which I discuss the main trends of change and also the continuity of tradition. The material for this is based on three short visits to Swaziland (1958, 1960, and 1961), but mainly on written documents: official publications, newspaper reports, articles in scientific journals, and private correspondence.

The position is not static. Developments after 1945 have brought whites and Swazi into new alignments. Economic investments by private companies and by the Colonial government are linking some of the most backward areas into the network of international finance; the granting of independence to various African territories has set up a chain reaction throughout the continent; in Swaziland, as in other nonindependent British colonies, efforts are being made to bring European and African inhabitants into a more "modern" democratic relationship. Within the Swazi state itself, political parties have emerged with goals different from those of tribalism or colonialism. I will show in the final chapter that the structure of Swazi society is less rigid than it appeared at the end of 1945.

1

From Clan to Colony

Traditional History

THERE ARE SEVERAL VERSIONS of traditional Swazi history because tribal historians, generally old men interested in the past, frequently contradict each other and themselves. Anthropologists are concerned less with the accuracy of remembered details or speculative reconstruction than with the way the past is perpetuated and sanctions existing institutions.

Kingship is hereditary in the proud Nkosi Dlamini clan, and Swazi historians recall the names of some twenty-five kings, though there is agreement on only the last eight, beginning towards the end of the sixteenth century with Ngwane II, the first king commemorated in modern ritual. For a reason no longer remembered, he and a small group of kinsmen and retainers left their home on the east coast and moved inland across the mountains, an achievement recorded in the royal song of praise "Nkosi Dlamini—You scourged the Lebombo in your flight." They finally settled in what is now southeastern Swaziland, known to the Swazi as the "Place of Burning," a name that some informants say refers to signs of previous habitation. There Ngwane died, and annual pilgrimages have ever since been made to the cave in the tree-covered hill where he and his royal male kin lie buried in state.

Swazi have no flag or national emblem by which to rally group sentiment, but the names of kings and such other verbal symbols as songs of praise and anthems serve a similar purpose. A limited number of royal names are given in irregular rotation, and the names of the old capitals are also repeated, serving as links with tradition.

Ngwane's grandson, Sobhuza I, came into conflict over garden lands with a powerful neighbor, Zidze, of the Ndwandwe clan, who was also building up a following. Sobhuza is remembered as a strategist who, at all costs, tried to avoid pitched battles against powerful opposition. Rather than fight against the Ndwande, Sobhuza moved northward with his group and established himself finally in the midlands at the foot of the Mdzimba Mountains, which remain to this day the area of most royal villages. The people who accompanied him are described as the "pure Swazi," "those who broke off with the Nkosi Dlamini, at The Place of Burning," and are the nucleus of the Swazi state.

The country they entered was already occupied by people of both Nguni and Sotho stock. The Sotho spoke a somewhat different language and practiced slightly different customs, but they were not organized for warfare and their level of culture was the same as that of the Nguni invaders. From all these people, described as "The Found Ahead," Sobhuza demanded allegiance. Some came humbly, offering tribute of food and maidens; others were defeated and plundered, but once their loyalty was assured, they were allowed to continue under their own recognized clan heads subordinate only to the Dlamini king. At least one group simply moved beyond his reach. "The Found Ahead" who remained and survived were incorporated as a second group into the growing state. From them, the Dlamini ruler acquired, among other things, new and powerful magic for rain, war, and cultivation, which bolstered his military conquest by extending his range of ritual. He further consolidated his position by diplomatic marriages, and sought as his main wife a daughter of his erstwhile enemy, Zidze of the Ndwandwe. He also sent two of his own daughters to the powerful Shaka, founder of the Zulu kingdom, and maintained his neutrality even when the Swazi princesses suffered the fate of all Shaka's queens and were killed when they became pregnant. On Sobhuza's death, he left his successor a strong kingdom, respected and feared by neighboring tribes, with a centralized political system controlling several thousands of people scattered over areas reaching far beyond the boundaries of modern Swaziland.

Throughout southern Africa in the late eighteenth and early nineteenth centuries, small tribes linked by kinship were being organized into strong military states under ambitious rulers. This important change in the structure of the traditional political units is primarily related to greater economic pressure on the land. Being peasants, their existence depended on the soil, and they moved when the yield was considered too low or the area too limited. But the tribal population was increasing, and land to the south, formerly open to African expansion, was being taken by the whites. Conflict between the tribes and between Africans and whites became inevitable.

Sobhuza's heir, Mswati, by his main wife, Zidze's daughter, was the greatest of the Swazi fighting kings. Probably influenced by the successful Zulu, he reorganized his army, which before had been on a local kinship basis, into centralized age regiments, and equipped his men with the short stabbing spear in addition to the long but less controllable throwing spear. To keep order over his vast domain, Mswati established royal homesteads as mobilizing centers for men in outlying districts, and these also served as military outposts from which to launch attacks on independent tribes. His armies' raids reached Southern Rhodesia, and the name of Mswati was the terror of the north. The warriors brought their plunder to the king, who redistributed most of it, giving preference to the heroes. Important captives were sometimes exchanged for Swazi prisoners of war. Destruction of the fighting forces of an enemy did not necessarily result in the permanent extinction of the vanquished group, or in their lasting hostility to the victors. The Dlamini king emphasized the sanctity and power of hereditary leadership, and as long as a chief or the heirs of a defeated people survived, he acknowledged him as a foundation on which the conquered groups might be rebuilt as part of the Swazi state. Thus, Mswati reinstated heirs whose allegiance was assured in the district of their fathers, and in this way both extended his domain and made staunch allies of once-powerful enemies.

The disruption of rival kingdoms magnified Mswati's power. Many survivors fled to his "armpit" for protection. His fame also attracted distant relatives of established tribesmen who were anxious for a protector in this period of intertribal conflict and unrest. Some were humble and insignificant and others were powerful; Mswati established loyal groups in sparsely populated districts under their own chiefs, he placed royal princes and nominees from commoner clans in control of clans that he trusted less. The immigrants became known as "Those Who Arrived After" and form a third category in the state. Of the present clan names, totaling over seventy, approximately one fifth are regarded as "True Swazi," one seventh are "Those Found Ahead" and the remainder are "Those Who Arrived After." About 70 percent of the clans are Nguni, 25 percent Sotho and 5 percent Tonga. Every clan has its history, and the combined history of all the clans gives the mandate of superiority to the Dlamini conquerors.

The Nkosi Dlamini did not attempt to enforce their culture, and even today there are local differences in dialect, architectural style, dress, food, utensils, and ritual. But considerable uniformity resulted from the method of absorption and the participation in national affairs granted to all subjects. The groups have intermarried, all are entitled to protection, to land, to bear the national mark—a slit in the lobes of the ears, to wear Swazi costume on state occasions, to serve together in the age regiments, and to speak in the council. These privileges and responsibilities of citizenship are conferred on everyone owing allegiance to the "twin" rulers—mother and son—and cultural homogeneity is greatest in the areas closest to these central authorities.

The Paper Conquest

The initial relationship between Swazi and whites was friendly and cooperative. Informants relate that Mswati's father, Sobhuza I, was forewarned of their arrival in a dream, even before cloth, beads, and guns substantiated their existence and before news of bloody battles between them and tribes to the south spread to his people. Early in Mswati's reign, which lasted from 1830 to 1868, Boer farmers from the Transvaal came in search of better grazing for their cattle, British traders from the east coast bartered their wares for ivory and skins, hunters shot the wild game that abounded in the bush veldt, and an English missionary worked for a while in the south. Several white men visited the king himself, who received them courteously.

Though the whites came as individuals, they were not isolated. They were members of two separate and antagonistic political communities—the Boer and the British—each struggling to establish itself in a country predominantly inhabited by non-whites. Initially, the Swazi were prepared to treat either or both white groups as allies, and Mswati appealed to the English for protection against the raids of the Zulu and sent an army to help the Boers defeat a hostile Sotho tribe to the north. In return for 150 breeding cattle and services (unspecified) he also signed his cross on two documents presented him by officials of the Boers; though these documents had no immediate effect, they ceded virtually his entire country to the whites and were the precursors of the spate of concession that led to the final subjugation of his people.

Mswati's death in 1858 was followed by a period of internal strife, centering on disputed succession. Rivalry between princes for the kingship had become part of the dynamics of traditional politics, but it gave whites the opportunity to further their economic ambitions by political intervention in the guise of "promoting peace." Mswati's heir, Ludonga, was a minor and Mswati's mother (the daughter of Zidze) and one of his half brothers were acting as regents. Ludonga died suddenly and mysteriously and suspicion fell on the male regent, who was clubbed to death. Ludonga's mother had only the one son, and his half brothers, sons by Mswati's other wives, wrangled and fought for the throne. Finally one group of princes agreed to appoint the motherless Mbandzeni in Ludonga's place to rule together with Ludonga's own mother. Thereupon the Boer Transvaal Republic sent a commando of 400 men to Mbandzeni's installation; after the ceremony the leader of the Boer troops had Mbandzeni make his cross on the document ratifying the concessions granted by his father, Mswati.

Boer and British expressed different interests in Swaziland. The Boers were predomiantly farmers searching for good arable land and also for a route to the coast which would enable them to establish their own port and avoid all contact with the hated British at the Cape. They were therefore anxious to annex Swaziland. On the other hand, Britain, following the loss of her American colonies and the rise of free trade, wanted to consolidate her empire rather than expand it, and had no desire to assume added financial responsibility. She was, however, reluctant to let the Boers gain control of a country of unknown promise or divert trade from her own southern ports. Her nationals were mainly interested in mining and commerce. In 1882, gold was discovered in the northwest and hundreds of European fortune hunters entered the country. They sought personal interviews with the king, to whom they gave cash, blankets, dogs, horses, guns, gin, and other products of the "civilized" world in return for the mark which he was asked to make on the documents they placed before him.

From the time of his selection, Mbandzeni's own position in the tribe was insecure. Hostility developed between him and the queen mother and culminated in a short civil war in which he sent his regiments against her. She fled with the rain medicines, but was captured and throttled. In her place, the king's supporters appointed another wife of his father, carefully choosing a woman with the clan name of his (Mbandzeni's) own deceased mother, and with no son of her own. On two subsequent occasions, Mbandzeni executed princes whom he found plotting aginst his person. Neither the British nor Boer governments had legal authority to restrain him, having guaranteed the independence of the Swazi in two conventions (1881 and 1884). But the internal tensions expressed in the rebellions were intensified by the presence of whites. They were in the country of the Swazi king, but were not his subjects; they did not serve him, yet they employed his men as their servants; their conspicuous wealth overshadowed his possessions and he complained that each white man behaved "like a king."

Though the sovereignty of the Swazi was frequently asserted, Mbandzeni had no constitutional control over the whites and a few lawless individuals, by-products of many a frontier situation, were a threat to all sections in the country. In an attempt to deal with the situation, Mbandzeni appealed to the British High Commissioner for assistance; when his request was refused he made use of a principle of government already developed among his own people: hereditary privileges in a trusted family. He turned to Sir Theophilus Shepstone, a proven friend of Swazi kings and a man who had supported the institution of chieftainship among the defeated Zulu, and asked him for one of his sons. Thus it came about that "Offy" Shepstone, who turned out to be a young adventurer, was installed by the Swazi king as paid "Resident Advisor and Agent" of the Swazi nation, with power to negotiate all matters affecting the whites. Swazi recall with great bitterness that it was during the period of his office that the majority of concessions were granted and validated.

The concessions were economic weapons representing a type of warfare beyond the traditional system. They included laws of land ownership that clashed with rights of customary usage, claims to minerals not yet exploited, the industrial developments of a machine age, the commerce and banking of an expanding capitalist economy. A leading councilor complained: "We hold the feather and sign, we take money but we do not know what it is for."

To assist him in his economic negotiations, "Offy" also introduced into Swazi government the principle of elective, as distinct from hereditary, representation, in which special interest groups, rather than the state as such, held the balance of power. He organized the concessionaires into a committee represented by fifteen elected property owners, with five additional members as king's nominees. To this committee, Mbandzeni gave, somewhat reluctantly, a charter of self-government, expressly reserving for himself the right to veto any decisions, emphasizing that he was "still the king." But in actual fact he had lost many of the powers associated with that position and when he was near death he mourned, "Swazi kingship ends with me."

Several textbooks blame Mbandzeni for the chaos that resulted from the indiscriminate granting of concessions, and condemn him as weak and dissolute, but he is remembered by his own people as a king of peace duped by unscrupulous whites. Judgments of personalities generally involve an element of self-identification. And it is left to the more impartial observer to point out that economic and political forces are more powerful than the qualities of any single individual in shaping the course of a country's history.

The death of Mbandzeni in 1889 was followed by a period of national unrest that was intensified, although superficially restrained by the presence of the whites. Swazi attribute death to sorcerers, and it was customary on the death of a king to kill all suspects. The British and Boer governments, despite their verbal recognition of Swazi sovereignty, had previously protested against this royal prerogative; when Mbandzeni died, the Swazi queen regent requested to be allowed "to destroy for just one day the evildoers who had murdered the king." Permission was refused, and this time the national leaders "resentfully submitted to the British queen's detestation of the practice." After heated discussion, but without bloodshed, the council selected as main wife and future queen mother, Gwamile Mdluli, a woman of unusual intelligence and ability, whose eldest son Bunu was a headstrong youth of sixteen years. A rival candidate was sent far from the capital. Sporadic violence continued. Stories of Swazi atrocities were headlined in the settlers' newspapers. There was a recognized increase in crime. To responsible Europeans settled in the country or with interests there, the necessity for a single administration became urgent. The white committee failed to exercise control, and was followed by a provisional government representing Boer, British, and Swazi, with "Offy" as the Swazi nominee. Torn by national and personal rivalry, it muddled along for over three years, during which period it "confirmed" 352 out of 364 concessions, but it had neither the organization nor support for effective executive action.

In 1894—without consulting the Swazi though knowing well it was entirely against their wishes—the two white powers, Boer and British, concluded a further convention whereby the country became a "protected dependency" of the South African Boer Republic, and powers of traditional rulers were circumscribed by the formula that they should be recognized only "insofar as they were not inconsistent with civilized law and customs." Among the powers the Republic bestowed upon itself was the right to impose a hut tax on the Swazi, a technique deliberately introduced in many parts of Africa to coerce peasants who had no cash crops into the labor market. Swazi objected to pay "money to keep the white man in the country," and as the time for collection approached, there were rumors that they would resist by force and that their rulers had summoned specialists in war magic to fortify the army. Tension was high, when a leading councilor who was sympathetic to the whites was executed at the capital. The Republican authorities summoned the young king, Bunu, to appear on a charge of murder. The nation mobilized. Bunu himself sought protection from the British magistrate in Zululand. "I have fled my country," he said simply, "because Boers are invading it and bringing in arms to kill me. I have stolen no sheep and shed no white man's blood." The British intervened and after a lengthy correspondence and a most unusual trial, Bunu was fined 500 pounds sterling (approximately 1400 dollars) and reinstated; at the same time a protocol drawn by both white governments radically curtailed criminal jurisdiction of future Swazi rulers. The "paper conquest" represented by concessionaires, but ultimately backed by superior military force, was complete, and the Swazi were no longer recognized as an independent state. When, in the following year (1899), the Anglo-Boer war broke out, the Swazi nation remained neutral.

The Period of Acceptance

In 1902, Britain reluctantly took over Swaziland as an added liability of a bitter military victory. Bunu died during the war and his mother Gwamile, and a younger brother, Malunge, acted as regents. The future queen mother, Lomawa, was chosen from among Bunu's widows because she was of the same Ndwandwe clan with which Sobhuza I had made so successful a marriage alliance. Lomawa had one baby boy, who had been named Mona (Jealousy); once she was appointed, the boy was given the royal title of Sobhuza II, and he is the present *Ingwenyama*.

The Swazi anticipated that the British would restore their sovereign rights and expel the troublesome concessionaires, but these hopes were soon shattered. However, in course of time, through economic and political developments, the Swazi recognized the whites as a vital part of their world and the years of friction merge with a period of interdependence and voluntary acceptance of British control. The machinery of a modern administration developed slowly, starting in 1902 with a little police force whose primary duty was to restrain the hostility of the Swazi and collect tax. Its personnel and duties were steadily extended. In 1906 Swaziland was placed under the British High Commissioner for South Africa, and, in 1907, a full administrative staff with a resident commissioner at the head and experts for different activities was appointed.

The government realized, however, that before there could be development or security in the new multiracial milieu, it was essential that the concession issue be finally settled. So the British appointed a commission and used its findings to proclaim that one third of every land concession be set aside for the sole and exclusive use of the Swazi and that two thirds remain with the white concessionaires, who could compel Swazi living in their area to move after a period of five years. Partition was organized by a skillful white administrator who divided the "Native Areas" into twenty-one separate blocks, but drew the boundaries in such a way as to create a minimum of disturbance in the more densely populated areas. The Swazi protested verbally and without effect. All arms and ammunition were taken from them.

Whereas Mbandzeni had attempted to control the whites by techniques established in the traditional system, Gwamile and Malunge strove to regain the rights of their people through methods introduced by the whites, within the framework of a domination they realized they could no longer overthrow by force. Gwamile openly expressed the belief that money and "books" were keys to the white man's power, and she imposed a cash levy on the Swazi for a fund to try to buy back the land, and also started a school for princes and sons of leading councilors, bringing in as the first teacher a colored man from Zululand. From the little local school she later sent Sobhuza II, together with a small clique of agemates and a sister to cook and sew for him, to a mission school in the Union (now Republic) of South Africa. Here he studied, until at the age of twenty-one she publicly announced him ready to assume the role of "Paramount Chief of Swaziland and King of the Swazi nation." In a letter written on her behalf in 1921 to the Resident Commissioner to inform him that she had handed over the reins of government, we read, "This is the day I have always longed for. It has now come at last like a dream which has come true. King Mbandzeni died in October, 1889, thirty-two years ago. As from that day my life has been burdened by an awful responsibility and anxiety. It has been a life full of the deepest emotions that a woman has ever had. Bunu died after only a very short life, leaving me with the responsibility of bringing up his infant son and heir. I rejoice that I now present him to your honor in your capacity as head 'of the administration of Swaziland. He is very young as your honor can see. He shall constantly require my advice. I and the the nation have every confidence in him. I have brought him up as a Swazi prince should be brought up. His spirit is in entire accord with the traditions and feelings and aspirations of his countrymen, and what is more, I have given him the opportunity to obtain the very best training which any native youth can obtain here in South Africa. Sobhuza II gets his name, title and position by the right of inheritance from his ancient house and kings who have ruled over the Swazi nation from time immemorial."

Sobhuza II's first national duty was to contest the concessions in the law courts of the white rulers. A special court of Swaziland gave judgment against him. In 1922 the nation sent him to appeal to the Privy Council in London. He was accompanied on this mission by a few illiterate elders, his private medicine man, an English-trained Zulu advocate, and a representative of the Swaziland administration. The Swazi nation lost the appeal on a technicality. In his judgment Viscount Haldane stated "this method of peacefully extending British Dominion may well be as little generally understood, as it is, where it can operate, in law unquestionable." The Swazii did not understand, but had to accept.

Though much of Swazi history is unique, the general outline for the past seventy-five years has been set by the wider economic and political interests of colonialism. Modern Swaziland is the meeting ground of two separate policies, that of the adjacent Republic of South Africa and that expressed by the British Colonial Office. The South African policy of *apartheid* is openly dedicated to the maintenance of white domination; the British proclaim the priority of African interests in their own territory. Provision has existed since 1910 for the transfer of Swaziland to South Africa, and the local Swaziland administration has been strongly influenced by economic pressure from the Republic and by the presence in the country of white settlers who have the colonial attitude towards the "natives."

Within the framework of white domination, a distinctive Swazi way of life persists. The imposition of the colonial system does not automatically eliminate an existing system of kinship or kingship. On the one hand, opportunities and inducements to change have been restricted by the whites; on the other, a conservative monarchy has attempted to resist the loss of its tradition-based identity.

White Swazilanders to whom I spoke in 1961 considered that the position of the Swazi had "improved considerably" in the postwar years. They mentioned development in communication, agriculture, mining, and industry and increasing investments in education, health, and welfare. Superficially, indeed, it seemed that the Swazi were better off and more Westernized. Nearly all the men and women wore Western dress, few were in traditional clothing or in ragged castoffs, a common sight in the urban areas two decades ago. At Lobamba the administration had installed a new office and taps for (cold) water. More families owned beds, chairs, and sewing machines and several had battery-powered radios.

But what of the attitude to the bearers of these gifts? Swazi appeared to show no corresponding increase in good will. There was less superficial courtesy and more openly expressed criticism. Very few gave the customary greeting and the open acknowledgement "we see you," accompanied by the hand raised in salutation, a greeting which before had been extended to anybody, white or black, along the roadside. Old friends who felt they could speak freely complained that the whites still held most of the good jobs, even though some of their own people were equally qualified. Although the administration, acting on instructions from England, was trying to hammer out a new political constitution, a section of the Swazi were becoming politically more aggressive (or progressive?) and anti-white.

The implication of the Swaziland situation is clear: economic aid alone, given without understanding of the society, may create greater antagonism than friendship and more destruction than construction. Effective control of the reaction of the people requires a knowledge of their past as well as present society and a recognition of what the people themselves want for their own future. Change is a process that may take a number of different directions; the anthropologist can offer no single formula for progress and must recognize that "happiness" is the most elusive of evaluations.

2

Kinship and Locality

Clan, Lineage, and Family

IN THE PREVIOUS CHAPTER we observed the historical process whereby people of different clans were welded into a centralized state, a political unit, by a conquering Nguni aristocracy. In this chapter we shall consider the working of the kinship system. In most small-scale personal societies, kinship by descent and ties by marriage influence behavior in a great number of situations; they determine where and with whom a person lives, his range of friends and enemies, whom he may or may not marry, the positions to which he is entitled.

The clan is the furthest extension of kinship, and when two Swazi meet for the first time they soon ask, "What is your *sibongo* (clan praise name)?" This is a major initial identification. Every Swazi acquires by birth his father's clanname, even if his mother is not legally married and her child is cared for by her own people. Women retain their paternal clan name on marriage but may never transmit it to their children.

Swazi clanship regulates marriage and, to some extent, political status. I will deal with the political aspects first, as I have already indicated that a centralized monarchy replaced the heads of autonomous clans. In the process of centralization, members of the royal clan spread throughout the territory and most clans are no longer distinct local groups.

Clans are graded roughly according to the relationship they have with the kingship and the position their members hold in the state. At the apex is the Nkosi Dlamini, in which the lineage of the king is pre-eminent and the closer the blood ties with kings, the higher the status of individuals; next in rank come clans described as "Bearers of Kings," that is, clans that have provided queen mothers who were as a rule chosen because they were the daughters of powerful chiefs. Third in rank are clans with their own local areas and hereditary chiefs, which have not yet provided queen mothers. Slightly below them are clans from which officials are selected for special ritual or administrative functions, and finally come clans with no coordinating clan ceremonies, no local centers, and no recognized national representatives.

The grading of clans is neither as precise nor as static as a caste system. Grading does not depend on differences of custom or occupation and is not maintained by endogamy (in-group marriage) nor sanctioned by the concept of ritual pollution. On the contrary, differences of customs are tolerated, there is no clan specialization of occupation, exogamy is the rule, and interclan contact is free and intimate. But the upper limits of promotion are set by the royal Dlamini clan.

Clanship is of primary importance in regulating marriage and succession. Marriage with a person of one's own clan is prohibited except for the king, the only man permitted to marry a clan sister. Inbreeding to the point of incest is a royal prerogative in many aristocratic societies; among the Swazi, incest between the king and a sister is both openly hinted at and condemned in one of the most moving of the sacred songs sung at the annual ceremony of kingship. At the same time, clan exogamy is recognized as an effective way of extending and creating social ties, and the king is expected to unify and centralize his position by taking women from all sections of his people. When he marries a clan sister, her father is automatically removed from the royal Nkosi Dlamini clan, and becomes the founder of a separate subclan. This also limits the number of Dlamini; a nobility always tries to maintain itself as an exclusive minority.

Subdivision of clans is a widespread process, dating from the early period of migration when brothers hived off, each with his own small group of followers who identified themselves through the name of their new leader or with an incident in their more recent history. The link between them and the parent, clan is retained in additional praise names (*sinanatelo*), and intermarriage is prohibited. Only among the Nkosi Dlamini do we find the deliberate creation of separate subclans for the purpose of intermarriage, but the king's clan sister will never be selected as his main wife; the future queen mother is always chosen from an outside clan.

Each clan contains a number of lineages in which direct descent can be genealogically traced over three to eight generations. Swazi lineages define legal rights and claims to various state positions, but do not provide the framework for the political structure as they do in certain segmentary societies, which have no centralised rulers. Kinship reinforces local ties but the two are not identical. Evidence of an original local basis to the clan and the lineage is found in the changing meaning of the word *sifunza*. In reply to the question "What is your *sifunza?*" Swazi usually give the *sibongo* (clan praise name), but when asked "Who is the chief of your *sifunza?*" they generally name their political chief, though his *sibongo* is different from their own, or they give the name of the man they consider the direct successor of the founder of their clan, even though he lives in another locality.

Swazi clan and lineage structure emphasizes the agnatic* kin as distinct

---

* Agnatic (noun agnates) is kinship through the male line only; sometimes termed patrilateral.

from the elementary family, in which relationship with both parents is recognised. However, kinship always involves some theory of descent, some explanation of conception. Certain matrilineal societies deny the physical role of the male, and interpret birth as the result of a sort of immaculate conception, or impregnation by a clan "spirit" or totem. This is not the case with the Swazi, who stress the physiological link between father and offspring and state emphatically that a child is "one blood with its father and its mother." The king in particular must have in his body "the blood" of kingship through the male line. The biological tie between father and child must be confirmed by law and ritual, for the physiological father (genitor) is not automatically the sociological father (pater).

Rights of fatherhood are acquired through *lobola,* the transfer of valuables, especially cattle, from the family of the man to that of the woman. If no *lobola* has been given or promised, the child remains with the woman's family while she, herself, may be separated from her offspring and given in marriage to a man other than the genitor. But the child retains the clan name of the genitor, the physiological father, who may among the Swazi—but not in neighboring tribes—*lobola* his offspring, even if he rejects its mother.

When a Swazi woman is in labor, she is asked the clan name of the baby's genitor. If she is not married she gives the name of her lover and the matter is fairly straightforward—either he gives *lobola* and takes her and/or the child, or the child remains with her parents and she is married elsewhere. But if the woman is married and she knows that the begetter of her child is not her legal husband, she must still confess. Otherwise it is believed that birth will be hard and may even prove fatal, for the child belongs "by blood" to the clan of the genitor, but by law to the man who gave the marriage cattle. Adultery by a woman was formerly punishable by death of both guilty partners, partly because it was a violation of the husband's basic rights over his wife, and partly because it was a threat to his group to "mix the clan names" through a woman acquired by the group.

The most important daily interaction takes place in the family environment of the homestead, where children are born and cared for, play and learn, and adults lead their private lives. The structure of the homestead is more flexible than that of clan or lineage and its composition fluctuates with births and marriages, deaths and migrations. Swazi distinguish between kinship ties and homestead ties. The homestead is an area of common living, and though ties of kinship and membership in a homestead usually reinforce each other, kinsmen trace connections through blood or marriage.

In control of the homestead is the patriarchal headman (*umnumzana*), whose prestige is enhanced by the size of his family and the number of other dependents. A conservative homestead may include the headman, his wives, his unmarried brothers and sisters, married sons with their wives and children, and unmarried sons and daughters, as well as more distant relatives. Among all southern Bantu, polygyny is regarded as a social ideal rather than a sexual extravagance, and because of the importance of payment of *lobola,* only the aris-

tocrats and wealthy (and often elderly) commoners are able to achieve many
wives. The king has the royal prerogative to take by force (*qoma*) girls he
desires who are not yet betrothed, but he must exercise his privilege with some
restraint. In 1936, Sobhuza, then thirty-five years old, had some forty wives;
by 1961 he had married eight additional women. Girls chosen by the king are
publicly recognized as future queens with political potential. Many wives are
primarily symbols of status, and their children build up the lineage of the father
and the size and influence of his homestead.

The Homestead Plan

The homestead is built according to a definite plan that reflects the
main interests of the occupants and their status relationships. In the center is
a heavily palisaded, unroofed cattle pen, and, if the lay of the land permits, its
main gateway should face the rising sun, a symbol in family and national ritual.
Men and boys have free access to the cattle byre but women may only enter on
special occasions. Dug into the cattle byre are deep flask-shaped pits for storing
the best grain from the fields. Informants state that the pits were devised in the
days of tribal warfare to hide food from the enemy, and the fenced cattle byre
served also as a stockade against attack. At present, siting the main granaries
in the byre enables the headman to keep some check on the food supplies used
by the wives.

The king's homestead follows the same basic principle as that of any
established polygynist but is on a larger scale and has a greater elaboration of
ritual symbols. The enormous cattle byre at the state capital is the meeting
place of all the people, and at the upper end is a sanctuary where the king is periodically "doctored." This doctoring insures his status—it bestows on him the
requisite personality, described by the word "shadow," and the ingredients required for the king are more potent (and secret) than those permitted to any
subject.

Grouped round the western end of the byre are the living quarters.
Among many southern Bantu there is a rigid placement of wives in order of rank,
but this is not the case among the Swazi. The only fixed point is the main enclosure with the "great hut" (*indlunkulu*) under the charge of the mother of the
headman, or, if she is dead, of a sister co-wife, or, in special cases, a wife who
is then raised to the status of "mother." The "great hut," often decorated with
skulls of cattle sacrificed to the headman's ancestors, is used as the family shrine:
in the rear, the headman offers libations of beer and meat. Places and things that
are sacred must not be approached by any person who is considered ritually "unclean"; among the Swazi, menstruating women, people in mourning, and
adults "hot" from sexual intercourse are never allowed to enter the *indlunkulu*.
The shrine is specifically dedicated to the headman's senior paternal relatives,
a category of kin towards whom younger female in-laws in particular must show
stereotyped respect. In some of the more conservative homes, the wives of the

headman make a detour to avoid passing in front of the doorway, or they deliberately avert their eyes and drop their voices when they approach. Though they may not enter the sacred hut, they are made conscious of its presence and of their own exclusion each time they gather in the yard of the "mother" (their mother-in-law) to perform common chores and discuss domestic routine. While daughters-in-law must avoid the "great hut" out of respect, their children may even sleep in it, entrenching the legal and religious distinction that is drawn between the patrilineal in-group and the women brought in from outside. The "great hut" at the capital, a magnificent structure, is periodically repaired by materials contributed by tribal labor and retains in its framework ropes and mats handed down from one reign to another. Inside, hidden by a reed screen, are sacred relics, including types of grain no longer grown; the huge dome is supported on heavy poles of ritually treated wood, and above the doorway are tiny holes through which the king spits in times of special celebration, symbolically radiating creative essence. Here, he and his mother speak to the royal ancestors on behalf of their subjects and perform the rites to bring rain.

Distinct from the huts of the "mother" are the quarters of the wives. In ordinary large homesteads, after a period of service to her mother-in-law each wife is given her separate sleeping, cooking, and store huts, which are shut off from the public by a high reed fence. Within her enclosure, spoken of as "the hut of so-and-so," she leads a certain private existence with her own children, who, although legally bound to the patri-kin and an integral part of the wider homestead, are emotionally most closely identified with their own mother whom they describe as "the mother who bore me." She is also allotted her own fields, and, if possible, cattle for her use, so that her "hut" is a semi-independent social and economic unit. Legal and ritual restrictions on a woman's rights are to some extent compensated for by the recognition of her economic and personal importance. A conservative headman uses his mother's hut as his daytime base and is expected to divide his nights equally between the wives. A modern headman generally has his own hut, to which he calls the women when he desires them. Among the co-wives there is frequently jealousy for which the Swazi, as other southeastern Bantu, have a special term—*ubukhwele*.

The arrangement of "huts" of the different wives facilitates the subdivision of a polygynous homestead. A headman may establish a smaller homestead for one or more wives, especially if they have grown sons, in order to obtain a wider choice of garden land, or to prevent friction between the women or (and this applies particularly to chiefs), to extend political influence. The mother's enclosure, with the "great hut," remains the main homestead, the place of ritual.

The king's wives are distributed at several royal homesteads that are strategically placed throughout the country. At the capital they live in a communal enclosure with a single narrow gateway in the high surrounding reed fence; instead of each wife having her own huts, a number of senior queens share their huts with attached junior co-wives. At the entrance of the royal harem is a hut associated with the king's marriage to his first two official wives—"the wipers away of his boyhood dirt." Like the shrine hut, this hut has been transformed from a profane to a sacred building by elaborate ritual, and it is also used as a guardroom by a trusted man especially appointed to look after the queens. The king has a personal sleeping hut deep in the harem, to which he summons his queens when he visits the capital.

Special sleeping arrangements are made for children in the homestead to conform with the expressed norm that the sex life of brothers and sisters and of parents and children must be kept separate. Young children sleep with the grandmother. Adolescent girls move into huts behind their own mothers and their brothers build barracks at the entrance of the homestead. A room of one's own is considered antisocial, and unattached individuals are always accommodated with people of their own age and sex. At the capital, the majority of the population consists of unrelated dependents who live in a double row of huts surrounding the quarters of the queen mother and of the queens. The inner row is occupied by men of rank and special office, the outer mainly by ordinary subjects who pay allegiance direct to royalty. Protecting all the civilians of the capital are men permanently stationed in regimental barracks.

Homesteads are so closely identified physically and spiritually with the occupants that the idea of selling or renting to strangers is new and repugnant to traditionalists. When a headman dies, he is buried at the entrance to the cattle byre. After a lengthy period of mourning the old site is abandoned, but the family home is revived (literally "awakened") in the vicinity by the main heir, whose duty it is to perpetuate the patrilineage. The old huts, apart from the death hut, are physically transferred to the new site and the spirit of the deceased is brought to the new family shrine. The old site, with its beacon of gravestones, becomes a treasured and fertile field for cultivating crops, which the new headman and his mother will disperse in hospitality.

Here is one example from the homestead of the late Prince Ndabankuku, an important chief in the south of Swaziland. In 1936, he had ten wives, six of whom were in his main homestead, Ehletsheni ("The Place of Whispers"), three at Mpisamandla ("Strength of the Enemy") and two at Enkungwini ("In the Mist"). Ndabankulu's mother was dead, but a co-wife of his father was in charge of the great hut. The women at Mpisamandla included Ndabankulu's first wife and her married son, but all important occasions were commemorated at Ehletsheni. Enkungwini was established to "waken" a homestead of Ndabankulu's own father, when one of his (Ndabankulu's) married sons wanted to move from Ehletsheni in order to obtain more land for cultivation. It was considered natural that the boy's own mother, La Simelane, one of Ndabankulu's senior wives, move with her son and daughter-in-law, and that they cultivate the fertile site of an ancestral homestead. Ndabankulu sent with La Simelane a younger wife, a full sister who had been "put into her marriage cattle" and given by the parents as *inhlanti* (junior co-wife) to her older sister. Ndabankulu died a few years ago and I am told that the council chose the senior Simelane sister as his main wife. It will behove her son to send some of his wives to "waken" Ndabankulu's other homesteads should they be left without close members of the family.

The king, in particular, must "waken" the main homesteads of his royal predecessors as well as inaugurate a series of his own. He perpetuates the old homesteads by sending some of his wives to live there, and one of their sons will become the chief prince of the area. In each reign the village of the ruling queen mother is the capital of the state; in relation to it, the king's personal homestead, established after he has taken his first ten queens, is described as the men's quarters or the "barracks."

The search for a site for a new homestead is guided partly by material considerations, the availability of adequate land, water and wood, and partly by social factors. A Swazi seeks friends, preferably kinsmen, as neighbors, and also seeks a chief with a good reputation. Should he find that he has chosen badly—as indicated by the unaccountable failure of crops or the sudden illness of his children, or unnecessarily frequent demands for his service—he will move with his family and his property to a more congenial social environment. Although his physical needs are important, it is even more essential for him to live among people whom he trusts. He does not necessarily sever his connection with the main branch of his kin, and he recognizes the heir as representative of the lineage, with the right to appeal to the ancestors on behalf of all its members.

Throughout Swazi areas, homesteads are said to be decreasing in size, partly because there is no longer the need for physical protection against man and beast and also because new interests, economic and religious, are cutting through the relatively closed and self-sufficient domestic groups of patri-kin. But the homesteads of aristocrats still tend to be larger than those of commoners, and the homesteads of non-Christians larger than those of Christians. In a sample area in the middle veld, the average number of occupants was over twenty-two in the homes of aristocrats and seven in commoners' homes. The largest homestead is obviously the queen mother's; the smallest I saw belonged to a Christian widow, living with two unmarried sons, far from their nearest kin. Such an isolated group, not even a single complete family, is a modern phenomenon. It is unusual, except in urban townships, for an elementary monogamous family to live on its own without contact with kinsmen in nearby homesteads. Similarly, it is only in European employment centers that unattached Swazi live anonymously outside a domestic circle.

Types of Marriage

Swazi marriage is essentially a linking of two families rather than of two persons, and the bearing of children is the essential consummation of wifehood. Swazi marriage is of so enduring a nature that should the man himself die, the woman is inherited through the custom of the levirate by one of the male relatives of the deceased to raise children in his name. Similarly, since the production of children is the essential fulfillment of the woman's part of the contract, should she prove barren her family must either return the cattle or, following the custom of the sororate, provide her with a relative, preferably a younger full sister, as junior co-wife to bear children to "put into her womb." For the second woman, no extra *lobola* need be given.

Divorce is rare in Swazi society and it is particularly difficult for a woman to be legally permitted to marry a second time. The reason for this is not to be sought in the amount of *lobola* but in the institutional complex of patrilocal marriage and the power of the patrilineage expressed through such customs as the levirate and sororate. High *lobola* is a symbol, not a cause, of the permanence of marriage. The amount of *lobola* varies with the woman's status. Twenty years ago, it ranged from twelve head for a commoner to as many as sixty for an important princess. Several hundred cattle are contributed by representative headmen throughout the country for the woman who is chosen as the main wife of the king.

Lobola is a controversial issue in modern Africa. Uninformed administrators and missionaries regarded it initially as "the buying and selling of women" and attempted to abolish it by law, but the tenacity with which Africans, including Christians, have retained the custom has led to a reinterpretation of it at a deeper sociological level. *Lobola* is generally translated as "bride price," but it is clear that a woman is not regarded as a commodity by the people involved. On the contrary, she is a valued member of the community, and her past status and future security are symbolized in the transaction. By giving *lobola,* her children are made legitimate and become entitled to the benefits of the father's lineage; by accepting *lobola,* her people are compensated for the loss of her services. Their emotional ties and ritual obligations towards her do not cease, and should she be ill-treated or find herself and her children destitute, she may appeal to the recipients of the cattle, who will be legally, as well as morally, obliged to assist her. The husband does not acquire a chattel, but a wife for himself and a mother for his children, and he and his kin owe her definite obligations of support and protection. In urban areas of southern Africa, money is being substituted for cattle; the mercenary aspect of the negotiations is being exploited by some unscrupulous parents who marry their daughter to the highest bidder and who, because they are remote from the extended kin, do not fulfill their traditional parental obligations. But even many educated urban women are not prepared to be married without the passing of token *lobola* in addition to Christian and civil marriage rites.

Swazi practice several types of marriage, and these are important in determining succession and inheritance in polygynous families. Selection of the successor, who is also the main heir, depends on the rank of the women in the harem. Among the Swazi aristocracy the first wife is never the main wife. Seniority in marriage brings certain advantages during the headman's lifetime, but upon his death other factors are considered. The most important is pedigree, and the daughter of a king or leading chief generally takes precedence over all other wives. There are also marriages with specific kin, of which the most important in Swaziland is marriage to a woman who has the clan name of the man's own paternal or maternal grandmother. The reasons for this will appear later.

These so-called "preferential marriages" are generally arranged by the parents, and arranged marriages, which are not necessarily forced marriages, always bestow a higher status than those based solely on individual choice. Swazi, however, recognize the power of personal attachment, and if a man informs his parents that he wishes to marry a particular girl, they may willingly send a representative "to beg a fire" from her people. Should they agree, the full marriage ceremony is performed, and her character may win her recognition as the main wife. The woman who has least chance of being selected is one who "makes love for herself" and runs to the man's home against her parents' will. Though the man's group claims her openly as a daughter-in-law, she is at a disadvantage because of the fact that her family opposed the marriage. If they did not accept any *lobola,* she may be given as wife to another man. Sometimes a grown son gives *lobola* for his own mother in order to legalize his status in the wider patrilineage.

The traditional marriage ceremony dramatizes an underlying tension between the two intermarrying groups and the necessity to create certain permanent bonds between them. Throughout the elaborate and formal series of rituals, the woman's family must display its reluctance at losing her. Her mother weeps and tells her to behave with restraint in the husband's home though she be subject to unaccustomed restrictions and accusations, and her father asks the ancestors to protect and bless her in the midst of her in-laws. She leaves her home accompanied by a group of supporters, including "brothers" and responsible elders appointed by the parents, who remain behind. The man's group receives the bridal party with warmth and friendliness, but the girl must neither smile nor respond. In one of the most dramatic moments of the ritual, she stands in the cattle byre of her husband and mourns in song the loss of her girlhood freedom and cries to her "brothers" to come and rescue her from her fate. They have been hiding and rush to her assistance in a demonstration of family loyalty and unity. In a mock battle carried out with much apparent fierceness, they rush off with her in their midst. But the girl knows, and they know, that she must finally accept the role of woman as wife and mother, and she returns when her future mother-in-law calls her back with a promise of a cow. Later she is smeared with red clay, signifying the loss of her virginity, and a child from her husband's group is placed in her lap as a promise of future motherhood. In the end, she ceremonially distributes gifts of blankets, mats, and brooms, brought from her home to the various in-laws whose favor is so necessary for her future happiness.

The marriage ceremony, which lasts several days, culminates in a feast at which an ox provided by the groom's group is divided, each family receiving half. When the bride's group returns, they leave with her a young girl to ease her initial loneliness, and the new wife is gradually introduced to the responsibilities of her new status. The following winter the groom's people bring the cattle for her marriage; her people pretend to drive the cattle back, but after this mock demonstration they make the "in-laws" welcome and may ever promise to send a second daughter as a junior co-wife. Once the bride has borne her first child, she is more often called "mother of so-and-so" than by her own distinctive clan name.

Basic Behavior Patterns

It is in the homestead that the main members of the Swazi family, husband and wife, parent and children, grandparents and grandchildren, brothers and sisters play out their roles in dynamic interpersonal relationships. Their behavior is patterned by the mating and kinship system; these—and not any psychological quality per se—account for the differences in the behavior prescribed for a Swazi father or mother and a father or mother in other societies.

Swazi classify kin into a limited number of broad categories, embracing with a single term relatives who, in more specialized and isolating societies, are kept distinct. Thus, the term "father" is extended from one's own father to his brothers, half brothers, and sons of his father's brothers. Similarly "mother" embraces his own mother, her sisters, her co-wives, and wives of his father's brothers. The children of these "fathers" and "mothers" are his "brothers" and "sisters," and their children are grouped in the same category as his own grandchildren. The use of a common term does not mean that a particular key relationship is unimportant. Indeed, within the category there are usually accurate descriptions of degrees of closeness. "The father who bore me" is distinguished from "my big father" (my father's older brother) or "my little father" (father's younger brother), but one's behavior towards all "fathers" is modeled on a single pattern.

A Swazi soon learns to separate in word and action the relatives of the father from those of the mother. They are two distinct legal groups, and so strong is the identification through one or the other parent that the word for father's sister is literally "female father," and the mother's brother is "male mother." Towards the "female father," a Swazi behaves with the respect and obedience associated with the word "father," and towards the "male mother" with the affection and familiarity evoked by "mother." The children of my "female father" and "male mother" are included in a single term, which can be translated as "cousins," and they are treated in a different way from "brothers" and "sisters." Each kinship term is thus like a mnemonic, reminding the person with whom he or she may sleep, eat, or joke, who must be respected and who avoided.

Implicit in the system of terminology is the assumption that kinsmen covered by a single term share a common social identity and, in some situations, can serve adequately as substitutes for each other in case of need, an assumption tenable only in societies where specialization is limited and where greater importance is attached to the kinship group than to the individual. This is the reality behind such customs as the levirate, in which brothers are regarded as equivalents, and the sororate, in which sisters may replace each other to fulfill specific wifely functions.

No equality is expected or desired between Swazi husband and wife. He is the male, superior in strength and law, entitled to beat her and to take other women. She must defer to him and treat him with respect. But a Swazi woman is not an abject and timid creature; she claims her rights as "a person" as well as "a wife." Should her husband maltreat her severely, she has no hesitation in berating him and, if necessary, running off to her people; she may, and very occasionally does, lay a charge against him before the "white man's court." Her people generally send her back for they are not prepared to return the marriage cattle, but they do inflict a fine on the husband for his offense. His behavior is also largely controlled by the constant supervision of his senior kinsmen, who are interested in the security and extension of their lineage, and by the pressure of his own mother, who depends on the services of her daughters-in-law. There is generally severe censure by a woman's kin as well as by her in-laws if she complains to the alien law of the whites.

An outstanding feature of Swazi kinship is the father's authority over his children. The term "father" is associated with someone who is both feared and respected. The headman is the "father" of the homestead. The king is the "father" of the country. The most direct and permanent power is wielded by a father over his own sons, who are legally minors even after marriage, until they establish separate homesteads, and formerly could not marry unless he provided the cattle for their wives.

Swazi men may never treat their sons as equals, even if they should wish to do so. Between father and son there is a conflict of institutionalized interests. A son is consciously recognized as a potential threat to the father's position, though, at the same time, he is necessary to perpetuate the father's name in the ancestral cult. Perhaps their relationship contains an element of the classical Oedipus complex, the unconscious rivalry for the woman as mother and as wife. The complicated rules of succession attempt to regulate the conflicting interests of father and son. The first son of a polygynous home is never the main heir. He is his father's confidant and helps him maintain authority. His mother takes precedence over later wives in such matters as distribution of food, but her son should never be allowed to challenge the father's position or to replace him. In polygynous families the heir is never publicly appointed until the father is dead. Conflict between the father's and son's generations impinges at the deepest levels—sex and life itself—and in many patrilineal societies there are institutional devices for minimizing contact. Among the Swazi, married sons are expected to live in the homestead of the father, but between the sons' wives and their father-in-law there is the strictest avoidance. They must not look each other in the face or use each other's names, and the women must use a special language of "respect" in order not to mouth any word with the name or even with the main syllable of the name of the father-in-law or of other senior male in-laws.

The legal authority of the father is in contrast to the more indulgent relationship with the mother, for whom Swazi men express affection and appreciation, as well as respect. A well-known riddle runs, "If your mother and wife were drowning, which one would you save?" The right answer is, "My mother. I can get another wife but not another mother." Swazi say, "The desires of men are satisfied by women but the satisfaction of women comes through their children."

In this patrilineal patriarchal society, there is even less personal intimacy between a father and his daughters than between him and his sons. Not only are they separated by sex and age, but a daughter leaves the home upon marriage and produces children for another lineage. The legal and economic aspects dominate the father's behavior, whereas the mother, herself an outsider, is said to "feel for," and to "share the sadness" of the girl and is expected to intercede on her behalf, both before and after marriage. In recognition of the mother's services, the family that is benefiting by her daughter sends with the *lobola* cattle a special beast known as "the wiper away of tears." This is the mother's private property; it is given for each daughter and is inherited by the mother's youngest son, a stereotyped darling.

Behavior between siblings, as this last point illustrates, is influenced by seniority and sex. Older siblings take precedence over younger, males take precedence over females. This is shown in the laws of inheritance. The main heir, who is always a male, inherits the bulk of the family property, including the cattle attached to the great hut, but the eldest son of each independent wife takes the *lobola* of his own sisters—except for the animals which belong to the youngest brother. Middle sons may inherit nothing, but they must be helped with marriage cattle before their juniors. The marked inequality of inheritance frequently causes rivalry between brothers and half brothers. Girls, who can never inherit family property, are less directly involved in family disputes. Swazi men have nothing to fear from their sisters and much to gain from them. It is their cattle that enable the boys to obtain their own wives; hence, when a sister visits her married brother, she must be treated as a most privileged guest and must be waited on by his wife, her sister-in-law, whose possessions she may use freely. The brother's children are told to fear this woman, the "female father," more than their own mother.

In addition to parents and siblings, grandparents are also integrated into the intimate world of the Swazi child. They teach the young to respect their parents, but their techniques are proverbially more lenient. Grandparents "scold by the mouth," parents "more often with a stick." Because marriage is patrilocal, children frequently grow up in the homes of the paternal grandparents, but, especially in cases of illness or tensions, children may be sent to stay for long periods with the mother's people. Lineage obligatons are reinforced by the paternal grandfather, the man whom the father himself must obey, while emotional protection is expected from the maternal grandparents who express their interest in the daughter's child, described as the "child of the calf," by a series of ceremonial gifts.

The conflict inherent in the parent-child generations is absent between grandparent and grandchild. Grandfather and grandson are, in fact, recognized as allies with mutual interests in curbing an overambitious and authoritarian individual, the son of the former, the father of the latter. Grandson and grandfather are culturally removed from sexual conflict, and the grandson is, to some extent, identified with his grandfather and given authority to regenerate him. This, Swazi say, is the reason that a marriage between a man and a woman of the clan of his grandmother is considered desirable.

We have already indicated that behavior between blood kin is different from behavior between in-laws. Patrilocal marriage separates a man from his wife's relatives, who live in their own homestead; but towards his senior in-laws, particularly his mother-in-law, he must show respect and avoidance, comparable to restrictions imposed on his own wife towards his senior male relatives. He may not eat, swear, or relax physically in the presence of his mother-in-law; but, being a male, he has certain privileges denied to a woman, and he is not restricted in language and movements to the same extent. On the rare occasions when he visits the village of his in-laws, he is treated as a distinguished guest and provided with all possible delicacies.

Behavior towards other members of the in-law group depends largely on whether they will be prohibited from marriage or permitted to marry. Thus, in sharp contrast to the avoidance enjoined between a man and his mother-in-law or his wife's brothers' wives, who are potential mothers-in-law, is the familiarity demanded of him toward his wife's sisters. Swazi say that the love between sisters overcomes the jealousy between co-wives; to take a wife's sister as a junior wife is provided for in the marriage ceremony itself.

In traditional Swazi society, kinsmen provide an ever-increasing network of social relationships, and in different situations people behave in stereotyped ways set by ties of blood or marriage. In the urban areas, where Swazi are isolated from the wider circle of kinsmen, they are still intensely aware of the need for people of "one blood" to assist in such crises as illness, accidents, or funerals. Clan brothers may then become substitutes for real brothers, and fictional kinship may be built up with people who come from the same neighborhood. The specialized interests that form the basis of association in more complex societies are still few in Swaziland, and it is mainly relatives who cooperate in work, ritual and government.

3

Political Structure

THE SWAZI were not conquered by force, and though the functions of traditional authorities were changed, the political system with its network of kinship was ostensibly allowed to continue under the British administration. It is only in very recent years that a deliberate effort has been made to integrate the dual monarchy into a Western democratic framework and to develop a single government for the entire territory of Swaziland.

The traditional statuses of the king and queen mother remain conspicuous in their daily routine. Both receive elaborate deference: their subjects crouch when addressing them and punctuate royal speeches with flattering titles. He is "The Lion," "The Sun," "The Milky Way," "Obstacle to The Enemy." She is "The Lady Elephant," "The Earth," "The Beautiful," "Mother of the Country," and so forth. Compared with them, the highest tribal officials liken themselves to "stars" and "ant heaps," and the average commoner speaks of himself disparagingly as "a dog," "a stick," "a nothing." The rulers are always accompanied by attendants and are set apart by unique regalia. The queen mother wears a crown of dark-brown wooden pegs, topped with a bright red feather of the flamingo, the rain bird, set between two lucky beans; around her ankles and wrists are tied small pouches of animal skins containing royal medicines. The king has less conspicuous insignia, except on special occasions when he appears in dazzling and startling robes. Both are regularly treated with "the medicines of kingship" to give them "shadow," (personality). The well-being of the nation is associated with the king's strength and virility, and he must neither see nor touch a corpse, nor approach a grave or a mourner. The major episodes in his life—birth, installation, marriage—are heaviliy ritualized. Death ceremonies, which always reflect the social status of the deceased, vary from the insignificant burial accorded the child of a commoner to the elaborate state funerals of rulers. The king, and the king alone, is embalmed by a primitive method known only to a clan that "broke off" with the Dlamini at the original home, the "Place of Burning."

The traditional Swazi constitution is complex, and, in some respects, extremely subtle. Superficially, all powers—legislative, executive, administrative, and religious—center in the *ingwenyama* and *indlovukati,* but tyrannical exercise of their powers is restrained by their own relationship, by a hierarchy of officials whose positions depend on maintaining kingship rather than on supporting a particular king, by a developed system of local government, by councils of state, and by the pressure of subjects who formerly could transfer their military strength and support to rivals. Among the neighboring and more military Zulu, hereditary succession was tempered with assassination. The structure of Swazi kingship restrained despotism.

The first check on the abuse of power and privilege by rulers is contained in the dual monarchy itself. The king owes his position to a woman whose rank —more than his own personal qualities—determined his selection for kingship, and between the two rulers there is a delicate balance of power. He presides over the highest court, and, formerly, he alone could sanction the death sentence, meted out for witchcraft and treason, but she is in charge of the second highest court and the shrine hut in her homestead is a sanctuary for people appealing for protection. He controls the age regiments, but the commander in chief presides at the capital. He has power to distribute land in the "native area," but together they work the rain magic that fructifies it. Sacred national objects are in her charge, but are not effective without his cooperation. He is associated with "hardness," expressed in thunder, she with the "softness" of water. He represents the line of past kings and speaks to the dead in the shrine hut of the capital; she provides the beer for the libations. He is revitalized in the annual ritual of kingship, which is held at her home. He is entitled to use cattle from the royal herds, but she may rebuke him publicly if he wastes national wealth. In short, they are expected to assist and advise each other in all activities and to complement each other. In the past, when the nation was more homogeneous and both rulers were "illiterate," their duties were evenly distributed, but today the king is educated and shoulders more of the administrative responsibilities, letting the burden of ritual fall primarily on the queen mother.

Conflict between the king and queen mother has always been recognized as a potential menace to national security and well-being, and certain rules, not always obeyed, have been formulated over the years in an attempt to minimize tension. Temperamental differences are appreciated in a society built on a personal kinship basis, and as the king is chosen by virtue of his mother's rank, there is a possibility that she might favor another son more than the heir. To avoid this, the rule for royalty states "A king is not followed by blood brothers," that is, the queen mother should have only one son. Once appointed, no matter how young she may be, the queen mother is prohibited from bearing additional children; and when her husband dies, she is excluded from the custom of the levirate that applies to all other widows. Direct conflict is also avoided by the compulsory spatial separation of the king's village from the capital. The queen mother is not allowed to move far from the national shrine, and she may spend weeks without a visit from the king. Diplomatic intermediaries carry messages between them, eliminating friction that might be engendered by face-to-face arguments.

Swazi assert, "A king dies young." His mother is expected to train her successor and hand over power when the new king reaches maturity. According to Swazi idiom, "The pumpkin plant lasts beyond the fruit"; that is, the queen mother outlives the king. In the present reign, this did not happen. Sobhuza has lived longer than most Swazi kings. His own mother, Lomawa, died in 1942 and was replaced by Nukwase, her full sister and co-wife. When Nukwase died, the tribe was in a dilemma, and the councilors finally appointed one of Sobhuza's own senior wives from the same clan as the two deceased "mothers." This woman is now called "mother," and is removed from all wifely relationship with him. Every society must adapt to the unexpected; it does not simply cease to function because of unforseen difficulties.

In the previous chapter, we showed that the elaborate system of succession was partly a means of protecting a man against the competition of his sons. The first son of a king is never his successor, and if he marries a woman of such high rank that she will obviously be the main wife, he only takes her when he is well on in years. Guardianship, as a means of transferring power from one generation to the next, is institutionalized at the national level in the regency.

Rulers maintain their position by delegating authority to trusted officials, related and nonrelated. Nepotism, the granting of privileges to kinsmen, is an accepted principle in Swazi government, and power radiates from the king to other members of the royal lineage, who are described as "children of the sun," "eggs of the country." The more important princes are sent to districts as chiefs and serve as members of the inner council of the state. They are expected to build up the prestige of the monarchy, to report significant rumors of dissension, and to see that subjects respond to summons to national services. But Swazi history repeats a tale familiar from the cycle of English kings: where hereditary monarchy is the accepted political system, the royal lineage itself provides rivals for kingship. Important princes should never settle too near the king and their ambition should be satisfied by granting them limited local autonomy. In Swazi idiom, "There is only one king." Not only should he have no full brother, but, in this polygynous society, he must be wary of half brothers by other wives of his late father. The princes may never enter the enclosure of the king's wives, may never touch his clothing, eat from his dishes, or use the "medicines of kingship." Their relationship with him is thus essentially ambivalent. On the one hand, it is in their interest to build up the Dlamini kingship, and on the other, to prevent the king from becoming too powerful. His senior male relatives, particularly his uncles and older half brothers, are among his main advisors and supporters, and also his most outspoken critics.

Protecting the king from royal rivals and other enemies are ritually created blood brothers known as *tinsila*, (literally, "body dirt" or "sweat"). The *tinsila* are always drawn from specific nonroyal clans. The first two *tinsila*, the most important, are roughly the same age as the king, and are chosen soon after his appointment so that they may participate with him in the ordeal of puberty, in the first marriage, and other rituals marking his growth in status. Some of the king's blood, together with special magical substances, is rubbed into incisions made on the bodies of these two men, and blood from their bodies is similarly transferred to him. Thereafter, these *tinsila*, who are also metaphorically described as the king's "twins," may touch his person, wear his clothes, and even eat from his dish. The two senior *tinsila* are called "father" by the people, including the princes, who may appeal to them to intercede with the king in personal difficulties.

"Blood brotherhood" is widespread in Africa but need not be symbolized by actual blood transfusion. It is frequently accompanied by acts of commensality and oaths of mutual help. Among the Swazi the medicated blood is sufficient, but the relationship it creates is not symmetrical: the *tinsila* benefit the king more than the king the *tinsila*. Swazi believe that any attack by evildoers against the king will be deflected by the *tinsila*, whose bodies serve as his "shield." He runs less risk of being endangered by their enemies because their position is less coveted. Yet, so close is the identification of the *tinsila* with the king that should they die before him, they are not recognized as sociologically dead, and their widows, who had been selected by the royal council and married with cattle from royal outposts, may not mourn their loss till the king himself dies.

In addition to the first two *tinsila*, a series of junior *tinsila* are appointed at different times to carry out routine and intimate ritual associated with the person of the king. Thus we have a series of individuals, drawn from commoner clans, who are brought into pseudokinship ties with the king to protect him from close physical contact with members of the royal lineage.

The female relatives of the king are political and economic assets and should be judically handled as investments. The more important female relatives (paternal aunts, sisters, and daughters) are given in marriage to foreign rulers and to non-Dlamini chiefs, in whose homes they are recognized as main wives. However, because they live in the homes of their in-laws, they are able to take little active part in the central government.

Although the political structure emphasizes the male agnates of the king, the close relatives of the queen mother also influence national affairs. Her brothers, who are the king's "male mothers," usually receive posts in the central administration, if they do not already hold them, and act as intermediaries for the maternal line in certain situations of crises. On the appointment of a new king, the maternal relatives of his predecessor may lose their direct influence—which is largely due to affection and not demanded by law—but they retain their social prestige and a connection with the princes. The wives of the ruling king are recognized as "mothers of the people," but they lead fairly secluded lives during the lifetime of their husband, though their families constitute his important group of in-laws. The harmony of royal homesteads depends to a great extent on the king's treatment of such relatives and their friendship towards him.

Swazi emphasize that the king's allies are unrelated commoners. A basic principle of Swazi government states, "A king is ruled by *tindvuna*" (councilors).

In each reign there is a *big* (that is, leading) *indvuna* with a special title, translated by educated Swazi as the prime minister, who generally resides at the capital where he hears cases, announces court judgments, advises on the temper of the people, and acts as their representative. The position tends to be hereditary in the senior lineage of a limited number of commoner clans, but the state appointment is not restricted to the main heir. The quality required of *tindvuna* is "respect for people," and though an appointment rests with the king, the big *indvuna* may be dismissed only by the king in council. Through his position, the big *indvuna* obtains so deep an insight into state secrets and so great a hold over national resources that he is drawn into a web of fictional kinship with the ruling clan and treated in some respects as a senior prince, and therefore as one who requires restraint. He is entitled to eat from the dish of princes and is not allowed to marry into the royal clan. His behavior to the queen mother is closely observed, for in the past he sometimes collaborated with princes and with the queen mother against the king, and sometimes with the king against the queen mother. But the big *indvuna* himself can never aspire to kingship: he is without the legitimizing claim of royal blood. Leading councilors have younger officials, also of commoner clans, to assist in the execution of the more physically arduous tasks.

Wisdom in tribal precedence and skill in debate are important qualifications for civil appointments, but the head of the military organization must above all, be able to maintain discipline. Since intertribal warfare has been stopped, the number of military personnel has been limited and civil authorities exercise more authority over the age groups that formerly constituted the regiments. In dealings with whites, Western education is recognized as an asset and young men with this qualification are being appointed to civil posts.

The final group of traditional officials considered essential for national security are the *tinyanga* (specialists in ritual), who are drawn from selected clans and are required to fortify the rulers and the nation as a whole. There is no single high priest or medicine man able to challenge the king whose inherited ritual power is enhanced by the training and knowledge contributed by representatives of several non-Dlamini lineages.

Swazi traditional officials, civil, military, and ritual, normally hold office for life and are only dismissed for treason or witchcraft. Incompetence, habitual drunkenness, stupidity, or weakness of character are criticized, but as long as a man is considered loyal, he retains his post, and the only way to counteract his defects is to appoint capable men as his assistants. No salary is attached to any traditional post, but the men receive sporadic rewards for their service and may make claims on the rulers for certain specific requirements.

In addition to individual officials, two organized traditional councils guide and control the rulers. The inner council (*liqoqo*) is a development of the family council (*lusendvo*) and hence is predominantly aristocratic. Here, senior princes, together with the great councilor, have an opportunity to vent their opinions and direct policy. The number of members is not fixed, and rulers must continue with the *liqoqo* of their predecessors, occasionally adding a member of their own choice. The people have no say in and do not know of these appointments, and it would be indiscreet of them to inquire who the members were or their qualifications. There are no regular sessions and no compulsory reports on activities. The rulers may consult individual members privately, but when an important decision is essential they are expected to summon the full *liqoqo* and abide by its decision.

The second council is the *libandla lakaNgwane* (council of the Ngwane nation), a larger and more representative body that is composed of all chiefs, leading councilors, and headman. Other adult males (not females) are entitled to attend but are not obliged to do so. Chiefs who cannot come in person are supposed to send deputies who act as their "eyes" but may not commit their superiors.

The national council which meets in the cattle byre of the capital, is opened by a spokesman for the *liqoqo*, who tells the people why they have been summoned; otherwise there is little formality—no agenda, no order of speakers, no time limit, no political parties, no vote. Speakers who make good points are applauded, others are heckled and may be told to sit down. There is considerable freedom of speech, and the aim is to reach agreement, not to break up into closed, opposing factions. The sanction of the *libandla* is required on all matters brought to it from the *liqoqo*, but neither council has any specific platform and there is no sharp cleavage of interest between the two. Both developed in a society where communication was slow and life sufficiently unchanging not to require many sessions, new decisions, or trained technicians. It is only in recent years that different occupational groups have arisen to put forward sectional interests and that a radical political minority has advocated a policy influenced by different political concepts.

Local Government

Tribal territory is divided into a number of districts, each of which is organized on principles similar to those underlying the central government. At the head is a chief (*sikhulu*), who is either a prince, a nominee of the king, or a hereditary head of a non-Dlamini clan. In his area, he centralizes law, economics, and ritual; if his mother is alive, she shares with him the responsibilities of control and is in charge of the main section of the homestead. The elaboration on this basic pattern varies with the historical background of each district, and ritual, in particular, is most conspicuous among chiefs who were established because of their own hereditary lineage.

Within each district there is a weighing of power between relatives and nonrelatives of the chief. Paternal kin living in the chief's district provide him with his local and family councils and, in turn, benefit from his position; his *tindvuna* on the other hand, are outsiders and represent the majority of his subjects. There is always a main *indvuna* who attends to law cases and supervises district labor, and minor officials who vary in number with the size of the district and population. Local headmen, some of whom are more active than others, constitute the *libandla* of each chief and may also attend the national council.

The districts are attached to the main royal villages, either directly or indirectly, through *tindvuna* of the royal homesteads. In each case, the arrangement depends on political considerations and not on geographical proximity. Local affiliations are evident in legal disputes, in the granting of land, in the acceptance of new subjects and in the organization of labor. Chiefs who come directly under the king or queen mother may have considerable local autonomy, but their powers over their subjects are restricted by their own officials who can, if necessary, appeal to the rulers for assistance, and who are expected to report subversion. There is no formula in Swaziland comparable to the "destooling" (deposing) of a chief found in West Africa, but a chief who flagrantly abuses his positon may be reported to the king and told "to rest," and another member of the lineage appointed in his place.

Knowledge of the principles involved in government is acquired by every adult male as part of his domestic experience. In the homestead, the smallest local unit recognized in the political structure, the headman exercises towards the occupants rights and obligations comparable on a smaller scale to those of the chief. As their legal head, he is responsible for the torts of the inmates. As trustee-owner of homestead property he controls the distribution of cattle and the allocation of land for cultivation; as councilor he represents his dependents in local politics, and as lineage senior he appeals on their behalf to the family gods. When he considers it necessary he consults senior kinsmen, who constitute his family council.

The relationship between a chief and his subjects, like that between a headman and his dependents, is essentially personal—albeit not intimate. The term "father," extended from the family to the head of the homestead and to the chief of the district, conveys in all these contexts a combination of authority, responsibility, protection, and ritual continuity. The chief is expected to know all the families on his lands and is related to many of them. Every birth, wedding, and death is reported to him. He mourns at the funerals of his subjects and drinks at their feasts. He does not live in a different type of home nor does he attend a different school or church. His power is paternalistic, not despotic.

Swazi political authorities are criticized by their subjects if they are aggressive and domineering. Qualities such as ability in debate, efficiency in organizing work, and knowledge of the law are admired, but they are not considered essential for a chief because it is expected that his councilors will provide them. He is constantly reminded that his prestige depends largely on the number of his followers, and he is aware that they have the right to migrate from his district if he does not fulfill demands that they consider legitimate. On the other hand, his followers realize that existing bonds should not be lightly broken. Before moving elsewhere they must take a formal farewell, thanking their "father" with a substantial gift for benefits they have received. Especially at the present time when land is limited, a chief is careful to investigate newcomers who offer allegiance (*kukhonta*) and may refuse to accept men with bad records.

A subject is not a slave. Formerly in a category different from that of ordinary subjects (*tikhonti*), who offer voluntary allegiance, were *tigcili*—mainly children captured in war. *Tigcili* were taken into the homes of the rulers and leading subjects, who were described as their "owners," but *tigcili* could not be sold or killed. Moreover, there was no barrier to intermarriage, and there is no section of the population today that bears any stigma of "slave descent." *Sigcili,* however, remains a term of contempt, indicating that a person is without the security of a kinship group and has limited independence.

Swazi make no mention of slave raiding in their traditional history, although Arab slavers on the east coast influenced much of African history before the arrival of Europeans. Chattel slavery was part of the economic structure of early white colonists in southern Africa, but it was abolished before the white man settled permanently in Swaziland. The closest existing analogy is the control exercised by white farmers in the Republic over squatters on their land, a control that stops short of the actual selling of a person and is more similar to feudal serfdom. The squatter must perform compulsory service for a set period, and has no freedom of movement. Freedom to move is a primary characteristic of the traditional legal rights of Swazi citizenship.

Law and Justice

Like all southeastern Bantu, the Swazi have a highly developed legal system and a graded hierarchy of courts that coincide roughly with the political structure. Swazi stress the importance of "the law" in regulating social relationships. Private matters ("dirt of the home") are dealt with by the headman, his mother, and his senior male kinsmen; disputes between unrelated people are discussed in the first instance by the family councils of the litigants; if they cannot reach a settlement, the complainant reports to his chief, who sends him with a representative to the chief of the defendant and the case is tried in public. If this court does not settle the matter satisfactorily, either party may appeal to a higher political authority. Certain cases may go direct to the capital, others to the highest tribal court, presided over by the *ingwenyama.* In every court, each man acts as his own advocate and any male present may take an active part in cross-examination and so influence the decision. Precedents are frequently quoted, but the main concern is to unravel the complicated interplay of interests involved in each dispute and arrive at a satisfactory settlement. No oath is administered, but a man may voluntarily swear by the name of a kinsmen or a ruler, and perjury is a recognized offense.

Swazi distinguish between private wrongs, for which compensation must be given to the injured party, and cases "with blood," in which compensation is given to the king as representative of the state. Theft, slander, adultery, and property disputes fall into the first category and are punished with fines; murder and witchcraft belong to the second, and usually carry the death penalty. The death sentence is immediately executed, and the possessions of the deceased confiscated ("eaten up"). An offense against the rulers, through their person or property, is more heavily punished than one committed against any ordinary subject.

Contact between Swazi and whites is accompanied by an efflorescence of new legislation that penetrates even the more routine activities. Not only are crimes and civil offenses that were formerly covered by traditional law formulated in terms of the dominant white culture but regulations are required for an entirely new range of situations—taxation, licensing, wage employment, fencing of land, inoculation of cattle, et cetera, et cetera! Some laws and regulations apply only to whites, some only to Swazi, others to both, and, since justice itself is relative to a particular culture and is never absolute, the same laws sometimes receive different interpretations. Liquor offenses, tax evasions, breach of masters' and servants' contract constitute the highest proportion of Swazi convictions by the courts of the white administration, but these acts are not morally condemned by the Swazi. Moreover, the diviner, or witch-finder, the superior detective of criminals in his own society, is himself defined as a criminal under the Witchcraft Ordinance and can be arrested as a murderer (see Chapter 7). Case records reveal points of social tension, and legal statistics indicate the extent of social maladjustment. Breach of law occurs in every society, and some form of social sanction is essential for the maintenance of an established order. In Swaziland—as in other colonial societies—law is also used to perpetuate and enforce racial pluralism.

Two distinct legal systems, traditional and Roman-Dutch, are administered through a series of parallel courts, which interlock at certain levels. In some cases, Swazi litigants may exercise choice of court; in others, the limits of jurisdiction are defined. The superiority of white courts is not automatically accepted. Disputes over property, eviction from land, and complaints lodged by women are believed to receive more sympathetic (but not more equitable) hearing in courts presided over by white magistrates. This can be illustrated by a summary of one of numerous cases I recorded in 1936 in the court of Chief Ndabankulu. An elderly woman, Velepi Hlatshwako, and a man, Alpheus Shongwe, were brought before the chief's court, charged with "soiling the law," and fined. It appeared that about twenty years before, Velepi had been given in marriage to a man named Isauk Mabuzo (who was also present). The marriage had been unhappy: he accused her of misconduct and laziness; she accused him of illtreatment. After a particularly violent dispute, he had "tied up her kit" and sent her from his home. This did not necessarily mean that he was relinquishing her altogether, but it was a demonstration of the extent of his displeasure: he wanted either the return of his cattle or the assurance that his wife would reform. Instead of returning to her father and reporting what had happened, in which case every effort would have been made to reunite the couple, Velepi "stole herself" and went to Alpheus Shongwe, who had been her lover before she married Mabuzo. Shongwe, the present defendant, was eager to keep her and sent a message to her parents offering bride price. They refused, saying they could not accept *lobola* twice. Her father (since deceased) and other members of his family council tried to persuade her to return to Mabuzo, but in vain. At that stage, Shongwe could have approached Mabuzo with an offer of cattle "to break the stomach" (that is, break his (Mabuzo's) relationship with Velepi), but instead Shongwe and Velepi moved to another district and let the matter ride. Mabuzo himself made no further effort to regain his wife until her daughter, fathered by Shongwe, was ready for marriage; then Mabuzo claimed both women under the terms of his original marriage payment. Shongwe, Velepi, and their daughter had become converts to the Wesleyan church, and, on the advice of the minister, went to the district commissioner to "state their case." The commissioner, a young man, summoned Mabuzo to the court house and publicly rebuked him for his "mercenary approach." Mabuzo went back to his chief, Ndabankulu. The chief and his court summoned numerous witnesses and unravelled the intricate details. This court agreed that Mabuzo was morally as well as legally in the right. Velepi had disobeyed her father and her husband, and she and Shongwe had gone "over the head of the chief" by appealing to the district commissioner. It was obvious that Mabuzo was entitled to any marriage cattle for the girl and that women like Velepi "soiled the law."

Knowledge of tribal law and court procedure is part of the normal experiences of most Swazi men, who are expected to attend discussions held in the yard of the chief's homestead, and to "talk cases" with friends and acquaintances. The formality and technicalities of the European court present a sharp contrast to tribal procedure; conservative Swazi have stated that in the former, the question of wrong and right is of secondary importance, that "the only way to win" is to have a smart lawyer.

Changing Alignments

The traditional Swazi constitution, which grew organically and is verbalized by elders, is deliberately being replaced by a new written constitution. Deliberate constitution making is not a fundamental innovation, but is restricted by the limits of a society in which there is no separate legislature and most changes come about unobtrusively through court judgments arising from specific conflicts. Swazi laws, rooted in precedents drawn from a relatively static society, are validated by reference to the past: "They were in the beginning" or "They were from the ancestors." Contact with the more heterogeneous society of whites created what has been described as "a legal vacuum" and formulae are required to deal with new situations in politics, economics, education, and health. This is part of a familiar pattern of social change in which a small-scale society, characterized by interpersonal relationships, must adapt to a more complex and anonymous outer world that requires greater specialization at both the local and international level. In all colonial systems power moves downwards, and British policy in Swaziland is directed from the Commonwealth Relations Office in Britain through a high commissioner (representing the Queen) in South Africa, to a local resident commissioner, who acts as the link between the Swazi on the one hand and the settlers on the other. From this point, power is divided between district commissioners and traditional chiefs, each with their associated personnel. Not until the late 1950s was there an effort to integrate the traditional authorities into a single bureaucracy.

The entire territory, occupied by whites as well as Swazi, is divided into three major districts and subdistricts. Unlike tribal subdivisions, these are units of administrative authority that have no essential political cohesion or loyalty, and their boundaries can be altered without consulting the inhabitants. The administrative officer in charge has no permanent roots in the country and no land to distribute to kin and followers. When he is transferred he leaves his house and his office to an unknown successor and relinquishes all ties with the people and the place. His office duties are both more general and more specific than those of tribal chiefs. He acts as a magistrate, revenue officer, tax collector, coordinator of various technical departments in the area, and as liaison officer between traditional authorities and white settlers. His post requires nontraditional qualifications—a relatively high standard of education, a knowledge of written law, a minimum of clerical efficiency, and administrative ability. Promotion depends mainly on individual achievement (academic or legal qualifications and some fluency in the vernacular) and not on claims of kinship and pedigree. Swazi draw a sharp distinction between "chiefs of the office" and their own "chiefs of the people." In Swaziland, "chiefs of the office" are white, and therefore—the argument runs—speak differently, act differently, live differently, and think differently from "the people," but not from "other whites." The majority of Swazi do not realize that even if the conspicuous difference of color did not exist, the duties and qualifications written into the position of "chief of the office" would create a bureaucratic officialdom distinct from the traditional chiefs.

Africans employed in the white-controlled bureaucracy have an ambiguous status and often conflicting roles. A few Swazi, mainly men of tribal standing, have been specifically recommended by the traditional rulers to serve as assessors to the "white" courts or as advisers to the district commissioners. They are paid by the administration, but their field is limited to matters affecting their own people and their primary loyalty is to the traditional society whose mores they must explain to the whites. In a separate category are clerks, teachers, agricultural demonstrators, cattle guards, and other technical staff that are selected, appointed, and paid by the white administration; their qualifications are formulated by Western standards, with the emphasis on education, training, and efficiency. Although these individuals derive their positions from the whites, their color keeps them outside the world to which their white colleagues return as the sun sets. Some accept this, but an increasing number resent it, and are among the more articulate of the emerging opponents of colonial rule.

Conflict is inherent in changing societies where hereditary chiefs are used as representatives both by their own conservative subjects and by the new administration, each of which represents different values. In other parts of Africa, the position has at times become sufficiently tense to prompt the colonial government to depose chiefs who expressed the opposition of their own people.

In Swaziland there has been less arbitrary action, but the position of the Swazi king *cum* paramount chief has long been the focus of opposing systems. In the first period of contact the whites exaggerated his rights and powers to obtain concessions for themselves; later, they curtailed the substance of traditional authority but used the king indirectly to act as the primary agent in bringing about his people's acceptance of innovations. At present, Sobhuza is still expected to be the first to improve his stock, use new agricultural techniques, employ demonstrators, encourage creameries and dairies, patronize schools and hospitals, and so forth. Until the early forties, he alone had regular and formal contacts with senior members of the white administration; these gave him a greater semblance of power than he actually wielded, with the result that his subjects tended to blame him for legislation for which he was in no way responsible and about which he was sometimes not even consulted. He and his mother were the only two members of the traditional hierarchy who were paid by the administration. He received 1250 pounds sterling (approximately 3000 dollars) per annum and she 500 pounds sterling (approximately 1200 dollars), which amounts were obviously inadequate for any national undertaking, but described by some Swazi as an attempt to "buy the kings."

During the war years, an effort was made to introduce the Swazi into fuller administrative, judicial, and financial control. The model selected was Nigeria, under the policy of indirect rule, and three basic proclamations—the Native Authorities Act, the Native Courts Act, and the Native Treasury Act—were eventually passed. But the Swazi situation was fundamentally different from that in West Africa where the European or white population was virtually restricted to an administrative cadre. In Swaziland, the country was owned largely by whites, and even when additional powers were granted to the Swazi by the British government, the white settlers remained a distinctive elite, with entrenched economic privileges, high status, and close ties to white officialdom.

4

Work and Wealth

The Work Cycle

SWAZI ARE TRADITIONALLY PEASANTS who cultivate crops, keep cattle and other domestic animals, hunt, and gather numerous wild fruits and vegetables. The main crops are maize and millet; in addition, every Swazi homestead produces subsidiary foods—ground nuts, gourds, sugar cane, and pumpkins.

Economic activities follow the rhythm of the seasons. The women begin by hoeing and sowing small plots along the river banks where the soil is generally moist and seeds germinate quickly. With the coming of the rains in September, men and women move to large inland fields which the men prepare with ox-drawn plows. Heavy rains are expected in the summer months, from November to January, and the last gardens must be planted. In midsummer, agricultural work is intensified and communal work parties, especially for weeding, are frequent. During the day, the homesteads are emptied of able-bodied adults, and even the young children toil in the fields, often returning home in the late afternoon. In autumn, from February through March, women cut the ripe maize and tie it into bundles, then carry it home on their heads, or the men cart it on ox-drawn sleds, the main means of transport. In winter, from April through July, after the last maize is harvested and the millet gleaned, the scene of activity changes again from the fields to the homes. Men and women rub and beat the corn from the cobs and thresh and winnow the millet, reserving the best quality for storage in the underground pits and using the inferior grain for immediate consumption and to reward workers with beer.

Other activities are fitted into the agricultural cycle. When the harvest is in, people have more leisure and sociability increases. Women take the opportunity to visit their parents and headmen attend more cases at the chief's courts or relax with beer drinks. Only in the dry season, once the danger of lightning is past, may new huts be built and old ones repaired. Winter is also the hunting season, and the time when government officials go on their tax-collecting tours—with a resulting increased exodus of recruits to white labor centers.

Many Swazi live at a precarious subsistence level; their food supplies fluctuate annually between plenty and a scarcity bordering on famine. Winter is the time of general satisfaction and physical well-being, but in summer, before the new crops ripen, comes the moon named "to swallow the pickings of the teeth." Maize and millet, the staple cultivated foods, are the main commodities purchased from trading shops; it is estimated that at least 25 percent of the Swazi do not grow enough for their domestic needs. Milk and meat are also prized, but the milk yield of Swazi cattle is low; milk, preferably soured and thickened in calabashes, is eaten primarily by children; beer from sprouted grain is the substitute in adult life. Beer and meat are considered an ideal combination, but cattle are seldom slaughtered. A wide range of wild leaf vegetables, roots and fruits, and various types of insects are enjoyed, but these are unreliable additions to the starchy diet. A few nutritious items of food are culturally excluded from the entire population or from specific sections thereof. Fish was never eaten by conservatives; specific birds and a few animals are taboo to associated clans; eggs must not be eaten by females; and a married woman may not take milk in any form in the husband's home unless a special beast has been allotted her. Christians do not follow the traditional food taboos and many women converts eat eggs, buy fish, and are prepared even to take milk in public; but on the whole, the diet is unimaginative and, according to nutritional standards, badly balanced. There is no difference in the quality of food available to different status groups and the desire is to feel (and *look*) replete.

Formerly, the Swazi were entirely dependent on the land for their livelihood, and the power the rulers wield over their subjects is still referred back to their rights to allocate land. Swazi say that land, the basis of subsistence, is "served" to the people by their political overlords, and every man has the right to eat. Individual ownership through freehold and leasehold are alien concepts; rights are secured by allegiance and usage, not purchase or rental. Should the subject leave the area for several years, his land reverts to the chief, but if their mutual relationship was good, it may be reclaimed when he or his sons return. In most of southern Africa, Africans are prohibited from buying land, and there is developing a class of landless peasants who live and work on white men's farms or whose homes remain in native area, but who obtain their food requirements with money wages. In Swaziland, it is still relatively easy to find adequate building sites, but there is an increasing scarcity of fertile, arable soil. Land is open for purchase, irrespective of color, though so far most purchases have been made by the nation, through a special fund. The majority of Swazi are still reluctant—or afraid—to own land individually and to exercise a power associated with chieftainship.

Swazi have a very limited knowledge of agriculture, and, compared with the peasants of Europe or some of the Bantu tribes in central Africa, are unenterprising farmers. They recognize a few types of soil, but are not very careful in their selection, and though they realize that cow dung fertilizes the ground, they do not bother to carry it to the gardens; they do not rotate crops or practice irrigation, and "doctoring of seed" and shifting cultivation are the limits of technological effort. Cultivation is not a prestige occupation, and, as among all southern Bantu, is left primarily to the women, whose main garden tool is still the iron hoe. The introduction of the plough was probably as radical an innovation into southern Africa as that of the horse among the Plains Indians. Since handling cattle is taboo to women, the plough drawn by oxen directly involved men in the essentials of cultivation, changing the division of labor and, in some areas, the attitude to agriculture itself. Swazi have begun to grow cash crops, especially tobacco and cotton, and to form farmers' associations. Group and areal differences in response to agricultural improvements can be related to both personal and structural factors, including the character of the local chief (conservative or "forward looking"), and the relationship with the local representatives of the agricultural department, especially the agricultural demonstrator. Land allocated to and cultivated exclusively by women is not regarded as a source of cash income.

Swazi have no objective measure of area, and the size of the plots attached to each homestead depends primarily on the supply of resident labor. Women, who receive their gardens from their husbands upon marriage, may obtain occasional assistance from work parties of kin and neighbors. The rulers have several "gardens of kingship" in different localities, cultivated for them by chiefs in the area, and they are also able to command the service of regimental age groups stationed at royal homesteads, a privilege shared by district chiefs over local contingents.

Sites for building and for cultivation are individually allocated, but grazing lands are communally used. The general approach of conservatives is that land which has not been specifically altered by the efforts of man remains under the control of the political authority for the use of his people as a whole. Hence, such materials as reeds for fencing, grass for thatching, and indigenous trees for firewood, are available to all people in the district. Hunting lands are similarly controlled by chiefs, who organize communal hunts.

Cultivation provides the staple food of the Swazi, but pastoralism is more highly rated. Swazi have the so-called "cattle complex" typical of many tribes in eastern Africa: cattle, in addition to their direct value as a source of food and clothing, serve as potent symbols in a wider range of situations, both economic and ritual.They are the conservative's closest approximation to currency, his highest reward for service, his means of ratifying marriage, the medium for propitiating ancestors, and essential requirements in various treatments for health and prosperity. Their physical presence is necessary for most national and family rituals; a man without cattle is therefore considered poor and insignificant and has been likened by informants to "an orphan without kin." The slaughtering of a beast, its division and preparation, is one of the most important social situations in which status and kinship bonds are literally carved in the carcass. Each portion of the animal is allotted to set groups of individuals in terms of sex, age, and relationship; there is no personal preference permitted for choice parts. The distribution and consumption covers several days, generally culminating in the cooking of a special dish made from the blood mixed with grain and shared between men, who eat in the cattle pen, and women, who sit in the yard of the hut of the headman's mother. The over-all importance of cattle is reflected in the language, which is rich in terms for hides of different colors, horns of many shapes, and organs of animal anatomy. Men are referred to in terms of cattle and cattle are praised with the praises of men. The king is "The Bull" of the nation.

Cattle are unevenly distributed, and although every Swazi has a claim to land, he has no equivalent claim to livestock. Formerly, men could obtain cattle through inheritance or the marriage of sisters or daughters, or as gifts in return for particular services. Rich men may lend beasts to people in need, who may use the milk and be rewarded with a calf when the other animals are required by the owner. At present any wage earner may gradually accumulate a herd, but the cattle of kingship, the cattle of the nation, still far exceed those of any single individual. This national revenue is derived from several sources —inheritance, death dues for important headmen, gifts accompanying requests for rain, "thanks" for favors received, fines, and especially the marriages of princesses, and also of daughters of unrelated subjects (often royal warriors) whom the king previously assisted with their marriage cattle. I calculated (in 1936) that the royal cattle numbered over 3,000; the total cattle owned by Swazi was counted as 334,000. Through its compulsory "dipping" against specific diseases, the white administration keeps accurate vital statistics of cattle (more accurate than of the human population), but the records do not reflect actual ownership; cattle of kingship are often registered in the names of special herdsmen, and poor men are registered as "owners" of borrowed cattle. In the past, national revenue was mainly derived from loot in warfare or from the "eating up of the cattle byre" of wealthy and ambitious subjects condemned as traitors or wizards. Several royal cattle posts were established by previous kings and represent capital investment of a pre-monetary period. Each cattle post has its own name, history, and place in government. The animals are used to feed the people at national gatherings, to obtain wives for princes, or to provide beasts for national sacrifices. There is one sacred herd to which mystical properties are attributed, and which provides fat used only for anointing the king, his mother and his first two ritual wives.

Cattle circulate primarily through marriage, and cattle and wives together are the traditional hallmarks of status and the indices of wealth. In Swazi society, wealth follows the curves of natural increase and may fluctuate considerably in a man's lifetime, not through the artificial manipulation of the exchange or as a result of training, concentration, thrift, and industry, but through "good luck" or "bad luck." Death and sterility are economic as well as social threats. Swazi political leaders, because of their favored position in a polygynous and aristocratic society, have more opportunities than their subjects to recuperate from economic misfortunes. The white administration, through its veterinary department, is attempting to reduce the numbers and improve the quality of Swazi-owned cattle by experiments in pasturage, cattle culling, and organized cattle sales. Some Swazi are responding, but conservatives remain reluctant to commercialize cattle. The conflict between the traditional and Western attitudes is subtly expressed in the remark of a fairly educated Swazi: "I only like to sell cattle when I speak English." In addition to cattle, Swazi also keep sheep, goats, dogs, chickens, and, in some areas, horses, but these have not the same importance in the ritual or economy. Informants state that their forefathers had fat-tailed sheep as well as cattle before the whites arrived, and it is significant that sheep is the animal that is taboo to all members of the royal clan. Animal husbandry in general is carried on at the expense of agricultural development. Until recently, approximately 75 percent of native area was devoted to grazing and only 10 percent to cultivation, the remaining 15 percent was not suitable for either purpose.

Division of Labor

Tribal (peasant) economy has little room for specialists, and the main criteria for division of labor are sex, age, and pedigree. Every man, irrespective of his rank, knows how to build, plow, milk cattle, sew skins, and cut shields; every woman is able to hoe, thatch, plait ropes, and weave mats, baskets, and beer strainers. Swazi attach value judgments to activities over which one or other sex claims a monopoly by reason of assumed psychophysical attributes. Specific "masculine" tasks that carry high status include warfare (possibly the *raison d'être* of original male mastery), animal husbandry, and hunting. Men are also the important public figures, the orators and councilors, and the family priests. A woman's life is restricted by domestic activities, the rearing of children, and the regular chores of grinding grain, carrying water, cooking foods, smearing the floors with cow dung. Men and women cooperate in agriculture and building, but the man's share is more spasmodic and energetic, the woman's more monotonous and continuous.

Age has a less defined influence on the division of labor. Children are encouraged to do the same work as adults and relieve their mothers of certain tasks in the home. It is only in relation to ritual that age becomes a primary qualification. Immature girls are required to help in the national rain rites, and in the ceremonies periodically organized to drive pests from the crops; old women are similarly considered ritually pure and given specific tasks.

Rank by birth cuts across distinctions of age and sex so that every Swazi does not participate to the same extent in manual labor. Aristocrats and leading councilors are responsible for providing suitable conditions for the success of the efforts of others rather than their own labor. They arrange for specialists to treat the land and seed; they summon men and women for work parties in district and national enterprises; they supervise the feeding and entertainment of workers when a task is complete. They are not, however, exempt from work with their subjects, and most of them perform a certain amount of service for the rulers. On occasion some chiefs have displayed long fingernails with obvious pride, but even the most noble women, including the queen mother, are expected to take part in cultivation.

Close personal relationship between the workers and the rulers as well as between the workers themselves contrasts sharply with the legal and economic behavior of employer and employee in Western industry. There are no fixed periods of work, no regular hours, and no stipulated pay. An age set may be summoned for several days in succession, but sometimes weeks will elapse without any demand for its services. No man is forced to work, though if he consistently shirks his obligations, his mates may reproach him and belabor him with sticks. It is frequently impossible for members of a homestead to do all the work required for their subsistence without extra help; as there is no special class of laborers, they rely on kinsmen and neighbors, organized into temporary labor associations. When members of both sexes are present, they are divided into two competitive groups, spurring each other to greater achievement. Swazi generally sing as they work, their movements coordinated through music and rhythm. Every joint economic activity has its own sets of songs, and the song leader is the closest approximation to a foreman or timekeeper. The number of work parties and their size depends on status and, to some extent, on the nature of the undertaking. There are occasional large-scale national enterprises, which require considerable planning and foresight and involve as many as a thousand workers on specific days. For the organizer, a work party is both an economic venture and an occasion for the enhancement of prestige. He or she—for women may also initiate the enterprise—must calculate whether supplies are sufficient to feed the workers. The reward of communal work in conservative homes is always food, beer, or meat, eaten at the home of the host. This is as integral a part of Swazi economy as money payment in European service. But the host, unlike an employer, offers sporadic hospitality, and the food is not regarded as a wage or a means whereby people hope to support themselves. It is a way of expressing thanks, a reward to be shared among the workers according to rank, age, sex, and locality. Individual effort or piecework is not considered. Some workers come early, others late. There are well-known shirkers who enjoy the feasting without having contributed their labor, but they are aware that if they shirk too frequently, they, in turn, will not receive assistance. The work party is, in some respects, the antithesis of a trade union, and an administrative instruction from the British government to introduce trade unions into Swaziland met with the criticism from conservatives that this was a device to compel laborers to work for a definite period of time at a fixed rate instead of on a personal and voluntary basis. Traditionally, there is no sharp division between employer and employee, and reciprocity was the most powerful sanction in maintaining Swazi economic organization.

Specialization

As a result of the economic homogeneity of Swazi society, each individual plies a number of crafts, but recognition of individual aptitude has led to a limited specialization within the general skills expected of each person. Some men are better than others at tanning the hides (used for shields and for skin skirts and aprons worn by conservative married women), and some women are more skilled than others at beadwork basketwork, and plaiting mats, and so may be asked to produce these, at a price, for the less skilled. There is a marked tendency for all goods to be commercialized at the present time. Prices vary, and bargaining is not part of the Swazi convention of exchange, as it is in oriental communities. The main source of income for women who have no special skill and do not have outside employment is the sale of home-brewed beer, on which the profit may be as high as 100 percent, but the smallness of economic venture is indicated by the fact that the capital involved, if the grain is bought, is seldom more than 30 shillings (less than 5 dollars!).

The term *tinyanga* is applied specifically to specialists in ritual—medicine men and diviners—but may be extended to smiths, woodcarvers, and potters, whose crafts tend to be specialized and hereditary and involve unusual "power," and risks requiring ritual protection.

The roles of medicine men and diviners and their relationship to the supernatural will be more fully discussed in Chapter 5. Here we are concerned with the economic aspect, for these *tinyanga* have the greatest opportunity of acquiring wealth by individual achievement. Payment varies with qualifications and the nature and success of the treatment. A medicine man of good repute receives an initial gift of a goat, spear, or other articles to "open his bags," and a further payment to make the medicine "shine." During treatment he receives the hide of any beast that is slaughtered, and he is liberally provided with meat. If the patient recovers, a cow is given in thanks, but if no cure is effected, there is no final fee. For other services, such as the "pegging down" of a homestead against evil-doers or the purification of a homestead after lightning has struck, payment may be a goat or a bag of grain. A diviner's fee depends on his technique and the seriousness of the situation, but generally specialist services receive no regular stipulated payment. Sometimes the amount is decided in advance; at other times new requests are made in the course of treatment. Not to pay an *inyanga* is dangerous because of the supernatural powers he may evoke if angered. As in other societies, payments incurred by illness can cripple a family for life, while successful medicine men flourish. The amount of time *tinyanga* devote to their practice depends on personal interest, but Swazi do not regard even this exclusive profession as a substitute for peasant farming.

Smithing, which includes both smelting iron from the rock and forging it into shape, was formerly the most exacting and remunerative of the crafts. The finished articles, especially iron hoes, knives, and different kinds of spears (the main weapons of war), were in great demand and short supply. Smithing was a hereditary occupation requiring long apprenticeship and surrounded by taboos. The smithy, with its flaming forge and elaborate bellows of goatskin, was built a distance from the homestead, and women were not allowed to enter. Rich iron deposits west of Mbabane are at present being exploited by white mining companies, and Swazi smiths find it more convenient to use scrap iron and to repair old articles rather than create new ones, which can now be bought at trading stations. Certain iron instruments are sacred, and these are kept for state rituals.

Swazi claim that at one time they also had specialists in copper and brass. Substantiating this are the large brass beads, handed down from one reign to the next, that adorn the skirts of the first ten wives of the king, and a copper bracelet that is also part of the royal insignia. But if the process of forging copper was once known, this knowledge has long since been lost.

Wood carving is limited to essentially functional objects, especially head-rests, milk pails, meat dishes, and spoons. There are no masks or sculptured figures, though the bushveld is rich in indigenous timber. The carver has no special status comparable to that of medicine men or even of smiths, nor is the appreticeship in any way restricted. Woodcraft is encouraged in the schools and a small tourist trade is being developed.

Pottery making survives as a special craft of women who, using the coil technique, produce different sizes and shapes of drinking and cooking vessels of considerable beauty and symmetry, decorated with simple geometrical designs. The kiln is a hollow in the ground, covered with dry brush; because it is difficult to control the heat, breakage is high. As in other situations where there is an element of risk and technical control is limitied, the Swazi potter resorts to various magical aids which in fact limit the development of effective technological improvements.

Markets comparable to those found in West Africa do not exist in Swaziland, but a certain amount of internal trade follows the irregular distribution of raw materials. Wood carvers, especially, are concentrated in bush country, and some of the best clay is found in riverbanks in the northwest.

With Westernization, a range of new, full-time occupational situations have been introduced. Some 12,000 Swazi males are employed mainly as unskilled laborers in farming, mining, building, and transport, and some 1,000 women are also in farming and domestic service. A much smaller number (under 500 men and 200 women) are teachers, clerks, and messengers, and there is a growing number of Swazi, mostly men, in "self employment" as shopkeepers, butchers, and "agents." New jobs associated with school education carry more prestige and a higher standard of living than those that do not require "writing." But as yet there is no economic class division, and the few educated men and women in financially good positions have not cut adrift from the extended family; the majority of their kin are both uneducated and unskilled peasants, and are often migrant laborers.

Wealth and Status

Accumulation of wealth is not conspicuous in traditional society, where rulers and subjects live in the same type of home, eat the same kind of foods, and use the same limited range of utensils and implements. The perishable nature of most Swazi products as well as the limited range of choice, make generosity the hallmark of achievement and the primary virtue of *ubuntfu* (humanity). From infancy, children are taught not to be greedy or to take too large a portion of food from the common pot, and they, themselves, soon enforce the rule of sharing. A mother who hides food for her own offspring will be insulted by co-wives and suspected of witchcraft, and the character of a headman is judged by his hospitality. A donor must always belittle his gift, while the recipient must exaggerate its importance and accept even the smallest article in both hands.

Begging has a connotation different from that expressed in the European milieu. Among conservatives it carries no shame. To beg is a sign of deference and to give is a token of superiority, enhancing status. It is the person who refuses a request who should suffer; to avoid inflicting shame, borrowers express their requests through intermediaries and the refusal should be couched in self-deprecatory terms. Something given in response to a request is a favor and need not be returned. It is totally different from objects that are specifically borrowed and also from those that are bought and for which there is an obligation to pay at a later date. A person is thanked for a favor by the further request, "Do the same tomorrow."

Inequality of wealth has always been acceptable but only within the aristocratic framework. Commoners who acquired too many wives or cattle were in danger of being "smelt out as evil doers," for whom death was the penalty and whose property was legally "eaten up" by chiefs. These drastic measures are prohibited by modern law, but in the rural areas there is still considerable restraint on ambition and ability. Rich conservatives divide their homesteads, lend out their surplus cattle, bury their grain in underground pits, and hide their money in the ground. The fear of witchcraft acts as a check on economic enterprise, and it is safer to plead poverty than to boast of wealth.

Although display of wealth is limited in traditional circles, a large range of trade articles has made economic differences more conspicuous, and a new, white-controlled, economic milieu has redefined status. Smart suits, record players, Western furniture, and sewing machines are the prized posessions of self-styled "progressives" while Sobhuza demonstrates a new "high" in aristocratic living. But the major obvious disparity in wealth is not between traditional and progressive or aristocrat and commoner, but between whites and non-whites.

5

Age and Education

Training the Young

IN EVERY SOCEITY age is a social, not an absolute concept, measured by artificial standards correlated more or less directly with the major physiological changes of infancy, prepuberty, adolescence, maturity, and the menopause. Generally speaking, in preliterate peasant societies increasing age carries increasing responsibilities, and elders, as "repositories of tradition," exercise considerable influence and command corresponding respect. The authority of age characterizes all Swazi behavior, and age is the main factor in group association.

Swazi distinguish, linguistically and ritually, eight periods of individual growth, from birth to "almost an ancestor." Until the third month of life a Swazi baby is described as a "thing." It has no name, cannot be handled by the men, and, if it dies, it may not be publicly mourned. It is recognized as being very weak and vulnerable (infant mortality is tragically high), and the parents perform various rituals to protect it against dangers emanating from animals, humans, and from nature herself. In the third month, the infant is shown to the moon and symbolically introduced to the world of nature. It is entered into the category of persons, and is given a name, which may be sung to it in its first lullaby. It remains a "baby" until it has "teeth to chew" and "legs to run." This stage, which lasts roughly three years, is traditionally terminated by the act of weaning. Until then the baby remains most closely attached to the mother, who carries it everywhere in a sling on her back, feeds it when it cries, and tends it with devotion. Other people, including the father, may also fondle it and deliberately try to teach it basic kinship terms and correct behavior.

Obedience and politeness are inculcated from the beginning of awareness. Little achievements meet with warm encouragement and such stereotyped praise as "Chief," or "Now you are really a man"—or "a woman." Toilet training is generally achieved within the first two years without much apparent conflict. The mother abruptly removes the baby from her back when she feels discomfort, but occasional lapses are treated with tolerance. Weaning, enforced,

286

if necessary, by the mother's rubbing bitter aloe or some other unpleasant-tasting substance on her nipples, is a symbolic as well as a real separation from maternal care.

The baby now becomes a toddler, who must begin to be independent and associate with his peers. When the mother goes to work in the fields or to gather firewood, she may leave him for many hours in the care of children not much bigger than himself, who play with him, sing to him, and teach him accepted rules of behavior. Disobedience or rudeness may provoke a sharp slap, but, as a rule, less drastic teaching by the play group appears sufficient to produce conformity. The threat of a beating is constantly uttered by both adults and older children for various "mistakes," but is seldom carried out.

Discipline becomes more strict and punishment more physical as the child grows older, but the over-all impression is that Swazi children are reared with unself-conscious indulgence, relatively free from constant adult supervision. They also learn unconsciously through riddles and verbal memory games, said to "sharpen the intelligence," and there are songs and dances to "make a person grow into a person." Most of the play of children is based on the activities of the adult world. Small boys model clay oxen (today some model automobiles) and indulge in stick fights. Girls pretend to grind and cook and do each other's hair. Children of both sexes build miniature huts near the homestead and act out the roles of kinsmen. In the evenings, the old women in whose huts they sleep after weaning recount tales and fables which, though ostensibly meant to entertain, frequently point out a moral. Legends dealing with clan and tribal history are recalled on specific ritual occasions.

At about the age of six, Swazi children have a small slit made in the lobe of each ear. They are no longer protected toddlers; they are now held more responsible for their own actions. Control of tears and laughter is part of the stereotyped process of growing up, and though the ear-cutting operation is quite painful, the children must bear it bravely. Thereafter they are encouraged to participate in economic and social activities insofar as their physical strength permits. The education of boys and girls is differentiated in accordance with the male and female roles in this society. The training of boys is directed towards hardening them physically and bringing them into public life. They must be severed from the womenfolk and "must not grow up under the skin skirts of their mothers." They go in small gangs to herd the calves in the neighborhood and are later promoted to the herding of the cattle, during which period they spend much of the day away from their homes, acquire a knowledge of nature, and learn to fend for themselves. The girls, on the other hand, are allowed less freedom of movement. They accompany their mothers or agemates to draw water or gather wood, or plant in the fields, and much of their time is spent working in the home where they help with the cooking and smear the floors. But a Swazi girl, like a Swazi boy, has an easy life before marriage, with much time for singing and dancing, recognized essentials of social life.

The attainment of puberty is a major landmark in individual development but is not publicly celebrated. Group circumcision of boys was practiced until the reign of Mswati when the custom was abandoned. It appears that the mortality was high and the military needs of the nation were considered more important than the ritual of personal transition. A symbolic circumcision, however, is still performed for the king as part of the ritual of his installation. There are no initiation ceremonies for girls, but menstruation imposes certain taboos on their public behavior and there is a conspicuous cultural difference between "little girls" and "maidens ripe for lovers." After puberty boys and girls are expected to enjoy sexual experiences, stopping short of full intercourse, before finally assuming marital responsibilities. Sexual morality is strictly defined as virginity, not chastity. Formerly, if an unmarried girl were found by her husband to have broken the law, her shame was indicated in a public ritual and the number of her marriage cattle was reduced. Today the ritual is discreetly modified, but there may still be a reduction in the number of her cattle, particularly if she has already born a child.

The period of relative sexual freedom is shorter for a girl, who is expected to marry a man several years her senior. The end of girlhood is marked by appropriate clothing and a change in hairstyle. A man should only marry when his age group receives permission from the king. Formerly, this was overtly symbolized by sewing on waxen headrings, but this was abandoned for the present king, whose grandmother, the Queen Regent Gwamile, considered it an unnecessary token of manhood for those who "put on hats" and had Western education. Very few headringed men survive, but marriage is still essential for the attainment of full tribal responsibilities and privileges. The married woman gains demonstrably in status with the birth of her first child, and reaches her highest position in the home of her married son. In old age, both men and women are entitled to veneration and care from the young; elders supervise the education of the young and lead the rituals.

Regimental Age Classes

Against these general age categories, individuals refer their own ages to important social episodes—wars, famines, epidemics, the arrival of important personalities, public celebrations—and, particularly in the case of men, to their age classes, or regiments (*emabutfo,* sing. *libutfo*).

The announcement of a new age class is made by the king when there is a representative gathering at the capital; it is the duty of those present at the gathering to inform others in their districts. The nucleus of the new group exists in the growing youths who already live in royal homesteads. A new age group should be formed every five to seven years when the last group is considered ready for marriage. The main dividing line between those groups permitted to marry and youths who may not yet "spill their strength in children" is drawn for purposes of ritual. When, in 1935, after a lapse of some fifteen years, Sobhuza II inaugurated the Locust Regiment at a public meeting, many in the "bachelor set" had already taken wives or given their lovers children. He later sent his messenger to collect a fine from these men for breaking the law, but the Christian Swazi, backed by missionaries, successfully objected to "interference" by a polygynous king in their private lives. This was one of the many situations in which the traditional political structure, sanctioned by ritual and ethics, conflicted with a new individualism and foreign religion.

Unlike other tribes in east and central Africa, the Swazi have no compulsory period of barrack life for every male. Each man is automatically recruited into a *libutfo,* but only a certain number reside more or less permanently in the public barracks attached to royal homesteads. These royal warriors (*emabutfo*) are distinguished from the rank and file (*emajaha*) who remain for the greater part of their lives in their own homesteads, or even in the homesteads of local chiefs, and who come to the royal centers only to perform specific services. *Emabutfo* have special titles, ornaments, songs and dances indicative of their higher status, and it is from this group that the king selects his most trusted messengers and attendants. Formerly men—especially if important—were eager that at least one of their sons should stay at state headquarters for some years, and family councils sent the heir to be educated in the etiquette and ways of the court. In addition to princes and sons of chiefs, poor commoners, who could derive few benefits from their own parents, offered their services to the rulers with the expectation that they would be suitably rewarded. The decision to become a "king's man" rests mainly with the individual; he need not obtain the prior consent of a father or guardian, for no one can prevent a subject from working for the king, the "father" of the nation. Thus, although every Swazi is automatically a member of an age class and there is no sharp distinction between civilian and soldier, the system makes a markedly different impact on individuals depending on whether or not they reside in a royal village.

Age classes are organized into distinctive units. The smallest is the squad (*siceme*) of eight to twenty men who stand together in the dance, an essential part of group activity, and form a recognized working team. Several squads join together to make a company (*licibia*), led by a prince, and each company has its own name, war cry, and decorations. The princes are subordinate to the regimental leader, or commander-in-chief—a commoner chosen by the king for his ability to maintain discipline, his military knowledge, trustworthiness, and loyalty. On national occasions he assumes control of all local contingents.

Age groups cut across the boundaries of local chiefs and across the bonds of kinship, incorporating individuals into the state, the widest political unit. Between members of the same regiment, and particularly those in permanent residence, there is a loyalty and camaraderie. They treat each other as equals, eat together, smoke hemp from the long hemp pipe that is part of their joint equipment, work together, and have a central meeting place or clubhouse in the barracks. They call each other "brother" or "my age mate," "my peer," and the ties between them are said to be stronger than those between kinsmen of different generations. Towards other age sets there is often openly expressed rivalry and occasional fights, usually provoked by disputes over beer or women, do occur. Young regiments resent the marital privileges of the older men who, in turn, attempt to keep the young from monopolizing as lovers girls old enough to become wives. To prevent feuds between the regiments national policy dictated periodic action against an external enemy.

Warfare was an essential function of the age classes, a clue to their former importance and present impotence. The Swazi, however, were never as aggressive as the Zulu in the period of military conquest, and though warfare offered the main opportunity for the display of individual courage and strength, Swazi leaders did not encourage reckless loss of life. When necessary, the regiments did not hesitate to retreat into their mountain caves; in battle formation the older regiments were strategically placed to control the younger and more foolhardy. The indoctrination of the army before it left for battle stressed both fierceness and cunning, and there were rituals for both national success and personal safety. Warriors who achieved a kill were decorated with medicated necklaces, and mimed their grand achievements in solo dancing at public gatherings. But they and their weapons were "cleansed of the blood" to prevent them from being infected with an obsessive urge to destroy.

Warfare was controlled so that it did not disrupt normal existence; the men usually left for battle only after they had completed the main work in the fields, and reserves always remained behind for economic and ritual duties. The regiments took no large quantity of food with them; they staved off hunger by smoking hemp and relied on obtaining meat from cattle looted from the enemy. During the warriors' absence, a strict supporting discipline was imposed on those who stayed behind. Wives and lovers in particular had to behave with special decorum, in the belief that if they were rowdy, drunk, or sexually "hot" they would subdue or "burn up" the strength of the warriors.

Death on the battlefield was considered a national sacrifice. Kinsmen were not allowed to mourn their dead who had fallen in battle and the king did not demand a beast for purification. Although warfare was extolled, the taking of life was considered fearful and dangerous. On its return, the army was "doctored" in a not always successful attempt to guard against the vengeful spirits of the dead. Warfare was considered an outlet for individual ambition and aggression but could not be allowed to become a menace to the peace of the state.

The last time the regiments functioned as traditional units was in the reign of Sobhuza's grandfather, but since then the Swazi have been indirectly involved in three major wars—the Anglo-Boer War, and the two world wars. In the Anglo-Boer War, the Swazi as a group remained neutral; in World War I, a small contingent served in France. In World War II, nearly 4000 were recruited by Sobhuza and sent to the Middle East where they built roads and fortifications, acted as stevedores, stretcher bearers, drivers, mechanics, and machine gunners. The whites have not, in practice, attacked militarism; they have not shown that fighting is bad, bloodshed in battle brutal, nor that nationalism is dangerous. They have increased rather than decreased the importance of armed strength as a source of national unity and individual security, but they have monopolized the power of force. Compared with the armaments of modern warfare, the traditional weapons (knives, spears, knobkerries, and shields) are antediluvian and the methods of using them have not even the superior strength of barbarism. A Westernized Swazi commented, "The whites have crushed intertribal war but they have introduced a false security of life and have stamped into Swazi culture the cheapness of individuals in an industrial economy."

Certain observances connected with warfare have been transferred to situations created by Western industry, especially deep-level mining. In conservative Swazi homes, women whose men work in the gold mines of South Africa follow the ritual precautions for protecting men engaged in battle; if a miner is killed in an underground accident his kinsmen do not have to pay death dues to the king. This transference of custom does not signify an identification of the value of death in the mines with that of death on the battlefield but an association of the two ways of dying through physical danger and attacks by hostile aliens.

The age sets were more precisely organized in the days of intertribal warfare than at present, but much of the structure survives for other than military purposes, which they continue to fulfill. When the regiments were not fighting they served as labor battalions, particularly for the aristocrats, and this remains one of their major duties. Their most intensive work depends on the agricultural routine of plowing, weeding, guarding the corn against the birds, reaping, and threshing; they may also be summoned to gather wood, cut leaves and poles for building, move huts, drive locusts off the fields, skin animals, run messages, fetch and carry. No matter how arduous a task may be, work begins and ends with the *hlehla,* a dance song in the cattle pen. During the performance, which always attracts children and often the women of the homestead, individual workers dance out of the group and sing short songs of their own composition, boasting of some achievement or exhibiting their artistic virtuosity.

During their period in royal homesteads, warriors are responsible for their own subsistence, but the rulers are expected to provide them periodically with beer and meat. Formerly, when cattle were raided from hostile tribes the men were better fed; the present rulers are less able to support financially a large permanent retinue, and this is one of the main reasons for the decline in the numbers of *emabutfo.* Those who stay lead a precarious hand-to-mouth existence, relying largely on the generosity of the women in the neighborhood for whom they do occasional jobs, in their spare time, and wandering from beer drink to beer drink. Moreover, money has become a necessity since every male over the age of eighteen is required to pay an annual "poll tax," ranging from 35 shillings (roughly 5 dollars) for the unmarried to 90 shillings (roughly 13 dollars) for men with four or more wives. The king pays the tax for a few selected warriors, but most of the others are driven to work for whites; for the younger generation, the prestige derived from living at court is challenged by the opportunities and excitement of the new urban and industrial centers.

The age classes are, however, still required for state ritual, and at the annual ceremony of kingship, designed to rejuvenate the king and strengthen the people, separate duties are allocated to the oldest regiments, to the regiment of men in full vigor of manhood, and to the youths who are considered sexually pure. Ritual is part of the educative process, a symbolic affirmation of certain social values, and in traditional Swazi society where specialized formal educational institutions are nonexistent, the age classes serve as the main channels for inculcating the values of loyalty and group morality. The emphasis is less on the content of a curriculum, and the acquisition of new knowledge than on traditional values. In the past, special "old people" were appointed as instructors; teaching was not a separate career and learning was a gradual and continuous process of consolidation. The warriors are expected to master the main skills associated with adult life—in the barracks they even perform tasks normally left to women—and to develop the qualities of "manhood," specifically those related to the code of sexual morality. When a girl accepts a lover, she and her friends are expected to visit his barracks in special courting dress, which is brief but elaborately decorated with beads, and to sing and dance to make the relationship public. Should she on a subsequent visit find him absent, it is the duty of his agemates to try to see that she remains faithful to their friend. They find her accommodations and provide her with food. Lovers of other regiments are considered fair game, but the man who steals a girl of his own agemate is beaten and ostracized. In some other societies, sharing of women is a right of group membership; among the Swazi the emphasis on sexual monopoly over a particular lover is related to the ritual obligations placed on each member of an age group. In the main annual ceremony of the state, every individual of the unmarried regiment is responsible for contributing "pure strength" to kingship. At the present time, lover relationships are often not public and participation in state rituals is frequently evaded.

Education has, in fact, become secularized—to the extent that it has been taken from the control of the Swazi state with its particular framework of ritual and transferred to the education department of the Western administration. At the same time 90 percent of the schools in Swaziland are mission controlled, and mission institutions are by definition opposed to traditionalist values. The conflict between Christian churches and the Swazi state is producing a cleavage in the Swazi people between Christians and traditionalists, a cleavage that does not necessarily coincide with the division between the educated and uneducated. In 1936 Sobhuza attempted to bridge the gulf by suggesting the introduction of a modified age-class system in all the schools. The idea, investigated by anthropologists, met with the approval of the (unorthodox) head of the local administration, but the missionaries, who obviously could not support a system directed by a polygynous king, head of a tribal religion, offered the Pathfinder Movement (Black Boy Scouts) instead. Sobhuza's scheme was finally applied in three schools and maintained and financed by the Swazi nation itself. For various reasons, however, it failed to achieve a unity—which the Swazi state itself no longer represented. I mention this experiment in misguided "applied anthropology" because it illustrates these points: first, the awareness of tribal leaders of the conflict between traditionalist and Western values; second, the extent to which these values are deep rooted in social institutions such as chieftanship or church; third, the interaction of institutions in a wider power structure —the military nation as compared with a colonial government with limited authority over whites as well as Africans. The Swazi age-class system represents a passing social order. It grew with territorial expansion and the need to maintain political independence and internal security. Its weapons proved ineffectual against conquest, symbolized by monopolistic concessions, Western industry, counterreligious institutions, and a bureaucratic colonial system.

Swazi women are also organized into age sets of married and unmarried, but these are less formal than those of the men and do not extend under a common name throughout the nation. They are essentially local work teams that engage in specific tasks for district or national leaders. Women are never stationed in barracks, and the age of marriage for a girl is sanctioned by her parents and her friends, not by the rulers.

Sometimes a group of teen-agers are brought together under the patronage of unmarried princesses or daughters of chiefs into a temporary association, for which they lay down laws regulating clothing, food, language, and morality. No member may be "touched by a male," a regulation from which not even the king is immune. Violation of the code is punished by fines, imposed and collected by the girls, and also by organized songs of ridicule. The association, which begins and ends with tribute labor, lasts from one winter to the next, and the older girls are then publicly recognized as ripe for marriage.

In tribal society a person is a meeting point of identities—the identity of siblings, the identity of the lineage, the identity of the age group. The modern Western system gives greater scope to the individual, male or female, young and old. When conflict breaks out in conservative homesteads between parent and child generations or between older and younger siblings, it is not a conflict of ideologies but of personality. Sons may covet the power of the father, but when he dies, they hope to exercise over their own sons the authority they themselves once resented. Young people are anxious to possess the privileges of their seniors, not to abolish the privileges of seniority; young brides may rebel against the way particular in-laws abuse the rights of age, but they agree to the principle that age and sex are entitled to those rights. At the present time, the social structure which gives power to the older generation is challenged by the money economy, a new legal system, and schooling for a literate society. A son is still dependent on his father and ultimately on his chief for the land on which to build his home, but he is legally permitted to move for working purposes into the European town and support himself on money wages. The manual occupations opened by Western enterprise require physical strength, for which the old are rejected, while the young and fit are in demand and able to contract in terms of their personal legal status. Formal education weakens the claim of the uneducated that the possession of the greatest knowledge is obtainable only through age. Books and classes, quick roads to learning, contradict the system of gradual education in which the major phases of physical development are correlated with responsibilities associated with the group of peers.

6

The Supernatural

The Spirit World

SWAZI CULTURE sanctions enjoyment of the material and physical: food, women, and dancing. It does not in any way idealize poverty or place a value on suffering as a means to happiness or salvation. To deal with the hazards of life—failure of crops, unfaithfulness of women, illness and ultimate death—the culture provides a set of optimistic notions and positive stereo-typed techniques that are especially expressed through the ancestral cult, the vital religion of the Swazi, and through an elaborate system of magic. The ancestors sanction the desires of their descendants; magic provides the techniques for the achievement of these desires.

In the ancestral cult, the world of the living is projected into a world of spirits (*emadloti*). Men and women, old and young, aristocrats and common-ers, continue the patterns of superiority and inferiority established by earthly experiences. Paternal and maternal spirits exercise complementary roles similar to those operating in daily life on earth; the paternal role reinforces legal and economic obligations; the maternal exercises a less formalized protective in-fluence. Although the cult is set in a kinship framework, it is extended to the nation through the king, who is regarded as the father of all Swazi; his an-cestors are the most powerful of the spirits.

Swazi believe that the spirit or breath has an existence distinct from the flesh. When a person dies, both flesh and spirit must be correctly treated to safeguard the living. Mortuary ritual varies with both the status of the de-ceased and his (or her) relationship with different categories of mourners. The more important the dead, the more elaborate the rites given the corpse; the closer the relationship through blood or marriage, the greater the stereotyped interest demanded by the spirit of the mourners. A headman is buried at the entrance of the cattle byre, and his widows, children, siblings, and other relatives are constrained to undertake different demonstrations and periods of mourning.

294

The widows shave their heads and remain "in darkness" for three years before they are given the duty of continuing the lineage of the deceased through the levirate. A wife is more expendable; the deceased woman is buried on the outskirts of her husband's home, and the mourning imposed on him is less conspicuous, less rigorous, and of shorter duration. The social order regulates overt demonstrations of grief, irrespective of the depth of personal emotions. Death, more than any other situation in Swazi culture, exposes the *social* personality of man, woman, and child in the fullest context of kinship. The living must, in turn, adjust to the loss by building new bonds on established structural foundations.

The spirit of the deceased is ritually "brought back" to the family in a feast that ends all active mourning; the spirit continues, however, to influence the destinies of kinsmen. It may manifest itself in illness and in various omens, or it may materalize in the form of a snake. Mambas are associated with kings; harmless green snakes are associated with commoners and women; and certain snakes are excluded from the ancestral realm because they '"never come nicely." An ancestral snake does not show fear and moves with familiar sureness within the hut. It is a bad omen if such a snake comes in and quickly leaves. The body of every Swazi is believed to have at least one snake, which is associated with fertility and health. It is somehow connected with the spiritual snake, but is not conceptualized in any elaborate theory of transmigration or reincarnation. The existence of an ancestral snake is simply stated as fact, with the emphasis on practical implications.

Illness and other misfortunes are frequently attributed to the ancestors, but Swazi believe that *emadloti* do not inflict sufferings through malice or wanton cruelty. The mean husband, the adulterous wife, the overambitious younger brother, the disobedient son may be dealt with directly or vicariously by the spirits, acting as custodians of correct behavior and tribal ethics. Ancestors punish, they do not kill; death is the act of evildoers (*batsakatsi*), who are interested in destroying, not in perpetuating, the lineage or the state. If an illness originally divined as sent by the *emadloti* later becomes fatal, evildoers are assumed to have taken advantage of the patient's weak resistance.

While each specific death is interpreted as an act of witchcraft, death is also recognized as universal and inevitable. In a myth, widespread throughout the southeastern tribes, death was imposed by the arbitrary and inconsistent nature of the "Great Great One," "The First Being," a vaguely conceived "Great Ancestor." He sent the chameleon to mankind with a message of eternal life, then changed His mind and sent the lizard with the message of death. To the African, the chameleon, with its peculiar mottled and changing skin color and its markedly protruding eyes that turn in all directions is quite distinct from the ordinary lizard, which glides along without changing color and has sleepy eyes that look only straight ahead. The lizard arrived before the chameleon, who had stopped to eat of tasty berries growing by the wayside. When the chameleon arrived and delivered his message, he was driven away—death had already become part of life. The Great Great One apparently did not again intervene in the affairs of men, and no prayers or ritual are associated with Him. Many Christian missionaries use the vernacular word for Great Great One as a translation of the Biblical God, but the ideas underlying the two deities are worlds apart.

Ancestors have greater wisdom, foresight, and power than the rest of mankind, but no spirit of a deceased ever reaches complete deification or is regarded as omnipotent. Swazi ancestors are approached as practical beings; there is no conflict between the ethics of the ancestral cult and the mundane desires of life. Swazi desire the ends they say the *emadloti* desire for them. Swazi are not concerned with the life led by the dead, but with the way the ancestors influence their lives on earth. No one inquires from a diviner if the *emadloti* are happy and satisfied, till they show they are unhappy and dissatisfied. Ancestral spirits, like witches and sorcerers, are thought of most when comforts are few and troubles are many.

Swazi have no class of ordained priests, and the privileged duty of appealing to the *emadloti* rests with the head of the family. The father acts on behalf of his sons; if he is dead, the older brother acts on behalf of the younger. In this patrilineal society, ancestors of a married woman remain at her natal home; they are approachable only by her senior male kinsman, but they retain a protective interest in the woman who has provided cattle through her marriage, and in her children who consolidated her position as a wife. Contact is usually made through the medium of food, meat, or beer, and the dead, who are said to be often hungry, "lick" the essence of the offerings laid at dusk on a sacred place in the shrine hut and left overnight. The family head addresses the dead in much the same way as if they were alive; appeals to them are spontaneous and conversational, interspersed with rebukes and generally devoid of gratitude. Recognition of the holy, as distinct from the profane, is, moreover, expressed on certain occasions through sacred songs. Each clan has a special song and there are a number of anthems reserved for rituals of state.

Each family propitiates its own ancestors at the specific domestic events of birth, marriage, death, and the building and moving of huts; in addition, the royal ancestors periodically receive public recognition. Every year before the rains are due cattle are sent from the capital to the caves in two tree-covered groves, where dead kings and leading princes lie buried in order of seniority. The groves, described as frightening and awe inspiring, alive with the sound of majestic voices and the movement of great snakes, are in the charge of important chiefs in the vicinity. They must see that no one enters without permission, and there is a current mythology concerning the doom of unfortunates who unwittingly intruded into the domain of the sacred. The ruler's emissaries report the affairs of the country to the dead and appeal for prosperity, health, and rain. Some of the cattle are sacrificed; the others are brought back to the royal village, where various taboos have been imposed on normal behavior. The cattle are brought in on a night when the moon is full, and the ordinary people are ordered to wait in their huts in silence while the king and his mother meet the returning pilgrims. Together they walk through the great cattle pen chanting a sacred song associated with major developments of kingship. That night the gates are left open, so that the ancestral cattle may wander freely through the village. The following day, there is the main sacrifice, in which each animal is dedicated to specific dead and eaten in a sacramental feast. So close is the identification between the animal and the human, that kinsmen who would have practiced avoidance of the person in life are prohibited from eating of the flesh of the sacrificial victim.

Subordinate to the ancestral cult, suggesting a separate cultural influence—another layer of tradition—is the recognition accorded the forces of nature. The sun, moon, and rainbow are personified, and though they are not appealed to directly, they are drawn into the orbit of human destiny. Swazi believe that the earth is flat and that the sun, the male, crosses the sky in a regular path twice a year. Each night he sleeps and wakens again strong and refreshed. The moon is the woman who dies periodically and is connected with the cycle of fertility. The rainbow is the sign of the "Princess of the Sky," associated with spring. All major rituals are timed by the position of the sun and moon. Ancestral spirits are most active at dawn and dusk, and ceremonies to mark an increase in status are generally performed when the moon is waxing or full; ceremonies that temporarily isolate a man from his fellows take place when it is waning, or "in darkness."

As previously stated, rain is in a different category from most other natural phenomena. It is believed to be controlled by medicines associated with kingship and is interpreted as a sign of ancestral blessing and good will. Knowledge of rainmaking is secret to the queen mother, her son and three trusted assistants, but every subject is aware that at certain times the rulers are "working the rain." The techniques they use increase in strength with the month and general climatic conditions, and move, if necessary, over a period of time from minor to more elaborate rites. Failure to make rain come has many explanations: disobedience and disloyalty of the people; breach of taboos; hostility between the rulers themselves, and other actions that evoke the prohibitive anger of the royal ancestors. The efficacy of the medicines is not doubted—rain eventually falls—and the belief in the rulers as rainmakers, a belief held even by many Christians, remains one of the strongest sanctions of traditional Swazi power. Lightning, on the other hand, is associated with the "Bird of the Sky," which lives in certain pools and can be controlled by particularly powerful evildoers. There are special lightning doctors to treat homesteads and people with antilightning medicines.

A rich body of folklore relates various places, plants, and animals to the world of men, but the Swazi have no store of sacred oral literature. The world of nature is of much the same order and quality as the world of man, and the animal kingdom in particular provides characters and situations that illustrate the aspirations, contradictions, and conflicts experienced by humans. No special tales based on the ancestral world or nature are accredited to divine inspiration. In the hierarchically structured but kinship-oriented society of the Swazi, articulate revelation is restricted to medicine and divination.

Specialists in Ritual

In all situations requiring "deep" (esoteric) knowledge, Swazi consult medicine men (*tinyanga temitsi*) and/or their colleagues, the diviners (*tangoma*), the main specialists in Swazi traditional society. Medicine men work primarily with "trees" (roots, bark, leaves) and other natural substances, and enter the profession of their own accord; diviners diagnose the cause rather than direct the specific cure and rely on spirit possession for their insight. Within the two major categories of ritual specialists several grades are distinguished on the basis of training and technique.

Every Swazi has some knowledge of "medicines" for common ailments and other misfortunes (poor crops, failure in love, sick cattle) and the lowest grade of ritual specialist includes people who, usually through personal experience, have picked up remedies for specific purposes and are not prepared to disclose their secrets without reward. They claim no inspiration from the ancestors and no tradition of belonging to a family of doctors. Behind their backs they are spoken of contemptuously as "crocodiles,"—the quacks—and they are said to be increasing in number since they have had the opportunity of acquiring medicines from men outside the country and from Western drugstores. Informants say that some of these self-taught specialists are skillful enough but insist that the ancestors must subsequently have agreed that their work meets with success.

More highly rated are the medicine men whose careers are destined from birth or sanctioned by the powerful dead. Knowledge of rituals and medicine bags are retained in certain families as an important part of the inheritance. The owner imparts them to a favorite son, a younger brother, or close kinsman, who is "pushed by the heart to learn" and need not be the main heir. Once qualified, he calls on the "father spirit" in each situation and periodically renews the power of the bags in ritual reaffirmation of his spiritual dependence.

Some *tinyanga* specialize very intensively and will treat only a single illness or misfortune; others have a very diversified practice and offer panaceas for an extensive and varied range of difficulties. Added tension and insecurity have multiplied the situations for which medicines are desired, and many illiterate Swazi apply the same principiles to get better jobs, make profitable beer sales, or "sweeten the mouths" of men brought before magistrates for breaking the "white man's laws." Specialists in ritual, unlike specialists in handicrafts, effectively resisted change, and while many mundane objects were easily replaced by trade goods, the range of "medicines" has been extended.

In Swazi "medicine" the material ingredients are emphasized more than the verbal spell. These ingredients are frequently chosen on the familiar principles of homeopathic magic—like produces like, and things once in contact retain identity even when separated by distance. Their names may indicate the purpose of the rite for which they are used and serve as abbreviated spells. Thus, in a love potion of a leading *inyanga,* the main ingredient is a resilient, everlasting leaf named "disobey her mother"; for the medicine to secure a homestead against evildoers, "pegs" are cut from a tree that remains firm in the thinnest soil on a precarious slope. In the treatment for success, instructions given by an *inyanga* must be implicitly obeyed and any pain he inflicts must be stoically endured. Most doctoring for even indirect benefits (household safety, protection against lightning, as well as personal quandaries—love, ill health) involve techniques such as injections, inhalation, and purgatives. In all but intimate sexual affairs, all people in the homestead must take part, for each member is recognized as interacting with others, and correct adjustment of social relationships is considered essential for a successful result.

The Swazi have no association of medicine men. Each *inyanga* works alone, drawing on a common stock of traditionally "proven" remedies to which he may add his own findings. Each *inyanga* is conspicuous by his "bags"— pouches, calabashes, and charms—and when consulted he proudly displays their contents and expatiates on their "strength." Success is also attributed to the innate "power" (personality?) of the practitioner, whose own life conditions should support his professional claims. Renowned medicine men are themselves men of substance, and the profession provides the main opportunity for the individualist of traditional society.

The diviners, often people of outstanding intelligence, are the most powerful and respected of specialists. Their nonconformity is sanctioned by the spirits. The first sympton of possession is usually an illness that is difficult to cure and frequently follows terrible physical or emotional experiences. The patient becomes fastidious about food, eats little, complains of pains in various parts of the body and strange sensations between his shoulder blades and in his head. After sacrifices and medicines have proved useless, an already established diviner may diagnose that the sufferer is troubled by a spirit that must be made to express itself. Inarticulate noises and wild behavior indicate possession by the wandering ghost of a stranger or of an animal, and treatment is directed to its expulsion, or exorcism, by "closing its road." On the other hand, possession by friendly humans, most frequently kinsmen, is considered socially beneficial and the patient is encouraged to become a diviner. This involves long and arduous training during which he wanders over the countryside, eats little, sleeps little, is tormented by fearful dreams—of snakes encircling his limbs, of drowning in a flooded river, of being torn to pieces by enemies: he becomes "a house of dreams." These dreams must be interpreted to forestall misfortune to himself and others. He is also purified with special potions and various medicines to enable him to hear and see the spirit that is guiding him. Each novice composes a song and when he sings it, villagers come and join in the chorus to help him develop his powers.

A master diviner may have several novices living at his home for varying periods, forming an embryonic ritual school. When he considers them to be fully trained he puts them through a public graduation ceremony. Spectators hide articles for them to discover and they are also expected to throw hints to selected members of the audience about their various predicaments. As in many transition rites, each novice is said to be "reborn" and is honored with gifts of goats, special clothing, and beads to mark the change in status.

Despite the prestige and power of diviners most people do not wish to become possessed. The reasons given express socially inculcated attitudes to this type of greatness. It is best to be normal, not to be limited all one's life by the special taboos on sex, food, and general behavior that are imposed by the profession, not to be exhausted by the demands of a spirit greater than oneself, not to have to shoulder responsibility for the life and death of others. There are men therefore, who try to stop the spirit even in cases of ancestral possession, but on the whole such tampering is considered dangerous since it may leave a person permanently delicate and deranged, an object of spite by the spirit he has thrust from him and of neglect by others, angered at the reception given to one of their kind.

Although very few Swazi women practice as herbalists, more women than men appear to be "possessed," and there are a large number of well-known women diviners. The difference in number of women herbalists and diviners is a consequence of the sexual division of labor and the relative statuses of male and female. A woman's duty is the care of home and children. An herbalist who must wander around the countryside to dig roots and collect plants is brought into intimate contact with strangers, and this is contrary to the norm laid down for female behavior. As a result, girls are rarely taught medicines by their fathers, the heir to the family bags is always male, and no husband encourages a woman to practice medicine. Possession, however, is in a different category. A woman does not fight against the spirit of an ancestor that wishes to "turn her around," and even her husband is afraid to interfere and must submit to her "calling."

Political leaders and other aristocrats are positively discouraged from becoming either medicine men or diviners, for this would interfere with their administrative duties and does not fit into their ascribed status. At the same time, they employ *tinyanga* of all types to bolster their powers, and the *ingwenyama* is himself believed to have "deeper" knowledge of medicines than any of his subjects and to be able to detect evildoers without preliminary possession by virtue of his unique royal medicines.

In most séances the clients sit in a semicircle on the ground, chant songs, and clap their hands while the diviner, in full regalia, smokes *dagga** and dances himself into a high pitch of excitement. He asks no questions but makes statements to which the audience replies, "We agree." Each statement is a feeler, a clue whereby he builds up his case, piecing together the evidence from the emotion behind the responses, until finally he gives the desired information. Diviners, often shrewd judges of human nature, have a wide knowledge of local affairs and their interpretations generally, perhaps unconsciously, confirm the suspicions or crystallize the unspoken fears of their clients. It is however, often considered desirable to consult other diviners who may use dif-

---

* *Dagga* is a potent drug, similar to marihuana.

ferent methods. An increasing number of modern diviners "throw bones," a technique associated with Sotho and Tonga influence. The "bones" may be the astragali of goats, cowrie shells found on the East Coast, or oddly shaped seeds. The diviner, pointing to the different pieces, interprets the combination of positions. Exceptional divinatory devices include the "talking calabash" (a ventriloquist trick), a rattle that shakes of its own accord, and a magic wand. Public séances to "smell out evildoers" are prohibited under the Witchcraft Ordinance, but continue secretly in the frontier regions. In Namahasha, high in the Lebombo between Portuguese and Swazi territory, I have seen a diviner in full regalia, "smelling out" with a magically impregnated hippo whip as he danced in front of a tense audience that had come from a homestead some fifty miles away to learn the "cause" of a sequence of misfortunes and deaths. The poison "ordeal" may be administered as the ultimate test: the innocent will not be affected, but the guilty will writhe, vomit, and confess. The poison is collected in Portuguese territory; as a rule, diviners from that area are asked to assist in its preparation, but its use must be sanctioned by the *ingwenyama*.

Over the years new techniques of divination have been introduced and integrated with traditional modes of thought and behavior. Allied to the traditional diviner are "prophets" who belong to certain Separatist churches and claim to be possessed by the Holy Ghost, in which guise they carry on both divination and exorcism with less fear of "white man's law." There have also been two associations, similar to those in other parts of Africa, that have been directed against witchcraft in general, and have reaffirmed the strength of divination.

Witchcraft

Medicine men and diviners, official supporters of law and authority, have as their illegal opposition the evildoers (*batsakatsi*). Swazi *batsakatsi* include witches, whose evil is both physiological and psychological, and sorcerers, who rely on poisons, conscious violence, or other techniques for the deliberate destruction of property or person. The propensity to witchcraft is transmitted through a woman to her children, male and female; a male does not pass it on to his offspring. The initial quality must, however, be further developed by injections and training, or the potential witch will be mischievous but ineffectual. Qualified witches are believed to form a permanent gang, within which they are ranked on the basis of evil achievements. They operate at night; during the day they gloat consciously on their nefarious activities. A sorcerer obtains his "poisons" from outside and acts individually in specific situations against personal enemies. To be effective he may seek assistance from a medicine man who, by collusion, also becomes an evildoer; the most powerful *tinyanga* are therefore sometimes feared as the greatest *batsakatsi*.

Batsakatsi may work through direct contact with the person by striking a victim through his food. The reality of the power of evildoers is considered self-evident; it is manifest in otherwise inexplicable misfortunes and confirmed by confessions at séances and ordeals. Moreover, at the end of every individual's life, sorcery or witchcraft turns up the trump card of death.

Murders for "doctoring" (so-called ritual murders) still take place in Swaziland, and fall into two main situational types: (1) agricultural fertility; (2) personal aggrandisement. The victim, referred to as "a buck," is innocent of any crime and is killed with as much secrecy as possible. An analysis of the European court records indicated that the characteristics of sex, age, and pigmentation of the victims showed no uniformity, and that different organs were selected from the corpse. Where the accused were found guilty of murdering for "medicine" to doctor the crops, capital punishment was carried out on the principals; others involved were sentenced to imprisonment with hard labor for periods ranging from fifteen years to life; in murders for personal aggrandisement the death penalty was invariably imposed, but in certain circumstances it was commuted to a long term of imprisonment. The men employing the "doctors" were generally important headmen, sometimes chiefs suffering economic or status insecurity. The average Swazi condemns murders committed in self-interest as sorcery, and places the ritual specialist who gave the instructions in a different moral and legal category from the diviner who, in his capacity as a witchfinder, may be responsible for the destruction of people publicly revealed as evildoers. The distinction is not accepted by Western law.

Swazi complain that batsakatsi are more common now than in the past and blame the law that has made "smelling out" by diviners illegal. They argue that "the white man's law protects women and witches. Bad men flourish and those who smell them out are hanged." But, in fact, any increase in sorcery, as in other types of magic, must be sought in additional situations of conflict, feelings of inadequacy and helplessness, financial uncertainty, rivalry for jobs, competition for the favor of white employers, and personal insecurity in an alien-dominated milieu.

Witchcraft and sorcery can be directed against anyone, but because they emanate from hatred, fear, jealousy and thwarted ambition they are usually aimed at persons who are already connected by social bonds. The social content is stereotyped by the alignments of Swazi society and indicates points of tension or friction, actual or anticipated. In the polygynous homestead, the umstakatsi is usually a jealous co-wife or an unscrupulous half brother who is ambitious of the inheritance; outside the homestead, suspected evildoers are blatantly successful and aggressive peers. Important men do not need to use sorcery against insignificant inferiors, nor are they suspected of doing so. Sorcery is an indication of status and of the ambitions for improvement of status that operate within the limits of the stratified traditional society. Thus, not all destructive ritual is condemned as the work of evildoers, nor do all "productive" medicines receive social approval. Judgment depends on the situation. It is legitimate to use retaliative medicine on the grave of a person whose death was attributed to an unidentified evildoer, or to doctor property so that a thief will be inflicted with swollen finger joints, or to inject into an unfaithful wife medicine that will punish her lover with a wasting disease. It is illicit to employ productive medicine for unlimited wealth or success. In short, the *umstakatsi* undermines the *status quo;* the *inyanga* struggles to maintain it. Wedged between the chief and the *tinyanga* on the one hand and the *batsakatsi* on the other, the masses are molded to accept a relatively unenterprising conservatism.

Christianity

Traditional Swazi religion is challenged by Christianity. In 1946 nearly 40 percent of Swazi were registered as "Christians" and more than twenty different sects were listed. In Swaziland, as in the Republic of South Africa, a growing number of converts belong to Independent or "Separatist churches," which vary greatly in organization and credo but share one common characteristic —independence from white control. These churches offer new opportunities for self-expression and power; many of the founders are men of unusual personality, and some are more highly educated than the average Swazi.

Largely because of tribal status and a vested interest in polygyny, Swazi male aristocrats have tended to resist conversion from the ancestral cult, but their mothers and wives have been more responsive. The Methodists were the first to establish a mission in Swaziland. The late Indlovukati Lomawa was a recognized supporter of the church, though the National Council ruled that full conversion—including the clothing in which it could be demonstrated— was incompatible with the ritual duties of her position. She was particularly sympathetic to the Zionist Separatist church, whose charismatic local leader had converted close members of her natal family, and, at the same time, had acknowledged the claims of hereditary kingship exercised by her son, the *Ingwenyama.* When she died, she was buried according to custom away from the capital in a former royal village, so that her son would not be weakened by contact with death or the dead. At her funeral—which her son was not permitted to attend— various church officials paid their respects. Despite the fact that leading councilors tried to follow traditional practices, the entire mortuary procedure was interrupted for a few hours when her sister, who later succeeded to the position of queen mother, found that the church membership cards of the deceased (described as her "tickets across the Jordan") had been left behind at the capital. These were fetched and placed beside the dead woman in a wooden coffin that had been specially shaped to hold her body which was bound in fetal position and wrapped in a shroud of black cowhide.

The traditional religion has been influenced by Christianity, and Christianity as practiced by the Swazi has, in turn, been influenced by existing traditions. The extent of adaptation by the white-controlled churches ranges from the eclectic approach of Catholics to the rigidity of extreme Afrikaner Calvinists.* The Catholic church, which began work in 1914, later than most churches in

---

* Afrikaner is the term for white South Africans who speak Afrikaans, a local language developed mainly from Dutch. Afrikaners tend to be culturally insular, and strongly racialist.

Swaziland, increased its enrollment more rapidly than any other white-controlled church. But the proselytizing influence of all white missions virtually came to a standstill in the late 1930s, when the nativistic African Separatist movement boomed on an upsurge of nationalism. Separatist "Zionist" leaders consulted with Sobhuza and decided to form the Swazi National Church, with a flexible dogma and great tolerance of custom. Sobhuza was thus to be ritually entrenched, both as head of the traditional ancestral cult and as priest-king of a new faith, a position different from that in neighboring areas where traditional chieftanship had been deliberately broken down or where the chief himself had been converted to Christianity. At the same time, separatist movements cannot—by definition—really create lasting unity. A church, planned as a memorial to the late Lomawa and designed by an imaginative European architect, was half-built when friction, accentuated by lack of funds, broke out between the leaders and construction stopped. So the walls remain roofless, symbolizing a religious and secular unity that is desired but does not exist in modern Swaziland.

The Annual Ceremony of Kingship

Throughout this study I have mentioned the annual ritual of kingship, the *Incwala,* a ceremony rich in Swazi symbolism and only understandable in terms of the social organization and major values of Swazi life. It has been variously interpreted as a first-fruit ceremony, a pageant of Swazi history, a drama of kingship, and a ritual of rebellion. This beautiful and complex ceremony is described and analyzed in great detail in *An African Aristocracy;* here, I can but outline some of the main sequences and characteristics.

The central figure is the king, the "owner" of the *Incwala;* performance of the *Incwala* by anyone else is treason, which, on two historic occasions, cost the lives of overambitious princes. The *Incwala* reflects the growth of the king and is thus not a static ritual. When the king is a minor, the ritual is less elaborate, the medicines less potent, the animals required for doctoring smaller, the clothing simpler. When he reaches full manhood and has his first ritual wife, the *Incwala* reaches its peak. All subjects play parts determined by their status: the queen mother, the queens, married and unmarried regiments, princes, the king's artificial blood brothers, councilors, ordinary commoners, and ritual specialists known as "People of the Sea," all have specific duties and receive appropriate treatment.

The *Incwala* is a sacred period set apart from the profane and mundane routine of normal life. It extends for roughly three weeks of each year, and is divided into the Little *Incwala,* which lasts two days, beginning when the sun reaches its southern summer solstice and the moon is dark, and the Big *Incwala,* which lasts six days from the night of the full moon. In the interim period, sacred songs and dances of the Little *Incwala* are performed in key villages throughout the territory. It is believed that wrong timing will bring national disaster that can only be circumvented by elaborate counter-ritual, a common cultural device to make people abide by tradition, yet not automatically accept calamity.

The *Incwala* involves considerable organization and preparation. Several weeks before the ceremony the "People of the Sea" are brought to the capital for initial arrangements, and are then sent out to collect the water and other ritual ingredients. They divide into two groups, one travelling through the forests to the coast and the other to the confluence of the main rivers of the country. They must draw "the waters of all the world" and also dig potent sacred plants to strengthen and purify the king. In every homestead where the priests rest, the host provides beer and meat, and from all strangers who cross their paths they demand a small fine, which will be burnt on the last day, the day of final national purification. At the capital itself, preparations are made by the councilors, who will also be held responsible for the correct timing.

The honor of opening the *Incwala* is bestowed on the oldest regiment. Thereafter, other participants join in, taking their places according to rank and sex. The stage is the open cattle pen of the capital, but the main rites are enacted in secret in the king's sanctuary. The public contributes by performing sacred songs and dances. As the sun sets in a moonless night, the formation of the dances changes from the crescent of a new moon to the circle of the full moon. Princes and foreigners are dismissed as the warriors chant a new song that is associated with other important events of kingship—a king's marriage to his main ritual wife, the return of ancestral cattle from the royal grave, the burial of kings. It is a key song of the *Incwala*.

> Jjiya oh o o King, alas for your fate
> Jjiya oh o o King, they reject thee
> Jjiya oh o o King, they hate thee.

Suddenly the chief councilor commands "Silence," and the singing ceases while the king spits powerful medicine, first to the east, then to the west, and the crowd is given the signal to shout, "He stabs it!" Informants explained that "Our Bull (Our King) had produced the desired effect: he had triumphed and was strengthening the earth." He has broken off the old year and is preparing for the new." This climaxes the opening of the ceremony. The people then sing a final song comparable to a national anthem, praising the king as "the Bull, the Lion, the Inexplicable, the Great Mountain." At dawn of the following day, the ceremony is repeated. Afterwards, warriors go to weed the queen mother's garden, for which service they are rewarded with a feast of meat. The Little *Incwala* is over, and the men may return to their homes until the moon is "ripe."

In royal homesteads, the songs and dances of the Little *Incwala* are rehearsed and the sacred costumes are prepared for the main ceremony. The words of the songs are surprising to Europeans, who are accustomed to hear royalty blatantly extolled, the virtues of the nation magnified, and the country glorified at national celebrations. Most songs of the *Incwala* have as their motif hatred of the king, and his rejection by the people. The actual words are few, mournful, and tremendously moving; they are reinforced by dancing, which mimes much of the drama. The beautiful clothing, including feathers of special birds and skins of wild animals, indicates differences in rank and also carrys deep magical and religious significance.

On the first day of the Big *Incwala,* the regiment of pure unmarried youths is sent to cut branches of a magic tree with which to enclose the king's sanctuary. Swazi believe that if the branches are cut by anyone who has violated the moral code of his age group, the leaves will wither. Such branches must be cast out and the culprit ostracized and even attacked, not so much for his sexual violations as for his willingness to endanger the well-being of the state. The tree is quick-growing, with leaves that remain green for many weeks, when cut by the virtuous. The cutting must begin as the full moon rises, to the rhythm of a new sacred song—a sacred lullaby—the theme song of the second stage of the drama. The qualities of quick growth, greenness, toughness, and fertility characterize most elements of the *Incwala* ritual.

On the morning of the second day, the youths return, bearing their wands proudly aloft and chanting the lullaby. The councilors surround the sanctuary with the mystic greenery, behind which the powers of the king will be symbolically reborn.

The main event of the third day is the "killing of the bull," the symbol of potency. The king strikes a specially selected black bull with a rod doctored for fertility and "awakening," and the pure youths must catch the animal, throw it to the ground, pummel it with their bare hands, and drag it into the sanctuary where it is sacrificed. Parts of the carcass are used for royal medicine; the remainder is an offering to the ancestors.

The "Day of the Bull" fortifies the king for the "Great Day" when he appears in his most terrifying image and symbolically overcomes the hostility of princely rivals. In the morning he bites "doctored" green foods of the new year; his mother and others follow suit, their medicines graded by status. Later in the day, under the blazing sun, all the people, in full *Incwala* dress, and with the king in their midst, dance and sing the *Incwala.* Towards sunset the king leaves them; when he re-emerges he is unrecognizable—a mythical creature—clothed in a fantastic costume of sharp-edged green grass and skins of powerful wild animals, his body gleaming with black unguents. The princes approach and alternately drive him from them into the sanctuary and beseech him to return. Behind them the people sing and dance. All members of the royal Dlamini clan and all "foreigners" (seen as potential enemies) are ordered from the cattle byre; the king remains and dances with his loyal supporters and common subjects. Tension mounts as he sways backwards and forwards. At the climax he appears holding in his hand a vivid-green gourd, known as the "Gourd of Embo" (the north), the place of Dlamini origin. Although picked the previous year, the gourd is still green. The king throws it lightly on the horizontally placed shield of a selected agemate, who must not let the fruit, sacred vessel of the past and symbol of continuity, touch the ground. The old year has been discarded; the king has proved his strength, and the people are prepared for the future.

Life does not immediately return to its normal routine; major rites of transition generally involve gradual readjustments. The whole of the following day the rulers are secluded and unapproachable, their faces painted dark with medicines, their bodies anointed with fat from the sacred herd. Subjects are placed in a condition of ritual identification and prohibited from many normal physical activities—sex, washing, scratching, merrymaking. There is a deep silence at the capital. The *Incwala* songs are closed for the year.

On the last day, the ointments of darkness are washed off the rulers, who are then bathed with foamy potions to make them "shine" anew. Objects used throughout the ceremony, and which represent the old year, are burned on a ritual fire. The king sets light to the wood (which must be without thorns) with ancient fire sticks and walks naked and alone round the pyre, sprinkling medicated waters. At noon, he and his people, dressed in partial *Incwala* clothing, gather in the cattle pen for the final scene. They perform a series of solemn, but not sacred, dance-songs; rain—the blessing of the ancestors—must fall, quenching the flames and drenching all the participants. If no rain falls, the people fear a year of dire misfortune. But the rains usually come, and in the evening the rulers provide vast quantities of meat and beer, and there is gaiety and love-making. Early the next morning the warriors collect in the cattle byre, sing ordinary march songs, and go to weed the queen mother's largest maize garden. The local contingents are then free to return to their homes, where they may safely eat of the crops of the new season.

Now for some brief comments on certain general features of the *Incwala*. Culturally, it is a dramatic ritualization of Swazi kingship in all its complexity—economic, military, ritual. The sacrament of the first fruits, an essential rite in a series of rites, relates the rulers to the productive cycle, and the timing links them mystically with the great powers of nature—the sun and the moon. Fertility and potency are stressed as essential qualities of social continuity and must be acquired by stereotyped techniques. Swazi (like all people) believe that the efficacy of ritual lies in correct repetition; certain changes have been made in the course of time but the tendency has been to add new items rather than discard old.

The *Incwala* symbolizes the unity of the state and attempts to maintain it. Fighting and bloodshed are recognized as possible dangers at a time when regiments from all parts of the country are mobilized at the capital. The men are prohibited from carrying spears and *assegais,* the main weapons of attack; only shields and sticks are incorporated in the costume. Emotional fervor is canalized in songs, and dances, obligatory acts of participation that induce the sacred pulse, the *tactus* of Swazi national life. Internal solidarity is frequently intensified by outside opposition; the king outshines his rivals and the nation is fortified against external enemies. In the past, the *Incwala* frequently preceded an announcement of war against a "foreign tribe."

The people committed to the *Incwala* represent the social groups that accept the authority of the traditional rulers; those who deliberately refrain from taking part indicate the limitations of their present acceptance. Certain missions prohibited their converts from dancing the *Incwala,* and those Swazi Christians who attend are mainly members of Separatist churches. It is significant that, since 1937, the leader of the main Zionist Separatist sect has travelled to the capital for the *Incwala,* thereby publicly demonstrating his support of Swazi kingship. Thus the *Incwala* serves as a graph of status on which the roles of the king, his mother, the princes, councilors, priests, princesses, commoners, old and young are mapped by ritual. The balance of power between the king and the princes and between the aristocrats and commoners is a central theme; the ambivalent position of a Swazi king and the final triumph and sanctity of kingship is dramatized in ritual. The groups and individuals who have no set roles in the present-day *Incwala* reflect the influence of European dominance and of a new basis of stratification.

References Cited

BEEMER, HILDA, 1937, "The Development of the Military Organization in Swaziland," *Africa*, Vol. X, No. 1, pp. 55–74, No. 2, pp. 176–205.

A detailed account of Swazi age groups.

CRONIN, A. M. D., 1941, "The Swazi," *The Bantu Tribes of South Africa*, Vol. VIII, Sec. 4. Cambridge University Press.

A fine photographic record with an introductory article by Hilda Beemer.

GREEN, L. P., and FAIR, T. J. D., 1960, "Preparing for Swaziland's Economic Growth," *Optima*, pp. 194–207.

A clear analysis of recent economic developments with excellent maps.

HUGHES, A. J. R., "Some Swazi Views on Land Tenure, 1962," *Africa*, Vol. XXXII, No. 3, pp. 253–279.

KUPER, HILDA, 1947, *An African Aristocracy*. London: Oxford University Press for the International African Institute.

A full study of the traditional Swazi political system and its economic and religious institutions.

———, 1947, *The Uniform of Color*. Johannesburg: Witwatersrand University Press.

A continuation of *An African Aristocracy*, analyzing the influence of Western civilization on the traditional society.

———, 1952, *The Swazi*. Ethnographic Survey of Africa, Daryll Forde (ed.), London: International African Institute. *Southern Africa*, Part 1, A concise survey of Swazi social conditions, political and economic structure, religious beliefs and practices, technology and art.

MARWICK, B. A., 1940, *The Swazi*. Cambridge: Cambridge University Press.

A useful ethnographic monograph.

THE NAVAJO

James F. Downs

University of Hawaii, Hilo

James F. Downs served in the U.S. Navy during World War II and the Korean War, worked as a newsman, professional horseman, and farmer. After conducting field research among the Washo of California and Nevada and the Navajo of Arizona, he received his M.A. and Ph.D. in anthropology at the University of California at Berkeley. He has studied oriental languages and conducted research on Tibetan culture in northern India in association with R. B. Ekvall, author of another case study in the series, *Fields on the Hoof.* He has taught at the University of Rochester, University of Wyoming, California State College in Los Angeles, and the University of Arizona. He is now professor of anthropology at Hilo College and the Center for Cross-Cultural Training and Research at the University of Hawaii.

Contents

Introduction

S PRAWLING OVER the northeastern corner of Arizona and into the neighboring states of Utah and New Mexico, the Navajo* Indian Reservation covers sixteen million acres, an area the size of West Virginia. One authority has described it as a fifty-first state within the boundaries of three other states. The Navajo tribe in cooperation (and sometimes in conflict) with the United States Government is governed by its own political bodies and maintains its own police force and courts to enforce tribal law. Navajo rangers build roads, dams, and other tribal works and operate a separate park service and tribal highway and works departments.

The citizens of this anomalous political body are the Navajo Indians, members of the largest Indian tribe in the United States. Approximately one hundred thousand Navajo live within the reservation boundaries or on lands immediately adjoining the reservation. Some small colonies are found in New Mexico completely separate from the reservation but still politically part of the tribe. In Los Angeles and in the San Francisco Bay area there are increasing numbers of Navajo who have immigrated to the cities. In the northern plain states of Wyoming and Idaho, semipermanent colonies of Navajo who work in seasonal agriculture have sprung up.

The arid and starkly beautiful scenery of Monument Valley in the northern part of the reservation is familiar to many millions of motion picture viewers as the background for such great films as *Stagecoach*, *She Wore a Yellow Ribbon*, and *Fort Apache*. The same viewers have seen the Navajo themselves appearing in great number in these and other films disguised as Sioux, Comanche, Apache, or some other tribe considered by screen writers to have been more "warlike" than the Navajo. Millions of people have become familiar with the more scenic parts of the

---

* *Navajo* is a word of mysterious origin and is often spelled Navaho. Although there are sound historical, orthographic, and linguistic reasons for this spelling, Navajo is used by the federal government, the Navajo Tribe, and all individuals who have had occasion to write letters to the author. To Westerners, the practice of pronouncing a "j" like an "h" is not disconcerting, and as a courtesy to the Navajo, this spelling is used throughout.

315

Navajo country through the media of railroad advertisements and post cards. On Highway 66, which passes along the southern boundary of the reservation, hordes of tourists have come into brief contact with the Navajo selling authentic rugs and jewelry and other novelties, often not so authentic.

The Navajo have been studied by anthropologists perhaps more than any other native people in the world. Over the past thirty years there has scarcely been a period when one or more anthropologists have not been engaged in research on one part of the reservation or another. Individual anthropologists have in some cases devoted their entire professional lives to the study of the Navajo way of life. Hundreds of others have cut their professional teeth in the field with the Navajo people. Unfortunately the bulk of this material has found its way into the relative obscurity of the professional journal, and in the main the Navajo people are scarcely known and often badly misunderstood by their closest neighbors, not to mention the mass of American people.

There are dramatic changes taking place on the reservation as communication, education, and economic forces gradually bring the Navajo closer and closer to sharing in the American society. But these changes are relatively new, and for several centuries the Navajo lived a distinct and separate life in high, arid country of the northern Southwest. Their system was well adapted to both the natural and social conditions of the region, and for many years they were the dominant military force in the Southwest and feared neither other Indians nor the Mexican and Anglo newcomers. Despite eventual military defeat of the Navajo, their style of life did not, as is the tragic case in so many Indian tribes, collapse. Instead it adjusted and adapted and expanded into a unique social and cultural system. That system is in large part now outdated, but it had within it the strengths to make even more changes and adjustments without too severely disrupting the tenor of life or the social identity of the individual Navajo.

This book will attempt to describe this special style of life developed by the Navajo in one community. In the more remote areas this life-style continues, and throughout the reservation it forms the foundation on which modern Navajo life is developing.* Much of the data was gathered by the author during 1960 and 1961 when he, his wife, and their son were privileged to live in the Black Mesa area of the reservation. This region was, at that time, remote and isolated and considered one of the most traditional areas in the Navajo country. Information not obtainable by direct observation could be recovered by questioning older men and women who remember, some of them, the first horse-drawn wagon that came into the region. Since then, the author has been able to return twice for shorter periods.

Because sheepherding has played such an important part in the history of the Navajo in general and remains the most important focus of the culture of Nez Ch'ii, the author has chosen to focus this book on the pastoral aspects of Nez Ch'ii society and culture. While the various elements of Navajo life are described, for

---

* The *ethnographic present* is a device developed to present a relatively static picture of a dynamic social situation. The description of Nez Ch'ii society then is a composite of Navajo culture as observed by the author, reported by other anthropologists, and described by older informants.

the most part they are treated within the framework of the ongoing and unending work required to keep sheep and cattle herds and maintain a social and cultural system based on this activity.

Black Mesa is only one part of a vast region with often dramatically different environments and historical circumstances, so the author has also drawn on the great store of research in the Navajo country that has been carried out since the beginning of this century and also on archaeology and historical documents to fill in the background of these remarkable people.

The reader should keep in mind that history never ends and that many changes have occurred since I first went into the Nez Ch'ii country. This book describes life as it was in that place at that time. On this foundation the present—and the future—stand.

The success or failure of any ethnographer's work depends on the willingness of his subjects and informants, who are, in the final analysis, his hosts, to suffer his presence. To the people of Black Mesa, who patiently bore my presence and my questions without fully understanding the reason for either and who gently instructed me to the limits of my ability in the art of being a Navajo, I owe this book, and to them it is dedicated.

Tuba City
August 1967

1

Evolution of the Navajo People

The Nadene Stock

THREE THOUSAND YEARS AGO—about the time Homer was composing the *Iliad* and the *Odyssey*, five hundred years after the fall of the civilization of the Indus Valley and the rise of civilization in China—a group of Asians separated from their fellows and crossed the Bering Straits into North America.

Some linguists believe that their language was ancestral to a family of Asian languages generally known as Sino–Tibetan. Since their entry into the New World, the immigrants developed a number of languages from the parent stock including Eyak, Tlingit, Haida, and the many variations and dialects of Athapaskan, which includes Navajo. By comparing the number of shared words in these various North American languages and some Asian languages, linguists arrived at the figure of three thousand years ago as a time when these languages were one. This common language, or stock, has been called Nadene.

What caused the Nadene-speaking people of Asia to migrate into the New World is unknown. This was a period of great turmoil in the Old World. All through Eurasia peoples from the interior seem to have been pushing toward the edges of the landmass. Perhaps this migration to the north and east is somehow related to this general situation.

It is difficult, perhaps impossible, to paint even the most brief picture of the physical appearance or the culture of these people. The fact that they were Mongoloids is certain. Dark hair, with very little curl or wave, is one Mongoloid characteristic. Dark eyes are another, and a yellowish brown skin is yet another. Facial characteristics were most probably like those of modern-day populations of Siberia, that is, more angular with narrower lips and more prominent noses than are common in Mongoloid populations farther to the south in Asia. Their babies frequently had, at birth and for several months thereafter, a dark blue pigmentation at the base of the spine, the so-called Mongolian spot, which is relatively rare among Caucasians but almost universal among Mongoloid peoples.

The culture that they brought with them into the New World is even more obscure, made the more so by the many cultural adaptations and adjustments evolved by their descendants. In surveying the known cultures of Nadene-speaking peoples, it is difficult to isolate elements that they may have brought from Asia to the New World from traits that they either borrowed from Indian populations already here or developed independently since their entry into the New World.

Two material culture items that they may have brought with them are the hard-soled moccasin and the strong, complex bow, both of which appear to have Asian origins. Certain elements of their mythology reflect Old World, probably Asian, origins. But this cannot be dwelt upon too heavily because it is a statement that can be made about nearly all American Indian mythologies. Persons who have associated with both Athapaskan, particularly Navajo and Apache, and Central Asian peoples such as Mongolians and Tibetans have often remarked at similarities of attitude and general behavior, but these conclusions are entirely subjective and difficult, if not impossible, to ever establish objectively.

The distribution of Nadene languages suggests that these newcomers, perhaps the last such group to enter the New World before its discovery by Europeans, penetrated or shoved aside a thin line of Eskimo culture along the Arctic Ocean and began to spread out into Alaska and western Canada. Eventually, descendants of this original language were distributed from the shores of Hudson Bay to the Pacific Ocean. In that environmental context, Nadene-speakers adapted to or developed a number of cultural types based either on the hunting of subarctic animals in the tundra and forests of the northwest or on the enormous fish and seafood resources of the coasts. These latter cultures, called Northwest Coast cultures, are distributed from southern Alaska to northern California and are shared by speakers of languages other than Nadene. They produced one of the most elaborate nonagricultural cultures to be recorded. The latter shared many cultural traits with the Algonkian-speaking peoples of northern Canada and are often listed among the more simple hunting cultures.

Students of North American culture history estimate that the original Nadene language or languages began to diverge from each other about two thousand years ago. On islands off the coast of Alaska and British Columbia two quite divergent groups, the Tlingit and the Haida, developed. The remaining languages are now called Athapaskan and are spread widely but not continuously over western North America.

The Athapaskans

The formation of distinct languages from a common parent stock is a consequence of the separation of peoples. The Haida and the Tlingit, for instance, occupied large islands well away from the coast of North America. Other Nadene-speakers spread east into the tundra and forests, while others moved south. In each of these new groups different language changes occurred, but, in general, they all remained recognizably related one to another.

After the first split-up of Nadene, the Athapaskan languages began to break up as well. Some groups, it is estimated between thirteen and sixteen centuries ago, settled in the extreme north of California where they participated in a form of the Northwest Coast culture, which was much influenced by the cultures of surrounding peoples of California who spoke several different languages. These include the Hupa and the Mattole peoples.

Some time between one thousand and thirteen hundred years ago Athapaskan underwent another schism. A number of peoples split off from the northern and coastal regions and moved into the American Southwest, through what are now the states of Arizona, New Mexico, and eventually Texas and northern Mexico. Although these languages are clearly related to the Northern Athapaskan languages, they have developed distinct enough differences to be given yet another name— Apachean, or Southern Athapaskan.

It is difficult to know what Athapaskan culture was in this period of southern migration or even what the route of the movement was. Some authorities feel that the migration was down the eastern slope of the Rockies. Others feel that it may have been along the western slope. Others cautiously admit that either or both possibilities might be correct and suggest that these wanderers may have come in several waves, or in many small wandering groups, along many routes. As yet, archaeological research yields no evidence that is indisputably Athapaskan in the vast area between Canada and the Southwest. Perhaps we should not expect that it would. Migrant people seldom leave monuments to their passing. And after two thousand years in North America, it is probable that much of the Athapaskan material culture would be shared by many other peoples in similar environments. But even without archaeological support, we can safely assume that the Athapaskans did come into the Southwest and there they developed a number of separate but related cultures and languages.

These newcomers appear not to have been agriculturists. They probably introduced the composite bow into the Southwest and with it the hard-soled moccasin. They may have come as raiders against the farming communities of the pueblo-dwelling people along the upper Rio Grande and elsewhere in the northern Southwest. They may have made a type of pottery characterized by a pointed bottom, but if they did, it was not an exclusive trait of the Athapaskans and was shared by a number of western tribes and perhaps a number of eastern groups as well.

The land into which they moved was peopled by a number of tribes with roots very deep in the area and with connections to the civilization of Meso–America farther to the south. In northeastern New Mexico along the upper reaches of the Rio Grande, the Eastern Pueblo peoples were living in villages, usually located on mesa tops for protection, and farming the bottom lands. Slightly to the west other villages were living basically the same pueblo life but speaking languages known as Keresian and Zuni. In northern Arizona there were, and are, a number of pueblo villages inhabited by Uto–Aztecan-speaking Hopi peoples who share the general patterns of Pueblo culture.

In earlier times these farming Pueblo cultures had been more widely distributed, with outlying communities in Nevada and Kansas and many more communities in the Southwest proper. The earlier communities were not invariably located on a mesa top. The withdrawal of Pueblo peoples into the Southwestern heartland and the movement of villages to easily defensible positions has been considered evidence of invasions of the Athapaskan-speaking peoples. This is not at all clear, however, because there is equally strong evidence that the Athapaskans entered the Southwest after the movement by the Puebloans had been completed.

In addition to the Pueblo people there were, to the west and north, various peoples of Uto–Aztecan and Yuman speech who were not as complex as the Pueblos. The Walapai and Southern Paiute, for instance, were generally hunters and gatherers, although some farming was practiced. On the banks of the Colorado there were Yuman-speaking tribes, noted for their warlike attitudes, who farmed the bottomlands of the river. In southern Arizona the Pima and their close relatives the Papago farmed the arid desert country and lived in villages. Most of these peoples appear to have had long histories of gradual development from hunting and gathering to farming. Crops and techniques suitable to the generally arid Southwest had been invented and developed, and, in general, relations between people were peaceful.

Into this land then came the Athapaskans, hunters rather than gatherers. The Southwest provided them with a stage on which to work out their cultural destiny. The northern Southwest is a variable land with deserts and mountains and almost all the possible environmental zones between these extremes. Inasmuch as the Puebloan peoples tended to exploit the limited areas where farming was successful, the Southwest provided many opportunities for a less sedentary people willing to live more directly off the land. As the environment provided various and different opportunities, the Athapaskans began to develop somewhat divergent styles of life and languages.

Precisely what their relations were with the Pueblo peoples with whom they were in contact, how their society was organized, and how much of their culture was absorbed from their more advanced neighbors we do not really know, but it is at this point that the Athapaskans first appear in history. The early travelers, explorers, and missionaries of Spain met them and gave them a new name—the Apache.

The Apaches

When Coronado probed into the Southwest, he met, east of the Pecos River in what is now Texas and New Mexico, small groups of wandering peoples whom he named the Tayas and the Querechos. These were hunting peoples, moving frequently in pursuit of the bison that lived on the plains in seemingly endless numbers. They may have been newcomers and explorers almost as much as the Spanish. Some authorities feel they entered this region only a few years before the Spanish. It is probable that these were the ancestors of the historic tribe of Lipan Apaches, who adopted the horse and became the southernmost representatives of the buffalo-hunting Plains Indian culture. Another such group, the Kiowa-Apache, an Athapaskan-speaking tribe that allied itself with the Kiowa, may also be a descendant of these early hunters.

Moving toward the west, Spanish explorers discovered the Pueblo people, a great disappointment because the Spaniards had been led to believe they would find great and rich cities. Nearby they made contact with roving people of a much different culture. These too appear to have been Athapaskan-speaking peoples who arrived in the area perhaps as late as 1500, certainly no earlier than A.D. 1000.

Anthropologists and linguists, seeking common elements that might be considered as reflecting the basic culture patterns that Apacheans brought from the north, have made detailed comparisons between the languages and the cultures of Northern and Southern Athapaskans. Such a reconstruction can only be tentative, but, to the degree that such patterns appear to be consistent with the environmental factors and the practices of other hunting and gathering peoples, they are worth considering as a base from which subsequent Southwestern cultures developed.

STYLE OF LIFE

The Apaches live a nomadic life, moving in search of game and plant foods through all the environmental zones of the Southwest. The basic unit of life was a small band of related peoples, probably related to bilateral* rules of descent (although they may have been in part matrilineal and matrilocal, a custom some writers suggest they imported from Asia).

The men, using the powerful sinew-backed bow, hunted the bison, elk, deer, pronghorn antelope, jackrabbits and cottontail, the wild turkey, porcupine, and probably any other game that came their way. Gathering of piñon nuts, grass seeds, berries, roots, and other plant foods was probably the responsibility of the women.

Housing consisted of a conical frame of light poles covered with brush, grass, or whatever else might be handy. Such structures are still to be seen among the modern Apaches in New Mexico and Arizona. Deer, elk, antelope, and buffalo provided skins for clothing, which probably consisted of little more than a skirt or kilt for both sexes plus robes and hard-soled moccasins. Shredded bark was used by the women to make short skirts after the manner of tribes in the Great Basin. They made relatively simple pottery and woven baskets and used the dog as a beast of burden.

Like most hunting and gathering peoples of western America, their religious life was centered on the person of a shaman, that is, a man or woman who was able to receive into his or her body the spirit and power of the supernatural and, while in that condition, to effect cures. The most important ceremony was in all probability that which was held on the occasion of the girl's first menstrual period.

A belief that they appear to have held in common with peoples throughout the northern hemisphere was a special consideration of the bear as a powerful and supernaturally dangerous creature. Beyond this brief sketch we can say little more about the Apacheans at the time of contact with Europeans. Whether, for instance, any of these people had begun to farm after the example of the Pueblos or whether their religion and social organization had begun to feel the impact of the more elaborate systems of the farming people we cannot as yet definitely determine.

---

* A descent system wherein a person reckons members of both his mother's and his father's family as equally related. *Matrilineal* systems are those in which a person reckons his descent in his mother's line. *Matrilocal* refers to the practice of the bridegroom's taking up residence with the bride's family.

Differentiation of Groups

However, it was from this basic form that all modern groups of Apaches and the Navajo were to spring. We should, therefore, consider the distribution of these peoples at or about the time of contact. The Pueblo peoples form a very rough and scattered curve that stretches from the upper reaches of the Rio Grande across west central New Mexico and terminates not far from the Grand Canyon in northern Arizona. To the east of them in historic times we find on the plains the Lipan and Kiowa-Apache, to the southeast the Mescalero, and to the immediate north the Jicarilla; directly to the south the Chiricahua and to the west, south of the Little Colorado, the various bands known as the Western Apache. Each of these peoples recognized its kinship with the other, but each was different from the other at least to the degree demanded by the different environments. In addition, the nature of the contact with the Pueblo peoples must also have affected the specific direction that each of these groups took.

This is particularly important in the case of one more group. The tribes mentioned above lived outside the curve of Pueblo peoples. One group, however, occupied the land within that curve and experienced more continued, varied, and intensive contact with the sedentary farming peoples of the area. In any event, the Spanish who established a settlement at Santa Fe in 1609 as well as a number of missions and colonies in the area began to differentiate between Apaches—wild, roaming, hunting, and raiding people who came into their settlements and those of the Pueblo people—and another group, the Navajo Apaches, or Apaches of the big fields.

The Navajo Apache

In 1630 the Spanish missionary Alonso de Benavides speaks of three kinds of Apaches—the Xila Apaches who lived by the hunt, the Vacquero Apaches of the buffalo herd, and the Navajo Apaches who were farmers. With this later group he had some extensive contact and provides us with our first dependable information on the lives of the people who must have been the ancestors of the modern Navajo.

Navajo, as used by Father Benavides, appears to mean "large cultivated fields." We can say that certainly by 1630 one group of Apachean peoples had learned agriculture from the Pueblos and had begun to adjust their lives to the new means of gaining a livelihood.

These farmers had abandoned their flimsy houses of poles and brush and adopted a semisubterranean house, that is, a hole excavated into the earth to form the walls and then a domed roof formed over it with timber and earth. Such dwellings are found throughout northeastern Asia and were also used in prehistoric times by the ancestors of the Pueblos. In addition to dwellings, the Navajo Apaches built special huts for storing grain.

Men still hunted, and perhaps entire families traveled into the mountains in certain seasons to hunt and gather. The adoption of farming had made it possible to produce enough food to support larger residential units. One consequence of this was the occurrence of polygyny, that is, one man marrying more than one woman. Benavides says they married as many as they could support. As family organization became more complex, so did political organization, and the Navajo Apache appeared to have had a definite feeling of possessing specific territory that they would defend against intruders. The details of their political structure are unknown, but Benavides met and negotiated with a number of men referred to as "captains," apparently the recognized leaders of particular areas.

The Navajo Apache, although very curious about the foreigner's religious ceremonies, were never successfully converted. They had a well-established system of trade with the people of Santa Clara Pueblo, which took the form of "fairs," large-scale visits of Navajo to the pueblos, during which time they traded dressed animal skins and mineral pigments (perhaps even turquoise) used by the Puebloans. That these trading affairs were peaceful seems certain because the Navajo Apaches brought their women and children with them. But all relations between the Pueblo and the Navajo were not peaceful. At least they had a mutually understood means of establishing peace negotiations after hostilities, part of which consisted of the sending of an arrow and some tobacco as a sign of peace.

Archaeological discoveries reveal the remains of Navajo communities from north central New Mexico (1491, 1541) to the Black Mesa region of northern Arizona (1622). However, Benavides' brief sketch gives us the only detailed information we have for nearly a century. Since the Spanish occupation of the Southwest was concentrated in the area of the Pueblos, attention was not regularly drawn to the more remote and mobile Apache groups. In 1680 an Indian rebellion in which both Pueblo and Apache peoples took part drove the Spanish from this region for nearly a decade. During this time there was much intimate contact between the two peoples. Some Puebloans, fearing Spanish reprisal, fled from their homes to live with the Navajo. Much of what we now think of as Navajo culture was born in this time. At any rate, for the period of the early 1700s history and archaeology provide evidence of a people quite distinct from the other Apache groups, a people we can now speak of simply as the Navajo.

The Early Navajo

ECONOMIC LIFE

The Spanish had introduced many new elements into the life of the indigenous peoples of the Southwest. For the Navajo the impact was double because they were absorbing much of the culture of the Pueblos as well. From their Indian neighbors they had learned farming and weaving, borrowed clothing styles and many religious ideas and ceremonies. The most important introduction made by the Spanish was domestic livestock. The Puebloan peoples had also been affected by domestic stock, but they tended to add herds of sheep, goats, cattle, and horses to their already established way of life. The Navajo on the other hand began to shape their lives around herds acquired from the Spanish. The high, arid country of northern New Mexico and Arizona is ideal for grazing sheep, although scarcity of water forces a herder to move rather frequently. This fitted into the roaming existence of the Navajo, who soon combined farming, in favorable locations, with extensive sheepherding. Living in relatively permanent villages or *rancherias* in the winter, they moved from one grazing ground to another through most of the year. Their winter houses were simple but substantial structures of log, stone, and earth, round in shape and often blending completely into the landscape. They are today called *hogans*, a corrupted form of the original Navajo term. In the summer, the Navajo lived in simple brush shelters or huts that were easily abandoned as they followed their herds.

Although they spoke the same language and in large part shared a common culture, there was no political unity among the early Navajo. In each area leaders appeared, informally selected for their wisdom. Their authority appears to have been limited according to the degree of willingness of people to follow their advice. Group activities such as hunting parties, war parties, or ceremonies were directed by men with special ritual knowledge considered necessary for the success of the activity so that power was dispersed among many individuals to be exercised only in specific contexts.

In some areas farming played a more important role in economic life than did herding, but these were considered by the Navajo to be unfortunate situations, and the people living there were said to be poor because they did not have large herds. Because herds of livestock can increase without increasing the demands for labor, many Navajo began to hold very large herds of sheep, goats, and horses. Some of these parcelled out parts of their herds to poor relatives and dependents and thus began to form a distinct upper class of *Ricos*, or "rich men" who had control, through economic ties, over many people. Still the major unit of Navajo life was a cluster of hogans, each housing a married couple and usually belonging to a number of sisters who lived in a matrilineal, matrilocal extended family. This extended family cared for a single herd of sheep made up of the animals of many individual related owners. Individual couples would farm fields sometimes located some distance away from the hogan cluster. Defense and nearness to a domestic water supply and wood for fires all played a part in determining the location of the homestead.

Decisions to shift grazing ground were made on an extended family, rather than a tribal or even district, basis, each group deciding for itself when it seemed best to move. Waterholes and springs were considered common property, but, in practice, the people living and grazing their stock nearby were the actual owners.

By the early 1800s the Navajo were beginning to be known for the long-wearing woolen blankets that were woven by the women and traded to the Puebloan people, the Spanish, and later to the Anglos. Raw wool was also sold and traded, and Navajo men appear to have spent much of their time hunting deer principally for their hides, which were an important item of trade. Women also made pottery that was much ruder than the fine ceramics produced by the Pueblos. Basketry was an old Navajo art, and Navajo baskets were also an important item of trade.

Corn, squash, beans, and watermelon are repeatedly mentioned as Navajo crops, and in some areas peaches were also cultivated.

RAIDS

Besides herding, weaving, hunting, and farming, the Navajo were also dependent on raiding for much of their economic well-being. Warfare was not a matter of honor and glory as it had become on the Great Plains after the advent of the horse. The Navajo were cool-headed, hard-fighting filibusterers who raided the Spanish and the Pueblos and sent parties well into northern Mexico. The Spanish and later the Mexicans sent frequent but seldom successful expeditions against them. The Puebloan peoples alternated between trading and fighting with the Navajo, while the Jicarilla Apache and the Utes to the north frequently raided the Navajo, often at the instigation of the Spanish and later the Mexicans and Americans.

Raiding parties were always formed by a single man calling on his friends and neighbors to join him. A successful war leader had to undergo a prolonged apprenticeship under an older man who knew any one of the several complex war rituals thought necessary for successful operations. Once ordained, a war leader could then call on his friends to launch a raid against some enemy. The most frequent goal was to capture livestock, sheep, and horses in particular. Often going to war on foot, with the expectation of returning mounted, and armed with bows, shields, hide armor and war hats, lances and war clubs, the Navajo were feared by all the people of the Southwest and northern Mexico. In addition to livestock, the Navajo sought slaves, particularly young men and women of enemy peoples and whatever other goods they might find. Enemy prisoners were often adopted immediately and treated as Navajo. Others served in a mild sort of domestic slavery. Still others were sold to the Mexicans and Spanish as slaves. The Navajo were themselves frequently victims of slave raiding and many of them were kept in New Mexico and Mexico proper. It is possible that many of the skills learned by the Navajo were brought to them by escaped slaves returning from the Spanish colonies.

Occasionally, larger war parties were formed to avenge the death of a Navajo at the hands of some enemy. These raids were often composed of many men, but still were entirely voluntary and inspired by individuals. And even when raiding for revenge the Navajo seldom neglected to take livestock, slaves, and movable goods. They never destroyed the economic base of their enemies by burning their homes or fields. One suspects they wished to come back again to harvest the fruits of war.

Although in regular contact with the Spanish and Mexican colonies of New Mexico, the Navajo were in reality just beyond the high water mark of Hispanic colonization. Expeditions, religious and military, did penetrate the Navajo country, but seldom for very long. Observations were sketchy and incomplete. We have no general picture of Navajo domestic life at this time. Polygyny was apparently common for the richer members of the tribe. A man might marry several sisters living together, or he might on the other hand have several wives living in different places that he visited regularly. This latter system, of course, gave a man with in-laws in several areas considerable influence.

Against their enemies, the Navajo, so effective in offense, had little defense. Hogans were located on mesa tops, in little out-of-the-way canyons, or other hard-to-find places. Structures were built so that they blended into the landscape. Lookouts were frequently stationed at high places to watch for the enemy and light warning signal fires if they appeared. But fortification appears to have been an unknown art and withdrawal into inaccessible places the most common defensive tactic.

All the Navajo were not at war with their neighbors. Certain captains and their followers strictly observed treaties made with the Spanish, Mexicans, and, later, the Americans. However, other Navajo did not, and they continued to raid. Unfortunately, the victims of these raids did not distinguish among Navajo, and the peaceful keepers of treaties often found themselves subject to attacks in retaliation for raids they did not conduct.

In 1846, as a result of the Mexican War, New Mexico and much of modern Arizona came under the control of the United States. The Navajo at first saw the newcomers as allies because they had been fighting the Mexicans. They soon learned however that the newcomers frowned upon raids on New Mexican communities or across the border into Mexico. The old pattern of hostilities continued. Some Navajo groups kept the peace. Others readily signed treaties during the periods when farming and herding would keep them busy and broke them when the raiding season began. Nor were the United States punitive expeditions any more successful than had been those of the Spanish or Mexicans. Even though Fort Defiance was established in what was virtually the heart of the Navajo country, the Indians remained powerful and independent. From 1846 to 1860 Navajo raiders stole nearly a half million head of livestock from the New Mexican colonies. It is interesting that when finally defeated the Navajo possessed most of these animals, which they kept in herds and tended. The other Apache bands had stolen nearly as many animals during the same period, but apparently had eaten them as they took them, since they had virtually no livestock when they were defeated.

THE CAMPAIGN AGAINST THE NAVAJO

The American Civil War provided a period of rest for many tribes on the frontier, as troops were withdrawn for fighting in the East. Not so the Southwest. The Union and the Confederacy contended for the area, and the presence of hostile Indians was a threat to both sides. As the early Confederate threat to the Southwest disappeared, local federal commanders found themselves with large forces of volunteers on their hands and no way to utilize them against the Southerners. Rather than see their commands melt away, as volunteer troops were so apt to do, a large-scale campaign was mounted against both Apache and Navajo.

Kit Carson, an illiterate but capable man who had explored the West with Fremont, lived as a mountain man in the days of the fur trade, pioneered on the freight routes into the Southwest, served as United States Indian Agent in New Mexico, was commissioned a Lieutenant Colonel under General Carleton and ordered to plan a campaign against the Navajo. Carson was friendly to the Ute, having once been married to a Ute woman, and enlisting their aid along with that of the Jicarilla Apache, he marched with the mixed force of volunteers, Indians, and regulars into the Navajo country. Too wise to attempt to force a pitched battle,

Carson attacked the economic base of Navajo life. Wherever his command rode, they burned cornfields, slaughtered livestock, cut down peach trees, and in short established a prototype for Sherman's famous March to the Sea. Finally the Navajo, starving and unable to grow food, withdrew into the almost impenetrable reaches of Canyon DeChelle in eastern Arizona. Here for a while they held out, but starvation did what battles could not, and they were forced to surrender. Beyond the high escarpment of Black Mesa in northern Arizona and in the western part of Navajo country, many bands were scarcely aware of the campaign and remained free during the next four years.

In 1863 the Navajo who had surrendered were taken to Fort Sumner at Bosque Redondo, New Mexico. Here the army hoped to get the Navajo to settle down and take up sedentary farming. The plan was a humanitarian one, but it was doomed by bad planning, the weather, and the determination of the Navajo not to be forced into settled life.

During the next four years the Navajo suffered a great deal. Even when they followed the army's directions and planted crops, bad weather ruined them. They were raided by the Comanche from Texas and raided them in return. An attempt to contain the Navajo with a band of Mescalero Apaches resulted in hostilities. Finally, what had been an ambitious and well-meaning plan collapsed, and the Navajo leaders requested that they be allowed to take their people back to their homelands. In 1868 the United States Government set aside roughly one million acres centered on Canyon DeChelle as a reservation for the Navajo, and the people began to return. By this time the captive Indians had virtually no horses, and the trip was made on foot. In Navajo tradition, it is referred to as the Long Walk. To help support the newly freed people, the government made grants of seed, farm. implements, and livestock and actively encouraged the Navajo to become self-sufficient rather than dependent on the government for food, as were an increasing number of tribes on the Great Plains. Arrangements were made for supervision and the building of schools. In this latter case, the government was not quick to make good its promise, nor were the Navajo eager to take advantage of education.

GRADUAL CHANGE

Reuniting with their fellows who had remained free, the Navajo began to reconstitute their lives. Despite the sufferings at Fort Sumner, they had learned many things and began to incorporate much of this into their culture. In the matter of clothing, for instance, the Navajo had gone to Fort Sumner wearing clothing styles heavily influenced by both the Spanish and the Pueblo. Women wore dresses made of two blankets joined at the shoulders and gathered at the waist with a sash much like Pueblo women. Men wore short, split-legged trousers made of buckskin following a Spanish style. They generally were bare above the waist and wore a kind of cloth turban or a skin or fur cap decorated with shells, beads, or feathers. At Fort Sumner they had to depend on gifts of unbleached muslin or cast-off Anglo clothing. Using these styles as models, women began to wear long wide skirts with a shirtwaist which soon came to be made of velvet or velveteen. Men adopted the shirtwaist and combined it with long muslin trousers. Increasingly the turban gave way to felt hats for men, although both sexes retained moccasins. Old style Indian saddles gave way to handmade copies of army cavalry saddles. Many items of food and styles of cooking were learned by the Navajo and incorporated into their lives. Most importantly, their defeat had caused them to realize that the power of the Anglo newcomer was such that they could never again hope to live by warfare. With a few minor exceptions, raiding parties were a thing of the past, and armed resistance to the Anglos was considered impossible.

But there were other ways to resist. The Navajo country was not particularly appealing to Anglos, and there was little pressure from settlers. The Navajo could remain in isolation. Living off their herds, they were able to move if they felt the need. With tens of millions of dry, sparsely occupied acres to the west, the Navajo were able to remain in virtual isolation for the next sixty years. Their own industry produced the things white men wanted from the region: raw wool, hides, rugs, livestock, and silver jewelry. Through the medium of traders, the Navajo could produce these things and in return obtain manufactured goods from the outside world with a minimum of direct involvement. No longer fearing raids from the Jicarilla or Utes, they could devote themselves even more wholeheartedly to the acquisition of wealth, and this they, in contrast to other Indian tribes, did.

Population increased from perhaps twelve to fifteen thousand in 1868 to nearly fifty thousand in the 1930s. From a handful of sheep and goats given to them in 1868, the Navajo increased their livestock holdings to well over a million head. Safe from excessive Anglo pressure in an area without roads or lines of communication, they expanded and developed what the Navajo have come to think of as the true old style of life. Until Arizona's entrance into the Union as a state prevented further expansion, the reservation was repeatedly increased from one to sixteen million acres in size and formed the foundation for the development of modern Navajo culture.

2

Primary Organization
and Physical Environment

The Reservation

ALTHOUGH NOT ALL NAVAJO today live on the reservation, nor have they ever done so, the reservation is the heartland of Navajo life. It constitutes the environmental and political stage on which Navajo culture has developed and is developing.

In American history and political life, the term *Indian reservation* has many meanings. An Indian reservation may be only a few acres of land deeded to an Indian family or band. It may be an area of contiguous plots of land owned by individual Indians, or it may be, as is the case of the Navajo Reservation, a large area with distinct boundaries controlled jointly by the tribal and federal governments. In some cases an Indian reservation is an integral part of the state in which it is located, with state and local laws applying to the Indians as well as to their Anglo neighbors. In yet other cases a mixture of tribal laws, local law, and federal law applies. This confusing situation is a result of shifting policies of the United States government toward Indian populations.

EARLY HISTORY

Prior to the 1870s Indian tribes, however vaguely defined, were considered as "domestic and dependent nations," sovereign in their control of certain lands and the application of custom or law. Their relations with the United States were directed by treaties which, more often than not, were violated or unilaterally abrogated by the government. After the 1870s Indians were considered wards of the government, and most of them lived on assigned reservations under the direct administration of the government. In the 1880s an attempt to detribalize and thus encourage assimilation led Congress to pass a law popularly known as the Allotment Act. Under the terms of this law, lands held by the federal government for Indians were to be parcelled out to individual Indians to hold in fee simple. The result was that in many cases, after individuals had received their allotments, great areas of unassigned surplus land reverted to the government to be opened for homesteading or put to other uses. Many Indians, entirely unacquainted with the concept of land ownership, sold their allotments for little or nothing and were left landless and destitute. Some authorities feel the entire allotment procedure was a cynical scheme to satisfy land-hungry settlers and speculators who resented the large Indian holdings. Others see it as a visionary dream gone wrong. Whatever the motivations, the results were that over the next several decades, millions of acres were taken from Indian control. Fortunately for many Indians, including the Navajo, the provisions of the Allotment Act were not applied, and they retained their reservations.

The administration of the Navajo Reservation has gone through many convolutions in the past ninety-eight years. At times the entire area was administered by a single agency staff; at other times it was divided into five or more separate agencies, each independent of the other. In the 1880s, with little planning or foresight, an area that was also claimed by the Navajo was set aside for the Hopi tribe; this led to a still unresolved dispute.

CURRENT ORGANIZATION

Today the Navajo Reservation is administered by a superintendent appointed by the Commissioner of Indian Affairs, himself a presidential appointee, under the Secretary of the Interior. The Bureau of Indian Affairs has overall responsibility for Indian reservations, although for nearly a decade the Public Health Service has assumed responsibility for Indian health. In addition to the Bureau of Indian Affairs (BIA), the Navajo tribe itself has gradually developed a political structure and has increasingly taken over the day-to-day management of reservation affairs. Federal law, enforced by tribal and federal policemen, obtains on the reservation. Major crimes are tried in federal courts. Minor crimes and misdemeanors are defined by tribal law and administered in special tribal courts. As citizens of Arizona, New Mexico, and Utah, the Navajo vote in the elections held in these states, not without some objection and resentment on the part of their Anglo neighbors. In Arizona various counties claim parts of the reservation, and a recent voter registration drive has revealed that a substantial majority of the people eligible to vote in those counties are Navajo who live on the reservation and thus are immune from the laws of the county which they might, theoretically, some day control. These many layers of government authority and anomalies of jurisdiction are relatively new. Over most of the reservation's history, the day-to-day life of the Navajo was only peripherally affected by such things. They lived and worked far beyond the end of the paved highway or the telephone and telegraph lines. Their connection with American society in general was tenuous and second-hand. Their attention was devoted not to the reservation as a political unit, but the reservation as land.

The Land

MYTHOLOGICAL SIGNIFICANCE

The wanderings of the Nadene-speaking peoples and Athapaskans through Asia and western North America are obscured in allegory in Navajo mythology that speaks, as do other Indian origin myths, of previous subterranean worlds in which people lived before emerging finally onto the surface of the world. Scattered legendary references to clothing and food habits suggest a past somewhere in the Great Basin, but little else. However, the coming of the northerners into the Southwest and the gradual separation of the Navajo from their Apache relatives is colorfully recorded in the elaborate mythology, which provides a charter for modern Navajo society and cultural patterns. The scene of the miraculous events from which Navajo society is felt to have evolved is *Dinetlah*, "the land of the People." *Dine* is the term used by the Navajo to refer to themselves and means roughly "The People," as contrasted to all other peoples who are, in all candor, somewhat less than acceptable in Navajo eyes. *Dinetlah* corresponds only in part to the present boundaries of the reservation. In earlier times, Navajo life was centered to the east and north in the valleys of the upper San Juan River. It extended—or, more precisely, extends—from there almost to the Grand Canyon along the Colorado line and the course of the Colorado River above the Grand Canyon. In the Southwest, the San Francisco Peaks near Flagstaff, Arizona, mark one of the corners of Navajo country. To the southeast, Mt. Taylor, New Mexico, marks another limit. Each of the corners and hundreds of peaks, mesas, creeks, springs, and other natural features of these areas are considered at least semisacred and are woven into the infinitely varied mythology of the Navajo. Within these confines the sacred curing ceremonies or "sings" are potent. Sacred minerals, salt, paints, and other materials can be obtained only within these boundaries. Although the reservation constitutes perhaps less than half of the ancient Navajo country, the Navajo have never given up the feeling that despite its occupation by foreigners, this land is essentially their own. Families and communities, holding lands under allotment as homesteaders or simply as squatters on large unoccupied railroad holdings, have continued to exist outside the reservation. Travel within these boundaries is relatively safe, easy, and familiar. Outside these boundaries is the dangerous land of foreigners where a person cannot call up the protection of traditional Navajo ceremony for security.

GEOGRAPHY

In general, the land is high, ranging from three thousand feet above sea level to nine thousand feet in the mountains in the center and west of the present reservation. Another condition which holds in all but a few favored spots is aridity. With the exception of the pine-covered mountain ranges, precipitation seldom exceeds ten inches a year and in many places is often considerably less. In the northwest and southwest the land is exceedingly dry, verging almost on true desert, marked only by small oases formed around springs or small rivers that sometimes are totally dry on the surface, although subsurface water serves to support cottonwoods and willows. Much of the country is marked by flat valleys studded with abrupt flat-topped mesas or dramatically shaped rock spires. The central portion of the reservation is often less scenic than the rest of the area, although more productive as range land. A general pattern of ridges, mesas, or low mountains separating long north–south running valleys dominates the geography. In the middle of each valley is a wash where the spring run-off from melting snow and the surprising floods of water that occur during summer cloudbursts drain. Such washes are often filled in little more than minutes and funnel off enormous amounts of water before it has a chance to sink into the soil. In low points of the valleys enough ground water accumulates to assure the production of crops; in other areas small flood plains or the apparently dry beds of seasonal rivers also serve as fields.

A typical area could be described as a valley that varies from three to five miles wide and is bordered by ranges of low mesas and mountains. Sloping gradually away from the deep-cut line of the central wash, the valley bottom is nearly flat and is covered with sage, greasewood, and numerous grasses. Here and there in the valley are spots of brilliant green where ground water settles, supporting lush crops of tumbleweed before it dries and begins its windblown seeding journey. From such plots there frequently spring cottonwoods or elms growing tall and straight with little limb development. Low, rocky hills may boast tiny micro-oases growing around miniscule springs. The hills and mesas rise out of a gradual alluvial fan which supports increasingly robust plant life and eventually relatively heavy groves of juniper trees before the rock walls rise straight up. In small box canyons and declivities in the mesa walls, numerous springs, often feeding into shallow caves, support small growths of willows and cottonwoods. On the mesa tops, juniper groves crowd out all other competing plant life. A dirt road or wandering wagon track usually parallels the route of the wash, and old-fashioned wind-driven water pumps, often broken and inoperable, mark the efforts of the Navajo tribe and the federal government to improve the water supply. To the traveler, the area appears without human habitation or inhabitants, but an alert traveler will notice networks of sheep trails which converge on small clusters of hogans, eight-sided structures built of mud-chinked logs and roofed with a dome of red–tan earth, or log cabins often plastered with mud and roofed with tar paper. The building materials and lack of any noticeable development near the homesite, save for a brush ramada (a kind of arbor) and a sheep pen made of juniper limbs, make these homesteads virtually blend into the landscape.

3

Society

SOMEWHERE IN SUCH A VALLEY as was described in the previous chapter the road will lead to what amounts to the center of a widely dispersed and ill-defined community: the trading post. On the edges of the reservation these enterprises may have been replaced by supermarkets, but in the interior they are often reminiscent of western motion pictures—a stone or adobe building with a windmill towering over it and a collection of pens and corrals surrounding it. Perhaps a Bureau of Indian Affairs school, a small post office building, a Protestant or Catholic mission building, often both, and the hogans and cabins of Navajo working for the trader, the school, or the missionary form the miniscule town. In some areas a modernistic chapter house where the people of the district meet with their representative on the tribal council adds a touch of the twentieth century. In other places a brush ramada serves this purpose. Here the people living in one or two million acres come to shop, sell their sheep, consult the doctor on his weekly visit, vote on tribal elections, and learn the newest programs and rules of the tribe or the government. Beyond this nucleus the community is composed of the isolated independent homesteads. Such a community is Nez Ch'ii.* It is typical of Navajo communities, retaining much of the flavor of the traditional past and yet possessing details which distinguish it from other communities on the reservation.

The concentration of buildings, people, and institutions that forms Nez Ch'ii is a new element of Navajo culture and society. Each building and the people working inside it represent a link with the nontribal world—the manufacturing centers of America, the federal government, the relatively new tribal government, and the health services—or, through the school, with American culture in general. Each supplies a need which has become important, even essential, to the continuation of Navajo life. But they represent developments less than a century old to which Navajo culture has made only partial adjustments.

---

* *Nez Ch'ii*, in keeping with common social science practice, is a fictitious name used to protect the identity of the individuals who so graciously cooperated with my investigations.

To the individual Navajo, traditional social institutions and forms play a more important role. These institutions take the form of the tribal society, a network of kinship and customary relationships centered in people rather than places.

Definition of the Navajo social structure has often frustrated anthropologists because it is so flexible. Having survived enormous changes through the past several centuries and able to adapt to a wide variety of environments, Navajo society has developed almost endless alternatives. However, certain tendencies or themes guide the choices made by the individual who lives in Nez Ch'ii or any other part of the reservation.

The Female Principle

In the nineteenth century, anthropologists postulated that one of the earlier forms of society was the matriarchy, that is, a society dominated by women. Today we are quite certain that no such society ever, as imagined by social theorists, existed. However the expanding ethnographic record has shown us that in many societies the role of women is quite different from that in American, western European, and Far Eastern civilizations.

Ideally, patriarchy can be defined as a condition in which the authority for all decisions is vested in the male. Among males the authority is vested in the father or his social equivalent, and in nonkinship areas of life the relationship of superior–inferior is viewed as a father–child relationship. The opposite of this, then, logically is matriarchy, a condition in which the authority for all decisions is vested in the female and where in nonkinship areas of life the relationship between superior and inferior is viewed as a mother–child relationship. Obviously neither of these conditions ever exists. Even in the most male-dominated societies certain areas are considered the exclusive domain of women in which the female has the authority to make decisions and take action without reference to, or in spite of, the male. Conversely, no society exists or ever appears to have existed in which women have had such an overriding domination of life. However, if these ideal types are placed at the extremes of a continuum and various societies placed between them, we could develop a gradation of social types based on the varying importance of the male and female in the total social picture. On such a continuum Navajo society would fall toward the matriarchal end of the scale; in almost all spheres of activity the principle of the importance of the female is expressed. Children, by and large, consider themselves as part of the descent group of their mother. There is a general tendency to want to live with one's mother after marriage, but more often than not the wife's desire to live with her mother overrides the husband's desire to remain with his. The relationship between brother and sister is important and often may override the relationship between husband and wife. One's sibling's children play almost as important a role in one's life as do one's own children, and the children of a sister are more important than the children of a brother.

The importance of the female and of relationships traced through the female line is constantly reinforced by the use of kin terms in daily life. Any woman, for instance, is privileged to greet any man of whatever age as *shiyaazh* ("my son").

In turn, any man can call any woman *shima* or *shima yaazhi* ("my mother" or "my mother's sister"—literally, "little mother"). However, were he to refer to any boy or man save his own sons as *shiye* ("male form of my son") it would at the best be in extremely bad taste and might well be considered as a grievous insult. When men greet each other, they have a choice of two terms, *shichee* ("maternal grandfather") or *shinali* ("paternal grandfather"); the former is always accorded to those with whom they have the closest relationship or to whom they wish to show the greatest respect. In addressing children, men frequently say *sitsoi*, which means "child of my daughter."

In Navajo mythology the most important figure is that of Changing Woman, who gave birth to the twin heroes who gained much of what the Navajo consider to be their special culture. In daily life the important social units, as we shall see, are those centering around a core of women—mother, daughters, sisters, and their sons and brothers. Affinal relatives* (usually husbands and sons-in-law) play an important but peripheral role.

Although most political roles are carried out by men, political action is not exclusively a male prerogative, and the individual is usually viewed as representing either his mother's family or that of his wife. In earlier times even warfare was not the exclusive prerogative of males, and there are relatively reliable traditional reports of women who became warriors.

Women are privy to religious and magical lore and can become practitioners. In the relationships between the sexes, women are often the instigators, as symbolized in the selection of dance partners by girls in the Squaw Dance and in the control over courting behavior exhibited by girls and women. In the words of a sixteen-year-old high school student when questioned about the selection of partners at an Anglo-style dance, "Well, sometimes the boys ask the girls but . . . in Navajo it's always the girl's choice." This same girl, who was suffering from being hit on the head with a rock by a boy attempting to avoid her attentions, was asked why she didn't let the boys chase her; her reply was that it had never occurred to her. This principle of girl's choice may well have a bearing on the remarkably low occurrence of rape on the Navajo Reservation, which is 9.7 per 100,000 of population as contrasted with 13.7 of general American rural population, although the Navajo average for murder, manslaughter, and aggravated assault is somewhat higher than the general rural average (Young, 1958: p. 139).

The discussion above should not be construed to mean that there is no division of labor along sexual lines, because of course there is. However, the opinions of women as to how and when work is to be performed is considered important and in many instances is *the* important factor in directing the activity of Nez Ch'ii society.

Although it would appear that this theme is an overriding one in Navajo society, we must expect its expression to vary and to be affected by any number of exigencies of day-to-day life, and so it is. Every individual does not consider himself a descendant of his mother's descent line, nor does every marriage result in the establishment of a new household near the bride's mother. Nor is it possible to

---

* Relatives by marriage.

assume that a man—brother, husband, or son-in-law—will in every case defer to the wishes of the women with whom he associates. Such departures, however, are variations on a theme, are recognized as such, and must be justified in practical terms if they are not to draw social criticism of some kind.

The Inviolability of the Individual

The importance of the network of kin ties that is essential to individual survival is balanced by another theme that is singularly important to the Navajo. Despite close and absolutely essential familial ties, the Navajo remain highly individualistic people. Their primary social premise might be said to be that no person has the right to speak for or to direct the actions of another. This attitude creates specific cultural and social responses. In childhood it permits, or rather enforces, the pattern of light discipline by persuasion, ridicule, or shaming in opposition to corporal punishment or coercion. Children, in a very broad sense, might be said to be herded rather than led by adults, inasmuch as adults tend to interpose themselves or some other object between the child and what it has set out to do, thus diverting it from an undesirable activity. The decision of a four-year-old that he stay home from, or go to, a Squaw Dance or to the store with the family is invariably honored, unless acquiescence is manifestly impossible. Often, adult plans are rearranged so that the child can stay home. Perhaps some extracts from my field diary will illustrate:

June 13
Ben and Maggie Yazzie Yaz went to the Squaw Dance at the Roan Horse homestead. Remained all night leaving Timmie, the youngest son (4 years), in the charge of Maggie's sister. Decided to go to Roan Horse's place on the following day. When we got into the car Timmie came running up and demanded a ride. Maggie's sister shrugged when we asked if it was all right and said, "If he wants to."
We stayed at Roan Horse's several hours. Through that time Timmie remained with us and played with Chris (our son) and other children. When we got ready to go he refused to get back in the car and shouted and cried that he wanted to stay with his parents. Although Maggie and Ben had clearly not wanted to take care of a child and preferred to devote themselves to card playing, they simply shrugged when we (expecting them to order him to return with us) told them Timmie wouldn't come and said, "It's O.K. if he wants to stay." They were clearly put out because we had been so stupid as to bring him in the first place.

In seven months' close association with seven nuclear families with a total of twenty-nine children below fifteen years of age, I observed a child struck on only four occasions. Only one of these chastisements, I might add, was for disobedience. All the blows involved were rather mild, even when compared with the spankings of the most "progressive" Anglo mother. Disobedient children are often threatened that an uncle or older brother will be requested to spank them.

Among adults this emphasis on individualism manifests itself in an unwillingness to make a statement that could be considered a commitment of another person. One learns quickly to phrase questions about other people so that an answer can be given by the informant without violating this rule. Brothers and sisters politely refuse to discuss the others' likes and dislikes, or husbands profess complete ignorance of whether or not their wives want to attend a Squaw Dance. This gives an outsider a first impression that the Navajo know very little about one another, an impression that later is seen to be manifestly false. It is simply a violation of Navajo mores to express an opinion for someone else.

The right of an individual to do as he wishes and to make up his mind creates what appears to an outsider to be a lack of concern about time. For instance, a Navajo may desire to see another about the purchase of hay, to request help in building a house, or to demand repayment of a debt. No matter how urgent the matter may be, there is a reluctance to press the issue or seek a confrontation. The person in question will speak repeatedly over a period of weeks about wanting to see such and such a person and his reasons for wanting to see him. He may even make a trip to see his friend in the hope that he might be home, but seldom would he make arrangements that would bind the other person to a definite meeting place at a definite time.

This individualism manifests itself in political activity to such a point that a council may or may not wait until the chairman is present to begin its business, nor does the chairman feel absolutely compelled to be on time. Moreover, one may, without feeling too much regret, fail to keep an appointment.

Even in the realm of curing and religion, where ceremonial payments must be shared by a large number of relatives, there are no directly coercive methods of enforcing payment. The fear of being accused of witchcraft or of engendering deep and perhaps irreparable family schisms usually enforces participation. When this attitude is confronted with the far more authoritarian and arbitrary attitudes of Anglo law, with its attendant coercive measures, it creates deep and bitter resentments that often manifest themselves in angry and nearly fatal attacks on policemen who must arrest violators, particularly drunks.

In summary, despite the importance of group ties in this area, it should be remembered that the group must and often does make major adjustments to fit the behavior of an individual.

The Primacy of Age

Yet a third theme weaves itself through the structure of Navajo society. That is the prestige of age, particularly age coupled with a life of hard work and the production of many children and grandchildren. Despite the fact that Navajo are very property-conscious and are all, in one way or another, seeking wealth, the possession of wealth does not in itself determine the power structure of the community. Although men of substance are members of chapter councils and make speeches at squaw dances in which they urge practicing good behavior, enrolling children in school, or participating in some tribal or government program, their position seems to be protected as much by their age as by their money. It is clear that old men and women are felt to be repositories of wisdom and should be considered in making decisions. Many young men attend tribal chapter meetings, but it is usually the old men who speak.

Within the homestead group or the nuclear family there is a clear deference to age, from the merest toddler to the oldest matriarch or grandfather. There is no doubt that an old man with a large sheep herd, a great amount of turquoise and silver jewelry, a number of horses, wagons, saddles and blankets, and other manifestations of wealth is an important man who must be listened to and considered when making community-wide decisions. If, however, he has few children or grandchildren, his position will not be as secure as if he were the grandfather (or perhaps the husband of the grandmother) of a large family. Conversely, a man with many descendents, however poor, must be listened to with respect. In part, this must stem from a prereservation time when such a man could count on the armed support of his nephews and grandsons and the husbands of his daughters and nieces. However, even the most destitute old man or woman living on the bounty of distant relatives and without a real family of his or her own is treated with kindness and consideration by those with whom he comes into contact, and should he choose to speak in public he will be heard out with patience and courtesy. His lack of luck and success may suggest that his advice may well not be very good, but his age will assure that his words are heard.

Reciprocity

Another important feature of Navajo society is the view that every debt incurred must be repaid and that the ledger of obligations and favors received should remain in balance. Within the domestic units of the Navajo there is a great deal of sharing, so that the ledger often becomes obscured by the overall obligation to support and assist relatives. Outside the network of kinship or even among kinsmen who are not closely related, *quid pro quo* is the rule. Often this takes the form of what non-Navajo might consider a blatant commercialism. Nonrelatives usually expect to receive money, food, or other recompense for their assistance. This is considered quite normal among the Navajo, who would be loath to accept a favor without making some return. Usually every attempt is made to settle a debt quickly, but, if it cannot be done, obligations are long remembered. Nor are they considered to be only the responsibility of the individual incurring the debt. Should a man be unable to pay a loan or repay a kindness or some important assistance, his relatives often feel obligated to see to it that the debt is paid.

The concern of one family over its debts can be seen in this series of entries in my field diary:

July 25
Drove to Fort Defiance and paid bail bond of Kee Beguey, who was arrested for being drunk at a Squaw Dance two days ago. Another Nez Ch'ii man, Eddie Yazzie, was also in jail. He asked if I would get him out too, which I did. He promised to repay me as soon as he could. Have my doubts, but it is a good investment in rapport.

August 5

Kee Beguey brought me twenty-five dollars, which he said Eddie Yazzie had given me to repay the bail bond debt. Immediately asked me if he might borrow the money. I agreed. Wrong about Eddie Yazzie. He is not working. Must have borrowed the money in order to pay me.

August 20

Two women whom I had never seen rode into camp today and spoke to Agnes. They were clearly talking about me. After they had left, Agnes, smiling at me, said they were Eddie Yazzie's mother and sister, who had ridden over from Signal Point to ask if he had indeed repaid me (must have borrowed from them). Satisfied that he had, they rode home. Signal Point is fifteen to twenty miles to the east. Thirty to forty mile ride to find out if the family debts were honored.

4

The Social Units

ECAUSE THE NAVAJO RESERVATION is large and offers a great many environmental alternatives to which society must adjust and because historical factors, economics, and so on, vary from place to place on the reservation, it is difficult to describe typical social units. However, over much of modern Navajo history the exigencies of a pastoral life have been important in shaping social organization, and it remains thus today in the Nez Ch'ii area, where animal husbandry is important both culturally and economically. The social units described then refer most specifically to the Nez Ch'ii, although the findings and opinions of other students of Navajo society have been included where pertinent.

The Family

The English word *family* is used in two ways among the Navajo of Nez Ch'ii. A man may occasionally refer to his wife and children as his family, but far more frequently his "family" means his mother, brothers, and sisters, and those people descended from them. Thus a man might answer the question, "Do you have any sheep?" by saying, "I run some at my wife's but I don't have any with my family." Similarly, a man living with his wife's parents may say, "I don't know about that. I'll talk to *the* family and tell you tomorrow." Or when asked about a sister's husband, a young man will say (most often with a not too thinly disguised hostility), "Him? No, he ain't no relation. He's just an in-law."

In keeping with anthropological usage I shall refer to the matricentered descent group as the *family*. When speaking of a man, his wife, and his children, I shall use, for lack of a better term, the expression *nuclear unit*.

The nuclear unit, then, consists of a man, his wife, and their, or more properly her, offspring. The tendency for children of dissolved marriages to remain with the mother usually means that most mature wives have children of at least two marriages in their households.

342

It is difficult to make a definitive statement as to which of the partners in a marriage is "head of the house." Clearly the role of the wife in decision making is important, but the husband appears to serve not only as primary wage earner but also as the representative of the nuclear unit outside the circle of immediate kinship. It must be kept in mind that emphasis on the individual in Navajo life colors the marriage relationship. Divorce is simple and the dissolution of marriage appears to create little social dislocation, nor does the justification for such dissolutions have to be great, that is, from the White point of view. Nonetheless, it should be pointed out that many Navajo couples display a great deal of affection for each other and appear genuinely to enjoy each other's company. Moreover, Navajo families become deeply involved in selecting a first husband for a daughter and go to great lengths to prevent divorce. However, should the girl refuse the family's candidate or the young couple reject reconciliation, their desires are accepted. It also appears that a woman's later husbands have less voice in the management of household affairs or economic decisions than do the husbands whom she married when she was young. This situation seems to stem in part from the fact that these later marriages tend to be marriages of mutual convenience for both men and women. Most often the woman has achieved a dominant position in relation to the larger kinship group; she commands, so to speak, several daughters and their husbands and possesses considerable property in her own right. A husband, then, serves to assist in the chores of living and becomes her legitimate sexual partner and representative to the nonkin world. For his part, an older man seeking a wife of mature years, unless he is a widower, may be a bad marriage risk because of connubial restlessness or poor economic position. He then accepts the role of husband with some gratitude, inasmuch as it gives him a share in his wife's herd as well as the general social and economic security stemming from an extended family situation. It should be pointed out here, however, that an unmarried man is not in the uncomfortable position of the bachelor in many other tribal societies. A young man can depend on his mother or unattached sisters for bed and board in return for his contribution to the family labor pool. An old man retains throughout life a claim on the services of his sisters for cooking and shelter, should he not have a wife to provide them. This relationship is clearly symbolized in the traditional responsibility of a man's mother, wife, or sisters for the neatness of his hair when it is worn in the traditional wool-bound queue. The Navajo say that you can tell if a man's wife *or* sisters love him by how neatly his hair is done. An unmarried man's hair is bound by his sisters, a married man's by his wife or sisters. Among more modern Navajo who have given up long hair in favor of the white man's haircut, it is most often a woman who wields the family clippers when her family needs barbering.

One cannot relate the nuclear unit directly to the livestock operation because of the individualism of ownership on the one hand and the wide dispersal of responsibility for maintaining livestock on the other. A husband, his wife, and any of the children may in fact own animals in the family herd. In an informal way, this unit assumes responsibility for its share of the work, but it seldom works as a unit in the sense that father, mother, and children take over a specific part of the livestock operation. More often, all the males take on one job, with the females doing another, while the children help at yet another. Despite this lack of emphasis on the nuclear unit in many phases of Navajo life, it serves as a vehicle for expressing the relationship between the father and his children through the symbolic and real presentation of wealth. Thus, although a man has a clear obligation toward his sister's children, it is not so great as to overrule his responsibility to his own offspring. A Navajo father is expected to give livestock and horses to his children, particularly his sons. A daughter receives a share of her mother's herd and traditionally can expect to remain with her mother's family, but a son, although he shares in his mother's herd, more often than not leaves her family to join his wife's. The livestock given to him by his father does not become part of his mother's herd and thus provides him with portable property of his own that he can leave with his mother's herd or take with him to his wife's family, but which in either case gives him a high degree of independence. It should also be pointed out here that it also permits him to establish, if he wishes, a neolocal household, making him essentially independent of either of his mother's or his wife's family.

Every man is expected to give a horse to his son. Grazing limitations and poverty often make this a difficult gift, but much effort is expended to bestow it, and a number of cultural subterfuges have developed so that the spirit if not the letter of the obligation is observed. It is not uncommon, for instance, for a man to give his only horse to his son, but to continue to use it himself. The obligation was expressed quite clearly by the informant from whom I rented a riding horse and a good saddle. "We're friends, and I'm treating you just like a father treats his son. I'm giving you that horse." The father is also responsible for feeding and clothing his wife and children, a fact that sometimes accounts for the wide range in condition of clothing found among children in the same family. The matter is felt to be entirely the concern of the nuclear unit as opposed to the family.

There is no clear-cut rule of inheritance except that the offspring of an owner have first claim on his herd. In the recent past, the claim of brothers and sisters was considered to have priority over those of the deceased's offspring; a wife, especially a second wife, could expect to receive little from her late husband's estate. In the case of a very old person it is more than likely that actual title to animals would already have been transferred to his offspring or siblings because the oldster no longer could contribute to caring for them. In practice this would mean very little because the older person would continue to be supported from the income of the herd. In this day of small herds it is unlikely that animals would be willed to persons outside the homestead group, for this would break up the herd.

Homestead and Outfit

The most important social unit in the Nez Ch'ii area is a kinship and residence group, locally called an *outfit*. This particularly western American term, referring to a cattle or sheep ranch, has an entirely different connotation among the Navajo and, it would appear, yet another connotation among anthropologists who work with the Navajo.

Kluckhohn (1947: pp. 62, 63) has described the outfit as a unit that is larger than an extended family and bound together by kinship ties and economic cooperation. The outfit is widely dispersed in a territorial sense, a community in its own right with a leader, usually the eldest male but with a matrilineal orientation (Sasaki and Adair [1952: p. 102] define it somewhat differently).

This definition, however, does not entirely apply in the Nez Ch'ii area. When Nez Ch'ii Navajo use the term *outfit*, they are usually referring to a much smaller unit. Essentially they are speaking of an extended family. Such a group is most often composed of a number of related females living close together and sharing the responsibility and benefits of a single sheep herd. The actual location of residences may be extremely compact, several nuclear families living within a hundred yards of each other, or somewhat more dispersed, with nuclear residences spread over perhaps half a mile.

To avoid confusion, I have used the term *homestead group* to describe this unit and *outfit* to describe the larger unit as defined by Kluckhohn. It might be pointed out here that the term *outfit* is unknown on some parts of the reservation, notably the Navajo Mountain area to the north and west of Nez Ch'ii. I suspect that the Nez Ch'ii usage may well be the result of changes in social structure that have taken place in the past two decades and that the outfit, as described by Kluckhohn, did exist in the area until very recently. Older Navajo tend to use the term *outfit* in a way closer to Kluckhohn's definition; younger people tend to say "our relatives."

Today, herds are so small that large-scale cooperation in livestock handling is no longer necessary, and any work on the herd can be carried out by the family, which has gradually taken over the title formerly given to the largest cooperative livestock group. Moreover, the end of warfare has probably reduced the demand for cooperation between related families. The *chapter system* of political organization that is in effect today with its elected tribal delegate and elected chapter council has supplanted informal councils of elders from the various outfits and placed all the chapter-area residents in a common political framework superseding the outfit. The tribal resource-development crews and the district grazing committees have also taken over what were functions of the older outfit. However, more extended sets of interfamilial relationships reveal themselves on social and ceremonial occasions and during communal sheep enterprises. The people who cooperate as hosts at a Squaw Dance are referred to as "relations." At a community sheep dipping, each extended family is usually joined in a casual way by a number of men who assist in driving sheep through the chutes and vat and who are also described as "relations." At least some of the same men appear associated at both events.

The homestead group, however, is clearly functional and easily defined in the Nez Ch'ii area. Most often the group consists of an older woman, her daughters, and perhaps younger sisters. In addition, the group will include the husbands of the married women. Not infrequently, one or more sons of the elder or dominant women will be part of the group together with their wives. The dominant woman may not be the eldest; an old grandmother or aunt may have a dowager position, although no longer able to contribute much labor to the group's maintenance. Essentially, then, this homestead group is a number of nuclear units related to each other by connection to the family of one of the spouses.

Additional and casual members may be relatives of one or more of the husbands or siblings, half-siblings, or cousins of the matrilineal core of the group. There appears to be a tendency for these casual members to be male rather than female.

The homestead group, however, is much more than a living expression of a kinship reckoning system. It might be described as the minimum unit of survival. In fact, it is safe to say that the survival of the nuclear family is impossible unless it has totally abandoned livestock keeping and exists either from subsistence farming or from income derived outside the area.

The homestead group is a residence unit, in addition to a kinship unit. It is not simply a number of related nuclear units living relatively close together and cooperating in certain economic activities. There are several levels of cooperation. (See Spatial Relations 1960–1962 and 1967 for makeup of one homestead.)

COOKING AND KITCHEN KEEPING

In theory, each wife is supposed to cook for her husband and children, which would suggest the existence of separate cooking arrangements for each nuclear unit. This is not the situation, however, and there is a tendency to share cooking responsibilities among several nuclear groups or, more properly, among several related women. The degree to which this is done, of course, varies with the number of nuclear units involved. The homestead I was able to observe most closely, which was occupied by seven nuclear units, generally used three cooking fires. One fire was that of the dominant woman in the group, who cooked for her husband (her third) and her children still living with her, ranging in age from four to seventeen. She was assisted at times by her husband and her eldest unmarried daughter, about ten years old. A second cooking fire was shared by the dominant woman's younger sister, a married daughter of the dominant woman, and the wife of her second eldest son. In addition, two teen-age unmarried granddaughters and a nineteen-year-old unmarried niece assisted their mothers. It was at this fire that the homestead's seventy-year-old grandmother ate and assisted as she was able. This fire was also shared by a second married daughter, whose husband worked off-reservation, and her children. A third fire was maintained at the house of a third daughter, who was currently unmarried but mother of five children, including two adolescent daughters. Her house and fire were shared by her eldest brother and his wife and children when they visited the homestead. In addition, she provided food and housing for her mother's brother, who lived at the homestead about one-half of the time in the summer. This arrangement of cooking fires resulted in a sharing of the kitchen duties by adult women and adolescent daughters.

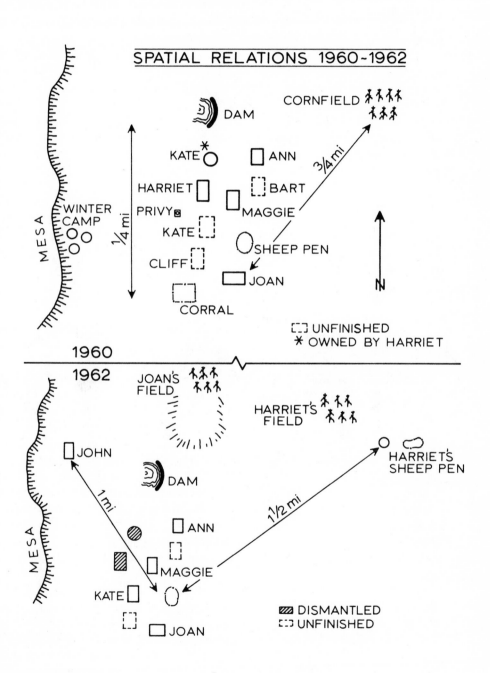

SPATIAL RELATIONS 1960~1962

CORNFIELD

DAM

KATE *

ANN

HARRIET

BART

PRIVY

MAGGIE

KATE

SHEEP PEN

CLIFF

3/4 mi

WINTER CAMP

1/4 mi

JOAN

N

CORRAL

[ ] UNFINISHED
* OWNED BY HARRIET

MESA

1960

1962

JOAN'S FIELD

HARRIET'S FIELD

JOHN

HARRIET'S SHEEP PEN

DAM

1 mi

1/2 mi

ANN

MAGGIE

KATE

DISMANTLED
[ ] UNFINISHED

JOAN

MESA

SPATIAL RELATIONS 1967

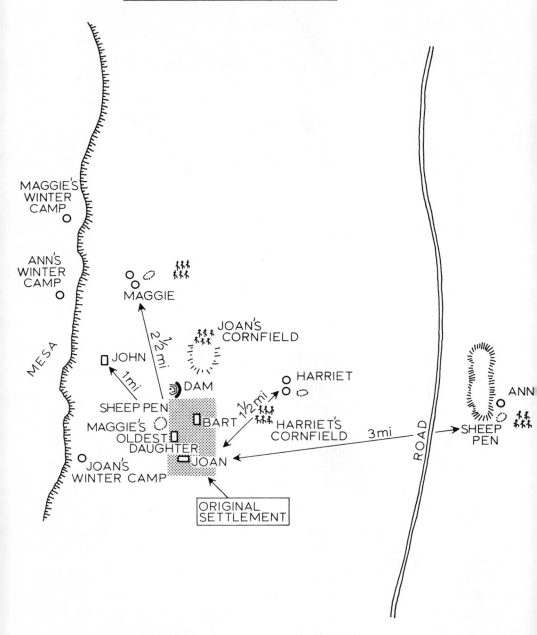

MAGGIE'S
WINTER
CAMP

ANN'S
WINTER
CAMP

MESA

MAGGIE

JOAN'S
CORNFIELD

JOHN

2½ mi

1 mi

DAM

HARRIET

½ mi

SHEEP PEN

BART

MAGGIE'S
OLDEST
DAUGHTER

HARRIET'S
CORNFIELD

3 mi

ROAD

SHEEP
PEN

ANN

JOAN

JOAN'S
WINTER CAMP

ORIGINAL
SETTLEMENT

AGRICULTURE

Each homestead has at least one cornfield. In homesteads with more than one cornfield there appears to be a tendency for certain nuclear groups to combine efforts in plowing, planting, cultivating, and harvesting, although the entire homestead group shares in the produce.

WATER AND WOOD

Providing water and wood is the concern of the entire homestead group. Water is drawn from a well or spring in either a wagon or truck by at least two men of the homestead group. The job of getting water devolves on whichever men are available when the supply is low. Water is usually kept in a central location in barrels or tanks and is carried to the various cooking fires as needed.

Wood may be brought into the homesite piecemeal from nearby supplies by one or two women, but it is more often cut in quantity by men. A wagon is driven into the nearby hills and a load of firewood brought back to be dumped in a common woodpile. Keepers of the fires may then drag a log or two closer to their homes and obviate the need for a long walk prior to each meal.

In hauling wood or water there seems to be no patterning of which men work together. Even brothers-in-law who are not fond of each other ride together willingly in these tasks. Younger boys tend to accompany their fathers or older brothers.

SHOPPING

As each nuclear unit has an independent status within the homestead, shopping is carried out independently by the women. However, food tends to be pooled within each cooking group, and a couple seldom go to the trader's by themselves because some other member of the group usually will take advantage of the occasion to hitch a ride.

RITUAL AND CEREMONIES

The most common ritual on a modern homestead is that of the male sweat-lodge. The lodge is usually located some distance from the homesite and, if at all possible, near a water source. Participation is entirely voluntary, but usually at least two members of the group take part, often all the males, including small boys. Men sweat once or twice a week or whenever one of the men of the group feels the need.

The second most regular ceremonial or socioceremonial activity is the summer Squaw Dance. Several homesteads must cooperate to supply the food for the feasting on the first night and the final morning of the three-day event. As suggested earlier, the homestead group joins other similar groups in the joint effort of acting as hosts. These homesteads are related to each other through the matrilineal principle (that is, members of the same clan). They are not, however, the only participating homesteads. Consanguineal or affinal relations of the family of the patient (that is, the person in need of a ritual cure for one reason or another) for whom the dance is given may well come from distant areas to take part.

Within the homestead group the nuclear units each contribute food, money, livestock, and labor to the affair.

CURING

The homestead group operates as a totality whenever one of its members holds a *sing*, or curing session. The patient may be expected to stand a large part of the cost, ranging from five to twenty dollars in cash, a ceremonial basket costing from three to six dollars, and food for the singer during his stay, which varies from one to five days. The rest of the group is expected to assist. More importantly, each member is expected to participate. This requirement binds even the most acculturated, who may openly disparage singing and singers but must attend certain parts of the ritual. At certain times all members of the group, including infants, must be present.

LIVESTOCK

The entire homestead shares the responsibility of and benefits from the sheep herd. Although individuals have title to individual animals, the work is shared and divided along the lines of sex and age rather than in terms of nuclear units.

The following account describes the working arrangements in a single homestead group as it prepared for and finally participated in the annual sheep dipping in mid-August. The animals are dipped in pesticide solution to kill insect pests and prevent mange. Marking was done in mid-July while the herd was penned at midday. Broken Foot, the eldest son of the dominant woman, assisted by his second sister and her children, did the marking job.

Three days before the dipping the entire homestead group assembled at the sheep pen. The job at hand was to attempt to separate the various classes of livestock—adult sheep, lambs, goats, kids, and rams—inside the pen and then move them in single file through the gate. At that time they were counted and the herd reassembled.

The separation in the pen was carried out by adolescents with the help of one or two adults. The actual counting was done by a single person; at first it was one of the adolescent girls who attended high school, but later the second oldest brother took over.

The sheep, already terrified by the separation within the pen, panicked completely at the gate and attempted to surge through en masse to rejoin their fellows. Keeping the stream down to countable proportions required that two adults assist the tallyman at the gate. All adults and adolescents were present, shifting from interested and vocal spectators to active participants, as the occasion demanded. All children able to walk were clumsily involved in herding.

The evening before the dipping day the herd was assembled and driven toward the vat about five miles away by all of the adolescents. The only exceptions

Sheep emerging from the dipping vats in the background. Sheep dipping is a time of homestead cooperation and often a display of clothing and jewelry by the women.

were two oldest girls, who were at that time living with a sister-in-law near the trading post, but who were summarily ordered home to help their mothers. Directing the herding operation was the dominant woman, her husband, her brother-in-law, and one of her adult daughters, who drove the wagon. This group remained camped by the vat during the night. In the morning they were joined by an older brother and a younger son who had not gone on the herding drive. The younger sister of the dominant woman, one daughter, and a daughter-in-law remained at the homesite to watch the youngest children who did not go to the dipping. It was at this point that the adolescent girls were called home to help with the cooking.

The adolescent boys riding the homestead's team drove the sheep home and then rode back to the vat so that the team could haul the wagon back to the homestead.

During the dipping, everyone—adults, adolescents, and children—assisted in holding the herd and separating them for vaccination against disease. When the sheep entered the chute, the men and boys took over the job of driving them and throwing them into the vat assisted by a number of male "relatives." The women and adolescent girls took up the community dipping-poles to move the animals through the vat and to see them into the dripping pen. This last step was supervised by one of the daughters of the dominant woman. The dominant woman had assumed the job of cooking for the entire homestead at a fire built near the wagon.

The Clan

Beyond the family, the outfit, the homestead group, or even the vague concept *relatives*, there is a larger social unit which serves to tie the Navajo together as a people. This is the clan.

Here, too, the female principle is paramount. Each person is considered to be a member of the clan of his mother. Experts differ on how many clans the Navajo people believe exist, but it is certainly more than fifty. Seldom are all clans represented in any one area. But, on the other hand, no area appears to be the exclusive domain of a single clan. Among some tribal peoples, the clan plays a singularly important role governing land tenure, ceremonial activities, and governmental functions. However, such is not the case among the Navajo. There are no clan councils or chiefs. In a given locality the most respected man of a clan may be considered something of a leader by his clan relatives, but in all probability his prestige extends beyond clan boundaries, and his authority, if such it can be called, is territorial rather than kin-based. Often a rather large area will be occupied almost exclusively by homestead groups representing a single clan, but such an area appears to be in fact simply the contiguous grazing lands of homestead groups which consider themselves to be quite independent. This situation develops rather frequently as homestead groups grow too large for efficient grazing and are unable to contain the tensions and frictions of a large number of people living close together. Particularly after the grandmother in such a group dies, there is a tendency for her daughters and their daughters to strike out and set up new homestead sites, thus forming the outfit. The clan affiliation remains unchanged, of course, but each new unit looks upon itself as sovereign. Because sons so frequently bring their wives to live in their maternal home and establish separate households when the break-up occurs, outfits seldom consist entirely of people of the original clan. The children of these daughters-in-law, of course, are members of her clan. The Navajo speak of being "born for" their father's clan and cannot marry these paternal relatives. Their relations to their cousins, then, even if of a different clan, are essentially those of "brothers" and "sisters." Thus, the flexibility of postmarital residence choices, coupled with the dynamics of the transformation of the homestead group into the outfit, precludes control of large areas by members of a single clan.

The clan seems to function largely to determine eligible marriage partners. The rules of the incest taboo extend to any person of the same clan, no matter how distantly related. One is also forbidden to marry a member of his father's clan. In some cases two or more clans, often because of their relationships at the time of their forming, which is recounted in the tribal origin myth, are considered to be related, and their members are forbidden to each other. Some clans practice minor eccentricities such as avoiding certain foods, but this is not the case for all clans. The formation of clans appears to be a process which has been continuous in Navajo society. Some clan names such as Nakai ("Mexican" or "foreigner") and Hopi clearly reflect the incorporation of foreigners into Navajo life. A person's clan affiliation can often be determined by certain idiosyncrasies of word usage or pronunciation.

When a Navajo is traveling in a strange part of the reservation, members of his clan are obliged to provide him with food and shelter if he asks for them. Clan mates are also expected to assist in various ways in ceremonial situations both ritually and financially.

Kinship and Kinsmen

A Navajo living in Nez Ch'ii spends his life among people he considers to be relatives. An informant in his early sixties described his childhood and youth as a period when he seldom saw people his own age save his "brothers" and "sisters." In his youth the land was less full, and homesteads were even more widely dispersed than they are today, but in a very real sense the situation has not changed.

GENERAL BEHAVIORAL GUIDELINES

The principles of social organization that have been described operate along a network of kinship ties, which are defined by kin terms that in themselves define how one person should act toward another in specific situations.

A Navajo is, as we have seen, a member of his mother's clan. This means that all other people of the same clan are considered kinsmen. The Navajo do not maintain complex and detailed genealogies as do some peoples. Rather, they simply classify entire groups of people in one category and apply a suitable term. A man you have never seen before, coming from perhaps a hundred miles away but claiming membership in your clan, is called *brother* or *mother's brother* and treated accordingly. But beyond that, a Navajo was "born for" his father's clan, and thus entire classes of people fall into similar categories because of their relationship to this line of descent. And because clans form the vague and unnamed coalitions or linkages mentioned earlier, yet further extensions of kinship can be made along these lines.

The kin term one uses to address another person indicates the way one acts toward that person, how much help one can expect in a crisis, whether they may or may not joke about sexual matters, the degree of authority one may exercise over the other, or indeed whether they can rightfully speak at all.

Of course, this is not a unique characteristic of the Navajo or even of tribal people. All societies use kin terms as guidelines for behavior. The love-sick American boy who is told by a girl that she thinks of him as a brother knows exactly what the young lady means; he is not, in her opinion, a competitor for her sexual favors. Priests are called "father" and nuns "sister" for precisely the same reasons.

Among tribal people, the Navajo included, the principles of kinship are more extensive and pervasive and may constitute the network of communications in which many decisions of a political, economic, or legal nature are made.

David Aberle's discussion of Navajo kinship (Aberle, 1961) sums up the general characteristics of Navajo kin behavior very nicely when he says there are two kinds of relatives: those with whom one is bashful and those with whom one is easy.

My informants did not use these terms, but the description fits very well. What this means is that there are a number of people in each person's life who are dealt with in very polite terms or perhaps approached through intermediaries rather than directly. Others can be approached directly and asked for assistance. These relatives with whom one is easy can also be joked with, often quite obscenely, with propriety.

The most notable bashful relationship is between a man and his wife's mother. Traditionally these two persons could not speak to each other, avoided looking at one another, and usually tried to avoid being in the same room with each other. This practice, which is not unique to the Navajo, is known as the mother-in-law taboo. Most authorities feel it is a way to avoid any possibility of conflict between mother and daughter over the sexual favors of the daughter's husband. However it might also be a simple means of avoiding the kind of son-in-law, mother-in-law relationship which is so much a part of our own domestic folklore. In Nez Ch'ii today, mother-in-law avoidance is gradually dying out. However there still is an air of restraint between these two relatives. In the past, old persons in this relationship could simply agree to give up the avoidance practices. If a man is a singer and must in some emergency sing over his mother-in-law, the avoidance is broken thereafter, and he uses another kin term toward her. And if, as was not uncommon, a man marries an older woman and later marries her daughter from a previous marriage, there is no avoidance requirement. Similarly, if he has sexual intercourse with a woman and later marries her daughter by another man, he does not practice avoidance. In Navajo eyes avoidance behavior is a sign of mutual respect and should be practiced by both parties, although in fact the burden is most often on the man.

Between parents and children there is some difference in behavior of children toward their mother and father. Children will usually approach their mother directly to ask for a favor or for help. However, girls particularly are a bit reluctant to approach their fathers, but rather use their mothers as intermediaries. Fathers and sons have a more direct relationship, one that may include fairly rough joking, which emphasizes the fact that a father and son are of different clans.

Between siblings, age is a great determiner of authority and attitude. The elder generally assumes authority over the younger throughout life, very much (in the case of women) as she did when the younger was a child and the elder assisted in caring for her.

Between brothers, the elder will generally approach the younger directly, and the younger may do the same, but he may ask his sister to act as intermediary. Not infrequently, when a mother or sister wishes to ask a favor of a married son or brother, they first approach his wife. A sister will sometimes have her children ask her brother in her behalf for a favor or for help. This, of course, symbolizes the relationship between a man and his sister's children. He would be much less likely to refuse them than he would his sister.

Although the relationship between siblings is very close, there is also an element of "bashfulness" or restraint between them. Joking about sexual matters is forbidden or handled with extreme delicacy, so circumspectly that an outsider would scarcely know what the subject of the discussion was. Generally a brother and sister never travel together alone, and in the past they were not supposed to hand objects to each other. The closeness of siblings can also be seen in the traditional attitudes toward distribution of a person's property at the time of his death. A man's was distributed, not to his spouse and children, but rather among brothers and sisters. Today, American patterns of inheritance, which are enforced by the courts, are causing much domestic unhappiness among the Navajo, who resent the fact that a spouse and children will inherit more than brothers and sisters.

The importance of women in the Navajo system is illustrated by the fact that a brother or sister often avoids asking a married brother for help directly, preferring to refer to his wife first. This is true when one asks a friend who is not a relative for help. If the friend's wife is present, she must be consulted before the husband can make a commitment.

In matters of authority and allocation of work or wealth the elder usually exercises authority over the younger in the case of siblings. However, a sister has far more extensive claims on a brother than does a brother on a sister. She can ask his help in farming or herding, request and expect gifts of money or food. A brother cannot generally deny these requests, although he can claim that his wife's family made demands that superseded those of his own family. One of Aberle's informants pointed out that in the case of conflicting requests he could hold his own family off by saying that his wife's family wouldn't let him comply. Because one cannot talk to a mother-in-law, one cannot argue or explain save through the intermediary of his wife.

I have mentioned elsewhere some of the obligations a father has toward his sons. In general, his role is one of authority and support. He is required to provide for all his children and to teach them properly. The mother's brother, who plays such an important role in many matrilineal societies, is not so important in Navajo society, unless the father is not present. However, he may be called upon to help discipline children and most certainly has a number of economic and ritual obligations toward them. Traditionally it was he, not the father, who helped arrange marriages, although the father would receive part of the gifts given by the bridegroom to the family of the bride.

Aberle sums up the general pattern of relating to kinsmen in this way:

In general, the communications of consanguine [or what we would call "blood"] kin and of husband and wife are direct and unimpeded. Age and generation differences sometimes produce asymmetrical patterns. Thus the mother is sometimes used as an intermediary when a junior consanguine needs leverage in asking the assistance of senior kin. No intermediary is used for the mother herself. Mother's brother–sister's son relations are handled directly. The direct communication of brother and sister is disrupted by marriage, and particularly by the brother's marriage. Then his wife or his sister's children serve as intermediaries.

A man's communications with both male and female affines are largely indirect, whereas a woman's with female affines are often direct. This asymmetry is not reflected in kinship terminology, it will later be seen. [Aberle, 1961: p. 162]

I have mentioned in passing the matter of joking. Among the Navajo of Nez Ch'ii, as elsewhere, with whom one can joke and what kind of jokes may be employed are determined largely by kinship relationships. Anthropological studies have emphasized this kind of interaction to the point that such patterns are often seen as the unique quality of primitive or tribal people. Of course that is not the case. If we examine our own lives, we will see that we joke with certain people in quite a different way than we do with others. And with some we do not joke at all. Generally we do not joke with parents about sexual matters, but we may well do so with cousins or with friends. The difference between ourselves and the Navajo lies only in the fact that so much more of their social universe is defined by kinship classifications.

A brother and sister may joke with each other, but such bandying must never have a sexual connotation. Either one may make derogatory jokes about the other's appearance or make funny remarks about the other's abilities and skills. Much the same pattern is observed between the children of sisters (that is, parallel cousins). As siblings get married and grow older, the formalities between them become more rigid and approach almost prohibition or avoidance relationship.

Joking with parents must also avoid sexual references and usually refers to membership in clans. A boy can for instance refer to his mother as "woman who married into my father's clan," and thus in a sense speak of her as an in-law (Aberle, 1961: p. 152). Such joking might be called a play on kinship just as we make plays on words. Such references are often a part of Navajo joking and considered a basis for much humor. They bring to mind the humorously intended song of a few decades ago which dealt with the supposed marital habits of hillbillies, I Am My Own Grandpa.

With his mother's brother, however, a young man may joke about sexual matters. Almost no subject seems taboo; genital size, rape, seductions and conquests the other is supposed to have made, as well as plays on their kin relationship, which is complicated by the fact that his mother's brother can marry a woman of his nephew's father's clan—which of course the younger man can not do.

Cross cousins—that is, the children of the mother's brother or of the father's sister are of different clans than are the mother and father's own children, and in fact are eligible mates. Between such relatives joking can be rough and obscene. Male cross cousins, according to Aberle, can make virtually any topic the subject of joking. In addition they may wrestle, race with each other, or in other ways demonstrate a kind of friendly (generally) rivalry between them.

Aberle sums up various styles of joking in this way:

> Members of a clan joke about the things that divide them: different paternal affiliations. Parents and children joke about their different affiliations. Brothers and sisters joke about their different fortunes and their marital ties, if in a rather cautious fashion. Cross cousins, whose affiliations are clearly different, joke about the delicacy of the marriage bond. Outsiders press home jokes centering about a person's paternal affiliations or his siblings'—not his own—in-laws. In-laws do not joke, according to Dapah, although Reichard says that father-in-law and son-in-law do. In general, the non-joking and avoidant relationships create the ties about which the jesting revolves. [Aberle, 1961: pp. 156–157]

KIN TERMS

Many anthropologists have studied Navajo kinship terminology, and generally one must conclude that it is a very complex subject. Not all authorities agree as to precisely what term is applied in what case. This diversity can be attributed to the differing memories of informants or variations among different areas on the reservation and different times during which the field work has been done over nearly half a century. Nonetheless, the main themes and patterns of Navajo kinship terminology can be demonstrated by examining the list below. Each of the items listed is prefixed with the term *shi*, which is best translated as "my," the Navajo having no way to express these names save in personal terms. This is also true of most Navajo nouns, which must be prefixed with a possessive to be intelligible.

CATEGORIES OF NAVAJO KINSHIP

Possessive	Term	Relatives included*
shi	ma	mo, *mosis*†
	ma yazhi	*mo sis*, mosisda, fasisda, elsisda
	ma-sani	momo, mafasis, momosis
	Ch'aii	mofa, mofabro, momobro, *mofabro*
	Nali‡	fafa, famo, famosis, famobro, fafabro, fafasis, brosoch, ownsoch, sisoch, mobrosoch, fabrosoch, *fafasisch*
	tsoi	brodach, sisdach, fasisdach, mobrodach
	bizhi	*fabro*, fasis, famosisch, fafabroch, fasissosoch, *fafasisch*, mosissoch
	d'ai	mofasisso, mofabroso, momosisso, momobroso, mobro
	k'ai	mofasisda, mofabroda, momosisda, *mosis*, mobroda
	zeedi	mobroda, fasisda
	maa'aash	mobroso, fasisso
	Naai	Elbro
	Tsili	yobro
	deezhi	yosis
	adi	Elsis

* For uninitiated readers, mo=mother, sis=sister, da=daughter, ch=child, el=elder, yo=younger, and so on.

† An italicized kin description indicates that alternate terms are applied.

‡ The term *-nali* is commonly extended in politeness to nonrelatives.

5

Residence, Mobility, and Land Tenure

S OME ETHNOLOGISTS have described the Navajo as nomads, while others have stated most definitely that they are not. The disagreement appears to arise from conflicting definitions of the term and from the sympathies of the ethnologists. One of the most common justifications of usurping Indian lands has been the argument that they were nomads and thus did not put the vast territories they used to proper use. Anthropologists and other friends of the Navajo thus were often pressured by their own sympathy for the people to deny the charges of the land-grabbers. In fact the Navajo do not and, it would appear, never have wandered aimlessly behind their herds in search of grass and water. Probably no such people has ever existed. Nonetheless, all authorities agree that the living patterns of the Navajo are, for the most part, extremely mobile. The life of the people in Nez Ch'ii supports such a description. In some parts of the reservation, natural or artificial conditions have made it possible to develop what can be best described as oases where regular crops of corn, melons, pumpkins, grapes, peaches, and grains such as oats, wheat, and barley can be produced and where the farmer can establish a permanent abode. However, over much of the reservation, a Navajo homestead group must be prepared to shift its location fairly regularly. For some, the shift comes twice a year as the herds are moved from the lowlands to the cooler highlands in the summer and, in some cases, from the snowy uplands to more temperate valleys in the winter. Such people generally fall into the classification of transhumants. In the Nez Ch'ii country such clearly defined movement does not occur, although during the summer a number of temporary sheep camps spring up as people from hotter and more arid regions drift into the area. For the permanent residents the pattern is more complex and entails consideration of grazing, water, wood supply, ritual beliefs, and the dynamics of the homestead group itself.

Traditional Use Area

For the most part, people in the Nez Ch'ii area answer a direct question about their mobility by saying they seldom or never move. However, more detailed questioning—asking an informant to point out on a map where he has lived during his lifetime—reveals a pattern of regular and frequent movement of the homestead group. One such informant, a boy of seventeen, could point out eleven separate locations where the homestead group had established itself in his lifetime. In addition, he recounted an annual move into winter quarters in the fall of each year and the establishment of separate mobile sheep camps during many summer periods. His experience is very much the same as those of his neighbors. The contrast between the claim that they do not move and the actual instance of movement appears to stem from the Navajo view about land tenure. Unlike many nomadic people in the Old World or the Plains Indians, the Navajo unit of movement is the homestead group or the nuclear family. Thus, no large-scale tribal or band migrations take place. Because the unit of movement is smaller, so is the size of the sheep herd. Thus, migrations in the Old World often are hundreds of miles long because the animals of the entire tribe are treated as a unit, and grazing lands must be sought for all of them. The Navajo, on the other hand, considers only the need of his own sheep herd and thus moves within a much more restricted area. Each herd, unless drought or another serious emergency forces other arrangements, moves within what has come to be called a *traditional use area,* that is, the land on which the family and its ancestors have regularly grazed their animals. Depending on the range, the water supply, and the weather, this use area may be quite small, and its efficient use may never require the moving of the base camp of the homestead group. In other instances, two areas, often widely separated, are identified with a single group that uses them alternately at different times of the year. Over most of the reservation, each homestead group will have a single contiguous use area. The condition of the range and the water supply in such an area means that an average herd must graze over an extremely large range in the course of the year, and, for convenience, the homestead must often be shifted. The most important factor in determining whether the land will support permanent occupation is the water supply. Inasmuch as the sheep herd is penned each night at the homestead, there must be adequate water sources near enough to permit the round trip to water and back. If these are limited in number, the repeated use of the same route will soon exhaust the grazing and force the homestead group to move so that the spring or well may be approached from a different direction. If a water source is so far away that the drive cannot be made and still allow time for grazing, the camp must be temporarily or permanently moved. In times past, it was often necessary for people from the Nez Ch'ii area to drive their animals in the summer to the Tuba City region, where a shallow canyon contains a river that provided permanent water for the herds. This annual migration was nearly eighty miles one way. Since the beginning of this century, the government has put down many wind-driven wells and assisted in the improvement of natural water sources, which have made such long trips unnecessary. However, until very recently, in some areas water was so limited that sheep were watered only every second or third day. Even a homestead which has several alternative water sources for its livestock is forced to move periodically, as the grass in all directions from the homesite eventually is eaten away.

As reservation lands have gradually filled with people, the traditional use areas claimed by each homestead group have grown smaller. In general, this has been a result of divisions of the original range utilized by a founding ancestor by his or her descendents. However, many homestead groups operate in an area of as much as fifteen thousand acres or more. The boundaries of such areas are recognized by the entire community, although it is often difficult for an investigator to draw a map from descriptions given by residents in the area unless the boundary is actually visited and the important landmarks demarking one grazing area from the other are pointed out. Often the boundary lines are disputed by neighbors, so that each area is surrounded by a vague zone of conflicting claims. In the past, such conflicts were resolved by shifting to new range. Today they constitute a matter of increasing social tension. Neither legally nor traditionally can these areas be considered private property. Only the right to graze sheep is effectively controlled by the homestead group. Free-ranging cattle and horses graze without reference to even these vague boundaries. Neighbors always have a claim on water sources if their own range does not have any. Trails cut directly cross country, often passing within a few feet of a hogan without reference to "ownership."

Factors of Mobility

WATER SUPPLY

If the water generally used by an outfit disappears during a drought, permission to water one's herd at a spring or well on the range of another grazer must be sought. Usually such arrangements can be made between related homestead groups. If the distance is too great to make the round trip in a single day, a temporary sheep camp will be established on the neighboring range, although the herd will be grazed on the home range as much as possible. In the past two decades a system of grazing permits issued by the tribe and government has attempted to limit overgrazing, and a committee of local grazers in each area has served to manage the range and communal operations such as branding, vaccination, and dipping. The committee often makes its decisions by articulating traditional range usages with the rules and regulations imposed from above.

Water for human use has become a less and less important factor in determining the location of a homestead since the introduction of wagons (later trucks) and barrels. Today and for several decades past, drinking water has been hauled from reliable water sources as much as thirty or forty miles away.

CROP LOCATION

The location of cornfields seldom influences the site of the homestead. If possible, it is desirable to live near one's fields, but because some areas are more suitable for crops than others and the demands of the herd are more immediate, fields may in fact be several miles from the homestead. At harvest time a temporary camp may be set up near the field to protect the crops.

FUEL SUPPLY

Fuel is a constant problem, but seldom does nearness of a wood supply influence the establishment of a homestead, save perhaps in the winter. One can use a wagon to haul large supplies of wood to the homesite rather than depend on daily foraging expeditions. In the winter, however, some consideration is given to nearby sources of fuel because it may be impossible, even with a wagon, to bring large fuel supplies through the snow drifts. Moreover, trees provide a modicum of protection from the often bitter weather.

SEASONS

The main site of a homestead is that generally occupied from early spring until the beginning of the cold season. This is seldom in the flat bottoms of the valleys, where sudden summer cloudbursts often create furious floods. Rather, the homesteads are located on the alluvial fan that spreads out around the base of the hills and mesas. The growth of juniper or piñon pine, which generally clusters

The winter camps are set up on the tops or flanks of the mesas to be near a fuel supply and to get some protection from the weather.

A typical hogan standing on the plain abandoned for the winter, while its occupants live in a more sheltered winter camp.

at the foot of the mesa itself, is often avoided because it spawns large numbers of viciously annoying flies in the hot months and is also more apt to be the habitat of snakes. Most generally, then, the summer homestead is located on the barren slopes; the surrounding grass and sage have been grazed to nothing, unprotected by trees. Shade is provided by building brush ramadas near the cabins or hogans. The various hogans and cabins may be set close together surrounding the sheep pen, itself a structure of untrimmed juniper and pine logs. More often, the homestead group will be dispersed with only one or two hogans together in one place, while other members of the group live up to a mile away.

When the winter sets in, the outfit draws closer together because the demands of the herd are much greater and require the cooperation of as many people as possible. Not infrequently, all the adults and older children must spend much of a winter day trudging on the range and stamping snow away from the scanty graze to provide feed for the herd. Winter hogans cluster close together and are usually smaller than the house at the main camp.

Temporary camps established in the summer are often nothing more than walls of brush set up against some natural object such as a standing rock or large bush. Perhaps a few blankets or pieces of canvas will be used to make the roof less porous.

The Changing Pattern of Mobility

The actual ownership of grazing lands on the Navajo reservation rests in the legal entity of the Navajo tribe and is held in trust for the tribe by the U.S. Government in order to prevent the tragic loss of land that accompanied the shifting of land to individual and tribal control among many Indian groups in the last century. Individual Navajo often strive to improve their grazing lands principally through making improvements on natural water sources. At the same time, the tribe and the Bureau of Indian Affairs attempt to maintain controls over range and water development, livestock grazing, and other matters. Income from leasing the rights to drill for oil or extract other minerals with which the reservation is richly endowed accrues to the tribe rather than to individuals. While individual families may move freely on and off the reservation and settle anywhere they wish, they must, if they wish to move their sheep herd, obtain permission from the tribal institutions involved in range management as well as secure concurrence of their new neighbors.

In the past, the long treks in search of water and grazing made the Navajo a clearly nomadic people, but the restrictions brought about by increased population, government and tribal regulations, and the increased availability of water have changed the patterns of their lives considerably. Nonetheless, they remain highly mobile people. In any year the individual will most likely live in two camps—summer and winter—and possibly more if the conditions call for the setting up of camps near the fields or a separate sheep camp. Always reacting to the demands of the sheep herd, which dominates his life as it did that of his grandfather, he will shift homesites many times during his lifetime within the scope of the traditional use area of his family. Finally, the death of a member of the family means the abandoning of his hogan and the entire homesite until the hogan has disintegrated. Other hogans in the homestead will often be dis-

One form of hogan made with upright wall logs.

assembled and transported to a new site. In recent years, because the Navajo have increasingly taken gravely ill persons to modern hospitals, their deaths in a hospital preclude the need to move.

The Adaptability of the Hogan

The core of the Navajo homestead is the distinctive hogan. Even families that prefer to live in a cabin or modern house usually build a hogan in which to have ceremonies. Many nuclear units have two hogans, one for storage. The hogan appears in a number of variations. Less frequently seen today is the oldest form, which consists of a number of logs set into the ground to form a point with a small alcove or gallery entrance constructed on one side. The wooden structure is then covered with earth. More common is one or another variation of a style called the "six-sided" or "eight-sided" hogan made of either horizontal logs chinked with mud and roofed over with earth and logs or shorter logs set into the ground in a rough circle and roofed in the same manner. Often the entire structure is covered with earth to form a dark room that is cool in the summer and warm in the winter, when a blanket or wooden hatch is used to keep rain or snow from entering the smoke hole.

6

The Animals

NAVAJO SOCIETY and culture was profoundly affected when the partially agricultural hunters and gatherers who were the ancestors of the modern Navajo chose to adopt livestock introduced by the Spanish. The older residents of the region, the Puebloan peoples, were too closely wedded to their agricultural past to exploit the potential of animal husbandry completely, although they did begin to maintain herds as an adjunct to farming. The other Apache groups, for various reasons, remained primarily raiders, seizing horses to ride in war and hunting and taking other livestock to eat. The Navajo, no less addicted to raiding for livestock, chose to maintain herds and place primary reliance on them. The general outlines of Navajo culture and many of its details then became those of nomadic or seminomadic pastoralists. Livestock—particularly horses, sheep, and goats—became the prime measure of wealth. Large herds were the goal of all Navajo, and the welfare of the herds became the central focus of Navajo life.

For the pastoralist, life must be oriented around the needs and habits of his animals. Daily and annual routines, attitudes, motor habits, and even social institutions must be planned in such a way that the demands of the herds are never left unmet. The following sections will describe Navajo society and culture from the point of view of the herds and the ways in which their owners live in order that they may be maintained.

Pastoralism gives a society greater potential for rapid territorial and population expansion than does agriculture. While the farmer must exploit enough land to feed his population, he on the other hand can seldom exploit much more than that because the amount of land to be worked is dependent upon the people available to farm it. The herder can handle two hundred animals with as much ease as one hundred, so that it is possible to expand wealth greatly without a corresponding expansion of population. However, his expanded herds demand grazing land and thus the pressure to extend territory is inherent in any pastoral society.

Before their defeat in the 1860s, Navajo culture combined raiding and herding, the former to increase the number of livestock and to obtain from

Europeans material goods that the Navajo could not produce himself. But a third element, trade, was becoming increasingly important even in these warlike times. Navajo trading parties loaded with heavy woolen Navajo rugs annually traveled to Fort Bridger in Wyoming. Wool, rugs, horses, and other livestock were readily traded for manufactured goods, often with the very people who had been raided only a short time before.

After the defeat, incarceration, and establishment of the reservation, the Navajo, in the main, abandoned warfare and raiding, at least against the dominant Anglo–American culture. Living in a land that held little attraction for American settlers but which was eminently suitable to the needs of the herdsman, the Navajo people developed a modified culture that for six decades provided a basis for expansion of population and territory and, overall, a generally satisfactory level of existence. Today, Navajo population has far outstripped the ability of the land to support it by herding. However, in Nez Ch'ii herding is still a primary activity, and the needs of livestock dominate patterns of thought and action. Nez Ch'ii today, as it was in the past, remains as the consequence of the complex interaction of men, animals, and land. The link between man and the land is the animals he keeps. It is useful, then, to look at the animals of Nez Ch'ii as a first step in understanding the Navajo who live in this region.

In general, animals can be divided into three types, based not on species but on the use to which they are put by man (*cf.* Downs, 1964, for a more detailed discussion).

Utilitarian Animals

THE HORSE

No Navajo in the Nez Ch'ii area feels comfortable unless he can speak of himself as the owner of a horse, but the discomfort is not entirely a matter of social status; a family without access to riding and draft stock is severely handicapped in the simple business of survival. Although perhaps a third to a half of the people today have some access to pick-up trucks, I did not discover a single homestead that did not have at least one, and usually two or more, horses. The wagon and the riding horse are still important methods of transport in the area. Particularly in periods of bad weather when most roads are impassable to automotive traffic, a wagon is indispensable for hauling wood and water and traveling to and from the trading store. To say a man is so poor he "don't even own no horse" is a comment not only on his social standing but also on his capacity simply to survive. However, the extension of the reservation system of paved roads into the Nez Ch'ii area is encouraging the purchase of trucks and automobiles, and the number of these vehicles nearly doubled in the year 1960–1961. The purchase of wagons and harness at the traders has dropped off considerably, as even those families without automotive transportation are looking forward to the day when they can buy an auto or truck.

The problems of the horse-keeper are not the same as those dealt with by the herder of sheep and cattle. First of all, the horse must be available for use. The degree of availability is determined by the distance one must travel to find a grazing

One of the last wagons to be sold in the Nez Ch'ii area standing in the back of the trading post. Few Navajo buy wagons today; they prefer to buy automobiles even in remote areas, where they save money against the day better roads are built.

horse and by the condition of the animal. Horses tend to drift rather far afield when they are turned out to graze, and they quickly learn that if they are close to the homestead they will be rounded up and used more often. If a man must walk ten miles to find his team, it will be used only when absolutely necessary. Some owners hobble their horses to limit their travels, and although Navajo horses are adept at moving while hobbled, the primary advantage is that an animal so handicapped can be caught more easily when finally located. At homesteads where there are enough horses available, one animal may be kept tethered to a post near the hogan, and saddled, ready for immediate use. This makes it possible to ride in search of the rest of the horse herd that has been turned out to graze. If such a surplus horse is not available, or if there is no nearby horse that can be borrowed, the homesteader must walk, often as far as ten or fifteen miles. Once the animals are located, it is customary to seek out a nearby hogan or sheep camp and borrow a horse to use in rounding up one's stock. Such loans may be made either willingly or reluctantly, but they always seem to be made.

Most homesteads boast a horse corral, but feed must be purchased for horses kept in the corral for any length of time, so such restrictions are kept to a minimum. If it is known that some member of the family will soon require a mount or team, the horses may be brought in and kept coralled for a day or two. If no hay is available, they may be turned out to graze with a boy to watch them or, in season, fed corn husks and ears (after the humans have eaten the kernels). Keeping horses in the corral creates the additional chore of driving them to water twice daily, a job usually usurped by the oldest boy in the homestead. The privilege of riding a horse is prized, and the prerogative of the elder is jealously guarded.

One factor working against the permanent corralling of horses is the Navajo belief, quite well founded in fact, that animals allowed to graze are in better condition for hard work.

Horse husbandry cannot be considered as simply a facet of the other herding activities of a family because the habits of the horse differ greatly from those of sheep and cattle. When turned out to graze, horses seldom if ever remain near the sheep herds. In fact, they generally move in the opposite direction, so that while a man is herding his sheep to the west his horses may be moving at a high trot toward a waterhole far to the east. Cattle, particularly those belonging to owners with only a few calves, often are content to remain with the sheep herd. Purchased as calves and placed with the sheep, they have been conditioned to their company. Horses, on the other hand, either are purchased as grown animals or, if raised by their owners, remain with their dams separately from the sheep. Thus animal husbandry comes to have a dual cycle, one for horses and one for sheep. If the cattle holdings are large enough, the cycle is trebled. Horses and cattle seldom graze together and when confronted with bad weather react in opposite fashions, horses moving into the storm, cattle moving with it.

The horse extends the area of a family herding operation farther than do either sheep or cattle, but the extension is not uniform in all directions. The horses of a particular family usually roam in the same general direction each time they are turned out, requiring the owner to have an intimate knowledge of the land in certain directions. Moreover, the owner thus becomes obligated to certain families whom he must often question as to whether they have seen the wandering horses or from whom he must borrow a mount. In addition, horses are generally to be found on the customary range of some other family, and such range utilization is rarely reciprocal because the family whose range is thus imposed upon may find its horses grazing on the land of yet another family. It is not surprising, then, that resentments and conflicts growing out of the grazing of horses are the most frequent livestock disputes encountered in the Nez Ch'ii area.

In periods of extreme drought, like the early summer of 1961, lack of nearby water and graze forces many families to do without their horses for long periods. At such times the animals are allowed to drift into areas where the summer rains have been more frequent, often as far as twenty or even thirty miles away. Owners of such straying stock are aware that they are taking advantage of the grazing rights of others but view this with a certain sly satisfaction at thus making profit on the better luck of a distant neighbor. Although the people thus imposed upon may grumble, they cannot—in the face of a drought—protest too loudly.

THE DOG

The other important utilitarian species is the dog. In both the scientific and popular literature it has been common to compare the Navajo shepherd and his dog to European shepherds and their sheep dogs. During my stay in the Nez Ch'ii area, however, I did not see a single dog that would be considered a sheep dog by any European or Anglo–American sheep owner. Navajo dogs usually accompany their owners into the field with the sheep, but their contribution to the control and direction of the flock is indeed limited. At best they move in the same direction as the herder and "chase" the sheep in the right direction. At worst, they remain totally uninterested in the sheep and spend their time chasing jackrabbits, digging in prairie-dog holes, or lying in the shade of a bush. Their function, however, must not be underestimated. In recent years the wholesale destruction of prairie dogs, the principal food of coyotes, and intensive campaigns of hunting and trapping have reduced the coyote population appreciably and thus the threat to the sheep herd. However, in the recent past, coyote depredations against grazing sheep were common and serious, and the primary duty of the dogs that accompanied the herd was to discover and pursue such herd-raiders.

Navajo dog training is largely limited to conditioning the dog to remain with the sheep herd. This is sometimes accomplished by keeping puppies in a box in the sheep pen and feeding them there. On occasion they are nursed by a ewe, or a goat or a ewe is milked to feed the puppy. A dog thus reared will usually stay with the herd whenever it leaves the homestead area. However, many dogs never receive such conditioning and simply learn to follow their masters when the herd is taken out. Usually a dog that refuses to join the herd is stoned, kicked, and otherwise abused if it remains near the homestead.

The dog's utility, at least in the eyes of his master, does not end with the sheep herd. Perhaps because of a history marked by raids from all directions by enemies, both Indian and White, Navajo prize their dogs as guards, a job they carry out admirably. The approach of a strange rider or wagon, or the passing of an automobile or truck, excites the dogs of a homestead into paroxysms of barking. Strange livestock, particularly horses, are also noisily announced. Of not inconsiderable importance is the belief that the dogs can sense the presence of wolf men.

Another role of the homestead dogs is that of scavenger, a function that is particularly important because of the informal toilet arrangements of the average Navajo home. Small children in particular relieve their bowels wherever they happen to be. The evidence, however, quickly disappears because a defecating child is immediately circled by several none-too-patient canines. Adults who withdraw from camp to defecate are usually followed by dogs. Dogs also consume fresh horse and cow dung that may be dropped in the vicinity of the living area, thus keeping the homesite relatively free of filth and flies.

Traditionally the Navajo have used dogs in hunting to locate animals and to track down wounded game. I did not find any dogs kept specifically for this purpose, but dogs with a proclivity for jumping rabbits and giving chase were not discouraged. One man who enjoyed hunting wildcats in the winter spoke of getting a hunting dog to assist him in tracking.

Most dogs found about a Navajo homesite are males, some of them castrated. Female puppies are usually fondled and petted for a few weeks and eventually killed to keep the population within bounds. Females that survive usually whelp in a cave or remote ravine and keep their puppies hidden until they can fend for themselves.

They haunt homesites to steal food for their broods and hunt rabbits and rodents as well. The litters seldom escape the eyes of bands of boys who roam the hills in play, and generally the puppies are brought home as pets.

Ownership of dogs, like that of other livestock, is individual. Each dog is associated with a nuclear family and is referred to as "Alta's dog" or "Kee's dog" in reference to the man or woman in the family. However, further inquiry usually reveals that within the nuclear group dogs have various owners, with each member of the group owning a dog if the family can afford it. The number of dogs varies, as a Navajo would put it, according to "whether you likes dogs or not," but everyone obviously feels that he or she should own a dog. The establishing of claims on a new litter of puppies is one source of friction within the extended family. Whether the bitch is owned by the homestead or not, puppies are usually "found," either abandoned by owners who do not want them or hidden by their mothers. The practice of killing unwanted puppies at birth seems unknown, and puppies are usually turned out near a well-traveled road, or at the trader's, or at a spring or well, so that someone will discover them and take them home. The discovery of a new litter immediately sets off competition among a number of children over the puppies. Not infrequently, the puppies are taken away from the mother and handled until they die. If they survive, there is a regular struggle between the family and the mother, who tries to relocate her brood and carry it away, although usually she will finally simply come in to feed the puppies periodically. If the puppies survive, adults who want a dog generally override the claims of children by appropriating the animal, usually when the child making the claim is absent. There may also be competition between adults, and such disputes sometimes lead to actual fist fights between adult women. Until the animal is fairly well grown and its ownership well established, the owner, child or adult, must be prepared to defend his or her claim against other members of the extended family.

Dogs encountered on the range away from any habitation may be shot, or shot at, if a gun is handy, but if the Navajo is mounted, it is very likely that he will uncoil his lariat and attempt to rope the animal. In such encounters there is a great deal of concern about the animal's ownership, a concern that is natural in any sheep-herding area because of the dread of packs of wild dogs. Such packs are perhaps the most deadly threat to sheep herders in America, their depredations far exceeding that of natural predators such as mountain lions, wildcats, wolves, eagles, or coyotes.

Navajo dogs are not starved, but they are forever hungry, which creates both advantages and disadvantages. There is little refuse left near a Navajo hogan because of the dogs' appetites, nor does the offal and waste from slaughtering survive long. On the other hand, dogs are always alert to snatch food, literally from the hands or the cooking fires of their masters, and when such forays are successful, a whole family may well have a night without food.

Although the Navajo consider their dogs important and real members of the group and view them affectionately, they seldom pet them the way Whites do. Dogs are allowed on the peripheries of the eating ground but driven severely from hogans, houses, or summer shades. In the Navajo view a dog should be devoted but remain distant, and common Navajo practice insures the distance. Dogs are often

called, patted briefly, then hit rather severely. Few Navajo can resist throwing a
stone at a dog, but although they can be amazingly accurate, they seldom hit the
dogs, thus belying their apparently vicious intent. There is general admiration for
a "tough dog," and generally the dogs of a homesite are subservient to a single
leader, which, as he grows older, must defend his position daily.

The Navajo tend to speak of their dogs in a kindly manner, and young men
speak with some pride of a dog that refuses to eat or otherwise demonstrates sorrow
at their absence or which refuses to be taken from their presence by another human.

A common occurrence is the killing of a dog by an adult male in the course
of a dispute with members of the family. A man frustrated and angry after a fight
with his wife may, particularly if the animal is a stray or does not belong to a
member of his family, shoot and kill a dog. An example drawn from my field notes
illustrates this:

May 10
    Tom and his wife have been quarreling all day. I think the problem is that
    she and his mother don't get along. She also has become very insistent that
    they move out of his sister's extra house and build one of their (really her) own.
    Just before dusk the bickering rose to a shouting quarrel, and Tom burst out
    of the house with a gun in his hand. He looked absolutely outraged. Before I
    knew what was happening, he shot a dog five times, killing it instantly. He
    seemed to calm down after that and went over to Harriet's cabin where he
    remained until dark. Don't know when he came home. The dog was not one
    of the regular homestead pack but had been hanging around the edges of camp
    for a couple of days. All of the others in camp disappeared into their cabins
    or hogans and stayed there, afraid.

May 11
    Asked Harriet's oldest daughter why Tom had shot the dog yesterday. She
    said, "Oh, he had been fighting with his wife. He was pretty mad. That's why
    he shot it." Today everything seemed back to normal. No quarreling at Tom's.

Although the owner of the dog may be both angry and sorrowful, he seldom takes
any direct action about such a killing. A man angry enough to kill a dog, in the
Navajo view, is not totally responsible, and moreover any angry person is considered dangerous and to be avoided.

Dogs are named according to the accidents of their acquisition, their individual peculiarities, or the whims of their owners. On the homestead where I lived,
the names included Wine, describing the light brown color (three other dogs of the
litter were named Whiskey, Beer, and Peyote); Bear, a reference to a burly build
and a short tail; Ringo, after a western outlaw currently popular on television in the
off-reservation boarding school; Johnny; and Supper—this last was said by some
members of the family to refer to the puppy's appetite, but others said it reflected
his size, which was "just enough to eat for supper." The people of the Nez Ch'ii
region view dog eating as both humorous and somewhat disgusting, and certainly
a trait of other and lesser Indians.

Dogs are considered the responsibility of their owners, insofar as there is
any control at all save the occasional flinging of a stone. If, however, a dog successfully raids the human food supply, its owner shares the guilt, although he is not

expected to make recompense. There is a high degree of anthropomorphizing in the attitude of Navajo toward their dogs. Dogs are described as tough, smart, and the like. The details of canine social and family structure are well known and remarks such as "that one—Johnny—he's Wine's son, so he always stick up for him in a fight" are common.

This attitude is in sharp contrast to that adopted toward a far more important animal, the horse. Some horses appear to be named, but usually their names refer to some characteristic, for example the "black horse," the "white mare" (gray horses are invariably spoken of as white), the "old horse," or they are identified by reference to the owner. Horses are also described as good or bad according to their ability to work, but no attributes of character are ascribed to them. White horsemen very frequently speak of a horse as having courage or loyalty, but such references are meaningless to the Navajo—except as they indicate the eccentricity of White men.

Dogs receive little or no medical attention, although their ailments are a matter of concern to their owners. The most common injuries are those incurred in fights. Often such wounds are extensive and serious, but lack of knowledge of first aid prevents treatment. A severely wounded dog is watched, and some attempt is made to keep other dogs from attacking a disabled member of the pack. Recovery from severe wounds is accepted as evidence of a dog's "toughness." If some aid is available, such as that offered by a visiting anthropologist, it is accepted gratefully and the treatment and recovery is apt to be a subject of repeated discussion.

The dog and the horse, kept in large part for their utility, present a distinct contrast in the demands their ownership makes and in the consequences their ownership has. The horse ranges widely and requires a wide extension of human relationships so that the owner may make use of him and at the same time support him by utilizing the natural range. This wide-ranging propensity of the horse is the basis of many interpersonal relationships, both friendly and hostile. In addition, in order to make the horse an effective part of the economic unit, a number of livestock artifacts must be obtained, which will be discussed in a later section. The horse also requires the expenditure of money for feed when there is extreme food shortage, when extended periods of hard work are required, and when travel is in areas where feed is not available. The dog, on the other hand, seldom ranges far away from its owner and thus seldom extends human relationships. Potentially, however, the dog is a threat to smooth human relations, inasmuch as it may raid the food supply of a neighbor, fight with and injure a neighbor's dog, or attack a neighbor's livestock. Also, the killing of a stray dog may lead to disputes with the owner. Very little effort is expended in maintaining dogs, although shepherds usually carry a gun in order to shoot rabbits for the dog to eat, and some of the animals killed in rabbit chases are given to the dogs.

Marketable Livestock

Animals in the category of marketable livestock include all species maintained for sale or consumption.

CHICKENS

Occasionally, homesteads have a few chickens wandering among the hogans. The birds are of indeterminate breed, scrawny, and often nearly featherless from some combination of ills. Occasionally, I was told, a bird will be killed and eaten, and eggs are sometimes eaten. The birds are not penned or otherwise housed in the summer. Occasionally a makeshift shelter referred to as a chicken house may be thrown up, or a covered dugout may be made, which helps the birds to survive the winter. The birds subsist on scraps from the preparation of human food and by pecking through horse and cow dung for undigested seeds. In this way they keep the homestead free of any garbage or offal missed by the dogs. The primary function of the birds seems to be to serve as targets for little boys practicing with a lariat, and as such they contribute to the development of human skills. In old literature on the Navajo the chicken is most commonly mentioned in connection with the Mexican equestrian contest of "chicken pulling." In this event a chicken is buried up to its neck, and riders attempt to seize the bird while galloping past it, a feat requiring a great deal of agility and skill. Informants in their fifties remember seeing this sport in their youth, but it has long since been abandoned. However, the Navajo word for rodeo is the same as the word for chicken.

SHEEP

Sheep dominate the livestock economics of Nez Ch'ii and the Navajo reservation as a whole. The social and cultural life of a family owning even four or five sheep is largely determined by this ownership. In part this is owing to cultural patterns built around sheep keeping as a way of life and supporting the patterns of sheep keeping as the "right" way to live. Also, the possession of even a few sheep requires certain activities that are only intensified if the number of sheep is increased. Sheep keeping also requires herding and tending every day, so that the activities of man are dominated by the needs of the herd. When the herd can provide man with his needs, the system remains in balance. In recent years, income from livestock cannot meet the needs of the Navajo, a situation that produces social and psychological tensions and sets the stage for major cultural changes.

Of all domestic creatures generally maintained by herding people, the sheep is perhaps the most thoroughly domesticated. It is doubtful whether domestic sheep could survive for a single winter without human assistance. Sheep are generally thought of, and rightly so, even by shepherds, as being unintelligent relative to other domestic animals.

HERDING INSTINCT   The most notable characteristic of the domestic sheep is its herding instinct. The need to herd, the compulsion to follow others of its kind, makes it easy for a single man with or without the assistance of dogs to control several hundred sheep. A moving sheep herd is seldom plagued with the consistent herd-bolter or bunch-quitter found in almost any herd of cattle or horses. A sheep separated from its flock is almost invariably doomed. If the almost defenseless animal is not killed by predators, it starves to death or dies of thirst. A herdsman can hope for the survival of an isolated calf or colt but seldom a lamb.

Moreover, the behavior of a sheep herd is such that it cannot be permitted freedom to graze at will. Watching a herd graze, one is struck by the fact that it is in constant, nervous motion, each animal reacting to the movements of the others. This motion sometimes leads the herd to good grazing, but it may also bring the herd to a full stop, each animal reacting to another and no single animal breaking the spell. Most Navajo herds have a few goats mixed in with the sheep, and these curious, active, and self-reliant animals initiate almost all the action in the herd. Sheep are easily conditioned into simple habits, so that certain surroundings or conditions evoke a repeated response. This enables the shepherd to move animals to a specific place and then ignore them, since he is certain that they will respond by going to water or following a certain trail or drifting back into the sheep pen. The fact that sheep are so easily handled and only have to be directed rather than driven makes it possible for anyone—man, woman, or child older than seven or eight—to assume the duties of herder. In short, a Navajo child may begin his life as a herder of sheep before he is ten and continue as a herder into very old age, stopping only when he or she is no longer able to walk. Sheep, then, require a maximum of care but are easily controllable, so that a great variety of people can take part in this care.

LAMBING   In the winter and particularly in early spring, sheep herding is far more arduous. The cold winds or snows usually keep the herd on the move to find grass and to avoid the worst of the weather. In the spring the problem is complicated by the lambing. Ewes are taken out with the herd and allowed to lamb in the field. This means that the shepherd must be alert to spot the ewes as they lie down in the sagebrush at the onset of labor. When the lamb is born, the herder, using a mirror, signals the homestead and someone comes out to take the lamb back. The direction of the sun in relation to the homestead is an important factor in herding at this time. If the homestead cannot be signaled or if several lambs have been born, the herder usually starts a fire and keeps the lambs warm until either he or someone else can take the animals home. His job is complicated by the fact that the ewes that have already lambed are also with the herd. These animals constantly attempt to leave the herd and return to the homestead where the young lambs are kept. As the season progresses and the number of lambed ewes increases, a major part of the herd may be constantly attempting to bolt for home.

HERDING METHODS   Anglo–American commercial sheep operations contrast with Navajo sheep herding, in which the sheep are regularly penned. Anglo–American methods fall into two classes, range techniques and fenced techniques. In the first, large herds are cared for by shepherds with the assistance of dogs. The sheep herd is moved slowly over a wide area, the herder accompanying the herd in a trailer home or tent. Movement is dictated by the condition of the range. When feed is exhausted, the herd is shifted to another range. Consideration must be given to the availability of water, but the primary pattern is the constant shift to new range that is grazed once each season. In certain areas and at certain times of the year, sheep may be maintained on fenced range without the constant surveillance of a shepherd or his dogs. Sometimes such operations are relatively small scale—a farmer maintaining a few head of sheep just as he keeps a few pigs, a head or two of cattle, and some chickens—but in other operations rather large numbers of sheep are kept under fenced conditions during lambing or in the process of fattening for market. Purebred sheep are often raised entirely in this manner.

Navajo herding methods combine close control with the open range. Perhaps because of a history of livestock keeping marked by raiding and counter-raiding, or perhaps because of the not inconsiderable fear most Navajo have of the dark, sheep are penned each night. The only exceptions to this in my experience were when herds were being moved and could not be penned, or when a herd was being held overnight near a dipping vat so that it might be dipped early in the morning. In both these situations the animals were closely herded and carefully watched. When it is necessary to pen sheep away from the homestead, they are penned if possible in an abandoned pen or a box canyon.

In addition to the nightly penning, sheep in the Nez Ch'ii area are penned during the heat of the day. This period begins when the sun is well up, about 9 A.M. in the summer and somewhat later or not at all in the winter. Although the heat in the Nez Ch'ii area is not intense, the Navajo here appear to be culturally conditioned toward an extreme sensitivity and consider it hot when the thermometer goes past 80°F. Their sheep react to heat by refusing to graze and by standing bunched together, each animal attempting to shade its eyes by sticking its head under its neighbor. It is virtually impossible for a shepherd to make a herd move once it has stopped. The shouts and blows of the herder, even assisted by dogs, seldom do more than force a few animals to shift position. Attacks on the flock by coyotes are reported to cause little disturbance. Thus, the Navajo has a choice of remaining with the herd throughout the day or getting it home and penned before the sun gets too high. The latter course is usually followed because it does not tie up the services of the herder during the midday meal. On cool days or when the herd is grazing near the homestead, it may not be brought in and penned but simply watched by whoever is around, or the younger children may be assigned to keep an eye on the animals. If, however, the herd is out of sight when caught by the sun, it is a matter of great concern, and the entire homestead begins searching until the animals and the herder are located.

The herd is generally taken out to graze just before dawn and kept on the range until the sun begins to get high, about 9 A.M. The animals are then penned through the heat of the midmorning and early afternoon and turned out for grazing again about 4 P.M. They are penned for the night shortly before sunset. On the long summer day, the herd is permitted to graze about seven and one-half hours out of the twenty-four. This patterning of grazing is, of course, determined by circumstances; for example, the pattern described above is the one followed on a homestead with a large water supply only a few hundred yards from the homesite. With slight modifications, it is the one followed by any herd that can be driven to water and back to the pen within the time limits. In some cases the herd must be held on the range during the still period in order to reach distant water that may be as far as from five to ten miles away from the homestead. Where the herd must go as far as ten miles for water, there is a strong tendency to shift camp because twenty miles in the course of a day is an extremely long drive for a sheep herd. A round trip of ten miles, however, is not at all unusual.

The shifting of the herd from the homestead to a sheep camp is not casually undertaken. Such a shift usually means that the herd must trespass on the grazing land of other families, and negotiation for permission must be undertaken. Usually this is done by a relative of the moving family who has married into the host family. For instance, if a brother is living with his wife on land that would be trespassed, he is asked to go to his father-in-law or mother-in-law to obtain permission for his family to camp near the water source. In addition, informal permission must be obtained from the grazing committee representative for the move. Once permission is obtained, one of the nuclear families is chosen to go to the camp. Invariably such groups isolated from the rest of the outfit express "fear" and report the appearance of wolf men, strange sounds, or very real intrusions of "drunkers." At the same time, the families remaining at the homestead often say they are "lonesome." Frequent trips between the homestead and the sheep camps are made on almost any pretext. Usually the first family is followed by yet another and as often as not the entire homestead will have shifted, in the course of a few days or a week or two, from the outfit to the camp. In addition, if a member of the outfit lives with his wife's family near the new location, he visits his relatives more often and perhaps brings his wife and family to live in the camp temporarily. At the same time, if intraoutfit frictions have developed, which frequently do during such periods of water shortage, the sheep camp provides a mechanism for increasing distance between quarreling members. Usually at least one family remains at the homestead to watch the property. With two such bases of operation, individual members can move back and forth to avoid conflict within the group.

My own observations and conversations with informants lead me to believe that the pattern of penning during the day is, and always has been, the preferred method of keeping sheep, but that in former times before the drilling of wells and creation of catchment dams, it was more often necessary to keep the herd out all day on the trip to water. Today, in times of drought when the windmill wells go dry and the dam water is exhausted, the long drive must be undertaken. In the winter when the days are shorter and the temperature is low, the herds are frequently kept out all day.

Today, under extreme drought conditions, the use of trucks to haul water makes it possible for at least some homesteads to weather the dry period without shifting camp. Informants estimated that a herd of two hundred and fifty sheep require about one thousand gallons of water daily. Their estimate was based on the number of fifty-five-gallon drums they hauled during the most recent dry spell. Under these conditions the entire effort of the homestead is required to graze and water the herd; two men were employed all day in hauling water, and the rest of the family was needed to water the sheep, which were released from the pen ten head at a time. It might be mentioned here that any operation that requires single sheep or small groups of sheep to be separated (for counting, drinking, vaccination, and so on) is extremely difficult. Such an operation calls for as many hands as can be mustered, so strong is the predilection of one sheep to follow another.

In the deep winter when the snow covers the grass, it is necessary for the entire homestead to devote its energy to uncovering feed for the herd. This means that all adults and older children spend the whole day with the herd and stamp the snow away from the grass.

This grazing and penning pattern quickly exhausts the range in two areas, the one immediately around the homestead where the herd grazes upon entering and leaving the living area and the one around water sources, dams, springs, or wells. Each of these areas is picked barren, with the greatest damage being done, of course, in the vicinity of water, for while the homestead can be and often is shifted, the water source cannot. However, some homesteads may not move because of the construction of permanent water facilities, or a desire to be near certain neighbors or the trading post. Around such homesteads the land is stripped bare, and even the sagebrush is reduced to stumps. In other areas of the reservation where the summer temperatures are higher and water scarcer, it is still common to move the herd into summer ranges and for at least part of the homestead group to live at a temporary sheep camp. In the Nez Ch'ii area few people are forced to do this because of relatively low temperatures, a fairly constant supply of grass, and a number of alternative water sources. However, a few families move into the peripheries of the Nez Ch'ii region from less-favored areas. Among the permanent residents there is a friendly contempt for these "sheep camps" but apparently no open hostility. To the east, around Nazlini Wash, almost the entire population vacates the area in the summer to move into sheep camps in the Lukachukai Mountains.

BREEDING   Generally speaking, sheep will breed at any time of the year. In practice, however, sheepherders attempt to prevent breeding before mid-October to insure the birth of lambs in the late spring. This gives the young the advantage of maturing during favorable weather. Early-born lambs are subject to the bad weather that may occur in early spring, and lambs born too late in the spring are not mature enough to survive the winter. The practice of keeping rams away from ewes until October is relatively new among the Navajo and is still not universally practiced. To separate the rams requires two herding and penning operations or the permanent penning of the males with the requirement that food must be purchased or collected to maintain them. One alternative method is to install an apron around the loins of rams that does not hinder elimination but covers the genitals of the ewe should she be mounted. In this way the rams can be herded with the rest of the herd, although, as with most methods of contraception, failures are frequent. Another alternative is for Navajo herders to use the rams supplied by the tribe from its experimental Ban N ranch and brought into the area at the proper time for breeding.

Government extension agents have advocated the late breeding of sheep to avoid the bad weather of early spring since they contend that lambs dropped later have a better chance for survival. Generally speaking, this is supported by the experience of sheepherders throughout the United States. However, the Navajo practice of early breeding and lambing may in fact not be as detrimental as the experts suggest. The structure of the Navajo extended family makes it possible for a great many man-hours to be devoted to caring for lambs. A regular night watch is maintained by each outfit; keeping a fire burning, members of the watch stay up all night in order to prevent the lambs from freezing and to care for any lambs dropped in the night. During the day, lambs are kept in the sheep pen and protected from the weather. If the weather turns bad, lambs are placed in small dugouts roofed over with branches and earth. Lambs that do poorly are fed with milk, either canned or surplus powdered milk. Canned milk of the Carnation or Pet brands is much preferred, the Navajo claiming that lambs do not like other canned brands or powdered milk. Although this kind of care requires a high investment of human effort under far from pleasant conditions, it results in a surprisingly high ratio of surviving lambs. Moreover, early lambing permits nursing ewes to take full advantage of the early spring grasses and the plentiful water supply of the season, and lambs beginning to graze enjoy the advantage of a large quantity of good spring grass. One of the major livestock problems on the reservation is the failure of many lambs to reach marketable weight (thirty-five to forty-five pounds minimum) in time for fall marketing. The tribe regularly purchases these unmarketable "peewee" lambs and later sells them at a loss in an emergency buying program. However, in the Nez Ch'ii area, where early lambing is still common, very few lambs fail to reach marketable weight, and the emergency purchases are limited to mature goats and barren ewes. This suggests that the traditional methods based on the structure of the Navajo family are better suited to the reservation environment than the "modern" methods advocated by the government.

The stock-reduction and the stock-improvement program have resulted in a general improvement of Navajo sheep, which were in the recent past notably unimproved and considerably less than efficient in meat and wool production. Indications of this unimproved blood are still to be seen in Navajo herds, particularly in remote areas. Most noticeable are the multiple-horned rams, having three, four, and occasionally five horns sprouting from their foreheads. Another sign of scrub blood is mixed-color wool. Many Navajo sheep are to be seen bearing wool of every shade from white to black, with many shades of grey, brown, and red. Such wool requires considerably more work to separate and is therefore less valuable in the market. Nevertheless, when hand-carded and spun, this wool is useful in the production of natural-colored Navajo rugs, which are sometimes made entirely without dye.

MARKETING   Spring, in addition to being the season for lambing, is also the time for sheepshearing and the sale of wool. Every effort is made to be on hand to assist during lambing at this time of year, and shearing requires the efforts of all members of the homestead group, except of course the children who are away at school or those members who must be absent in the course of work. At this time the wool is marketed, most of it going directly to the Indian trader for cash or credit.

The late spring and summer is a period during which the sheep herd is counted, dipped, and vaccinated, and, as the summer progresses, any animals to be marketed are selected. There is no clear-cut market period. Late in the summer the trader announces he is purchasing sheep and cattle, and the animals are brought in individually or in small bunches by their owners. Several such sales may be made during the fall by a single owner as he needs money. When the trader has collected a number of sheep, a commission agent hauls the animals away to feed lots to be fattened prior to marketing. However, the trader will usually purchase sheep at any time during the year, although his prices may be so low as to discourage very many offerings. In addition, the trader maintains on feed perhaps a dozen head of sheep (often old and barren ewes, sold because they are not productive), and from time to time he slaughters one of these animals for sale at his own butcher counter.

Navajo father sharpening his shears before beginning to shear a sheep in the early spring.

GOATS

Goats are in most respects the social and cultural equivalent of sheep. They are herded with the sheep, dipped, vaccinated, and sheared at the same time and, except at counting times, considered simply as part of the sheep herd. However, there are notable and important differences between goats and sheep. Despite the similarity of the animals, the goat is far more independent of man and, as has often been proved, quite able to survive without man's protection. The goat is curious, active, and far more adventurous than the sheep. Goats are usually satisfied with rougher food and are able to subsist on all sorts of brush that sheep prefer not to eat except when driven by hunger. The goats in a sheep herd, and there are always a few, act as both the sentinels and leaders of the herd, and the sudden dashes from food source to food source that often mark the progress of the herd are invariably led by goats. Goats add to the burden of pen building because they are more determined in their efforts to escape and because they climb and jump with amazing agility. Some pens are constructed with a stile that permits the goats to leave and enter at will but keeps the sheep contained. This device in a way symbolizes a vaguely expressed difference in attitude toward the two species on the part of the Navajo. The herd, for instance, is always spoken of as the "sheep herd," or "the sheep," although in fact most of the animals may be goats. This attitude is difficult to describe exactly—the Navajo simply appear to be less interested in goats. It may stem from the fact that sheep are viewed as the food animal par excellence, and mutton is surrounded with all the connotations of home, comfort, and good living. Mutton hunger is a recognized condition of Navajo who must live away from the family herds. "I want some fresh mutton," means that the speaker in fact does want some mutton to eat, but it also carries the connotation of homesickness and, I suspect, an allusion to young, unsophisticated back-country girls. Goats are eaten, but much less often than sheep. At Squaw-Dance feasts the ratio of goats to sheep is perhaps one to four. Goats are occasionally milked, and possibly in the past cheese was made, but I found no evidence of cheese making at the time of my visit. Until perhaps three decades ago most goats were of nondescript milking breeds, and goat milk was an important part of the Navajo diet. The shift to angora goats in an attempt, not particularly successful, to raise cash income has adversely affected nutrition, especially that of children.

Goats supply mohair and are most often of the angora or long-haired type in colors ranging from white through pale tans and browns to mixed colors and pure black. Mohair is currently selling for a higher price than wool. However, most Navajo do not seem inclined to increase the number of goats in their herds at the expense of their sheep holdings. The most common reason is that the long goat hair makes it extremely hard for the animals to winter in the snow-bound uplands. The tightly curled greasy wool of sheep tends to insulate them from the cold, but goat hair gathers mud and snow in frozen balls, threatening the animals with immobilization and freezing. (It might be pointed out that the cropping of sheep's tails is done to prevent the balling of mud and snow, which will literally anchor an undocked sheep in bad weather.) The final special problem in goat husbandry, although minor, is extremely annoying to the owner. The brush and leafy tree-limb roofing of the summer shade under which a great part of the life of the Navajo is carried out is unfailingly attractive to goats, which strip the shade and the shade roof if not watched. The sight of a goat peacefully browsing on the roof while his owners try to dislodge him with thrown sticks and stones is a common summer scene.

CATTLE

Cattle are the only other animals kept for economic or marketing purposes. Without exception, the animals are beef cattle, and with only a few exceptions they are the common "whiteface" of the Western cattle industry. A "whiteface" is in fact a grade animal descended from the introduction of Hereford and shorthorn blood into the herds of Texas or Mexican cattle common in the West until the 1880s and 1890s. There have been infusions of most other beef brands into this range pool, but the Hereford characteristics of red body contrasted with white belly and face mark the majority of Western range cattle, including those of the Nez Ch'ii area.

It is a rule of thumb that it requires a breeding herd of 150 cows to maintain an adequate income in the United States. In 1957, there were 665 mature cattle grazing in the Nez Ch'ii area. Of these, "over a hundred" were reportedly owned by a single owner near Hard Rocks and "almost a hundred" by another wealthy man (by Navajo standards) who lives near the trading post. Other herds are appreciably smaller, with twenty to thirty head being considered a "lot of cattles" by the Navajo of the area. Many cattle owners boast only one, two, or three head. Most of these animals are breeding stock, that is, cows that produce calves for market and / or female calves to be kept to enlarge the breeding herds. As mentioned earlier, if an owner possesses more than a single cow, his livestock operation takes on another dimension in addition to the horse and sheep complex described above. Cattle are often obtained as weaned calves, perhaps six or eight months old. Not infrequently, such animals are what is colloquially called "dougy" (dogy) calves, that is, they do not have mothers, or the mother cannot feed them. Such animals may simply be turned out with the sheep herd of a small owner and become quickly conditioned to the environment; they seldom wander far from the sheep and goats and become part of the herd for all practical purposes. However, if the number of cattle increases beyond one or at the most two, the picture changes, and the two or three head form a cattle herd inasmuch as they require special allocation of time and effort on the part of the herdsman.

GRAZING PATTERN   It is part of the folklore of the West that·cattle and sheep will not occupy the same range or use the same waterholes and that the entry of sheep into a cattle range drives the cattle off. This generalization, of course, is untrue as an unqualified statement, but there are differences in the range utilization by the two species. In part because cattle are kept under less restraint and in part because they require four times the range per head, they range far more widely than do sheep and goats, although not so far as horses. Sheep can and do graze ground-cover much more closely than do cattle and are able to consume many plants not normally considered palatable for cattle. This means that a sheep herd can remain for a longer period on the same ground and still benefit. Cattle, having grazed an area as closely as they can, move on, so even if sheep and cattle were herded together, they would gradually separate as the cattle ranged farther and farther afield while the sheep remained on the original ground. Observations made of a single herd suggest that five miles from the homestead is generally the normal limit of cattle wandering. The wandering of cattle, like that of horses, is not random but tends to extend itself in specific directions according to the distribution of food plants and the availability of water. Only the herd conditioning of a single calf raised with sheep would keep it relatively close to the sheep herd. If the calf had the company of another of its kind, the cattle would soon separate from the sheep and drift off on their own. To prevent this would require that the sheep herd constantly move or that the herder continually drive the cattle back to the sheep herd. What happens in fact is that cattle are treated differently and considered apart from sheep. Although two or three cows or calves may be penned at night with the sheep and moved away from the homestead at the same time and in the same direction as the sheep, the herder does not keep as close a watch on them; he seldom expects them to come back to the pen at midday and in fact is not too concerned should they fail to return for a day or two. A constantly operating livestock-locating network is likely to keep him informed of the whereabouts of both his cattle and horses for many days without his actually seeing them. For example, a rider passing through the homestead or a friend met at the trader's mentions that he saw the owner's stock at a certain place as he was traveling. If the reports suggest that the animals are straying too far, or if no reports come in for several days, the owner or a relative may conduct a desultory search, usually on horseback.

If such a preliminary search does not discover the cattle somewhere on or near the owner's grazing land, he expresses real concern and sets out to search in earnest. A larger herd will probably receive more constant surveillance but generally will be expected to find water for itself, except during periods of drought when the animals must be driven to different watering places.

BULLS   The few bulls owned in the Nez Ch'ii area constitute a special problem because they are viewed as particularly dangerous (a contention not without foundation but greatly exaggerated by the Navajo), and a wandering bull is apt to create serious friction between outfits. The appearance of a bull, threatening or not, disrupts the life of an outfit, as invariably the women and children retreat to the shelter of a hogan while some of the braver men attempt to drive the animal away. In the summer of 1961 a bull belonging to a tribal policeman became a local cause celebre, as the animal became a focus for resentment toward its owner. The

The owner, in light shirt and hat, standing, supervises the branding of one of his calves at the community branding.

animals depredations were daily reported to the policeman or his family, together with threats to kill the bull. More often than not, the bull was reported in several places at one time. It was considered an excellent joke to suggest that this bull be offered to a man who was being asked to become host of a Squaw Dance, as it was rumored he did not want to accept the "honor" in return for the traditional present of four sheep, but preferred a cow instead. Finally, the policeman in desperation kept the bull in a pen and fed him hay. The situation was all the more ludicrous when one observed the children of the policeman's family playing with the bull, which had become little more than a pet and which "raided" the neighbors only out of a desire for human company.

THE ROUNDUP   The most important time in the cattle owner's year is in late summer, after the community sheep dipping, when a series of community roundups are staged. The tribe supplies no working crew for the roundup, and the work is carried out by owners, members of the grazing committee, and men who are interested in cattle or, more properly, in being cowboys. It is notable that the festive air of a sheep dip is completely absent at a cattle roundup, and, in contrast to the former occasion, there are almost no women present.

At the roundup, bull calves and colts are castrated by a man who travels with the grazing committee chairman, who supervises the roundup. The most important job is that of branding the unbranded stock. Each owner has a registered brand consisting of a number indicating the grazing district and a number indicating his own herd. In addition, a Bar N is branded on the shoulder of all Navajo cattle and horses.

The roundup takes place during or shortly before the livestock-buying period at the trader's. Because most herds are extremely small and many owners

An elder looks on while younger men castrate a horse.

keep cattle only to increase their holdings, animals are usually bought one at a time; barren cows, bull calves, and steers make up the bulk of the salable animals, as they do anywhere. One or two large owners sell a number of cattle directly to commission agents. The purchased animals are held in the trader's corrals until a sufficient number have been gathered for shipping.

Occasionally, in response to the urging of his White clerks and the rest of the beef-hungry non-Indian population, the trader will butcher a beef for sale, but most of the animals are shipped out to feeders. Once branded, counted, and registered by the tribal brand inspector, the cattle are driven back to their home range. Any sale, either between Indians or off the reservation, must be registered by the brand inspector of the tribe.

SPECIAL PROBLEMS   As stated before, most herds are small and not considered as income property at present but are being kept to breed and increase by hopeful owners. To increase the size of a herd is very difficult because of grazing restrictions. Even the purchase of an animal from outside the district, although within the reservation, creates a good deal of friction and resentment. Thus, an owner builds his herd as someone else reduces his, and the overall number of animals in the district increases slowly.

Although cattle, unlike sheep, do not require the day-to-day care that is more and more resented by younger men, they present some special problems. During the winter, cattle are less able to subsist on the surviving forage than are sheep and goats, and cattle owners must often find means of obtaining some additional winter feed. One of the more common sources, if funds are available, is hay from other Navajo who live in areas where field agriculture is practiced, particularly where irrigation projects have made alfalfa production possible. In the past, during periods of heavy snow the tops of trees were cut to supply browse for both sheep and cattle, and, at least sometimes, cattle were driven into lower areas where snow was less of a problem.

There would appear to be more resentment of a large cattle herd than of a large sheep herd, perhaps because cattle are almost never slaughtered for food and thus represent a "rich man's" economic activity. It is whispered that the area's single rich man, who owns a large number of cattle, is able to maintain his large herd by "stealing" water from other people, that is, by driving his stock to springs, dams, and wells that are traditionally used and maintained by others. He is said to do this at night when other people aren't about. It is interesting, however, to compare the resentment directed toward this man, who is noted for his miserliness and who has only one child, with the attitude toward a man at Hard Rocks who is said to have even more cattle. The latter owner seems to be the target of no resentment, at least among his more distant neighbors, because "he has lots of kids."

STEALING   One other aspect of the cattle complex should be mentioned—cattle stealing. There appears to be relatively little stealing of animals by members of the district from other members of the district; the discovery of such larceny would be almost inevitable. However, there are some families living along the boundary between Navajo and the Hopi reservation who are said to make their living by stealing Hopi cattle. The informant offered this intelligence tentatively and carefully waited to judge my reaction before elaborating. Further questioning made it clear that neither he nor his neighbors felt such activities were particularly reprehensible as long as they were carried out by Navajo against Hopis, which reflects the long history of Navajo raiding against the mesa-top villagers.

The single case of cattle stealing that I was able to establish occurred in the summer of 1961 when the adopted son of the local rich man, with the help of two friends, butchered one of his father's cattle. This was considered an out-and-out theft by the Navajo, who excused it to a degree because the thieves were drunk. It was also considered excusable because the victim was rich. The thieves were three well-known ne'er-do-wells of the area, whose only occupation in the summer was to move from one Squaw Dance to another, taking advantage of the plentiful food supply at such affairs and contributing little besides their presence and singing ability. The local Navajo and the police looked briefly for the culprits but soon gave up the search. About three weeks after the incident all three men were once again seen in the area. It is possible that they had agreed to recompense the owner for his loss, an act that in the Navajo view would have closed the case. On another occasion, a woman demanded and received ten sheep from a young man who, while drunk, had stolen a blanket and some jewelry in order to buy liquor. In addition, my informants reported that because of the drought many people were suffering hardship and occasionally killed a cow from the rich man's herd. This was considered as theft but not a serious crime because the animal was killed for food and the victim was rich.

Thus we see in the livestock complex of the Nez Ch'ii region three distinct subcomplexes of land use, each requiring different techniques and bringing into play different sets of human relationships.

The Tools and Techniques of Livestock Operations

Domestication involves much more than the presence of an animal under the control of human beings. A domesticating society must have at its disposal a complex of tools, techniques, attitudes, and knowledge. Each species of animal brought under control increases the number of tools and techniques needed and expands the knowledge required. A good shepherd is not necessarily a good cowboy. Neither the shepherd nor the cowboy, by virtue of his competence in these fields, is automatically a good horse wrangler. Among the Navajo, who have adopted all three of these grazing animals into a single socioeconomic and cultural complex, it has been necessary to develop or borrow techniques to carry out the livestock operation. It might be pointed out here that in the European tradition there is at least a strong tendency for specialization in livestock operations. Although it is common for a single economic unit, such as a large ranch, to have sheep-, cattle-, and horse-raising operations contributing to its income, they tend to be definitely separated. Different sets of specialists work with different animals, and different parts of the range are used for each operation.

The Navajo have combined these three complexes rather closely. This combination is due in part to the generally small units of livestock held by an individual (herds of even a thousand or two thousand sheep are not considered very large in the American sheep-raising industry). Therefore it has been necessary for the Navajo to develop a generalized skill as herder, shepherd, cowboy, and horse wrangler in one. Being a jack-of-all-husbandry-trades has served the Navajo well, but he is often considered less than excellent when he is employed in the far more specialized husbandry of White men.

What has happened in the two hundred to two hundred and fifty years of the Navajo livestock industry is that White techniques have been borrowed and adapted to fit the Navajo situation. The basic techniques of Navajo husbandry are Spanish colonial, not Anglo–American. They were borrowed and adapted some hundred or hundred and fifty years before the Anglo–Americans in Texas began to learn the Mexican techniques of cattle- and sheep-raising, which were more useful in the West than were the techniques of the eastern United States. Thus, Navajo husbandry represents an independent development from basic Iberian techniques separate from and somewhat earlier than the Anglo–American development. In the last few decades the Navajo and Anglo–American traditions have become more closely associated, and the former is beginning to take on some of the specific techniques and much of the coloring of the latter.

SHEEP AND GOAT TECHNIQUES

Sheep and goats in the herd situation are generally easy to handle as long as the herder remains alert and plans what he intends to do with the herd before the leaders are committed to another action. The direction of a herd requires only that the leaders be turned, and the rest of the herd will follow. On the other hand, if a single leader gets past the turning point, the rest of the herd follows with a determination that can be thwarted only by physical restraint of the individual animals or by a fence. Thus, in the normal course of events a single herder, often a child, can watch and direct the herd grazing quite competently. But on occasions when the herd must be broken down into individuals for counting, marking, vaccinating, or shearing, the participation of every available hand is required. In such situations where the herd becomes individualized and the animals separated from each other, sheep in particular become totally confused, frightened, and unmanageable except by manhandling. The confusion grows worse as various animals are separated from the group in the course of counting, and one feels as if he is somehow involved in keeping apart two opposite magnetic fields determined to reunite.

HERDING   The primary technique for sheep herding, then, is a knowledge of herd behavior and an alertness to the movements of the leaders. The single herdsman may find himself in difficulty if his attention wanders too far from the herd because he may not be aware of some movement of the leaders until they are committed to a course past the possibility of being diverted. When the "sheeps get away" from the herder in this way, he can only wait until they have made their movement and then set out to extricate them from the bottom of a dead-end ravine or some such impossible place. The most common mischances on the range are when the herd moves into a space from which the leaders cannot escape without going back through the herd or when two herds drift together while grazing. The danger in the first case is that the animals cannot be induced to move before the sun is high, when they simply refuse to move and the herder must remain with them until the cooler part of the day. (This is a common occurrence when youngsters are herding sheep.) In the latter case, the two herds mingle and, in what seems almost a chemical reaction, catalyze into a single large herd. The owners must devote the rest of the day, and sometimes longer, to separating the two herds. The difficulty of this job without the aid of corrals, chutes, or pens, and with perhaps only two herders working is almost impossible to describe. It is considered one of the major and most serious inconveniences of the range. A few Navajo dogs have developed the ability to prevent such accidents by attacking the strange herd.

Sheep are timid animals, and the herder's methods are molded to fit this. Generally a herder directs the herd by simply standing up suddenly and moving in the desired direction. This usually sets the leaders off and the herd moves. Directions may be augmented with gentle sounds such as the breath expelled between the lips, low whistles, and so on. Although most families have abandoned ritual methods in sheep handling, such as the singing of a particular sheep-protecting song timed to begin with the first sheep out of the pen and to end with the last, snatches of song are often sung at this time, and one suspects that the ritual played an important role in moving sheep in the past. The song, sung regularly each morning, probably served as a signal for the easily conditioned animals to get to their feet and keep moving through the gate.

Although sheep herding seems a relatively simple task, a novice soon learns that the degree of alertness that has to be exercised is great, although the observed behavior of a Navajo herder might belie this. Despite frequent stops to watch passing hawks or eagles, a readiness to shoot a startled rabbit, or a willingness to chat with a companion, a herder is constantly watching his animals and is aware of any movements of the leaders that might commit the herd to an undesired course.

SHEEP DIPPING   On occasions when the animals must be actually controlled rather than directed, the gentle herding techniques of the range are replaced by sharply contrasting methods. Sheep dipping, which is carried out in midsummer in order to rid the sheep of ticks and other pests and partially wash excess dirt out of the wool, is a scene of frenzied activity and noise. The sheep are held in separate herds outside the pens, then moved into a holding pen where they can be examined and vaccinated. From there they are driven into chutes that terminate at the dipping vat. From the vat the animals are pushed into dripping pens, where most of the water drains onto the ground and eventually back into the vat. The greatest danger is that herds being held before or after dipping may become mixed, and, to prevent this, as many people as possible are called in to help with the herd. Standing a few feet apart, they keep the animals bunched by making a continual noise with their lips, a number of tin-can lids on a wire loop, or by beating a can or flapping a paper box. In addition, switches of brush or lariats are constantly swung toward the animals. The most difficult part of the process is moving the animals, by now terrified and confused, through the chutes and into the vats. At this point noise reaches a crescendo—tin-can rattles are shaken furiously, boxes are beaten to pieces, ropes are banged against the wood or wire fencing, animals are hit, and finally, in the last few feet, one or two people must stand in the chute literally wrestling the woolly current in the right direction as the animals panic and try to retreat down the chute in the face of their oncoming fellows. Often this leads to "plugs" of animals absolutely unable to move and requires the animal-by-animal search for the "keystone" so that the dam can be broken, the animals straightened out, and the dipping continued. Once in the pen at the mouth of the chute, the sheep are picked up and thrown into the vat, a back-breaking, finger-tearing job that requires the strongest men in the group.

Once in the vat, the sheep swim its length with the aid of women and children and a few men who stand along the sides of the vat with long crooks. In the past these poles were usually forked sticks, but in recent years these sticks have been replaced by iron piles with crooks welded on the end. The use of these crooks appears deceptively simple, but in the hands of a novice they are devices that may well drown a sheep or two. They are used properly either to push the animal down for total immersion or to lift it up and help it along the vat.

Before the dipping, the animals must be branded to identify them for the count and to prevent loss of animals in the confusion. Sheep brands are put on with paint. The usual applicator is a wire twisted into the proper shape and wrapped with wool or string to hold the paint. This is dipped into a can of commercial house paint of any color to suit the fancy of the owner, although blue and black are most common, and planted on the rump of the animal. This is a leisurely process carried out when the animals are held in the pen during the midday break. A number of people of the family lend a hand in keeping the animals bunched and in running down the ones that have escaped the brand.

SHEEPSHEARING   In the spring the wool is sheared. Until 1870 the Navajo sheared with knives, pieces of glass, tin cans, and the like. But in that year, at the suggestion of the agent, a shipment of commercial sheep shears was supplied, and these tools have entirely superseded the more primitive makeshifts. Shearing is an art understood by nearly all adults.

Sheep are usually sheared by the individual owners or, if the owners are children, by their parents, and shearing constitutes one of the few sheep operations carried out by the nuclear rather than the extended family. Goats are usually sheared first because the early prices for mohair are high. The need for cash generally forces the owner to shear at least some animals before the rest. However, there is a tendency for the family to cooperate to some degree when the major part of the herd is sheared.

In the process of shearing, the animals are thrown, tied by their ankles, and sheared, with the shearer either squatting beside the animals or standing up and bending over. The ground on which the shearing takes place is swept with a broom or some branches and a piece of canvas, if available, is spread on the ground. Hand shearing is a slow process, taking as much as an hour for a single animal, and even the most expert shearer clips the wool or hair at different lengths, thus lowering the grade of wool or mohair. Because of the danger of cutting the animal, a shearer using sheep shears usually does not cut as short as one using machine clippers, so much wool is wasted. The tribe and government have encouraged the use of machine clippers, but even the simplest of these devices is too expensive for the average Navajo.

SLAUGHTER   The slaughter of sheep is most frequently the job of women, except at a Squaw Dance when the number of animals and the demands of the cooks for mutton may force an old man to lend a hand. In slaughtering, the sheep is bound by its ankles and thrown on its side, its neck over a bucket, frying pan, or other vessel. The neck is then cut to the back bone with a short knife that would be referred to as a paring knife in a modern kitchen. The blood is drained into the vessel for use in sausage or blood pudding (the process seems always to be attended by a ring of wide-eyed little girls), and the animal is skinned and butchered. This can be done on the ground, or the animal may be hoisted by its hind legs to a limb or post. The skin is then pegged down, scraped slightly, and covered with dirt to absorb the blood and fat.

HERDING CATTLE AND HORSES

THE ROPE   The most important tool in handling either cattle or horses in the West is, of course, the lasso or, as it is referred to in the Southwest, the lariat or simply "rope." But there are several differences in the way it is used by the Navajo in contrast to White herdsmen. Although a few older men still make and use rawhide lariats, the most common types found today are of commercial rope of hemp or nylon. These cost from ten dollars to fifteen dollars, and often men who cannot afford these prices use makeshifts of cotton rope or other material. Navajo ropes are usually shorter than one finds in Mexico or in the West generally, in part because animals are seldom roped on the run on the open range and are therefore never more than a few feet away from the man who is trying to catch them. Cattle are seldom roped except at branding time or in order to drag a single animal into the back of a truck for transport to market. In either case, the roping is done in a corral. When it is necessary to catch grazing horses, they are most likely to be driven to nearby corrals or empty sheep pens or perhaps into a box canyon, or if several people are present, they may be simply surrounded and held. It is notable that these corrals lack a snubbing post, a post three or four feet high set in the ground in the center of the corral. These are common if not universal in corrals, particularly those used for horses, throughout the West. They allow the cowboy to rope his mount from the ground and snub his rope around the post to keep the animal from dragging him off his feet. The Navajo, as noted early in this century by the Franciscan fathers, simply allow the animal to drag them. In addition, I seldom saw a single rope being used on unbroken horses or cattle; while one member of the roping team was being dragged, others were closing in to add their ropes to the animal's neck or legs. Horses that are accustomed to being roped and ridden generally attempt to avoid the rope in the corral by milling and circling but are conditioned to stop the instant they feel a rope, whether or not it has actually encircled their neck.

Cattle are handled in much the same manner as horses. At branding time a herd is held in a pen and several Navajo cowboys on foot cut out a single animal, rope it by the neck and legs, and throw it to the ground. Once the animal is down, another man brings the branding irons from a fire outside the pen and brands the animal while the ropers hold it by leaning on the ropes.

The few occasions on which I have seen animals roped on the open range have been, to say the least, less than expert performances. On one occasion a young man, formerly a champion rodeo cowboy, roped a cow and was nearly thrown because his saddle was not cinched tight enough for roping. On yet another occasion when three Navajo and I attempted to catch and transport a range cow, the two mounted ropers lost their ropes, and the operation degenerated into a hurly-burly scramble on foot until the cow, exhausted and panic stricken (but nonetheless able to wound two of her tormentors and very nearly terminate my field investigation) was simply manhandled into a truck. Most roping is limited to rodeo performances, and the proficiency of Navajo ropers in rodeo events is not particularly great. Roping from the saddle is clearly an innovation in Navajo herding. The old-style handmade saddles that I have seen do not have a horn, which is essential for roping from the saddle. Occasionally a Navajo will rope a sheep from horseback or, in a spirit of bravado, try to rope a stray dog. Their lack of accuracy from horseback contrasts sharply with their uncanny ability on foot.

The term *cowboy* is used among the Navajo to refer, not to men who work with cattle, but to men who perform in rodeos. Methods of roping from the ground are not the same as those employed by Anglo–American or Mexican cowboys. In either of these latter traditions a man makes a loop and allows it to spread, while dragging it along the ground as he locates his target, and then launches the loop with a single overhand or side-arm motion. The Navajo, on the other hand, opens his loop and, making a few running steps, whirls the loop around his head; he depends on centrifugal force and the twisting action of the wrist to keep the loop open until he launches it with a short chopping motion of his already extended arm. Whirling a loop, of course, is characteristic of the Mexican or Anglo–American roping technique when the roper is mounted.

Cattle or horses are not generally herded on foot in the United States or Northern Mexico; they form a less compact group when moving than do sheep and move much faster, and individuals in a herd are not so loath as are sheep to quit the group and strike out on their own. Thus, although Navajo *may* herd sheep on horseback, particularly if the trip to water is a long one, they *must* herd horses and cattle while mounted. Such herding is usually done only when it is necessary to move the herd to water or from one pasture to another, and, once the trip is made, the control is removed and the animals are simply kept under periodic surveillance. The driving of cattle or horses appears to be far more relaxed among Navajo than among White cattlemen. The pace is slower, the latitude permitted individual cattle greater, and all in all the process is much more like driving a herd of sheep. Cattle are seldom, if ever, handled on the range, and if it is necessary to hold the herd while working it, the animals are run into a corral or pen. This contrasts with the Mexican and American practice of holding the herd on the open range, where mounted men continually circle, keeping the animals together while other riders cut the desired animal from the herd and drive it near the branding fire where it is roped, tied, and branded.

It should be noted that the handling of cattle by the Navajo appears in many ways to be an extension of techniques originally learned in sheep husbandry.

At the same time, younger men do not hesitate to rope a sheep or goat, an unthinkable practice by White standards.

THE BRANDING IRON   The other principal tool of the cattle herder is the branding iron, which is usually owned by the tribe. Each iron represents a letter or a number that can be applied in combination with other irons to make the individual brand. Occasionally an owner will have his own iron and will bring it to the community branding.

Since both bull calves and colts are castrated, the knowledge of the operation is essential to the keeping of livestock in this area. The technique used requires the opening of the scrotum and removal of the testes entire rather than crushing or tying the organs. The operation is performed by a specialist. One such man, an elderly gentleman who is the father of the tribal resource development chairman, is hired to work at the community brandings. In other instances, an older member of an outfit will do the castrating for all his relatives. The castrator's instruments consist of a well-sharpened penknife and a can of patent astringent powder. The fact that older, traditional males seem to have a monopoly on the operation suggests that they are perhaps considered to have horse medicine or curing power, but I observed no ritual in connection with the operation. Sheep tails are docked by applying an elastic band that allows the tail to atrophy and drop off. This practice, now nearly universal, was introduced during World War II.

RIDING AND DRIVING HORSES

THE SADDLE   Although Navajo riding increasingly tends to follow patterns found among Whites and Mexicans in the West, there are still distinctive patterns to be observed. The saddle is always the so-called Western saddle, itself a modification of Mexican stock saddles that in turn have developed from the war saddle and stock saddle brought from Spain. In the recent past the Navajo manufactured their own saddles, but this practice has been nearly abandoned. There are a few old men who still know the craft, and occasionally a homemade saddle is seen in use. The process is hedged with a number of restrictions and taboos discouraging younger men from learning the craft. Today, saddles and bridles are purchased at the trader's or from stores in Gallup, Holbrook, or Flagstaff. Saddles are usually made in the medium-low-cantled "association" style, well decorated with leather engraving and perhaps having a foam rubber seat. Old men still ride the more conservative, high-cantled, narrow-pommeled models, and almost any homestead has one or more of these models—broken and patched, with stirrups held on by rope or rawhide—which are used by women and children.

The most distinctive Navajo riding trait is one that has been noted by travelers, explorers, anthropologists, and horsemen as characteristic of most Indians of the Plains, Southwest, and Plateau-Basin areas. Compared to the American, the Navajo rides with an extremely short stirrup. In the vernacular of the West, "Indians ride like Chinamen," and in fact they do. It is far more significant perhaps that an Indian rides essentially like a Spanish soldier of the sixteenth century trained to ride *a la jineta*, the short stirrup style brought to Europe by the Moors. The difference is less marked today because younger Indians interested in rodeo events tend to lengthen their stirrups somewhat. At the same time, Western riding habits are being influenced by the "scientific" schools of European and Eastern American riding, and cowboys and rodeo performers have begun to make their own stirrups shorter than they were, let us say, half a century ago.

THE QUIRT   The Navajo, like the Plains Indian but unlike the Papago and Pima, does not wear spurs. Instead he uses a quirt, and few Navajo ride far without one or without some substitute for one. This habit has given rise to statements that Indians are horse-beaters. As a matter of fact, it appears that the Navajo, at least, are seldom horse-beaters. They do keep their quirts in almost constant motion as they ride, but most of the blows fail to land, and those that do are gentle indeed. The quirt constantly urges the horse forward, substituting for the signals given with the legs or heels by White riders. In fact, many Navajo horses do not seem to respond to any leg signal save for a vigorous kick in the ribs, but work perfectly if leg signals are abandoned and a continual rain of light taps with a quirt are used. Quirts can be purchased at the trader's, and one does see them being used. However, plaited rawhide is still common, and many makeshifts such as stripped branches, sticks, rope, or strips cut from worn-out auto tires are used.

THE HOBBLE   Hobbles, used to contain horses within a limited area, can also be purchased at the trader's. Homemade rawhide hobbles appear to be most common, although makeshifts of soft cotton rope are not unusual. Many Navajo do not hobble their horses but prefer to keep a horse picketed if it is necessary to keep one on hand. It is usually picketed with a short rope that prevents its grazing, and if the animal is picketed for a long time, it must be fed hay or grain or allowed to graze periodically and must be taken to water from time to time. A hobbled animal, on the other hand, can forage for itself, and the tendency is to let horses graze with hobbles at functions such as sheep dippings or dances.

MAKESHIFT EQUIPMENT   Although certain items of equestrian equipment are considered necessities, the Navajo display a great willingness to use any makeshift if the choice is between riding or not. Riders using saddle blankets belted on with a surcingle,* or the surcingle alone for something to grasp in emergencies, are common sights. Almost any Navajo man will leap on a bareback horse in a situation calling for quick action, and he will ride with considerable skill. Similarly, bridles are used and considered essential, but if one is not available, it will be contrived by looping a rope over the animal's nose or through its mouth.

CARE   Contrary to many popular statements about Indian cruelty or lack of concern with animal welfare, the Navajo appear to be very considerate of their horses. It must be kept in mind, however, that no amount of social symbolism alters the fact that horses in Nez Ch'ii are working livestock, maintained because they are needed from the day-to-day exigencies of existence in this isolated and virtually road-less area. Considerations for the comfort of a horse, therefore, must come after considerations of the job the animal is required to do. Horses are prized and rated according to their ability to work but certainly are never pampered with stalls,

---

* A strap that is passed around a horse to hold the saddle or saddle-pad on the animal's back.

blankets, and the other paraphernalia that are thought so essential by White pleasure-riders. Old horses are never expected to undertake a job they cannot do, but this is less from any principle of kindness than from a practical view. Pregnant mares are gradually ridden and worked less as parturition draws near. Supplemental feed is supplied to working horses, but animals not being worked must fend for themselves.

Mature animals in good condition are required to work extremely hard on occasion. The process of carrying the "stick" from the ceremonial hogan to the site of the first night of a Squaw Dance is literally a race among the younger and bolder riders, who proceed in as near a straight line as the topography will permit and as fast as possible. Sometimes this trip covers between ten and twenty miles at a lope and gallop with only brief halts to allow the horses to blow. The final morning's dash from the second night's site to the original site, which culminates in the ceremonial circling of the hogan on horseback, is equally a race. The problem of watering the overheated horses does not present itself because the animals are usually simply hobbled and turned out to graze and therefore must make their way to water rather slowly. Horses are seldom "walked cool," but after a long run such as those described above or during a rabbit hunt, the riders will pause for a few moments to chat and dismount while the animals cool off before proceeding to water.

It is common to strip the saddle at this time and bathe the horse whenever the water hole is of sufficient size to permit it. For the rider who still has some way to ride before he can unsaddle, the alternative is to ride his mount up to its belly into a pond or dam.

After a hard run, the horses are turned out to graze and allowed to rest for several days. During this period the animals are stiff and sore and their muscles work unwillingly, and the Navajo usually avoids using the horse at such times unless it is absolutely necessary. Such practices are clearly related to a time when the individual Navajo had many more horses available than he has today, when the periods of rest for a tired horse caused no inconvenience because other animals were available. Today these same patterns are maintained, sometimes with the result that for several days after a Squaw Dance or rabbit hunt a horse owner must walk. It should be noted that the occasions of greatest effort for horses are related to social or religio–social events such as rabbit hunts, Squaw Dances, and rodeos. In actual work on the range, horses are used rather gently. Because cattle are seldom roped on the range, the hard usage often accorded White cow horses is avoided, and the most that is demanded of the Navajo cow pony is only occasional short bursts of speed. Generally, herding methods are so relaxed as compared to White techniques that horses seldom get out of a walk.

The most common gait for Navajo horses is either a rather long swinging walk or lope. This pattern is the same throughout the West and wherever the basic equestrian techniques are Spanish. The trot is a difficult and uncomfortable gait to ride unless the rider posts, and posting, which was in fact developed for riding on roads, has its disadvantages in rough country. The lope, which is no faster but much more comfortable for both horse and rider, is used whenever a Navajo is traveling any distance.

Navajo women ride often and well, although perhaps not as vigorously as the men. The only general concession to sex is that a blanket is often thrown over the saddle when a woman rides. This serves as a decoration but also protects a woman's legs and inner thighs from chafing.

TRAINING   Training of horses is gradual and informal. Colts and fillies run with their dams until weaning. They follow adult horses when they are ridden or driven and become completely accustomed to the presence of human beings. It is common to see colts lying asleep by their dams who are still harnessed to the wagon and waiting to be driven home from a Squaw Dance, while hundreds of people walk, dance, and sing within a few feet of them. As a colt begins to get its growth, the process of breaking is undertaken rather informally by young boys. Already used to humans, the animal generally does not resist when youngsters climb on it and ride for short distances. Such early mounting does not seem to have adverse effects on the development of the back because the riders are light and the periods of mounting short. By the time the horse has reached full growth, it is already "green broken"—that is, used to having riders on its back and not likely to buck vigorously. The horse is taught to accept the process of saddling and bridling and learns to respond to rein signals.

Training beyond the elementary stages is not generally undertaken except by young men interested in competing in rodeos. The two classes of competition requiring a trained horse are roping and bulldogging. Navajo horses do not seem to be particularly well trained as roping horses. The primary requirement in roping is that the horse must remain facing the roped animal and must back away, keeping the rope taut and preventing the calf from regaining its feet while the rider dismounts and ties the calf's feet. Of the several dozen roping horses I saw during my stay, only a few were able to carry out this part of the job with any degree of efficiency. Training for this skill appears to be based first on an observed talent in the horse for such work and then by the rider's roping from the animal in the hope that practice will somehow make it perfect. Bulldogging requires a horse to run straight and very close to the target steer so that the rider can lean forward and grasp the animal's horns before leaving the saddle. It was my impression that the number of animals that jibbed (swerved off course), causing their riders to miss altogether and sprawl face down in the dust, was considerably higher than one sees in White rodeos.

Beyond this, very little specialized training is required of any Navajo horse. Most horses can be driven as well as ridden; however, a particularly good riding horse is usually not driven, and there are always a few horses that drive calmly but react violently when ridden.

The Navajo are particularly fond of horse racing, and a fast horse may be kept largely for that purpose. Most racing is informal, and matches are often made at Squaw Dances. Some rodeos have more formal competitions, usually half-mile dashes. Young light riders mounted bareback or with only a surcingle often serve as jockeys.

Although any horse may be pressed into service on a rabbit hunt, certain animals show a distinct talent for spotting rabbits and following them closely without direction from the rider, much as a good polo pony becomes accustomed to following the ball. Such animals are prized, but no special training methods are used to develop such talent.

ATTITUDE TOWARD FALLING   One significant aspect of Navajo horsemanship is the casualness with which a fall from a horse is accepted. Among White riders a fall is considered a sign of inexpertness, and although it will be laughed off by the one who falls, it is nonetheless not taken lightly. Experienced riders tend to minimize falls with statements like "If you haven't been pitched off a few times, you're not a rider."

The Navajo, on the other hand, do not seem so concerned with a fall as a sign of inexpertness. The willingness to ride whatever horse happens to be available, with or without saddle, and the abandon with which such activities as rabbit hunting and racing are carried out means that falls are to be expected, and they are frequent. On one rabbit hunt, for instance, in which eight adults were riding, there were four falls in the course of an hour—exclusive of the rather spectacular fall I had. All the riders were experienced and skillful and had been riding since childhood. It was clear that no one felt such falls were signs of inexperience but simply part of the expected course of events. It was equally clear, however, that a fall had to be treated lightly by the man who fell. One of the few occasions on which I witnessed a Navajo child being struck was when a twelve-year-old boy refused to get up after he fell from a horse and instead lay on the ground sobbing.

THE TEAM   All Navajo appear to know how to drive a team and hitch it to a wagon. However, such work is usually performed by men if any are present. No particular driving skill is displayed or required today in the Nez Ch'ii area because the hitches are limited to a simple two-horse hitch, and the pace is either a walk or a very slow trot.

Harness is purchased from traders, as are wagons. However, the price of a wagon and harness, presently about five hundred dollars, has led to a high degree of expertness and ingenuity in repairing and maintaining this equipment. Harness is most often repaired with rawhide or, in recent times, with strips cut from old automobile tires and riveted together.

Wagons are repaired with scrap lumber; worn wheels are rounded out with strips of rubber tires and re-tired in iron. Often nothing of the original wagon remains except the metal work, hub, and felloes.* On some part of the reservation many wagons are constructed from an auto or truck chassis, wheels, and tires, but these are uncommon in the Nez Ch'ii area largely because they are too low to negotiate the rough wagon tracks in this region. All wagons can be fitted with bows† and covered to keep off the sun, and they usually are when used to transport people or livestock. The cover is removed for hauling wood, barrels of water, or brush for the roofing and siding of shades.

COMMERCIAL COMPETITION   In the past, saddles and bridles were made of rawhide, and Navajo smiths fabricated bits. However, bit making seems to have disappeared in the face of the competition of manufactured articles. Some Navajo

---

* Shaped wooden rims of the wheels.
† Curved wooden slats used to support a canvas cover on a wagon.

silversmiths still make ornate silver-decorated headstalls for on-reservation sale and for sale to White tourists, but they are expensive and few Navajo can afford them.

Saddle blankets are often old bedding, but many people, particularly on festive occasions, use Navajo saddle blankets. This is the only domestic use of Navajo weaving. A few old men still cherish buffalo-hide saddle blankets, and, for their part, a few young men prize factory-made saddle pads.

VETERINARIAN SKILLS   The most common ills of the horse—those involving strains and bruises of the feet and legs, stone bruises of the frog (the elastic horny pad in the sole of the foot, splints (a bony enlargement on the upper part of the cannon bone), and bowed or strained tendons—are difficult to treat under any circumstances, and among the Navajo they usually appear to be left for time to heal. A horse disabled in this manner is generally turned out to rest and not worked until it improves. However, most Navajo men know a traditional form of treatment for "knocked" shoulder that demands a degree of surgical skill, inasmuch as it requires incisions to drain off surplus fluid that collect between the flesh and the hide. Most Navajo men also claim competence in removing lampers, the horny growths that often develop in the roof of a horse's mouth when the diet contains large amounts of rough or thorny matter. The fact that both these operations are described by the Franciscan Fathers indicates that knowledge of them is not particularly recent. For more severe injuries the Navajo have recourse to the same curing techniques traditionally available to humans—curers with supernaturally sanctioned powers. These men form a loosely organized association of horse doctors sharing esoteric and ritual knowledge concerning the treatment of horses. During my stay in the area, one horse was severely injured in the ceremonies on the third morning of a Squaw Dance. The animal ran into the ceremonial hogan, which had been hurriedly constructed and had a number of snags jutting from it, one of which tore a large wound in the animal's shoulder. The blood was staunched by the application of mud, and then the animal was turned over to several men reported to know how to cure horses.

HUNTING

Hunting is discussed here because it has such a close relationship to livestock husbandry. Hunting is actually only a sport among the people of Nez Ch'ii, although the game taken may constitute a welcome and sometimes essential addition to the diet. However, hunting is justified by them in terms of its relation to agriculture and animal husbandry as well as being simply "fun."

In the past fifty years deer have been hunted in the mesa tops in the northern part of this region, but it has been many years since any have been reported.

Bears are still fairly common in the Lukachukai Mountains, but none have been reported for many years in the Nez Ch'ii area. Thus, the only game in the area is limited to two species of rabbits—cottontail and jackrabbit—prairie dogs, and a number of smaller predators.

Rabbits are taken in mounted hunts by means of sticks hurled at them by the pursuing riders. Such hunts are primarily social in nature, and informants state that since the inception of rodeo contests a few years ago, such hunts have become smaller and are held less often because the daring young riders prefer rodeos to rabbit chasing. The recreational aspect of such a hunt is quite clear in the English sentence, "Some boys are coming over tomorrow and we gonna have fun." However, the hunts are also justified in terms of the damage that rabbits do the corn fields, and they are held most frequently during the period when the corn is most easily damaged. When the snow in the winter is about three inches deep, impeding rabbits but not horses, rabbit hunts are also regularly staged.

Prairie-dog hunting was, until the population of these animals was reduced, common and popular, particularly with boys and young men, who lured them into the opening of their dens with a mirror and killed them with a barbed arrow. The hunters also took them by waiting near a "town" and shooting them with small caliber rifles.

In the winter, wildcats are tracked in the snow and shot, as are badger and fox if they are encountered. These winter hunts are described as "real fun" but justified, in addition, in terms of the potential damage these animals, particularly the wildcat, may do to sheep herds.

Many birds are killed, but seldom for food. Eagles are taken whenever they are encountered because of their value in Navajo ritual. An eagle skin with all the feathers is worth about twenty-five dollars. Bluebirds and owls also can be sold alive or dead to medicine men. Buzzards are shot at for sport, and a species of jay is killed because "it pecks at the corn." A variety of large swallow (bize) is occasionally killed in the summer because the act is said to bring rain.

UTILITY FOR LIVESTOCK OPERATIONS   One important function of the hunting complex and of the avid interest in hunting and killing animals displayed by most Navajo men and boys in that it trains Navajo males in a number of skills of singular importance to their livestock-raising activity.

Successful livestock operations in this area require an extremely detailed knowledge of a relatively limited area. The location of springs, seeps, and wells must be known, as well as sites of potentially good grazing and places where stock might become confused or lost. This knowledge could theoretically be gained from observation during actual herding operations or from more formal instruction. However, the amount of time spent with the herd by any one youth is a relatively small part of his life, considering the system of rotation of duty that exists within the homestead group. The remainder of his waking time is usually devoted to the pursuit of animals of all sorts and sizes with a sling-shot made of inner tube, a crude bow and arrow, or perhaps an ancient small-caliber gun that is usually kept secreted in a cave or tree out of sight of adults. This constant hunting develops the required knowledge that will later be put to good use in tending livestock.

Moreover, hunting develops the Navajo skill of tracking animals on the often dry, hard, and unyielding soil, a skill that is essential to the successful conduct of livestock operations on an open range. The ability of Navajo men and boys to follow the track of a single jackrabbit over ground recently churned by horses, perpetually marked by sheep hooves, and traced and retraced by numerous other jackrabbits is truly amazing. This skill is often put to the test in tracing down stray horses and cattle or seeking out lost sheep. The ability not only to follow a trail but also to identify a particular animal's hoof print is a requirement for any Navajo herder. Thus, the combined knowledge of terrain and tracking that is developed by boys and men is essential to their livestock operation, conducted as it is without fences on overcrowded but extremely rugged range. To some degree women share this knowledge, but it seldom appears to be as highly developed in them as it is in males. Nonetheless, most Navajo women are what we might term "track conscious" and seldom miss any obvious signs left in the earth by passing animals or humans. A Navajo woman was able to give a fairly accurate account of my own wanderings on foot and horseback from her observation of my week-old tracks.

RITUAL BEHAVIOR   Aboriginal hunting was highly and rigidly ritualized and has been described in much detail by Hill. Today, much if not all of this ritual is absent in hunts staged by Navajo men. However, certain behavior that I observed reflects the ritual strictures of aboriginal life.

In keeping with the mythological view that wild animals and man are products of the same act of creation, that animals once shared language, culture, and society with man, and that today they offer themselves as a volunteer sacrifice to man, no animal was killed without reason during my stay. Whenever an animal was killed, or an attempt was made to kill one, a reason was offered. Jackrabbits were killed to be eaten or fed to the dogs or because they ate the corn; bluejays were killed because they could be sold to a medicine man or because they picked the corn. An owl could be used to supply arrow feathers. A swallow killed in midsummer would bring rain. On one occasion my companion, who usually carried a rifle, stopped to shoot a buzzard. The act was quite without justification, as buzzards are inedible and their feathers are useful only in a single ceremonial context. Nonetheless my friend claimed, until he had fired and startled the bird into flight, that he was shooting at an eagle, extremely valuable for arrow feathers and in ceremonies. I am sure that his sudden lack of discernment was simply a cover to allow him to shoot at a living creature for pleasure.

Certain animals such as the coyote and the rattlesnake are not supposed to be killed because of their supernatural power. In conversations with Navajo men about hunting, it was pointed out that despite these ritual prohibitions both the coyote and rattlesnake were regularly killed *because they were a threat to humans and livestock.* In other areas where black bear are common and a threat to sheep, the Navajo, wherever possible, ask a White trader to kill the marauder in order to escape any possibility of revenge by the bear spirit. Members of the various deer clans are reluctant to kill deer or eat venison except on special occasions.

It is interesting in light of the reported behavior toward wild animals to note the casualness with which a wandering dog is killed or shot at. No explanation or excuse was ever offered for killing a stray dog. Nor is there any ceremony involved in the slaughter of a sheep or goat. The job is done in a casual manner, usually by two women who gossip and joke while they quickly slit the animal's throat and proceed to butcher the carcass.

Another stricture of Navajo hunting ritual required hunters to concentrate entirely on hunting. Only hunting was discussed, dreams of blood and killing were hoped for, and hunters were cautioned to keep their thoughts on the job at hand.

Today there is no formalized requirement for such concentration, but actual behavior follows the pattern closely. When a group of men have decided to hold a rabbit chase and have ridden away from the homestead, hunting dominates their thoughts and conversation. They discuss the hunt to come, where rabbits may be lying, rabbits they have seen recently, past hunts, the virtue of their horses as rabbit-chasers, whether or not the sticks they have cut are good rabbit clubs, and so forth. After each chase each detail of the run is discussed and analyzed over and over again. Any attempt to introduce some other subject into the conversation is either ignored or curtly rejected.

On one occasion I had ridden into the mesas with two brothers to search for owls to provide arrow feathers. In the course of our search we had casually killed a number of bluejays (because they picked the corn) and one cottontail (for dinner). Moving into the flatlands again, the brothers decided to have a rabbit chase. The casual air of the trip suddenly evaporated as we cut sticks and spread out in line. The chase ended successfully after less than two minutes. The discussion of the chase continued without interruption for the next thirty minutes until we had dismounted at the homestead.

The contrast between the single-mindedness of a hunter and the apparent casualness of the same man when herding sheep is interesting. Although always alert to the movement of the herd, the shepherd willingly discusses any subject that crosses his mind, engages in target shooting, undertakes brief stalks after rabbits (with the attendant critique of rabbit behavior), or simply enjoys nature.

Learning the Techniques of Herding

One might draw a comparison between the cultural and individual foundation of livestock herding among the Navajo. The livestock culture of today rests on the aboriginal hunting-and-gathering culture of the past, and in the same way the individual's basic knowledge of herding skills depends to a significant degree on the hunting for its continuation. However, there are many details of livestock herding that must be learned directly by young Navajo. This section will deal with the methods of teaching employed.

Because children are required to assume herding responsibilities somewhere between their eighth and tenth year, the skills must be taught early and taught well enough for youngsters to be entrusted with the herd with a fairly high degree of confidence.

Just as Navajo horse training is rather unstructured and informal, so is the training of Navajo children to work with animals. Most of the herding skills are developed as part of childhood play and not through any formal teaching programs.

The children live in a world very close to animals. The house or hogan is seldom more than a few dozen or hundred yards from the sheep pen or the horse corral. A horse is often tied from dawn to sunset within a few yards of the hogan, and the ubiquitous dog is constantly present. Toddlers less than two years old are apt to attempt to ride a dog or wrestle it and pull its ears until it flees. Chickens receive the same kind of attention from tiny children, although they are seldom incautious enough to fall into an infant's grip. Thus, children grow up with little or no fear of animals, and by the time they are two years old they fearlessly confront any stray sheep, goat, or cow that comes near, with shouts and arm wavings. They soon learn that most animals react quickly to such demonstrations. Certainly before their first birthday they have been taken up on the saddle by their father or an uncle and already experienced their first horseback ride.

EARLY INITIATION   By the time a child is three, he or she is allowed to participate in herding activities about the homestead. While one or two adults and several older children handle the sheep as they are being marked in the pen, children of three, four, and five are also in the pen "helping." Although their misguided and enthusiastic pursuit of sheep often hinders the operation, they are seldom made to stop, nor are they corrected. After a time an older child may take over the task of moving a sheep toward the marker and thus leave a youngster in screaming frustration. Only if there is real danger would a child be forcibly removed from the pen. In fact, children so young as to be clumsy on their feet may be used in herding when their father, uncle, or older brother places them on the ground at some gap in the sheep-pen fence; from that position, they serve to drive away the animals seeking to escape while the herd is being handled for one reason or another.

In herding it is quite common for the sheep to be allowed simply to drift into the pen by force of habit after they have been brought within a few hundred yards of the homestead. (A herd is often spoken of as "good" if it finds its way home without straggling.) If they desire, four- and five-year-olds may then take over the task of penning the sheep. Imitating their elders as best they can and often forced to combine forces to pull a stubborn ram by his horns until he faces the right direction, the youngsters drive the animals to the pen and close the gate. The adults appear to pay no attention to these efforts but do covertly watch to prevent the youngsters' enthusiasm from starting a stampede.

By the time a boy or girl has reached six or seven, he or she may accompany the herder with the herd onto the range, particularly if the herder is one of the older children, but seldom if the herder is an adult other than a parent.

THE ROPE   Toys are few in a Navajo household and those few are shared by all the children in the homestead. Girls usually have manufactured dolls, but boys' toys are most often makeshifts, the most common and most prized of which is a piece of rope fashioned into a lariat. From about the age of three, roping practice begins, usually with a piece of string and shifting, and continues, as the boy's expertness and discrimination develops, with the best rope he can find. Youngsters rope continually, using any object as a target, including dogs, chickens, sheep, each other, and younger siblings. Navajo children are generally retiring with strangers, and even when they have become friendly they may lapse into dumbness if suddenly confronted with a direct question about themselves. However, boys are invariably eager to show their skill with a rope.

Skill with a rope is an important factor in establishing one's prestige in early manhood. Almost without exception, boys and young men yearn to participate in rodeos in which calf roping is considered, along with saddle bronc riding, as an honored event. A family that includes a male who has a reputation as a "cowboy" basks in his glory, and his status as a "cowboy" far outweighs any other accomplishments he may possess.

Because roping is by and large a technique of cattle herding, it is less commonly a skill of women, although most women appear capable of lassoing a horse in a corral. However, so ubiquitous is the "roping complex" that a woman preparing a meal may fashion a loop in a piece of string and casually lasso a pot or a pan and drag it to her rather than rise or even lean forward to get it.

PLAY   The most common games played by Navajo children are those involving an imitation of herding activities. Older siblings willingly play horse for toddlers. Older children frequently draft younger siblings as "horses" to be led by a rope. The family wagon is a focus of much play whenever it is not in use. Two children play the role of horses, pawing, snorting, and buck jumping, displaying considerably more spirit than the average Navajo team, while another serves as driver for the rest of the children crowded into the wagon bed. At other times somewhat older children will pair off and play bucking bronco, or one will take a rope in his or her mouth while the partner "drives."

RIDING   Learning to ride is a gradual process, progressing from being taken up on the pommel by a father, uncle, or older brother to riding behind an adult or older child until, between nine and twelve, a child begins to ride the less fractious horses by himself. In fact, he seldom is completely alone because the youngsters' demand for animals to ride far exceeds the supply. A boy almost always has a younger sibling or cousin riding behind him, or two boys of about the same age ride and walk alternately. In their early teens, boys generally take over the job of driving horses that have been penned at night to water. A strict precedence of age is observed in carrying out this popular job, which usually permits a bit of galloping and rope waving. Before he is completely entrusted with this job, usually in his twelfth year, a boy is often taken on rides by his father or uncle. Although these rides are seemingly casual, the older man is carefully watching the boy's behavior. Not infrequently the trip includes a ride to the top of a high mountain or past some sacred spot. Generally such trips end in a "race," with the son's being allowed to ride the better horse and win. Once trusted to ride off by himself on horseback, a boy is considered an adult. It is at this time he receives a lariat, often purchased at no little sacrifice. It is also the time when he is given a horse if it is at all possible. He is no longer expected to come home every night and is felt to be old enough to cope with the dangers of large gatherings—that is, he is expected to take care of himself in the presence of drunken people.

Girls sometimes ride when they herd sheep, and if no older boy is present to herd the horses, they may occasionally take over the job. However, they ride for "fun" whenever they can. They take advantage of the special brother–sister relationship to importune their brothers, a situation that often results in a Navajo boy's walking home from some function to which he had ridden because he could not in good conscience deny his sister the use of the horse. However, female ambition in equestrian skills is thwarted by a lack of opportunity for expression. Older teen-age girls are faced with a choice of marriage on-reservation, the possibility of employment on-reservation, or of going off-reservation to seek employment; in any case, their ability as expert riders is not significant beyond their riding well enough to help with the herding. Rarely, a girl enters in one of the gymkhana classes of the rodeo such as the barrel race. This is not considered entirely good behavior by the Navajo, and such entrants are more likely to be Hopi girls.

By the time a Navajo child has reached his or her late teens, all the basic skills of livestock handling have been acquired. Special skills such as horseshoeing, operating for lampers or hide-bound shoulders, vaccinating, castrating, and de-horning may or may not be learned in adult life. Relatively few Navajo in this area shoe their horses since it is cheaper to rest a horse with sore feet than to purchase commercially made horseshoes or even, assuming the possession of the skill, to buy iron for making horseshoes.

Ownership, Benefit, and Responsibility

Livestock raising in the Nez Ch'ii area is often a family or communal enter-prise, but actual title of each animal is retained by an individual. The ultimate right to alienate any animal rests with the person considered to be the animal's owner. There are distinct patterns of ownership in the various classes of livestock, and perhaps more important than ownership is the benefit from the sale or slaughter of an animal. Many people besides the owner are involved in the care of the utilitarian and marketable animals, and many people besides him receive some share of the income.

Moreover, with certain classes of livestock there *is* an element of communal ownership involved. An individual Navajo will identify all the animals in a herd as "his" when he is speaking in general terms but if pressed for details will break down the herd according to the members of the group who actually hold title to the individual animals. It should be remembered that this is a social rather than a legal title. The institution of the grazing-permit system created a number of special problems inasmuch as permits were issued to individuals, although the herd may have in fact belonged to a number of people. Occasionally single animals are considered as jointly owned, but this situation is rare and may be limited in application to horses, or perhaps cattle, purchased with pooled funds. Only once did I hear an animal referred to as belonging to more than one person; this was a horse, and it belonged to a sister of the informant and her husband. The animal may have belonged in fact solely to the husband, but there is a strong tendency to identify a sister's husband with the sister and make claims on her property through her.

SHEEP AND GOATS

The sheep and goat herd usually is composed of animals owned by the individuals of a matrilineal group—that is, a woman, her daughters and sons, and perhaps even her brothers who live elsewhere with their wives. A husband may, if he wishes, buy sheep or bring sheep to be added to the herd at the time of his marriage. These sheep do not constitute a marriage payment but remain his property. However, a payment in sheep and jewelry is usually made to the bride's parents.

Children are usually given sheep and goats by their father, although his brothers or their mother's brothers may also give them sheep. The occasion for such gifts is in the spring during lambing season. In addition, a husband will often make his wife a present of several lambs at this time. Once the gift has been made to a child, the adults defer to the child on the question of disposing of the animal.

Every effort is made to save the sheep belonging to a boy or girl so that each child will have the beginning of a herd of his own when he or she is old enough to marry. However, when older children go to off-reservation schools for long periods and cannot contribute to the care of the herd, their animals are not infrequently slaughtered for food. The rationale seems to be that this is recompense for having cared for the animals while the owner was away. This is not always considered unfavorably by younger Navajo who have been educated. The lack of sheep relieves them of the arduous task of herding when they are home on vacation.

Responsibility for sheep and goats, however, is clearly that of the entire homestead group. The duty of herding the sheep is rotated from adult to adult when there are enough adults. If not, young adults and children either share the responsibility as helpers or assume full responsibility if adults are busy with other chores. It seems equally clear that liability for the sheep herd is shared by all the homestead group, and when the herd does not come home as expected, the entire group becomes concerned and begins to search. However, the members most closely related to the herder usually start searching first and continue longer than the other members of the group.

Jobs such as counting and dipping the sheep require the active participation of the entire homestead group. Some members must make the drive with the sheep and camp near the vat to hold the herd at night. Others remain at home until morning and then join the herders at the vat to assist in handling the sheep. At the same time, at least one adult woman or older girl must remain at the homestead to watch the infants and toddlers who do not go to the dipping.

When an animal is slaughtered for food, it is the property of a single individual but at the same time is shared with everyone present. Slaughtering for food seems to follow an informal rotation so that each individual suffers about the same drain on his or her holdings. If, however, as sometimes happens, one of the family comes home with a mutton hunger and demands meat, one of his animals will be killed. If he returns home to get meat to take away from the homestead and not to share with the rest of the group, it is his sheep that will be slaughtered.

The sale of sheep is also an individual activity. Members of the group select stock from among their own animals to sell at a time that is convenient to them. The proceeds of such sales are the property of the seller.

CATTLE

Cattle are much less a group enterprise. Women by and large show little interest in cattle operations, although occasionally a woman may buy a calf to raise. Cattle handling is considered to be a man's job and one that women cannot or will not do. More often than not, the cattle belonging to a homestead are the particular property and concern of one or two men of the group. Although the group will assume general responsibility for the animals, such as seeing that they are watered, it is up to the owner to find them if they are lost, to round them up and herd them to branding, and to assist in the branding. He may have the help of a brother-in-law or brother, particularly if he has a younger brother who is interested in being a "cowboy," but such help is considered a favor and in some way should be repaid.

Proceeds from cattle sales are the property of the owner of the cattle. The close relationship of Navajo brothers and sisters usually means that a man can count on a sister to look after his cattle interests if he has to leave home to work.

The distinctly different attitudes evidenced toward sheep and cattle are the foci of a pervading conflict in homesteads of the Nez Ch'ii area. Many young men who object to the demands placed on them by the sheep—the continual care, the repeated penning, the duty of herding—and who are conscious that for the past decade cattle have been the more profitable enterprise want to give up sheep husbandry and concentrate exclusively on cattle. However, women—wives, sisters, and mothers—and the more traditional men resist such moves vigorously. This resistance is probably due to the women's important role in sheep husbandry as herders, butchers, and shearers; they can handle sheep in the course of their domestic duties, and the wool from the sheep also provides them with material for rugs, which often constitute an important income source. If sheep were abandoned, women would no longer have such a central place in the economic system, and in all probability their overall influence and security would be weakened. For instance, no Navajo woman need endure mistreatment, or even boredom, from a husband because she is economically unable to leave him or, more properly, to order him to leave. A shift to cattle economy would place the economic reins more fully in his hands because even if she owned the cattle, it would be essential that a man be available to herd them.

HORSES

Horses are owned individually but they are shared within the homestead group. There is an informal but seldom violated precedence of horse usage, with the owner always having first choice of riding the animal he owns. In his absence or with his acquiescence, the riding privilege descends to his brothers and sisters, then to their spouses, then to other more distant relatives, and finally to the younger children who operate according to a precedence of age without reference to nearness of relationship. However, the rights of the owner must sometimes be tempered by the welfare of the homestead group, and his horse must be hitched to the wagon even though he would like to go on a ride or search for his cattle. Nevertheless, if he should insist on his right, the entire group will acquiesce, displaying only a very restrained resentment, and wait until he is through with the animal. This precedence of ownership does not extend to the children if actual title rests in a child, which is not infrequent. Having received a horse from his father, a boy may experience several years of frustration while his father usurps the animal and the use precedence descends from his father through the adults until it finally shifts into the children's system where the "owner" may have precedence if he can prevail over the demands of the older boys and his demanding sisters.

PRESSURES TOWARD COLLECTIVITY

The individualistic tendencies in stock ownership are clearly tempered by the dependence on others that is so essential for survival. The decision to sell stock or slaughter sheep is not completely unilateral and seldom is made without informal conferences. At the very least, such decisions are usually made with the knowledge that the action will not be greatly resisted by others.

How strong these collective pressures on the individual are can best be illustrated by the case of Crooked Fingers, who is thirty-eight, seldom refused by his family or in-laws, and tends to be charmingly overbearing. He is consumed with a desire to raise cattle, but in his own words, "My mother and sister won't let me." This female opposition prevents him from buying more cattle openly. However, he often buys calves secretly and gives them to friends to keep for him. When his mother and older sister left the reservation to weed and harvest crops in Idaho, he immediately began to bring his calves into the homestead knowing that economic prudence would prevent the women from taking any action to remove these valuable animals when confronted with a fait accompli. His scheming was not impeded by his adoring younger sister, although she was fully aware that the other women would be angry when they returned.

The Family and the Herd

The relationship between the family and the herd is one tinged with rather deep emotion and a great deal of symbolism. Sheep are not only wealth in an objective sense but serve as a measure of family well-being on a more abstract level of discourse. One is quickly impressed with the identification between "the family" and the "sheep."

This is most clearly seen whenever any unusual activity with the herd is planned. Thus dipping, shearing, shifting of pastures, or emergencies such as droughts, during which water is hauled to the herd, require the presence of as many members of the family as possible. Never are all the members pressed into service. Nonetheless, while those actually working the herd are busy, the others remain standing or sitting nearby carefully watching the operation. Often the preparation of meals is delayed while the women sit near the sheep pen watching the men bring the animals out to water. In fact, it would be considered somewhat less than proper if one of the women did not join the others at a time like this. At sheep dippings, members of the family not resident at the homestead usually appear to assist the family casually and to talk to their relatives. This is most often done in the sheep pen or near it. On several different occasions Navajo living at a distance from the family home where the sheep were kept asked me to drive them there, and in most instances the reason they gave for wanting to take the trip was to "see the sheep." "I haven't seen the sheep for a long time" was considered sufficient explanation for wanting to visit one's homestead. On one occasion, having taken a woman and her husband to visit one of her sisters, we found that the sheep were still grazing. After waiting for perhaps an hour we were forced to leave before the herd was brought in because of a sudden snow storm. The woman's complaint, "I sure wanted to see them sheep," could be compared only to a White relative who had missed seeing a favorite niece or nephew during a visit.

Quite often, particularly in the winter and spring, the sheep pen serves as a center of social intercourse for the women of a family. Generally keeping to their hogans in the daytime, they emerge some time before the herd is due to return and assemble in the sheep pen. There they fondle the lambs (and their children, quite without distinction) and discuss the affairs of the day, all the while holding hands, caressing each other casually, or otherwise expressing the Navajo trait of tactile assurance in face-to-face interpersonal relationships. This period is looked forward to all through the day as a time of relaxation and gratification and, even under the most miserable of weather conditions, is a time of gentle laughter and joking. When the sheep arrive, the women help herd them into the pen and assist the lambs in finding their dams before dispersing to prepare the evening meal.

However, when the family is torn by interpersonal tensions or openly expressed hostilities for any reason, the care of the sheep herd drops off noticeably. The animals are simply turned out of the pens and left to fend for themselves, with only a casual watch being kept. As often as not, they will not be driven to water until necessity forces the move. Once penned in the late morning, they may not be taken out in the afternoon at all. The job of herding may be assigned entirely to children, with an attendant series of derelictions. In short, as a focus of cooperation the sheep herd serves as a means of expressing both affection and hostility toward one's close relatives. It also serves as an anchor for members of the family not normally resident. Such relatives may periodically come back to the family homestead and insist on herding the sheep for a few days, thus establishing their relationship symbolically as well as creating an obligation on the part of the family. School-age boys often insist on herding sheep during the last few days of their summer vacation. On one occasion a young man came all the way from a summer job in Wyoming to spend a few days with his family before the school year started. In those few days he spent a goodly part of his time with the sheep on the range. Similarly, his older brother, who is employed by the Bureau of Indian Affairs, spends most of his vacation periods herding sheep at the family homestead.

These are examples of behavior, emanating from an attitude that is clear but difficult to describe, that links the sheep herd to the matrilineal family. Extremely old men point with pride to animals in the herd that are descended from the original animals issued by the government after Fort Sumner. Families will tell with pride how their immediate ancestor or ancestress began life with only a few sheep but increased the herd through perseverance, the proper exercise of ritual power, and right living.

The word *love* is used frequently to describe a Navajo's feeling toward his sheep. To quote from a letter written by one of my informants, "It's hard to make a living out here with our sheeps and cattles but we love them and will keep on trying no matter how hard it is."

Many observers of the Navajo have commented that in large part their resentment of the stock reduction program was a result of the government's allowing thousands of sheep to die in holding pens or en route to the railroads. Such behavior, perfectly understandable in White economic terms, was viewed as utter barbarism by the Navajo and is still spoken of in Nez Ch'ii. The fact that lambs, kids, and colts running with their mothers were worth nothing to stock reduction buyers was keenly resented not only in economic terms, but also as an insult to the persons of the animals.

Thus the Navajo is linked to his herds both in a simple economic relationship and by deep emotional ties in which he and his family's continuity and well-being, as well as his own self-image, are symbolized by his herds.

7

The Crops

THE NAVAJO learned to farm from the Pueblo peoples and adopted the native crops of corn, beans, pumpkins, melons, and squash that had been developed in the New World. They were also quick to adopt European crops such as peaches, oats, wheat, and barley. Except in a few well-watered areas, the Navajo were never enthusiastic farmers. Herds of animals, not large fields, constituted the basis of wealth and prestige.

In the Nez Ch'ii area, farming is particularly difficult. Rain is infrequent and unpredictable. There is never any certainty of making a crop. Water sources are too limited and uncertain to permit the development of irrigation.

Nonetheless, every homestead group works one or more fields to supplement its diet. Unlike the herd, which is tended communally, the cornfield is spoken of and managed as the individual project of a nuclear family. It is always identified with the wife rather than the husband, especially if the couple have taken up matrilocal residence. Occasionally two sisters may join efforts on a single field. This is particularly true if one of them is widowed or separated.

The common crops are corn, squash, and pumpkin. Regular efforts are made to maintain peach trees, but usually the seedling plants die from lack of water or from being stripped by grazing sheep. Occasional and sometimes successful attempts are made to grow potatoes, but the uncertainty of moisture often brings about failure. In as many as one out of three years even the cornfield fails to produce a crop because of lack of rain. Nonetheless, each year the crop is put in and the land worked in hope.

Fields are usually located on the traditional use area of the homestead group but often as much as several miles from the home of the farmer. At different periods of intense activity a brush shelter may be built near the field so that the nuclear unit can camp there to avoid a long round trip each day.

In the past the Navajo were noted for planting their fields in a peculiar spiral plan. However, with the introduction of the plough, after the return from Fort Sumner, this system was abandoned and with it much of the ritual associated with agriculture. The land is turned in the late spring after the snow has melted but hopefully while at least some moisture remains in the soil. Because no fertilizer is used, the fields quickly exhaust themselves, so that new ones have to be cleared by ploughing and burning every two or three years. The corn seeds are planted very deeply and very widely spaced and with them the seeds of watermelon, pumpkin, and squash. Once planted, there is little more that can be done save warding off birds that might steal the seeds before they sprout. If the rains are adequate, there may be some weed development that requires work in the midsummer. Frequently rain is so lacking that the corn stalks stand for weeks without apparent growth in fields absolutely barren of any other plants. If late summer rains come and are not so heavy as to wash out the field altogether, the almost dormant crops suddenly begin to mature, and by early September—late August in some places, October in others—the crops are ready for harvest.

The Navajo diet is singularly lacking in fresh vegetables, and many recipes for preparing unripe corn and pumpkins have been developed. In this way the farmer need not wait until the end of the growing season for vegetables and is also able to salvage something of a crop that has failed to mature completely. Roast green corn ears are extremely popular, as are green pumpkins, sliced and boiled in deep fat. Because the climate in this area is so inconsistent, crops in fields only a few miles apart may mature at different times. During the late summer, Navajo carry on an active trade in vegetables from fields that have matured and are later repaid in vegetables from fields that have not yet matured. By summer's end, vegetable-starved Navajo undertake long trips to obtain a few ears of corn from the field of a relative.

The techniques of farming are not complex, nor are farming skills of much importance in building personal prestige. The crops provide a small amount of extra food and help stay the family over the hunger-filled winter. After the fresh vegetable period, surplus corn is dried, hung on strings, and later ground on a stone slab into flour that is used as the basis for fried bread and mush. However, the fields of the Nez Ch'ii area are not able to produce anywhere near the amount of food needed for the present population, so increasingly the Navajo have become dependent on food purchased from the trader, principally wheat flour and potatoes.

Despite the fact that agriculture does not play an important role and, compared to livestock husbandry, is decreasing in importance with each generation, one product of agriculture is singularly important to the Navajo. Corn pollen is considered perhaps the most sacred of all the substances of the universe. It is carried as an amulet in small buckskin bags, is used to bless persons, animals, and hogans, and is a part of every Navajo ritual. This reflects the important influence the Pueblo peoples, who also revere corn pollen, have had on Navajo religious and ritual life.

Learning To Farm

The techniques of farming are few and simple. As a matter of course both boys and girls learn how to harness a team for ploughing. Men generally do the ploughing, and one male in the homestead group may in fact plough all the fields for his sisters or sisters-in-law. But he takes no special pride in a straight furrow or the other traditional signs of competence so proudly displayed by White farmers. Beyond the ploughing there is only the placing of the seeds and the unskilled business of hoeing weeds and picking the crop. What little has to be learned is learned casually by children helping their parents.

Today most fields are fenced to keep out livestock, and perhaps fence making, not a very popular art among the free-ranging Navajo, should be included as one of the agricultural skills learned by young men from older men who themselves may have picked up the art from watching or working with White men.

An interesting aspect of Navajo agriculture is the making of scarecrows. Among the nearby Hopis, birds are frightened away by draping lengths of cloth on frames or on the limbs of trees. The Navajo on the other hand are apt to display considerable ingenuity and wit in constructing human figures by using sticks and old clothes. Often family groups—men, women, and children—will be placed in the field in attitudes of work or waving at passersby. They seldom discourage birds but they add an element of whimsy to an otherwise tedious, hot, and not too rewarding activity in an often bleak landscape.

Gathering

Although hunting provides a basis of skills useful in herding, gathering seems little related to farming. In the past, we believe, the Navajo were gatherers as well as hunters. Recent traditions describing the thin days after the return from Fort Sumner describe extensive gathering activities. Today these have all but disappeared. In the spring, herders or children playing may dig up small bulbous root plants and eat them on the spot but never bring them home or gather them in amounts large enough to be considered as part of the family food supply.

Most women know a number of plants used to make native dyes for weaving and, with their daughters in attendance, go on collecting expeditions during the spring and summer. A number of plants used for herbal remedies are also collected, but, aside from this, gathering plays almost no part in Navajo life save in the case of the piñon.

In the northern reaches of the Navajo country the piñon pine, which bears large crops of fat seeds in small easily opened cones, grows in profusion. In the past, collecting piñon nuts for food was done by the Navajo just as it is by most of the tribes of the Great Basin (cf. Downs, *The Two Worlds of the Washo*). However, in Nez Ch'ii there are few such trees, and the piñon is not important. In other parts of the reservation relatively large sums of cash can be made by gathering piñon nuts for sale to traders who then sell them to confectioners. Only rarely does a Navajo from Nez Ch'ii undertake such work.

Farming and the Nuclear Unit

The herds symbolize the unity of the homestead groups and the continuity of the various matrilines. The fields would appear to have important symbolic relation to the nuclear unit.

As noted before, farming is the responsibility of nuclear units rather than the homestead group. As such, it constitutes the basic element of survival for the nuclear unit. A man and wife without relatives are hard pressed to manage more than a few sheep. As a team, however, they and their children can put in and harvest a crop. The most vigorous and industrious farmers are apt to be people unfortunate enough to be separated from their relatives by circumstances of death. Similarly, poverty in the Navajo sense is often symbolized by devotion to one's corn crop as a final desperate attempt to survive through one's own efforts. Hard work is a positive value among the Navajo, and a poor man who works hard in his fields is admired but pitied. In the past, the Navajo who maintained large and prosperous farms in Canyon DeChelle were considered unfortunates because they did not have large herds.

Another occasion on which farming is emphasized is when a large homestead group begins to fragment. This most frequently takes place after a period of disagreement and at least minor quarreling. As the individual nuclear units begin to separate from the original homestead group, they take with them their sheep, each to form the nucleus of a new herd. Usually such herd fragments are very small and not in any sense economical. As each unit reestablishes itself, its members devote themselves wholeheartedly to clearing new fields and planting a new crop. Consciously or not, they seem to respond to the new situation in which for the time being at least, they do not have the cooperative support of the other members of the homestead group interacting around the combined sheep herd. In short, the herding operations of Nez Ch'ii tend to extend and elaborate interpersonal relations, while the farming activities are oriented toward smaller units and fewer relationships.

8

Religion

ERHAPS NO OTHER ASPECT of Navajo life has been so thoroughly studied as has Navajo religious practices and beliefs. The consequence of this emphasis on religion has been the development of a somewhat out-of-focus view of the Navajo. Laymen, in particular, are apt to see the many works on religion and ritual as representing the priorities of Navajo culture and gain an impression of a people totally immersed in the holy and the sacred and somehow isolated from the mundane and profane. Nothing could be further from the truth. The Navajo, being hard-headed and pragmatic, is as able to judge objective reality as the next man and can be just as concerned about material comfort and social status as others are. However, unlike us, his "being religious" does not preclude his acting in an everyday way. In short, the Navajo view of the supernatural does not really make that distinction. The universe is of a single piece; it is all natural, and man is a part of that universe and must adhere to its many laws. The laws, however, are known—if not in detail to every Navajo, in general; he knows how to behave from time to time and situation to situation so that he may keep the universe in order and balance. To put his shoes on the wrong feet, as a very minor example, will bring about his death, not because putting shoes on the wrong feet is a sin but because the order of the world has been for an instant shaken. Old men believe that the lack of rain in recent years is due to the fact that young men are cutting their hair after the fashion of the White man. Long hair encourages rain; it is the natural order of things, and the results are inevitable and understandable. To deny this order is as wrongheaded to a Navajo as it is to argue that the earth is flat in our own world.

The famous anthropologist Bronislaw Malinowski suggested many years ago that primitive magic was a kind of science or ancestor to science. Many people, perhaps most, have not agreed with that view totally, but in a sense the Navajo support this idea. For us, science, with its laws of motion and gravity and its knowledge of germs and microbes, provides a background of explanation for our actions and for the things which happen around us—rain storms, hurricanes, earthquakes, and the like. For the Navajo, his religion is the explanation not only for what happens but for what one must do in order to keep the universe in order.

We, with our nuclear weapons and pollutants, have only recently accepted the notion that we are responsible for destroying ourselves and our environment. The Navajo has for centuries lived with the idea that he, by some careless act, some small failure to observe proper behavior, could upset the balance of the world and create disaster. Thus his religion, if we may call it that, is a matter of constantly observing the laws of the universe rather than the commands of God. He has little real theology but much wisdom that can be applied to everyday life. There are many Navajo ritual practitioners but no body of Navajo priests. Some men speculate and imagine, while others do not, being satisfied merely to carry out the prescriptions of ritual. Thus, following models of religious study formulated in their own history, scientists and scholars of another culture impose the sort of order on Navajo theology that is implied even in this brief section. For instance, those who study the religion in depth have had great difficulty in distinguishing various mythological figures that appear, disappear, and reappear in Navajo mythology. This difficulty troubles us, but it does not seem to bother the Navajo, who are no more concerned with the incongruities of their origin story than the fundamentalist Christian is troubled by incongruities in Genesis.

The Myth

Dine, the Navajo term for themselves, means literally "People of the Surface of the Earth." The origin myth of the Navajo describes the ascent of the ancestors of the People of the Surface of the Earth to the surface and the adventures and miraculous happenings that led to the establishing of traditional Navajo life. It could be considered an allegory describing the wanderings of the Athapaskan-speaking peoples and their eventual arrival in the Southwest. It incorporates elements of mythology that are almost universal in the New World. Some themes even appear to have relations to myth elements common in Asia. Certain aspects of myth and ritual reflect association with other Southwestern people, especially the Hopi and other Pueblo tribes. Still other things are unique to the Navajo or at least to the Southwestern Athapaskans.

Before there were Earth Surface People, there were, and are, the Holy People who once lived in the lowest of twelve worlds below the present surface of the earth. The Holy People are holy because they are powerful—not because they are perfect. It was in each instance some act of mischief or malice that forced the Holy People to move into a higher world. Usually one among them practiced witchcraft against the others and forced the move. In each world there were adventures and events that still have effect on the people of today. Practices were established, knowledge was created, and even special types of people appeared. For instance, in the third or fourth world (there is disagreement in the different versions of the myth) there appeared hermaphrodites or transvestites, men who dress and act like women. Such people today and in the past are somewhat venerated by the Navajo and considered to have potential supernatural power. In the last world but one, men and women quarreled bitterly and decided to live separately, each sex on the opposite side of the river. The men, according to the myth, lived quite harmoniously, learning the skills of women and even inventing some important household implements and techniques. The women, on the other hand, after getting off to a good start, were unable to suppress their sexual urges. Details vary, but it would seem that they engaged in homosexual intercourse and also had intercourse with monsters. From these relations there sprang a whole series of monsters who were to plague the Navajo for a long time—some of them even today. Eventually the sexes reached a rapprochement and rejoined each other to live in traditional harmony. But soon a great flood began to fill the eleventh world, and the Holy People were forced to scramble up through a hollow reed to the surface of the earth.

On the earth, the natural objects were formed, the landscape shaped either by powers of the universe or by the Holy People themselves. Death appeared for the first time.

Prominent among the Holy People were First Man and First Woman, who were created from two ears of corn and who are felt by some to have created the Universe (or at least First Man is given that honor). But their important role is that of mother and father of Changing Woman, the most important figure in Navajo mythology. Her conception and birth were miraculous affairs, but the original pair raised her and trained and allowed her to mate with the Sun and with Water. This mating or matings (it's difficult to know) produced two sons, twins, who grew up to seek out their father the Sun and receive from him weapons and knowledge that allowed them to slay the monsters plaguing the earth and The People. The record of their victories is written in the landscape of the Navajo country. Prominent mountains, lava flows, and other natural features are identified with the carcasses of slain monsters.

The Twin Monster Slayers are considered by some students of the subject to be War Gods, and their lives serve as a model for traditional Navajo male behavior.

Their mother, however, is more properly thought of as a personification of the earth itself, for she is forever growing old and withered only to emerge again, as does the earth in the spring, as a young and beautiful woman.

These figures are certainly not the only ones in Navajo mythology. There are dozens of Holy People, and it is often hard to distinguish one from the other. Is White-Shell-Woman, for instance, a sister of Changing Woman, or is she Changing Woman herself in a different form? Each of these Holy People, or *Yei* as they are called in Navajo, is associated with specific natural features of the land, with other *yei*, and with aspects of the weather, vegetation, mineral deposits, and with certain animals. Perhaps one illustration of these complex relations is needed before we discuss religion as it is acted out in day-to-day life. In her book *Navajo Religion* Alice Riechard describes the relations of a single *yei*, Talking God. His direction is the west; color, yellow; mountain, Mt. Humphreys. He is related to the sunbeam, yellow clouds, and a yellow light in the evening. Among things used as jewels, he is the abalone shell. Among the birds he is symbolized by the yellow warbler, and as vegetation he is black or yellow corn. Other *yei* who live on Mt. Humphreys are

White Corn Boy, Yellow Corn Girl, Evening Light Boy, and Abalone Girl. Dark Clouds, male (?) rain, yellow corn, and wild animals are also associated with this *yei*.

Every Navajo does not know or understand such a systematic approach to the *Yei* who today live at the various points of the compass and at zenith and nadir. However, practitioners are supposed to understand such symbolism so that they will not make errors in rituals. The *Yei* are not in our sense gods, although we often translate the word that way. They can misbehave, make errors, and act with malice. At the same time, they can be controlled and coerced as well as persuaded by proper ritual acts, and it is these acts that form a network of behavioral guideposts for Navajo life. We cannot discuss them in detail but will simply examine some of the more important aspects of ritual and belief.

Daily Activities

It is customary for the eldest male of a Navajo homestead to begin the day at sunrise by singing a sacred song and dropping corn pollen, a singularly sacred substance in all Navajo and Hopi ritual, in the four cardinal directions. Throughout the day that follows, the routine is accompanied by endless and almost unconscious acts of ritual. A sacred song is frequently sung as the sheep herd is taken from the pen for grazing, and snatches of songs often semisacred in nature are heard throughout the day. The manufacture of various tools and utensils is accompanied by often elaborate ritual. The anthropologist Harry Tschopik has suggested that one reason that the Navajo so quickly abandoned native handmade utensils and tools such as baskets, pottery, saddles, and so on is that the ritual involved had become too elaborate and time-consuming, and when alternatives appeared in the form of manufactured goods, they were quickly accepted. Even the flat baskets used as part of the ritual payment to singers and medicine men in virtually all ceremonies are seldom made by the Navajo but instead purchased and repurchased from the local trader who, by long and complex routes, has received them from the Southern Paiute. The making of a bow and arrows is another activity requiring not only technical but also esoteric knowledge. Without the latter, the former would be useless, and the weapon would not perform satisfactorily.

Even such mundane acts as cooking are governed by characters from the mythological past. The simple act of baking a mud-covered prairie dog in the ashes of the cooking fire is explained in the humorous story of Badger and Coyote.

> Badger was hunting prairie dogs and had killed a bunch when he met Coyote. Coyote was hunting, too, but he hadn't caught none of them prairie dogs. He saw all them prairie dogs that Badger had and he tried to figure out how to get them. He said to Badger, "Let's us have a race around that mesa, and the one who wins will get to eat all the prairie dogs." Badger he say, "O.K., but let's put them in the ashes of the fire to cook so they will be ready when we get back." So they built a fire and put the prairie dogs in the ashes with just their tails sticking out, and then they started to race. Well, Coyote was real fast, and pretty soon he was out of sight, and Badger he knew all the time that he

couldn't run faster than Coyote. So when Coyote went behind the mesa, Badger he just run back to the fire and pull them prairie dogs out by their tails and ate them. And then he put just the tails back, sticking out of the ashes, and then he went off and hid. Pretty soon Coyote come around the mesa all tired and panting, and he figured he won the race, and so he ran over to the fire laughing about how he'd tricked Badger and grabbed them tails and pulled them out, but there wasn't nothing but tails, and old Badger he laughed and laughed, and that's why we cook prairie dogs the same way Badger and Coyote cooked them.

This story provides an example of how even the most minor aspects of Navajo daily life are shaped and influenced by references to the Navajo cosmology. Like most other American Indians, the Navajo mythically recall a time when men and animals shared a single society, culture, and language. It is difficult to separate the mythical prototypes of modern animals from the actual animals or to understand clearly in what form the actors in such stories appear.

Throughout their daily life, the Navajo also weave a network of sacred or semisacred songs. From the ritual singing at sunrise and while the sheep are being driven from the pen to the singing in the cornfields and during wood gathering, weaving, or spinning, the Navajo homestead is full of song. Sung softly to one's self or in loud self-confident tones, which are always startling in such a barren, generally silent country, the songs call up blessings or bring down protection on the singer, his herds, his family, or the enterprise in which he or she is involved.

One important combination of the sacred and the mundane is the ritual of the sweat-bath. An integral part of each Navajo homestead is a semisubterranean structure that is perhaps two feet deep, three or four feet above ground, and eight to ten feet wide. It is covered over with earth and entered through a very small door that is closed with blankets. This forms an almost airtight sweat room that can be heated to seemingly unendurable temperatures by placing heated rocks in one corner. Usually once a week, sometimes oftener, the men of a homestead take a sweat-bath. The process is a long one requiring the collection of a large wood supply that is used to heat the sweat-rocks. When the rocks are properly heated, the fire-tender calls his companions, and, using a shovel, places the rocks in the sweat-house. Modern Navajo usually take a washtub filled with water as well as soap with them to the sweat lodge. All adult males are required to tie a string around their prepuce before entering the sweat-lodge. To fail to do this would be a very dangerous act. One of the signs of a boy's acceptance as an adult occurs when his father or uncle instructs him to use a prepuce string before entering the lodge. Such a boy is always looked upon with a great deal of envy by his younger contemporaries. Once the rocks are in place, as many men as the small room will hold crowd into the lodge and call to the fire-tender to cover the door. They then begin a round of songs calling for good health, fine healthy animals, good crops, rain, and wealth. The songs are sung in groups of four, and sweating continues through a complete cycle of four, eight, sixteen or even more, depending on the stamina of the sweaters and the size of their repertoire. When the song cycle is finished, the blankets are pulled away, and the sweaters emerge. They dry themselves by rolling in the dust, while praying softly to themselves, and then rinse off with water. Often two groups take turns, or individuals return for yet another cycle of sweating and singing. The sweat bath serves at one time the functions of cleanliness and worship. It can also, as do all other Navajo rituals, include a curing element. Minor ailments are often taken to the sweat-bath. Certain plants that are said to be good for stomach trouble or headaches are carried into the sweat-lodge. Less frequently, and always after sunset, the women of the homestead go to the sweat-house to use the rocks already heated by the men. This use, however, appears to have much less ritual content. Men must stay well away while the women are sweating, and female laughter can be heard for miles across the steppes.

Other aspects of religion and ritual that occur almost incessantly and casually are such things as a constant attention to omens and small personal ritual invocations for health, success, or rain. Regarding omens, one is always alert to signs of danger, the sounds of certain birds or animals, forgetfully putting one's moccasins on the wrong foot (an omen of death), and so forth. An example of a ritual invocation is picking up a horned toad, rubbing it over one's neck and chest, and freeing it along with a prayer to be carried to the forces of nature requesting good health. Also, rain can be encouraged by shooting a variety of swallow that appear in the Navajo country at dusk. It is considered good luck for a traveler to place a stone or a bit of shell or turquoise on cairns established along trails throughout the Navajo country and to say a prayer. These cairns, standing visible for miles in the flat steppelands, mark well-traveled trails and often are as high as a man on horseback.

A stone trail marker on top of a hill indicates older travel routes. The telephone pole marks the route of the automobile roads.

Sings and Singers

The acts described above constitute the daily, casual aspects of Navajo religion. The core of Navajo religious activities, however, is the person of the *hatli*, or "chanter," and the ceremonies (generally called "sings" in English) over which they preside. All ceremonial activities are based on special prayer songs, and one can make only an arbitrary distinction between sings and the ceremonies that will be discussed in the next section.

The Navajo chanter, frequently called a medicine man, is a person who has, through apprenticing him- or herself to an older person, learned certain sacred prayer songs connected with the origin myth. Song is considered an especially powerful force in Navajo life, and many persons have personal songs or know parts of sacred songs, which they sing for their own benefit. Only a recognized practitioner, however, can sing to effect a cure of another person. Singers do not constitute a separate caste of people. They live normal lives and are involved in herding and farming, although a popular singer may have little time for these activities, owing to the demands for his services.

There are many classifications of sings and chants developed by students of Navajo religion; however, we need only consider them in terms of length, elaborateness, and associated activities. In all cases, the expressed purpose of a sing is to cure. The ailment may be an obvious physical complaint or a vague feeling of uneasiness, or it may be overindulgence in drink, gambling, horse racing, marital infidelities, or laziness. There are many dozens of chants and songs and accompanying rituals, and one must know the proper one to use. For this purpose, a diagnostician is called. The singer is a skilled workman who has learned a song and its associated ritual. The diagnostician is a person with certain special talents for divining the basis of the complaint. Some diviners, as they are often called, can handle such mundane matters as finding lost articles and animals. Others have the power to understand what is the cause of a patient's complaint and recommend the proper song, ritual, or chant to effect the cure. Some diviners even specialize in getting to the bottom of domestic problems such as quarreling between members of an outfit.

Once a special song-ritual has been recommended, the patient and his family must send an intermediary to seek out a singer who knows the song, has the ritual paraphernalia, and who is willing to work for them. Sings vary from one-day to five-day affairs. Some may be performed only in a hogan of traditional design. Others can be performed even in the houses of White men. For others it might be necessary to remove the door from a log cabin or White-style house (called *kin* in contrast to the *hogan* or traditional-style dwelling). Still others may require that a special structure, in which the ritual can be performed, be built of brush. The shorter the sing, the fewer are the people involved. A one-night sing—actually taking place in two parts, one in the daytime and the other late at night until dawn—is attended only by the relatives residing in the homestead. But often in such cases it is not considered effective unless all the residents are present at certain parts of the ritual. In almost every instance, a sand painting or design of colored sands, earths, and pollens is made as the beginning step of the ritual, which ends hours later after a night of continuous singing and intermittent ritual directed at the patient. The effectiveness of the performance is based on the skill of the singer, who must know the proper songs in word-for-word perfection, as well as the ritual acts.

Such semiprivate family affairs may last from one to five days, and the larger and larger groups of relatives who often attend the longer sings are asked to share some of the expense of paying the singer. Certain traditional payments are made, such as ears of corn and a flat basket and frequently a tanned deerskin, but, in addition, food stuffs, blankets, sheep, and money are also required.

A singularly important family sing which reflects both the strong matriarchal orientation of Navajo culture and the relationship between Navajo and other Western American tribes is the Girls' Sing. This four-day ceremony is held to announce and celebrate a girl's first menstrual period. The Navajo believe that, during the period of her transition, a girl is particularly sensitive to influences that will affect her later life. She is, in fact, seen as an almost plastic being who can be easily injured and at the same time easily shaped into a proper mold. For four days, then, she remains quiet within her hogan and ventures out during the day only in the earliest dawn to collect wood, run, and act out other virtues of womanhood that reflect hardiness, energy, and a will to work. During each of the four nights she is the center of continuous ceremonial singing by her relatives and friends. The more guests who attend and the more vigorous their singing the more assured is the girl's future. Meanwhile the girl's mother or maternal relatives prepare a large cake of ground corn meal, flavored with sugar and dried fruits and baked in an earth oven. On the morning of the last day, the young woman emerges from her seclusion, and the cake is distributed to all the visitors who come through the faint dawn to congratulate her and her family with their presence.

Public Ceremonies

In contrast to the essentially private, family-oriented sings, there are a number of public ceremonies that include entire communities, in fact, the entire Navajo people. They are, however, not in any sense communal ceremonies. At the base is the same rationale as for the simplest of sings, the need of a person to find a cure for a physical, psychological, or spiritual complaint. In essence there is no difference, save in complexity, between the sings and chants discussed above and the larger ceremonies. The primary emphasis is one of curing, and any ceremony must have one or more patients as a focus of the ritual. However, two types of ceremonies have accumulated a superstructure of social activities, which make of them something far different than a simple curing sing. There are two classes of these ceremonies, depending on when they are performed. The actual chants and rituals performed during the ceremony may differ according to the diagnosis and the skills of the chanter employed.

THE SQUAW DANCE

Perhaps the most famous and most frequent of these ceremonies is the so-called Squaw Dance, which refers to the social, not the religious, aspects of the occasion. This can be performed only during the warm months, usually after April, although occasionally Squaw Dances have been held as early as March. Originally the Squaw Dance centered on ritual aimed at removing evil influences from the persons of warriors returning from a raid. The association with foreigners, the exposure to death, and the ultimate danger of actually having killed, placed a returning fighter in an extremely dangerous position. Such a purification required four days and nights of ritual overseen by a medicine man familiar with complex chants, sand paintings, and other rituals. To be properly effective, it requires the participation of as many people as possible to lend their assistance to the medicine man and to increase the strength of the ritual through their presence and singing. Paying the chanter and his assistants and feeding the assembled visitors then becomes an undertaking too expensive to be supported by a single homestead group. To meet these expenses the hosts—that is, the family of the patient—call on the most distant of relatives in the matrilineal group as well as groups related through marriage. Guests are also expected to make contributions of food or money, although this is not required and hospitality is extended to anyone who appears. A Squaw Dance given by a rich person or by a family with many connections then may entertain several hundred and sometimes more than a thousand guests. Although the ritual is overtly directed at individual patients, the entire ceremony takes on a communal aspect inasmuch as it requires the cooperation of many people in its planning and execution. Moreover, it also has a spatial dimension, as the ceremonies and attendant social activities take place at three different locations during the course of the four days.

The decision to have such a ceremony rests originally with a single individual who feels ill or suspects that a ritual cure might relieve him of a feeling of despondency or depression, stop his excessive drinking, solve domestic problems, or simply improve his luck. A consultation with the diagnostician confirms his need for a dance, and discussions with the members of the homestead group explore the economics and logistics of such an occasion. Often a poorer family must delay the event until money can be saved and relatives convinced of the necessity of the ritual.

Once the decision is firm, the homestead group of the patient begins making arrangements with nearby consanguinal relatives. A series of meetings are held and arrangements made as to where the three different locations will be; the secondary hosts are requested to cooperate, and arrangements are made to pay them, usually in livestock, for their trouble. Because the original ritual site and the secondary site require the building of elaborate structures and preparing food for large crowds, the second-night host is usually an affinal relative of the patient. In this way, members of the patient's clan are required to assist in the construction of one site, while the members of an affinal clan are involved in the other. Another factor in the planning is the availability of a chanter or medicine man who knows the recommended ritual. There are many rituals suitable for the Squaw Dance, but not all medicine men know them all. Many remain only memories and are no longer practiced because no one remembers the proper procedures.

The actual ceremony itself begins at the site selected by the host, where a special brush hogan is constructed for the medicine man and his assistants and where, more or less continuously, various phases of the ceremony are performed over the four-day period. In addition, wood for cooking and lighting is collected in large amounts, barrels of water assembled, and a large brush ramada, where the women of the host clan prepare food, is constructed. Sheep and cattle are collected from relatives and held ready for slaughtering as needed. Quantities of flour, coffee, and other foods are purchased from the trader and delivered to the hosts.

The activities for which the ceremony is popularly named has nothing to do with the ritual being performed and is entirely social. The returning of warriors in the past was seen as a good time to announce the readiness of young women for marriage. These young unmarried women, dressed in their best clothing and displaying their wealth in turquoise and silver, appeared each night to select partners to join them in a simple shuffling dance. The primacy of women in Navajo life

Almost merging with its background, a brush hogan stands abandoned after a Squaw Dance. The ceremonial aspects of the event take place largely in this kind of structure.

is again reflected in the etiquette of the dance. No young man, once selected, can refuse to dance with a girl unless he can prove that he is a member of the girl's or some other ineligible clan. Should a man refuse, the girl's mother, aunts, and older sisters may well descend upon him and drag him into the center of the circle of wagons and campfires that forms each night. If a young man does not want to carry the affair further, he must make some small payment at the end of the dance. Should he refuse to pay, he binds the young woman to be his partner through the rest of the dance. If she has second thoughts about her choice, she is trapped unless she can steal his hat, blanket, or some other possession and ransom it, thus receiving the payment necessary to free her.

In addition to the courtship dance, which is the focal point of a great deal of good-natured ribaldry and not a little jealousy because girls can select married as well as unmarried men, there are round dances performed by both men and women, married and unmarried, and team singing. The singing teams form quite casually and are made up of men of all ages, who, while swaying back and forth, sing traditional and often spontaneously composed "Squaw Dance songs," accompanied by a small pottery drum. This gives rise to the term *swaying songs* often used to describe these compositions. Navajo vocal music is particularly distinctive because it is performed with great throat tension and with an emphasis on high-pitched

One of the principles in the Squaw Dance mounting his horse to lead the procession to the site of the second night of ceremonial singing and dancing. The decorated cedar branch is the focus of the four-day ceremony.

nasal sounds. The newcomer who is not familiar with Navajo music generally assumes that women are singing until he sees the crowds of young men.

In the days between the night dances, while rituals are being conducted by the medicine man, the visiting families camp near their wagons, visit relatives and friends, gamble, stage horseraces, and continue diffidently the courtships that began the night before.

On the final day, the arrival of young warriors is reenacted and presents of bread, cakes, candy, and fruit are thrown to the crowd. If the host can afford it, the events of the day may also be enlivened by young men who, disguised with simple masks and daubed with mud, act as clowns and terrorize the crowd by seizing hapless individuals and dumping them in the mud or otherwise harrassing them. The clowns also confer some benefits of health by seizing a person and, while chanting, carrying him on a blanket. Persons suffering minor or chronic ailments or those seeking a change in luck volunteer for the treatment.

Although the orientation of the Squaw Dance is familial and individual in practice, it involves all, or at least a large part, of the community, by defining relationships, establishing obligations, and providing the opportunity to pay off old ones. It is an occasion of social display—wearing one's best clothing and jewelry, displaying one's horses and wagons (and in later years trucks and autos), initiating courtship, and engaging in illicit liaison. Failure to take part in a family's Squaw Dance is tantamount to admitting a serious breach within the structure of the family. At the same time, a well-known or powerful family entertains visitors who "drop in" from throughout the reservation as a symbol of friendship and support. Relatives absent from the community are informed and expected to return home to take part, even, and this is often the case, if it means giving up off-reservation employment. At the same time, the collection of livestock and other food stuffs, the presenting of gifts to the host, the payment of the chanter and his assistants, the feeding of participants and guests, the exchanging of money and goods in gambling, and the purchase of supplies from the trader mean that each Squaw Dance has an enormous impact on the economic life of the community.

The flexibility within prescribed patterns that characterizes Navajo social structure can also be seen in ceremonial life. Since the defeat of the Navajo, the military aspect of Navajo culture has gradually disappeared. However, the ceremonies surrounding the warrior's life were extended to serve as protection for anyone exposed to foreigners—children returning from school, women working as domestics off-reservation, traders, Bureau of Indian Affairs officers, or anyone else suffering from what might be diagnosed as dangerous contact with foreigners. After World War II, returning veterans almost without exception were the focal point of a Squaw Dance to ward off the evil influences of their wartime experiences.

In the past, the Squaw Dance ceremonies appear to have been held less frequently than in recent years, perhaps only a few each summer on the entire reservation. In modern times, especially since World War II, hundreds of such ceremonies are held each summer throughout the reservation area. This may be a result of the greater felt need as a result of increasing contact with outsiders. On the other hand, the gradually deteriorating economic conditions on the reservation may be the basis for more frequent attempts to correct whatever supernatural evil has befallen individual families. There is also a distinct element of competition in the staging of Squaw Dances in any given area. The occurrence of one dance almost always is followed by another and yet another, until it would seem that the psychic and economic energy of a community is exhausted. In part, this is the consequence of each homestead group's wishing to display its status by staging the most impressive dance possible. In part, too, the decision to hold a dance may be motivated by the knowledge that as more and more dances are held the ability of relatives and friends to contribute is reduced, so each family considering the possibility of a dance speeds up its decision. In the Nez Ch'ii area in the summer of 1960, thirteen such events occurred within a radius of about twenty miles. The summer before, only two dances were held, as a response to real physical illnesses, and in the following year only four dances were held. A dance cycle such as the one in 1960 is particularly exhausting physically and economically to persons of influence and political aspirations and those who have many lines of kinship in a given area. One such man, the chairman of the local grazing committee, felt obliged to appear at every dance, to make speeches and participate in the ceremonies for which he always received a gift of tanned buckskin, food, or a plush shirt; ruefully contemplating yet another dance, he said, "I hope them people don't give me no nice presents. I can't afford no more presents." His problem was that the giving of presents anticipated a reciprocal act that he could no longer afford. Yet, to maintain his position in the community, he felt required to repay each gift even if it meant going into debt at the trading post.

Yeibeichai DANCES

The mobile nature of the summer Squaw Dance reflects perhaps the mobility of Navajo life in the summer as well as the network of relationships within which each homestead group rests. The winter ceremonies on the other hand are not mobile and for a number of reasons are less frequently performed. Again, a great number of separate chants and rituals can be performed in the winter, but the general class of ceremonies at which they occur are called the *Yeibeichai* dances. The fact that the *Yei* are represented by masked men and can appear only in the winter months suggests that they may, in part, at least, represent religious figures borrowed from the neighboring Pueblo peoples, with their colorful cycle of *Kachina* dances. In any event, a *Yeibeichai* dance is even more expensive and complex than the Squaw Dance, inasmuch as nine days and nights of ritual are required in order to complete it. Because chanters who know the entire complex ritual of a nine-day ceremony are rarer than Squaw Dance medicine men, because the feeding of large numbers of people for nine nights is exceedingly expensive, and because travel is more difficult in the winter, thus preventing the kind of enjoyable socializing associated with the Squaw Dance, the *Yeibeichai* dances are not as frequently performed. However, in the event of some disaster or illness which cannot be otherwise treated, there is no alternative. The dances, with costumed dancers or the social Fire Dance in which fire brands are whirled and thrown into the darkness, are more spectacular than the night performances at a Squaw Dance, and in a sense the rituals associated with the *Yeibeichai* are considered more powerful simply because they are more complex. Some of these chants are associated with the bear, and the dances are never held before the traditional time when the bear goes into hibernation. In the past, particularly ambitious medicine men have attempted to use live bears or bear cubs in the ceremonies, but the results have often been disastrous and dangerous, so that the animal, particularly fearsome and sacred to the Navajo, is represented only in symbol.

Of the actual rituals performed in either the Squaw Dance or the *Yeibeichai* dances we will probably never have a complete accounting Some of them, associated with activities no longer important to the Navajo, such as antelope hunting, remain memories but are no longer practiced. Others have fallen into disuse because the medicine men who knew the correct chants and rituals have died without passing on their knowledge.

The rituals, skills, paraphernalia, and songs necessary to conduct such a ceremony are exceedingly complex and require years to memorize under the tutelage of a practicing medicine man. This must be paid for with personal service or wealth in livestock, food, or money. Learned in any other way, without payment, the knowledge would be of no value because it would, in effect, be stolen and thus not the true property of the practitioner.

Among the neighboring Hopi, the rituals and ceremonies follow a pre-destined pattern through the year in a cycle of dances that mark different phases of the year and assure in each ceremonial step that the rains will fall at the right time and the crops will come to fruition when they are expected. The role of each man and woman is determined in relationship to the community, his clan, or cult membership; the ceremony is not the function of a family but of the entire community.

The Navajo ceremonial complex is equally as symbolic of the structure of his society as is that of the Hopi, and it reflects the flexible nature of Navajo life and the importance of the homestead group on which each Navajo, in the final analysis, must depend for survival. Thus, while each Hopi plays a predetermined role in each ceremony according to his status in the community, the Navajo participates in terms of his relationships to the host family. If his homestead is the sponsor, his duties and responsibilities are many and often onerous. If, on the other hand, the sponsor is a distant relative or a friend, the individual Navajo may or may not be expected to contribute and participate heavily. Thus, while a person might take part in as many as a dozen ceremonies in a single year, each ceremony will present itself from a different perspective and emphasize the person's relationship, not to the community as a whole, but rather to each homestead unit that makes up the community. Only an understanding of all the complex interrelations provides a definition of community.

Death and the Dead

The people of Nez Ch'ii, like most other Navajo, do not fear death any more or less than do other people. However, like many Western Indians, notably those of the Great Basin, they do fear the dead. The dead are dangerous because the ghost of a dead man may return to trouble the living. There are no good ghosts in Navajo life. A ghost is the evil part of a total man. It may return because its property has been mishandled or expropriated or because of ritual failures. It is possible for a ghost to harm the living by entering their bodies. Thus it is best to avoid the dead, lest one is exposed to such a visitation. There is great danger in being near the dead, whether they are former friends or former enemies. To escape the danger that such association raises one must undergo long and expensive ritual treatment.

Thus, when a person has died in a hogan, for instance, the structure is abandoned. The body is often left inside with its belongings. Burial is rapid and without much ceremony, and, in the past at least, a person's favorite valuable possessions were buried with them. Early traders and missionaries were often tolerated by the Navajo because they would volunteer to bury the dead, thus freeing the Navajo from the fearsome task. Similarly, hospitals were used as a place where one could take an obviously dying sick person so that the hogan did not have to be abandoned; this was perhaps also done to confuse the ghost so it could not return to plague the living. The consciousness of the presence and danger of ghosts is expressed in fear of the dark and a reluctance to go out at night, as well as in avoidance of funerals and of obviously dying people.

Witches, Werewolves, and Society

The power of Navajo songs, chants, prayers, and ritual is compulsive. A prayer is not a supplication but the activation of natural forces, the outcome of which is a foregone conclusion. An error in manipulating these forces, a mistaken word in a chant, an error in the preparation of a sand painting, or the omission of some act renders the ritual ineffective and sometimes can be quite dangerous for the patient, the practitioner, and the community. Errors of course can be set right, but if an error in ritual can be dangerous, what of deliberate error? Navajo logic holds that chants sung backwards or ritual deliberately performed improperly can bring disaster to the community or to individuals. They further believe that just as there are good medicine men who have labored and paid to learn blessing chants, there are others who have labored and paid even more to learn evil chants. These witches, both male and female, can bring illness and disaster on enemies, and their influence is constantly feared. It is a fear of coming under the spell of a witch that makes Navajo careful and wary in large crowds. Seldom does a person go to even purely Navajo affairs without the support of familiar company, preferably relatives or close friends. Nor does a Navajo relish staying alone, particularly at night. One seldom sees women alone, even in the daytime, and although men may travel alone in the daylight, they try to find company before nightfall. Particularly when going to a large gathering, a Navajo wears charms and amulets, often simple bags of sacred corn pollen, to protect himself from danger.

NEGATION OF NAVAJO ETHIC

Despite the strong belief in witches and witchcraft and extensive study by anthropologists, witchcraft is an elusive subject. Almost anyone who has gained the confidence of Navajo people has heard endless stories of witches and "wolf men" and heard vague accusations against one or another person, usually a non-relative living at some distance from the accuser. In addition, he has been told how the death of one or another person close to the teller has been traced to the evil influences of a witch. Navajo can describe in detail the initiation of witches to a coven, the murder of relatives, and incest and nakedness in mixed groups. All of these are violations of the most important strictures of Navajo morality. Murder brings down danger on the murderer and the community as a whole. Incest, of course, is a singularly dangerous act abhorred by even the most depraved. And while the Navajo are relatively casual among themselves about nudity above the waist, exposure of the genitals by even the youngest of children, particularly girls, is a serious breach of etiquette. In short, the witch presents a reverse picture of what a good Navajo should be and a negative emphasis of the Navajo ethic. Whether or not there are people who actually undergo the initiation of witches and believe they can perform evil deeds through evil chants and ritual is a matter of conjecture. The individual Navajo believes that such people exist, and he governs his behavior accordingly. A person suspected of witchcraft, particularly if he or she is suspected of directing his power against one's person or relatives, may, if all other means fail, be killed in self-defense. Such killings, officially unexplained by White law, still occur. A less drastic cure is to seek the aid of a chanter who knows the proper rituals to counteract evil spells. Although seldom declared outright, this is often a reason for holding a Squaw Dance or *Yeibeichai* ceremony.

THE WOLF MAN

The most frightening figure among Navajo witches is the "wolf man." Such a person is felt to be able to transform himself into a wolf or coyote and, while in this form, bewitch his enemies by sprinkling a magic substance containing ground parts of human infants through the smoke hole of a hogan. Few Navajo attain adult status without having some experience that they interpret as having to do with wolf men. A man riding alone at dusk and spotting a stray dog near the trail will spur his horse into a gallop and ride into the homestead wide-eyed and breathless, convinced that the animal was a wolf man. Any unusual sound in the night is explained as being made by the wolf man. A sudden paroxysm of barking by the homestead's dogs is considered a sure sign that a wolf man is prowling in the darkness. If it persists, the men of the homestead arm themselves with all the weapons the family can muster and fearfully probe into the darkness. A wolf man can be killed by ordinary bullets, and many stories circulate about the tracks of a wounded coyote suddenly changing into the tracks of a wounded man. Killing a wolf man is a dangerous event because the killer will most certainly be the object of vengeance on the part of the wolf man's relatives, who in all probability are themselves witches.

Jimmie Yazzie, he was married to my sister. He was a good man and worked hard and took care of his kids. In the winter he was hunting—looking in the snow for tracks. It was getting pretty dark, and then he saw this coyote or wolf or dog, and it was real close and he shot it. He knew he hit it, but all of a sudden it was gone. So he went home, and the next day he went back to where he had shot that thing, and he found the tracks and blood, and they went to a place under a tree, but they never went away from the tree. The trail away from the tree was a girl's tracks, and they went over to the west toward where an old man and woman lived with their granddaughter. And we heard that she came home one night, and she had been shot and died the next day. So we knew what it was. And that Jimmie Yazzie, he died six months later.

FEAR AS CULTURAL REINFORCEMENT

The complex of mythology, omens, and ritual that make up the "good" aspects of Navajo religion all function to reinforce the structures and attitudes essential to the survival of Navajo society. Stressing the "evil" aspects is no less important in confirming the proper behavior in the Navajo individual.

Many observers have noted that Navajo child training, in keeping with general Navajo interpersonal relationships, is generally lacking in coercive practices. That is, whipping and other corporal punishment to enforce proper behavior does not occur as frequently as it might in a non-Navajo family. However, Navajo make skillful use of terror to instill in their children, and reinforce in adults, the most important attitude in Navajo life—dependence on the immediate relatives of the homestead group. As mentioned earlier, the Navajo seldom travel alone, always preferring to be in groups and preferably groups of relatives. The most innocent departure from this norm is met with great emotion. Members of a family are constantly worried lest some other member "run away" from the family. Even a casual walk by oneself is considered a suspect act. In fact, a desire to be alone and to go for lonely walks is evidence to the individual and to his or her family that something serious is the matter, probably the evil influence of a witch.

To instill this dependence on the group, the Navajo not only encourage loyalty to the family through positive admonition, but also through fear. From infancy, children are exposed to frightening experiences from which they can be extricated only by their mothers or older sisters. A common practice for older children is to dress up in old clothes, often using a coyote or wildcat pelt, and to paint their faces with charcoal and other pigments and appear suddenly to terrorize infants and very young children. The frightened youngsters flee to the arms of their mothers, who usually let them continue their frightened outbursts for several minutes and often add to the fright by pretending fear on their own part. Only when the infant is nearly hysterical with fear does the mother cover its eyes and comfort it and protect it from the horrible monster. Such experiences can only suggest to the infant mind that safety exists solely in relation to mother. The costumed monster may be related to the similar but much more complex institution among the Hopis. The use of fear to instill family adherence is also practiced through the telling of stories about wolf men, witches, and other fearsome beings. Again, as with so many Navajo institutions, there is little formality in the behavior involved. Only after repeated exposures is it possible to realize that what seems like a casual childish prank is a regular activity and is intimately linked to the structure of the society as a whole. Almost every evening, the older children, from eight through twelve years of age, begin to tell stories about evil beings to the younger toddlers and soon have them in a state of abject fear. During this performance, older children and parents watch and listen with much amusement and only in the final extreme of infantile terror offer protecting arms and comforting words. But the cycle does not stop with infants. The teen-age children and adults join in the recounting of tales of witches and wolf men and soon reduce the eight- to twelve-year-olds to states of terror as abject as that of the infants they were previously tormenting. In the telling, the older children and adults usually manage to frighten themselves, and by full dark entire families, fearful of the unknown dangers of the dark and feeling safe only in the protection of their family are crouched in their hogans. Thus, the network of beliefs works from infancy to adulthood to reinforce the idea that only with one's close relatives can one feel safe and only to them can one turn for comfort, aid, and protection. In short, the homestead group is emphasized and reemphasized as the single refuge in an otherwise hostile world. Its needs transcend all others, and its loyalties are more lasting and dependable than all others.

9

Wealth and the Traders

DESPITE THE SCHOOL BUILDINGS, the missionary chapels, the glaring white medical station, and the chapter house, the dominant structure in Nez Ch'ii is the Nez Ch'ii Mercantile Company. In an area where buildings, both native and foreign, tend to be built low, the trading post stands ten feet above the hard packed earth that forms a "town square." Built of native fieldstone in 1918, the trading post has grown over the years to include a cluster of cabins and modern house trailers, a building in which the diesel electric generator rumbles and pops, a wool shed, a service station and garage, the local post office, a small restaurant, and a tangle of holding pens and corrals. A well-shaded wooden porch, fitted with benches, stretches across the front, where double doors open into a gloomy interior.

Although the federal government and the Navajo tribal government and missionaries have had their impact on Nez Ch'ii, their presence is a foreign and dissident element in the community. The trading post, however, stands as an accepted, almost indigenous, institution essential to Nez Ch'ii life. Without the trading post, Navajo culture could never have developed as it has. The role of the trader is as real and as important to Navajo life as is that of the shepherd or the medicine man, and yet the trader is not a Navajo. He is, as are most traders on the reservation, a member of a family that has roots three and more generations deep in the reservation and in Navajo society and that has developed the institution that links Navajo life with the rest of the world.

Status Symbolism

In the popular mind, tribal people are unencumbered by considerations of wealth and status symbolism that so plague the modern American or European. Unfortunately, such an idyllic picture seldom, if ever, exists in reality. It is true that some societies have made adaptations to their environment in such a way that technical and material considerations are minor. In many cases, their level of existence is too low to support competition for food and instead emphasizes sharing. But in almost every case competition for prestige, for control over the activities of other men, is symbolized by a struggle for something. Often the symbols of wealth or importance are not recognized by people unfamiliar with the patterns of foreign cultures. In some cases it may be as ephemeral as supernatural power, acquired fortuitously from the spirit world. Perhaps finely chiseled but totally nonutilitarian blades of obsidian, ornamental plates of copper, the scalps of woodpeckers, elaborate tattooing, or a large number of wives are the goals for which various tribal peoples contend. To a money-oriented modern man such things seem unimportant. The Navajo, however, recognize as wealth much of what their White fellow citizens also consider important. They strive to acquire things that make life easier, more comfortable, or more secure, or that are important enough to influence in their own favor the actions of other men in return for some of these goods. Nonetheless, Navajo economic life has always been one in which men expended efforts in order to secure the necessities rather than amass capital. Many Navajo attitudes about sharing and accumulation of wealth tend to restrict unrestrained accumulation by individuals.

Pressures to share one's good fortune with relatives and a fear of being accused of acquiring wealth by means of witchcraft both restrain the acquisitive impulse, although they most certainly do not suppress it altogether.

For well over a century, the Navajo have been acquainted with and able to handle money. Their own language uses the Spanish term *peso* (Navajo, *beso*) to mean money, and the Navajo counting system reflects experience with various currencies. However, money is not the basis of the traditional Navajo concept of wealth. Money serves only to buy real wealth, that is, "goods."

There are two kinds of "goods" considered to be wealth by the Navajo—hard and soft. Hard goods include silver and turquoise jewelry, saddles, silver horse gear, wagons, and other durable materials. Soft goods include blankets, good clothing —especially plush shirtwaists and satin skirts—tanned buckskins, special flat hand-woven baskets of traditional design, hats, and other less durable items. In describing a person's wealth, a Navajo speaks with awe of a man who owns "eight hats he don't never wear," as well as the number of spare saddles, mule collars, wagons, and shirts he possesses.

The basis of all wealth, however, is livestock. Not only is it possible to trade livestock for any other valuable object or to sell it and obtain money to buy wealth, but animals in and of themselves are wealth and visible symbols of wealth. Traditionally, the Navajo made little distinction in value between individual animals, particularly sheep. Older Navajo speak a bit resentfully of what they consider the unfair, new, and somewhat demeaning practice of weighing individual animals and paying for them by weight. They much prefer a flat "per head" price, even though it might result in a monetary loss overall.

In the past, most certainly the difference in worth between an old and decrepit horse and a fast racer was recognized and the price set accordingly, but nonetheless a horse, any horse, was wealth and a living symbol of its owner's prosperity and importance. Because of this attitude, the Navajo tended to collect great herds of horses, often composed largely of undesirable and unusable animals, but the owning of such a herd conferred too much prestige to ever permit culling it. Similar attitudes toward the mere size of sheep and cattle herds affected the quality of Navajo livestock. This attitude, of course, worked to the disadvantage of the Navajo when articulating with the economy of the rest of the world. Ill-bred sheep had poor wool, which they often shed in large amounts before shearing time. Moreover, it grew in various colors and required laborious separating, thus lowering the price received for wool. The hardy, shaggy near-wild "Navajo" sheep brought virtually no price in the livestock markets, and, consequently, today many live-stock contracts in the Southwest contain a clause guaranteeing that no "Navajo" sheep are present in a lot offered for sale. Similarly, Navajo horses, often under-sized and useful only to a man who had dozens of animals from which to draw, had almost no value to outside traders except as dog food.

Establishment of the Trader

As low as the price might be, Navajo wool did have a value, as did Navajo rugs, sheep pelts, cattle hides, and jewelry. To make a profit on these items the traders began to appear in the Navajo country even before the time of military defeat and incarceration.

These earliest traders were enterprising Mormons pushing into the northern Navajo country from the expanding Mormon settlements in Utah. After the Navajo returned from incarceration, the Mormons began to establish more permanent posts in the northern and western areas of the reservation. In the east, where many Navajo had been forced to depend on government rations during the early years of their return, another type of trader developed. The disbursement of rations was generally in the hands of civilian contractors attached to the army as sutlers.* Always alert to a profit, these men began exchanging surplus rations for whatever wool, hides, or other valuable goods the Navajo might have. Soon, as the Navajo economy became more and more vigorous, the sutlers left the army to establish posts throughout the eastern and central portions of the reservation. Nearly one-half of the over two hundred posts now operating in or near the reservation are operated by the descendents of perhaps a dozen families, Mormon or gentile, that pioneered the trading business among the Navajo.

In order to make a profit, the trader has developed a unique business. He learned quickly that if he was to trade with the independent and haughty Navajo, he must adapt himself to the practices of his customers. A kind of pidgin Navajo called "trader" Navajo was developed to enable the Indian and the White man to do business. He found that he must provide any number of services for his customers for which he received no recompense. The distasteful and dangerous job of burying the dead was often left to the trader. Perhaps a rampaging, sheep-killing bear threatened the herds. More often than not, the trader would be informed, and his customers would then retire and wait for him to kill the animal and thus incur the dangerous wrath of the Bear Spirit. Or perhaps the trader would be called

_____
* Those who provide provisions for an army post; often established in a shop on the post.

upon to represent the local Navajo before the government agent or in court. In later years the trader assumed the role of hiring agent for the railroads as they sought Navajo workers. As such, he also supervised unemployment, injury, and pension claims. In recent years he has begun filling out the income tax returns of those of his customers whose earnings are high enough.

From the trader the Navajo was able to obtain the material goods of the outside world without becoming personally exposed himself to the dangerous presence of foreigners on his homeground. A taste for coffee had been acquired at Fort Sumner, along with a need for sugar. Commercial ground flour was both easier to use than the hand-ground corn flour and available at the trader's when the supply of corn ran out. Manufactured saddles, bridles, harnesses, wagons, ploughs, and yard goods from which to make the new styles of clothing—all served to attract the Navajo to the trader. As the years have passed, more and more items of White material culture, from kerosene lamps to sewing machines, have become irreplaceable to the Navajo and have formed a material foundation for Navajo culture. The Navajo were able to supply the trader with a number of profit-making commodities in exchange, almost all of which were produced by the herds.

WOOL

Wool is clipped in the spring. Even before the snow has melted, the needs of the individual owner may force him to begin shearing. At this time the activity is carried out by the nuclear family of the owner. Later in the spring the entire homestead group cooperates in shearing the bulk of the herd. The wool of individual owners is sold separately in order that their accounts at the trader's may be kept properly. The sale of wool is the first opportunity the Navajo have to earn money each year, and much of the price is used up immediately in settling credit accounts that have built up during the winter.

LAMBS

In the late summer or early fall, the lambs that were dropped in the spring have matured to market weight and are sold to the trader. The trader holds the lambs in his own corrals until large enough numbers have accumulated to sell them to commission agents. In the recent past the combined herd was driven overland to the railhead, but today livestock trucks haul the animals away. Cash and credit from lamb sales provide an economic buffer against the winter. At this time the trader tries to get all credit accounts brought up to date because there will be little income in the Nez Ch'ii area until the following spring.

HIDES

Much of the actual value of the sheep herd must be reckoned in terms of the contribution that it makes to the family food supply. Sheep are killed for home consumption throughout the year. As the hides accumulate, they are taken to the trader and sold as wool pelts. When a large enough number are collected, the trader in turn sells them to agents who eventually resell them to specialized wool-pulling companies that strip them of wool.

RUGS

In most families, some of the spring wool clip is withheld for use in making rugs. The Navajo rug is a distinctive and well-known item, considered part of the ancient tradition of the Navajo. In fact the Navajo were not weavers until they came into contact with the Pueblo peoples who wove cotton cloth. The Navajo adapted their new skill to wool and for the most part turned the job of weaving, which was a male occupation in the Pueblo villages, over to the women. From their own wool they began to weave rough, long-wearing blankets that served as clothing, especially for women, and robes. Old-fashioned Navajo blankets of this sort were known throughout the West. They were, along with buckskins, the principal item of trade between the Navajo and the Pueblo. Until the 1860s, expeditions of Navajo loaded with blankets were a regular feature of the trading year. Apparently, extensive trade was carried on with the Plains tribes with whom blankets were exchanged for buffalo hides, some of which are still prized heirlooms and used for saddle blankets.

The Navajo rug of today, woven in elaborate designs, is very different from early-day blankets. In the 1890s, traders attempting to develop more profit-making products among the Navajo encouraged the weaving of rugs and the use of both traditional and manufactured dyes. In response to the high prices offered, the Navajo quickly abandoned the older blankets and developed an enormously productive rug-weaving industry.

In Nez Ch'ii almost all adult women are weavers, and the rug trade is an important element in the economic life of the area. The standard rug sizes are single and double saddle blankets, that are either approximately 30 × 30 inches or 30 × 60 inches. Larger sizes are regularly woven by the more expert or ambitious weavers. Rugs measuring up to eighteen to twenty feet are occasionally offered. Such an enterprise often requires the work of two or more women and takes more than a year to complete. When contemplating such a rug, the weaver first consults the trader. If her reputation at her craft is good, he arranges to subsidize the work until the rug is brought in, its value being weighed against trade goods advanced and the difference paid in cash or kind. Such rugs often cost the trader from one to two thousand dollars in trade goods and sell on the outside for upwards of four thousand dollars. Although most weaving is done in the summer when the weather is mild enough to allow the weaver to work outside, rugs are produced throughout the year. A homestead group boasting a few able and energetic weavers is fortunate in having a source of regular although not very high income. A saddle blanket can be finished in a day, but larger rugs require weeks or months, so the hourly income of a weaver is not at all high. Girls learn weaving in the same informal manner in which other skills are taught, by watching their mothers and aunts and older sisters. They may be taught to card wool when still toddlers, be instructed in spinning before they are ten, and begin experimenting on small looms well before they reach puberty. When their work is judged adequate, it is taken to the trader. No matter how uneven and badly made the rug may be, he is wise to make an offer and thus not offend a supplier.

The Navajo themselves use only the smaller rugs as saddle blankets. Large rugs and the bulk of the saddle blankets are made entirely for sale and are never used by the Navajo themselves. The Navajo rug is almost a symbol of the relationship between the people and the trader. Distinctly Navajo in style and technique, it is a product of the combining of the traditions and needs of the Navajo and the Americans, and its utility to the Navajo depends on the trader's acting as agent of its sale. Ironically, when a Navajo wants a soft, colorful "Indian Blanket" to wear, he purchases one made in a factory and sold at the trader's.

JEWELRY

The Spanish and Mexicans taught the Indians of the Southwest how to work silver, most frequently combined with the traditional turquoise. Today silver and turquoise, like the Navajo rug, are considered by most people to be traditional Indian crafts. Many Navajo did in fact become silversmiths, selling or trading their products to other Navajo. However, in the Nez Ch'ii area there have been no smiths for many years, and most jewelry is purchased from trading posts or from smiths elsewhere, particularly among the Pueblo people who practice the art much more intensively than the Navajo.

Both men and women wear jewelry—earrings, necklaces, bracelets, leather and silver wrist guards, rings, belt buckles and belts, and silver buttons and plaques sewn to clothing.

Jewelry is prized for its beautifying and decorative effect, but its primary function is as a repository and visible symbol of a person's wealth and status. Public occasions such as sheep dippings, brandings, Squaw Dances, rodeos, and so on are deemed proper occasions for the display of all the family's jewelry. Competitions or disputes between families is often marked by the sudden appearance of all the jewelry that can be mustered, and it is displayed on every occasion over a period of weeks until one or the other of the disputing parties ends the contest and tacitly admits defeat. Jewelry can be used to buy anything in exchanges between Navajo, but its primary economic function is to insure credit. All trading posts are also pawn shops and receive in pawn almost any item—saddles, guns, spurs, watches, boots, blankets—but the most common article of pawn is jewelry. Pawned for cash or to build a credit reserve to be drawn upon, especially during the winter, jewelry serves to meet economic emergencies and provide some buffer against the lean months of the winter. Most traders hold pawned jewelry long after the legal limit has expired, and many do not sell expired pawn belonging to regular customers without first asking if they intend to redeem the piece in question. When pawned jewelry is not redeemed, it is first displayed in the trader's store for sale to other Navajo or finally sold to large jewelry-buying firms, operating from Gallup, New Mexico, and from there transferred into the marketplace.

Thus, while jewelry generates a great deal of economic activity, it cannot really be considered a product of the area because it was first purchased from the outside before entering into the economics of Nez Ch'ii. In the past a person's jewelry was buried with him when he died. Rich men were often accused of grave robbery as an explanation of their good fortune. However, today most jewelry is passed on to offspring or siblings before the death of an old person so the family does not lose this important capital investment.

RITUAL TRADE

The Nez Ch'ii trading post stocks and displays several thousand items of food and merchandise. Of these, only some pieces of jewelry and rugs are of Navajo manufacture. There are, however, two other items of Indian origin regularly stocked by the trader as part of his traditional service to the community—buckskins and baskets.

Both the flat handwoven basket and the tanned buckskin are prized, often required payment in certain ritual contexts. The baskets, particularly, are required in the course of curing ceremonies and as part payment to the singer. In neither case is there any utilitarian or real commercial value attached to the items. To serve his customer, the trader keeps a number of baskets of varying size and quality and a number of buckskins on hand. He sells these at a standard price to Navajo, and usually the day after the ceremony buys them back from the singer's wife at a slightly lower price. The baskets and hides circulate and recirculate in the area, the trader earning a few dollars at every exchange. The baskets are usually acquired from the northwestern portion of the reservation where there are a number of "Navajoized" Paiute families that retain the art of basket weaving, which has, by and large, been abandoned by the Navajo. Buckskins occasionally are brought in by men who have been successful in hunting expeditions off-reservation. The hides, tanned by traditional methods, bring a good price at the trader's, but the appearance of a new hide in the system is very rare.

The Store

The pace of commerce in Nez Ch'ii is leisurely. Inside the high-ceilinged main salesroom of the Nez Ch'ii Mercantile Company, one or two White and several Indian clerks move from customer to customer waiting along the counter. Sitting directly in front of the "pawn room" on a high stool behind a glass display counter with the cash is the trader, supervising the issuance of credit, receiving payment of accounts, and evaluating rugs and jewelry for purchase or pawn. Behind him, the pawn room is festooned with thousands of items of turquoise jewelry, guns, saddles, hat bands, even an occasional bow and arrow set offered in pawn by an old man, and perhaps a medicine bundle pawned by a desperate singer. To serve an old customer and on the off chance a museum or collector might want such items the trader accepts them. The pawn room, in all traditional stores, is made solidly of rock and cement and entered through a safe vault door.

The Navajo does not hurry his shopping. The store is the focal point of the community; it is a place to chat with friends, catch up on the news, flirt with girls, or negotiate with the informal prostitutes who generally operate near the store. Here, too, he can contact the bootlegger and with a few friends buy some illegal wine for a drinking party in back of the trader's corrals. On days when people have other reasons to come to Nez Ch'ii, such as Tuesday when the doctor makes his weekly visit or on days when unemployment checks or federal wool-incentive payments arrive, the store is packed from eight in the morning until well after dark. The trader, who is also the postmaster, already knows which of his customers has received a check and has prepared his accounts in advance, attempting to settle outstanding debts and at the same time encumber remaining funds. Even in these times of pick-up trucks or automobiles, a trip to the store is seldom short. A half-day seems to be the least time one spends in chatting, bargaining, and buying, no matter how small the purchase.

CREDIT

Like most general stores in rural areas, the Nez Ch'ii Mercantile Company operates largely on credit. Goods are advanced against seasonal income, wool, rugs, lambs, and, increasingly, seasonal wage work. During much of the year very little cash changes hands over the counters of the trading post, and the trader virtually finances the social life of the region for much of the time. In a very real sense, the survival of the Navajo people depends on the willingness and ability of the trader to extend credit. His own credit operations are dominated by the willingness of large wholesale companies off-reservation to extend credit to him and by the surety that eventually his customers will pay their bills in cash or products.

At the same time, the trader must maintain a relationship with his customers that insures that once they have settled their accounts, they will continue to charge merchandise at his store. To this end he must conduct a continuous public relations campaign attuned to the tenor of Navajo life. Even the most heavily indebted Navajo must, in all probability, be given more credit to finance a sing or assist in financing a Squaw Dance or *Yeibeichai* dance. Certain products brought in by Indians and sold will be exchanged for cash, even though the seller has a large account outstanding. In some areas, rugs brought in are not charged against credit, although they are in Nez Ch'ii. The trader is also expected to make contributions in the form of extra food to families staging Squaw Dances. And when his other customers buy candy and fruit as gifts for the hosts of a Squaw Dance, a wise trader makes sure his clerks throw an extra measure into the bag. Ceremonial requirements also affect the trader's inventory in other ways. Skeins of colored wool are important as gifts and for the decoration of horses, wagons, and, in recent times, automobiles and trucks during the "race" on the first evening of a Squaw Dance. A trader caught short of wool not only misses many sales but seriously disturbs his customers.

IMPORTANCE OF TRUST

Since the turn of the century, at least, Navajo material and economic culture has been dependent on the trader. Until recently, each trader had by virtue of extended credit and isolation a virtual monopoly in this area. For some of these men, the temptation to exploit his often illiterate customers by holding them in debt peonage, issuing his own currency redeemable at his store only, manipulating accounts, and overcharging and underpaying, was too great to resist. Today, government and tribal regulations prohibit these practices, and the increasing education and sophistication of the Navajo limit the ability of the sharp dealer. However, most traders have been honest and responsible figures in Navajo life and have related to the Navajo not only as customers but also as clients. The trader too amenable to sharp practice or unable to adjust to the very special style of business expected by the Navajo found that his apparently secure monopolistic position was not as secure as it had seemed. The Navajo needed not any particular person as trader but rather the trading post itself, operating in an expected and accustomed manner. More than a few traders have gone bankrupt because the Navajo, preferring to make long trips to other stores or tighten their belts and do without, simply refused to do business with them. Faced with such a boycott, such traders had little to do save sell out at as little loss as possible and move to another field. The continued successes of the dozen or so old-line trading families on the reservation must be credited in large part to their willingness to accept and adjust to the Navajo style of life, which they often do not understand.

Just as the Navajo must feel a rather personal confidence in the trader, he also must feel trust in the trader's products. Building an inventory for a trading post is a far cry from the popular view of collecting shoddy and cheap merchandise to be palmed off on unsuspecting "natives." Rather, the Navajo is a hard-headed customer, stubbornly loyal to products that have served him well and generally suspicious of new products. In a largely illiterate population, familiar and unchanging labels are of great importance. Carnation and Pet brands of condensed milk are purchased even though other brands might be cheaper. In 1960 an attempt of a new milk company to introduce its products by pricing them far below the market tempted many traders to stock them in the hope that the low prices would bring in customers. Some of the low-priced milk still remains unpurchased on traders' shelves. High quality, able to stand up to the rough usage of Navajo life, is demanded of housewares, riding gear, boots, and tools. Shoddy material may be sold once, but seldom will it be purchased again, and a trader known for such merchandise will soon find his customers going elsewhere.

Agent of Change

Today, paved roads and motor vehicles have made it possible for the individual Navajo to shop by visiting other trading posts and stores in off-reservation towns. The trading post is increasingly becoming a counterpart of the off-reservation department store, with cash sales predominating. However, in Nez Ch'ii and other remote areas such as Shonto and Navajo Mountain, the trading post remains as the central feature of the economic life and the physical nexus of social interaction.

The trader has been the most effective agent of change among the Navajo, much to the chagrin of the missionary and government agent. However, his impact has been in the material and economic fields. His success, in all probability, rests on the fact that he has made no attempt to challenge basic Navajo beliefs and practices and has exerted no pressure against Navajo social organization. Even today, the Navajo tribe feels compelled to consult with the trader's associations when it plans large-scale or dramatic programs or actions that might affect the economic life of the reservation.

References

ABERLE, DAVID F. "Navajo." In David M. Schneider and Kathleen Gough (Eds.), *Matrilineal Kinship*. Berkeley: University of California Press, 1961.

————. *The Peyote Religion among the Navaho*. Chicago: Aldine, 1968.

DOWNS, J. F. "Animal Husbandry in Navajo Society and Culture." *Anthropology*, Vol. 1, No. 1. University of California, 1964.

————. *The Two Worlds of the Washo*. Case Studies in Cultural Anthropology. New York: Holt, Rinehart and Winston, 1965.

FRANCISCAN FATHERS. *An Ethnological Dictionary of the Navajo Language*. Navajo Indian Mission, St. Michael's, Arizona, 1910.

KLUCKHOHN, CLYDE, AND DOROTHEA LEIGHTON. *The Navaho*. Cambridge, Mass.: Harvard University Press, 1946.

REICHARD, ALICE. *Navaho Religion*. Bollingen Series. New York: Pantheon, 1950.

SASAKI, TOM, AND JOHN ADAIR. "New Land To Farm." In E. H. Spicer (Ed.), *Human Problems in Technological Change*. New York: Russell Sage Foundation, 1952.

YOUNG, ROBERT. *The Navajo Yearbook*. Navajo Agency, Window Rock, Arizona, 1958.

THE VICE LORDS: WARRIORS OF THE STREETS

R. Lincoln Keiser

Wesleyan University

R. Lincoln Keiser first developed an interest in Black ghetto culture while working as a caseworker for the Cook County Department of Public Aid in 1962–1963. During this time he gathered the material for *Hustler! The Autobiography of a Thief* (1965)—the life history of a small-time criminal who operated on the streets of one of Chicago's Black ghettos. Later he worked as a court caseworker in Boys Court North, a Chicago Municipal Court, and through this work first met members of the Vice Lords. He has his Ph.D. from the University of Rochester. He has conducted field research in the Hindu-Kush Mountains of northeastern Afghanistan. He is professor of anthropology at Wesleyan University.

Preface

The Vice Lord Nation is a large federation of street-corner groups whose home is the streets, alleys, and gangways of Chicago's major Black ghettos. Groups such as the Vice Lords—generally called delinquent gangs—are a popular subject for both the urban press and social scientists of various disciplines. In reading the scientific and popular literature on delinquent gangs one finds little attempt to provide a clear picture of the social and cultural systems of these groups. The aim of the press is to report news, while that of many sociologists and social psychologists interested in delinquent gangs is to construct theories explaining delinquent behavior. However, all groups and associations have structure, systems of organizations, and sets of commonly held values, and it is apparent from the hints found in the academic and popular literature that the so-called deviant or delinquent groups are no exception to the general social rule. What we classify as delinquency is only a part of a larger behavioral system, and if we are going to understand it, we have to understand the system as a whole. Thus, a study of a delinquent gang in its own right seemed worth the effort. I chose the Vice Lords for two reasons: the Vice Lords were reputed to be one of the largest and best-organized delinquent gangs in Chicago; and by chance I was able to establish a friendship with several Vice Lords who were willing to help with the research project. The first part of the research consisted solely of work with informants. It was conducted in 1964–1965 while I was employed by the Social Service Department of the Municipal Court of Chicago. In the summers of 1966 and 1967, after graduate training in social anthropology, I conducted field research in the Lawndale area of Chicago's West Side ghetto with a subgroup of the Vice Lords known as the City Lords. Through a Vice Lord I had known previously, I approached the leaders of the club, explained that I wanted to write a book about the Vice Lords, and offered to share any royalties with the club. The proposal was put before the club in a meeting and a majority of the members gave their approval.

The major purpose of this book is to provide a systematic description of the Vice Lord way of life. Actually constructing such a description, however, presents difficulties. In any field study an anthropologist observes wide variations in behavior that must be organized and interpreted in written form. In this study, culture and social system are basic organizing concepts. There are many ways to define these concepts, and the definitions used in this study are not necessarily the only correct ones. However, they did prove useful to me in making sense out of the wide behavioral variations I observed in Vice Lord life. The definitions of culture and social system provided by Clifford Geertz are followed in this study.

One of the more useful ways—but far from the only one—of distinguishing between culture and social system is to see the former as an ordered system of meaning and symbols in terms of which social interaction takes place; and to see the latter as the pattern of social interaction itself. . . . On the one level there is the framework of beliefs, expressive symbols, and values in terms of which individuals define their world, express their feelings, and make their judgements; on the other level there is the ongoing process of interactive behavior, whose persistent form we call social structure. Culture is the fabric of meaning in terms of which human beings interpret their experience and guide their action; social structure is the form that action takes, the actually existing network of social relations. Culture and social structure are then but different abstractions from the same phenomena. The one considers social action in respect to its meaning for those who carry it out, the other considers it in terms of its contribution to the functioning of some social system (Geertz 1957: 33–34).

Rather than give examples here from my observations of the behavior of the Vice Lords to illustrate these concepts, I will let my applications of them in the case study following speak for themselves.

However, it must be granted that the terms "culture" and "social system" are abstractions. They help the anthropologist to organize his observations. I have attempted to enliven the analysis and bring it closer to the reality of life among the Vice Lords by providing anecdotal observations of specific situations, events, and people. My observations, my selection of anecdotes, and surely my interpretations of what I saw and heard are consistently colored by my own biases, known and unknown. In order to provide some correction for these biases, I have turned to an individual, who sees the events, people, and situations I have described from an outsider's point of view, from the inside. In the last section of this book, after the culture and the social system of the Vice Lord Nation have been described, we shall view the Vice Lord world from the standpoint of the individual actor through the means of autobiography of one named Cupid.

It is impossible to adequately describe Vice Lord life without designating individuals by name. For their protection, therefore, no one has been designated by his real name. However, the names have not been made up by me, but are those actually used by members of the Vice Lords and other rival groups.

This book could not have been written without the help of others. I owe my greatest thanks to my wife Lynn for her constant encouragement and suggestions. I also profited from criticisms made by the faculty and graduate students of the Department of Anthropology, University of Rochester, and other friends. Specifically, thanks are owed to Marie Asnes, Warren Barbour, Dan Bauer, Arnold Green, Jane Guyer, David Jacobson, Sue Jacobson, Ghislane Lecours, Karl North, March Plume, Charles Scruggs, and George Scruggs, all of whom read and criticized various parts of the manuscript. Naturally, however, I bear all responsibility for the final version of the work.

R. Lincoln Keiser

Middletown, Conn.
August 1969

Contents

1

Vice Lord Development

EFORE BEGINNING OUR DISCUSSION of the Vice Lords' social and cultural system, it would be useful to look at the origin and subsequent growth of the group. The Vice Lords originated and have become differentiated and elaborated in an extremely short time. The "facts" presented in later chapters will make more sense if viewed against the background of Vice Lord development.

The description in this chapter is not presented as "historical fact." My aim is not to describe what happened, but what Vice Lords believe happened, for these beliefs affect Vice Lord behavior in the present. The data were gathered from a number of informants, and their accounts did not always completely correspond. Nevertheless, there was general agreement about broad lines of development.

It is generally stated that the Vice Lord Nation—referred to by Vice Lords as a "club," not a gang—originated in 1958 in what is usually called "Charlie Town," the Illinois State Training School for Boys at St. Charles, Illinois. In St. Charles the inmates live in what are called "cottages." The Vice Lords began in Harding Cottage, which housed the toughest boys in the institution. The club was started in the Lawndale area of Chicago in the fall of 1958, following the release of several members.

Lawndale has long been a breeding ground for "delinquent" groups primarily organized for fighting. Even before the area became predominantly Black, Polish and Jewish groups in Lawndale engaged in fierce gang fighting. (Short 1963:xxvi) After the area changed from White to Black, the fighting-gang pattern was continued by Black groups. One of the early Black fighting gangs in Lawndale was called the Clovers. At the time the Vice Lords first returned to Chicago from St. Charles, the Clovers were breaking up. Its members were getting older (approaching 20), and the group came under increasingly heavy pressure from a newer club called the Egyptian Cobras.

The Cobras had originally started in the Maxwell Street open-market area of Chicago's Near West Side known as "Jew Town." Later, a branch of the Cobras was initiated in a part of the West Side ghetto to the west of the Clovers called "K-Town" (because all the street names begin with K), and therefore this particular branch was called the K-Town Cobras. The K-Town Cobras soon increased in power and came into conflict with the older, more established Clovers. A boy living in the Clovers neighborhood who later became an important member of the Vice Lords tells the following story about the gang war between the Cobras and the Clovers:

> See, there was this humbug [fight] between the Clovers and the Egyptian Cobras. A boy got killed in that humbug. A Clover, a stud named Walker, got his head burned [shot] off with a shotgun, Jack! See, the Clovers, they was pretty old then. They had been out a long time, and they had their name. But the Cobras had just come out that summer [1957]in K-Town. And they started to fight the Clovers. The Clovers, they were established. They had their reputation. Now if the Cobras had fought them a couple of years before, they couldn't have done nothing with them. But by then all the Clovers were old and tired. So the Cobras hurt them, and that's when the Cobras first got their name.

In the fall of 1958 the members of the newly created Vice Lords moved into a section of the Clovers' old neighborhood vacated during the decline in Clover power. At this point there is a major divergence between accounts. One informant stated that many of the original members of the Vice Lords had previously belonged to a group known as the Imperial Chaplains located to the east of the Clovers. When the members of the Vice Lords returned to Chicago, they decided to start their own branch of the Imperials called the Imperial Vice Lords. The Imperial Vice Lords did not remain a branch for long. Friction developed between the two groups, and fighting broke out at a party at which both were present. Although the Lords were outnumbered, they won the fight, injuring several Imperials in the process. This established the Vice Lords as a group completely independent of the Imperials, and from then on the club was known as the Conservative[1] Vice Lord Nation.

Another informant told a different story. He said that the Vice Lords never were a part of the Imperial Chaplains. When the members of the Lords returned to Lawndale from St. Charles, they decided to continue the group as a small club organized for social (sponsoring parties) purposes. The original Lords had been members of many different fighting gangs—the Apaches, the Thunderbirds, the Golden Hawks, the Vampires, and the Imperial Chaplains. At first the club's activities consisted solely of giving parties, and hanging together. Slowly, the group grew until, almost inevitably, fighting developed with both the Cobras to the west in K-Town and the Imperial Chaplains to the east. It is my feeling that this latter version is probably closer to the actual fact, since (1) it is corroborated by other accounts; and (2) the informant who gave the account actually took part in this period of the group's development. The earlier version came from a Vice Lord who was in St. Charles during this time, and who was repeating stories told to him.

The first big jump in Vice Lord membership came from an alliance with a club called the El Commandoes. The El Commandoes was later completely absorbed by the Vice Lords. Like the early Vice Lords, the El Commandoes was primarily a

---

[1] Conservative refers to a reserved manner of dressing and acting.

social rather than a fighting group. Cave Man, one of the original Lords from St. Charles (and reputed by some to be the actual founder of the club), had previously been a member of the El Commandoes. When he returned to Lawndale, the alliance was made between the two groups. At first Cave Man's mother allowed the club to use the basement of her house for meetings and parties, but after several fights, the group was forced to give its parties in small rented halls and other basements. At parties such as these the group giving the affair furnishes something to drink, often a weak punch, and charges a small admission fee of 25 or 50 cents. The group usually makes a small amount of money which is used to finance future parties.

Social groups organized by a small group of friends to give parties are common in the Black ghettos of Chicago, and most do not develop into large federations of street-corner groups. That the Vice Lords developed in this direction can, I feel, be attributed to the power vacuum created by the decline of the Clovers. As the Cobras to the west, and the Imperial Chaplains to the east grew in strength, pressure was exerted on unorganized boys living in the Clovers' territory. This pressure consisted of shakedowns, demands that nonaffiliated individuals join one of the two groups, attempts to monopolize girls in the neighborhood, and fights and threats against the unorganized boys. It was probably inevitable that some group would become the rallying point for resistance against this pressure.

The Vice Lords became the rallying point following two incidents. The first began at a dance at which both Vice Lords and Cobras were present. During the course of the evening a Vice Lord and a Cobra argued over a girl. At the time the argument was considered inconsequential, but later, it took on major importance. Following the dance the Vice Lords went to a restaurant and by chance met a group of Cobras. The Vice Lords were wearing their special club capes, and each boy had an earring in one ear. The curiosity of the Cobras was aroused, and when the Vice Lords were asked why they were dressed in this manner, they explained it was the uniform of their new club. At first the Cobras suggested that the Vice Lords merge with them, but this offer was refused, and the Cobras decided to fight. The excuse the Cobras used was the argument that had taken place at the dance. The Cobra who had first been involved recognized the Vice Lord he had argued with and began to insult him. The Vice Lord, a boy named Bird (who later became supreme war counselor) hit the Cobra with a chair, which started a fight between the two groups. The Vice Lords claimed that the Cobras were not able to win—which may, or may not, be true. In any case the Vice Lords' claim that they had evenly matched the Cobras was the story spread throughout their neighborhood.

The second incident took place at a dance given by the Imperial Chaplains. Following is a Vice Lord's account of this incident:

> There was only a few of us there at this dance, and the Imperials, they jumped on [jump on, beat up] us for something, and this was when we first started fighting them. Like I said, there wasn't very many of us, but we made such a good fight at this showing that our name went out. See, a lot of the Imperials got hurt, and there was just us few. That's where we got our rep [reputation] from . . . you know, when we're outnumbered and still whupping ass.

After these incidents more individuals in the neighborhood joined the group and it grew to about 25 members. The original members still felt, however, that the club should remain primarily a social group. Their feelings began to change after the Cobras delivered a threatening message that the Lords had "only one more night left to live." Soon after, when several Imperial Chaplains broke into the basement of Cave Man's house (still used for club meetings), tore the furniture apart, and set fire to the basement, many of the Vice Lords decided that some kind of retaliation was necessary. A meeting was called to decide on a course of action. While many members did not feel the club was strong enough to fight either the Imperial Chaplains or the Cobras, a few of the more influential leaders had decided that the group could no longer remain simply a social club. According to one of the Lords present at this meeting:

> Everybody said, "Man, what can we do . . . against clubs as large as the Cobras and the Imperials?" So Bird said, "Well, one thing we can do is when we get ready to come down on any club, we send twenty guys home—tell them to go anywhere—watch TV. The five of us left will come down with guns, and after we shoot up a couple of studs we'll go back to our neighborhood and go home. We won't stay there and fight, we'll just go home . . . period! And when they come back through our neighborhood, they won't find nothing. We got to stop them from hurting us. We can't go on like this." So that's what we decided to do.

At this point in the Vice Lords' development, there was no institutionalized formal organization. There were no formal leadership positions and no formally recognized cleavages within the group. However, there were recognized leaders whose power stemmed from personal charisma. These leaders recognized that if the Vice Lords were to withstand both the Cobras and the Imperial Chaplains, they would have to increase their membership, for only with a larger group could they (1) control their neighborhood and thus protect themselves from surprise attacks; and (2) more evenly match their opponents in gang-fighting encounters.

The Vice Lords approached the task of recruiting new members in several different ways. Both the non-affiliated boys and other existing small clubs were potential sources of new members, but each posed different problems in recruitment. The methods used to recruit nonaffiliated boys were explained to me as follows:

> What we did, we did a survey of the neighborhood. We found out that there was fellows that was not accepted by any club for one reason or another—maybe a guy was disliked 'cause he had jumped on somebody, or because he wouldn't join some club. So we approached him from a different angle. First, instead of trying to scare him into becoming a part of our group, we tried to gain his friendship. See, what a lot of clubs didn't realize is that if a guy's your friend, he automatically be with you in a humbug [fight]. But what they would come through with, "You either join our club or we'll do this or we'll do that." We didn't do that. We said, "Well . . . ah . . . the Imperials are falling down on us, the Cobras are falling down on us. We got to do something about this, man! We can't keep being abused by these clubs. What we going to do, we going to get together and look out for our hoods [neighborhoods]."
>
> Now see, by him being tight with us, when the Cobras or the Imperials fall down on us, they going to fall down on him too. By making him our friend, automatically we make him the enemy of the other group. He only have one support, and that's to stay within the body that's with him.

Different tactics were necessary in recruiting new members from the smaller clubs located in various West Side neighborhoods. Many of these clubs were engaged in gang wars with stronger rivals. The Vice Lords supported these groups in their wars, and in return these clubs became subgroups of the Vice Lords. In other instances the Vice Lords entered alliances with groups which were also under pressure from the Cobras and Imperials, and slowly these groups began to consider themselves Vice Lords. According to my informants, a club called the Spanish Counts, with about twenty to twenty-five was absorbed into the Vice Lords in this manner. Although this club was small, several Spanish Counts had well-known gang-fighting reputations, and the Vice Lords' prestige was enhanced by the addition of these members.

Following the alliance with the Spanish Counts, the Vice Lords began a systematic attack on a club called the Imperial Knights, a group located between the Imperial Chaplains and the Cobras. While this group had previously refused all overtures for an alliance with the Vice Lords, the combined strength of the Spanish Counts and the Vice Lords was now too great for them, and finally, after a prolonged period of gang warfare, they agreed to become Vice Lords.

Possibly these various clubs would not have successfully merged if it had not been for intensified pressure from both the Cobras and Imperials. Both these groups renewed their threats to crush the Vice Lords, and began an all out attack. By this time it was too late. The addition of new members gave the Vice Lords added strength, and the increased prestige of the group continued to bring in new members—many with established gang-fighting reputations. In talking about this stage in the club's development one of my informants gave the following account, which reads something like the catalog of warriors in the Iliad:

From the Imperial Knights we got guys like Fresh Up Freddie, Wade, Lil' Bull, Pole Cat, Napoleon, Goat, Duck; from the Clovers we got Cherokee, Prince G.G., Peanut, Hawk, and the Satisfier; from the Camancheroes came Sonny Boy Brown, Willy B., Blinkey; and from the Braves came Carlos, Zenith, and Blue Goose. Now all of these guys had reputations all around the West Side, and when other guys got together you could hear them talk about it. You could walk past (because they didn't know whether you was a part of the Vice Lords or not), and you'd hear them say, 'Those Vice Lords got some terrible guys in they group. You going to have to put up some strong resistance to stop them!'

Even with this increase in strength, however, the Vice Lords would have been at a definite disadvantage if the Cobras and the Imperials had been able to cooperate successfully. During a battle with the Vice Lords, however, the brother of the Cobras' president was accidentally shot by an Imperial, and a gang war between the Cobras and the Imperials resulted. This placed the Vice Lords in an advantageous position, since the Cobras now blamed Vice Lord attacks on the Imperials, while the Imperials blamed them on the Cobras.

In 1962 the Imperials began to break up, and from then on were less of a threat to the Vice Lords. In contrast, the war with the Cobras intensified, and in 1961 and 1962 flared out in numerous battles in which members of both clubs were killed. This is how a Vice Lord describes one of the early battles in the war with the Cobras:

One night we really found out whether or not we was ready. Almost every Cobra from the South Side, down Jew Town way, K-Town, and some of the King Cobras from the North Side all came over to the YMCA. We was in the gym playing ball—there was about fifty of us in there. They had gave what is called a bunking party. All the fellows would come over, play sports, eat, and at night they'd lock the doors and you'd sleep there. So both the Cobras and our fellows was there. And Lil' Herk in our club and Lil' Herk in the Cobras, they got to arguing about something that happened between them and a broad. So Herk said, "Well, man . . . I don't want to see all the fellows fighting, so what we'll do, me and you just go." So they took they shirts off, and they got ready to humbug. But Crazy Horse, they president, he came over and said, "No! If one Cobra fight, we all fight!" And Rico, he was in there at the time. Rico was one of the original seven in the Lords. So when the fight starts, Rico and Crazy Horse took over the picture, and everybody stop—just watching them, more or less. But when the real force of the Cobras come up from downstairs to fight, that's when the humbug really broke out. See, we got the best of that fight 'cause really, the Cobras that had they guns was stuck outside because the door was locked and they couldn't get in.

Following the growth in the Vice Lords' membership, there was a corresponding institutionalization in organization: (1) groups of Vice Lords from various parts of the West Side formed into distinct subgroups called "branches" which were joined in a loosely knit federation; (2) within each branch leadership became institutionalized in specific positions; (3) age categories were set up which crosscut the branches; and (4) within branches, particular groups were given specific duties. We have already mentioned that many of the smaller clubs which the Vice Lords absorbed became distinct branches. In other instances groups of Vice Lords occupying neighborhoods some distance from the club's core territory also became separate branches. Following the establishment of branches, the original group centered at 16th and Lawndale became known as the City Lords, since they controlled that portion of the club's territory called Vice Lord City. Other important branches were: the Monroe Lords on Monroe Street, the Maypole Lords on Maypole Avenue, the California Lords, the Sacramento Lords, the 5th Avenue Lords, and the Albany Lords.

Within each branch, and for the club as a whole, leadership was institutionalized in positions. This development was a conscious response by the Vice Lords to the high probability that particular leaders would be arrested. The police approach to the problems posed by fighting clubs is to jail the leaders in hopes that the group will then dissolve. The Vice Lords solved this problem by developing leadership positions which provided an effective mechanism for replacing leaders jailed by the police. With the Vice Lords' newly gained size, there were many boys with leadership ability, and when a particular leader was arrested, another individual was chosen to occupy the vacated position.

Each branch was subdivided into age groupings called "Seniors," "Juniors," and "Midgets." In some branches there were even "Pee Wee" Vice Lords. Many of these formed particular subgroups within branches, each electing their own set of officers. In other instances these were social categories rather than functional groups. The age criteria of these groupings varied from branch to branch, and in any case were never completely rigid.

Writing the club name on a wall.

Branches were further subdivided into what I call cliques, some of which were entrusted with particular responsibilities. These groups were composed of a small number of individuals who "hung" together. An example of a clique entrusted with a specific responsibility is the Spy Patrol. This group never took part in gang fighting, but watched other clubs' activities, and reported what they saw to the president of the City Lords. At the time I did my research the Spy Patrol was no longer functioning, and my informants were not able to give more specific details about this group.

In 1962 the war with the Cobras reached its peak, and then began to wane. This was due to a variety of factors. The YMCA, through its detached worker program, was successful in reaching leaders of both the Vice Lords and the Cobras, and detached workers were often able to head off gang fights. Further, Black Nationalism began to influence boys in each group, and this acted as a check on gang fighting. According to several informants, after the sniper killing of a Black high school student in South Lawndale, a predominantly Polish neighborhood, both Vice Lords and Cobras united in retaliatory raids. Following is a Vice Lords account of this particular incident:

What happened, this guy was coming from school and he was shot and killed. It was in a gray hood [White neighborhood]. There was mostly Polish living over there. I guess they killed him 'cause he was a Negro. He wasn't doing nothing, just walking down the street coming from school . . . with two other studs. And the Man [the police] didn't know who did it. Anyway, he say he didn't. I guess it could have been anybody in the hood.

And when this happened . . . well, I don't know just exactly how it was, but everybody just thought the same way. The Lords decided to go on over there, and some kind of way we ended up with the Cobras too. It was just that everybody was out there, all the groups on the West Side. And we went through the high school over there, and the neighborhood every day and every night after that! And we dusted everybody we saw, Jack—tearing up property—we turned over cars—we did everything!

You know, before that, any time we went over there—in South Lawndale—we almost always would get dusted, or maybe even killed. But now they think twice . . . especially the older people because they have more at stake. Now you get some young studs, they might do it. You always got fools anywhere you go . . . that don't care really. But they'll think twice before they do it now. And that's why I say like Malcolm X, "Violence sometimes serves its purpose."

However, fighting between the Vice Lords and Cobras continued to flare up intermittently, and even during the time of my field work fights between groups of the two clubs still occurred.

After 1962 definite signs of stress in the Vice Lord organization began to show. During this time there were several feuds between various subgroups within the Vice Lord federation. Some of these feuds were between branches, while others were between individuals competing for the leadership of a particular branch. Following the imprisonment of many of the older boys who had been important leaders in the club's early days, the solidarity of the Vice Lord federation weakened even further. There was little communication between branches, and many branch leaders did not even know one another. Further, the original branch, the City Lords, became divided into what were called "sections." These sections were cliques which had developed into subbranches. Each section had a different name and set of officers. One section called the St. Louis Lords tried to gain even more autonomy from the City Lords by changing their name from Conservative Vice Lords to Mighty Vice Lords, and even went so far as to start their own female auxiliary known as the Supreme Queens. All girls connected with the club had previously been called Vice Ladies.

Sometime during 1963, the Imperial Chaplains completely broke up, and a short time later a new club, called the Roman Saints, was formed in a part of the Imperials' old neighborhood. It was not long before various branches of the Vice Lords became involved in gang fights with this new group. However, the fighting between the Vice Lords and the Roman Saints was never as intense as that between the Vice Lords and Cobras, although intermittent conflicts with the Roman Saints continued to the time of my field work.

In the summer of 1966 there was a new development in the Vice Lords' organization. This was brought about by several circumstances. First, the jail terms of many of the original leaders terminated. These individuals were no longer boys, but ranged in age from about 23 to 26. Rather than give up their gang membership, they decided to stay in the group. They also brought new members, other men their age, into the Vice Lords. Second, the Blackstone Rangers, a fighting club located on the South Side, began to receive newspaper publicity due to a gang war with the Devil's Disciples. In fact, one of Chicago's daily newspapers ran a week-long series on this group. In this series it was stated that the Blackstone Rangers were perhaps the toughest, best organized gang Chicago had seen for some time. In reaction to this series I heard comments from Vice Lords about how the group was falling apart; how they used to have an organization, but it was going downhill. Finally, after the riots which occurred on the West Side in the summer of 1966, the feelings of many Vice Lords turned away from Black Nationalism. I was told that some Black Nationalist groups had made promises to the Vice Lords that were not kept. At this time there was also an increase in hostile incidents between groups of Vice Lords and Roman Saints and Cobras. A meeting was called to discuss the future of the club. Although I was not present, I was told later that Bull, who was a member of a militant Black Nationalist organization, had spoken out against a resumption of gang fighting. He felt that all the clubs on the West Side should stop fighting among themselves and unite against the Whites. Others thought that the club's first responsibility was to protect its own members. I was told that, in answer to Bull, another Vice Lord said, "The Cobras may be my 'brothers,' but if one of them mother fuckers jump on me I'll bust a cap in his ass [shoot him]!" The overwhelming number of Vice Lords felt that the group should reorganize to protect themselves and their neighborhoods from hostile clubs, and to re-establish the reputation lost to the Blackstone Rangers. According to my informant, Bull might have been jumped on for his views if he had not left the meeting early.

The decision was made to reorganize the club, and the responsibility for working out the details was given to a group composed of representatives from each branch, along with the older individuals that had just been released from prison. The most important element in the new organizational scheme which resulted from the discussions of this group was the creation of an administrative body called the "board" to deal with matters affecting the entire Vice Lord Nation. Further, regular weekly meetings were instituted with representatives from all the subgroups present. Finally membership cards were printed with the Vice Lord's insignia—a top hat, cane, and white gloves. Every Lord in the Nation was required to pay an initial membership fee of 1 dollar, have his nickname written on the club's rolls, and carry his card with him at all times.

In the fall of 1968 I visited the Lords in their new business office on 16th Street, a few doors west of 16th and Lawndale. There had been numerous changes since I had done my first field work. The club was now legally incorporated, and had received a substantial grant from government sources to undertake self-help projects. The group had started a restaurant called "Teen Town," begun an employment service, and opened a recreation center named "House of Lords." They had entered into agreements with both the Cobras and the Roman Saints, and all three of the clubs had cooperated in community help projects. The Vice Lords were strongly involved in Black pride and Black consciousness programs. A staff of both Whites and Blacks was working in the Vice Lord office on legal problems faced by

The new Vice Lord restaurant on the corner of 16th and Lawndale.

members of the Lawndale community. In the short time I was there, however, it was impossible for me to get more than a few hints as to the basic changes the club had undergone. There were still various Vice Lord branches, but sections no longer functioned within Vice Lord City. Everyone I talked with, including friends who no

A group of Vice Lords outside their recreation center.

longer took part in any of the club's activities, said that gang fighting had completely stopped. If this is true, then it is clear to me that the Vice Lord social and cultural systems must have undergone basic and radical changes. The inflow of a large amount of money from government sources coupled with the complete termination of gang fighting must have had a profound impact on the group. Unfortunately, I was unable to go into any of this in the few hours of my visit. It will be fascinating to see what happens to the Vice Lords in the future.

In this chapter we have discussed the Vice Lords' origin and subsequent development. While this sketch is only an outline, most of the major developments in the club's growth have been highlighted. In the following chapters we shall turn from historical developments, and look more carefully into the club's social and cultural system as it existed at the time of my fieldwork in 1966. I will use the "ethnographic present" in my description, meaning that I will employ the present tense, even though the events occurred in the past, during the time I did the fieldwork.

2

Features of the Vice Lord
Social System

WHEN VICE LORDS DISCUSS THEIR CLUB, references are often made to particular features. Certain of these figured in the previous outline of Vice Lord development, and all are important to the discussions in later chapters. Here our concern is to introduce and briefly describe these features so that the arguments in later chapters can be followed.

Branches

The Vice Lord Nation is divided into "branches." Each branch has its own particular name, set of officers, and territory. At the time of my first period of field-work, Vice Lords said that the following branches existed—the Albany Lords, the California Lords, the 5th Avenue Lords, the Lake Street Lords, the Lexington Lords, the Madison Lords, the Maniac Lords, the City Lords (that is, those from Vice Lord City), and the War Lords. However, I cannot verify that all of these branches actually exist, for not every individual could name every branch, and leaders could not always be designated for the branches named. The Vice Lords who gave me information were from Vice Lord City, the Albany Lords, and the Monroe Lords. In addition I met Vice Lords from the Maniac Lords, the Sacramento Lords, and the War Lords. This indicates that the club is divided into at least these six branches.

Everyone I talked with agreed that the City Lords is the original branch; it is the largest and probably the most powerful subgroup in the Vice Lord Nation. The Vice Lord Social Center was located in Vice Lord City, the territory of the City Lords. Before it closed for lack of funds, the Center was a meeting place for all the Lords in the Nation. Vice Lords stated that each branch, while autonomous, generally acknowledges the seniority of the City Lords. Prior to the latest change in organization, the leaders of the City called the infrequent meetings of the entire Nation, decided what was going to be discussed, and ran the actual meeting. The members of the City were in charge of maintaining order. Although some branches may have been feuding, no fighting was allowed during these meetings.

The number of branches is not constant—old branches break up, and new ones are formed. One of the ways branches are formed is through alliance and subsequent absorption. The formation of the Monroe Lords provides a good example of this process. A club known as the Ambassadors started fighting a club called the Imperial Burpies. The Ambassadors lost fight after fight, and finally agreed to become a part of the Burpies. When the Vice Lords contacted the leaders of the Ambassadors and agreed to help them if the fight with the Burpies was renewed, the Ambassadors withdrew from the Burpies, and the two groups again began fighting. With the help of the Vice Lords, the Ambassadors won this war and broke up the Burpies. The Ambassadors and the remnants of the Burpies became the Monroe Lords.

In other instances branches are formed when groups of boys decide to start a Vice Lord branch in their own neighborhood. After hanging with the Lords on 16th and Lawndale—the "capital" of Vice Lord City—and proving themselves to be regular fellows, the leaders of the City Lords allow them to set up their own branch and to use the Vice Lord name.

Toward the end of my field work I witnessed the formation of a branch by this process. Some of the boys living in a neighborhood that was part of the North Side ghetto were jumped on by a group of older boys who lived several blocks away. The younger boys reacted to this in the standard ghetto way—they formed a club for mutual protection. Some of these boys were friendly with a woman in the neighborhood who offered them the use of her basement for their club meetings. This woman was a good friend of several Vice Lords, and one afternoon they decided to visit her. She suggested to one of them that he talk to this group about becoming a branch of the Vice Lords. When this individual showed the boys his Vice Lord membership card and described how powerful the Lords were, they decided to try to become a part of the club. That weekend these boys sponsored a dance, and several Vice Lords from the West Side came to help in case enemies of the group might try to break it up. I was told that later the boys would be taken to the West Side to meet other leaders of the Vice Lords, and after a short time, would probably be accepted as Vice Lords by the leaders of the City.

Finally, new branches are formed as a result of the high rate of spatial mobility found in the ghetto. As members of various branches move out of a neighborhood, they often start new branches in their new neighborhoods. Since they are already known as Vice Lords, it is not necessary for them to prove themselves further.

According to various Vice Lords, branches are often connected by ties of alliance which become activated during interbranch conflicts. These alliances are based on individual friendships: Particular alliances often stem from the maintenance of friendship ties between members who move away and join or found new branches, and those who remain. When a conflict develops between two branches, others are drawn in through the operation of ties based on friendship. An example is provided by a feud between the Maypole and Monroe Lords. A Monroe Lord gives the following account of the early phases of this feud:

> This was one of them come-and-go fights. We strike and they strike. They were coming over in our neighborhood and jumping on the little boys and taking their money. Now we kept a strong neighborhood. We didn't do this, and we didn't allow it to go on. And the little kids looked up to us. They knew we were real bad, but they still thought we were nice.
>
> So one day some of the Maypole Lords came across Garfield Park and took some money from Jesse's little brother. Jesse, he was one of the heavy [important] Monroe Lords. We had to do something. We had told them not to come over robbing anybody. So we caught them in this little restaurant one night . . . unaware. And that's when the fighting broke out. We had quite a little humbug.

Fights between the Monroe and Maypole Lords continued, and other branches became involved. The Madison and California Lords supported the Monroe Lords, while the City Lords were allied with the Maypole branch. The following account by a member of the City Lords illustrates the principle of reciprocal friendship on which alliances between branches are based:

> The Maypole Lords, we dug them, but we didn't like the Monroe 'cause they was kind of funny—they was kind of bourgeois. They would give sets [parties] and stuff, and wouldn't let the City and Maypole know about it. We would find out afterwards. So why didn't they tell us? Then they'd go around talking about us. They said, "Well, we don't want them fools out here!" They didn't want Tankson and them from Maypole around 'cause they were stone fools. As far as I was concerned they were real mellow, but Monroe didn't dig them. And then we got the idea that Monroe was just using our name . . . to keep other people off them. And when Monroe started fighting the Maypole Lords, well quite naturally we going to come into it. Cave was out [of jail] then, and Cave more than likely would take the Maypole's side. Monroe didn't dig this. See, the Maypole, they was our boys. That stud Tankson, the president, he was a mellow stud. They were out of sight, and we dug them.

While branches may engage in feuds, they unite when threatened by an enemy club. The Monroe and the Maypole Lords united against the Racketeers even while their feud was in progress:

> Now while this [the feud between the Monroe and Maypole branches] was going on, the Racketeers was steady coming over. They were throwing gas bombs, and they had got pretty good at it. But we united with the Maypole Lords and trapped them over in Douglas Park . . . which they weren't expecting. They had done wrong, and they knew they had done wrong; before they knew it, we were on them! This was both us and the Maypole Lords. It was about two days after we had got the Maypole Lords in the restaurant. But the fight between us was still going on. We were still mad with them, and they were still mad because we had beat up a lot of them, and tore up their hangout.

In feuds between branches Vice Lords state that fighting should be limited to fists, although other weapons are sometimes used. In wars between clubs, in contrast, there are no limitations set on the legitimate use of weapons.

Sections

Within each branch there are various other kinds of subgroupings. The City Lords is the only group, however, that is divided into subgroups called sections. The sections that City Lords named are: the 15th Street Lords, the Ridgeway Lords, the St. Louis Lords, and the Trumbull Lords. At first glance these groups seem to be identical to branches. However, when asked about this, City Lords insist that sections are not the same as branches, but are subdivisions of one particular branch—the City Vice Lords. We shall look at sections in greater detail in the next chapter. Here all that need be noted is that (1) sections claim to control particular parts of Vice Lord City; (2) sections had a distinct set of offices before the recent reorganization, while after it they had only one office; and (3) the leaders of sections are considered more subordinant to the leaders of the City Lords than are those of other branches.

Age Groups

As stated in chapter 1, almost every branch of the Vice Lord Nation is divided into a set of subdivisions which Vice Lords call "Seniors," "Juniors," and "Midgets." Some branches even have "Pee Wee" Vice Lords. There is no cover term to refer to such groupings, but since age is an important basis for distinguishing between them, I have chosen to call them age groups.

In most branches each age group has its own set of officers. In the City Lords, however, this is not the case at the present time. Before the development of sections within the City Lords, each age group did have its own officers, but at the time of my field work such groups had no internal organization.

Membership in age groups varies between branches. In the City Lords the Midgets are usually 12 to 15, the Juniors are 16 to 17, and the Seniors are 18 and over. In the Monroe Lords the situation is quite different. Generally, the Midgets are boys 16 years of age and older who are small in size, the Seniors are boys 16 and older who are large, and the Juniors are all those under 16, regardless of size. However, individual choice is the most important consideration in age group membership. In the Monroe Lords an individual is usually free to join whatever age group he chooses as long as that group will accept him. If at a later time he wishes to change his age group affiliation, he is free to do so providing the members of the other group will accept him.

A comparison of age groupings among the Monroe and City Lords following the development of sections shows definite differences. In the Monroe Lords age divisions form distinct social groups, that is, they are internally structured. In contrast, at present these are only social categories in the City Lords. This is reflected in the way Vice Lords discuss events concerning the club with each other. In conversations I heard between individuals in the Monroe and Albany Lords, and between members of the City Lords who were talking about events that took place before the development of sections, particular people were often identified in terms of the age group to which they belonged, and events discussed in terms of age groups which had taken part in them. One of the older members of the City Lords who was talking about the "old days" provides an example.

> The roughest boys I ever met, they was between the ages of 13 and 15—Lil' Lord, Rough-head and them. They was the Midgets—the Midget Lords. And these were the baddest boys I ever went up against! What happened, they beat up one of the Senior Lords, a stud called Dough Belly. And Cave Man wouldn't even mess with the Midget Lords' cause they had so many guns. We didn't know where they got the guns from, but they used to bring them around and give them to us.

In contrast I never heard any of the City Lords allude to age groupings when discussing contemporary events. In these instances individuals were referred to in terms of their section membership.

The Vice Ladies

The Vice Ladies is the name of the female auxiliary connected with the Vice Lords. My information concerning the Vice Ladies comes from Vice Lords only, and, therefore, is incomplete. I was told there is a Vice Lady group attached to each branch. At one time there seem to have been Vice Ladies connected with certain sections of Vice Lord City, but this is not the case at the present time.

It is said that each Vice Lady group is independent of the Vice Lord branch to which it is connected. Vice Lady groups elect their own sets of officers, hold their own meetings, and make their own group decisions. There is no norm that Vice Lords should monopolize sexual rights in Vice Ladies—many Vice Ladies are said to go with Cobras, and some Vice Lords say their girlfriends are Cobraettes, the Cobra female auxiliary. On the other hand, this independence is not always complete. In Vice Lord City the girl who goes with the president of the City Lords is generally considered to be the head of the City Vice Ladies. There is often strong hostility between Vice Ladies and Vice Lords, and in several instances this has taken the form of actual fighting.

> Every once in a while we used to fight with the Vice Ladies. They was boss humbuggers, Jack! [Boss—very good, humbuggers—fighters.] I remember one night we had a fight with them and they got us. Jesse was out there at the time— Jesse Clayborn. Jesse's a stone fool! He was out there rolling a tire—playing with this broad Rose. I don't know what was wrong with her. She was in the Vice Ladies, and she had a quick temper. She high at the time anyway. So they was rolling a tire back and forth. Jesse rolled the tire, and Rose missed catching it, and it knocked her down. Now Rose was high and crazy, and Jesse crazy too. Rose got mad. She jumped up and pulled out a knife . . . long knife, Jack! And Jesse got a stick. You know, he going to bust her in the head with that stick! So all the girls jumped up. They not going to go for this. One of them said, "Look at him! Got a big stick after that girl!" Jesse said, "She got a knife! If she try to cut me with that knife, I'll bust her in the head with this stick!"

So all the Vice Ladies started picking up bricks and carrying on. They going to help Rose. By then I had grabbed Rose around the waist. I was holding her, and Shotgun was holding her. Killer, he had on a pair of leather gloves, so he took the knife out of her hand.

But Rose said, "That don't mean shit! That ain't nothing!" and Jesse and her started going from the cuff. They was actually out there boxing. So Rose, she was so tore up [high] that she accidentally hit another one of the fellows named Lonzo, and he hit her back. That really got the Vice Ladies shook up. So when he hit Rose, this girl Ella Mae, she hit Lonzo with a stick . . . yeah, in the head with a stick. So Lonzo picked up a brick. He going to hit the broad with a brick. And everybody started picking up weapons off the ground—anything they could lay their hands on. Half the fellows wanted to go on and dust the girls, but the other half were going with them, and quite naturally they didn't. So while the fellows were arguing among themselves about what they should do, well, the girls were popping us in the head with sticks and bottles and bricks. I got hit myself . . . right in the eye. Rose hit me. They really messed us up that night.

Offices

Formal offices are found in various branches, age groups, and sections of the Vice Lord Nation. Before the latest reorganization, there were seven named offices, although all were not found in every subgroup. These offices are: president, vice-president, secretary-treasurer, supreme war counselor, war counselor, gunkeeper, and sergeant-at-arms. The information I was given concerning these offices can be summarized in the following manner:

1. The president conducts meetings, in some cases makes the decision whether or not to fight another group, and is responsible for leading successful raids. He symbolizes the group's power, and in feuding and warfare his injury is the prime objective of enemy force.

2. The vice-president is the president's assistant. He has few formally recognized duties. When the president has been arrested, or otherwise cannot or will not fulfill his duties, the vice-president succeeds to the office of president.

3. The war counselor is the president's main assistant when the group is involved in fighting. He is specifically charged with the responsibility of deciding whether or not to begin a fight in a confrontation between two rival groups. No one is supposed to begin fighting until the war counselor throws the first punch, or, as the case may be, fires the first shot. In the Albany Midgets there are three war counselors: a supreme war counselor and two regular war counselors. The war counselors, along with the president, form a war council which decides whether or not the group will fight when one of its members has been attacked by individuals outside the group. All decisions have to be approved by a majority of the council. If a decision to fight is made, the supreme war counselor organizes and leads the raid. Much of the fighting that informants discussed followed accidental encounters between enemy cliques, and in such cases war counselors have no institutionalized responsibilities.

Cliques

Branches and sections are subdivided into a set of what I call cliques that are basic units in the Vice Lord social system. In the jargon of the streets a group of individuals in a clique are referred to as "running partners." These groups are important in warfare, political power struggles, and social activities. Membership in cliques sometimes crosscuts age groups, but never sections or branches. Within cliques, in contrast to branches, sections, and in some instances, age groups, leadership in not institutionalized into a set of formally recognized offices. For example, in one clique in the City Lords before the development of sections, one of the leaders was secretary-treasurer of the Seniors, while another was president of the Juniors. Within the clique itself, neither was considered to outrank the other.

Many cliques have their own name and status in a ranked hierarchy. In Vice Lord City a few years ago the "Magnificent Seven" was the most powerful. Another powerful group was known as the "Rat Pack." At present in the Sacramento Lords the most important of these groups is called the "Gallant Men."

Cliques play a crucial role in power struggles within the branch organization. According to Vice Lords, cliques sometimes fight one another in support of rival leaders vying for positions of power within the branch. The following story was told about a fight between the Rat Pack and the Magnificent Seven:

What happened was whenever one of these civic groups give a dance they would invite Cave Man, and he would bring a couple of the fellows, he would get some of these new fellows that had just got in the club. So I told Cave Man, I said, "Cave, why don't you get a couple of older fellows and take them around?" And the YMCA was having some of the fellows be field assistants and consultants, and Cave Man was picking out the guys, but he was picking out the wrong fellows. So I told him about it . . . at the club meeting. I said, "I'm about to give it up . . . seeing how you all running everything. I'm tired of this! I got so many fellows with me, and Cool Fool got so many with him, we could start something of our own." I said, "Cave, you just one man, and there's a whole lot of us. We really are the backbone of the club." So those dudes in the Magnificent Seven, Cave and them, they got mad.

Now when I first got in the club, I was real small dude, but I had put on a little weight, and I had got tall. The next day we was all in the pool room over on Roosevelt. So a dude called Fresh-up Freddie, he was in the Magnificent Seven, he said, "Just because you've got big, I bet you believe you can whup me." I said, "I didn't say nothing like that, but I . . ." He said, "Come outside!" So we went outside and we started boxing. He couldn't touch me, so I said, "I quit," and I dropped my guard. That mother fucker, he hit me in the nose, hit me in the mouth, and my mouth started bleeding.

Now Cool Fool had my jive [gun]. I said, "Fool, gimme my jive!" and Fool, he gave me my gun. I said to Fresh-up, "I ought to shoot you!"

Now Fresh-up got the intention of snatching the gun. He done snatched three or four guns out of different fellows hands, and he started walking at me. He said, "Shoot me if you want to. I don't believe you going to shoot me." I knew what he's going to do when he got close, he going to grab the gun. I didn't want to kill him so I shot him in his arm. I had to shoot him. You see, if I hadn't done it, he would of took my gun away from me. So I went straight home. Cool

Fool and the rest of our fellows, they stayed around the pool hall. There was a boss humbug.

New Organization

Under the new organization, each branch remains fairly autonomous. However, there is an executive body of 8 members that deals with problems affecting the club as a whole. This group, known as the "board," is made up of representatives from each major branch along with some of the older members from various branches. The board is headed by a president chosen from among its members. A council of about 20 members from various branches backs up the board. If a member of the board is arrested, it is planned that his replacement will be chosen from this group.

The board is supposed to function as an advisory rather than a decision-making group. As we have seen, under the old organization the president or war council of a particular branch decided whether the group would fight. In matters pertaining to a war involving all the branches, in theory the president of the City Lords had this power. Under the new organization, however, it is the group as a whole which carries the responsibility for making such a decision. The board would bring the problem to the group during a weekly meeting, and the group would decide what course of action to take. Vice Lords give a definite reason for making the group rather than the president responsible for such decisions.

> We noticed that it put a lot of pressure up on one guy to make a decision alone. Like, for instance, just think what would happen if we having trouble from some guys—the Cobras or the Roman Saints—and Cave stood up and said, "Well, we fight them." The minute he says this, then this means he gave the order to start it. But when you put it to a board, the board don't say, "Well, we fight them." The board ask the group, "What is your decision about this?" and they make their own decision. The board say, "Well, we with the fellows." Then no one guy had made no decision. See what I mean, the group has made the decision, and ain't no one man have the responsibility. In other words, this is the way to eliminate the problem of the law. In the past when somebody got killed or hurt they could come and pick up one man, and actually charge him with the murder 'cause he gave the order. This way they just have to come and get the group, and they can't do that. So they just have to pin point the man—the one who actually pulled the trigger. But this is almost impossible to do.

Within Vice Lord City the sections were abolished as formal semi-independent subdivisions. Nevertheless, the individuals who had formed sections were to choose leaders, called "lieutenants," to be responsible in gang wars for mobilizing their group, defining a particular part of Vice Lord City, and leading their group in attacks on the enemy.

Finally, three individuals were chosen to comprise what is called the "death squad." If a Vice Lord is attacked by another club, and the group as a whole does not decide to go to war, then a member of the death squad is given the responsibility for organizing and leading a small retaliatory raid.

Membership

It is extremely difficult, if not impossible, to determine the size of the Vice Lord Nation. The leaders themselves do not have a really accurate idea of how many members the club has. I received estimates from various individuals ranging from 600 to 3000. One way to get a figure would be to do a census of each branch. However, the size of their group is one of the things branch members are most reticent to talk about, and I was only able to do a census on the section of the City Lords called the 15th Street Vice Lords. In any case a census of all the branches would still fail to produce a completely accurate figure, for it is not always clear in what sense particular individuals are members of the club. For instance, a person may get a job, start supporting a family, and cease to take part in most Vice Lord activities. Occasionally, however, he may come out on the corner, drink wine, and shoot craps with other Vice Lords. While he is on the corner, he acts like and is treated by others as a Vice Lord. It then becomes problematical whether one would wish to count this particular person as a part of the club. A possible solution would be to count as members those individuals who are defined by others as Vice Lords. In many cases, however, there is real disagreement concerning whether a particular person is actually a member. Further, an individual himself may claim to be a part of the group in one instance, but deny he is a member at other times. Given the changes in organization, theoretically it should be possible to obtain a fairly accurate figure of the group's size since everyone in the club is supposed to have a membership card and his name placed on the club rolls. In actuality I found that certain individuals did not have membership cards, did not have their names on the rolls, but were still considered by some to belong to the club in certain situations. When I asked Vice Lords about these inconsistencies, the matter was shrugged off as essentially unimportant.

Ignoring this problem for the moment, one can make a very rough approximation of the Vice Lords' size, although I doubt whether in the final analysis it is even a meaningful undertaking. The 15th Street Lords have at the least thirty members. If we assume this to be typical of the other sections in Vice Lord City, then the City Lords probably number at least 150. Counting the other branches, the total number of Vice Lords may fall somewhere between the figures of 600 and 3000 given by the Vice Lords.

According to all accounts, the Vice Lords have no standard initiation for new members. Initiation varies both among the different subgroups in the club, and among the various individuals involved. In some cases a boy simply moves into a neighborhood which has a Vice Lord group and hangs with members of the club. He participates in certain activities with them, "runs" with them on the streets, and gradually takes part in more and more of their activities until finally he is considered a member.

Sometimes a boy will commit some act that gives him prestige in the eyes of club members and he will be asked to join. An example of this is a boy called Mad Dog. Mad Dog moved into Vice Lord City. His first day in the neighborhood he was challenged by two younger brothers of one of the club's "heavy" members. In

Herzel School located on 15th Street. In the past Vice Lords often used the school grounds at Herzel for meetings.

the fight that followed he not only "whupped" the two younger brothers, but the older brother as well. He was then invited to join the group. First, however, he was required to box with Cave Man, at that time the president of the City Lords. Following this, Cave Man and Mad Dog stood back to back and fought off other members of the club who came at them from all sides in what is called a free-for-all. Mad Dog fought until his jaw was dislocated. Since he had won the respect of the club members, he was considered a full-fledged member.

In most cases, however, becoming fully accepted as a member occurs over a period of time. The president of the 15th Street Lords gives the following account of how an individual becomes a member of his particular group:

Like you a new member, and you join the 15th Street Lords. Now you haven't got no name or nothing, and we haven't exactly got one right off hand so we'll look at the chart. See, we have a chart of all the nicknames—Emp, Roughhead, Bat Masterson, Windy, Chico, Pico, Rico. Then I asks the group, "Who want this man to be named after him?" And one of the fellows raise their hand and say, "He can be named after me." So I'll say, "Your name is little Tico, and this Big Tico." Now Big Tico supposed to make sure you do everything right. He show you how to do it . . . take you around, introduce you to the neighborhood. He let you see the neighborhood, how it is, how we got it arranged and everything. But all the while Big Tico doing this he not going to take you to the regular hideout 'till about three weeks after you joined. And all the three weeks you being watched—to see where you go; when you leave the house; what neighborhood you go in; who you be walking with and what time of the day. We checking you out in other words. We don't know, you might be a Cobra.

Territory

Vice Lords call the space they control "territory." It is that part of Chicago in which there is little chance that a Vice Lord will be attacked by an enemy group, but a significantly larger chance that a member of an enemy club will be attacked by a group of Vice Lords. Any Vice Lord, regardless of clique, section, age group, or branch can go into any part of the territory controlled by the Vice Lord Nation and he will not be attacked by a Vice Lord group. For example, if a member of the City Lords has a girlfriend who lives in the territory of the Albany Lords, he knows that he will not be jumped on by a group of Albany Lords when he visits her. If a member of the Albany Lords also goes with this girl, then there may be a fight between the two concerning the girl. However, this should be a "man-to-man" fight, and other Albany Lords should not take an active part. If other Albany Lords did take part in such a fight, with the result that a City Lord was beaten by a group of Albany Lords, this would constitute a repudiation of the Albany Lords' membership in the Vice Lord Nation. It would signal that the Albany Lords now considered themselves to be separate from, and an enemy of, the rest of the Vice Lords.

Branch territory is not contiguous. Branches are spatially separated from one another both by territory of enemy clubs and by segments of the ghetto that are not controlled by any club. Within Vice Lord City particular sections are also linked to territory. Section territories, unlike branch territories, are in some cases contiguous. Not all of Vice Lord City, however, is claimed by particular sections. The heart of the City—the corner of 16th and Lawndale—is the meeting place and hangout for all the members of the City Lords, and is not a part of any section. There are other parts of Vice Lord City which are of no particular significance, but are also, like the corner of 16th and Lawndale, not thought to belong to any section. The outline map below shows both territorial divisions of Vice Lord City and boundaries with enemy clubs. The map below shows Vice Lord City as forming a distinct, bounded territorial unit, but this picture is somewhat misleading. Vice Lord territory is that part of Chicago where Vice Lords (but not members of other clubs) are relatively free from attack. The map shows the territory claimed by the Vice Lords, but Vice Lords are not equally free from attack in all portions of that territory. As one approaches the boundaries of other clubs, the chance that a Vice Lord will be attacked by an enemy group increases. At an actual boundary with an enemy club there is roughly an equal chance that a Vice Lord will be jumped on as there is that a member of the enemy club will be jumped on. If the boundary is crossed, then the chance that a Vice Lord will be jumped on is greater than the chance that members of the enemy club will be jumped on by Vice Lords.

I first began to understand how Vice Lords think about territory in listening to a discussion concerning the Central Park—a movie house located on Central Park and Roosevelt Road (12th Street). A number of 15th Street Lords were discussing whether to go to the show. In the discussion it was mentioned that the Vice Lords used to "have" the Central Park show, but that it now "belonged" to the Roman Saints. This was answered by, "Yeah man, we owned that Central Park show!

Looking south on Pulaski, the boundary between Vice Lord City and K-Town.

The northwest corner of 16th and Lawndale.

The southwest corner of 16th and Lawndale.

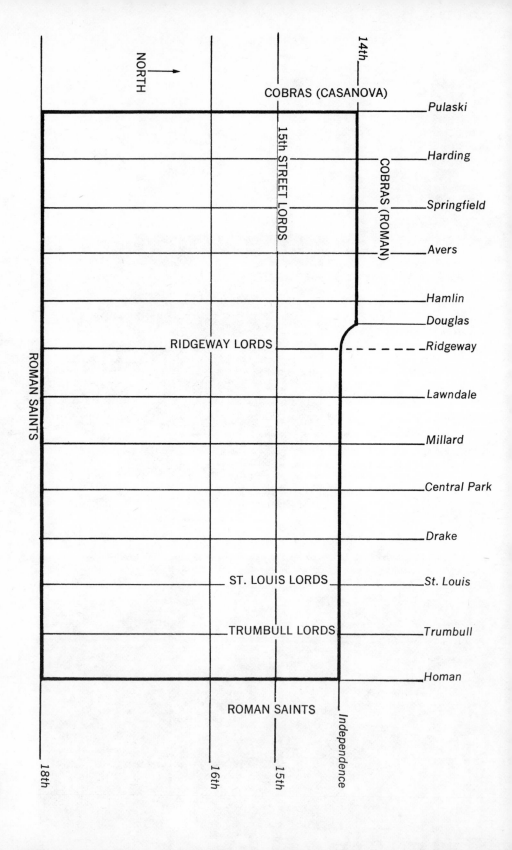

Couldn't none of them Roman Saints come. They was afraid, Jack! They knew we'd whup their ass!" The discussion concluded with the admission that Vice Lords had lost the Central Park show to the Roman Saints, and unless it was worth risking a gang fight, it would be better not to go to the show in a group. When I matched this with how particular Vice Lords had explained the concept of territory to me, the way Vice Lords think about territory became clear:

> The 15th Street Lords' territory is from 15th and Ridgeway all the way to Pulaski. This is our territory 'cause can't nobody come through—no off-brand clubs.

> The territory of the 15th Street Lords is from 15th and Ridgeway to 15th and Pulaski. We have mostly all of it up tight. This means that no other groups can come down in our hood and start nothing. If we didn't have it up tight we'd have to try and get it up tight—get it organized. If we didn't have it up tight, then dudes could come by and jump on us and the other people in the neighborhood.

This discussion of territory shows how Vice Lords distinguish their own territory from that of enemy clubs; but what distinguishes between the territory of different sections? To illustrate an important point, I will digress a bit and include several interviews in which I was trying to find out how various section territories are distinguished. In working with informants the most difficult task is to formulate the right questions. However, in order to be able to ask the right questions, one has to have a fairly accurate idea of what the right answer might be. In these particular sessions, my idea of what the right answer might be was so inaccurate that it kept me from perceiving the significance of what I was told.

R. L. K.:   What's the territory of the Ridgeway Lords?
Duck: Ridgeway, all the way from 18th to Independence.
R. L. K.:   Where do most of the Ridgeway Lords hang out?
Duck: On 16th Street. There be very few on Ridgeway.
R. L. K.:   If they all hang out on 16th Street, why aren't they considered 16th Street Lords?
Duck: 16th Street just a hangout for everybody.
R. L. K.:   When you say that's the territory of the Ridgeway Lords, what do you mean? What does it mean that you have that territory?
Duck: Everybody got their little section where they hang out at. It's just different street names. They just go by street names, that's all.
R. L. K.:   Well, is it because they live on that street, or is it because they hang out on that street?
Duck: They hang out on that street, and most of them live on the street, but you don't have to live on the street.
R. L. K.:   O.K., suppose you live on Ridgeway, and you're in the Ridgeway Lords, and you move away; does that change your membership, or can you still belong?
Duck: You can still belong.
R. L. K.:   But if you start hanging around with the group where you live now will that change your membership?
Duck: Not exactly. I keep telling you we all the same. You can belong to one group, but you can hang out wherever you want.

I had assumed (almost unconsciously) that section territory was differentiated in terms of rights, and it was this idea that directed my questioning. However, after this interview I was obviously no closer to understanding the basis for section territorial distinctions. I failed to realize that my questions were based on an incorrect assumption about what the right answers might be, and in the next interview I worked from the same direction. Therefore, I not only missed an important clue but also thought I found the basis for the distinction which was, in fact, not the case at all.

R. L. K.:   As a member of the Ridgeway Lords, what is the difference between my territory and your territory?

Earl: They trying to keep the Roman Saints from falling down on us, and we trying to keep the Cobras from falling down on them. We got two different groups coming from two different ways. From the east its the Roman Saints, and from the west its the Cobras. We trying to hold the Cobras back far as we can so they won't get closer to 16th and Lawndale, 'cause 15th Street is the back door to the City.

R. L. K.:   What I'm trying to get at is the difference having a particular territory means for individuals in different groups. Now I don't know if this is the case, but are there certain things that Ridgeway Lords can do in their territory that they can't do in your territory.

Earl: You right there. Like some of the 15th Street Lords might go over there—they ain't got no business jumping on no one over there, and they ain't got no business coming over to our hood and jumping on somebody.

The first answer should have given me a clue as to how Vice Lords distinguish between section territories, but because I assumed there must be differences in rights, I failed to see its significance. When I asked Earl to give me an answer in terms of rights, he did. This simply led me further along a blind alley. It was not until the interview with Big Otis that I finally understood the basis for territorial distinctions between sections. I started this interview with the same assumption. Fortunately, Goliath, one of my best informants, closest friends, and roommate for the summer, was present. He saw at once what I was trying to find out, and why I was getting nowhere. Goliath provided the right questions to ask as well as the right answer.

Goliath: What advantages do you have in your own territory?

Big Otis: We know all the gangways and rooftops, and we know just about everybody in the streets.

Goliath: Do you use your territory also like a meeting place? Like for instance all the fellows get together to go someplace and take care of business [get together for a raid], could you all meet in this same area, could you get together right away, like could you contact everybody?

Big Otis: Yeah, you know where to find them at. You know where all the places they be at.

Goliath: In other words, you wouldn't have to worry about the Cobras coming down and whupping you in your territory.

Big Otis: No, we know it before they get down there.

R. L. K.:   How is this different from the territory of the Ridgeway Lords?

Big Otis: It's no different.

R. L. K.:   Why isn't the territory of the Ridgeway Lords your territory? What makes it different?

Goliath: See, everybody in one box, like for instance Roach and them, they be on 15th Street, so they make sure don't nobody come down Ridgeway that we don't know. This way you block off the whole area, and there always be somebody around. If you can't handle it, then you get help.

Big Otis: Yeah, if the Cobras coming from one end and the Saints coming from another its our job on 15th Street to stop the Cobras.

It is apparent that the distinction between section territories is based on differential responsibility rather than differential rights. Sections have the responsibility of protecting particular parts of Vice Lord City from enemy attacks. A section's territory, therefore, is that particular part of Vice Lord City for which it is responsible in case of enemy attack. In order to fulfill this responsibility, section members must have a good knowledge of how their territory is laid out—where gangways lead, how to gain access to rooftops, what alleys are dead ends, and so forth. It is advantageous, if not necessary to have such knowledge when section members must actually defend their territory against enemy raids.

Our outline of the Vice Lords social system poses a particular problem. I have described a set of groups and positions within the club that are significant to Vice Lords, but in what sense do these form a system? In the following two chapters I shall attempt to answer this question.

3

The Social System—Groups

O UR PROBLEM IN THIS CHAPTER is to demonstrate how Vice Lord social behavior constitutes a system. A social system has been previously defined as the pattern of social interaction actualized in the ongoing process of interactive behavior. (Geertz 1957:33–34). In attempting to describe the pattern in Vice Lord social behavior we shall identify forms which emerge in social interaction and principles on which social behavior is based.

In observing Vice Lords in action over a period of time one finds a recurring series of situations in which behavior follows a particular pattern. Situations like this are generally called "social contexts" by anthropologists, but could just as well be called "happenings"—to borrow a particularly apt term from the hipster. Vice Lords themselves recognize certain social contexts, or happenings, as being distinct, and refer to them in certain ways. Some are given particular names, for example, "gangbangs," "sets," and "meetings." Others are designated by the kinds of activities that occur within them, such as: "pulling jive," "shooting craps," "hustling," and "wolf packing."

If we look at the behavior that takes place within social contexts, certain patterns emerge. One kind of pattern takes the form of what can be called "social roles." Social roles are both specific social identities and the particular kinds of behavior considered proper between individuals who assume these identities.

Another kind of pattern which emerges from interaction taking place within social contexts relates to social groups. In the last chapter we outlined the ways Vice Lords talk about various social groupings within their club, and we found that individuals are simultaneously members of a series of groups. But what gives these groups meaning? When, for example, is an individual's branch, as opposed to his age group, affiliation of significance? The answer is that Vice Lord social groups have meaning in terms of particular social contexts, for it is through interactive behavior which occurs within social contexts that social groups are given substance. Part of the pattern in the Vice Lord system is that similar kinds of social contexts

470

give form to similar kinds of social groupings. In other words, we can find regularities in the particular social groups that emerge from the interaction taking place within particular social contexts.

We have identified three aspects of the pattern of Vice Lord social interaction: (1) There are recurring sets of behavior that are recognized by Vice Lords as forming distinct social contexts or "happenings"; (2) particular social roles systematically emerge from the interaction that takes place within these happenings; and (3) this interaction systematically gives form to particular social groups. In this chapter we are primarily concerned with social groups, while in the following chapter we shall focus on social roles.

In looking at the relationship between social contexts and social groups there are several observations that stand out. We find in some instances a direct correspondence between a particular social context and the group affiliation that is significant within that context. For other contexts there is a limited range of significant group affiliations—that is, certain social contexts limit the range of possible group affiliations that can be of significance to individuals acting in those contexts. Within this range the actual activation of any potential group affiliation is a function of choice. Nevertheless, it is possible to find regularities in such choices, and, therefore, principles can be isolated which specify what group will actually emerge in any given instance.

We shall be dealing mainly with data from the City Lords in our discussion of patterns in social interaction since most of my research was with this particular branch. However, I did gather some information on other branches which will also be brought into the discussion.

The Gangbang

The social context of a "gangbang" (gang fight) is considered by Vice Lords to be one of the most important social happenings in street life. How individuals behave in gangbangs is a constant topic of conversations, and is a crucial determinant of status and prestige. In a later chapter we shall look at the gangbang as a cultural scene, and consider the norms and values which are important to it. Here we are concerned with the relationship between gangbangs and the activation of group affiliations.

Among the City Lords we find three kinds of group affiliations that are activated in gangbangs—membership in a section; membership in the branch; and membership in the Vice Lord Nation. Clique and age-group affiliation are never meaningful in this context. In other branches that do not have sections, age group, as well as branch and Nation, affiliation can be significant.

What principles underlie the choice of one of the possible group affiliations in a gangbang rather than another? To answer this we first have to distinguish between variations in the range of situations Vice Lords call gangbangs, for this variation is related to the principles which generate choices of group affiliation. Gangbangs can occur in several ways. A collection of Vice Lords may accidentally encounter several members of an enemy club at a party, a dance, or a movie, and a gang fight results. In explaining gangbangs a Vice Lord gave the following account of this kind of gang fight.

> There are these accidental fights. Say you walking down the street with some of the fellows and you meet the Cobras. You're not really looking for them, but when you run up on them you go down [fight]. Or say, for instance, we going to a set [party] and it's out of our neighborhood. We really not looking for no fight, but we ready. So the Cobras decide to come too. You all might get along 'til just about time the party's over, and then boom—everything goes down.

Gangbangs also result when Vice Lords either raid an enemy club, or when an enemy club raids them. In the first instance Vice Lords mobilize for attack, and the ensuing gangbang materializes as a Vice Lord raid on enemy territory. In the second instance Vice Lords mobilize for defense, and, in the resulting gangbang, defend against raiders from an enemy club. Gangbangs which do not result from accidental encounters usually stem from instances where one or two members of a club are jumped on by a large number of individuals from another club. If Vice Lords are jumped on by members of another club, various Vice Lord groups often mobilize for attack, while if a group of Vice Lords jump on members of another club, the Vice Lords will usually gather for purposes of defense. A Vice Lord explained this to me in the following way:

> If the Cobras come down and hurt one of the fellows and the president say "fall," we got to fall. When the president say "fall" that means that all the fellows supposed to get together and go down there [to the Cobra's territory]. Just say we going to fall tomorrow. The president and the vice-president get together, they talk, they say we going to fall at a certain time, and to meet at a certain place. When everybody meet, we all split up and go different ways. But we don't arrange to meet another club at a certain time or nothing like that.
> If the Cobras coming down in our hood, we be prepared for them. Like if we jumped on a Cobra and he hurt, this is what he going to do. He going to go down and tell his fellows. He going to say, "The Vice Lords jumped on me!" This is what they going to do. They done get mad and all riled up. They going to say, "We going down there on the Vice Lords!" When they come, we prepared. They come down 15th or maybe 14th. What we do, we lay back . . . maybe in just a couple of gangways, and when they fall out, we fall out on them.

Gangbangs can also result from fights between an individual Vice Lord and a member of another club. If the Vice Lord wins such a fight, the Vice Lords may be attacked by the other club, while if he loses, there may be a decision by a Vice Lord group to retaliate against the other club.

We have made the following distinctions in the situations that Vice Lords call gangbangs—gang fights that result from accidental encounters between Vice Lords and members of an enemy club, gang fights in which Vice Lords defend their territory against an enemy raid, and gang fights in which Vice Lords raid the territory of an enemy club. When we look at these distinctions in terms of group affiliations, it is possible to isolate the principles which generate the kind of group affiliation that will emerge as meaningful in any given gangbang context.

Accidental Encounters

In instances where gangbangs result from accidental encounters between Vice Lords and members of an enemy club we find the following principle determines which group affiliation will be significant: if the Vice Lords involved in the gang-bang are members of the same section, then it is section membership that will be significant; if the Vice Lords are members of different sections, but the same branch, then it is branch membership that will be significant; and if the Vice Lords are members of different branches, it is club membership that will be significant. In branches that do not have sections, the principle works in a similar manner except that age groups replace sections as the narrowest group that can take on significance.

Vice Lords Defend

My information for gangbangs in which Vice Lords are defenders is limited to the City Lords. For the City, there are two kinds of groups which are mobilized for purposes of defense—sections, and the branch. Before proceeding further it is necessary to review the way Vice Lords think about territory, for territoriality is crucially related to ways group affiliations are given meaning. As we recall, the territory of the Vice Lord Nation is comprised of the noncontiguous territories of each branch. Vice Lord territory is that part of Chicago in which there is little chance that a Vice Lord will be attacked by an enemy group, but a significantly larger chance that a member of an enemy club will be attacked by a group of Vice Lords. Within Vice Lord City particular sections are linked to particular territories. "Section territory" is that part of Vice Lord City that sections are responsible for defending in case of enemy raids. Now let us return to the problem at hand.

In some cases an enemy attack is aimed at the territory of a particular section. In instances like this, section membership becomes meaningful. For example, late one night I came to the corner of 15th and Hamlin with Tex, the president of the 15th Street Lords. We had been standing there for about five minutes when Bat Man walked up and told us that there had been a fight earlier that evening between Shotgun and Excell. Excell was in the Roman Cobras, while Shotgun was one of the important members of the 15th Street Lords. Shotgun had won the fight, and it was felt that the Cobras might decide to "fall," that is, make a raid. Tex immediately started to organize for the defense of the territory. Bat Man was given instructions to find other 15th Street Lords who lived outside the territory and meet at a particular place at a certain time. Tex then went around the 15th Street Lords' territory collecting members of the section and placing them in strategic positions. Although the raid never materialized, a certain group of Vice Lords had been mobilized in terms of their responsibility to defend a particular segment of Vice Lord City. It was section membership that was significant in this instance.

There are other instances where Vice Lords feel an enemy raid is aimed at penetrating to the heart of Vice Lord City—the corner of 16th and Lawndale. In cases like this, both section and branch membership become significant. I observed a situation in which it was thought the Roman Saints were planning to attack 16th and Lawndale. Both the St. Louis Lords and the Trumbull Lords were mobilized for the defense of their territory since it was suspected that the Saints would come through that segment of Vice Lord City in order to get to 16th and Lawndale. (See map on page 24.) Thus certain members of the City Lords were mobilized in terms of their section membership for the defense of their territory. However, the rest of the City Vice Lords who gathered at 16th and Lawndale were organized for the defense of the corner by the leader of the branch. For these Vice Lords branch membership was significant.

The significance of group affiliation in cases where Vice Lords are defenders is based on differential responsibility for the defense of the branch. The group affiliation that will actually be significant depends on assessments of the enemy's aims. If it is believed that an enemy club plans to attack the territory of a particular section, then for those Vice Lords who have potential membership in that section, this membership is activated. If, however, it is believed that an enemy club plans an attack on the branch, for example, the corner of 16th and Lawndale, then section membership is activated for some, while branch membership is activated for others. The actual section membership that becomes activated depends on what enemy club is believed to be planning an attack, and from what direction it is thought the attack will come.

Vice Lords Attack

When a Vice Lord is beaten up by members of another club, certain Vice Lord subgroups are mobilized for retaliatory raids. In some instances sections form the raiding parties, while at other times branches, and even the entire Vice Lord Nation, may be mobilized for retaliation against an enemy club. This presents us with a set of problems. First, how can we account for instances in which Vice Lords actually retaliate when a member is jumped on by an enemy club, in contrast to instances when there is no retaliation? Then, looking only at the cases in which there is retaliation, how can we explain differences in the kinds of groups which function as raiding parties?

Although Vice Lords state that when a member is jumped on there should be retaliation, most admit that this does not always happen. Actually, retaliation depends on a variety of factors. If there has been a series of incidents (such as arguments and individual fights) between Vice Lords and members of another club, retaliation is likely. Competition for leadership within Vice Lord subgroups also affects the probability of retaliation. Strong competition for leadership increases the probability of retaliation, while lack of competition decreases it. Vice Lords feel that a rep as a brave warrior is a necessary qualification for occupying leadership positions, and thus the rep of competitors is highly valued political capital. If a competitor fails to call for retaliation when a member of the group is jumped on by an enemy club, his rival can accuse him of lacking "heart" (that is, roughly, bravery). Such an accusation can seriously weaken an individual's rep, and place him at a disadvantage vis-à-vis his rival. Therefore, leadership competition makes it politically expedient for contestants to uphold the norm of group retaliation for wrongs committed by an enemy club against its members. The result is that, other things equal, the probability of retaliation is higher when leadership is contested than when leaders are secure in their positions. A third factor affecting the incidence of retaliation is the status of the person who was jumped on. If the person is of low status—if he is neither a leader nor an important follower of a leader—then often some excuse will be given for not retaliating. In contrast, if the person is a highly respected leader, or an influential member of a particular Vice Lord subgroup, then retaliation is likely.

The status of the Vice Lord beaten up by an enemy club is also the crucial factor in determining which subgroup will be mobilized for retaliation. If the person jumped on is an influential leader in a section or strongly allied with an important section leader, but is not allied with any of the important branch or Nation leaders, then the group that may be mobilized for retaliation would be the section; if he has high status in a branch, but not the Nation, then the branch may be mobilized; and finally, if he is considered one of the "top Lords" in the Nation, then the entire Vice Lord Nation may be mobilized for the purpose of retaliation. There have been a few times when the entire Nation gathered for carrying out attacks. One such incident was a gang fight between the Vice Lords and the Imperial Chaplains (also known as the Commanches). I collected several different accounts of this fight—one is included in Chapter 6. It is striking that in all the accounts it is stated that the Vice Lords decided to attack the Imperials only after several of the most important Lords in the Nation had been jumped on by the Imperials. The following account provides a good example of how the status of the Vice Lord jumped on is crucially related to the kind of Vice Lord subgroup mobilized for retaliation. In reading this account it should be recalled that Cave Man is alleged to be the founder of the Vice Lords, and has always been the most influential person in the entire Nation. Even when he was not the actual president of the Nation he was the leader with the most *de facto* power.

It was about seven o'clock on Saturday when I came to 16th Street, and there was about forty or fifty boys on the corner. They were hollering and shouting and carrying on, Jack! So I asked them what was happening. They said that Cave Man, Tree Top, and a couple a more of the top Lords had went into the Imperials' neighborhood, and Cave had got hit across the eye with a stick. And someone started hollering, "You go over on Maypole! You get those fellows over on Maypole! You go out South, get the fellows out South! You go up to Albany and Monroe, and get those fellows! We'll meet back here at 16th and Lawndale in an hour and a half!" So I went home to get my shotgun.

We really messed them up that night, Jack! I cut three of them myself. What happened, I walked across the street and before I know, I got down [to get down is to do something really well]. It was Ghengis Khan, Big James, and Big House Willy. The first one ran into me . . . and I cut him. It was Big James. Ghengis Khan ran into me, and I cut him. Willy seen the knife, and he ran across the street.

We have discussed two aspects of gang fights in which Vice Lords attack an enemy club. First, we looked at the problem of instances in which Vice Lord groups retaliate against an enemy club, in contrast to instances in which there is no retaliation. We found that there are several factors that affect the probability of retaliation. If there have been a number of incidents between Vice Lords and an enemy club—such as arguments and fights between individuals—then the probability increases that the Vice Lords will retaliate when one of their members is beaten up by an enemy group. If there is strong competition for the leadership of a Vice Lord subgroup, the chance also increases that Vice Lords will retaliate when a Vice Lord is jumped on. Finally, the status of the individual who is beaten up affects the probability of retaliation. If he is influential, then there is a greater chance for retaliation than if he is a member of low status.

The second problem dealt with concerned the kind of group that is mobilized for purposes of retaliation. We found that the status of the Vice Lord jumped on is crucial in determining the kind of subgroup that will function as a raiding party. If the person is an important member of a section or has influence with an important section leader, then the section will function for retaliation; if the person has high prestige in the branch or influence with a member of high prestige, then the branch will be the retaliatory force; and finally, if the individual is one of the top Lords in the Nation, then the Nation will be mobilized for retaliation.

Other Contexts

We have identified "hustling," "wolf packing," "pulling jive," "meetings," and "shooting craps" as social contexts that form an important part of Vice Lord street life. While Vice Lords do not feel these contexts are as important as gang-bangs, they are far more frequent in occurrence. Most of Vice Lord street life is comprised of such happenings.

Clique membership is the only affiliation that is actualized in the context of "hustling" and "wolf packing." "Hustling" is any activity other than legitimate employment that is aimed at making money. Begging in the streets, gambling, and stealing are common kinds of hustling activities. Although begging in the streets and gambling are usually individual activities, stealing often involves groups. Strong armed robbery, a form of theft, is often used in the ghetto to make money. While individuals do strong-arm alone, it is more usual for this to be done in groups since it increases the chances for success. Too large a group, however, would attract attention, and also cut down on individual profits. Thus a group between two to four is felt to be best suited for hustling purposes. Successful group strong-arming is also dependent upon teamwork. There is a division of labor—each person is allocated a specific task: for example, stopping the intended victim (usually by asking him for a cigarette, or for the time); grabbing hold of the victim; keeping the victim from struggling by threatening him with a weapon or striking him; and taking the victim's money and other valuables. Since teamwork is so important, individuals most often hustle with their closest friends—people whose abilities and limitations they know well. Therefore, it is clique affiliation that becomes actualized in hustling contexts.

"Wolf packing" is somewhat similar in form to strong-armed hustling. However, the aim is different. Strong-armed hustling is concerned with making money, while wolf packing is primarily for enhancing a rep. Wolf packing was explained to me in the following way: "Wolf packing—like for instance me and some other fellows go out and knock you down 'cause we feel like it. That's what it is. I might take your money, but I really want to kick some ass anyway, so I decide to knock the first thing in my way down." Vice Lords feel that for wolf packing, as for hustling, one must be able to trust the actions of others in the group. For this reason close friends usually wolf pack together. As one Vice Lord put it, "You pick peoples you know you can depend on—your close partners. See, if you pick someone you don't know, he liable to trick on you [tell the police], or run on you." Thus clique affiliation becomes actualized in wolf packing contexts, as it does in hustling contexts.

In the context of "pulling jive" (drinking an alcoholic beverage—usually wine) Nation affiliation is actualized. "Pulling jive" is one of the most frequently occurring social contexts in Vice Lord street life. Vice Lords pull jive before and after gang fights, following successful hustling, and while they are hanging on the corner. There is a certain pattern to the way Vice Lords drink wine. We shall look at this more closely in a later chapter. What is important here is that in the form of pulling jive which is the same for all Vice Lords, the unity of the Vice Lord Nation is symbolically stated. Before any wine is drunk, a portion is poured on the ground in the letters CVL. Vice Lords say that this is for all the Lords who have been killed or who are in jail. Further, a study of incidences of pulling jive shows that

Shooting crap in an alley off 15th Street; three of the boys belong to the 15th Street Lords and two are Ridgeway Lords.

any Vice Lord who happens to be present, regardless of clique, section, age group, or branch affiliation is offered some wine to drink, and, therefore, takes an active part in the drinking activity. Thus it is apparent that Nation membership is the crucial group affiliation in the context of pulling jive.

"Meetings" are a social context in which Nation, branch, section, and age group affiliation may be significant. Clique membership is never actualized in this context. There are regular periodic meetings of the entire Vice Lord Nation that are presided over by the most important leaders of the club. Any Lord in the Nation can come to these meetings. At meetings of the Nation that I attended there were between a hundred, and a hundred and twenty-five Vice Lords present. Branches, sections, and age groups also hold meetings at various times. However, there is no regularity to these meetings. Usually, they are held only during times of crisis—for example, following some kind of incident that could lead to a gang fight.

Although "shooting craps" is a frequent Vice Lord social activity, it forms a social context in which Vice Lord street life cuts across the more inclusive street life of the Lawndale community. While Vice Lords most often shoot craps with other Vice Lords, membership in the club is not significant in this particular context. Anyone with money, regardless of clique, section, age group, branch, and even club membership is welcome to take part in the game. In crap games I observed there were middle-aged men, as well as Vice Lords, actively participating. A Vice Lord explained this to me in the following way:

> Whenever everybody get some money, we get together and shoot some dice. I mean the whole hood. This don't mean just the Vice Lords, it means anybody in the neighborhood—anybody got some money, women, babies, kids. If you got some money, we'll know you.
> So we get a crap game on 15th Street, and somebody else got one on 16th. You, me, him, we all over on 15th Street. We going to shoot dice among each other. And if one man bust all of us, he know there's a game on 16th, and he going down there and try and bust them. See, you go anywhere the money is.

In this chapter our interest was focused on one aspect in the pattern of Vice Lord social interaction—the relationship between social contexts and groups. We had previously noted that Vice Lords belong to a series of groups. We then asked when is membership in one, rather than another, of these groups activated? We found that the activation of group membership is systematically related to particular social contexts. This systematic relationship forms part of the pattern of the Vice Lord social system. In the following chapter we shall look at another part of this pattern.

4

The Social System—Roles

AN IMPORTANT PART OF THE PATTERN in Vice Lord social life is comprised of what can be called social roles. In our study of Vice Lord roles we shall use a theoretical framework to help organize and bring sense to the data. Dr. Allen Hoben has written a concise explanation of the role concept in a community study guide for Peace Corps volunteers. Part of this will form a section of our framework, and that portion of his work is included here.

Hoben identifies three general aspects of social roles:

First, there are in any society a number of well-defined and publicly recognized social personalities or identities. Father, son, teacher, pupil, employer, and employee are examples of social identities in our own society. It should be stressed that these are not different kinds of people, but different social identities. The same individual is called upon to assume different identities in different situations.

Second, in any society only in certain social identities can people interact with one another. There are very definite rules of combination—a sort of grammar of possible social interaction. For example, father-son, father-daughter, husband-wife, teacher-pupil, and employer-employee are grammatical combinations of social identities in our own society. Father-pupil, employer-son, daughter-teacher, and son-wife are not. A single social identity (father or professor) may have a grammatical relationship with several other identities (father-son, father-daughter, or professor-student, professor-professor, professor-chairman of department).

Third, there are in any society, for each grammatically possible combination of social identities, agreed-upon rules concerning appropriate modes of interaction. This means, for example, that father and son, teacher and pupil, employer and employee are aware of the behavior they expect from one another [Hoben 5–6: n.d.].

If we focus on the third aspect—the "agreed-upon rules concerning appropriate modes of interaction"—differences in kinds of rules are found:

1. There are formal rights and duties limiting the behavior of individuals in identity relationships. A Vice Lord who assumes a particular identity expects certain

rights, and owes certain duties to the Vice Lord who assumes the alter identity in the relationship. If either party fails to fulfill his duties, sanctions are imposed.

2. There are modes of behavior that are considered proper between individuals in social relationships. These we can call social etiquette.

3. There are modes of behavior that signal which identities are being assumed.

The final point in our framework concerns role distribution. If the distribution of roles in relation to social contexts is studied, important differences in contextualization are found. While Vice Lords assume some identities in a few contexts, there are, in contrast, other identities that are assumed in a wide range of social contexts.

Vice Lord–Vice Lord

The role Vice Lord–Vice Lord is found in a wide range of social contexts. Whether hanging on the corner, drinking wine, or gang fighting, individuals in the club often assume the identity Vice Lord in relationships with each other. There are a certain set of rights and duties that regulate behavior between individuals assuming this identity. When my informants discussed the way Vice Lords should behave toward one another, the idea of mutual help was a constantly recurring theme. As one person put it, "We may get to arguing and then humbug [fight], but soon as it's over we buy a drink, and we back together. See, the way we see this thing, we all out to help each other . . . really."

Mutual help can be divided into two kinds—help with regard to material things, and aid in fighting and other dangerous activities such as strong-arming. Vice Lords state that members of the club should help each other in any kind of dangerous activity. If a Vice Lord is jumped on by members of another club, all other Vice Lords present should help, regardless of personal risk. Also, if a Vice Lord asks another to help in hustling, he should not turn down the request. When I asked if most Vice Lords actually do usually give physical help to each other, the answer was an emphatic "yes." For example, I asked one Vice Lord what one should do if he saw another Lord getting jumped on. The answer was, "Help him! You not supposed to do this, you going to do this! You a Lord . . . Lords don't fear nothing but God and death. I never seen a Lord cop out [chicken out]—not a true Lord." When pressed, however, some informants admitted that not all Vice Lords act in this manner. Those who don't, however, are strongly sanctioned. A person who does not fulfill the obligations of physical support is derisively referred to as a "punk," or a "chump." According to one informant, if one is judged a punk, other Vice Lords will refuse to have anything to do with him: "They say he's a punk—tell him to go on away from them; tell him to go home; tell him to stop hanging with them." Another Vice Lord stated that a person would actually be physically sanctioned if he "punked out": "Most of the time when a fellow punks out they wait until the person get out of the hospital, get his side of the story, see did the dude really punk out. If

A group of Vice Lords "hanging" on the northeast corner of 16th and Lawndale.

the guy say he punked out on him they usually jump on him . . . or take him in Cobra territory and put him out."

It should be pointed out, however, that the obligation of physical support is similar to the commandment "Thou shall not kill." Although this commandment is supported by sanctions, there are certain circumstances when it can be broken with impunity. Sanctions are not imposed for killing in self-defense, or during a war. Similarly, sanctions are not always imposed on Vice Lords who do not give physical aid to other Vice Lords. For example, if a small group of Vice Lords is attacked by a much larger enemy force, it is felt that one Vice Lord should run and get help rather than stay and help the others. Also if a Vice Lord sees another member being beaten up by an enemy group, he can try to get a weapon before helping in the fight. Even if he returns with his weapon after the fight is finished he will not normally be sanctioned for punking out. There are also situations where a Vice Lord's obligations to help other Vice Lords in hustling activities is put aside. For example, at 3:00 A.M. one morning two drunk Vice Lords came to the house of Doughbelly and yelled in his window asking him to help them hold up somebody. Because of the noise they created Doughbelly's mother told him he could no longer live in her house. He became enraged at the two drunk Lords for getting him "thrown out," and told them he would not help them, and further, if he saw them again he would kill them. It was never suggested publicly that Doughbelly had punked out for refusing to help in this situation, and no sanctions were imposed.

Since there are sanctions imposed for failing to fulfill the obligations of physical support, it seems clear that these are part of the rights and duties of the Vice Lord-Vice Lord role. A Vice Lord has the duty to give physical support to other Vice Lords and the right to physical support from other Vice Lords. This set of rights and duties, however, can be tempered by particular circumstances.

The rights and duties of mutual help regarding material things presents a more complicated picture. Although Vice Lords say they should lend money and clothes, share food, and should not try to "beat" (con) each other out of their possessions, many individuals admit that most do not usually act in this way. In fact when I asked if Vice Lords usually do give material help, the answer was often hoots of laughter. In my observations I found that Vice Lords frequently tried to beat each other out of things, and saw many cases where individuals refused to lend things to other Vice Lords. There were no group sanctions imposed for failing to live up to this ideal, and when questioned, my informants stated that it was the responsibility of the individual who felt he was wronged to take what action he felt necessary. Can it be said that mutual help with regard to material things is not important in the Vice Lord-Vice Lord role? I don't think so. It is generally felt that individuals who refuse to live up to the ideal of mutual help should not deny the validity of the ideal. Further, there are situations when most Vice Lords usually will extend material help to other members of the club. If they are convinced that a member is really in need, then he usually will be helped. An individual may have been thrown out of his home by angry parents and have to fend for himself on the streets, or he may have recently returned from jail with no money and nowhere to live. In such cases other Vice Lords usually give whatever help they can. I observed an instance where material help was given to a Vice Lord in need. A set had been planned by the 15th Street Lords. Throughout the prior week, the set was a constant topic of conversation. The clothes that were going to be worn and the girls that were going to be present were repeatedly discussed. The evening of the set I met a group of 15th Street Lords at the house of Tex, the 15th Street's president. Everyone was dressed and ready for the set except Old Dude. Old Dude was one of the least important members of the 15th Street Lords. He was thought by everyone to be "light upstairs" (not too intelligent), and he did not have a rep for gang fighting. His family was extremely poor, even by ghetto standards, and his mother gave all her attention to another brother. One of the fellows asked Old Dude, "Say man, why you ain't dressed for the set?"

"I ain't got no pants. It's my own fault. I knew about the set all week, but I just ain't got no pants."

Tex said, "Damn Jack! You should've asked us. You a Lord—we take care of you." Tex then asked his mother to press one of his extra pairs of pants, and another of the fellows went home to get a clean shirt for Old Dude to wear.

It is interesting that in this context Vice Lord sanction individuals who will not help a club member in need. Such a person is referred to as "stingy" and becomes the topic of derogatory conversation. Certainly anyone with leadership aspirations could not afford to be classified as stingy. From this we can conclude that material help is a binding obligation when it is thought an individual is in real need.

Looking now at the rights and duties regarding mutual help, a clearer picture emerges. Mutual help, both material and physical, is a binding obligation when Vice Lords feel real need is involved. If a Vice Lord is jumped on by members of an enemy club, he is in danger of serious physical injury. When a Vice Lord has nowhere to live and nothing to eat, he is also in need. The obligations of mutual help become binding in such situations. We can now better understand why Vice Lords feel that even when an individual is not in real need, it is still necessary to uphold the value of mutual help. Life in the ghetto poses many risks; the rights and obligations of the Vice Lord-Vice Lord role provide a kind of social insurance. No one knows when he may find it necessary to bring into play the obligations of mutual help. Thus the ultimate legitimacy of such obligations must be jealously guarded. Publicly denying that these obligations are legitimate would threaten the well-being of all Vice Lords. Therefore, it is felt that individuals should not deny the legitimacy of a request for help, although the request does not always have to be granted.

There are certain forms in the interactive behavior of individuals who assume the Vice Lord identity that can be called social etiquette. Standardized greetings are one example. When individuals pass one another on the street there are two greetings that are used. In some cases the right hand is raised to the side, the hand balled into a fist, and the arm raised and lowered two or three times. In other instances the club name is yelled out as a greeting.

Upholding the legitimacy of the obligations of mutual help is also a part of Vice Lord social etiquette. For example, if a Vice Lord were asked to loan money to another member and answered, "No man! I ain't your daddy. I ain't going to give you nothing!" this would be a breach of good manners, that is, it would go against social etiquette. It would also be interpreted as a hostile act—a signal not only that he was refusing to assume the identity Vice Lord vis-à-vis the asker but also that he was assuming an identity as a protagonist. The individual who asked for the money would then have the legitimate right to retaliate by starting a fight, that is, public opinion would support his starting a fight. In contrast, if the person asked for the loan couched his refusal in the form of an excuse, and in a friendly tone, this would constitute proper social etiquette. It would not be interpreted as a hostile act, and public opinion would not support the asker if he started a fight. I observed an instance that provides a good example.

A meeting of the Nation had just occurred, and groups of Vice Lords were standing around talking. I was with Goliath, my major informant, and a few other Vice Lords. While we were talking, Tico walked up and said to Goliath, "Hey man, give me a quarter. I get paid Tuesday, and I'll take care of you then, but I got to get me some jive [wine] tonight." Goliath answered, "Yeah man, I'll take care of you," and turned around and started talking to another Vice Lord who was standing with us. After a few minutes Tico again asked Goliath for the money. "Damn Jack, what about the quarter?" Goliath answered, "Yeah, I'll turn you on." This continued for a short time—Goliath kept assuring Tico he was going to give him a quarter, but made no move to actually do so. Finally he reached into his pocket, pulled out some change, and began counting it intently: "Let's see, I need forty cents for a Polish [sausage], twenty-five for a . . . "

"Shit man, we Vice Lords. We supposed to be brothers. Come on, Jack, I gotta get me a taste."

"I'll take care of you. You know that. Now I need forty for a Polish, twenty-five for carfare, fifty to get my baby some milk . . . shit! I'm fifteen cents short. Say man, can you loan me fifteen cents?" Tico shook his head, and walked away in disgust.

I should note that Goliath did not need 15¢—he had $10 in his wallet—but this was used as an excuse rather than denying that he should loan the quarter. Goliath was, therefore, observing the proper social forms of the Vice Lord-Vice Lord role. (Incidentally, Tico did not need the quarter. I saw him later that evening with $2.

Street Man–Street Man

Another role that is found in a wide range of contexts is what I call the Street Man-Street Man role. The social identity Street Man is one that all male Blacks living in the ghetto assume at various times. Vice Lords often assume this identity in their relationship both with other members and those who do not belong to the club. The essential element in the Street Man-Street Man role is manipulation. It is expected that persons who assume the Street Man identity will try to manipulate (or, as Vice Lords say, "beat") each other out of as much as possible. This manipulation, however, has certain bounds set to it. An example will illustrate.

While driving down 16th Street, Cochise was hit by a woman who had gone through a red light. She did not have insurance, but agreed to pay $40 for damages. After two weeks she still had not paid Cochise, and he decided to get the money himself. He asked Jesse, another Vice Lord, to accompany him and help out in case of any trouble. Jesse was to get a share of whatever was collected in return for his help. Jesse and Cochise broke into the woman's house and took a television set, radio, and toaster. Cochise kept the toaster and radio. Jesse got the television set, but gave Cochise $20 so that each would have a fair share. Later Cochise and Jesse were on the corner of 16th and Lawndale disucussing what had happened. Cochise mentioned that he was going to take the radio home and then try to sell it the next day. Jesse said, "No man, don't do that. The Man liable to come in your house, and if he find the radio he'll bust [arrest] you. Now I know an old building, ain't nobody in there. You can leave it there." Later, when I mentioned this incident to Goliath he laughed and said, "You know why Jesse said that?" I said, "No."

"Well, if Cochise took that radio home, Jesse couldn't go in his house and get it, but if he put it in that old building then Jesse'd sneak back at night and get the radio hisself."

In this instance Jesse was attempting to manipulate Cochise in order to beat him out of the radio. According to the expectations of the Street Man-Street Man role it was acceptable for Jesse to attempt this. However, there are limits to the ways it could be done. If Cochise had taken the radio home, it would not have been acceptable for Jesse to have taken it from there. Stealing from the home of a close acquaintance is considered wrong behavior by Vice Lords, and few individuals would have much to do with a person known to act in this way. On the other hand, if Jesse could have talked Cochise into leaving the radio in an abandoned building, he would have been free to go back and get it for himself. Successfully manipulating others is called "whupping the game." If Jesse had been successful in whupping the game on Cochise, his prestige with other Vice Lords would have increased. It is now possible to isolate at least one of the rights and duties of the Street Man-Street Man role. Individuals who assume the identity Street Man have the right to expect others in the alter identity will follow the rules which set limits to manipulation, and have the duty to follow these rules themselves. The sanction of public opinion supports this right and duty.

The social etiquette of the Street Man-Street Man role consists of greetings, farewells, and forms of ongoing social interaction. There are two greetings that are generally used. An individual may say either "How you doing?" or "What's happening?" Sometimes "man" or "Jack" is placed at the end of the greeting—for example, "What's happening, Jack?" The person who begins the exchange has the option to choose the greeting he wishes. When one of these greetings is used to initiate a social exchange, the other is usually the response. To terminate a social episode most individuals say simply, "Later."

A form of behavior that is a part of ongoing social interaction is hand slapping. In hand slapping a person puts his hand out with the palm up, and another person touches the open palm with his own hand or arm. Although this might seem somewhat similar in outward form to shaking hands, as we shall see, it has radically different social significance. (Vice Lords do not usually shake hands like most middle-class Americans.)

A hand-slapping exchange can begin in two ways. In some cases during the course of a social episode an individual puts his hand out with the palm raised. The proper response is to touch the raised palm with a hand or arm. Other times a hand-slapping exchange is initiated by a person raising his hand with the palm down. The proper response is to put out the hand with the palm raised. The first individual then slaps the outraised palm. In the first kind of hand-slapping exchange there are several kinds of responses to an outraised palm that are considered proper. Some, but not all, of these have different social significance. A person can respond to an outraised palm by slapping it with his own palm either up or down. This has no particular social significance. Touching the outraised palm with the arm or elbow is also a possible response. Further, an individual can vary the intensity of his slap. These last two differences—touching the palm with an arm or elbow rather than the hand and varying the intensity of the slap—do have significance.

In general, when a hand-slapping episode occurs during social interaction it emphasizes agreement between the two parties. If an individual has said something, or done something he thinks particularly noteworthy, he will put out his hand to be slapped. By slapping it, the alter in the relationship signals agreement. Varying the intensity of the slap response indicates varying degrees of agreement. A Vice Lord may say, "Five Lords can whup fifty Cobras!" and then put out his hand, palm up. Another club member responds by slapping the palm hard, thus indicating strong agreement. The first Vice Lord might then say, "I can whup ten Cobras myself!" and again put out his hand. This time, however, the second individual may respond with a much lighter slap. This indicates that he does not emphatically agree with the statement. If he barely touches the outraised palm with a flick motion of the wrist he indicates disparagement. However, if he touches the outraised palm with his arm or elbow this shows that he respects the person, but does not feel his statement is either particularly true, or else particularly important. If the second individual raises his hand before the first puts out his hand, this not only emphasizes agreement, but also expresses esteem.

It is considered a serious breach of social etiquette to purposely ignore the initial moves of a hand-slapping episode. I was told that to do so is a serious insult. While I observed several instances in which Vice Lords indicated disparagement by lightly touching an outraised hand with a flick of the wrist, I never saw anyone refuse to respond at all in some appropriate way.

Vice Lord–Enemy

The social identity, Vice Lord, has a grammatical relationship with the identity I call Enemy. An individual who is a member of the Vice Lords can assume either the identity Street Man or Vice Lord in social interaction with males who are not members of the club. If he assumes the Street Man identity, the grammatically proper identity for the alter to assume is also Street Man. However, if he assumes the Vice Lord identity, then the alter is automatically defined as an Enemy. Both parties in such a relationship have an initial option as to which identity they will choose, but if either chooses the identity which defines the situation as one of enmity, then the other must choose the grammatically matching one. In other words, if the individual who is not a member of the Vice Lords assumes the identity Street Man, then the person who is a Vice Lord has an option. He can assume either the identity Street Man, or that of Vice Lord. If he assumes the latter, then the first individual must act as Enemy. In contrast, if the first individual assumes the Enemy identity rather than that of Street Man, then the second person must assume the identity Vice Lord.

Although there is insufficient information to discuss the Vice Lord-Enemy role in terms of rights and duties and social etiquette, I did find both behavioral expectations between individuals interacting in this role and regularized forms of behavior that signal the assumption of the identities in question. There are two kinds of behavior that are expected in situations of enmity. Vice Lords call these "whuffing," and humbugging. Whuffing is the exchanging of insults and challenges to fight, while humbugging is actual fighting. Not all situations of enmity end in humbugging. Individuals who assume the identities Vice Lord and Enemy, respectively, can play out their social interaction solely in terms of whuffing.

People who intend to assume the identities which define a social situation as one of enmity do not signal this simply by initiating physical violence. There are certain verbal formulas which indicate a person is assuming the enmity identities. One of the most common is to demand a sum of money—for example, "Hey man, gimme a dime!" When put like this, it is not an actual request for money. If a dime were given, then a demand for more money would be made until finally the individual would have to refuse. Refusing the demand is the cue that the alter is assuming the grammatically matching identity of enmity, and from there the relationship can be played out in terms of whuffing or humbugging.

Another formula for signaling the assumption of an enmity identity is to start an argument. Individuals often argue in the course of social interaction, and these arguments do not always signal enmity. However, when an individual starts a violent argument over something that is considered extremely inconsequential, it does function as such a signal. For example, an individual may be talking about the kind of clothes he likes the best. If another person begins to vehemently argue with him, it is a sign that he is assuming an enmity identity. Of course it is not always clear whether an argument is "consequential" or not, and there are other subtle cues which also indicate if an identity of enmity is being assumed. My informants, however, could not verbalize about these. They said, "Man, you just *know* . . . that's all." Unfortunately, during the time of my field work I was not able to make a systematic study of these subtle cues. Possibly, they consist of such things as facial expressions and certain qualities and tones in the voice. Not all people are as adept at appropriately responding to such cues as others. Being adept at responding properly is one of the things that constitutes "knowing what's happening," or, as Cupid puts it in Chapter 6, "knowing how to live on the streets."

Leader–Follower

There are several named leadership identities that are assumed in a few social contexts. We have already discussed these in Chapter 2, and it is not necessary to deal with them in detail here. However, in order to be eligible for these identities—for example, President, War Counselor—one must be what Vice Lords call a "Leader." We can, therefore, discuss a Leader identity without necessarily specifying a formal political position. Vice Lords define a Leader as a person who has followers. To a person outside the world of the fighting clubs this may seem overly simplistic, but what defines one as a Leader or Follower is self-evident only to Vice Lords. There are several reasons for this. Leadership is highly contextualized—that is, there are few contexts when an individual's identity as Leader emerges. Further, the same person may assume identities of both Leader and Follower at different times.

A few definitions would help clarify the discussion. A Leader is one who exercises power. Power is the ability to get others to do one's will. The exercise of leadership is thus the exercise of power. Among Vice Lords a person is recognized as a Leader when he has the ability to get others to do his will. In some societies power is often a function of force. Individuals exercise leadership through the use, or threat of use, of physical or mystical force. This fits the popular conception of the gang leader. Among Vice Lords, however, power is not based on force. A Leader exercises power through what we can call influence. Vice Lords follow others because they like them, or respect them, or because they think they will gain something by doing so, but not because they fear them.

What are the contexts in which the Leader and Follower identities are relevant? There are two kinds of contexts when people assume Leader and Follower identities—that is, there are two kinds of contexts in which power is exerted. The first kind includes situations that demand physical action. Some obvious examples are: gangbanging, wolf packing, and hustling. An example from the 15th Street Lords provides a good illustration. I had met Tex, the President of the 15th Street Lords, several times before I found out how important a person he was. Observing Tex riding in a car, hanging on the corner, or drinking wine, there was no clue that he was a person with power. He was not particularly assertive, and when demands were made of him, he usually complied. If there was an argument over who was going to sit by the window while we were riding, Tex usually lost. If there was an argument over who was going to buy cigarettes, Tex usually lost. At a party one evening a group of 15th Street Lords stole a large sum of money from an individual who was not a member of the club. When Tex tried to get them to return the money, he was completely ignored. Then one evening there was a fight between a 15th Street Lord and a member of the Cobras. Everyone expected the Cobras would attack 15th Street territory. In this situation Tex's identity as a Leader became relevant. He immediately took charge of planning for the defense of the territory. Not only were his orders obeyed without question but individuals sought him out to ask what they should do.

I observed other instances which also demonstrated the pattern. Crow was one of the top Leaders in the Nation. Next to Cave Man, he was considered to be the most influential Vice Lord. I was on the corner of 16th and Lawndale one night with Pico talking to Crow. There had been an outbreak of fighting between the Lords and the Roman Saints that evening, and it was expected that the Roman Saints would attack 16th and Lawndale. Pico suggested that he lead a group of Lords into Roman Saint territory, but Crow felt he should stay and help protect the corner. Pico did not even put up an argument, but simply said, "Yeah man, I guess you're right." Another time I was riding with Pico down Lawndale. We pulled up to a corner where there was a group of Lords. Crow was standing in the group, and Pico wanted to talk to him. Pico yelled out the window, "Hey Crow, you skinny mother fucker, get your ass over here!" Crow smiled and said, "What's happening man?" and walked over to the car.

These two examples help us better understand how Vice Lord leadership works. Both Tex and Crow assumed the identity Leader in the gang-fight context, but at other times assumed different identities. The casual onlooker observing their behavior at these other times might think they were not Leaders. He would be wrong. Both Tex's and Crow's failure to exert power in these situations was unrelated to their identities as Leaders since these were social contexts where the Leader-Follower role was irrelevant.

The second kind of context in which leadership identities are relevant are those defined by public decision making. Some decisions which affect the club are made during discussions between Vice Lords while hanging on a corner or in an alley. Usually, however, public decision-making takes place during club meetings. These meetings form an arena for leadership competition and demonstrations of power. A major objective of individuals who either are recognized Leaders or have leadership aspirations is to prove they have power—that is, to demonstrate that others will follow them. Many times the particular decision under discussion is secondary to this objective. For example, Cave Man had long been president of the Nation. During the summer of 1966, however, a group of the Senior Lords met and decided it would be best for the club if someone else took over. Cave Man agreed to step down and let Lonzo be the new president. At this time the executive board was instituted. Cave Man was not even given a place on the board, but was relegated to the formal position of a regular member. However, Cave still had considerable power, and lost little time in demonstrating it to the new officers. A group of social workers and clergymen from the West Side contacted Lonzo, the new president, to request permission to attend a meeting. They desired to get Vice Lord participation in a project. Several board members told them their request would be submitted to the club, but that the board would support it. When the meeting began, it was evident there was considerable opposition to this group. Cave Man had been hired by the YMCA to help control gang fighting, and had worked in close cooperation with a social worker who was part of this group. At the meeting, however, he was the loudest voice in the opposition. He said, "What have them social workers ever done for us? Shit man, we don't want them in here!" Cave Man became the rallying point for the opposition, and was able to marshall enough support so that the group was not allowed in the meeting.

After the formal part of a meeting it is customary for Vice Lords to congregate on 16th and Lawndale to drink, sing, and recount past exploits. After this particular meeting, Cave Man called out to Vice Lords who were standing around in small groups:

> Come on! We're going to tear up this West Side! We're going to tear down all these signs! [Someone had painted "Black Power" on several buildings.] We're going back to the old days! We're going to gangbang! Those Cobras and Roman Saints, They ain't shit! We're going to run 'em out of the West Side! Vice Lord! Vice Lord! Terrifying, terrific Vice Lords! This whole West Side belongs to the Vice Lords! Come on, let's go!

With that, Cave started out for 16th and Lawndale, and about 25 other Vice Lords fell in behind echoing his yells and shouts.

Cave Man's actions, both during the formal meeting and immediately after, can be understood in terms of the way Vice Lord leadership operates. He opposed allowing the YMCA worker to attend the meeting even though he was getting money from the YMCA and had in the past closely cooperated with this same person. He stated that social workers had never done anything for the club, but he had been instrumental in getting Vice Lords to cooperate with YMCA programs. For some time he had been working to limit gang fighting, but after the meeting called for a resumption of gang wars. All this makes sense if we look at Cave Man's position at this time. He needed to demonstrate that while he was no longer a formal officer, he was still a Leader—that it, a person with power. He needed to show that others would still follow him. An important segment of the new officers had tacitly agreed to letting the outsiders attend the meeting, but many members were against it. This gave Cave Man his opportunity. By mobilizing the resistance and successfully opposing the new officers he convincingly demonstrated his power to everyone. His later behavior is also understandable in these terms. Arriving at 16th and Lawndale in full view, at the head of a large group, further emphasized Cave Man's ability to gather a following. I do not believe he seriously intended to lead Vice Lords in a new gang war. He simply used an appeal to gang fighting values that are seldom, if ever, publicly questioned to gather a following and validate his identity as a Leader. After Cave Man reached 16th and Lawndale at the head of this group, he made no further move toward initiating gang fighting.

Some Vice Lords who are considered Leaders sometimes assume Follower identities in certain situations. There is a formal hierarchy of leadership positions that partially accounts for this. For example, the president of the Nation is thought to be a higher position than president of a branch. Therefore, the president of the Nation assumes the identity Leader in certain situations, while presidents of branches are Followers. The *de facto* distribution of power, however, fits only partially with the formal hierarchy of political positions. The incident just discussed involving Cave Man provides a good example. Bat Man was a Leader and vice-president of the 15th Street Lords. In the meeting of the Nation he opposed allowing the social workers to attend. Cave Man, even though he had no formal political position at this time, assumed the identity Leader in the meeting and Bat Man, who was a vice president, assumed that of his Follower. After the meeting, Bat Man joined the group that followed Cave Man to 16th and Lawndale.

The composition of a Leader's following changes in various situations. One time a Leader may join the following of another Leader (and bring his own following with him), but another time oppose that same Leader. Thus Vice Lords never know ahead of time exactly who will be allied and opposed in any particular instance. In other words, the strength of an individual's power is subject to constant fluctuation. We can now better understand why situations in which public decisions are made are contexts for the exercise of power. Power is based on the number of one's followers, but a Leader's following is constantly changing, and the exact extent of a person's power is not usually known. In situations where public decisions are made, however, lines of opposition are drawn, and power becomes crystallized. In the decision-making process individuals make the choice whether to assume a Leader or Follower identity. Those who choose the latter make the further choice as to whose following they will join. Through these choices power is actualized, and claims to the Leader identity are validated.

In this chapter we have concentrated on social roles—one aspect in the pattern of Vice Lord social behavior that comprises the social system. We have identified certain social roles and discussed these in relation to a particular theoretical framework. In the next chapter we shall switch our concern and look at Vice Lord behavior in terms of a cultural system.

5

The Cultural System

V ICE LORDS DEFINE THEIR WORLD and guide their actions in terms of a particular ideological framework. This constitutes Vice Lord culture. Our concern in this chapter is to describe some of the beliefs and values comprising this framework, and to show how they relate to social behavior. I found four general ideological sets which constitute Vice Lord culture. They can be designated: heart ideology, soul ideology, brotherhood ideology, and game ideology. Each of these sets functions to divide Vice Lord reality into a number of compartments we can call cultural scenes, and to guide and judge behavior within these scenes.

Heart Ideology

A Cobra swung on one of the fellows, and he come down with his knife out. That means he's not scared to take that man's life if he wished to. That's what you call a lot of heart—not scared to go to jail and pay whatever the consequences is.

If a group of boys say, going to break into a store or truck, and I tell this boy to do it and he does it, the people say he got a whole lot of heart—he not afraid of anything. He'll just go on and do everything the other person tell him to do.

A person who got heart, he not scared to do anything. Like we break in a liquor lounge or something, he not worried about being busted. He's game for it. Or like we in a fight, and we outnumbered say four to two. This man will stand up there and fight with you no matter what. If you all go down, he there with you. You all both go down together.

If you don't show heart people call you a punk, and they don't want to hang with you. A punk is a person who like get into a fight with somebody and he don't fight back. Or like if say me and you and somebody else, we going to rob somebody, and one of us be scared and won't do it. Then they say he punked out.

From these explanations we can understand what Vice Lords mean by "heart." It is apparent that generally "heart" means bravery, but it means more than just this. It also means bravery in terms of being "game," that is, being willing

491

to follow any suggestion regardless of personal risk. Having heart contrasts with punking out. A person who acts in a cowardly way—that is, who is not "game" for any suggestion—is a punk. Vice Lords believe that having heart is good, while being a punk, or punking out is bad. Heart, in other words, is one of the values of Vice Lord culture.

The heart-punk contrast defines a particular segment of Vice Lord reality. If we look at the explanations given by Vice Lords, it is apparent that the heart-punk contrast is relevant to situations where there is personal risk. Individuals are judged in terms of heart ideology only in situations which involve personal risk, and thus these situations are set off as distinct segments of Vice Lord life. A further look at our Vice Lords' explanations shows a division in risk situations—those involving fighting, and those involving robbing. Vice Lords call fighting humbugging, and robbing hustling. Humbugging is further subdivided: fighting between rival clubs is gangbanging, fighting between individuals is humbugging, and fighting which results when a group of club members goes out to jump on anyone they can find is wolf packing. We can show this more clearly by constructing a typology comprised of contrast sets.

Personal Risk Situations				Other Situations
Humbugging$_1$			Hustling	
Gangbanging	Humbugging$_2$	Wolf packing		

Personal risk situations contrast with other situations. Within the former, humbugging$_1$ contrasts with hustling. Within humbugging$_1$ situations, gangbanging, humbugging$_2$, and wolf packing all contrast. I should explain the difference between humbugging$_1$ and humbugging$_2$. Vice Lords refer to all kinds of fighting as humbugging. A fight between a boy and his father, a fight between males and females, a fight between rival clubs, or any other kind of fight can be referred to as a humbug. However, Vice Lords further distinguish between kinds of fighting. Gangbanging refers only to fights between enemy clubs. When individuals wish to distinguish between fights involving two individuals and fights involving rival clubs, they refer to the former as humbugs and the latter as gangbangs. Thus humbugging means any kind of fighting when contrasted with hustling, but means only fighting between individuals when contrasted with gangbanging. Therefore, I have used humbugging$_1$ to designate fighting in general and humbugging$_2$ to specify fighting between individuals.

Situations which involve humbugging$_2$, gangbanging, wolf packing, and hustling form distinct segments of Vice Lord reality that can be called cultural scenes. The use of scene is an analogy to the scenes of a play. As the action of a play is divided into scenes, so the action of Vice Lord behavior is structured into units we can call cultural scenes. My data on humbugging$_2$, wolf packing, and hustling is too limited to provide a detailed description of the pattern of action that takes place within these scenes. We can, however, study the cultural scene gangbang in greater detail. In Chapter 3 we made the distinction between gangbangs that resulted from accidental encounters between members of an enemy club and those that involved prior planning. Here, we are concerned with the latter.

There are four phases in a gangbang. The first we can call the prefight gathering. Before actual fighting begins, Vice Lords meet in their territory to plan strategy. During this phase there is drinking, singing, shouting, and bragging. Besides planning strategy Vice Lords are emotionally preparing to face the dangers of actual fighting. The second phase is the confrontation between enemy clubs. During the confrontation the groups stand facing each other, while the two rival war counselors are in between exchanging threats and insults. When the rival war counselors begin fighting, the third phase begins. This we can call the encounter. During the encounter the actual fighting takes place. The final phase is the postfight gathering. During this phase Vice Lords again gather in their territory to drink and brag of their exploits. The following account illustrates in greater detail what happens during the second and third phases.

> Now a fight like this really looks funny when it starts, but it turns out to be terrifying. When it's just coming night is when most of the fighting occurs so if the Man come, then everybody can get away.
>
> You get a stick, or maybe a knife, or a chain. And some fools got shotguns. What you really do, you stand there and the counselors are the first ones up. You stand back and you wait and see if they come to an agreement and talk. Now everybody standing there watching everybody else to see what's going to happen. And all of a sudden maybe a blow will be passed, and if it is, a fight start right there. Let's say this is what happened. Now nine out of ten you know everybody in your club, or everybody who came with you. You standing just like you'd met in a crowd and you were talking. It's really almost a semicircle. You just standing there and you're looking—you're watching the counselor. And if a blow pass, automatically the first thing you do is hit the man closest to you. After that if things get too tight for you then you get out of there. If it look like you getting whupped, you get out. It's all according to your nerve. The first who runs, that's it right there. Naturally if you're standing there and you're fighting, and you see half the club starting to run, you know the other half going to run soon. All it takes is one to run and the whole crowd breaks up. That's how a club gets its rep—by not running, by standing its ground.

The beliefs and values of heart ideology underlie the action of the gangbang scene. Esteem among Vice Lords corresponds to rep. Rep, in turn, depends on how others judge one's behavior in relation to heart ideology. These judgments are made on the behavior that takes place during the second and third phases of the gangbang scene. Heart ideology is also important in the first and third phases of a gangbang. Here, the beliefs and values of heart are reinforced through expression in ritualistic behavior. The basic tenets of heart ideology are contained in a poem composed by several of the original members of the club:

> From back out to south came the King of the Gestapoes, Lord of the Sabotage, Ruler of the Astronauts, knocking down fifty-sixty lanes.
>
> I say, for any man make attempt to take a Vice Lord down, he got to first find a rock to kill Goliath, overturn the pillars of Sampson, name the stone that David stood on, name the three little children that walked the burning fires of hell, stand in front of the Lord and say, "I have no fear."

For the Vice Lords, I say for all Vice Lords, sixty-two across the chest, don't fear nothing, God and death, got a tombstone opportunity, a grave-yard mind, he must be a Vice Lord 'cause he don't mind dying.
Vice Lord! Mighty Vice Lord!

During the first and third phases of a gangbang this poem is repeated by members of the club. The group divides intself into sections and each repeats alternating phrases. The final refrain—"Vice Lord! Mighty Vice Lord!"—is said by the entire group. In this manner the beliefs and values contained in the poem are given public expression, and heart ideology is reinforced.

Soul Ideology

There are several aspects to the Vice Lord concept of "soul." In one sense it refers to a general sort of Negritude. One who acts in a "hip" manner is said to have soul. However, it means more than this. Soul also refers to a way of doing something. When someone puts real effort into what he is doing, he is said to have soul. Stripping away superficiality and getting to the essence (or, in ghetto jargon, getting down to the real "nitty-gritty") is also involved in soul. Thus, for example, someone who sings with real effort and real feeling, and in so doing succeeds in capturing the essence of Black experience, has soul. His musical ability as such is irrelevant to the amount of his soul. Charles Keil has made an intensive study of the soul concept among Blacks in Chicago, and his research shows that the Vice Lord meaning of soul is the same as that found in ghetto culture as a whole. For a deeper analysis of the soul concept the reader is referred to Keil's monograph *The Urban Blues*. For our purposes, however, it is only necessary to note these three elements—Negritude, intense effort; and stripping away superficiality, or getting down to the real nitty-gritty—for Vice Lords base their judgments of soul on these elements.

Vice Lords value soul. To tell someone he has soul is a compliment, while to say he has "a hole in his soul" is a definite criticism. There are certain social situations in which judgments are made in terms of soul. These are contexts involving music. Music is an extremly important part of Vice Lord life. Vice Lords closely follow the music from Chicago's Black radio stations, and are constantly singing the songs that are broadcasted there. Many have formed their own singing groups which hold regular practices and perform at certain times. Dancing is even more important in Vice Lord life. Almost all Vice Lords take intense pride in their dancing ability, and lose few opportunities to demonstrate it.

Vice Lords judge one another's singing and dancing in terms of soul ideology, and thus that segment of Vice Lord life in which singing and dancing is found is set off from other social situations. Singing and dancing are important activities in two Vice Lord scenes. These are called by Vice Lords sets and hanging on the corner. A set can be translated as a party. Vice Lords usually display their dancing ability in this scene, and it is here that judgments are made in terms of soul. Singing takes place in many situations. Riding in a car, or meeting at a member's house, are a few examples of when singing occurs. However, judgments about singing are

"Pulling jive," the person in the striped shirt is about to pour out a portion of the wine in the Vice Lord letters.

usually made during performances that take place while hanging on the corner. When large groups of Vice Lords gather on the corner of 16th and Lawndale, for example, various groups demonstrate their singing abilities, and soul judgments are made on these performances.

Brotherhood Ideology

We noted in the last chapter that the idea of mutual help is an important value in the Vice Lord cultural framework. Vice Lords often express this in terms of brotherhood. "Man, we're just like brothers" is an often-heard phrase. One Vice Lord scene in which the values of brotherhood are especially relevant is drinking wine. There is a special ritual to wine drinking, and through this ritual the values of brotherhood are expressed and reinforced.

A wine drinking scene is initiated when a small group of Vice Lords gathers and someone suggests having a taste, or pulling some jive. The next phase is gathering the money. The individual who made the first suggestion usually acts as collector. Everyone in the group donates what he feels he can afford. Often it is necessary to go around the group several times before enough money is collected. Vice Lords passing by are also asked to contribute money and join in the wine drinking activities. After the money is collected and the wine is purchased, the next phase of the scene begins. This consists of "cracking the bottle." The bottle of wine is given to one of the group, who points it toward the ground and strikes the bottom of the bottle two times with the palm of his hand. This cracks the seal. Next, a small portion of the wine is poured out on the ground either in the letters CVL, or simply the letter V. This is interpreted as a symbolic gift to all the Vice Lords who have been killed or who are in jail. Finally, the bottle is passed around to everyone in the group, and each drinks the same amount regardless of how much money he contributed toward buying the wine.

There are two aspects of the wine drinking scene that give expression to brotherhood ideology. The first is the wine that is poured out in the Vice Lord letters. Vice Lords place a high value on wine, and pouring out even a little is a form of sacrifice. This sacrifice is interpreted as a symbolic giving to other Vice Lords in need. Vice Lords who are dead and in jail can't get wine for themselves, but this way there is symbolically something for them to drink too. The second aspect that reinforces brotherhood values is the way the wine is distributed and the way it is drunk. Every person in the group is entitled to an equal amount of wine regardless of the amount of money he contributed. Each gives whatever he has or whatever he can afford, but all, as Vice Lords put it, "share like brothers" in the consumption of the wine. Further, the wine is drunk from the same bottle. Each person does not take his portion in a separate glass, but everyone drinks from the same bottle. To Vice Lords this sharing further symbolizes the unity and brotherhood between members of the group. Thus the wine drinking ritual expresses and reinforces the values of mutual help—the values of brotherhood.

Game Ideology

In our previous study of the Street Man–Street Man role we noted that in certain situations the ability to successfully manipulate others, or, as Vice Lords say, "whupping the game," is an activity which sets off a particular part of Vice Lord life. We can call this segment a "game." The way individuals behave during a game scene is judged by other Vice Lords in terms of game ideology. Individuals who are thought to be good at whupping the game are said to have a "heavy game," while those who are judged to be poor at this activity are said to have a "light-weight game." The technique one uses in whupping the game is called a "front," and the quality of various individuals' fronts is often a topic of conversation.

Various Vice Lords often tried to whup the game on me with various degrees of success. A few examples will help illustrate the kinds of situations that constitute the game scene. Washington was known for having a lightweight game. He was seldom successful in beating anyone out of anything, but was often taken himself for various items of value. His attempt to whup the game on me consisted of simply requesting money: "Hey man, can you give me a quarter?" My answer was, "Sorry Washington, I don't have it today." This exchange constituted a game scene in Vice Lord life.

Blue Goose, in contrast to Washington, was known to have a heavy game.

Once he convinced me that a group of older men who were not members of the Vice Lords were planning to jump on me. He assured me, however, that I had nothing to fear because he would see to it that they did not bother me. He made a big show of chasing two old wineheads who he purported were plotting against me down the street. A little while later he asked me to loan him 50 cents and a shirt so he could make his "gig" (job) the next day. Of course, in gratitude, I was more than glad to help in any way possible. Later I learned I had taken part in a game scene and had been the victim of a successful front.

References

GEERTZ, C., 1957, "Ritual and Social Change: A Javanese Example," *American Anthropologist,* Vol. 59, No. 1.

HOBEN, A., N.D., *Community Study Guide,* a mimeographed pamphlet for Peace Corps Volunteers in Ethiopia.

KEIL, C., 1966, *The Urban Blues.* Chicago: University of Chicago Press.

SHORT, J. JR., 1963, "Introduction to the Abridged Edition," in *The Gang* by Frederic M. Thrasher. Chicago: University of Chicago Press.

Further Reading

We have selected a few books and articles for each of the case studies included in *Cultures Around the World* that can extend your knowledge of the culture. You should also note the titles contained in the References Cited list at the end of each study. We will not repeat such titles below.

THE TIWI

BERNDT, R. M., AND C. H. BERNDT, 1952, *The First Australians*. Sydney: Ure Smith.
A sound attempt to summarize the life of the Aborigines for the general reader.

GOODALE, JANE C., 1971, *Tiwi Wives*. Seattle: University of Washington Press.
This is a study of the women of Melville Island, from the woman's point of view. It develops what for beginners in anthropology may seem like a fairly technical analysis of social structure and marriage. Study of this book will prove rewarding, however, for it both extends and departs from the analysis by Hart and Pilling. This book also contains further useful bibliography on the Tiwi.

HART, C. W. M., 1970, "Fieldwork among the Tiwi." In *Being an Anthropologist: Fieldwork in Eleven Cultures*, edited by G. Spindler. New York: Holt, Rinehart and Winston.
This is very nearly must reading. You will understand *The Tiwi* much better and will acquire insights into the nature of anthropology and of anthropologists.

SPENCER, BALDWIN, AND F. J. GILLEN, 1972, *The Arunta* (2 vols). London: Macmillan.
The Arunta live in the interior desert region of Australia and are quite different than the Tiwi, but they are one of the classical cultures of aboriginal Australia, perhaps *the* classical culture, for many anthropologists.

TONKINSON, ROBERT, 1974, *The Jigalong Mob: Aboriginal Victors of the Desert Crusade*. Menlo Park, Calif.: Cummings.
This book is also about desert people. It is particularly valuable as a contribution to the anthropology of colonialism and as a study of the ways in which a people may keep their ethnic identity despite great odds.

ULITHI

LESSA, WILLIAM A., 1950, "Ulithi and the Outer Native World." *American Anthropologist* 52:27–52.
The place of Ulithi in the Yap empire.

————, 1961, "Tales from Ulithi Atoll: A Comparative Study of Oceanic Folklore." *University of California Publication: Folklore Studies* 13.
A vast analysis of certain Ulithian tales and motifs, and their cognates throughout all of Oceania, with attention to cultural influences.

————, 1964, "The Social Effects of Typhoon Ophelia (1960) on Ulithi." *Micronesia* 1:1–47.
How a devastating typhoon hastened incipient social change in Ulithi.

————, AND MARVIN SPIEGELMAN, 1954, "Ulithian Personality as Seen through Ethnological Materials and Thematic Test Analyses." *University of California Publications in Culture and Society* 2,5.
A description of Ulithian personality traits as seen from an analysis of 99 TAT protocols and from field observation.

On the Pacific as a Whole

GARDINER, LYNDSAY, 1957, *Pacific Peoples*. London: Longmans, Green.

OLIVER, DOUGLAS, L., 1951, *The Pacific Islands*. Cambridge, Mass.: Harvard University Press.

THE SWAZI

(See References Cited for the Swazi)

General Reading on the Culture Area

BEATTIE, JOHN, 1960, *Bunyoro: An African Kingdom*. New York: Holt, Rinehart, Winston (Case Studies in Cultural Anthropology Series).

An excellent case study of a people in East Africa with a political system somewhat similar to that of the Swazi.

BEIDELMAN, T. O., 1971, *The Kaguru: A Matrilineal People of East Africa*. New York: Holt, Rinehart and Winston (Case Studies in Cultural Anthropology Series).

Livelihood, cosmology, clans, marriage, neighborhood, life cycle, and the impact of the Christian mission are described and interpreted.

FORTES, M., AND E. E. EVANS-PRITCHARD (eds.), 1940, *African Political Systems*. London. Oxford University Press.

Describes the political structure of eight African tribal societies, of which five are Bantu and one is Zulu, the Swazi's powerful neighbors.

GLUCKMAN, MAX, 1952, *Rituals of Rebellion*. Manchester, England: University of Manchester Press.

A stimulating interpretation of rituals, including the Swazi ritual of kingship.

READ, MARGARET, 1968, Children of Their Fathers: Growing Up among the Ngoni of Malawi. New York: Holt, Rinehart and Winston (Case Studies in Education and Culture Series).

The Ngoni of Nyasaland retain many similarities with the Swazi despite separation in space and time.

THE NAVAJO

DYCK, WALTER, 1938, *Son of Old Man Hat*. New York: Harcourt.

The autobiography of a Navajo beginning shortly after the return from Fort Sumner.

KLUCKHOHN, CLYDE, AND DOROTHEA LEIGHTON, 1956, *Children of the People*. Cambridge, Mass.: Harvard University Press.

A companion volume to *The Navajo*, by Clyde Kluckhohn and Dorothea Leighton, dealing with the individual and the formation of personality. Kluckhohn devoted much of his life to the study of the Navajo.

SHEPHARDSON, MARY T., 1963. "Navajo Ways in Government." *American Anthropological Association Memoir* No. 90.

An outstanding discussion of the institutionalization of modern political structure among the Navajo.

VOGT, EVON Z., 1961. "The Navajo." In *Perspectives in American Indian Cultural Change*, edited by E. H. Spicer. Chicago: University of Chicago Press.

An excellent review of Navajo prehistory and history.

THE VICE LORDS

ASCHENBRENNER, JOYCE, 1975. *Lifelines: Black Families in Chicago*. New York: Holt, Rinehart and Winston (Case Studies in Cultural Anthropology Series).

A very different view of Black life in Chicago, focusing on family, kin, and social relationships other than those occurring on the street.

HERSKOVITS, MELVILLE, 1947, *The Myth of the Negro Past.* Boston: Beacon Press. Important background reading. Although at times the author seems to underestimate the importance of the American experience in the development of Black culture, his evidence for African survival is impressive.

KUNKEL, PETER, AND SARA SUE KENNARD, 1971, *Spout Spring: A Black Community.* New York: Holt, Rinehart and Winston. (Case Studies in Cultural Anthropology Series). The ethnography of a Black community in the Ozarks. Also contrastive; a very different life style than that described in the *Vice Lords.*

KEISER, LINCOLN, 1970, "Fieldwork among the Vice Lords of Chicago." In *Being an Anthropologist: Fieldwork in Eleven Cultures,* edited by G. Spindler. New York: Holt, Rinehart and Winston. Tells the story, and an interesting one, of Keiser's fieldwork upon which *The Vice Lords* is based.

SPEAR, ALLAN H., 1967, *The Making of a Negro Ghetto* 1890–1892. Chicago: University of Chicago Press. An historical account of the Great Migrations and the development of social and political institutions in the Black ghettos of Chicago.

WHITTEN, NORMAN, JR., AND JOHN F. SZWED, 1970, *Afro-American Anthropology: Contemporary Perspectives.* Beverly Hills, Calif.: Free Press. Also important background. A collection of essays.

WHYTE, W., 1943, *Street Corner Society.* Chicago: University of Chicago Press. A study of a street-corner group based on anthropological field research. A classic in the field of urban studies.

YABLONSKY, L., 1962, *The Violent Gang.* New York: Macmillan. Provides capsule versions of major theories of gang delinquency.

Useful Reading

TEXTS DESIGNED AS COMPANIONS FOR CASE STUDIES

BEALS, ALAN, WITH G. AND L. SPINDLER, 1973, *Cultures in Process*. New York: Holt, Rinehart and Winston.

OTTERBEIN, KEITH, F., 1977. Rev. Ed. *Comparative Cultural Analysis: An Introduction to Anthropology*. New York: Holt, Rinehart and Winston.

SCHUSKY, ERNEST L., 1975, *The Study of Cultural Anthropology*. New York: Holt, Rinehart and Winston.

SPINDLER, GEORGE D., ed., 1970, *Being an Anthropologist: Fieldwork in Eleven Cultures*. New York: Holt, Rinehart and Winston.

FROM THE BASIC ANTHROPOLOGY UNITS SERIES
(edited by G. and L. Spindler and published by Holt, Rinehart and Winston)

FRIEDL, ERNESTINE, 1975, *Women and Men: An Anthropologist's View*.

GAMST, FREDERICK C., 1974, *Peasants in Complex Society*.

GARBARINO, MERWYN, 1977, *Sociocultural Theory in Anthropology: A Short History*.

HOSTETLER, JOHN A., 1974, *Communitarian Societies*.

LANCASTER, JANE B., 1975, *Primate Behavior and the Emergence of Human Culture*.

LUSTIG-ARECCO, VERA, 1975, *Technology: Strategies for Survival*.

NORBECK, EDWARD, 1974, *Religion in Human Life: Anthropological Views*.

SCHUSKY, ERNEST L., 1974, *Variation in Kinship*.

SPINDLER, LOUISE, 1977, *Culture Change and Modernization: Mini-Models and Case Studies*.

Each of the units above ties in closely with the Case Studies in Cultural Anthropology Series.

Index*

---

* Italic letters before page numbers indicate the case study for which pages are given: *T* (Tiwi), *U* (Ulithi), *S* (Swazi), *N* (Navajo), and *VC* (Vice Lords).

505